LOUISIANA'S JEWISH IMMIGRANTS
from the
BAS-RHIN, ALSACE, FRANCE

CAROL MILLS-NICHOL

JANAWAY PUBLISHING
Santa Maria, California

Copyright © 2014, Carol Mills-Nichol

ALL RIGHTS RESERVED.
No part of this publication may be reproduced, stored in a
retrieval system, or transmitted in any form or by any
means whatsoever, whether electronic, mechanical,
magnetic recording, or photocopying, without the
prior written approval of the Copyright holder
or Publisher, excepting brief quotations
for inclusion in book reviews.

Published by:

Janaway Publishing, Inc.
732 Kelsey Ct.
Santa Maria, California 93454
(805) 925-1038
www.janawaygenealogy.com

2014

Library of Congress Control Number: 2014950869

ISBN: 978-1-59641-340-5

Made in the United States of America

With my deepest gratitude to my husband, Jack, who suffered through the writing of another book. To the Cavaliers, Rascal, Barbie and B.J.; the terrier, Lily, and our rescue, Winston, who all vied for some attention.

To my dear friend, Daniel Lubrez, who helped me with my research in France and Germany, and selflessly spent his time promoting my first book.

Finally, to anyone who reads this and finds a long lost relative, I wish you many more happy years of genealogical discoveries

TABLE OF CONTENTS

Introduction vii

Acknowledgements xi

List of Illustrations xiii

PART I Researching Your Jewish Ancestors From The Bas-Rhin 1

PART II Case Studies 21

PART III – Format and Abbreviations used in this book 37

PART IV Jewish Emigrants from the Bas-Rhin to Louisiana 41

PART V – Illustrations, Maps and Indices 397

    Map of Bas-Rhin region in France 423

    Location of Bas-Rhin in France.. 424

    Index of towns in Bas-Rhin appearing in this book 425

    Parish Map of Louisiana 431

    Index of towns in Louisiana appearing in this book 433

INTRODUCTION

This book is devoted to the exclusive study of immigrants who came to Louisiana from the Bas-Rhin, that part of France which shares a border with the former German state of Bavaria, also called the Pfalz, the Rheinland-Pfalz, or the Rhineland-Palatinate, to the north, and a border with the French districts of Moselle, Meurthe-et-Moselle and Vosges to the west. To the east, and across the Rhine River, sits the German state of Baden. The Bas-Rhin, which is the northernmost half of what we know as Alsace, is a relatively small part of France which, by itself, is comparable in size to the state of Texas. The Bas-Rhin has an area of 1869 square miles (4793 sq. km) and is just three hundred square miles larger than Rhode Island, our smallest state. Immigrants arriving from this part of France, who settled in Louisiana, found themselves in the thirty-first largest state in the union, with an area of 51,840 square miles (134,265 sq. km) and a very different semi-tropical climate.

The Jewish men and women who came to Louisiana before the Civil War in a first wave of immigration in the 1840s left the Bas-Rhin for many reasons. Times were especially hard for the bourgeoisie and the poor, including many Jews living in the Bas-Rhin. In France the 1789 Declaration of Rights of Man which had granted equality to all citizens had not changed the lives of the French Jew very much at all. The majority of them still lived in small towns and continued to work as merchants or cattle dealers, as most other professions were still closed to them. Young Jewish men were educated in small Hebrew-run establishments where the basics of French and other disciplines, along with the tenets of their religion, were taught. In order to curb the non-Christian population, some towns even had marriage restrictions for Jews, allowing only the eldest son to take a wife. The younger boys had to wait until an elderly male member of their community died, or move on to another village where they might be accepted as residents. Men, reaching the age of conscription, often found it unthinkable to fight for a country where they were, in many ways, second class citizens. A Christian, with money, could pay a substitute to do his military service. Most poor Jews could not. After the fall of Napoleon in 1815 France was rocked by years of political unrest, sporadic street fighting, high unemployment, bad harvests, and a crumbling infrastructure which exacerbated an already hostile climate of class warfare. This social upheaval culminated in the Revolution of 1848. The freedom and political stability that America seemed to offer these early immigrants was enough for them to overcome the fear of an arduous six week sea voyage.

For Jews from the Bas-Rhin, antebellum Louisiana was an attractive destination. It was cheaper by one third to take a ship to New Orleans although the voyage was one third longer than to alternative northern ports such as New York. Moreover, French was widely spoken in Louisiana. It is also important to note that almost every immigrant to Louisiana knew someone else who had preceded him to America. Earlier Jewish arrivals often kept in touch with the "old country" encouraging other townspeople from the Bas-Rhin to follow. Moreover, they were inclined to pay the passage for their relatives to join them. Eventually some men of means even brought over brides for themselves or for other single Louisiana Jews of their acquaintance. Usually starting out their American experience in antebellum New Orleans, a bustling metropolitan port city even then, these new arrivals from the Bas-Rhin were like fish out of water. Some stayed and adapted to city life but many more fanned out into the countryside to work as peddlers in order to make enough money to open up a general merchandise establishment in a small town or village, or to manage a plantation store for a large land owner. It is not surprising that thousands were willing to travel half-way across the world to settle in towns and villages that closely resembled their previous homes.

Although immigration to the United States was virtually halted during the American Civil War, many Jewish immigrants who had fled their homes in Louisiana during the hostilities between the North and South and had travelled back to France, returned to America to start life anew as soon as the war was over. A second large wave of immigration was precipitated by France's defeat in the Franco-Prussian War in May 1871, which cost the residents of Alsace and parts of Lorraine their French citizenship. Ordered to accept German nationality or leave, thousands did just that, fleeing their comfort zone in the countryside to inhabit the larger cities of France, especially Paris. Many, however, chose to come to America instead, often following other relatives and friends who had come to the Gulf South a generation before. This second wave of immigrants from the Bas-Rhin, unlike those who had come before the American Civil War, generally entered the country through the port of New York

Many Jews from the Bas-Rhin remained for years in the small towns and villages in the outlying parishes of Louisiana, despite the lack of a socio-religious support network. Only eighteen of the sixty-four parishes which make up Louisiana had a Jewish Cemetery. Only ten parishes had one or more synagogues. While some early Jewish immigrant men often married outside the faith, others travelled to New Orleans to pick a bride amongst the young Jewish women who had made the journey to America alone or with relatives or friends from the same village. A small number of Jewish men, especially in the early 1850s, had families with persons of color. Upon finding a suitable Jewish bride, these first racially-mixed families were often abandoned. Rabbis travelled from New Orleans or Baton Rouge to officiate at weddings hundreds of miles away. Many times, with no available rabbi, a Jewish elder, in a small town would serve as a spiritual guide for the handful of Jewish families in the neighborhood and lay-led services would be held in private homes. Oftentimes Jews simply lived as their Christian neighbors did, and were, for the most part, readily accepted. Jewish women in small towns often joined Protestant or Catholic social welfare organizations or clubs. Some even attended regular church services. Jewish families stuck it out in the parishes through hurricanes, floods, epidemics, and economic downturns well into the twentieth century. Many even prospered. As they aged, and their children scattered, some retired to New Orleans or Baton Rouge to the comfort of a larger city with a nearby place to worship and a Jewish Cemetery. Louisiana's small-town Jewish residents were only driven out en masse when the state's cotton crops were decimated by the boll weevil blight which spread from Texas in 1905, culminating in the disastrous harvest season of 1913. As the local farmers drowned in a sea of debt, the Jewish merchants who kept them supplied with the necessities of life were no longer able to pay their own creditors in New Orleans. Bankruptcy was often the result. Some merchants fled north while others relocated to New Orleans to go into other businesses. This agricultural disaster, however, had really only precipitated the inevitable. Many of the sons of prosperous Alsatian Jews had, as early as the 1860s, been sent away to college. They had been trained as doctors, dentists, pharmacists and teachers and would not have returned to small-town life in any case.

I have been researching immigrants from the Bas-Rhin to Louisiana for more than ten years. After I completed my first book which concentrated on the Jewish residents of Avoyelles Parish, I decided to investigate as many families as I could find in other parishes across the state, and to write small biographies of each family. Because there were so many Jewish immigrants to Louisiana, I narrowed my search to those coming from the Bas-Rhin. While doing this research I decided that I needed to include some tips about how to go about tracing one's French Jewish ancestors. The first pages are devoted to an explanation of how to go about one's research, and especially what pitfalls to avoid. I have included four case studies where I have outlined step by step how I uncovered information about certain immigrants including their towns of origin, dates of birth, their parents' names, their dates of immigration, where they settled in Louisiana, if and when they married, how and where they died and where they were buried. The remainder of this book is devoted to the stories of over six hundred immigrants from the Bas-Rhin to Louisiana whose lives that I have studied. Treated alphabetically by last name, I have attempted to capture the essence of their lives in both France and Louisiana. Each biography is meant to serve as a starting point for any future research conducted by the descendants of these immigrants.

The book ends with a collection of photographs, mostly tombstones, on which is written the town in the Bas-Rhin from which these emigrants came. It is a clear indication of their pride at having been born in the Bas-Rhin, and a desire to remind others, even in death, from where they had come. There are many thousands more memorials just like these all over the United States that mark the graves of proud Alsatians.

ACKNOWLEDGEMENTS

I would like to thank the people who have helped me in my quest to research the lives of the Jewish men and women who came to Louisiana from the Bas-Rhin, France. First and always, Randy Decuir, who told me that I was Jewish, and who, as the editor of the *Marksville Weekly News*, and a genealogist, himself, gave me access to his historical newspaper files, through which I was able to discover details about the lives of many Jewish men and women who are the subject of this book. I also owe a special debt of gratitude to Steven Mayeux, author of *Earthen Walls, Iron Men: Fort DeRussy. Louisiana, and the Defense of Red River*, whose expertise in the Civil War history of Avoyelles Parish, LA, led me to the discovery of the French and American Claims Commission files held by the NARA, an invaluable source of information about our Jewish merchant ancestors. Information on Avoyelles Jewish families was generously given by Barbara Escudé Lemoine, Judith Ann Siess, Joseph and Bill Friend, Lorraine, Seiss, Felicia Seiss, Juanita and Yolanda Barbin, Arlene Barbin, Jim Levy, the late Lenox Leopold Siess, Jr, the late Mary Nell Davenport, and the late Donald Clement. Haas family researchers, Alice Holland and Brad Fanta contributed to my knowledge of the Haas brothers from Rothbach.

The story of the Rapides Parish Jewish families was previously told by Rabbi Martin I. Hinchin, DD, in his book *Fourscore and Eleven, A History of the Jews of Rapides Parish 1828-1919*. His work proved to be a great help for me in many ways during the course of my research. The support and encouragement of Arnold Task, Rabbi Emeritus of Temple Gemiluth Chassodim in Alexandria was also invaluable.

Micheline Gutmann, president of GenAmi, (l'Association de Généalogie Juive Internationale), who discovered the fate of the immigrant ship *Luna*, provided me with vital information which cleared up mysteries not only for the Siess family, but for the Loeb and Ehrmann ancestors who perished in the English Channel, while en route to join relatives in Louisiana.

Much has already been said about the variety of internet sites that provide information which facilitate genealogical research in the twenty-first century, and without which many discoveries might never have been made. I have listed the sites which I have found to be the most helpful on pages 15-20 of this book. Some have a subscription fee, but the amount of money charged is far less than one would spend to travel to courthouses in America and to archives abroad.

Finally I own a special debt of gratitude to my friend and fellow researcher, Teri Downs Tillman, CG,. As an expert on the lives of the interconnected Goudchaux-Kahn-Weill families of Brumath, Schirrhoffen and Riedseltz, Bas-Rhin, she was an invaluable resource. Teri was always able to decipher the old German script that was used in original records from the Bas-Rhin before 1810 and after 1871, when I could not. Moreover, she was happy to read my entries as they were written, and to offer suggestions and corrections, both genealogical and stylistic. If I hit a "brick wall" in my research of one or another of my entries in this book, she would often come up with that one little fact which would provide a breakthrough in the case at hand.

LIST OF ILLUSTRATIONS

Unless otherwise noted, all images are from the author's collection.

Tombstone of Caroline Aaron from Bouxwiller 397
Tombstone of Raphael Block fromHerrlisheim 398
Tombstone of Ernest Block of Duttlenheim 399
Tombstone of Miriam Blum from Dettwiller 400
Tombstone of Babette Dahlman from Brumath 401
Tombstone of Louis Geerst from Niederbronn-les-Bains 402
Tombstone of Charlotte Hirsch from Niederroedern 403
Tombstone of Rachel Klein from Hoenheim 404
Tombstone of Adolph Klotz from Lauterbourg 405
Tombstone of Édouard Levy said to be from Lauterbourg 406
Tombstone of Israël Levy from Bouxwiller 407
Tombstone of Samuel Levy from Lauterbourg 408
Tombstone of Simon Levy from Lauterbourg 409
Tombstone of Emily Meyer from Drachenbronn 410
Tombstone of Isaac Meyer from Lembach 411
Tombstone of Justine Meyer from Schweighouse-sur-Moder 412
Tombstone of Louis Meyer from Lembach 413
Tombstone of Moses Rosenthal from Oberlauterbach 414
Tombstone of David Siess, said to be from Lembach 415
Tombstone of Nochim Weil from Surbourg 416
Tombstone of Simon Weil from Bischheim 417
Tombstone of Leon Wolff, said to be from Ingwiller 418
Lep Sommer's Leader Store at Torras, Pointe Coupée Parish,
    LA 419
Photo of Leopold "Lep" Sommer 419
Mr. Godchaux, Mobile Merchant at Waterloo,
    Pointe Coupee Parish, LA 420
Interior of Lep and Sylvan Sommer's Leader Store, Torras,
    Pointe Coupée Parish, LA 421
Map of the Bas-Rhin, Alsace, France 423
Location of Bas-Rhin in France 424
Parish Map of Louisiana 431

PART I

RESEARCHING YOUR JEWISH ANCESTORS FROM THE BAS-RHIN

A WORD OF CAUTION: While Jewish genealogy has its particular problems, working with the French and German records from the region, which are readily available on-line, presents another set of difficulties, especially if one is not conversant in both languages. Original records always trump information taken from tombstones, census records and on-line genealogies. Since researching one's ancestors has become, of late, a national obsession it is best to be very careful when relying on unsourced material. The most important thing one can have is simple common sense. If your ancestor died in 1910, do not conclude that a person with the same name who arrived in New York City aboard a ship in 1920 is your ancestor back from the grave. There are thousands of people who share the same name, but who are not related to one another. Research itself can be a very tedious process, and if not done correctly, and with a bit of thought and a large measure of critical thinking, can yield disastrous results.

IS ALSACE-LORRAINE JUST ANOTHER NAME FOR THE BAS-RHIN? When we talk about "Alsace-Lorraine" here in the United States, we are referring to three separate and distinct districts in France. Alsace is made up of two parts: the Bas-Rhin or Lower Rhine region, which geographically sits atop the Haut-Rhin or upper Rhine region. Lorraine, on the other hand, is situated to the west of Alsace, and is made up of the regions of Moselle, Meurthe-et-Moselle, Vosges and Meuse. There are many surnames which are unique to Lorraine which one does not often see in the Bas-Rhin whose residents were more faithful to their Germanic roots. While standard Jewish surnames like "Abraham," "Bloch," "Jacob," "Levy," "Salomon," "Samuel," "Simon," and "Weill" are common to all regions, names like "Altroff," "Amsel" "Coblentz," "Dennery," "Jochil," "Lion," "Morhange," "Picard (Bickart), "Tuteur," and "Zins" are peculiar to Lorraine. You may also, with some exceptions, see "Cahen, "Caen," "Cain"" or "Kahen," in Lorraine, while "Kahn" or "Cahn" is the usual spelling in Alsace."

JEWISH SURNAMES IN FRANCE .Before 1808 relatively few Jewish families in France used a surname. This was almost universally true in the Bas-Rhin, and to a much lesser degree in the Haut-Rhin and in Lorraine. A Jewish boy or girl would be given a first name and then use the first name of his/her father as a second name to distinguish him/her from all other persons using that first name. So a boy born "Feisel" to Baruch Isaac would be known as "Feisel Baruch." On 20 July 1808 the Emperor Napoleon promulgated a law which was known as the "Décret de Bayonne." All Jews living in France were required, within three months from the law's publication, to take and to register a first and last (family) name, at the local Town Hall. Heads of households were permitted to register themselves, their wives and children. Those Jews who were already using last names were not exempt from this law, and were required to report as well, and to put their names on the record. No one was allowed to take a family name from the Old Testament, or to use the name of a town as their family name, except those who had used those names before the law was written, and were well-known by that name. Moreover, any Jew immigrating to France, who did not have a fixed family name, was required to take a name within three months of arriving in the country.

Each town preserved a record of Jews who had formally adopted surnames in 1808. This list was kept with all the other civil records at the Town Hall. The *Recueil des déclarations de prise de nom patronymique des Juifs du Bas-Rhin en 1808*, was published in 1999 by the Cercle de Généalogie Juive, and edited by the late Pierre Katz. These volumes contain a collection of records from each town in the Bas-Rhin that had taken this census of the Jewish families who were residents there. What is singularly important is that these lists provided not only the newly adopted first and last name, but the old name used by the person before 1808, his/her relationship to the head of household, and, occasionally, even a date of birth. The following are two examples of why this collection of records with both sets of names might be important when doing research:

(1) In the town of *Bischheim*, Baruch Isaac, head of household, registered his first name as "Baruch" and took the family name "Fleischmann." His wife, Scheinel Kahn, took the first name "Jeannette" and kept the last name "Kahn" as it had formerly been used as a surname by her father. Baruch and Jeannette had two children, a son, formerly known as "Feisel Baruch," who became "Ulric Fleischmann," and a daughter, "Reichel Baruch," who took the name "Rosette Fleischmann." Since these children were born before 1808,

their births would have been recorded using their former names, so looking for the name "Fleischmann" would have produced no results.

(2) The birth certificate of **LEON BLUM** from *Bischheim*, who was born in 1815 listed his mother's name as "Breinel Levi." Since he was born that early in the century, it was probable that his father, Marx Blum, and mother, Breinel Levy, would be listed in the 1808 Jewish name-taking records. There were fourteen Blum families in *Bischheim* in 1808, and two men using the name "Marc" Blum. The first was Meyer Isaac who was said to be absent in the military, the second, a head of household with no children who chose the name "Marc Blum," but who was formerly "Meyer Aron." His wife's name was Pauline Kling, whose previous name had been "Breinel Gerson Levy." So the mystery of which Marc Blum was Leon Blum's father was solved, by the discovery of the mother's former name on the birth record. When Marc Blum's wife died, her death record was indexed under the name "Kling, Pauline," not "Levy, Breinel" or "Blum, Pauline." In France, unlike the United States, a woman's maiden name is, almost without exception, used on legal documents, including vital records, even after marriage.

THE PROBLEM WITH CERTAIN TOWN NAMES: There are quite a few French towns with very similar names, which can cause difficulty in trying to locate an ancestor's vital records:

BISCHHEIM is in the Bas-Rhin, BIESHEIM is in the Haut-Rhin

BOUXWILLER, a town in the Bas-Rhin, was called *BUCHSWEILER* between 1871 and 1918. The town of BUSCHWILLER is in the Haut-Rhin

INGENHEIM: There are two different towns with that name, one in the Bas-Rhin, which is very small, and another in Rheinpfalz, Germany, many of whose residents immigrated to the Gulf South. The German town is now called Billigheim-Ingenheim.

MULHAUSEN is in the Bas-Rhin and MULHOUSE is in the Haut-Rhin.

SOULTZ-SOUS-FÔRETS is in the Bas-Rhin, while SOULTZ is in the Haut-Rhin

STRASSBURG W.P. is the town of Strassburg in West Prussia (now in the Ukraine). This is not the same as *STRASBOURG*, Bas-Rhin, France. The Prussian town was founded by Alsatians fleeing from the destruction that the Napoleonic Wars had brought to their homeland.

WINTZENHEIM-KOSCHERBERG is in the Bas-Rhin, while WINTZENHEIM is in the Haut-Rhin.

IS THE BAS-RHIN IN FRANCE OR GERMANY? In the 1850, 1860 and 1870 federal census records our ancestors from the Bas-Rhin usually indicated that they had been born in "France." Occasionally they used the designation "Alsace," "Alsace-Lorraine," and very infrequently "Bas-Rhin" or "Lower Rhine Region." After France's defeat by Germany at the conclusion of the Franco-Prussian War in May 1871, many former residents of the Bas-Rhin, when questioned by an American census enumerator in 1880, 1900 or 1910, stated that they had been born in Germany even if they had actually been born in the Bas-Rhin at a time when it was a part of France. A few, however, continued to use France as their place of birth. After the return of the Bas-Rhin to France at the conclusion of World War I, its former residents usually said that they had been born in France.

Because Alsace was both a part of France, and later a part of Germany, many town names in the Bas-Rhin have both German and French spellings. Some can be very different. Town names ending in the French "house," in German will be spelled with a final "hausen" For example, Schweighouse is the French spelling, while Schweighausen is the German version. French town names ending in "willer" become "weiler" in German. Ingwiller became Ingweiler after 1871. Beware of the town of Marmoutier, however as the German spelling is "Maursmünster!" The village of Obernai, originally Obereinheim in 1784, became Obernai ca. 1808 and remained so until 1871, when it reverted back to the name Obereinheim. At the conclusion of World War I it was once again Obernai. Similarly the village of *Niedernai* became *Niedereinheim* during the time that it was a part of Germany. We have provided both French and German spellings in the index of towns in the Bas-Rhin which appear in this book.

FRENCH CIVIL RECORDS 1787-1815: So many researchers, especially novices, are confused when they see a reference to their

German ancestor having been born in France between 1797 and 1815. Many towns and villages in the Rheinpfalz region, which is now a part of Germany, were under French control following the French Revolution until the Congress of Vienna in 1815. The author's own ggg-grandmother, Mindel Löb, was born in one of these towns: Heiligenmoschel, commune of Niederkirschen, canton of Otterberg, Département of Mont Tonnerre, France. Her birth was registered on 11 June 1806, in a document, written in French. Technically she was born in France. In 1815 her birth town, Heiligenmoschel, reverted back to German control as part of the Rheinpfalz, where it remains today.

THE TROUBLE WITH TOMBSTONES: When examining tombstones for clues about our Jewish ancestors, it is wise to note that the information written on them is not always correct. This is true especially for dates of birth which may be off from a few days to several years. Fortunately those who immigrated after the Franco-Prussian War in 1871 seem to have been more accurate with their dates of birth. Towns of birth may also be incised on tombstones in error, and are often misspelled. Either the surviving relative did not know the town, or mistook the last location their immigrant ancestor had lived for his town of birth. As for the date of death, which one would think should be correct, be advised that occasionally the date of interment is used instead. Verify the date of death on a tombstone by searching for a date of death on a death certificate, in a published obituary, or in the Social Security Death Index where applicable. To summarize: grave marker information is not always written in stone. Take a look at the photos starting on page 397 and you will see what I mean.

NAMES AND THEIR PITFALLS: Given names are very susceptible to change, this is especially true for females, although it does happen occasionally to men. Many immigrants changed their first names, some multiple times, before coming to America. My ggg-grandmother was born Mindel Löb. In 1808 the name she was given was "Marthe Dalsheimer." She was married to Salomon Lehmann in Lembach using the name "Amalie Dalsheimer." In the 1851 census at Lembach, she was enumerated as "Minette Thalsheimer." When she was shipwrecked and died, the name on the manifest was "Nina Lehmann." "Pauline" Bloch was born in *Mertzwiller* as "Caroline" Bloch, enumerated in 1851 as "Jeanne" Bloch, and finally in 1861 as "Pauline" Bloch. Jacob Levy ran away from home, came to America and, taking his mother's maiden name, became Jacob Mayer. Later he Americanized his first name from Jacob to John, becoming John Mayer. Such changes make the search for an ancestor extremely difficult, and are more common than one might think. When it doubt about a person's first name it is always best to check the census records which are available for most all the towns in the Bas-Rhin for the years 1819, 1836, 1841, 1846, 1851, 1856, 1861, and 1866. These records are located on-line, and may be searched free of charge at the Archives départementales du Bas-Rhin [Departmental archives of Bas-Rhin] (ADBR), Listes nominatives numérisées du Bas-Rhin–Ellenbach [digitized census enumerations of Bas-Rhin–Ellenbach] They are located at: http://population.bas-rhin.fr/ellenbach/index.php. Unfortunately there may be one or more of each census year missing for each town. Be aware that the 1819 census, if there is one, is similar to the early U.S. census records between 1790-1840. It lists only heads of household and the number of people living there broken down by sex and age. The Jewish name-taking records for 1808 are an invaluable tool and the originals appear on-line with the vital records at http://archives.bas-rhin.fr/ . In 2000 the Cercle de Généalogie Juive published *Les Communautés Juives du Bas-Rhin en 1851 relevés du recensement de 1851*, compiled by Pierre Katz. The author extracted a list of the Jewish families from the original 1851 town censuses, which are now on-line. There is also an index of surnames at the end of the volume, and the name of each town where this surname appears. The book, and especially the index, is an invaluable tool because it provides the researcher with a short-cut to finding a surname of interest in 1851, without having to plough through the entire census on-line. Both the 1851 Jewish Census of the Bas-Rhin as well as the two volume 1808 name taking census are available for purchase on-line at www.genealoj.org/fr.

DOUBLE LETTERS: In the nineteenth century little attention was paid to whether a name was spelled with a single or double "N" or "L" at the end. Is it Heyman or Heymann; Kaufman or Kaufmann, Weil or Weill, Seligman or Seligmann? It is best to pay little attention to the single or double letter problem and think only of a name's pronunciation, not how it is spelled. There is a similar problem with the given name "Aron" or "Aaron" which may also appear as a surname. As for "Kaufman," also used as both given and surname, while the single or double "n" is a problem, the "f" can appear either as a single or double letter as well.

GIVEN AND SURNAMES: The following are some other given and surnames which have alternate spellings. It is worth noting that when examining original vital records on-line you will see that many of the Jewish men reporting births, deaths, and marriages, especially before 1850, signed in Hebrew, not French. Since local civil recorders in the Bas-Rhin were seldom Jewish themselves, they often took information down from the father, who did not how to write in any language other than Hebrew. Ultimately, the town's recorder simply wrote what he heard, and adopted a spelling which he thought was correct. Hence, there are many variations in spelling even the simplest of names. "Levy," for example, is often written "Levi," or "Lewi." On the whole such small differences in spelling do not matter. It is even common to find slightly different spellings of the same name within the same family group. American census takers and transcribers were faced with similar difficulties, and could often become very creative. Faced with people speaking many different languages, many of whom could not read or write, the census taker simply wrote down what he heard. Twentieth-century transcribers of these records, many of which have faded over time, were left to try to interpret what they saw written down, sometimes in a handwriting that was bordering on illegible. The following are some names that always cause problems.

BAER is a simple name but can be spelled variously as BER, BAER, BIER, BEER, BAEHR and BEHR in France as well as in the United States. American census takers and those who transcribe their work can be even more creative. Samuel Baer was transcribed as Samuel "Bau" in one on-line record. When searching for a name like "Baer," it is sometimes better to search a first name, or the first name of a spouse or child. If faced with a common first name, add, an approximate date of birth, or country of origin.

BLOCH is often anglicized as "Block." Unfortunately it is more often than not, transcribed in error as "Black" which can make a search more difficult because it does not show up when using a "soundex" search.

BOLLACK is sometimes spelled "Pollack" here in America as well as in France.

BRAUN: Because the German and French pronunciation for this name sounds like "Brown" it is often spelled as "Brown" in American census and vital records. This makes searching "Braun" difficult because of the huge number of "Brown" families there are in the United States.

CAROLINE is a very popular name in the Bas-Rhin. You cannot always depend upon the Caroline you find in Louisiana to have been born "Caroline" in her native town. She could have been born "Gertrude," or "Jeannette," "Julie," or "Henriette." Jeannette/Henriette often started out as "Hanne/Hanna, or even "Anne." Females are very likely to change their names, or have them changed for them. You can often spot these name changes according to the ages given for the children in a particular family as you go through the various census records taken at five year intervals between 1836-66.

CERF or HIRSCH: Cerf is the French word for "deer," while HIRSCH is the German equivalent. These names are sometimes used interchangeably in records. Samuel Cerf Netter may also be known as Samuel Hirsch Netter. Both "Hirsch" and "Cerf" are common surnames in the Bas-Rhin. When searching for "Hirsch" in American census records look for "Hirsh," "Hersch," "Hersh," or even "Kirsch." "Cerf" may be transcribed as "Serf."

DAHLMAN also appears in France as THALMAN. The final "n" may be single or double at the whim of the recorder.

DALSHEIMER may also appear as "Thalsheimer," "Dalheimer," or "Thalheimer" in France. It is sometimes simplified to "Dalsimer" in America.

FLEISCHMAN may be written and/or indexed in American census records as "Fleshman," "Flashman," or "Flyschmann." The final "n" may be single or double.

GODCHAUX or GOUDCHAUX: The first spelling is more common to the Haut-Rhin region. The second is more commonly found in the Bas-Rhin. In France this name can have any number of spellings: GOTSCHO, GUTHSCHO, GUTSCHAUX, GUTSCHLER, GUTSCHER, GOUTSCHO, GUTSCHO, GOTTSCHALK. In Louisiana, the spellings may be equally inventive; Godcheany is probably the most unusual. The Leon "Godchaux" family who were immigrants to New Orleans from the Lorraine region of France, became very rich and well-known. The Leopold "Goudchaux" family, originally from Brumath, Bas-Rhin, who inhabited Central Louisiana, were often thought to be related, but were not. Furthermore, because of the prominence of the "Godchaux" family, the "Goudchaux" family often had the initial "u" stricken from the spelling of their surname by those transcribing census data or by civil registrars recording vital records.

HENRIETTA, which is "HENRIETTE" in French, is often found spelled the French way in Louisiana records. There are many nicknames associated with "Henrietta," the most common one being "Harriet." However, "Hattie," "Ettie," "Nettie," and "Retta," may also be found.

HEYMAN may be spelled with a single or double "n". The name itself, in American census records, may also appear as "Hayman," "Heiman," or "Hyman."

JACOB often appears as JACQUES in French records. Many men originally called "Jacob" adopted "Jacques" as their name in Louisiana.

KAHN may be spelled CAHN, so when searching the Bas-Rhin indices (Tables Décennales) look under "Cahn" as well as "Kahn." Such a simple name can cause trouble for census takers in America. "Kahn" may be found in census transcriptions and other vital records as "Kalm," "Kann," "Conn," "Cann," or even "Chan." Several members of the "Kahn" family from Schirrhoffen adopted the spelling "Cohn," in Louisiana which was occasionally misspelled as "Cohen."

KLOTZ appears in French records occasionally as "Glotz." This spelling is rarely, if ever, used in Louisiana.

LEON, is a simple first name, but is often spelled or transcribed as "Lean" in American census records which makes it difficult to find. Many a "Leon" was born "Leopold" or even "Lion" in the Bas-Rhin. If the old Hebrew equivalent was used, look for "Leyser" or "Leiser." Many who bore the name "Leopold" shortened it to "Leon" or even "Leo after coming to America.

MARX as a first name often appears in its French version, "Marc," in French records. In America this name may appear also as "Marcus,"

"Mark," "Marks," or "Max." As a surname "Marx" may also appear as "Marks."

MAYER, MEYER as both a given or surname are often used interchangeably, especially in American census records, making it tricky to find the right person. Often the family itself, who may have started out as "Meyer" in France will become "Mayer" in Louisiana, or vice versa. Sometimes even members of the same family will use different versions of this name, which may also appear transcribed in some records as "Meier" or "Myer."

MATILDA is usually spelled in the French way as "Mathilde," or even "Mathilda" in Louisiana. The nickname "Tillie" is quite often found, replacing the full formal name.

MOÏSE is the French equivalent of MOSES or MOSE and is seen frequently in Louisiana records.

MOOG is also spelled MOOK in French records, and over the years some families have adopted the spelling MOCH or MOCK.

POLLACK and BOLLACK are variations of the same name. When searching indices both spellings should be checked.

UHRY is a fairly common name in the Bas-Rhin and has a variety of spellings: "Uri," "Uhri," "Ury," "Ori," or "Oury." In America it is most often spelled "Uhry."

WEIL presents a few problems of its own. Because there is no "w" sound in the French language, the name "Weil" is pronounced "Veil." American census takers have been known to write the name with a "v." This was especially true in earlier censuses when the person offering the information might not have been able to spell. "Weil" may also be spelled with a double "l." While there are some families who differentiate the two spellings, many use either. Both spellings are used by civil recorders or census takers at their own whim.

WEISS is often spelled "Weis" or even "Wise" especially in American census records. In French birth records the name appears either with a single or double "s" according to the choice of the recorder, or the parent.

WELSCH, which was a surname of many Jewish families in the Bas-Rhin, was often changed by Louisiana census enumerators to "Welsh." Some families eventually adopted this new spelling, dropping the "c" for convenience.

DEATH RECORDS IN LOUISIANA: New Orleans death records start in 1804, but are only sporadic until the early 1850s. The keeping of death records in the Louisiana parishes did not become mandatory until 1914, but church and cemetery records can provide information for the nineteenth century. Obituaries which appeared in New Orleans and local parish newspapers can also fill in that gap. While many death records and tombstone transcriptions are now available on-line, there have been times in Louisiana's history when it was simply impossible to find out the fate of one's ancestor. Record keeping, even in New Orleans, was difficult during the Civil War 1861-1865. Moreover, the years when there were large outbreaks of yellow fever presented the most challenges. Many of the immigrants from the Bas-Rhin contracted yellow fever, which the local creole population called the "stranger's disease." While scientific research eventually pinpointed its insect-borne source, the disease was a mystery to the average nineteenth century inhabitant of Louisiana. It was not always the fatal malady that everyone suspected. Many local residents had had very mild forms of the illness in childhood which had gone unnoticed. Even this mildest form provided antibodies that immunized that person from ever falling prey to the sickness again. Consequently, recent immigrants from Europe, who had never had an "immunization," were ordinarily the first persons to fall ill, hence the name "strangers" disease. It may often be difficult to ascertain if an ancestor succumbed to yellow fever. Occasionally it was inscribed on the person's tombstone. The names of victims who died were also often listed in the daily papers. In years when the outbreaks were particularly virulent, especially 1853 and 1878, the disease often outran peoples' ability to accurately record it. In some cases mass graves had to be dug and the dead were buried without regard to religion. There have been cases when a victim's family would chose to spirit the body out of the city to be interred in some small town cemetery just so that person could be laid to rest according to his religion and with a proper memorial.

Since many Jewish men started out in Louisiana as peddlers, travelling on foot or horseback from town to town in the outlying parishes, it is worth noting that some may have died far from any town or village. The weather and terrain were vastly different from conditions back in France. Diseases such as cholera, dysentery, diphtheria and other fevers were common. Many young men simply disappeared. Some drowned in the many rivers, streams, and bayous. Nineteenth century local Louisiana newspapers frequently carried stories of the discovery of the body of an unidentified person on a riverbank, in a bayou or wooded area. The remains were usually buried in the local churchyard without any attempt at identification.

HOW TO SEARCH FEDERAL CENSUS RECORDS: Expect any possible spelling of your ancestor's name (especially a phonetic representation), and check a record no matter how unsure you are that it might be his/hers. Due to a high degree of illiteracy, names were often spelled according to how the census taker thought they should be written, not how the person being questioned thought his name should be spelled, if he could have actually spelled it. The questioning of people with heavy foreign accents often resulted in surprising interpretations of the actual surname. While census enumerators were often guilty of spelling a name inaccurately, the twentieth century transcriptions were many times done by people unfamiliar with foreign names, leading to more confusion. It is important to note that the original 1870 census was so replete with errors that it was taken a second time. Unfortunately the second version was not much better.

Children from a first marriage were not always listed with the correct surname. They were often enumerated under the step-father's last name. Hyphenated last names may appear indexed under the first or second name in the hyphenation, so look for both. If you cannot locate someone using the last name, try their first name, the first name of the wife or the children. Start with the most unusual given name, as looking for Mary, for example, in the 1900 census in a particular state is an overwhelming task. If the name is too common try narrowing it down by including a place of birth and/or a year of birth, choosing a window of two to five years if using the latter. Always be aware that the person giving the information to the census taker, may not know or remember the most accurate details about other family members living in the same household. Expect a lot of mistakes, because there are usually many of them.

The following is an example of a search for a New Orleans resident with a hyphenated name at *Ancestry.com*: I was unable to find

Ulysse Haim Lopez-Silva in the 1870 federal census. Nothing came up for Lopez-Silva or for the names "Lopez" or "Silva" individually. I did a soundex search for Ulysse, and found Ulysse Sylvain a forty-five-year old book keeper from France. Looking at the record I found, Mr. "Sylvain" living with his thirty-six-year-old wife, Celia, a native of France, a twelve-year-old daughter, Celia, a nine-year-old son, Edward, and two more daughters: four-year-old, Lydia, and two-year-old Leah. I already knew the names and ages of the Lopez-Silva children who were all listed in the "New Orleans, Louisiana Birth Records Index, 1790-1899" at *Ancestry.com*. I recognized that the last four entries listed in the "Sylvain" household were, in fact, the Lopez-Silva children, based upon their first names and their respective ages. With the exception of "Ulysse" and "Leah," the first names were not, however, spelled accurately. Ulysse's age matched the age given in the 1860 census, plus ten years. His wife's name, "Clelie" was close, but not correct, but her age was accurate. She was thirty-six in the 1870 census and twenty-six in the 1860 census. Charles Salomon, a child from her first marriage, was not in the 1870 census because he had died in 1864. He had been enumerated in the 1860 census as Charles Silva, using his step-father's surname. The first child, Celia, age 12, I knew from records was "Sarah Zelia" born in 1858. She had appeared as two-year-old Zelia in the 1860 census. The next child, Edward, said to be nine years old, was the Edouard (French spelling) listed in the 1860 census as being one year old. The slight age discrepancy was not unusual for the time. Four-year-old Lydia was "Lilie Mariam," born to the couple in 1866. The last child, two-year-old Leah, born in 1868 had been registered in the "New Orleans, Louisiana Birth Records Index, 1790-1899" with the same name and spelling as the census record. Ulysse "Sylvain" was unquestionably Ulysse Haim Lopez-Silva listed with his wife and four surviving children.

HOW TO NAVIGATE SHIP'S RECORDS: If your Jewish immigrant ancestor came between 1830 and 1845 he/she was likely to have entered the U.S. at New York. From 1845 through to the beginning of the Civil War in 1861, he/she was more likely to have come directly to New Orleans. During and after the Civil War, he/she probably came into the port of New York. There are, of course, many exceptions to that, so it is vital to search both New York and New Orleans records. Early entries, before the late 1880s rarely give us much more than a name, age, sex, occupation and place of origin. Many times the information was incorrect or incomplete. Since many early immigrants could not spell their names, a phonetic representation of what the person who recorded the information had heard at the time was entered on the ship's manifest. When those manifests were made available on-line, transcribers often lent to the confusion by writing down their own interpretation of what had been written many years previously. It takes a lot of patience to find even the simplest name. Once you have found a likely candidate you will be frustrated to know that it is many times impossible to know with one hundred percent certainty that you have found the right person. If you find a pair of siblings, or a whole family who immigrated together you canbe confident of your information. Before you start searching for a ship's record it is better to try to get an approximate date of arrival from other sources. Such information was commonly given in the 1900 and 1910 federal censuses, if your ancestor lived long enough to have been recorded at the time. Naturalization records and passport applications may also yield clues to the year of immigration, although there are many errors and omissions contained within those records as well. I was amazed at how often information about the date of arrival and name of the ship was recorded incorrectly on an immigrant's later application for a U.S. passport. When searching ships' records it is sometimes necessary, to leave out everything except an approximate date of arrival, or birth date and a last name due to the incredible number of spelling errors contained within the records themselves and their subsequent transcriptions. Passenger arrivals beginning in the late 1880s are much more informative and usually give the destination of the immigrant as well as the name and location of a relative who would welcome him to America. The record may even give the last place the immigrant lived in France, as well as his nearest relative. It can often take a very long time to find the exact search parameters which will lead you to that missing ship's record. So do not be discouraged. Keep looking periodically until the mystery is solved.

WHEN ALL THAT IS LEFT IS SUPPOSITION: There are occasions when an ancestor, having been in America for such a short time, has left you nothing but a tombstone, if you are lucky. This was the case of several members of the BLUM family from *Bischheim*. Leon Blum, his wife, Mathilde, and five of their children came to Louisiana during or after one of the most difficult times in its history, the Civil War. Three of the seven family members died in 1867. The last French civil record for the Blum family at *Bischheim* was the August, 1861 birth of their son, Samuel, scarcely four months after the start of the American Civil War. Although news did not travel very fast in those days, it was highly unlikely that Leon would have taken his wife and five children into a war zone, so I suspected that Leon might have immigrated during the final days of the conflict, and his family had followed soon after. I found a tax assessment record at *Ancestry.com* for a Leon Blum, working as a retail dealer in Opelousas, St. Landry Parish, LA, ca. June 1865. Since the name Leon Blum was not one of those unique combinations of names, I could not be certain if it was Leon Blum from *Bischheim*. Moreover tax records did not include the age or birthplace of those who paid taxes making a positive identification impossible. There was a ship's record for a Leon Blum who arrived in New York by himself from Le Havre on 15 May 1865 aboard the vessel *Europe*. There was also a Leon Blum working in Donaldsonville, Ascension Parish, LA, dated 1866, which listed him as a retail dealer in town. Since I knew that Leon Blum from *Bischheim* died in Donaldsonville in 1867, I was certain I was on the right track. Because the ship's record showed that he had come alone, when did his wife and children arrive? Two children, who lived to be adults, indicated, in different state census records, different households, and different years, that they had immigrated in 1866. Since their parents and a sibling died in 1867, only a year later, it would seem that the time of their immigration to Louisiana, followed by three such tragedies would have been etched in their minds. Unfortunately using every surname spelling, and the first name of each person immigrating, I was unable to find any ship's record for the arrival of Leon's wife and children. Using the information I had, I reconstructed their American lives as follows: Leon immigrated in May 1865, travelled to New Orleans, spent perhaps a few months at Opelousas, then moved on to Donaldsonville, where he welcomed his family in 1866. He died in May 1867. His wife died in October 1867. Ten days later, one of his children, an eleven-year-old son, died as well. The four remaining children were sent to the Jewish Widow's and Orphan's Home in New Orleans. See entry for **LEON BLUM** from *Bischheim* for further details.

ON-LINE RESOURCES are the first place to go to begin researching your family. *Ancestry.com*, a subscription site, as well as *Familysearch.org*, and *Rootswweb.com* which are free, are the three major genealogical sources that I use on a daily basis. There are, however, some specialty sites which you will find to be invaluable as you continue your research:

Archives départementales du Bas-Rhin [departmental archives of Bas-Rhin] (ADBR), État civil numérisé du Bas-Rhin-Adeloch [digitized civil registrations of Bas-RhinAdeloch] (http://archives.bas-rhin.fr/index.php)

If your French is poor, here is how to work with these records: After you access the web address, look down at the bottom of the page and check the box after the phrase "J'accepte ces conditions." A new screen will appear. Single left click onto "Accéder à la version graphique." An on-screen typewriter will appear. Using your mouse, enter the name of the town in the Bas-Rhin whose records you wish to access. Single left click onto each letter, until the whole name appears above. Once it does, a single left click on the whole name will bring up a screen which resembles a bookshelf. At the bottom there is a slide bar. With your mouse, move the slide bar to the area with the maroon color. You will see volumes labeled "TD" (Tables Décennales or Ten Year Tables) with the years covered at the bottom. The volumes usually start with 1793-An X,* An XI-1812, 1813-1822, 1823-1832 and so on. If a volume is missing it will be in a light color, not the dark maroon of the volumes containing the information. Double left click onto the volume you would like to access. These Ten Year indices are arranged with "births" (naissances) first, listed in alphabetical order by last name. Occasionally some of the larger towns will break the entries down by year for each letter of the alphabet. Following the births are "marriages" (mariages), and finally, "deaths" (décès). Note: there is a peculiarity with the 10 year tables for 1863-1872. Because of the French defeat in the Franco-Prussian War, the Bas-Rhin fell into German hands. Consequently the 1863-1872 index may be divided into two parts. Births, marriages and deaths which occurred between 1863-1870 are indexed first, followed by births, marriages and deaths that occurred in 1871-72. To look through any volume, you may go page by page using the right-pointing arrow to go forward, and the left-pointing arrow to go backwards. Once you have found the name of the person for whom you are looking, the date of the document will appear after his/her name. Jot down the date, then, at the top of the screen you will see tabs. Left-click onto the one labeled "retour." This will bring you back to the volumes. Use the slide bar at the bottom of the screen to see the single year volumes. Each year will have at least four volumes. The first labeled "N" is the births for that year. The second is marked "PM" and contains marriage banns and other paperwork given by the married couples. The third is labeled "M" and is the volume containing the marriage records. The fourth volume is marked "D," and contains the deaths for that year. Double click onto the volume you wish to open. Turn the pages using the arrow at the bottom or else the slide bar which is faster if you are searching for a record which occurred towards the end of the month. You may manipulate any of the open pages by placing your mouse on the image, holding the left click down. If you wish to print a record, look at the tabs at the top. The first one is marked "imprimer" Center the record that interests you on the screen and left-click on "imprimer." A white screen will appear with the record you wish to print. You may manipulate its position using your mouse until it is visible the way you want it to appear on the page. You may, if you wish, annotate your document by typing in the white area labeled "annoter votre document." Left-click onto "valider" to print your document. After printing, you can return to the original screen by left-clicking onto "retour." Note: You cannot download any of the images. You must print them if you wish to have a copy.

* Note: When you see years designated by roman numerals, you are dealing with the French Revolutionary Calendar which was adopted in 1793 and used until the end of 1805 in France, lasting almost thirteen years. In order to distance the new French Republic, which was highly secularized and virulently anti-Catholic, from its dependence on the Gregorian calendar established by the church, the Revolutionary government invented a new calendar with ten-day weeks called "decades," and twelve months, with the year starting on 22 September. Each month consisted of three decades. The days of the week were: primidi, duodi, tridi, quartidi, quintidi, sextidi, septidi, octidi, nonidi and décadi. The months were: Vendémiaire, Brumaire, Frimaire, Nivôse, Pluviôse, Ventôse, Germinal, Floréal, Prairial, Messidor, Thermidor and Fructidor. Five supplementary days were added at the end of Fructidor and a sixth extra day, called the "Jour de la Révolution" was added each leap year. Napoleon abolished this calendar in September 1805 and the country reverted back to the Gregorian calendar on 1 January 1806. Unfortunately these date from the Revolutionary calendar were used in records between 1793-1805. There is a Republican/Gregorian Calendar converter at:
http://www.napoleon.org/en/essential_napoleon/calendar/index.asp
It explains the Republican calendar concept, its "décades" and months. It also lists every day of the year, each of which was given a different name. This calendar, as you can see by names of each month, was based on the cycles in nature, with the beginning of the year starting at

the autumn equinox. To use the converter, type in the "Republican" date, for example: 12 floréal, an XII and click onto "Gregorian" and you will see that it was equivalent to 2 May 1804.

Archives départementales du Bas-Rhin [departmental archives of Bas-Rhin] (ADBR), Listes nominatives numérisées du Bas-Rhin–Ellenbach [digitized census enumerations of Bas-Rhin–Ellenbach] http://population.bas-rhin.fr/ellenbach/index.php
These census records work exactly the same way as the vital records above. After you access the town you need, you will see volumes marked with the years 1819-1836-1841-1846-1851-1856-1861-1866. Many towns do not have records for 1819, in which case the volume will be gray in appearance. All volumes which have records will be black. The records for 1880 and 1885 were unavailable at the time the others were digitized, but may be added later. The handwriting on these records may be challenging, but the ability to enlarge the records using the "plus" icon next to the magnifying glass make things easier to decipher. There are no indices, so you must search for a family page by page. Remember that these census records include everyone who lived in the town, not just Jewish residents.

Findagrave.com has literally millions of entries, and many photos of actual tombstones. It was started in 1995. Anyone may contribute information and photos. Always double check any printed information accompanying the entries, as errors do creep into it. As has been pointed out before, dates of birth and death recorded on tombstones are not necessarily accurate. It is always best to double check by consulting a civil birth or death record.

Fold3.com Is subscription only, but may be accessed as well by purchasing an all-inclusive membership from *Ancestry.com*. Fold-3 specializes in military documents. Civil War documents are especially well represented. Even if your Jewish ancestor did not serve in the Civil War, he may appear in either the Union or Confederate Citizens' files if he sold goods to the army, or if he petitioned an army officer in writing on behalf of himself, another person, a cause, or complaint.

Fulton History.com, managed by Tom Tryniski, can be very useful if your Louisiana relative eventually moved to New York. There are thousands of pages of New York State newspapers, which are searchable. Occasionally an article which may have appeared in a Louisiana paper will be carried in a New York edition.

Genealogybank.com contains newspapers, historical documents, the Social Security Death Index, and recent obituaries It requires a subscription, but is, perhaps, the most valuable I have found, especially for Louisiana newspapers. New Orleans and Baton Rouge papers are very well represented. It is searchable by name and date and its pages may be downloaded.

Geneanet.org – While some records and searches on this site are free, you must pay the price to get the most out of it. In the long run it can be worth it, if someone before you has researched a family which interests you. Since most of the contributors are French, it is likely that they will not have tracked down someone who has immigrated to America, but it is helpful for finding parents and grandparents of immigrants. If you find an ancestor at *Geneanet.org*, and his town of birth is included, your next step is to go to the original record on-line to verify the information.

Italiangen.org is a free website which is not only for people of Italian descent. It has a collection of vital records for everyone who was born, married or died in the five boroughs of New York City during the periods indicated at the website. By using information given there, it is possible to order vital records from the city of New York. It usually takes five to six weeks to get a document back from them.

Jewishgen.org has free access to most of its data. The on-line burial registry (JOBR) may be the most helpful. (The JOBR is also accessible through *Ancestry.com*, although ancestry requires a subscription.) Jewishgen also has many family trees which are available to search as well as specialized mailing lists called "sigs" (special interest groups) You may wish to register for the French and Early American lists at: http://www.jewishgen.org/JewishGen/sigs.htm You will receive daily posts and may submit questions to the list.

Newspapers.com is a subscription-only newspaper site, which may also be accessed through *Ancestry.com* if you elect to get an all-inclusive membership. It has some newspapers that are not available at *Genealogybank.com*.

SWLR (*Southwest Louisiana Records, 1750-1900*) compiled by Rev. Donald J. Hébert may be purchased by single volumes or in CD-ROM form. The many volumes of Rev. Hébert's books, contained in the 2001 release of SWLR CD 101, have church and civil records from the current thirteen civil parishes of southwest Louisiana: Acadia (originally part of St. Landry Parish until 1886), Allen (originally part of Calcasieu Parish until 1912), Beauregard (originally part of Calcasieu Parish until 1912), Calcasieu (part of St. Landry Parish until 1840), Cameron (originally part of Calcasieu & Vermillion parishes until 1870), Evangeline (originally part of St. Landry Parish until 1901), Iberia (originally part of St. Martin & St. Mary parishes until 1868), Jefferson Davis (originally part of Calcasieu Parish until 1913), Lafayette (originally part of the old St. Martin Parish until 1823), St. Landry (established in 1805 and originally the largest parish in Louisiana), St. Martin (created in 1811 from Attakapas County and split into two parts when a surveyor's error created Iberia Parish in 1868), St. Mary (created in 1811 from Attakapas County) and Vermillion (originally part of Lafayette Parish until 1844). Although the majority of the records are from the many Catholic Churches in the region, there are also records from the various parish courthouses, where you will find marriages, successions, and occasionally even birth records of the Jewish men and women who settled in these parishes. The courthouse location, book and page numbers for each entry are included so that you will have enough information to be able to contact the various clerks of court if you wish to get a copy of the original record. Note: In 1807, soon after Louisiana was purchased from France, the eastern territory was divided into 19 parishes, with part of the southwestern half still called the neutral territory, an area disputed by Spain. There are now 64 parishes which make up the state of Louisiana. Many parish boundary changes have occurred over the years.

Google.com – When all else fails, it never hurts to "google" a name. Many things will show up if you try this search, including entries from *Ancestry.com*, *Rootsweb.com*, newspapers and periodicals. You just might find the little gem which has eluded you. If searching for a common name, try adding a place of birth or usual residence, a date of birth or death in order to narrow the field.

PART II

CASE STUDIES

While in the process of compiling this book, I concluded that it might be useful to gives some examples of the processes that I use when researching a Jewish ancestor. I have included four case studies which illustrate how a person may be found and eventually identified. Some are certainly triumphs of dogged determination. One, however, must be put aside as "yet to be solved" pending the discovery of new information.

CASE STUDY #1 - JACOB/JACQUES STEIN (*Oberlauterbach*) –I ran into problems trying to trace Jacob/Jacques Stein, although he had given his place and date of birth in a 1900 application for a U.S. passport. I found his birth record right away in *Oberlauterbach*. He was recorded as Jacques Stein born 17 November 1846 to Isaac Stein and Nanette Bloch. His birth record did not include his father's birthplace, only that his parents were residents of the town. Since Isaac was twenty-nine years old at the time of his son's birth, I looked for an Isaac Stein born ca. 1817 in *Oberlauterbach*. While "Stein" is a common name in the U.S., it is not common in the Bas-Rhin. In 1851 it appeared in census records for only eight towns. I found Isaac Stein born in *Oberlauterbach* on 2 April 1818 to Leopold Stein and Catherine Hertz. However this "Isaac Stein" may not have been Nanette Bloch's husband. I turned my attention to Nanette Bloch to find her place of birth. Bloch is a very common name in the Bas-Rhin, so a search of individual town records would have been very time-consuming. Since Nanette was already thirty years old in 1846, I hoped I could find her death record in *Oberlauterbach*. I searched for her in the "Tables Décennales" (Ten Year Tables) starting with the 1843-1852 volume containing death records. Since these were French records, even though she was married to a "Stein," she would appear in the index as "Bloch, Nanette." A woman's maiden name appears in all vital records in France, unlike here, where after marriage a woman is always known by her husband's last name. It was also possible that a variant such as "Anne" or "Hanne" might appear in lieu of "Nanette," which might make a search for her very difficult. Occasionally the compiler of the death records will include, "wife of" or "widow of" after the name. Nanette Bloch, widow of Isaac Stein, had died on March 1, 1888. Upon examining her 1888 death record I discovered that she had been born in

Trimbach. I double checked the *Trimbach* records, examining those Ten Year Tables to look for the marriage of an "Isaac Stein" to a "Nanette Bloch." In the 1843-1852 volumes I found "Anne" Bloch married to Isaac Stein. I checked the original marriage record which had taken place on 8 June 1843. Not only did it confirm that "Anne" Bloch had been born in *Trimbach*, but her groom, Isaac Stein, to my surprise, had been born in *Salmbach*, a very small town on the Franco-German border. At the time of his marriage he had been a resident of *Oberlauterbach*. The *Salmbach* records confirmed that the Isaac Stein, who married Anne Bloch, had been born there on 4 April 1817 to Jacques Stein and Caroline Weil. To double-check this information I would need to locate the death record for Isaac Stein. Since Nanette had died a widow, Isaac had to have died before her. He was listed in the Ten Year Tables as having died on 10 December 1884. His wife's name was given as "Johanna" Bloch and his parents "Jacob" Stein and "Carolina" Weill, all acceptable variants for the names previously found on other records. Looking at birth records for some of their other children, I had seen that Nanette was also known as Jeannette. She was "Anne" on her marriage certificate and "Johanna" on her husband's death certificate, names also used more or less interchangeably by our Jewish ancestors. *Oberlauterbach* had erroneously been given as Isaac Stein's birthplace on one of his children's birth records. By double-checking marriage and death records for Jacques/Jacob Stein's parents, I had avoided repeating an error that had been made by one French civil recorder. This case was closed.

CASE STUDY #2 - JULES BERNHEIM (*Kuttolsheim*) – Jules Bernheim stated in a passport application that he had been born on 28 January 1878 in *Strasbourg*, France. Unfortunately, many Alsatians will give *Strasbourg* as a place of birth, not the city of *Strasbourg*, but a geographical area called an "arrondissement," or under German rule a "Kreis," much like a county, which has many small villages within its borders. Before tackling the French records I had found Jules Bernheim's World War I draft registration which listed his next of kin as Fernand Bernheim of Lafourche Parish. I found Fernand's death record at *Ancestry.com* which gave his birth as 18 April 1875. Armed with this information I consulted the *Strasbourg* Ten Year Tables. Neither Fernand nor Jules had been born there. In the back of *Les Communautées juives du Bas-Rhin en 1851*, published by the Cercle de Généalogie Juive, there is a list of surnames, and the towns in which these names appeared. Bernheim was not a common name in the Bas-

Rhin. Using the list in the book, I searched the Ten Year Tables for 1873-1882 for each individual town where a Bernheim had lived in 1851. When I got to *Kuttolsheim*, I found both Jules and Fernand in the Ten Year Tables for 1873-1882. I looked up their individual birth records and found their parents were Gustav Bernheim and Regina Levy. My next step was to trace the parents and find out where they were born. I needed to find their parents' marriage record to ascertain their dates and places of birth. They had not been married in *Kuttolsheim*, but might have been married in the bride's home town, or in a town where both had been working. This meant that I would have to search every town for a Regina Levy marrying a Bernheim between 1863 and 1882. I had determined their approximate date of marriage working backward from the date of birth of the first known child, Ferdinand, born in 1875. Fortunately I remembered that Jules Bernheim had been living with his uncle, Simon Abraham, in Lafourche Parish in 1900. I had already found Simon Abraham and knew that he had been born in *Reichshoffen*, so I searched there to no avail. But I also knew that Simon Abraham's mother was Eve Levy from *Wingersheim*. Hoping that there was a connection between Eve and Regina Levy, I searched the *Wingersheim* Ten Year Tables and found a 25 February 1868 marriage for Emmanuel Bernheim and Rachel Levy. The names were close, but was it a match? I located the marriage record and found that the groom's full name was Emmanuel Goetsch Bernheim and he had been born in *Kuttolsheim*. His bride, Rachel Levy, was a native of *Wingersheim*. The fact that Rachel also used the name Regina was not unusual. Many girls called Rachel adopted the name "Regina," "Régine," or "Reine." Contained in the marriage record was Emmanuel's date of birth, 11 January 1837, so I looked up his birth record in Kuttolsheim. He had been born Emmanuel Goetsch Bernheim to Emmanuel Bernheim and Marie Goetz an unmarried couple. So the only logical conclusion was that Emmanuel Goetch Bernheim was now using the name "Gustave" a French "equivalent" of his Hebrew middle name. His 1837 birth date matched approximately his age given in the birth records of his two children. This case was closed.

CASE STUDY #3 - ROSALIE LEVY (*Westhouse*) - Often in birth records, while the father's place of birth may be mentioned in his child's birth record, the mother's rarely ever is. If the couple was married in the father's home town, the wife's date and place of birth will be in the marriage record, along with the names of her parents, if they are still alive, and if not, the death dates for her parents will be given. A problem arises when there is no marriage record in the father's town of birth. The next step to take is to look for the mother's death record, which will also contain her place of birth. She will be listed under her maiden name in the Ten Year Tables. She may or may not also be identified as "the wife of" as well. However, if your subject is having children in the 1860s and 1870s chances are she will have died after 1883 where most on-line records run out, although a few have been digitized through 1912. So if you cannot find a death record, here is an alternative which helped me. Rosalie Levy, wife of Seligmann Weyl, had not been born in *Westhouse*, nor had she been married there. I had found the following children: Caroline Weyl born 31 July 1868, Marie Weyl, born 13 January 1875 and Hyeronimous (Jerome) Weyl, born 13 October 1877. I needed to find out when Rosalie and Seligmann's first child was born: I started working backwards from the first child known to me to have been born, Caroline in 1868. I did not use the Ten Year Tables, but instead went year by year going backwards from 1877. There is usually an index on the last page of each year in question. I found Simon Weyl born to the couple on 7 March 1866, then Isaias Weyl born to them on 28 April 1864 and Berthe Weyl born to them on 26 February 1863. At the time of Berthe's birth, Seligmann was twenty-nine years old and Rosalie was twenty-one. I checked for more children in 1862, 1861 and 1860, and finding none, concluded that they had to have been married between 1860 and 1862, but still did not know where. In the on-line records at http://archives.bas-rhin.fr/ there is a section before the Marriages (marked "M"), which is marked "PM" (Marriage Publications). More often than not it is missing. Luckily those for *Westhouse* were intact. The year 1862 had 58 pages of various documents pertaining to the brides and grooms, their parents, as well as a transcription of the marriage banns. Even though Seligmann and Rosalie had not been married in *Westhouse*, there had to have been banns posted in the town because it was Seligmann's place of birth. On image 30 of 58 for the year 1862, I found their banns published on the 5th and 12th of January 1862. Rosalie had been born in *Mutzig*. So I searched the Ten Year Tables for *Mutzig* to verify this information. Their marriage had taken place there on 5 February 1862. But what if the banns had not been saved at *Westhouse*? Two genealogy websites, *Geneanet.org* and *Ancestry.com*, both of which require subscriptions, may be of help. The former has thousands of French family trees submitted by amateur genealogists. Be very careful when using someone else's work and always verify information when possible by consulting the original records. While some information is accurate, some may have been copied from unreliable third parties. If no clues are unearthed at either website, take out a map of the Bas-Rhin. Locate *Westhouse*, and using it as a starting place, spiral out checking each town's Ten Year Tables for marriages taking place between 1853and 1862. This can be time consuming, and even frustrating, but had I done that, I would have had to check the Ten Year Tables in about thirty-five towns before I reached *Mutzig*, which is, after all, only about fifteen miles northwest of *Westhouse*. This case was closed.

CASE STUDY #4 – CAROLINE WEILL (*Bischheim*) - While searching at *Genealogybank.com* for subjects to include in this volume, I found a death notice in the New Orleans *Daily Picayune* for Caroline Weil, the wife of Frank Sharp. According to the brief notice which announced her death on 12 August 1909, she was a sixty-one-year-old native of *Bishsheim* [*sic*], Alsace, who had been a resident of the city for forty-three years. The names of towns in the Bas-Rhin are often misspelled in American newspaper articles, as it was here. Caroline was apparently a native of *Bischheim*. I looked for "Caroline Sharp" living in New Orleans in 1900, the last census in which she would have appeared before her death. There was no listing for a "Caroline Sharp," but I found Frank Sharp in the 1900 census index with no trouble. Frank was a sixty-year-old Hungarian immigrant, who had been married for eleven years. His wife, Carrie, was a fifty-year-old immigrant from Germany, who was the mother of one living child. There were no children, however, enumerated in the household. Frank and Carrie were living at 125 South Robertson, the address which had been mentioned in Caroline Weil's obituary as the location of her funeral. Since the couple were said to have been married for eleven years, I searched for a marriage record. There were two: the first was for Frank Sharp, who married "Widow Hy. (Henry) Cohn" on 1 August 1891, the other, for Frank Sharp, who married Caroline Weill on 1 August 1891. Both entries referred to the same record from Vol. 15, page 369 of the "New Orleans Marriage Records Index" at *Ancestry.com*. I ordered a copy from the Secretary of State, Vital Records, Baton Rouge, LA, hoping that it would include her parents' names. However it did not. So, at the suggestion of Ms. Teri Tillman, a registered genealogist, I requested the corresponding license from Baton Rouge which, unfortunately, did not give her parents' names either. It was clear, however, that Caroline had been married before. I decided to go back to the New Orleans newspaper records at

Genealogybank.com to see if I could find an article about her wedding. I did a search for "Caroline Weil," narrowing it to 1880-1899 in Louisiana and came up, not with a description of the marriage in 1891, but with an interesting bit of news. An article had appeared in the 20 February 1891 edition of the *New Orleans Daily City Item* entitled "The Bonzano Will Contest." Hubert Bonzano had died on 31 January 1891 leaving his entire estate to "Mrs. Caroline Weil." Since Hubert left no direct heirs, his siblings, contested the will, alleging that they were entitled to the estate which was valued at over $40,000. They stated that Caroline had lived with Hubert for eighteen years, and not only had he left her everything in his will, he had given property to her during his life which exceeded ten per cent of the value of the entire estate which he was not legally entitled to do. The first question I had to ask myself was whether the "Caroline Weil" who had lived with Hubert Bonzano for eighteen years was the same "Caroline Weil" who had married Frank Sharp just months after Bonzano's death. I searched for "Bonzano" in the index for the 1880 federal census for New Orleans and found fifty-three-year-old H. Bonzano living at 14 South Robertson Street with "Caroline Wild," a twenty-eight-year-old immigrant from Alsace who was his "servant." "Wild," was a common enumerator's misspelling of the name "Weill," so the only problem now remaining was how to be sure that Caroline Wild/Weil, companion of Hubert Bonzano, was the same Caroline Weill who married Frank Sharp.

An article about Bonzano's life had appeared in the New Orleans *Daily Picayune* published on 1 February 1891. Hubert was described as the leading Custom House broker at the Port of New Orleans for over half a century. Hubert had never married. He and his brother, Dr. Max Bonzano, immigrants from Swabia, Germany, had thrown in their lot early with the Union cause, and after the defeat of the Confederate army, had garnered much favor with the military government of New Orleans. At his death Hubert had controlled a major part of the Custom House and internal revenue brokerage business in New Orleans. He had also been co-owner of a sugar plantation in St. James Parish. There was no mention of his "companion," Caroline Weil in the article. A description of his funeral which appeared in the 2 February 1891 New Orleans *Daily Picayune*, listed a large number of friends who had attended the wake at 14 South Robertson. It was reported that he had been buried in Metairie

Cemetery in New Orleans. Once again there was no mention of Caroline Weill.

I had also found a real estate transfer he had made to Caroline Weill in 1883. It consisted of one lot with improvements bounded by Robertson, Canal, Claiborne and Gasquet Streets, and from its description, appeared to be his residence at 14 South Robertson. A South Robertson address sounded familiar because Caroline Weil Sharp's address had been listed as 125 South Robertson at the time of her death in 1909. I knew that street addresses had undergone a change in 1894-95, having been converted at that time to the "hundred block system." For a time the "old" addresses were used in the New Orleans city directories which were published annually. The *New Orleans City Directory* for 1895 had a listing for Frank Sharp at "old 14 South Robertson," the same address from where Hubert Bonzano had been waked. Frank Sharp, who lived at Hubert Bonzano's former address, was an auctioneer, a fact which had been mentioned in another article about his life. So Caroline Weill, companion of Hubert Bonzano, was apparently Caroline Weill, wife of Frank Sharp. The discovery of a 24 June 1893 article in the New Orleans *Daily Picayune* left no doubt as to her identity. A "peculiar robbery" had been reported at the home of Frank Sharp, auctioneer, at No. 14 South Robertson. Taken was $700 in cash, six mortgage notes, a ladies diamond wristwatch, and a man's gold watch. The robbers left behind at least $100 in cash, assorted papers and deeds, some broken jewelry worth $200, and a dozen solitaire and diamond cluster rings valued at $1000. Mrs. Sharp, it was said, had always kept her jewelry in a safe deposit box at the local bank, but several months previously, had removed it and put it in an iron safe at home for which, it seems, everyone in the household had access to the key. Living there at the time was Mrs. Sharp's sister and nephew, as well as the owners of the residence. Mrs. Sharp had first accused her husband, then her nephew of the theft, and the detectives sent to investigate doubted that a burglary had even been committed. The last paragraph of the article identified Mrs. Sharp as the "widow" of M.H. Bonzano, the "custom-house broker," who at the time of his death had left her much of his fortune.

Since Caroline Weill's companion, Hubert Bonzano, and husband, Frank Sharp, were men of means, I thought I might find copies of their wills. The Jesus Christ of Latter Day Saints "LDS" website, *Familysearch.org*, which charges no fee, had put the "Orleans

Parish, Louisiana, Will Books 1805-1920" on line in 2013. I knew that Hubert Bonzano had died in January 1891, so I located his name in the index for Volume 24 which contained wills filed between 1889 and 1891. Hubert had bequeathed all his effects, real and personal "to my faithful and beloved friend Caroline Weill, native of Bischheim, near Strasburg, Alsace, and for the past twenty years, my constant attendant in sickness and health, and devoted to me to the day of my death. To her in token of my appreciation for all her constant devotion and constant care, I leave all I possess in this world to her. This is my last and only will." Caroline Weil presented the will to the civil district court judge on 4 February 1891 where it was declared to be valid. The contents of this will was proof positive that Caroline Weill Sharp from *Bischheim*, who died in 1909 was the same Caroline Weill, native of *Bischheim*, who had lived with Hubert Bonzano for twenty years.

Frank Sharp's will told us even more about Caroline Weill. Frank had been married before he wed Caroline, and was the father of eight children who would inherit the bulk of his estate. He had been, for many decades, an auctioneer, who sold off the estates of the deceased for the benefit of the heirs, but he was also the auctioneer for the city of New Orleans, which gave him the inside track on properties which might go up for sale for delinquent taxes. As a consequence, he owned houses and land all over the city and his wealth was estimated at half a million dollars. Two years after Caroline Weill's death, Frank had married again, no longer wanting to live with one of his daughters. He had contracted one of those May and December marriages through a local matchmaker that is so-often fodder for the press. His was no exception. On Tuesday, July 25, 1911, a headline in the New Orleans *Daily Picayune* read "Octogenarian Outwits Family and Weds Young Woman at Hotel DeSoto." Thirty-seven-year-old Sarah Forsyth who ran a small grocery store and had recently been divorced from Jacob Bernstein, had wed eighty-one-year-old Frank Sharp the previous afternoon. Frank's children were furious. None had been invited to the wedding which was performed by Rabbi Dr. Bergman. In a contract, signed several days before the nuptials, Frank had provided for a gift to his bride of $10,000 upon his death. Several weeks later the couple again made headlines when the matchmaker, Bachel Tulbowchez, demanded payment of $500 which he said he was owed for having provided Frank with a bride which according to his own wishes should neither be "rich, fat, nor tall, but rather short, pleasingly plump and, above all, young." Those requirements having been met, Bachel, the matchmaker, had only been paid $50 by the chagrined bride who had pleaded with her husband to pay the man off. Whether or not Bachel got his money may never be known. Frank died six months later on 24 February 1912. In his will he left to Sarah Forsyth, his wife, the houses at 120, 124 and 126 South Claiborne. In addition he left $500 each to Caroline Weil's brother and sisters, and $2000 to the "Jewish Orthodox Synagogue on Carondelet Street between Terpsichore and Euterpe," to be used in equal parts on the anniversary of his death and his late wife, Caroline Weil Sharp's death, to fund "kaddish" prayers (prayers for the dead). The residue of his estate, twenty-two prime New Orleans properties, was auctioned off by Ramsey and Danziger in May 1912 for the benefit of his children.

Caroline Weill's will was also on-line at *Familysearch.org*. She had predeceased her husband Frank Sharp, dying at the age of sixty-one, on 12 August 1909. In her will, filed at New Orleans on 17 August 1909, I discovered that she had left $6000 to her son, Rudolph Weil. Rudolph had never been enumerated in New Orleans with his mother either in the household of Hubert Bonzano, or of Frank Sharp. In the 1900 federal census Caroline or Frank had provided information to the census taker that she had borne one child, and that he/she was still alive. The residue of Caroline's estate went to her husband at death, Frank Sharp. The will revealed one more thing about Caroline Weil who had been the companion/wife of two powerful New Orleans residents. She was unable to write, so she had signed the document using "her ordinary mark." The question now was how to trace Rudolph Weil.

There was one more clue to mention which gave us an entrée into Caroline's early life. At the time of the infamous "robbery" in 1893, which appeared to the police to have been an "inside job," it was reported that Caroline Sharp's sister and twenty-one-year-old nephew had been living with the Sharps after having recently come to New Orleans from Mobile, AL. In my quest to unravel the life of Caroline Weill from *Bischheim*, I had sought the help of Teri Tillman, a registered genealogist. She discovered several Weill families in Mobile, Mobile Co., AL, who had been born in *Bischheim*, whom she thought might be related to Caroline. I had not seriously considered these possible connections until I read that newspaper article which identified a sister and nephew who had lived in Mobile. Moreover, I had assumed that her child's last name would be "Cohn," and that he was the son of her first husband, Henry. What had become of this man? Was Rudolph his child, or a son born out of wedlock to an unknown father? Caroline had been married to Frank Sharp as the widow of Henry Cohn. But why had she never married Hubert Bonzano, who was a single man all his life? It was time to have a look at the Mobile, AL connection.

Ms. Tillman discovered that a "Caline Ville," transcribed as "Caline Uelli, " in the 1870 federal census was living in Mobile, AL, in the household of Abram Moog. A search at *Findagrave.com* turned up quite a few burials for the Moog family at Springhill Avenue Temple Cemetery in Mobile, Al, including Aaron and Lippmann Moog whose tombstones gave their town of birth as *Niederroedern*, Bas-Rhin. Lippmann' wife, Judithe/Julie Weill's stone gave her birthplace as Bisheim [sic]. The Lippmann Moog family was also enumerated in the 1870 federal census at Mobile. If Judithe/Julie Weill was Caroline Weill's relative, then finding Caroline in the household of a Moog family in 1870 in Mobile, AL, was surely no coincidence. "Alabama Marriages 1809-1950" were available on-line at *Familysearch.org*. Ms. Tillman found a marriage record for "Caroline Weil, over 18 years old" and "Sam'l COHN" which took place in Mobile, on 7 January 1871. One of the bondsmen was "Emanuel Weill." Searching the Mobile, AL census records, Ms. Tillman had found that Emanuel Weill of *Bischheim* and his wife Rosalie had been living in Mobile at the time of the 1860 federal census. Further research determined that Judithe Weill, wife of Lippmann Moog, was Emanuel Weill's niece, born to his brother, Salomon Weill and the latter's wife, Sarah Metzger, on 18 September 1845 in *Bischheim*. Could Caroline have been Judithe/Julie Weill's older sister, and thus, another niece of Emanuel Weill? Forty-six-year-old Emanuel and his thirty-six year-old wife, Rosalie, were childless. Failing to find them in Mobile or anywhere else in 1870, the couple had reappeared in the 1880 federal census for Mobile with a fourteen-year-old "son" Rudolph Weil. At the time of this census, Emanuel was sixty-five years old and his wife, Rosalie was fifty-seven. It was unlikely that the couple, childless for so long, were Rudolph's birth parents. Emanuel Weill had been a bondsman at Caroline Weill's marriage to Samuel Cohn. Had this older couple agreed to raise Caroline's child so that she could find employment in New Orleans? If we are to believe Rudolph's date of birth as reported in 1880, he had been born ca. 1866. However the 1900 census gave his birth date as ca. 1872. Rudolph died on 12 January 1911 at forty-six years of age. All that could be said was that Rudolph was born between 1865 and 1872, probably between 1866 and 1868. Samuel Cohn, was most likely not Rudolph's father. Had Rudolph been born to her in France? Probably not, since all records for Rudolph showed that he had been born in Alabama. Efforts to find Samuel Cohn, or "Henry Cohn" as he had been identified by Caroline at the time of her 1891 marriage to Frank Sharp, were fruitless. If Cohn had died or deserted Caroline while she was living in Mobile, it is possible that she could have been living in New Orleans with Hubert Bonzano as early as 1871, after having left her son in the care of her uncle, Emanuel Weill. What is certain is that Caroline Weill rarely, if ever, had lived in the same household as her son, Rudolph.

A search of the *Bischheim* records to locate Caroline Weill's birth record proved to be even more frustrating than untangling her life in Louisiana. It was even difficult to ascertain when she had been born. The earliest American record for Caroline, the 1870 Federal census where she was living in the household of Abram Moog, gave her age as twenty-nine years. Hence she would have been born ca. 1840-1841. This might be the most reliable record, because a younger woman would have been less likely to lie about her age. Ten years later, Caroline "Wild" showed up in the 1880 federal Census for New Orleans, LA, as a twenty-eight year old servant living with Hubert Bonzano. She was said to be forty-three years old at the time of her 1891 marriage to Frank Sharp. Her date of birth was recorded as March 1850 in the 1900 federal census. When Caroline died in 1909 she was said to be sixty-one years old. Consequently all that can be said is that she had been born between 1840 and 1850 in *Bischheim*. Whether she has been born as "Caroline" Weill or had been given another name at birth created another problem. There were four girls born as "Caroline" Weil between 1839 and 1852. Caroline, born 18 September 1839 to Felix Weil and Pauline Salomon, died as "Elizabethe" Weil on 2 June 1841. Caroline, born on 24 September 1839 to Samuel Weil and Babette Stern, died on 23 January 1845. Caroline, born on 16 February 1845 to Simon Weil and Rebecca Blum, died on 3 October 1845. We were unable to trace Caroline Weill born 22 April 1852 to Barbe Weill of Ingwiller and an unknown father. However, since Caroline Weill lived amongst Weil relatives from *Bischheim* while in Mobile, AL, and was said to have a brother and sister according to Frank Sharp's 1912 will, it is doubtful that she could have been the illegitimate Caroline Weill whose mother was from another town.

Having exhausted the supply of girls born as "Caroline," we had to turn to children born as "Jeannette," "Julie," "Henriette," "Pauline," and "Marie." There were eleven candidates:

1. Jeannette Weill born 27 February 1841 to Simon Weill and Sara Uri (called Nanette in 1851).
2. Julie Weill born on 13 April 1841 to Salomon Weill and Rosette/Sara Metzger who was legitimized by their 11 Aug 1841 marriage at *Bischheim*.
3. Jeannette Weill born 14 July 1841 to Felix Weill and Pauline Salomon (called Babette in 1851).
4. Henriette Weyll, born 21 August 1843 to Michel Weyll and Dina Blum, died on 21 December 1843.
5. Babette Weill born on 25 February 1844 to Felix Weil and Esther Salomon.
6. Babette Weill, born 26 April 1848 to Leopold Weill and Julie Blum, died on 20 September 1849.
7. Jeannette Weil, born 7 May 1848 to Felix Weil and Esther Salomon, married Moïse Salomon on 22 June 1880 in Bischheim.
8. Pauline Weill, born 2 August 1848 to Michel Weill and Dina Blum, died on 20 May 1849.
9. Judithe Weil, born on 3 December 1850 to Felix Weil and Pauline Salomon, died on 9 May 1857.
10. Marie Weil born on 24 September 1851 to Isaac Weil and Marie Weil.
11. Pauline Weil, born to Malken Weil and an unknown father on 1 February 1852, died on 29 September 1852.

Five of the girls had died as children and one had married in Bischheim. We were left with five candidates. Jeannette, born 27 February 1841 to Simon Weill and Sara Uri; Jeannette, born 14 July 1841 to Felix Weill and Pauline Salomon and Jeannette's half-sister, Babette, born on 25 February 1844 to Felix and his second wife (and former sister-in-law) Esther Salomon; Julie born on 13 April 1841 to Salomon Weill and Rosette/Sara Metzger; Marie, born 24 September 1851 to Isaac Weil and Marie Weil.

It was time to re-examine some of the Weil families in Bischheim, to see if any had immigrated to the United States, and what, if any relationship they might have to the five remaining candidates. Abraham Weill and his wife Sara Blum, a native of *Quatzenheim*, had two children born in *Bischheim*. Their daughter, Jeannette, married

Adam Salomon. Jeannette and Adam's two daughters, Pauline and Esther Salomon, were both married to Felix Weill. Felix Weill's daughter, Jeannette (b. 1841) had not been accounted for and was still a candidate to be Caroline Weill, wife of Frank Sharp. However, no one from his immediate family was known to have immigrated to America.

Abraham and Sara Blum Weill's son Michel Weill had numerous children with his wife, Babette Katz, of Cernay, Haut-Rhin. Michel Weill's eldest son, Emanuel Weil (b. 1816), married Rosine/Rosalie Schwab on 7 November 1848.in *Bischheim*. Emanuel and Rosalie had been enumerated in the 1851 census for *Bischheim*, living by themselves. Emanuel was enumerated in the 1860 federal census in Mobile, Mobile Co., Al, with his wife Rosalie Schwab. Michel Weill's third child, Nannette (b. 1819), had married Jacob Dreyfus in Warren County, MS, on 29 April 1854. Michel and Babette's second son, Salomon (b. 1817), had married Sara Metzger. Salomon and Sara's first child, Julie, born 13 April 1841, was a candidate to be Caroline Weill, the wife of Frank Sharp. Salomon and Sara's second daughter, Judithe (b. 1845), had immigrated to Mobile, AL, between 1861and 1866. She had married Lippman Moog from *Niederroedern*, Bas-Rhin, on 19 Feb 1868 at Mobile. Judithe was always called "Julie" or "Julia" in Alabama. If Caroline Weill Sharp was, indeed, Julie/Judithe Weill's sister and Judithe had decided to use the name .Julie. or "Julia" in America it stands to reason that, in order to avoid confusion, Julie might have decided to adopt the name Caroline. Salomon and Sara's son, Samuel (b. 1852), had immigrated to Alabama as well. He married Jeannette Moog in Mobile on 18 December 1878. In short, two of Michel's children, Nannette and Emanuel, and two grandchildren, Judithe and Samuel, had immigrated to Alabama. If Salomon's daughter Julie (b. 1841) was Caroline Weill Sharp, then she would have been the fifth of the descendants of Michel Weill to make the trip to America.

Was there a further connection between the Moog and Weill families of *Niederroedern* and *Bischheim*? A quick search of the 1851 census for *Niederroedern* revealed that Abraham, Bernard, and Aron Moog were all children of Isaac Moog. The two eldest had been born to his first wife, Madeleine/Madel Reiss, a native of *Bischheim*. Aron was born to Isaac and his second wife, and former sister-in-law, Pauline Reiss, who had immigrated to Alabama after the death of her husband in 1859. Abraham, Bernard and Aron Moog were all enumerated in the

1870 federal census for Mobile, AL in the same household as "Carline Villé." The Moog siblings other brother, Liebman/Lippman, was enumerated in the 1870 federal census at Mobile, AL, with his wife Judithe/Julie Weill, daughter of Salomon Weil and Sara Metzger. I was becoming more and more convinced that Caroline might be "Julie" born to Salomon Weill and Sara Metzger, sister of Judithe, who had married into this same Moog family. Moreover, when "Caroline Weil" married "Samuel Cohn" in Mobile, AL, on 7 January 1871, one of the bondsmen had been Emanuel Weill who, along with the groom, had pledged $200 to secure the marriage. Emanuel Weill and Salomon Weill were brothers. If Caroline Weill was born "Julie" in 1841 to Salomon Weill and Sara Metzger, then Emanuel was standing for his niece at her marriage in Mobile.

Failing to find an immigration record for any Caroline Weill who could have been our candidate, I searched for the entry of a "Julie" Weil into the United States. Sixteen year old Julie Weil had arrived in New Orleans, Orleans Parish, LA, on 26 December 1857, from Le Havre, France, accompanied by thirty-year-old Rosalie Schwab, aboard the ship *Ann Washburn*. Rosalie Schwab (b.1822), a native of Rimbach, Haut-Rhin, France, had married Emanuel Weill in Bischheim on 7 November 1848. Emanuel and Rosalie had been enumerated in Mobile, AL, in 1860 living together. A check of the entire passenger list revealed that forty-year-old Emanuel was not a passenger on the *Ann Washburn*. A further search revealed that he had arrived on 27 January 1857 at New Orleans from Le Havre, France aboard the ship *Wurtemberg*. But his wife, thirty-four year old Rosalie Schwab, had accompanied him on the voyage. Had she come and then gone back to fetch a relative? While it was not very likely, it was possible. I was constantly astonished at how many times some immigrants had made the trip back and forth, and at a time when the voyage itself took between five and eight weeks. A quick check of the 1861 census for *Bischheim* showed that Julie Weill, who had appeared with her parents, Salomon and Sara Metzger Weill, in the 1856 census as a fifteen-year-old girl, was no longer living in the household five years later. There was a sixteen-year-old "Julie" Weill living there in 1861, but this was the daughter born "Judithe" in 1845, who would marry Lippmann Moog in Alabama in 1868. This 1857 immigration record made it possible to tentatively eliminate two more women from our list of five candidates for Caroline Weill. Babette, born in 1844, was still living at home in *Bischheim* as late as 1861, so if Frank Sharp's wife had really immigrated in 1857 aboard the *Ann Washburn*, Babette (b. 1844) was not a candidate. The same could be said for Marie (b. 1851), as she would have been only six years old, not sixteen, at the time of her immigration. There was one more problem with this discovery. If Julie Weil had arrived in 1857 aboard the *Ann Washburn*, why was she not living with Emanuel Weill and his wife Rosalie Schwab in 1860 in Mobile? We could not find Julie/Caroline Weil anywhere in any 1860 federal census.

Caroline Weill Sharp's association with the Emanuel Weill family did not end with this perplexing immigration record, or Emmanuel's participation in her 1871 marriage. Emmanuel Weill and Rosalie Schwab were living in Mobile, Al, in 1880 with Caroline Weill Sharp's son, Rudolph Weil. The enumerator listed him as Emanuel's son, however, Caroline Weil had recognized Rudolph Weil as her son in her last will and testament, at which time she had left him $6000 from her estate.

Not satisfied with the information given in Caroline's and Frank's wills filed in 1909 and 1912 respectively, I decided to order the case papers which had been microfilmed and were available from *Familysearch.org*. All I learned from Caroline's case papers was that her son Rudolph had collected his $6000 bequest and had signed a document indicating that he did not contest his late mother's husband's right to the residue of her estate. While reading the one hundred or so pages in Frank Sharp's file, I had hoped to discover the identity of Caroline Weill's brothers and sisters, three of whom were each left $500 from the proceeds of Frank's estate. This bequest was only mentioned one time in a list of debts incurred by the estate. It read "brothers and sisters of Caroline Weil Sharp $1500." The three siblings were never mentioned by name, nor were there any receipts in the file indicating that they had ever received any money.

As it stands now, this case is not closed. While I believe that Caroline Weil, wife of Frank Sharp, was probably born "Julie" Weil on 13 April 1841 to Salomon Weill and Sara Metzger of *Bischheim*, Bas-Rhin, France, I am still waiting for that one single clue which will seal the deal. Note: Caroline Weill's name was often spelled with a single "L" in Louisiana and Alabama. In French records the Weil(l) families at *Bischheim* had their names spelled occasionally with one

"L," other times with two, so no determination could be made by ruling out the children whose names were originally spelled with one "L."

I have devoted the rest of this book to brief biographical sketches of more than six hundred men and women who immigrated to Louisiana from the Bas-Rhin. Some lived only briefly, leaving no descendants. Others married and had large families. These are the stories of people who were never famous or extraordinary. They were merchants and farmers, owners of public gins and saw mills, slave masters and Confederate patriots, jayhawkers and prisoners of war. They were members of the Police Jury, mayors, constables, and postmasters. They founded towns and promoted railroads. They grew cotton and cane, raised cattle, and struck oil. Whether they stayed for ten years or a lifetime these Jewish immigrants left their mark on Louisiana, helping it to grow and develop its resources.

These brief biographies are not meant to be complete, but are offered to the novice researcher as a starting point for his/her own genealogical discoveries. By examining these entries it is my hope that it will show the reader how to reconstruct the lives of long-lost relatives from vital records, census and tax records, city directories, wills and newspaper articles.

PART III

FORMAT AND ABBREVIATIONS

The names of immigrants to America from the Bas-Rhin are written in boldface capital letters. Names of spouses who are not from the Bas-Rhin are written in capital letters. Bas-Rhin town names are always written in italics. If both spouses are from the Bas-Rhin, the wife's information will be found in the husband's biography. She will be included in the alphabetical listing with a notation to see the husband's entry. At the end of each biography, enclosed in parentheses, are abbreviations which represent the sources used in the research. Below is a key to these abbreviations:

A - *Archives départementales du Bas-Rhin* [departmental archives of Bas-Rhin] (ADBR), *État civil numérisé du Bas-Rhin–Adeloch* [digitized civil registrations of Bas-Rhin–Adeloch] http://archives.bas-rhin.fr/index.php

AL - *Alsace Immigration Book, Volume I*, Cornelia Schrader-Muggenthaler, compiler, Apollo, PA: Closson Press, 2011

AL2 - *Alsace Immigration Book, Volume II*, Cornelia Schrader-Muggenthaler, compiler, Apollo, PA: Closson Press, 1991

AN – www.ancestry.com

AP – *The Forgotten Jews of Avoyelles Parish, Louisiana*, Carol Mills-Nichol, Santa Maria, CA: Janaway Publications, Inc., 2012

B –*The Foreign French – Nineteenth-Century French Immigration into Louisiana* Carl A. Brasseaux, Lafayette, LA:The Center for Louisiana Studies, University of Southwestern Louisiana, Lafayette. Volume II, covering 1840-1848 published 1992; Volume III, covering 1849-1852, published 1993.

BC – Brian Costello – Pointe Coupée Historian

BR – *Images of America – The Jewish Community of Shreveport*, Eric J. Brock, South Carolina:Arcadia Publishing, 2002

B1784 – *Dénombrement des Juifs d'Alsace 1784*, Cercle de généalogie juive, Paris, No date. This book is searchable on-line at http://www.genami.org/listes/alsace/denombrement-1784-Alsace.php

B1808 - *Recueil des déclarations de prise de nom patronymique des Juifs du Bas-Rhin en 1808,* Ed. Pierre Katz, Cercle de généalogie juive, Paris, 1999.

B1851 - *Les communautés juives du Bas-Rhin en 1851* , Ed. Pierre Katz, Cercle de généalogie juive, Paris, 2000.

C – *Les mariages juifs en Moselle 1792-1892*, Jean-Louis Calbat, Paris, France: Cercle de généalogie juive, 2001.

CA – The Library of Congress - Chronicling America – Historic American Newspapers – http://chroniclingamerica.loc.gov/

E - *Archives départementales du Bas-Rhin* [departmental archives of Bas-Rhin] (ADBR), *Listes nominatives numérisées du Bas-Rhin–Ellenbach* [digitized census enumerations of Bas-Rhin–Ellenbach] http://population.bas-rhin.fr/ellenbach/index.php

ES- Kaplan, Benjamin. *The Eternal Stranger.* New York: Bookman Associates, 1957.

F – www.familysearch.org

F3 - www.fold3.com

FPC – Old Fulton Postcards (Tom Tryniski's site) http://www.fultonhistory.com/Fulton.html

FS – *Fourscore and Eleven – A History of the Jews of Rapides Parish 1828-1919*, Rabbi Martin Hinchin, D.D., Alexandria, LA:McCormick Graphics Inc. for Congregation Gemiluth Chassodim, 1989

G – www.findagrave.com

GB – www.genealogybank.com

GN – www.geneanet.org

GW – The Goldring-Woldenberg Institute of Southern Jewish Life http://www.isjl.org/history/archive/main_la.htm

HJL – *History of the Jews of Louisiana*, published by Jewish Historical Publishing Company of Louisiana, 1903

I – www.italiangen.org

J – Jewishgen On-Line Worldwide Burial Registry

L- Louisiana State Board of Health Records, available at Secretary of State, PO Box 94125, Baton Rouge LA 70804-9125

M – *Recueil des déclarations de prise de nom patronymique des Juifs de Lorraine en 1808 – Moselle, Meurthe-et-Moselle*, Ed. Pierre Katz, Paris, France: Cercle de généalogie juive, 1999

N – New Orleans (Louisiana) Justice of the Peace Marriage Records Index, 1846-1880, on-line at http://nutrias.org/~nopl/inv/jpmarrindex/jpmarrindex.htm.

NP www.newspapers.com

R – www.rootsweb.com – Rootsweb World Connect Project

SWLR – *Southwest Louisiana Records (1750-1900)* Rev. Donald J. Hébert, compiler CD-ROM

TL – *Terrebonne Lifelines* - A quarterly publication of the Terrebonne Genealogical Society, Houma, Terrebonne Parish, LA

TT - MS Teri Downs Tillman, CG

USGW - http://www.usgwarchives.net/

PART IV

EMIGRANTS FROM THE BAS-RHIN TO LOUISIANA

AARON, CAROLINE, was born on 27 March 1842 in *Bouxwiller*, Bas-Rhin, France, to **ELIE AARON** and his wife, **SARA BENJAMIN**, both natives of the town. Caroline and her brother, **MEYER AARON** (See entry) immigrated to New Orleans, Orleans Parish, LA, arriving on the ship *Bolivian* out of Liverpool, England on 7 November 1865. Caroline married DAVID LEVY, a native of Sarrebourg, Moselle, France, on 7 June 1866. David, a junk dealer, and Caroline were the parents of six children, all born in New Orleans: Isaac (b. 1867), Brunette (b. 1869; died 1874), Elias (b. 1871), Jeannette (b. 1874; died 1875), Moses (b. 1876), and Petroline (b. 1878; died 1882). David Levy died on 5 April 1888 in New Orleans, at the age of forty-eight. He was interred in Gates of Prayer (Joseph Street) Cemetery in the city. Caroline died on 15 January 1921, and was buried in the same cemetery. (**A, AN, G**)

AARON, MEYER, was born on 19 April 1847 in *Bouxwiller*, Bas-Rhin, France, to **ELIE AARON** and his wife, **SARA BENJAMIN**, both natives of the town. Meyer and his sister **CAROLINE AARON** (See entry) immigrated to New Orleans, arriving on the ship *Bolivian* out of Liverpool, England, on 7 November 1865. Meyer married HENRIETTE/HARRIET JOSEPH, a native of Louisiana, on 12 February 1873 in New Orleans, Orleans Parish, LA, where Meyer was working as a butcher, with a stall in the French Market. They were the parents of three children: Brunette (b. 1874), Estelle (b. 1875), and Elias (b. 1880). Meyer and his family relocated to Houston, Harris Co., TX ca. 1881, where he was listed as a vegetable dealer at the City Market in the *Morrison & Fourmy Houston Directory* for 1882. We have not been able to locate any further records for him, and have concluded that he died in Texas ca. 1882. His widow, Harriet, married MARX GREENBLATT, also a butcher, in Harris Co, TX, on 2 January 1883, and had two children, Leon Aaron Greenblatt (b. 1884) and Jacob Seligman Greenblatt (b. 1885; name changed to Jac S. Greene). Harriet Greenblatt died at the age of thirty-four from chronic nephritis in New Orleans on 3 June 1890. We were unable to find burial records for either of them. (**A, AN, GB, L, TT**)

AARON, SARA (*Bouxwiller*) – See entry for **HENRY GRADWOHL**

ABRAHAM, EUGENE, was born on 19 October 1854 in *Reichshoffen*, Bas-Rhin, France to **DAVID ABRAHAM**, a native of the town and his wife **ÈVE LEVY**, born in *Wingersheim*, Bas-Rhin, France. He immigrated to America, arriving in New Orleans, Orleans Parish, LA from Bremen, Germany, on 27 February 1872 aboard the SS *Koln*. He went to work for his brother-in-law, **ABRAHAM KLOTZ** in Klotzville, Assumption Parish, LA, as a clerk in the general store. .He continued to live with and work for the Klotz family even after Abe's death in 1907. Fifty-seven-year-old Eugene Abraham was enumerated in the 1910 federal census as an unmarried dry goods salesman who was boarding with Edmond, Klotz, his nephew, and **ALPHONSE WEIL** (See entry), the bookkeeper for the Abraham Klotz store in Klotzville. Eugene died on 28 March 1916 on a trip to Hammond, Lake Co., IN. According to the March 8, 1916 obituary of his sister, Pauline Abraham Klotz, Eugene had been living in St. Louis, MO, before his death. His remains were returned to New Orleans and were interred in Hebrew Rest Cemetery # 1. (**A, AN, G, GB**)

ABRAHAM, JULIA, (*Reichshoffen*) – See entry for **ABRAHAM KLOTZ** (born 17 February 1832).

ABRAHAM, PAULINE, (*Reichshoffen*) – See entry for **ABRAHAM KLOTZ** (born 17 February 1832).

ABRAHAM, RAPHAEL, was born on 20 November 1849 in *Reichshoffen*, Bas-Rhin, France, to **DAVID ABRAHAM**, a native of the town, and his wife, **ÈVE LEVY**, born in *Wingersheim*, Bas-Rhin, France. We were unable to find a reliable record for his entry into the United States. In 1870 and 1880 he was enumerated in the federal census for Klotzville, Assumption Parish, LA, as one of two brothers-in-law working as a store clerk for the town's founder, **ABRAHAM KLOTZ** (See Entry). He returned to France after 1880 and married **MINETTE WELLHOFF** on 20 January 1886. Minette was born on 10 June 1856 at *Odratzheim*, Bas-Rhin, France, to **ISAAC SALOMON WELLHOFF**, a native of *Odratzheim*, and his wife, **BARIS/SARAH LEVY,** born in *Westhoffen*, Bas-Rhin. Raphael and Minette were the parents of five children, all of whom were said to be born in Nancy, Meurthe-et-Moselle, France: Edmond (b. 1887), Jeanne (b. 1889), Lucie (b. 1892), Robert (b. 1893) and Georgette (b. 1895). Raphael Abraham may have died in Paris on 21 July 1900, at the age of fifty. When his sister, Pauline, the second wife of Abraham Klotz, died on 7 March 1916, he was not listed as a survivor. Only Simon and Eugene Abraham were mentioned, so it has always been presumed that he had died before this date. **(A, AN, G, GB, GN, N)**

ABRAHAM, SIMON, was born on 28 January 1848 in *Reichshoffen*, Bas-Rhin, France, to **DAVID ABRAHAM**, a native of the town and his wife **ÈVE LEVY**, born in *Wingersheim*, Bas-Rhin. He immigrated to Louisiana ca. 1868 and started out working for his brother-in-law, **ABRAHAM KLOTZ** (See entry) in Klotzville, Assumption Parish, LA. In 1876 he partnered with a cousin to open a country store in Raceland, Lafourche Parish, LA. Simon Abraham married FANNIE SCHWARTZ, a New Orleans native, in April 1884. Four children were born to them: Therese (b. 1885), Jeanne (b. 1886), Raoul (b. 1887) and Lucille (b. 1889). S. Abraham Co. was not only a general store but sugar planting operations as well at Brickhern and Theresa Plantations, in Lafourche Parish. Simon also later bought a partnership in Melrose Plantation, in Natchitoches Parish, which made him a fortune. He became director of the Raceland Bank and Trust, and was, for a time, the postmaster of Raceland. After the turn of the century he moved his family to New Orleans, but he divided his time between the city and his interests in Lafourche Parish. He died on 2 January 1939 in New Orleans and was buried there in the Jewish section of Metairie-Lakelawn Cemetery. His wife, Fanny, died on 28 December 1942, and was interred there as well. **(A, AN, G, GB, NP)**

ACKER, ROSA, was born **RÉGINE ACKER** on 18 October 1843 in *Lembach*, Bas-Rhin to **JACQUES ACKER,** a native of *Lembach* and **JULIE BLUM,** born in *Billigheim*, Germany. According to the 1910 Federal Census, she immigrated to Louisiana ca. 1872, a record for which we were unable to find. She joined her brother, **SOLOMON ACKER** (See entry), in Shreveport, Caddo Parish, LA, and married LOUIS MORITZ, a native of Speyer, Rheinpfalz, Germany on 29 January 1873 in the city. Their only child, Milton, was born on 7 November 1873 during the yellow fever epidemic, which had taken his uncle Solomon Acker's life six weeks before. Milton lived only one day due to the weakened condition of his mother, who was also stricken with the fever. Milton was buried in Hebrew Rest Cemetery #1 (Jewish Section of Oakland Cemetery). The couple remained in Shreveport where Louis was a grocery clerk. Before the 1930 Federal Census Louis and Rosa went to live in the B'nai B'rith Home in Memphis, Shelby Co., TN. Louis died there on 23 September 1930, and Rosa followed on 3 November 1932. They were buried in Temple Israel, formerly Congregation Children of Israel or CC of I Cemetery in Memphis. (**A, AN, TT**)

ACKER, SOLOMON, was born on 26 July 1848 in *Lembach*, Bas-Rhin to **JACQUES ACKER,** a native of *Lembach* and **JULIE BLUM**, born in Billigheim, Germany. He emigrated from Le Havre, France arriving in New York on the SS *Helvetia* on 30 July 1866. He made his way south to Shreveport, Caddo Parish, LA, where he was enumerated in the 1870 federal census as a twenty-two-year-old unmarried man who was working as a grocer. Solomon married EMMA COHN in Shreveport on 27 February 1871, and died there during the yellow fever epidemic on September 20, 1873. He was buried in Hebrew Rest Cemetery # 1 (the Jewish Section of Oakland Cemetery) in Shreveport. [**A, G**]

BAER, ADOLPHE, was born **ADOLF BAER** on 23 October 1876 in *Bischwiller*, Bas-Rhin, France, to **MICHEL BAER**, a native of *La Walck*, Bas-Rhin, France, the brother of **ISAAC BAER** (See entry), and Michel's wife, **ROSALIE WEIL**, born in *Soultz-les-Bains*, Bas-Rhin. In a 1900 application for a U.S. passport, Adolphe wrote that he had immigrated to New York aboard the SS *Friesland* from Antwerp, Belgium, in August 1890. We were unable to verify this information using existing available ship's records. He traveled to Monroe, Ouachita Parish, LA, where his uncle, **ISAAC BAER** (See entry), ran a dry goods store. He was naturalized on 21 June 1899 in Ouachita Parish. Adolphe became a traveling salesman for the I. Baer Co., dividing his time between Monroe and New York City, where many of the firm's suppliers were located. Adolphe never married. He moved permanently to New York City ca. 1930, when he retired from business. Fifty-three-year-old Adolphe was enumerated in the 1930 federal census for Manhattan, New York, living as a guest in the Plymouth-Mayflower hotel. He died on 21 January 1962 in Paris, France. His last known address had been the Hotel Ansonia, 2109 Broadway in New York City. He was interred on 25 January 1962 in Montparnasse Cemetery (Cimetière du Sud). His niece, Mme. Albert Henri Victor, née Paulette Picard, also a resident of Paris, with whom he had been residing, took charge of the arrangements. (**A, AN, GB, GN**)

BAER, ARMAND, was born on 15 March 1878 in *Bischwiller*, Bas-Rhin,France, to **MICHEL BAER**, a native of *La Walck*, Bas-Rhin, France, the brother of **ISAAC BAER** (See entry), and Michel's wife, **ROSALIE WEIL**, born in *Soultz-les-Bains*, Bas-Rhin. Sixteen-year-old Armand Baer immigrated to America, arriving in New York on 11 September 1893 from Le Havre, France, aboard the SS *La Gascogne*. He went to work for his uncle, Isaac Baer in Monroe, Ouachita Parish, LA. In August 1909 Armand was shot and wounded in Monroe when an African-American man, who purchased a shotgun and buck shot which fortunately turned out to be bird shot given him by mistake, took aim at white citizens, wounding twenty-nine of them. Armand was shot in the back, arm and hand. He retired from business several decades later and was enumerated with his brother as a guest in the Plymouth-Mayflower Hotel in the 1930 federal census for Manhattan, New York. Armand never married and eventually returned to France. He died on 22 May 1958 at Neuilly-sur-Seine, a suburb of Paris, France. (**A, AN, GB, GN**)

BAER, ISAAC, was born **ISAAC BAEHR** on 14 June 1853 in *La Walck*, Bas-Rhin France, to **ABRAHAM/RAPHAËL BAEHR**, a native of the town, and his wife, **ANNE/HENRIETTE LITT**, born in *Dettwiller*, Bas-Rhin. According to the 1910 federal census, Isaac arrived in Louisiana in 1873 and was naturalized there in 1876. Although there were four possible ship's records for an Isaac Baer's arrival in America we believe that the nineteen-year-old "Isaac Behr" who arrived in New York on 19 September 1871 from Hamburg, Germany aboard the SS *Thuringia* is the most likely. He first appeared in U.S. census records in 1880 where he was enumerated in Oak Ridge, Morehouse Parish, LA, as a twenty-four-year old immigrant from Alsace, working as a dry goods merchant. He married MAUD MARX, of Port Gibson, Claiborne Co., MS, in her home town on 4 September 1889. The couple returned to live in Monroe, Ouachita Parish, LA. They were the parents of four children, all born in Monroe: Peola (b. 1890), Rosalind (b. 1891), Alvin Harry (b. 1893) and Raphael (b. 1901). The couple also raised Isaac's niece, Ernestine Langfelder, after the death of his sister **PAULINE BAER** (See entry) in 1895. Isaac was the president of the business he founded in Monroe, I. Baer, Co., Ltd., which dealt in wholesale dry goods and notions. In addition, he was vice-president of the Union Bank and Trust Co. and the People's Warehouse Company, both local Monroe businesses. Isaac moved his family to Manhattan, New York, ca. 1912 where he took an apartment on Riverside Drive. He turned over the presidency of his Monroe firm to M.H. Marx, his brother-in-law, but retained the vice-presidency for himself. He died on 4 January 1922 while on a business trip back to Monroe. His body was returned to New York, where it was buried in Woodlawn Cemetery in the Bronx, Bronx Co., NY. His wife, Maud, died on 29 December 1929 in Manhattan, NY. She was buried next to her husband. (**A, AN, F**)

BAER, LEOPOLD, was born on 16 March 1862 in *Dettwiller*, Bas-Rhin, France, to **ABRAHAM/RAPHAËL BAER**, a native of *La Walck*, Bas-Rhin, France, and his wife **ANNE/HENRIETTE LITT**, born in *Dettwiller*, Bas-Rhin. According to his own recollection in a U.S. passport application, Leopold stated that he entered the United States in October 1881, and was naturalized in Louisiana in 1888. He may have been the seventeen-year-old [*sic*] Leopold Baer, a German immigrant who arrived in New York from Rotterdam, Netherlands, on 25 July 1881 aboard the SS *Rotterdam*. Leopold settled in Monroe, Ouachita Parish, LA to be near his brother, **ISAAC BAER** (See entry), where they operated a retail dry goods store. Leopold married CARRIE V. STEINAU, a native of Mississippi, whose Bavarian born parents had relocated to Monroe in 1878. Leopold and Carrie were married ca. 1890, the record for which could not be found. They were the parents of two children: Adrian Steinau (b. 1893) and Hylda (b. 1895). Leopold worked in the wholesale liquor business for a time, but soon returned to work for his brother, Isaac, as a traveling salesman. After Isaac's departure for New York, Leopold and his family remained behind to take a hand in the family business. Upon retirement from business ca. 1933 he went to live with his daughter Hylda Klotz in Napoleonville, Assumption Parish, LA. A year later, he was hospitalized at Touro Infirmary in New Orleans, Orleans Parish, LA, and died there on 20 November 1934. His body was returned to Monroe, where he was buried in Rosena Chapel Jewish Cemetery. Carrie Baer died on 26 March 1957 in the Jessica Nursing Home in New Orleans. She was buried with her husband in Rosena Chapel Jewish Cemetery in Monroe. (**A, AN, G**)

BAER, PAULINE, was born on 10 December 1856 in *Dettwiller*, Bas-Rhin, France, to **ABRAHAM/RAPHAËL BAER**, a native of *La Walck*, Bas-Rhin, France, and his wife **ANNE/HENRIETTE LITT**, born in *Dettwiller*, Bas-Rhin. She immigrated to Louisiana following in the footsteps of her brothers, **ISAAC** and **LEOPOLD BAER** (See entries). We believe that twenty-seven-year-old "Pauline Bayer," a German national, arrived in New York on 26 May 1883 from Amsterdam, Netherlands, aboard the SS *Zaandam*. We know that she was married to MARK/MARCUS MARKS/MARX briefly before 1889 because she was listed as his widow at the time of her marriage to ADOLPH LANGFELSDER on 12 March 1889 in New Orleans, Orleans Parish, LA. Adolph had emigrated from Zakopcie in the Austro-Hungarian Empire (now located in Slovakia), taking the steamer *Hannover* from Bremen, Germany, which arrived in New Orleans on 22 November 1878. Adolph and Pauline returned to Monroe, Ouachita Parish, LA, to live near her brother Isaac and his wife, Maud Marx. Pauline and Adolph were the parents of a daughter Ernestine, born in September 1894 in Monroe. Pauline died on 26 October 1895 in Monroe and was buried there in Rosena Chapel Jewish Cemetery. Her brother Isaac took charge of Ernestine and raised her until she married. Adolph continued to live in Monroe, working first as a book keeper, then as a bartender in a local saloon, while living in a series of boarding houses. He died in Monroe on 29 April 1911 and was buried there in Rosena Chapel Jewish Cemetery with his wife. Note: Mark/Marcus Marx was Isaac Baer's brother-in-law. Marcus and his sister Maud were enumerated with their family in Macon, Noxubee Co., MS in the 1880 federal census. (**A, AN, G, GB**)

BAUER, ACHILLE SALOMON, was born **SOLOMON BAUER** on 10 September 1861 in *Romanswiller,* Bas-Rhin, France, to **HEYMAN BAUER** and his wife, **JEANNETTE GEISSMAR**, both natives of the town. He immigrated as twenty-six-year-old "Salomon Bauer," arriving in New York from Le Havre, France, on 4 June 1886 aboard the SS *Westphalia*. He worked for several years in Lambertville, Hunterdon Co., NJ, after which he moved to Alexandria, Rapides Parish, LA, where he worked as a clerk for Bauer & Weil. In 1894 he went into business as a retail grocer. Three years later he decided to concentrate on the wholesale grocery business, becoming one of the most successful men in Alexandria. He married HORTENSE SCHMALINSKI, the Alexandria born daughter of Samuel Schmalinski, a Prussian immigrant, and his wife, Elise Weil, a native of Ingenheim, Germany. Three children were born to them: Camille Salomé(b. 1896, died as a child), Sylvan Ashton (b. 1897), and Melvin Bloom (b. 1902). Hortense died on 17 December 1914 in Alexandria and was interred in the Jewish Cemetery in Pineville, Rapides Parish, LA. Achille died on 17 February 1927 at New Orleans, Orleans Parish,

LA, while on a business trip for his firm. He was buried in the Jewish Cemetery in Pineville with his wife. Achille was a second cousin to **FELIX BAUER** (See entry). **(A, AN, FS, G)**

BAUER, FELIX, was born on 13 July 1855 in *Romanswiller*, Bas-Rhin, France, to **SALOMON BAUER**, a native of the town and his wife, **HENRIETTE KAUFFMANN**, born in *Bouxwiller*, Bas-Rhin. In an 1899 application for a U.S. passport, Felix stated that he had come to America, arriving on the steamer *St. Laurent,* on or about 20 September 1872. In searching for his actual arrival we have concluded that he probably arrived under the name of "Salomon Bauer" at New York, from Le Havre, France, on 19 July 1872 aboard the SS *St. Laurent*. There are no other likely arrivals for a "Felix Bauer" that could be found in existing available ship's records. Felix was a merchant in New Orleans, then Cottonport, Avoyelles Parish, LA, where he was the victim of a series of anti-Semitic attacks which cause his removal to Alexandria, Rapides Parish, LA. He partnered there, for a time, with Bertrand Weil in a general merchandise store, known as Bauer & Weil. He remained in the United States until 1896, whereupon he sold his interest in the store in Alexandria and returned to France. At the time of his 1899 application for a U.S. passport, he had been living in Le Havre, France for three years. He retained his American citizenship and returned occasionally on business, the last record of which was in 1911. We have not been able to trace him after that date.**(A, AN, AP, FS)**

BAUER, RAPHAEL, was born on 20 September 1830 in *Romanswiller*, Bas-Rhin, France, to **ABRAHAM BAUER,** a native of the town and his wife, **RÉGINE BLUM,** born in *Offwiller*, Bas-Rhin. We believe that Raphael may have immigrated to the United State as twenty-two-year-old Raphael Baer [sic], arriving at New York on 30 June 1854 from Le Havre, France, aboard the ship *Elizabeth Kimball*. He married MARY STEINHART**,** a Prussian national, in New Orleans, Orleans Parish, LA, on 2 November 1861. Raphael became a successful grocery merchant, moving after the war, ca. 1866 from his store on Old Levee Street in New Orleans to the Third Ward, Plaquemines Parish, LA, at Pointe à la Hache He and Mary were the parents of six children: George (b. 1862), Abraham (b. 1864), Theodore (b. 1866), Regina (b. 1869), Seraphine (b. 1871) and Lazard (b. 1873). Raphael died on 28 November 1889 at Pointe à la Hache. He and his wife, Mary, who died on 9 December 1892, at St. Sophie, Plaquemines Parish, LA, were buried in Hebrew Rest Cemetery # 1, in New Orleans, LA (**A, AN, GB, J**)

BECKER, BENJAMIN PAUL, was born on 30 April 1891 in *Schweighouse-sur-Moder,* Bas-Rhin, France, to **NATHAN BECKER** (See entry), a native of the town and his wife, **PAULINE WEILL**, born in *Schirrhoffen*, Bas-Rhin. He immigrated with his parents to New Orleans, Orleans Parish, LA, via New York, on 22 May 1894 aboard the SS *Chester* out of Southampton, England. The family settled in White Castle, Iberville Parish, LA. By 1910, nineteen-year-old Paul B., or Paul Ben as he was called in Louisiana, was helping his father in a family grocery store. They moved briefly to Morgan City, St. Mary Parish, LA, in 1912, where Paul was in partnership with his father in N. Becker & Son, manufacturers of moss for mattresses. After his father's suicide in July 1914, he and his mother returned to White Castle, where he worked first as a clerk in a local store, then as a picture frame salesman. He also worked for a time in Marrero, Jefferson Parish, LA as a commissary clerk, but soon returned to be with his mother in White Castle. Paul never married. He died on 8 July 1954 and was buried in Bethel Cemetery in Logansport, Desoto Parish, LA. (**A, AN, G, GB**)

BECKER, NATHAN, was born on 2 March 1861 in *Schweighouse-sur-Moder*, Bas-Rhin, France, to **HERMANN/ HEYMANN BECKER**, a native of *Minversheim*, Bas-Rhin, France and his wife **CÉCILE WOLFF**, born in *Herrlisheim*, Bas-Rhin. He married **PAULINE WEILL**, born on 18 September 1860 in *Schirrhoffen*, Bas-Rhin, France, to **JOSEPH WEILL**, a native of the town, and his wife, **SARA/RACHEL SAMUEL**, born in *Trimbach*, Bas-Rhin. Nathan and Pauline were wed on 6 November 1888 in *Schweighouse-sur-Moder,* where their only surviving child, **BENJAMIN PAUL BECKER** (See entry) was born. According to information that was given in both the 1900 and 1910 federal census enumerations, the family immigrated together to Louisiana in 1894. Nathan, Pauline and Paul Becker arrived at New York, on 22 May 1894 aboard the SS *Chester* out of Southampton, England. They settled in White Castle, Iberville Parish, LA, where Nathan opened a grocery store. They chose White Castle because **GUSTAVE/GODCHAUX WEILL** (See entry), Pauline's brother lived in White Castle, and her aunt **HENRIETTE WEILL NETTER** (See entry for **EMILE NETTER**) lived in nearby Lutcher, St. James Parish, LA). In 1912 Nathan opened up a moss ginnery for the manufacture of mattresses in Morgan City, St. Mary Parish, LA. He committed suicide two years later by slashing his own throat on 24 July 1914. He was buried in the Morgan City Cemetery and Mausoleum the next day. Pauline and Benjamin returned to White Castle, where her son continued to work at various sales jobs. Pauline died there at the age of ninety-one on 18 July 1946. Her body was returned to Morgan City where she was buried in the Morgan City Cemetery and Mausoleum. (**A, AN, G, GB**)

BEER – See **BER**

BEHR, EDMOND, was born **EDMUND BAEHR** on 13 September 1888 in *Neuwiller-lès-Saverne*, Bas-Rhin, France, to **JULES BAEHR**, a native of the town, and his wife, **BABETTE BRAUN**, born in *Ingwiller*, Bas-Rhin. Edmond immigrated to America, arriving in New York on 17 January 1910 aboard the SS *La Lorraine*. He was recorded on the ship's manifest as a twenty-one year-old clerk from Germany whose next of kin was his father, Jules Behr, a resident of *Neuwiller*, Germany. His destination in the U.S. was recorded as Cincinnati. He was, however, first enumerated in the United States in the 1920 federal census in New Orleans, Orleans Parish, La, where he was living as a boarder in the household of **LEON** and **ARMAND BRAUN** (See entries). He was employed as a millinery salesman. Edmond was naturalized on 29 April 1920 and immediately applied for a passport to return to France to visit his parents. A letter containing his request was written on Grossman Bros. Millinery Co. stationery. He intended to sail from New York as soon as he received his passport. Edmond married JEANNE SCHWAB, a native of Paris, France, ca. 1922. There is no record for the marriage in New Orleans. It is possible that the union was arranged and celebrated in France before Edmond's return to the United States. The couple had a daughter, Jacqueline Behr born ca. 1923. Jeanne Schwab Behr died in New Orleans on 3 June 1928. She had been living in New Orleans for barely six years. Jeanne was buried in Gates of Prayer Cemetery #2 (Joseph street). Her mother, SARAH/CÉLÈSTE SCHWAB, was enumerated with her son-in-law Edmond and grandchild Jacqueline in the 1930 federal census. Edmond, a widower, was still working as a millinery salesman. After his mother-in-law returned to Paris, he was forced to put Jacqueline in the Jewish Children's home on St. Charles Avenue ca. 1935. Seventeen-year-old Jacqueline was enumerated there in the 1940 federal census. Her father, who traveled extensively for his job as a representative for Grossman Bros., the largest millinery company in the south, was enumerated in 1940 as a guest at the Victoria Hotel in Andalusia, Covington Co., AL. Upon reaching her majority, Jacqueline and her father were reunited under the same roof. She was married to WILLIAM BERMAN of Mobile, Mobile Co., AL in 1953. Edmond Behr took a second wife, Betty Grohn (b. 1928), of Sour Lake, Hardin Co., TX, after his daughter's marriage. Edmond died on 25 April 1962 in Beaumont, Jefferson Co., TX. His remains were returned to New Orleans where they were interred in Gates of Prayer Cemetery #2 (Joseph Street) next to those of his first wife. (**A, AN, F, G, GB, TT**)

BENJAMIN, LAZARD, was born **LAZARE BENJAMIN** on 12 February 1829 in *Bouxwiller*, Bas-Rhin, France, to **LEYSER/ LEOPOLD BENJAMIN**, and his wife **ZERLEN MOSES/SARA HELLER**, both natives of *Ettendorf*, Bas-Rhin. We believe that twenty-three-year-old Lazare immigrated as "Benjamin Lazare," his first and last names having been reversed in error, to New Orleans, Orleans Parish, LA, arriving on 18 March 1853 from Le Havre, France, aboard the ship *Wurtemberg*. Lazare married **BABETTE LEVY** on 9 October 1855 in the city. **BABETTE** was born **BABETTE LEVI** on 11 December 1829 in *Bouxwiller*, Bas-Rhin, France, to **ISRAËL LEVI** (See entry), a native of the town and his wife, **ESTHER WOLF**, born in *Büswille*r, Bas-Rhin. The couple had one child, Charles Lazare (b. 1856). Lazard owned a dry good store on St. Andrew St. (Between Constance & Laurel) for many years. Just after the 1880 census he moved to Opelousas, St. Landry Parish, LA, to start a business with his son, Charles, who married ADELE CERF, the Mississippi born daughter of **ISAÏE CERF** (See entry) and his wife ROSINE HILLER. Lazare's son, Charles, and father-in-law, Isaïe Cerf, died in Opelousas and were buried there in the local Jewish Cemetery. Lazare and his wife returned to New Orleans. Lazare died on 22 August 1902 and was buried there in Gates of Prayer Cemetery #2 (Joseph Street). Babette died on 11 November 1910 in New Orleans and was buried with him. (**A, AN, G, GB**)

BER, DELPHINE, (*Harskirchen*) See entry for **ABRAHAM HEYMANN**

BER, MATHILDE, was born **MATHILDE BEER** on 16 June 1846 in *Harskirchen*, Bas-Rhin, France, to **SAMUEL HIRSCH BEER** (See entry), a native of the town, and his wife, RACHEL LEVY, born in

Moselle, France. Two year-old Mathilde arrived on 7 November 1848 in New Orleans, Orleans Parish, LA, with her mother and two siblings on the ship *Espérance* out of Le Havre, France. She married JOSEPH MANN, a native of Hesse-Darmstadt, Germany, in New Orleans on 3 February 1868. Mann was her father's partner in the clothing store, Baer and Mann, which Joseph continued to operate after his father-in-law's death in 1898. He moved the store from the Third District to the French Market and finally to Rampart Street. Joseph and Mathilde had eight children: Simon (b. 1868), Jenny (b. 1871), Fannie (b. 1874), Delphine (b. 1877), Hattie (b. 1879), Michael (b. 1882), Bertha (b. 1885) and Mayer/Myer (b. 1887; died at three months). Sixty-eight-year-old Joseph Mann died in New Orleans on 11 November 1905. His wife followed on 4 June 1926. They were both interred in Hebrew Rest Cemetery # 1 in New Orleans. **(A, AN, G, GB, N, TT)**

BER, MICHEL, was born Michel Beer on 22 October 1844 in *Harskirchen*, Bas-Rhin, France, to **SAMUEL HIRSCH BEER**, a native of the town, and his wife, RACHEL LEVY, born in Moselle, France. Three-year-old Michel arrived on 7 November 1848 in New Orleans, Orleans Parish, LA, with his mother and two siblings on the ship *Espérance* out of Le Havre, France. He did not appear in the 1850 or 1860 federal census enumerations with his family in New Orleans. Efforts to locate any other records have failed to turn up any information. We assume that he died as a child. His final resting place is unknown. **(A, AN, G)**

BER, SAMUEL, was born **SAMUEL HIRSCH BEER** on 9 March 1812 in *Harskirchen*, Bas-Rhin, France, to **ABRAHAM BEER**, a native of Reningen (Reinange), now part of Volstroff, Moselle, France, and his wife JEANNETTE LEVY, probably also from the Moselle region. He married RACHEL LEVY, from Niedervisse,Moselle, France, on 8 December 1840 in Grosbliederstroff, Moselle, and the couple returned to *Harskirchen* where Samuel was a second hand dealer. Three children were born to them in France: Dauphine/Delphine (b. 1842;-See entry), Michel, (b. 1844; See entry), and Mathilde, (b. 1846; See entry). If we are to believe a ship's record for the *Rockall* which departed Le Havre, France, arriving in New Orleans, Orleans Parish, LA, on 17 May 1848, Samuel, whose age was correct, but whose place of origin was listed as Prussia, arrived six months before the rest of his family. He was enumerated in the 1850 census as a thirty-six-year-old French dry goods merchant, living with thirty-year-old "R. Ber," eight-year-old "D. Ber," and four-year-old "M. Ber," the latter three all females. On 2 October 1850, a son, Adolph, was born to the couple in New Orleans. Another daughter, Seraphine, was born on 9 July 1859. After the Civil War Samuel went into partnership with JOSEPH MANN and the two sold dry goods at the corner of Spain & Royal Street. Samuel and his family lived above the store. Mann eventually became his son-in-law, marrying **MATHILDE BER** (See entry). Samuel's wife, Rachel died in New Orleans on 17 May 1887 and he followed on 11 March 1898. They were buried there in Hebrew Rest Cemetery # 1. (**A, AN, G, GB, L, TT**)

BERNHEIM, FERDINAND, was born **FERNAND BERNHEIM** on 18 April 1875 in *Kuttolsheim*, Bas-Rhin, France, to **EMMANUEL GOETSCH/GUSTAVE BERNHEIM**, a native of the town and his wife, **REGINA/RACHEL LEVY**, born in *Wingersheim*, Bas-Rhin. Ferdinand immigrated to New York arriving on 8 October 1890 from Antwerp, Belgium, aboard the SS *Friesland*. He settled in New Iberia, Iberia Parish, LA, where he was naturalized on 30 September 1898. He was enumerated in the 1900 federal census in Houma, Terrebonne Parish, LA, as a twenty-five-year-old immigrant from Germany working as a clerk in a store. He was still working in Houma when he became engaged to marry SADYE KERN, a Louisiana native, on 19 June 1910. Efforts to find their exact marriage date have proved elusive. Sadye and Ferdinand made their home in Donaldsonville, Ascension Parish, LA, where other Kern family members were living. Ferdinand became a traveling salesman for a New Orleans firm, Alaynick Manufacturing Co., which made skirts, pants, coats and shirts in their Decatur Street factory. Sadye and Ferdinand were the parents of four sons: Gustave (b. 1911), Berthold (b. 1914), Florian (b. 1916) and Sadrian Kern "SK" (b. March 17, 1921). A New Orleans *Times-Picayune* article announced the death of "Mrs. Ferdnand Burnheimer" [*sic*] who had given birth to a daughter and died the same day on 17 March 1921 at Touro Infirmary in New Orleans, Orleans Parish, LA. The "daughter," was Sadrian, a boy, given a male version of his dead mother's first name. Sadye's remains were returned to Donaldsonville where she was buried in Bikur Sholim, the local Jewish cemetery. Ferdinand Bernheim died on 19 February 1928 in Donaldsonville and was buried with her. The children were sent to Lexington, Holmes Co., MS, to live with their grandmother, Flora Kern. They were all enumerated there together in the 1930 federal census for Lexington, MS. Ten years later, nineteen-year-old Sadrian Bernheim was enumerated in the 1940 federal census living with his mother's sister, Agathine Kern Applebaum, also a resident of Lexington. Note: There is an astonishing number of ways to misspell the name Bernheim: Burnheim, Burnheimer, Bernheimer, Bernhimer. The most unusual spelling was found in the 1920 federal census index for Donaldsonville. Ferdinand Bernheim was dubbed Fernand Remheim. Doing a "Sadie" search in Ascension Parish was the only way we were able to find the family. (**A, AN, GB**)

BERNHEIM, JULES, was born **JULIUS BERNHEIM** on 29 January 1878 in *Kuttolsheim*, Bas-Rhin, France, to **EMMANUEL GOETSCH/GUSTAVE BERNHEIM**, a native of the town and his wife, **REGINA/RACHEL LEVY**, born in *Wingersheim*, Bas-Rhin. In a 1913 application for a U.S. passport, Jules wrote that he immigrated to the United States aboard the SS *Bourgogne* which arrived in New York in August 1892. We believe, however, he was more likely to have arrived as fifteen-year-old "Jules Bernheim" on 18 May 1891 from Le Havre, France, aboard the SS *La Bourgogne*, a full year earlier. He had also mistakenly alleged on his 1913 passport application that he had been born in Strasbourg, France. Jules made his way to Thibodaux, Lafourche Parish, LA, where he was enumerated in the 1900 federal census working as a clerk for his uncle, **SIMON ABRAHAM** (See entry). He was naturalized on 26 May 1902 at Thibaudaux. Jules registered for the World War 1 draft in 1918 in New Orleans, Orleans Parish, LA, where he had become a traveling salesman for the Morais-Hiller Jewelry Company. Jules married **EULA BOSSIER**, a Mississippi native, ca. 1920, a record of which we were unable to find. Jules and Eula had no children. She died on 2 November 1936 in New Orleans and was buried in Cypress Grove Cemetery in the city. (Note: The record shows "Cerla" Bernheim). Jules remained in New Orleans and became the proprietor of his own jewelry shop. He died on 9 April 1977 at the age of ninety-nine years. He was buried in the Hebrew Rest Mausoleum located in Hebrew Rest Cemetery #1 in the city. (**A, AN, G, GB**) See also pp 22,23

BIGART, ALBERT, was born on 1 April 1867 in *Muttersholtz*, Bas-Rhin, France, to **BENJAMIN BIGART**, a native of the town, and his wife, **MINDEL BADER**, born in *Dambach-la-Ville*, Bas-Rhin. In an 1890 application for a U.S. passport Albert wrote that he immigrated to the United States aboard SS *Labrador* from Le Havre on 24 September 1884. In truth he was the "Mr. Bigart" who arrived in New York from

Le Havre, France, aboard the SS *Canada* which arrived in New York on 18 September 1884. Albert settled in Shreveport, Caddo Parish, LA, where his brother, Judas, was a partner in Kahn & Bigart, a retail dry goods firm. Albert was naturalized on 14 April 1890 in Shreveport. A month later he booked passage out of New York to return to France to see relatives. He arrived back in New York on 8 September 1890 aboard the SS *La Champagne* and returned to Shreveport, only to die there on 13 August 1893 at the age of twenty-six. He was interred in Hebrew Rest Cemetery # 2 (Texas Ave.) in Shreveport. (**A, AN**)

BIGART, JUDAS/ "L.J,", was born on 8 May 1858 in *Muttersholtz*, Bas-Rhin, France, to **BENJAMIN BIGART**, a native of the town, and his wife, **MINDEL BADER**, born in *Dambach-la-Ville*, Bas-Rhin. He immigrated to the United States, arriving in New York as "Mr. L. Bigard, " a nineteen-year-old clerk from Germany, aboard the steamer *Pereire* on 6 September 1877. He was enumerated as "L. Bigart" in the 1880 U.S. federal census for Shreveport, Caddo Parish, LA as a twenty-five-year-old unmarried man working as a clerk. He was associated with Kahn Dry Goods retail store and soon became a partner in the establishment. On 2 November 1885 Kahn & Bigart's was closed by attachments and $35,000 in stock and fixtures were sold at a sheriff's sale. "L.J. Bigart," the name he was always known by in Shreveport, was soon back in business with his brother, **ALBERT BIGART** (See entry), as Bigart & Co. managing a 3000 square foot dry goods store on Texas Street. On May 14, 1896 Bigart & Co. moved down the block to a modern 12,000 square foot establishment with electric lights, and every other modern convenience. It was briefly the leading dry goods establishment in the city. On 23 December 1898 a fire broke out at Bigart's, reported to have been from improperly insulated electric wiring, which not only destroyed the store's entire contents but the holdings of four other buildings, including Kahn Dry Goods, two millinery houses and a cigar company. The Phoenix Hotel was also badly damaged. L.J. Bigart filed for voluntary bankruptcy on 4 March 1899 citing $100,000 in liabilities with no assets. L. J. Bigart had made frequent trips back to France between 1894 and 1899 and had applied for four passports under the name of Judas Bigart. He sailed, however under the name of L.J. Bigart, and once under "Lehmann" Bigart. His last application for a passport was made on 1 December 1899 from New York City. We have been unable to find any more information about him under any of the names he used. It is possible that he never returned to the United States. (**A, AN, GB, NP**)

BLOCH, ARNAUD, was born on 31 December 1865 in *Schirrhoffen*, Bas-Rhin, France, to **LEHMAN/LEON BLOCH**, a native of the town, and his wife, **LOUISE MEYER**, born in *Herrlisheim*, Bas-Rhin. Arnaud Bloch immigrated aboard the SS *La France* as seventeen-year-old "Arnould Bloch," arriving in New York on 23 May 1883.(Note: The transcriber erroneously noted his age as eleven years.) He settled in Donaldsonville, Ascension Parish, LA, where he opened a dry goods store several years later known as the Dollar Store. He married LEONORA GOLDSTEIN, born in Berwick, St. Mary Parish, LA, to Bavarian immigrants, ca. 1894. We were not able to find a marriage record for the couple. They had two children: Sophie Bertha (b. 1895), who married **MARCEL HIMMLER** (See entry), and Leo (b. 1904).Arnaud employed two of his nephews, Maurice Bloch's children, Leon and Marcel, in his dry goods store. In 1910 they could both be found boarding with him as well. Arnaud maintained his dry goods establishment, which by the 1930s, had attained the status of a department store in Donaldsonville. Arnaud died on 23 Jan 1934. He was buried in Bikur Sholim Jewish Cemetery in town. His wife, Leonora, died on 27 December 1946 and was buried in the same cemetery. **(A, AN, G, GB)**

BLOCH, AUGUSTE, was born on 8 May 1807 in *Duttlenheim*, Bas-Rhin, France, to **SOLOMON BLOCH**, born in *Krautergersheim*, Bas-Rhin, France, and his wife, **SARA FRANCK**, a native of *Duttlenheim*, Bas-Rhin. He married BEYERLÉ/BABETTE WEIL, born in Schmieheim, Baden-Württemberg, Germany, on 11 February 1841 in *Duttlenheim*. Babette had already given birth to their child, **SIMON BLOCH** (See entry), the year before. Babette died in *Duttlenheim* on 21 March 1849. Auguste married **SARA FALK** on 3 July 1849 in *Duttlenheim*. Sara was born on 21 August 1823 in *Duppigheim*, Bas-Rhin, France, to **HEYMANN/HERMANN FALK**, a native of the town, and his first wife **JEANNETTE/HANNA LEVI**, born in *Odratzheim*, Bas-Rhin. August and Sara were the parents of three children born in *Duttlenheim*: Charles (b. 1850; See entry), Marc/Mathias/Maurice (b. 1851; See entry) and Cécile (b. 1853; See entry). Auguste left for Louisiana at some time between the birth of his last child in November 1853 and the taking of the 1856 town census for *Duttlenheim*. We were unable to find a ship's record for him. Sara Falk Bloch was listed as an indigent head of household in that census record, along with her sixteen-year-old stepson Simon, and her three children: Charles, Marc, and Cécile. She immigrated with her step-son, Simon and her three children to New Orleans, Orleans Parish, LA, on 9 January 1857, from Le Havre,France, aboard the ship *Mortimer Livingston*. She was accompanied by her cousin, **CAROLINE FALK** (See entry). Sara joined her husband, Auguste, who was a peddler, working in New Orleans. The couple were the parents of another child, Raphael, who was born in the city on 25 May 1858. The family, with the exception of Simon, was enumerated in the 1860 census living in New Orleans. An 1866 entry in the New Orleans Directory listed Auguste Block [*sic*] as a dry goods dealer. Auguste died on 9 September 1866 in the city. We have been unable to find his place of burial. He may have been interred in the old Gates of Mercy Cemetery which was razed in 1957. The widow, forty-five-year-old Sarah Block [*sic*],was enumerated in the 1870 federal census at New Orleans with her two sons, nineteen-year-old Mathias and twenty-year-old Charles. She was working as a retail grocer with the help of her sons who were clerks in the store. Sarah and her two sons, Marc/Mathias and Charles, moved to nearby Plaquemines Parish later on in the decade to be near her cousin, **SOLOMON FELIX FALK** (See entry), where she and her sons operated a grocery store. By the time of the 1880 federal census, Sara had retired to St. Charles Parish where she lived with her stepson, SIMON BLOCH, who was a forty-year-old, single, store keeper. Sara Falk Block [*sic*] died on 12 January 1885, She was probably interred near other FALK/FELIX relatives in the old Tememe Derech Jewish Cemetery, now Gates of Prayer Cemetery #1 (Canal Street).Note: See entry for Sara's brother **MARX FÉLIX (A, AN, E, TT)**

BLOCH, CAROLINE, was born **GERTRUDE BLOCH** on 4 February 1824 in *Saverne*, Bas-Rhin, France, to **LAZARD BLOCH**, born in *Odratzheim*, Bas-Rhin, France, and his wife **BARBE DANHEISER**, a native of *Saverne*, Bas-Rhin. She immigrated to Louisiana in the late 1850s, a reliable record for which we were unable to find. Caroline married JOSEPH LEUMAS, a native of Hellimer, Moselle, France, on 28 Febraury 1859 in Vermilionville, Lafayette Parish, LA. In the 1808 census for Hellimer, a person we suspect to be Joseph's grandfather, Joseph Samuel, took the surname LEAMUS, an anagram of "Samuel." Here in America, the name became LEUMAS, the two final vowels having been switched. In 1860 the couple were living with their seven month old son Samuel (later called Joseph), and Caroline's brother **JACQUES/JACOB BLOCH** (See entry). A second son, Lazard, was born to the couple in 1862. The Leumas family apparently returned to France during the Civil War, because their third

57

son, Jules, was born on 29 April 1864 in Paris, France, according to an affidavit supporting his request for a 1903 passport. The family returned to Donaldsonville, Ascension Parish, LA, in 1870 where Caroline's niece, **CLARA/CLAIRE BOMPET** (See entry), was living with her husband LAZARE LEVY. Caroline's husband, Joseph Leumas died soon after their return on 1 October 1870 and was buried in Bikur Sholim Jewish Cemetery in Donaldsonville. Caroline Bloch Leumas remained in Donaldsonville with her sons to operate a dry goods store. In 1880, Caroline, called "Josephine" in the census, was living with her three sons, Joseph, Lazard and Jules, as well as her elderly brother, **JACOB /JACQUES BLOCH**(See entry), who was a peddler. Caroline Leumas died on 6 March 1903 and was buried with her husband in Bikur Sholim Jewish Cemetery in Donaldsonville. (**A, AN, G, M**)

BLOCH, CÉCILE, was born on 14 November 1853 in *Duttlenheim*, Bas-Rhin, France, to **AUGUSTE BLOCH**, a native of the town, and his second wife, **SARA FALK**, born in *Duppigheim*, Bas-Rhin. She immigrated with her mother and siblings to New Orleans, Orleans Parish, LA, arriving on 9 January 1857, from Le Havre, aboard the ship *Mortimer Livingston*. She was accompanied by her mother's cousin, **CAROLINE FALK** (See entry). Six-year-old Cécile was first enumerated in Louisiana in the 1860 federal census living with her parents and siblings in New Orleans. In 1880, she was enumerated as an unmarried niece living in the household of **ISAAC RAAS** (see entry) and his wife Sara Kauffmann. Cécile's uncle, **MARX FÉLIX'S** wife, Rebecca Kauffmann, and Isaac Raas's wife, Sara, were members of the Kauffmann family from *Gundershoffen*, Bas-Rhin. Cécile married ROBERT STIFFELL on 25 August 1886 in New Orleans. Robert, whose father was Austrian and mother was German, was born in Louisiana in 1843. He had clerked in Shreveport, Caddo Parish, as a young man, and subsequently moved to Galveston, Galveston Co., TX. He married Cécile Bloch on 25 August 1886 in New Orleans. They were the parents of four children: Cornelia (b. 1887), Asher (b. 1889), Isaac (b. 1891), and Charles (b. 1894). Cécile and her four children were enumerated in the 1900 federal census in the household of her brother, **MARC/MATTHIAS/MAURICE BLOCH** (See entry) in Waco, McLennan Co., TX. Although she was enumerated as a married woman, she was evidently living apart from her husband. Cécile died on 26 September 1902 in New Orleans. She was interred there in Gates of Prayer Cemetery #1 (Canal Street). After her death Robert Stiffell moved to Shreveport, Caddo Parish, LA, where he died on 11 April 1924. He was buried in Hebrew Rest Cemetery #2 (Texas Ave.) in Shreveport. (**A, AN, G, TT**)

BLOCH, CHARLES, was born on 13 July 1850 in *Duttlenheim*, Bas-Rhin, France, to **AUGUSTE BLOCH**, a native of the town, and his second wife, **SARA FALK**, born in *Duppigheim*, Bas-Rhin. Charles immigrated with his mother and siblings to New Orleans, Orleans Parish, LA, arriving on 9 January 1857 from Le Havre, France aboard the ship *Mortimer Livingston*. He was accompanied by his mother's cousin, **CAROLINE FALK** (See entry). Charles was enumerated with his family in the 1860 federal census for New Orleans, Orleans Parish, LA. Twenty-year-old Charles was enumerated in the 1870 federal census in the household of his widowed mother, forty-five-year-old Sarah Block [*sic*] and his nineteen-year-old brother, Marc/Mathias. He and his brother were working as clerks in their mother's grocery store. Sarah, Charles and Marc/Mathias moved to nearby Plaquemines Parish later on in the decade to be near her cousin, **SOLOMON FELIX FALK** (See entry), where she and her sons operated a grocery store. We have been unable to trace Charles Bloch any further in Louisiana, or in Texas, where his brother **MARC/MATHIAS BLOCH**, and sister **CECILE BLOCH** (See entries) had moved before the turn of the twentieth century. We believe that Charles may have died before the 1894 birth of his sister Cécile Bloch Stiffel's last child whom she named Charles. It would have been customary for her to name her son after a recently deceased relative. (**A, AN, GB, TT**)

BLOCH, CHARLES, was born on 22 August 1856 in *Duttlenheim*, Bas-Rhin, France, to **MOÏSE BLOCH**, a native of the town, and his wife, **NANETTE DREYFUS**, born in *Duppigheim*, Bas-Rhin. According to the 1900 federal census he immigrated to New Orleans, Orleans Parish, LA, in 1872. We believe that he may have been the eighteen-year-old [sic] "Charles Block," a French citizen who arrived in New York on 6 August 1872 from Le Havre, France, aboard the SS *Russia*. His sister, **MELANIE BLOCH** (See entry for **SOLOMON FELIX FALK**), was already living in the city. He may have spent his first years in Louisiana in Marksville, Avoyelles Parish, LA, where he was enumerated in the 1880 federal census as an unmarried twenty-three-year-old merchant. He married **JULIE HIRSCH** in New Orleans on 29 September 1880. Julie was born on 13 June 1856 in *Hatten*, Bas-Rhin, France, to **HERMANN/ HYMAN HIRSCH** (See entry) and his wife, **BABETTE MOOCK/MOCK**, both natives of the town. Because she was the youngest of the Hirsch children, Julie probably immigrated to New Orleans with her parents, brothers **THÉOPHILE** and **JACOB HIRSCH** (See entries), and sisters **HARRIET** and **NANETTE HIRSCH** (See entries), ca. 1861, a date offered by both Harriet and Nanette at the time of the 1900 federal census. While we were unable to find a likely immigration record for Julie, she and three of her siblings, Jacob, Théophile, and Nanette, all from *Hatten*, appeared on a list of emigrants preserved at the archives at *Wissembourg* who left the canton before 1/1/1866. This information was recorded in *The Alsace Immigration Book, Volume 1*, compiled by Cornelia Schrader-Muggenthaler. Julie lived with her parents in New Orleans until her marriage to Charles Bloch, who worked as a butcher. Charles and Julie settled down in New Orleans where their only child, Beulah, was born in 1881. Julie's unmarried sisters, Harriet and Nannette, lived with the Bloch family in New Orleans until their deaths. Charles Bloch died on 13 February 1927 in New Orleans and was buried there in Hebrew Rest Cemetery #2. Julie Hirsch Bloch died on 30 January 1936 and was buried with her husband. (**A, AL, AN, F, GB**)

BLOCH, DAVID, was born on 13 August 1847 in *Riedseltz*, Bas-Rhin, France, to **HENRY BLOCH**, a native of the town, and his third wife, **RACHEL KLOTZ**, born in *Soultz-sous-Fôrets*, Bas-Rhin. David followed an older half-brother, **JOSEPH BLOCH** (See entry), to Louisiana ca. 1875, a reliable record for which we have been unable to find. David settled in Lake Charles, Calcasieu Parish, LA, where he was a dry goods merchant and a prominent member of Masonic Lodge 165. He married ESTELLE MICHEL (See entry for **MEYER MICHEL**), a native of Waterloo, Pointe Coupée Parish, LA, in New Orleans on 9 May 1883, and took her back to Lake Charles to live. They were the parents of three children: Ruby (b. 1884), Henry M. (b. 1886), and Rosa (b. 1887). After the turn of the twentieth century, David went into the insurance business with his son, Henry, in Lake Charles. His wife, Estelle, died on 26 January 1915 in Lake Charles and was buried there in Graceland, the Jewish section of Orange Grove Cemetery. David then moved to North Alexander Street in New Orleans, Orleans Parish, LA, where he lived for a few years until his death on 17 March 1918. He was buried in the Masonic Cemetery on City Park Avenue in New Orleans. (**A, AN, G, GB**)

BLOCH, DAVID, was born on 9 October 1894 in *Schirrhoffen*, Bas-Rhin, France, to **EMANUEL/MAURICE BLOCH** (See entry), a native of the town, and his wife, **MARIA/MADELEINE HIMMLER,** born in *Gundershoffen*, Bas-Rhin, France. He preceded his parents to Louisiana ca. 1912, a reliable record for which we were unable to find. David went to work for his uncle, **ARNAUD BLOCH** (See entry), at the Dollar Store in Donaldsonville, Ascension Parish, LA. After his parents arrived a year later, they all settled down in Donaldsonville in a house on Iberville Street. In 1930 David Bloch was still unmarried. He lived with his widowed father, Maurice Bloch, and worked in the Bloch store in town. He married **YVONNE HIRSCH** ca. 1932, a record for which we were unable to find. Yvonne was said to have been born on 4 April 1905 in *Haguenau*,Bas-Rhin, France, to **SAMUEL HIRSCH** (See entry), a native of *Batzendorf*, Bas-Rhin, France, and his wife **JEANNE/JOHANNA BLOCH**, born in *Saverne,* Bas-Rhin. Her place of birth is, to date, still unverified. Records beyond 1892 are difficult to obtain. There is no trace of her birth in *Saverne*, the town in which her parents were married which does have available vital records through 1912. Thirty-seven-year-old David Bloch and his twenty-seven-year-old wife, Yvonne, landed in New York on 23 September 1932, arriving from Cherbourg, France, on the SS *Berengaria.* Included with the ship's record was the information that David had been naturalized in Baton Rouge, East Baton Rouge Parish in November 1921, and Yvonne had been naturalized in New Orleans in June 1932. We have not been able to verify these naturalizations using any existing available records. David and Yvonne had one child, a daughter, Claudette (b. 1938). David Bloch and his brother, **MARCEL BLOCH** (See entry), took over the day to day running of the Bloch Department Store after the retirement of their Uncle **ARNAUD BLOCH** (See entry). Yvonne's parents, Samuel and Jeanne Hirsch, and her brother, **GASTON HIRSCH** (See entry), followed Yvonne to Louisiana arriving in New York on 15 June 1936 on board the SS *Normandie.* The Bloch-Hirsch extended family lived together in Donaldsonville until death took them one by one. In 1940 David, Yvonne, Claudette, David's father Maurice, and his in-laws, Samuel and Jeanne Bloch Hirsch were all enumerated together in Donaldsonville. As the Jewish population dwindled, David took over as caretaker of Bikur Sholim Jewish Cemetery in the town, a position which he held until ill health took its toll. He passed the mantel to his brother-in-law, **GASTON HIRSCH** (See entry). David died on 21 September 1973 in the local hospital and was buried in Bikur Sholim Jewish Cemetery. Note: Since there are no vital records available for *Schirrhoffen* after 1892, David's date of birth was taken from the Social Security Death Index. After the death of her husband in 1973, Yvonne moved to Roswell, Fulton Co., GA to live with her daughter, Claudette Bloch Solomon. Yvonne died in Roswell on 23 June 1994. Her remains were returned to Louisiana and were interred with those of her husband in Bikur Sholim Jewish Cemetery in Donaldsonville. (**A, AN, G, GB**)

BLOCH, ERNEST, was born on 17 January 1877 in *Duttlenheim*, Bas-Rhin, France, to **SAMUEL BLOCH**, a native of the town, and his wife **JOHANNA FALK**, probably born in *Duppigheim*, Bas-Rhin, a fact we have been, as yet, unable to verify. Ernest immigrated to America arriving in New York on 4 March 1895 from Boulogne-sur-Mer, France, aboard the SS *Veendam*. He was listed on the manifest as a seventeen year old clerk from Germany, whose destination was New Orleans, Orleans Parish, LA. Ernest worked as a dry goods merchant in Crowley, Acadia Parish, LA, where he was naturalized on 12 March 1900. Shortly after the 1900 federal census where he had been enumerated at Crowley, he moved to Alexandria, Rapides Parish, LA. He died there of typhoid fever on 7 January 1902. Ernest Block never married. He was buried in the Jewish Cemetery in Pineville, Rapides Parish, LA. (**AN, F, FS**)

BLOCH, JACOB/JACQUES, was born on 23 March 1813 in *Saverne*, Bas-Rhin, France, to **LAZARD BLOCH**, a native of *Odratzheim*, Bas-Rhin, France, and his wife **BARBE DANHEISER**, born in *Saverne*, Bas-Rhin. Thirty-seven-year-old Jacques Bloch was enumerated with his parents in *Saverne* in 1851. He was still unmarried. We believe he arrived in New Orleans, Orleans Parish, LA, on 23 September 1853 aboard the ship *Ashland* from LeHavre, France. Jacob remained unmarried, living off and on with his sister, **CAROLINE BLOCH LEUMAS,** in Vermilionville (now Lafayette), Lafayette Parish, LA. In 1866 he was listed as paying a special tax in Donaldsonville, where he was working as a "peddler third class." The fee was $15. He rejoined the Leumas family upon their return from France in 1870, and was enumerated with his widowed sister and her children in Donaldsonville in the 1880 federal census. He moved to New Orleans, Orleans Parish, LA, ca. 1885 where he died on 26 September 1891 at Touro Infirmary. We have been unable to locate his final resting place. (**A, AN, B1851, G, L**)

BLOCH, JEANNE/JOHANNA, (*Saverne*) - See entry for **SAMUEL HIRSCH**

BLOCH, JOSEPH, was born on 13 May 1833 in *Riedseltz*, Bas-Rhin, France, to **HENRY BLOCH**, a native of the town, and his first wife, **JULIE STRAUSS**, born in *Gundershoffen*, Bas-Rhin. We believe that he was the "Joseph Block" who arrived in New Orleans, Orleans Parish, La, from Le Havre, France, on 31 May 1858 aboard the ship *Zenobia*. He settled in Ascension Parish, where he worked as a clerk in a dry goods store. By 1860 he had moved to Opelousas, St. Landry Parish, LA, and was associated with **SOLOMON FIRNBERG**, a native of Mannheim, Germany, in the merchandising establishment of Block, Firnberg & Co. He married **BERTHA KAUFMAN**, a native of Rheinpfalz, Germany, on 27 December 1865 in New Orleans and brought her back to Opelousas. Six children were born to the couple: Albert Jonathan (b. 1867), Eugene S. (b. 1869), Julia (b. 1871), Edgar H. (b. 1873), Lucille (b. 1880), and Percy Argyle (b. 1887). Going out on his own after the Civil War, he built up a retail merchandise business and by 1891 he was taking in more than $50,000 annually. He was president of the School Board in Opelousas and a prominent Mason, as well as President of the Hebrew Congregation in Opelousas. Joseph was instrumental in the development of Crowley, Acadia Parish, LA, and also had real estate holdings in Lake Charles, Calcasieu Parish, LA. He moved to New Orleans with his wife in 1897 and died there on 25 January 1900. He was buried there in Hebrew Rest Cemetery # 1. Bertha died in Manhattan, New York, on 23 September 1916 and her remains were returned for burial with those of her husband. (**A, AN, G, GB**)

BLOCH, LÉON, was born **LEOPOLD BLOCH** on 5 June 1861 in *Trimbach*, Bas-Rhin, France, to **SAMUEL BLOCH**, a native of the town, and **NANETTE/JEANNETTE MARX**, his wife, born in *Surbourg*, Bas-Rhin. This identification was made, unfortunately, not from any evidence gleaned from documents here in America, but was based on Leon's choice of residence in Louisiana, a witness to his wedding, the naming of one of his daughters, his lifelong association with members of the Goudchaux family, and his first choice of an occupation in Evergreen. The names Leopold and Leon were often used interchangeably in Jewish families and, indeed, in the 1866 census of Trimbach, the household of butcher Samuel Bloch and his wife, Nanette Marx, included four children: a daughter, Henriette, and three sons, Charles, Aron, and five-year-old Leopold enumerated as Léon. According Leon's naturalization petition, filed at the Avoyelles Parish Courthouse at Marksville, LA, on 26 September 1886, he arrived in Louisiana ca. June 1880. We believe that he was the twenty-one-year-old [*sic*] "Leon Bloch" who arrived in New York from Bremen, Germany, on 27 March 1880 aboard the SS *Main*. He went directly to the town of Evergreen in Avoyelles Parish, LA and was enumerated there on 19 June 1880 as a resident in the household of **MOÏSE LEVY** (See entry). Nineteen-year-old Leon was employed as a clerk in a store. Before long he had saved up enough money to open up a butcher shop, an occupation which, according to his obituary published on 12 January 1945 in a local newspaper, *The Bunkie Record,* was the origin of his nickname "Butch." He married MATHILDE/MAUDE LEVY on 6 March 1895. Rabbi **MARX KLEIN** (See entry) performed the service which took place in Avoyelles Parish. Maude was the Louisiana-born daughter of Moïse Levy of Evergreen, with whom Leon had boarded when he first arrived in Louisiana. Moïse Levy and **LAZARD GOUDCHAUX** (See entry) were witnesses to the marriage. We believe that Lazard's presence was significant. His brother **LEOPOLD GOUDCHAUX** (See entry) had married **FLORA MARX** (See entry for **LEOPOLD GOUDCHAUX**) twelve years earlier in New Orleans. Flora Marx's father, **MORTIER/MARX MARX,** and Leopold/Leon Bloch's mother **NANETTE/JEANNETTE MARX** were siblings, thereby making Flora and Leon first cousins. Leon took his bride, Maude Levy, to nearby Bunkie, Avoyelles Parish, LA, to live. The town, founded in 1882 in conjunction with the arrival of the Texas and Pacific Railway, was, by the turn of the century, a bustling place with over 900 residents. The Goudchaux and Haas families headed by Leopold Goudchaux and **SAMUEL** and **ALEXANDRE HAAS** (See entries), had, by the beginning of the twentieth century, enriched themselves to the point where they controlled most of the banking and commercial enterprises in both St. Landry and Avoyelles Parishes. They staffed their enterprises with relatives and in-laws, many of them immigrants from Alsace. Leon Bloch and William David Haas, son of Alexandre Haas, opened a livery stable called the Bunkie Carriage Company. Leon was president and Haas, the secretary-treasurer. Leon became the leading dealer of horses and mules in the little town. He and Maude were the parents of three children: Leon Jr. (b. 1898; died nine days later), Annette (b. 1902), and Rosalie (b. 1905). Rosalie had been named for her maternal grandmother, **ROSALIE MEYER**. We believe that Annette was named for her paternal grandmother,

NANETTE/JEANNETTE MARX. The Blochs lived in Bunkie for the rest of their lives. When horses and buggies were replaced by cars, Leon became an agent in the oil and gas business, probably still working for the Haas and Goudchaux families, who had extensive mineral holdings in the area. Leon and Maude last appeared in the 1940 federal census living with Maude's brother, Ben Levy, on Holly Street in Bunkie. All three were retired from business. Leon died on 8 January 1945 in Bunkie. A funeral service was conducted the same day by a Baptist minister at the First National Funeral Home in Bunkie. Leon was buried in the Jewish Cemetery at Pineville, Rapides Parish, LA. Rabbi Alfred Dreyfus of Shreveport officiated at the service. Significantly, one of the pall bearers was Mose Firnberg, husband of Leopold Goudchaux's granddaughter Leona. Maude died on 27 March 1947 and was interred with her husband. **(A, AN, AP, G, GB, TT)**

BLOCH, LÉON, was born on 26 September 1889 in *Schirrhoffen*, Bas-Rhin, France, to **EMANUEL/MAURICE BLOCH** (See entry), a native of the town, and his wife, **MARIA/MADELEINE HIMMLER**, born in *Gundershoffen*, Bas-Rhin. Fourteen-year-old "Leo Bloch" arrived in New York from Le Havre, France, on 29 August 1903 aboard the SS *La Lorraine*. He was headed for Donaldsonville, Ascension Parish, LA, to work in his uncle Arnaud Bloch's dry goods store. He lived with **ARNAUD BLOCH** (See entry) until he went back to France to bring his parents back to Louisiana in 1913 where the whole family was reunited in Donaldsonville. Leon married JULIE LABÉ, whose mother, Gertrude Block, a native of Louisiana, was of Swiss, Alsatian, and Jewish origin ca. 1924. Julie had lived with her widowed mother and her two uncles, Leon F. and Adolph Block, most of her life in Thibodaux, Lafourche Parish, LA. Leon and Julie lived in Donaldsonville where their two daughters: Julie (b. 1925) and Frances Leone (b. 1929) were born. In 1933 Leon and his family moved to Thibodaux where he opened up a dry goods store. Julie Labé Bloch died on 11 June 1950 and was buried in Bikur Sholim Jewish Cemetery at Donaldsonville. Leon later married FLORENCE BACH, the widow of Dr. Julius Isaacson, the record for which is unavailable. Leon died in Birmingham, Jefferson Co., AL while visiting his daughter, Leone Bloch Risman on 3 January 1969 and was buried in Bikur Sholim Jewish Cemetery at Donaldsonville with his first wife. **(A, AN, G. GB)**

BLOCH, /MARC/MATTHIAS/MATTHEW was born **MAURICE BLOCH** on 15 November 1851 in *Duttlenheim*, Bas-Rhin, France, to

AUGUSTE BLOCH (See entry), a native of the town, and his second wife, **SARA FALK**, born in *Duppigheim*, Bas-Rhin. He arrived with his mother and siblings at New Orleans, Orleans Parish, LA, on 9 January 1857, from Le Havre, France, aboard the ship *Mortimer Livingston*. They joined his father, Auguste, who had preceded them to Louisiana. They were all enumerated in New Orleans in the 1860 federal census. Nineteen-year-old Maurice Bloch was enumerated as "Mathias Block" in the 1870 federal census for New Orleans where he was employed in the family grocery store which was now being run by his widowed mother. A few years later he, his mother, Sarah, and brother, Charles, moved out to Plaquemines Parish to be near other members of the Falk family. Matthew Bloch eventually moved to Waco, McLennan Co., TX, where he worked as a butcher. He was enumerated in the 1900 federal census with his widowed sister, **CÉCILE BLOCH** (See entry), and her four children He never married. On 10 September 1906 Matthias Block, who had become a wealthy purveyor of groceries and meat in Waco, was set upon by a robber who crushed his skull with an ax as he dozed in a chair in his store. Three hundred dollars was taken from the cash register. Matthias was buried as "Matt Block" at Hebrew Rest Cemetery, in Waco, McLennan Co., TX. The perpetrator of the crime, Jesse Washington, one of Block's employees, was convicted of the murder and later executed. **(A, AN, GB, TT)**

BLOCH, MARCEL, was born on 20 November 1891 in *Schirrhoffen*, Bas-Rhin, France, to **EMANUEL/MAURICE BLOCH** (See entry) a native of the town, and his wife **MARIA/MADELEINE HIMMLER**, born in *Gundershoffen*, Bas-Rhin, France. Fifteen-year-old Marcel Bloch immigrated to Louisiana to work in his uncle Arnaud Bloch's dry goods store in Donaldsonville, Ascension Parish, LA, arriving from Bremen, Germany, on 5 September1906 in New York aboard the SS *Kaiser Wilhelm der Grosse* with his cousin, **MARCEL HIMMLER** (See entry). He lived and worked with **ARNAUD BLOCH** (See entry), and his brother, **LEON BLOCH** (See entry) until his parents arrived in 1913. In 1930 Marcel was still unmarried was enumerated in the federal census with his widowed father, Maurice Bloch. At the time, he was still working in the Bloch Department Store. On 11 March 1934, Marcel wed MARIE BARBARA LINKS, a native of Kosciusko, Attala Co., MS, in New Orleans,Orleans Parish, LA, with his father as best man. Barbara, a teacher, came with her mother Bettie Simon Links (b. 1865 in Alabama) to live with Marcel in Donaldsonville. Marcel and

Barbara had no children. Eventually he and **DAVID BLOCH** (See entry), another brother, became the proprietors of the Bloch Department Store. Marcel died on 12 October 1947 in Donaldsonville and was buried there in Bikur Sholim Jewish Cemetery. He shares a headstone with his mother-in-law, Bettie Simon Links who died in 1957 and his wife, Barbara, widowed in a second marriage to Marx Cohen. Barbara died on 22 January 1970. (**A, AN, G, GB**)

BLOCH, MARIE, (*Diebolsheim*) See entry for **BENJAMIN DREYFUS**

BLOCH, MARX, was born on 24 February 1830 in *Ingwiller*, Bas-Rhin, France, to **LAZARE BLOCH** and his wife, **LÉA MARX**, both natives of the town. He married **BRUNETTE DREYFUSS** on 21 January 1861 in *Mertzwiller*, Bas-Rhin, France. BRUNETTE was born **GERTRUD DREYFUSS** on 25 March 1834 in *Mertzwiller*, Bas-Rhin, to **ISAAC DREYFUSS**, a native of the town, and his wife, **JEANNETTE/ESTER/SCHEINEL JOSEPH,** born in *Neuwiller-lès-Saverne*, Bas-Rhin, France. The couple had three children all born in *Ingwiller*: Léon (b. 1863), Moise (b. 1865) and Cécile (b. 1867). We can find no trace of his family, or him, for that matter in Louisiana other than his tombstone, which has his exact date and place of birth. Nor could we find any reliable record for his immigration to the United States. There is, in addition, a photo of him in a book on Shreveport Jewry, indicating he was a pioneer merchant in the region. He died in Shreveport, Caddo Parish, LA, during a yellow fever epidemic on 10 September 1873 and was buried there in Hebrew Rest Cemetery # 1 (Jewish section of Oakland Cemetery). There are no other Bloch family members buried in Shreveport. It is possible that he immigrated ahead of his family, and died before they could join him in Louisiana. (**A, BR, G**)

BLOCH, MAURICE/ MORRIS/ MORITZ, was born **EMANUEL BLOCH** on 12 September 1861 in *Schirrhoffen*, Bas-Rhin, France, to **LEHMANN BLOCH,** a native of the town, and his wife, **LOUISE MEYER**, born in *Herrlisheim,* Bas-Rhin. He married **MARIA/ MATHILDE HIMMLER** on 8 February 1888 in *Gundershoffen*, Bas-Rhin. Mathilde was born **MARIA HIMMLER** (with a marginal notation in German written in 1888 that her name was "Mathilde") on 14 July 1863 in *Gundershoffen*, Bas-Rhin, France, to **MICHEL HIMMLER**, a native of the town and his wife, **THERESE/DINA**

DREYFUS, born in *Mertzwiller*, Bas-Rhin. Maurice and Mathilde were the parents of three sons, all born in *Schirrhoffen*: Leon (b. 1889; See entry), Marcel (b. 1891; See entry), and David (b. 1895; See entry). Maurice and Mathilde Himmler Bloch followed their sons who were earlier immigrants to Donaldsonville, Ascension Parish, LA. Their son, Leon, returned to France to accompany them on their trip. They all arrived in New York on 17 September 1913 from Cherbourg, France, aboard the SS *Kaiser Wilhelm II*. The family was enumerated together in the 1920 federal census for Donaldsonville. Mathilde died on 12 March 1929 in Donaldsonville and was buried there in Bikur Sholim Jewish Cemetery. Eighty-three-year-old Maurice, a retired dry goods merchant, died on 25 December 1944 in Donaldsonville and was buried with his wife. Note: Maurice and **ARNAUD BLOCH** (See entry) were brothers. **MARCEL HIMMLER** (See entry) was Mathilde Himmler Bloch's nephew. **(A, AN, G, GB)**

BLOCH, PAULINE, was born **CAROLINE BLOCH** on 21 May 1842 in *Mertzwiller*, Bas-Rhin, France, to **JOSEPH BLOCH** and his first wife, **ROSINE STORCK**, both natives of the town. There were several BLOCH families living in *Mertzwiller*, and, at least four daughters born to these couples around the 1840s, but no one was given the name "Pauline" or "Baulina" at birth. Following "Caroline" through the available census records for the town of *Mertzwiller*, she was enumerated as JEANNE in 1851, age nine, and finally "Pauline," age eighteen in the 1861 census. We believe that twenty-three-year-old Pauline Bloch immigrated to the United States, arriving on 22 June 1866, at New York, from Le Havre, France, aboard the SS *Lafayette*. Her final destination was New Orleans, Orleans Parish, LA. Pauline married JACOB FARRNBACHER, a widower with eight children, born in Furth, Bavaria, who was a merchant in Baton Rouge, East Baton Rouge Parish, LA. They were wed on 18 March 1872. Two children were born to them: Delphine (b.1872; See entry for **MAURICE LEVY**) and Isidore (b. 1874). Pauline died on 24 February 1898 in New Orleans, and was interred in the Jewish Cemetery in Baton Rouge. Jacob died on 24 April 1918 and was buried with her. Note: Pauline's birth town is inscribed on her tombstone. **(A, AN, E, GB)**

BLOCK, RAPHAEL, was born **RAPHAEL BLOCH** on 11 September 1864 in *Herrlisheim*, Bas-Rhin, France, to **MARX/MARC BLOCH**, a native of the town, and his wife, **MINETTE/MONIQUE**

BRAUN, born in *Offendorf*, Bas-Rhin. He immigrated to the United States, arriving in New York on 9 August 1882 aboard the SS *St. Laurent*. Raphael married CECELIA STEEG, a native of Louisiana, on 10 October 1899 in New Orleans, Orleans Parish, LA. The couple settled in St. James Parish, LA, where they were enumerated in 1900 along with a brother-in-law, Jacob Steeg. Raphael moved shortly thereafter to Sellers, St. Charles Parish, LA, where he operated a general store. The couple had one child, Mervin Steeg Block, born on 4 September 1900. Raphael died on 6 April 1919 and was buried in Hebrew Rest Cemetery #1 in New Orleans. Cecelia stayed on in Sellers to operate the store with the assistance of several young men from Alsace, including **ARMAND** and **RENÉ BRAUN** (See entries), two of her late husband's cousins. Cecelia Steeg Block died on 14 May 1954 in New Orleans and was buried with her husband in Hebrew Rest Cemetery #1. (**A, AN, G, GB**)

BLOCH, SAMSON, was born **SELIGMAN ARON BLOCH** on 7 frimaire, an XIV (28 November 1805) in *Saverne*, Bas-Rhin, France, to **LIBERMAN ARON (LAZARE BLOCH** after 1808), born in *Odratzheim*, Bas-Rhin, France, and his wife, **BEILE HERTZE (BARBE DANHEISER** after 1808), a native of *Saverne*. When Samson's son, Marx, applied for a U.S. passport in 1919, he stated that his father had immigrated to Louisiana in 1842 and had lived in Franklin and then in Patterson, St. Mary Parish, LA, for thirteen years until his death. We believe that he may have been the "Samson Bloch" who arrived in New Orleans, Orleans Parish, La, on 27 January 1840 from Le Havre, France, aboard the ship *Christophe Colombe*. Samson married **BABETTE ISRAEL** on 21 April 1845 in Franklin, St. Mary Parish, LA. Babette was born on 4 April 1821 in *Romanswiller*, Bas-Rhin, France, to **SAMUEL ISRAEL**, a native of the town, and his wife **MALGY/MARIE LEVY**, born in *Duttlenheim*, Bas-Rhin. We were unable to find an immigration record for Babette. Samson and Babette were the parents of five children: Samuel (b. 1845), Florette (b. 1848), Marx (b. 1850), Clara (b. 1852), and Lazare (b. 1855). Samson died in Franklin, LA, on 4 July 1855 and was buried there in the local cemetery. His tombstone identifies his place of birth and his date of death. After her husband's death Babette Israel Bloch appears to have returned to France ca. 1865 with her children. Both Marx and Lazare Bloch indicated on their U.S. passports that they had lived in France between 1865 and 1872, where they had gone to school. Moreover, their purpose for a 1919 return visit to France was to see their sisters, one of whom was very ill. (**A, AN, F, G, GB, L, SWLR**)

BLOCH, SIMON, was born on 29 August 1840 in *Duttlenheim*, Bas-Rhin, France, to **AUGUSTE BLOCH** (See entry), a native of the town, and **BEYERLÉ/BABETTE WEIL**, born in Schmieheim, Baden-Württemberg, Germany. Auguste and Babette were married on 11 February 1841 in *Duttlenheim* and she died on 21 March 1849. Auguste married **SARA FALK** on 3 July 1849 in *Duttlenheim*. Sixteen-year-old Simon was enumerated with his step-mother, Sara Falk Bloch, who was listed as an indigent head of household, and his three step-siblings in the 1856 town census for *Duttlenheim*. Sixteen-year-old Simon Bloch immigrated with his step-mother, Sarah and her three children to New Orleans, Orleans Parish, LA, arriving on 9 January 1857, from Le Havre, France, aboard the ship *Mortimer Livingston*. Nineteen-year-old Simon was not enumerated with his family in the 1860 federal census for New Orleans. He was however, boarding elsewhere in New Orleans with another young man from France and was working as a baker. We were unable to find him in the 1870 federal census. He was enumerated in the 1880 federal census as an unmarried thirty-year-old [*sic*] storekeeper in St. Charles Parish, living with his mother, Sara Falk Bloch. Efforts to trace him any further have yielded no results. (**A, AN, E, F, TT**)

BLUM, ADELE, was born on 19 August 1829 in *Dettwiller*, Bas-Rhin, France, to **MARX/MARC BLUM**, a native of the town, and his second wife, **MADELEINE WEIL**, born in *Schwenheim*, Bas-Rhin. One of five Blum sisters to come to Louisiana, she may have been the Adele Blum who arrived in New Orleans, Orleans Parish, LA, on 15 January 1855 from Le Havre, France, aboard the ship *Gosport*. Adele was married to ABRAHAM LEOPOLD, a native of Biedesheim, Rheinpfalz, Germany, ca. 1855, a record of which we have not been able to locate. Thirty-four-year old Abraham and twenty-seven-year-old Adele were enumerated in the 1860 federal census in New Orleans with eleven-year-old Harriet and nine-year-old Rose, children from Abraham's first marriage, as well as the couple's first two children, Benjamin (b. 1856) and Bertha (b. 1858). Three more children were born to the couple: Manasses (b. 1861), Simon (b. 1865), and Henry (b. 1867). Abraham worked in New Orleans as a master tailor and later as a "huckster," before moving to Berwick, St. Mary Parish, LA, where the family was enumerated in the 1880 federal census. Abraham opened a retail grocery, which he ran until his death on 30 July 1898 at Berwick. He was interred in New Orleans at Gates of Prayer Cemetery #2 (Joseph Street). Adele continued to run the grocery with the help of her unmarried son, Manasses, until her death at Berwick on 29 June 1910. She was interred there in the Hebrew Cemetery. Note: See entries for her four sisters: **MARIE**, **JEANNETTE**, **PAULINE** and **SARA BLUM** (A, AN, G, GB, TT)

BLUM, ADELE, was born on 23 December 1854 in *Strasbourg*, Bas-Rhin, France, to **LÉON BLUM** and his wife **MADELEINE/ MATHILDE HIRSCHMANN**, both natives of *Bischheim*, Bas-Rhin, France. She came to Louisiana ca. 1866 with her mother and siblings, following her father who had arrived the year before. We could find no reliable record for their entry into the United States. Adele and her family settled in Donaldsonville, Ascension Parish, LA, where her father, Léon, was a merchant. Her parents and brother, Sylvain, died in 1867 and were buried at Donaldsonville. Thirteen-year-old Adele and her three surviving siblings, **SAMUEL**, **ISAAC** and **PAULINE BLUM** (See entries), were sent to the Jewish Widows and Orphans Home in New Orleans, Orleans Parish, La, where they were enumerated together in the 1870 federal census. From here on the records are sparse. We believe that she was the same Adele Blum who appeared in the Galveston, Galveston Co., Directory in 1881 and subsequently married SOLOMON J. HIRSCH on 8 November 1885 in Harris Co., TX. Nothing is known of Sol Hirsch except what can be found in Houston, Harris Co., TX, directories. In 1884 he was listed as a streetcar driver, in 1886 as a clerk for J. Seligman, in 1887 as a salesman for Sam Stein, and in 1892, as a clerk for Frank Dunn. He may have died in Texas between 1892 and 1895. We know that Mrs. Adele Hirsch, sister of Pauline Stein, was living at the Stein Hotel in Monroe, Ouachita Parish, LA on 22 June 1895, the day her brother **SAM BLUM** (See entry) shot and killed his brother-in-law, SIMON STEIN. Adele subsequently appeared as a witness at the coroner's inquest held at Monroe in an attempt to exonerate her brother. Not long after the shooting incident, Adele Hirsch, her sister Pauline Stein, and Pauline's four children moved to Galveston, TX. Both Adele Hirsch, listed as the widow of Solomon, and Pauline Stein, listed as the widow of Simon, appeared in the 1896 Galveston directory living at 2002 Avenue K. Two years later, both widows were recorded in the 1898 Galveston directory living at 1821 Broadway. While Pauline and her children remained in Galveston, surviving the devastating 8 September

1900 hurricane which killed between 6,000 and 12,000 people, Adele Hirsch moved back to New Orleans. She was listed in the 1902 and 1903 New Orleans directories first, as an assistant, then as an employee at the linen room at Touro Infirmary. She was enumerated in the 1920 federal census at the Julius Weis Home for the Aged, where she died on 30 July 1923. She was interred at Dispersed of Judah Cemetery in New Orleans. (**A, AN, G, GB, TT**)

BLUM, ARON (aka. **AARON BLOOM**), was born on 10 July 1819 in *Rothbach*, Bas-Rhin, France, to **LAZARE BLUM** a native of *Mulhausen*, Bas-Rhin, France, and his wife **JUDITH FRAENCKEL** born in *Rothbach*, Bas-Rhin. He immigrated to Louisiana along with his prospective wife, **MADELEINE/MINETTE/MINA BLUM**, from Le Havre, France, on the ship *Oxnard,* arriving in New Orleans, Orleans Parish, LA, on 4 October 1847. Madeleine was born on 28 July 1820 in *Gundershoffen*, Bas-Rhin, France, to **ISAAC BLUM,** a native of the town, and his wife **ROSINE VOGEL**, born in *Gunstett*, Bas-Rhin, France. Aron and Madeleine married on 25 February 1849 in New Orleans. Aron became a dry goods merchant in Bayou Goula, Iberville Parish, LA, where four of their five children were born: Isadore (b. 1850), Rosalie (b. 1852), Phillip (b. 1856), and Abraham (b, 1857). By 1860, with the birth of their fifth child,Henriette, the family was established in Baton Rouge, East Baton Rouge Parish, LA. Aaron started out there as keeper of a coffee house, joined the Confederate Army as a Second Lieutenant in Company B, 4th LA Infantry in 1861, and, upon return, became a retail grocer. Minette, as she was more commonly known in Louisiana, died on 25 October 1864, and was buried in the Jewish Cemetery in Baton Rouge. Aron Blum remarried ca. 1865, taking CAROLINE HABER, a native of Oberlustadt, Bavaria, Germany, as his second wife. Six children were born to them: Theresa (b. 1866), Samuel (b. 1868), Lea (b. 1870), Lazare (b. 1872, Joseph (b. 1873) and Henry (b. 1877Aron Blum died in Baton Rouge on 4 March 1894 and was buried there in the Jewish Cemetery. Caroline Haber Blum died on 24 November 1901 in Baton Rouge and was buried with her husband. (**A, AN, G, TT**)

BLUM, GABRIEL, was born on 5 April 1851 at *Quatzenheim*, Bas-Rhin, France, to **EMANUEL BLUM**, a native of the town and his second wife, **PAULINE/ROSINE RECHT**, born in *Schaffhouse-sur-Zorn*, Bas-Rhin. Gabriel immigrated to Louisiana, arriving on 1 September 1872 aboard the Steamer *Washington.* He started out as a merchant in Fayette, Jefferson Co. MS, where he was naturalized in 1877. He soon moved to St. Joseph, Tensas Parish, LA, where he made his permanent home. He was enumerated there in the 1880 federal census as an twenty-seven-year-old unmarried immigrant from Alsace working as a merchant. His half-brother, **OSCAR LEVY** (See entry), and a cousin, **JOSEPH LEVY** (See entry), were enumerated with him in St. Joseph, Tensas Parish in 1900. At age forty-nine, Gabe was still unmarried. He and Oscar were running a general store in the town. We could find no other records for him in Louisiana. Note: His name was often misspelled as "Bloom." (**A, AN**)

BLUM, ISAAC, was born on 10 March 1859 in *Strasbourg*, Bas-Rhin, France, to **LÉON BLUM** and his wife **MADELEINE/MATHILDE HIRSCHMANN**, both natives of *Bischheim*, Bas-Rhin, France. He arrived in Louisiana ca. 1866 with his mother and siblings, following his father, who had emigrated from the Bas-Rhin the year before. In the 1920 federal census, Isaac gave his date of immigration as 1866. He and his family settled in Donaldsonville, Ascension Parish, LA, where his father was a merchant. His parents and a brother, Sylvain, all died in 1867 and were buried in Donaldsonville. Eight-year-old Isaac and his three surviving siblings, **SAMUEL, ADELE,** and **PAULINE BLUM** (See entries), were sent to the Jewish Widows and Orphans Home in New Orleans, Orleans Parish, La, where they were enumerated together in the 1870 federal census. Isaac Blum became a successful cotton merchant in Brookhaven, Lincoln Co., MS, with a residence in New Orleans. He was also the manager of Newburger & Levy at Meridian, Lauderdale Co., MS. Isaac married JENNIE/JANE L. MOSES, a native of Louisiana, on 30 December 1901 in Cincinnati, Hamilton Co., OH, the former home of her parents. The couple returned to Mississippi where they made their home in Meridian. The couple had one child, Eleanor J. Blum, born in 1909 in Meridian. Although we have not been able to ascertain the death dates of either Isaac or Jennie, they were enumerated together in the 1940 federal census for Meridian where they were still living. An Isaac Blum was buried in Beth Israel Cemetery in Meridian, however no dates were given. His daughter, Eleanor died on 7 July 2011 in Urbana, Champaign Co., IL, at the age of 102. She was buried there at Mount Hope Cemetery and Mausoleum. Eleanor never married. (**A, AN, G, GB, TT**)

BLUM, JEANNETTE, (*Dettwiller*) See entry for **EDOUARD LEVY**

BLUM, JOSEPH, was born on 10 October 1830 in *Gundershoffen*, Bas-Rhin, France, to **LEOPOLD BLUM**, a native of the town, and his wife, **BALINA/PAULINE WEYL/WEIL**, born in *Reichshoffen*, Bas-Rhin. Joseph immigrated to New Orleans ca. 1861, although we were not able to find a definitive record for his arrival in America. He lived for over a decade in New Orleans, Orleans Parish, LA, before marrying **SARAH RAAS** on 24 May 1871. She was born **SARA RAAS** on 9 November 1844 in *Niedernai,* Bas-Rhin, France, to **ELIE RAS**, born in 1800 at *Mutzig*, Bas-Rhin, and his wife, **ROSINE HIRTZ,** a native of Wintzenheim, Haut-Rhin, France. Sara followed her older brothers, **ISAAC** and **SAMUEL RAAS** (See entries), to New Orleans where she married Joseph. Their first child, Pauline, was born in Opelousas, St. Landry Parish, LA, in February 1872 where Joseph was working as a dry goods salesman. Shortly thereafter, Joseph moved his family to Calvert, Robertson Co., TX, where their children Rachel (b. 1876), Julia (b. 1879) and Leopold (b. 1883) were all born. Sarah died in Calvert, TX on 28 August 1889 at the age of forty-four. She may be buried in the small Jewish Cemetery in that town, although, there seems to be no record of it. Joseph returned to Louisiana with his children. His eldest daughter, Pauline, went to live with her uncle, **ISAAC RAAS** (See Entry), in Lake Charles, Calcasieu Parish, LA. In 1900, Rachel, Julia, and Leopold were living together as boarders in New Orleans, where they worked and attended school. Their father, Joseph, was living in Carencro, Lafayette Parish, LA, where he worked as a dry goods salesman. He died there on 28 April 1902. His body was brought back to New Orleans and was buried there in the Hebrew Rest Cemetery # 1. (**A, AN, G, GB, TT**)

BLUM, LÉON, was born on 4 December 1815 in *Bischheim*, Bas-Rhin, France, to **MARX/MARC BLUM (MEYER ARON** before 1808), born in *Ettendorf*, Bas-Rhin, France, and his wife, **BREINEL LEVI (PAULINE KLING** after 1808), a native of *Dauendorf*, Bas-Rhin. Leon married **MADELEINE/MATHILDE HIRSCHMANN** on 28 December 1858 at *Bischheim*. Madeleine was born on 8 April 1831 in *Bischheim*, Bas-Rhin, France, to **ZACHARIE HIRSCHMANN (SELIGMANN SAMUEL** before 1808) and his wife **ZIBORA/ FRANÇOISE HEMMERDINGER (FRADEL HEMMERDINGER** before 1808), both natives of *Bischheim*. Léon and Madeleine were the parents of six children, all born in *Strasbourg*, Bas-Rhin, France: Adèle (b. 1854; See entry), Samuel Silvain (b. 1856; See entry), Charles (b. 1858;died 1859), Isaac (b. 1859; See entry); Pauline (b. 1860; See entry), and Samuel (b. 1861; See entry). Leon may have immigrated to the United States by himself on the ship *Europe*, which arrived in New York from Le Havre, France, on 15 May 1865, just after General Robert E. Lee's surrender to Union forces on 9 April 1865. According to this ship's record, Leon Blum was a forty-nine year old merchant whose destination was New Orleans. Although his ethnicity was listed as "American," this could have been an error since he was grouped with ten other men who were said to be American as well. Although there is a tax assessment list for a Leon Blum who was working as a retail dealer in Opelousas, St. Landry Parish, La, in June 1865, we cannot be sure that this is Leon Blum from Bischheim. There is, however, a tax assessment list record for Leon Blum in August 1866 which showed him as a retail dealer working in Donaldson[ville], Ascension Parish, LA, the place of his death. Two of Leon's children who survived to adulthood, Isaac and Pauline, remembered, in different federal census records, that they had immigrated in 1866. We conclude from this that Mathilde and her five children arrived in Louisiana in 1866, although, we have not been able to find any ship's record for them. Since their arrival was followed the next year by three family tragedies, we believe that Isaac and Pauline were accurate in their memory of their immigration to America which had been fixed in their minds by the life-changing events that occurred in 1867. Their father, Leon Blum, died on 26 May 1867 and was buried in Bikur Sholim Jewish Cemetery in Donaldsonville. Mathile [*sic*] Hirschman Blum died on 20 October 1867, and was buried near her husband. Ten days later, on 30 October 1867 the deceased couple's eleven year old son, Sylvain (See entry) died as well. There was an epidemic of the "fever" reported in the Thibodaux, LA *Sentinel* published on 12 October 1867 and carried in the New Orleans *Daily Picayune* which told of the spread of yellow fever into the river parishes that month. It is possible that father, mother, and son, recent immigrants with no immunity to the pestilence, were its victims. The four surviving Blum children were sent to the Jewish Widows and Orphans Home in New Orleans, Orleans Parish, LA. (**A, AN, G, TT**) See also pp 3, 14, 15

BLUM, MADELEINE/MINETTE/MINA, (*Gundershoffen*) See entry for **ARON BLUM**

BLUM, MARIE/MARY/MARIAM, was born **MARIE BLUM** on 10 January 1840 in *Dettwiller,* Bas-Rhin, France, to **MARX/MARC BLUM**, a native of the town, and his second wife, **MADELEINE**

WEIL, born in *Schwenheim*, Bas-Rhin. According to a notation in the 1900 federal census, Mary immigrated to the United States in 1855, the same year as her older sister, **ADELE BLUM** (See entry), one of the five Blum sisters who eventually settled in Louisiana.(See also entries for **JEANNETTE, PAULINE,** and **SARA BLUM**). We have not found a likely ship's record for her arrival. Mary married HYPOLITE PAUL FORTIN/FORTUNE, a native of Canada, ca. 1859, probably in Louisiana, although no marriage record has yet been found. The couple's 1900 federal census record reported that they had been married for forty-one years. Hypolite Fortin/Fortune was an engineer on steamboats, so it is not surprising that the couple's first child, Bertha Elizabeth, was born in July 1861 in Cincinnati, Hamilton Co., OH, at the beginning of the Civil War. Cincinnati is located on the banks of the Ohio River where steamboats made their way down to Cairo, Alexander Co., IL. There the Ohio River flows into the Mississippi, gateway to the South. H.P. Fortin, or Captain Fortin, as he was known, joined the Confederate cause in 1862, enlisting as a private in Company B, Louisiana Militia, Chalmette Infantry Regiment, where records show him working on Confederate gunboats in March of that year. The Fortin/Fortune family settled in Patterson, then relocated nearby Berwick, St. Mary Parish, LA. Berwick, located on the Atchafalaya River, a main tributary of the Mississippi, which flows west of it down to the Gulf of Mexico, was a perfect location for Captain Fortin, who worked as a marine engineer well into the twentieth century. Hypolite and Marie were the parents of seven more children, all born in Louisiana: Moïse/Morris M. (b. 1867), Henry B. (b. 1869), Rose (b. 1872), Cécile (b. 1875), Mathilda (b. 1878), Joseph A. (b. 1880; died 1898), and Edward M. (b. 1882). Both Morris and Edward followed in their father's footsteps. Morris became a river pilot, and Edward, was chief engineer on river steamers. Marie Blum Fortin died on 17 February 1907 at Berwick and was interred there in the Hebrew Cemetery. Her grave marker, which appears on the front cover of this book, is the largest in the cemetery, the majority of whose occupants are descendants of the five Blum sisters from *Dettwiller*. Marie's husband, Captain H. P. Fortin, died on 3 March 1915 in Berwick and was interred with his wife. Note: The family was recorded using the last name "Fortune" in the 1870, 1880 and 1900 U.S. censuses. Some Texas descendants of Morris M. Fortin continue to use the name "Fortune."(**A, AN, G, GB, TT**)

BLUM, MARX, was born on 28 August 1834 in *Niederbronn-les-Bains*, Bas-Rhin, France, to **SAMUEL BLUM**, a native of the town, and his wife, **RACHEL MOCH**, born in *Mommenheim*, Bas-Rhin. He arrived in Louisiana ca. 1860. Unfortunately we were unable to find a reliable ship's record for his entry into the United States. Marx started his mercantile career in Donaldsonville, Assumption Parish, LA. On 13 September 1861 he volunteered for the Confederate Army, signing up as a private in Captain Landry's Donaldsonville Light Artillery, Company C. He was discharged from service in April 1864 account of a disability. He married Fannie (b. 1850), whose maiden name we were unable to ascertain, ca. 1866, and settled in Shreveport, Caddo Parish, LA, where he was a dry goods merchant. Marx, often called "Max" in Louisiana, and Fannie had no children. According to the 1900 federal census Fannie had come to America in 1860 at the age of ten, so she probably would have been with her family or with older siblings. At her death, she was said to have been a resident of Shreveport for fifty years. Marx Blum died on 11 November 1904 in Shreveport and was buried in Hebrew Rest Cemetery #2 (Texas Ave.). Fannie died on 8 August 1912 and was buried in the same cemetery. (**A, AN, G, GB, TT**)

BLUM, PAULINE, was born on 2 May 1845 in *Dettwiller*, Bas-Rhin, France, to **MARX/MARC BLUM**, a native of the town, and his second wife, **MADELEINE WEIL**, born in *Schwenheim*, Bas-Rhin. In the 1900 federal census for Berwick, St. Mary Parish, LA, Pauline reported that she had immigrated to America in 1860, a fact which we could not verify using an appropriate ship's record. She settled in New Orleans, Orleans Parish, LA, where her older sister **ADELE BLUM LEOPOLD** (See entry) was already living. Pauline married JOSEPH L. JACOBS, a New York native, ca. 1868, a date calculated from the registration of the birth of their first child, Amelia/Emelia at New Orleans on 30 June 1869. A second child, Henry, was born on 2 November 1870, also in New Orleans. Pauline's third child, Charles Jacobs, however, was born in Pattersonville, St. Mary Parish, LA, in June 1873. Pauline's sister, **MARIE BLUM** (See entry), was living there at the time with her husband, Hypolite Fortin/Fortune. The fate of Pauline Blum's marriage to Joseph L. Jacobs is unknown. We could find no death record for him, or any reliable information that he lived past 1873 to start a new life elsewhere. Pauline was enumerated in the 1880 federal census with her second husband, CHARLES WILSON, at Berwick, St. Mary Parish, LA, where the five Blum sisters, Adele, Marie, Pauline, Jeannette and Sara (See entries), had all eventually settled. Charles Wilson, also a shadowy figure, was a forty-one-year old sailor from Hamburg, Germany. His thirty-three-year-old wife, Pauline, and his three step-children, Amelia, Henry, and Charles Jacobs lived with him on Pacific Avenue in Berwick. Charles and Pauline were the parents of two children: a daughter, Martel [sic], born in January 1881, and a son, Milton H., born in March 1883. We have found no record of a marriage between Charles and Pauline or a death record for Charles. The 1900 federal census for Berwick, where Pauline appeared with her two children by Charles Wilson, and her daughter, Amelia Jacobs, recorded the presence of yet another mate, D. R. Thompson, a fifty-five-year-old Scottish locomotive engineer, to whom she had been married for six years. Ten years later there was no sign of D. R. Thompson. Pauline Wilson was enumerated at Berwick as a sixty-five-year-old widow with her daughter, Mimi Wilson, age forty-one, who according to her age, was , in fact, Amelia Jacobs. Pauline's son, twenty-six-year-old Milton Wilson was also living in the household. Milton married Mena Wormser, the widow of his first cousin, Simon Leopold, on 20 September 1915 in New Orleans. The couple raised Mena's three children at Berwick where Milton became the town marshal. Pauline Wilson died on 7 June 1919 at Berwick and was interred there in the Hebrew Cemetery. (**A, AN, G, GB, TT**)

BLUM, PAULINE, was born on 29 April 1860 in *Strasbourg*, Bas-Rhin, France, to **LÉON BLUM** and his wife, **MADELEINE/ MATHILDE HIRSCHMANN**, both natives of *Bischheim*, Bas-Rhin, France. She arrived in Louisiana ca. 1866 with her mother and siblings, following her father who had emigrated the year before in order to prepare for the arrival of his family. While we could find no ships record for her, her mother, or her four siblings, she remembered having come to America in 1866, a fact which was recorded in the 1900 federal census for Galveston, Galveston Co., TX, where she lived with her children. She and her parents settled in Donaldsonville, Ascension Parish, LA, where her father was a merchant. Her parents and brother, Sylvain, all died in 1867 and were buried in Donaldsonville. Seven-year-old Pauline and her three surviving siblings, **ISAAC**, **ADELE** and **SAMUEL BLUM** (See entries), were sent to the Jewish Widows and Orphans Home in New Orleans, Orleans Parish, La, where they were enumerated together in the 1870 federal census. We believe she was enumerated ten years later in the 1880 federal census in New Orleans as a twenty-year-old unmarried woman who was working as a servant. Pauline married SIMON STEIN, a native of Asselheim, Rheinpfalz,

Germany, on 4 January 1881 in Farmerville, Union Parish, LA. Simon and his brother, Daniel Stein, had been in partnership in the mercantile firm of D. Stein & Co. at Farmerville. After his marriage, Simon purchased a general merchandise store at Stein's Bluff, Union Parish, LA, where he and Pauline had five children: Caroline (b. 1882), Leon (b. 1883; died 1884), Mathilde (b. 1885), Esther (b. 1886), and Daniel (b. 1888). Simon's brother-in-law, Samuel "Sam" Blum, worked at Stein's Bluff as a cotton receiver. In 1892 business reverses caused Simon Stein to leave Stein's Bluff and settle in Monroe, Ouachita Parish, LA, with his family, where he purchased the Verandah Hotel, renaming it Stein's Hotel. On 22 June 1895 at approximately 10:00 AM Simon Stein was shot and killed by his brother-in-law Sam Blum. Sam claimed self-defense and alleged that he was protecting his sister from Simon who, when sober, was a good man, but when drunk, was dangerous. Simon was said to have been drinking heavily for about twelve hours, and had threatened to kill his wife. Simon's body was returned to Union Parish where it was interred in the Farmerville Cemetery with other members of the Stein family. Pauline quickly relocated to Galveston, Galveston Co., TX. Pauline Stein, listed as Simon's widow, appeared in the 1896 *Galveston City Directory* living at 2002 Avenue K. Two years later, the 1898 Galveston directory showed her residence as 1821 Broadway. She and her children were enumerated in the 1900 and 1910 federal censuses for Galveston. Pauline and her children survived the 8 September 1900 hurricane which devastated that community, killing thousands of residents. Pauline died at Galveston on 9 June 1932 and was buried there at the Hebrew Benevolent Society Cemetery. (**A, AN, G, GB, TT**)

BLUM, SAMUEL, was born on 10 April 1821 in *Niederbronn-les-Bains*, Bas-Rhin, France, to **JACQUES BLUM**, a native of the town, and **ADELE LEVY**, born in *Haguenau*, Bas-Rhin. In the 1851 census for *Niederbronn*, thirty-year-old Samuel was enumerated with his father and mother. He was unmarried and working as a second hand dealer. He immigrated to New Orleans, Orleans Parish, LA, a year later, arriving on 26 October 1852 aboard the ship *Pyramid*. He married **BABETTE VOGEL**, the widow of Meyer Mayer, on 8 April 1854 in Donaldsonville, Ascension Parish, LA. **BABETTE** was born **JEANETTE VOGEL** on 20 September 1818 in *Niederbronn-les-Bains*, Bas-Rhin, France to **DANIEL VOGEL**, a native of the town and his wife, **MARY ANNE KLEIN** born in *Pfaffenhoffen*, Bas-Rhin, France. Babette married **MEYER MAYER,** ca. 1843, a record for which we were unable to discover. Their daughter **MELANIE MAYER** (See entry) was born in *Niederbronn* on 16 May 1844. Babette was enumerated without her first husband in *Niederbronn* in the 1846 town census. Babette and Melanie immigrated using the last name "Vogel" on the ship *Oxnard* which arrived in New Orleans on 4 October 1847. A son, Elie, was born to Babette in 1849, whose paternal identity is in question, although he used the name Blum. Babette and Samuel's son, Jacob Blum, was born in 1856. A ship's record shows Samuel, Babette, Melanie, Elie and Jacques/Jacob returning from France once more on 27 November 1858 aboard the *New Hampshire*. Babette and Sam Blum were shown in the U.S. federal census records of 1860, 1870, 1880 and 1900 living with their children, and in 1900 with their grandchild, Jacob, Melanie's son, in Donaldsonville, where Sam retired as a dry goods merchant. Babette died on 16 July 1909 in Donaldsonville, and was buried there in Bikur Sholim Jewish Cemetery. Her tombstone indicates she was born "Babette Fogel." Samuel died in Donaldsonville on 8 October 1915 at the age of 94 years and six months. He was buried in Bikur Sholim Jewish Cemetery with his wife. **(A, AN, B1851, E, F. G, GB)**

BLUM, SAMUEL "SAM," was born on 6 August 1861 in *Strasbourg*, Bas-Rhin, France, to **LÉON BLUM** (See entry) and his wife **MADELEINE/MATHILDE HIRSCHMANN**, both natives of *Bischheim*, Bas-Rhin, France. He immigrated to Louisiana with his mother and siblings ca. 1866, following his father who had arrived the previous year. Two of his siblings, Pauline and Isaac, remember having arrived in 1866, and Sam's 1902 obituary reported that he had lived in Louisiana for thirty-seven years. Sam's family settled in Donaldsonville, Ascension Parish, LA, where his father was a merchant. His parents and brother, Sylvain, all died in 1867 and were buried in Donaldsonville. Six-year-old Sam and his three surviving siblings, **ISAAC**, **ADELE**, and **PAULINE BLUM** (See entries), were sent to the Jewish Widows and Orphans Home in New Orleans, Orleans Parish, La, where they were enumerated together in the 1870 federal census. After his sister, Pauline's marriage to Simon Stein, Sam worked at Stein's Bluff, Union Parish, LA, as a cotton receiver and shipper for his brother-in-law. After the Stein store fell on hard times in 1892 and Simon and his family moved to Monroe, Ouachita Parish, LA, Sam stayed behind, but could not make a living at the bluff. In 1893 he sought employment on a river packet, the *Belle of D'arbonne* where he worked as a bartender. The *Belle*, built in Monroe, Ouachita

Parish, LA, and launched from there in April 1893, plied the waters between Farmerville and Monroe, where she carried passengers and as many as 500 bales of cotton at a time. When at Monroe, Sam stayed at the Stein Hotel. On 22 June 1895 Sam shot and killed Simon Stein at the hotel. He claimed self-defense and said he fired to protect his sister, who was being threatened by a drunken husband. Initially acquitted by the coroner's jury, he was jailed and tried three times for murder. He was found guilty of manslaughter at the first trial, but appealed, account one of the jurymen had left the jury room after sequestration to attend to one of his children who had been accidentally shot. The second trial ended in a mistrial. The third which was convened in April 1898 must have brought an acquittal. Two years later Sam Blum was enumerated as a boarder in Kenner, Jefferson Parish, LA with **REBECCA FELIX** (See entry for **MARX FELIX**). He worked as a clerk for her at her local dry goods store, Felix & Block. Sam died on 20 November 1902 at Touro Infirmary in New Orleans, Orleans Parish, LA, and was interred there at Dispersed of Judah Cemetery. He was forty-one years old and had never married. (**A, AN, G, GB, TT**)

BLUM, SARAH, was born **SARA BLUM** on 31 October 1847 in *Dettwiller*, Bas-Rhin, France, to **MARX/MARC BLUM**, a native of the town, and his second wife, **MADELEINE WEIL**, born in *Schwenheim*, Bas-Rhin. The youngest child in her family, and the last to arrive in America, she was one of the five Blum sisters who eventually settled in Louisiana. We have not found a likely ship's record for her entry into the United States, which was variously reported by her in three separate census records as 1880 or 1881. Sarah "Bloum" married "John William De Puiseau" (JAN WILLEM WAUBERT DE PUISEAU) on 16 November 1885 in St. Mary Parish, LA. The marriage was filed in New Orleans on 6 December of the same year. There are few records for John/Jan who was difficult to locate due to his unusual surname which was spelled differently in every record we have found. He was naturalized as "John Waubet De Puiseau" in New Orleans, Orleans Parish, LA, on 27 September 1878, and was said to have emigrated from Holland in 1855. John and Sarah had no children. According to an unverified, on-line entry for the Waubert de Puiseau family of the Netherlands, Jan was born on 13 June 1839 in Lemsterland, the Netherlands, and died on 13 December 1893 in Berwick, LA. Sixty-nine-year-old [*sic*] Sarah was enumerated as Sarah "Buriseau" in the 1900 federal census at Berwick, St. Mary Parish, LA, living next door to her sister and brother-in-law, Hypolite and Mary Fortune, (See entry for **MARIE BLUM**). Sarah was a childless widow born in France, living in her own home. Her occupation was recorded as "capitalist" and her date of immigration as 1881. She was enumerated as Sarah "Dubisson" in the 1910 federal census for Berwick as a sixty-five year old widow from Germany with no children, who had immigrated to America in 1880. Ten years later, still living in Berwick, she was enumerated as Sarah "DePuison," a seventy-five-year-old widow from France, who had immigrated to the United States in 1881. Sarah died in Berwick on 20 November 1921 and was buried there in the Hebrew Cemetery. Her epitaph reads "Sarah De Puysean, Born in Dettweiler, Alsace Oct. 31, 1847, Died in Berwick, LA Nov. 20, 1921." We have not been able to locate a place of burial for her husband. (**A, AN, G, TT**)

BLUM, SIMON ELIE, was born on 1 February 1852 in *Hochfelden*, Bas-Rhin, France, to ARON BLUM, a native of Ingenheim, Rheinpfalz, Germany, and his wife, **AGATHE/JULIE HIRSCH**, born in *Niederroedern*, Bas-Rhin. He emigrated from Le Havre, France, arriving in New York on 12 September 1872 aboard the SS *Washington.* He was naturalized in Baton Rouge, East Baton Rouge Parish, LA, on 27 March 1879. Simon was first enumerated in Louisiana in 1880 as "Simon Bloom," a twenty-eight-year-old unmarried store clerk in Madison Parish, LA, sharing a house with his first cousin, **THÉOPHILE HIRSCH** (See entry). Simon married JULIA BEER, a Mississippi native ca. 1885, a record of which we were unable to locate. Simon worked as a travelling liquor salesman. The couple's first two children, Abraham (b. 1886; died on 10 Dec 1886), and Agatha (b. 1888), were born in Tallulah, Madison Parish, LA. Their son Maurice J. Blum was born in 1889 in Evergreen, Avoyelles Parish, LA, where, we suspect, Simon had been working. Their daughter Marie Blum was born in 1891 back in Tallulah, LA. She died the following year. Shortly thereafter the couple moved to Mississippi, where their son Louis J. Blum was born in 1893 in Satartia, Yazoo Co., MS, and their last child, Dayve B. Blum was born in 1896 in Vicksburg, Warren Co., MS. The Blum family settled down in Natchez, Adams Co., MS, where they were enumerated there together in the 1900, 1910 and 1920 federal censuses. Their son Louis Blum was also enumerated in the 1920 federal census, but he was living in Denver, Denver Co., CO, as an "invalid" at the National Jewish Hospital for Consumptives. He died in Denver in August of the same year probably from tuberculosis. Simon, Julia and their three surviving children:

Agatha, Maurice and Davye, moved to Denver, Colorado, ca. 1920, shortly after the census, which was taken in Natchez on 2 January of that year. Simon died in Denver on 26 December 1921 after a short illness. He was interred at the Congregation Emanuel Cemetery in Denver, Arapahoe Co., CO near his son, Louis. Julia died in Denver on 9 September 1938 and was buried with her husband. (**A, AN, G, GB, TT**)

BLUM, SOLOMON, is said to have been born on 2 May 1824 in Alsace, according to what is engraved on his tombstone However, efforts to locate him in Alsace have been unsuccessful. He married **FANNY BOMPET** on 15 November 1858 in Ascension Parish, LA. Fanny was born **FANNY POMPET** on 13 August 1838 in *Saverne*, Bas-Rhin, France, to **MOÏSE POMPET** and his wife, **SARA BLOCH**, both natives of *Saverne*. She immigrated as nineteen-year-old "Fany Pompette" to New Orleans, Orleans Parish, LA, arriving on 26 December 1857 from Le Havre, France, aboard the ship *Ann Washburn*. Solomon and Fanny were enumerated in the 1860 federal census with their first child, Samuel (b. 1859) in the town of New River, Ascension Parish, LA. Two other children, Leon (b. 1864) and Julius (b.1866) were born there as well. They later moved to Thibodaux, Lafourche Parish, LA, where they remained the rest of their lives. Five more children were born in Thibodaux: Jennie (b. 1869), Louis (b. 1870), Arthur (b. 1872), Isidore (b. 1875) and Stella (b. 1879). Solomon ran a dry goods store in town. He died on 2 November 1906 in Thibodaux and was interred in the Morgan City Cemetery and Mausoleum in Morgan City, Saint Mary Parish, LA. His wife, Fanny Bompet, followed on 23 November 1915, and was buried by his side. Note: Fanny's two sisters **CLAIRE** and **PAULINE BOMPET/ POMPET** came to Louisiana as well. (**A, AN, G**)

BLUM, SYLVAIN, was born **SAMUEL SILVAIN BLUM** on 19 September 1856 in *Strasbourg*, Bas-Rhin, France, to **LÉON BLUM** (See entry), and his wife, **MADELEINE/MATHILDE HIRSCHMANN**, both natives of *Bischheim*, Bas-Rhin, France. He came to Louisiana with his mother and siblings ca. 1866, following his father who had emigrated the previous year. Two of his siblings who survived to adulthood, **ISAAC** and **PAULINE BLUM** (See entries) remembered their immigration date as 1866. Eleven year old Sylvain died in Donaldsonville, Ascension Parish, LA, ten days after his mother on 30 October 1867 and was buried there in Bikur Sholim Jewish

Cemetery. There was an epidemic of the "fever" reported in the Thibodaux, LA *Sentinel* published on 12 October 1867 and carried in the New Orleans *Daily Picayune* which told of the spread of yellow fever into the river parishes that month. It is possible that both mother and son, recent immigrants with no immunity to the pestilence, were its victims. (**A, AN, G, GB, TT**)

BOLLACK, ADOLPH, was born **ADOLPHE BOLLACK**, a twin to **JONAS BOLLACK**, on 6 January 1841 in Riedseltz, Bas-Rhin, France, to **JOSEPH BOLLACK**, a native of the town, and his second wife, **JUDITHE ROOS/ROS (JUDITHE WOLF** before 1808), born in *Wissembourg*, Bas-Rhin. Adolph Bollack immigrated to New Orleans, Orleans Parish, LA, from Le Havre, France, arriving on 31 January 1857 aboard the ship *Manchester*. He was enumerated in the 1860 federal census, working as a clerk for his former neighbor in *Riedseltz*, **JOSEPH BLOCH** (See entry), who was partners with SOLOMON FIRNBERG, a native of Mannheim, Germany, in the mercantile firm of Bloch, Firnberg & Co., in Opelousas, St. Landry Parish, LA. During the American Civil War this firm, along with Isaac Levy & Co. out of Alexandria, Rapides Parish, LA, operated a brisk smuggling trade from Louisiana through Texas and into Mexico. Cotton had to be shipped out through Mexico after the fall of New Orleans to Union troops in April 1862, and any goods from Europe had to return to Louisiana via the same route. We assume that young Adolph was stationed along the Texas-Mexico border to facilitate these shipping arrangements, because he stayed in Texas for a good part of his life. He was enumerated as Adolph Pollack in Brownsville, Cameron Co., TX, in 1870, with his younger brother, **HENRY BOLLACK**, born **HENRY POLLACK** on 21 January 1843 in *Riedseltz*. Adolph was running a dry goods store and Henry was his clerk. Adolph married YETTA FELLMAN, a native of Germany, on 22 February 1871 in New Orleans. They were the parents of four children: Celina (b. 1872), Isaac (b. 1875), Joseph (b. 1877), and Julia (b. 1882). At least two of their children, Celina and Isaac, were said to have been born in Louisiana, although Isaac's death record states otherwise. The family spent the rest of their lives in Brownsville. Yetta died on 27 March 1927 and was interred in the Hebrew Cemetery at Brownsville. Adolph died weeks later on 22 April 1927 and was buried with her. Note: We believe that Henry Bollack remained in Brownsville, and despite a discrepancy in his date of birth incised on his tombstone, was interred in the Hebrew Cemetery at Brownsville in April 1934. (**A, AN, FS, G**)

BOMPET, CHARLES, was born on 14 October 1851 in *Brumath*, Bas-Rhin, France, to **CASIMIR ALBIN JOSEPH POMPET**, a native of *Kuttolsheim*, Bas-Rhin, France, and his wife **ROSINE GOUDCHAUX**, born in *Brumath*. Bas-Rhin. Charles immigrated to America after the Franco-Prussian War, a record for which we were unable to find. He settled in Millikin's Bend, Madison Parish, Louisiana and worked as a clerk in a dry goods store. He married **HATTIE BLOCK**, a native Louisianan, on 7 June 1877 in Madison Parish. Four children were born to them, Rachel/Raye (b. 1878), Florence (b. 1880), Ida (b. 1882), and Julius (b. 1883), before Charles died from meningitis on 24 May 1885. He was buried in Anshe Chesed Jewish Cemetery in Vicksburg, Warren Co., MS. His widow, Hattie, married **MAURICE/ MARX HEYMAN** (See entry) another immigrant from *Brumath*, Bas-Rhin, in 1897. Note: All members of the BOMPET (originally POMPET) family are descendants of Eliezer "Lazare" Wolf and his wife Yentele "Jendel" Elyakoum who married in *Kuttolsheim*, Bas-Rhin, France on 3 Feb 1751/52. The name POMPET was given to the couple's three sons at the time of the 1808 name-taking census of Jews at *Kuttolsheim*, Bas-Rhin. In America the most frequent spelling is "Bombet" (**A, AN,G, J**)

BOMPET, CLARA, was born **CLAIRE POMPET** on 30 October 1836 in *Saverne*, Bas-Rhin, France to **MOÏSE POMPET** and his wife, **SARA BLOCH**, both natives of *Saverne*. She immigrated to the United States after her second cousin, **MICHEL BOMPET** (See entry), who arrived in America in 1850. We were unable to find a reliable record for her entry. She married **LAZARE LEVY,** a native of Baden, Germany, at Donaldsonville, Ascension Parish, LA on 31 July 1854. They raised seven children: Henriette (b. 1860), Moïse (b. 1862), Émile (b. 1864), Coralie (b. 1866), Bella (b. 1867), Irma (b. 1869), and Florence (b. 1875) in Donaldsonville, where Lazare was a horse trader. Clara died on 18 January 1902 in Donaldsonville, and her husband, Lazare, followed on 10 December 1908. They were buried in Bikur Sholim Jewish Cemetery, in Donaldsonville, Ascension Parish, LA.(**A, AN, F, G**)

BOMPET, ESTELLE, (*Hochfelden*) See entry for **JOSUÉ DREYFUSS**

BOMPET/POMPET, FANNY, (*Saverne*) See entry for **SOLOMON BLUM**

BOMPET, MICHEL, was born **MICHEL POMBET**, on 16 August 1832 at *Hochfelden*, Bas-Rhin, France, to **HILAIRE SALOMON POMBET**, a native of *Kuttolsheim*, Bas-Rhin, and his wife, **AGATHE BLUM**, a native of *Hochfelden*. Eighteen-year-old Michel arrived in New Orleans, Orleans Parish, LA, on 14 June 1850 aboard the ship *Pyramid*. He settled in Shreveport, Caddo Parish, LA, where he worked as a merchant. He fought for the Confederacy as a 2nd Lieutenant in the 21st Louisiana Infantry, Company D. Michel never married. He was killed at the age of 48 on 2 March, 1881, when a brick wall from an adjacent burning building in Shreveport fell on top of him. Michel was buried in Hebrew Rest Cemetery # 1 (the Jewish section of Oakland Cemetery) in Shreveport, LA. [**A, F, B, J**]

BOMPET, PAULINE, was born **PAULINE POMPET** on 6 September 1840 in *Saverne*, Bas-Rhin, France, to **MOÏSE POMPET** and his wife, **SARA BLOCH**, both natives of *Saverne*. She followed her sisters, Clara, and Fanny, to Louisiana after the Civil War, a reliable record for which we were unable to find. She married **ABRAHAM HEYMANN**, a native of Gommersheim, Germany, on 4 January 1869 in New Orleans, Orleans Parish, LA. Abraham was a dry goods merchant in the city. The couple raised four children in New Orleans: Fannie (b. 1869), Carrie (b. 1871), Maurice (b. 1873), and Julia (b. 1879). Abraham Heymann died in New Orleans on 11 November 1904, and Pauline followed on 27 February 1921. They were buried in Gates of Prayer Cemetery # 2 (Joseph Street) in New Orleans. [**A, AN, G**]

BOMPET, ROSALIE, (*Hochfelden*) See entry for **MOÏSE LEVY** from *Niederseebach*

BOMPET, SARAH, was born **SARAH POMBET** on 16 March 1836 in *Hochfelden*, Bas-Rhin, France, to **HILAIRE SALOMON POMPET**, a native of *Kuttolsheim*, Bas-Rhin, and his wife, **AGATHE BLUM**, born in *Hochfelden,*Bas-Rhin. Seventeen-year-old Sarah immigrated with **MALINE GOUDCHAUX** (See entry) on the ship *Belle Assise*, arriving in New Orleans, Orleans Parish, LA, on 8 November 1854. Sarah married **ADOLPH GROS** on 13 June 1864 in New Orleans. Twenty-two-year-old Adolph Gros arrived with twenty-nine-year-old Henry Gros at New Orleans from Le Havre, France, on 15 April 1850 aboard the ship *Espindola*. We could find no other information about Adolph Gros or his wife, Sarah Bompet. **(A, N)**

BRAUN, ARMAND, was born on 23 July 1881 in *Offendorf*, Bas-Rhin, France, to **EMANUEL BRAUN,** a native of the town, and his wife **ROSALIA BLUM,** born in *Gundershoffen*, Bas-Rhin. In a 1920 application for a U.S. passport, Armand stated that he had immigrated to America, arriving from Antwerp, Belgium, on 1 September 1906. In reality he arrived in New York on 11 September 1906 from Antwerp aboard the SS *Kroonland*. He went to work in his cousin Minette Braun's son **RAPHAEL BLOCH**'s general store in Sellers, St. Charles Parish, LA (See entry for **RAPHAEL BLOCK**). Armand stayed several years after Raphael's death to help his widow, Cecelia Steeg Block, run the store. After she moved to New Orleans, he joined his brothers, **LÉON** and **HENRY BRAUN** (See entries), in the city as a partner in Braun Bros., a confectionery and bakery located on Dryades Street. Several years later, ca. 1918, he relocated to Reserve, St. John the Baptist Parish, LA, and went to work for Charles Alltmont and Bro., General Merchandise Company, where he ultimately rose to the position of Assistant-Manager. He married DENISE MARIE BOUTITON, a native of Reserve, who had been widowed in 1916 in her first marriage to ALLEN BOURG. The couple wed ca. 1926. They had no children. Denise Boutiton Braun died at Hotel Dieu in New Orleans, Orleans Parish, LA, on 10 May 1942. She was buried in St. Peter's Cemetery in Reserve. Armand died on 5 October 1948 in Reserve and was buried with his wife. **(A, AN, GB)**

BRAUN, ARMAND, (b. 1905 *Oberschaeffolsheim*) See entry for **HENRY BRAUN**

BRAUN, GERMAINE, (b. 1906 *Oberschaeffolsheim)* See entry for **HENRY BRAUN**

BRAUN, HENRY, was born **ABRAHAM BRAUN** on 17 October 1876 in *Offendorf*, Bas-Rhin, France, to **EMANUEL BRAUN,** a native of the town, and his wife, **ROSALIA BLUM,** born in *Gundershoffen*, Bas-Rhin. He married **LUCY DREYFUS** ca. 1904 in France. She was born **LUDMILLA DREYFUSS** on 12 August 1874 in *Oberschaeffolsheim*, Bas-Rhin, France, to **MOÏSE DREYFUS,** born in *Rosheim*, Bas-Rhin, and his wife, **JULIA BLUM,** a native of

Quatzenheim, Bas-Rhin. We were able to find Lucy's place of birth because a brother, Leon Dreyfuss, of Vancouver, Canada, was mentioned in her obituary. Since he had resided in the Philippine Islands, then in Canada, we located a ship's record which listed his birthplace. Henry Braun immigrated to America, arriving in New York on 23 February 1908 aboard the SS *La Touraine*. His wife, Lucy, and children Armand (b. 1905) and Germaine (b.5 December 1906) arrived in New York on 17 October 1908 from Le Havre, France, aboard the SS *La Savoie*. Armand was listed as Edmond on the ship's manifest In 1910 the family, enumerated as "Henry and Lucy Brown" [sic], lived in New Orleans on Terpsichore Street, with **LEON BRAUN** (b. 1855 in *Offendorf*; See entry), a dealer in horses. Another child, Bertha Rose, was born to Lucy and Henry in New Orleans in 1910. Henry was a baker and confectioner in New Orleans, a business which he had operated with his brothers **ARMAND** and **LEON** (b. 1880) **BRAUN** (See entries) until they went on their own. Henry died on 23 March 1931 in the city and was buried in Gates of Prayer Cemetery #2 (Joseph Street). Lucy died on 22 July 1944 in New Orleans and was buried with him. Note: Bertha Rose married Ralph F. White. She died on 27 May 1984 and was buried in St. Roch Cemetery, after a mass of Christian burial. Germaine married Harold C. Amrhein, an employee of the Falstaff Brewing Co. She died on 15 June 1978, and was buried in Hope Mausoleum, following a service conducted by a Lutheran minister. Armand Braun (b. 1905) left Louisiana to join his maternal uncles, Jules and Leon Dreyfuss, in the Philippines, where a record of his marriage to Maria Teresa Freire was registered in Manila on 5 June 1933. He is believed to have been engaged in the banking business there. We have not been able to verify when and where the children of Henry and Ludmilla Dreyfus Braun were born, but believe, based on information given on the manifest of the SS *La Savoie*, that their last known address had been in *Oberschaeffolsheim*, Bas-Rhin. (**A, AN, G, GB, TT**)

BRAUN, LÉON, was born **LÉOPOLD BRAUN** on 2 January 1855 in *Offendorf*, Bas-Rhin, France, to **LAZARUS/ELÉAZAR BRAUN**, a native of the town, and his wife, **THÉRÈSE BLUM**, born in *Brumath*, Bas-Rhin. His immigration date to Louisiana, as reported in various census documents, may have been as early as 1873 or as late as 1898. We could not find a reliable ship's record for him under either "Leon" or "Leopold." We did find a fifteen-year-old [sic] "Leonhard Braun" who arrived at New York on 10 August 1872 from Bremen, Germany, aboard the SS *Smidt* which could possibly be his arrival. Léon first appeared in a federal census record for New Orleans, Orleans Parish, LA in 1900, where he was recorded as a forty-five-year-old bachelor, in a boarding house who was working as a horse trader. In the 1910 and 1920 federal census records he was enumerated with **HENRY BRAUN** (See entry), a relative who had immigrated with his family to New Orleans in 1908. In both instances his occupation was recorded as horse dealer or trader. Léon never married. He died on 8 February 1922 in the city and was buried in Gates of Prayer Cemetery #2 (Joseph Street). (**A, AN, G, GB**)

BRAUN, LÉON, was born on 31 January 1880 in *Offendorf*, Bas-Rhin, France, to **EMANUEL BRAUN,** a native of the town, and his wife **ROSALIA BLUM,** born in *Gundershoffen*, Bas-Rhin. He immigrated ahead of his brother **ARMAND BRAUN** (See entry), arriving in New York from Le Havre on 6 September 1904 aboard the SS *La Savoie*. He travelled to New Orleans, Orleans Parish, LA, where he went into business with his brothers **HENRY** and **ARMAND BRAUN** (See entries) in a confectionery business known as Braun Bros. on Dryades Street. He married JEANNETTE DREIFUS, a New Orleans native, on 6 January 1915. Jeannette is sometimes referred to as Jeannette Dreifus Diamond. Her mother, Leonora Gretzner, was widowed by Emanuel Dreifus, shortly after Jeannette's birth. In 1899 Leonora married Osias Diamond with whom she had several children. Léon and Jeannette moved to Kenner, Jefferson Parish, LA, where they opened a family grocery store. Two children were born to the couple: Emanuel D. (b. 1916) and Meyer Gus/Rex (b. 1921). Politically active, Léon became the tax collector for the town of Kenner. In the 1930s he was also in partnership with several other men in retail gasoline and kerosene sales. Léon died on 14 June 1945 in Kenner and was buried in Gates of Prayer Cemetery #1 (Canal Street) in New Orleans. Jeannette died on 21 December 1959 in Houston, Harris Co., TX, where both of her sons had settled. Her remains were returned to New Orleans, where they were interred with those of her husband. (**A, AN, G, GB**)

BRAUN, RENÉ, was born on 29 May 1894 in *Offendorf*, Bas-Rhin, France, to **HERMANN BRAUN**, a native of the town, and his wife **CAROLINE DREYFUSS**, born in *Rosheim*, Bas-Rhin. He immigrated to New York, arriving on 12 October 1911 on the Hamburg America Line SS *Cincinnati*. He joined a cousin, ARMAND BRAUN (See entry), at Sellers, St. Charles Parish, LA, where they both worked in the general store owned by **RAPHAEL BLOCH** (See entry), whose mother, Minette, was a member of the Braun family of *Offendorf*. After Raphael's widow, Cecelia Steeg Bloch, closed the store, René moved to New Orleans and entered the printing business, eventually opening the Braun Printing Company, of which he was the president. René married FANNYE BERNSTEIN, a New Orleans native, on 20 October 1935 in the city. The couple had one son, Paul Herman (b. 1938). René died in New Orleans on 24 November 1966 and was buried in Gates of Prayer Cemetery #2 (Joseph Street). Fannye died on 11 December 1984 and was buried with him. (**A, AN, G, GB, TT**)

BRAUN, VALERIE, was born on 4 May 1852 in *Schirrhoffen*, Bas-Rhin, France, to **ABRAHAM BRAUN** and his wife **REISSEL "RACHEL" WEILL**, both natives of the town. She married **ADOLPHE SOMMER**, also a *Schirrhoffen* native on 10 February 1874 at *Schirrhoffen*. After the death of her husband in 1880, and of her third child, Lidia, in 1889, she had thoughts of following her two sons, **LEOPOLD** and **SYLVAN SOMMER** (See entries) to America. Her son, Sylvan, made the trip back to Alsace in 1905 to marry nineteen-year-old **MARGUERITE KAHN**, also a *Schirrhoffen* native. Valerie accompanied her son and his new bride back to America, arriving with them in New York on 22 November 1905, aboard the SS *Kaiser Wilhelm der Grosse*. She lived seven years in Torras, Pointe Coupée Parish, LA with her son, Leopold, and his family until the town was wiped out in the great Mississippi River flood of 1912. The Leopold Sommer family relocated to Baton Rouge, East Baton Rouge Parish, LA, where Valerie spent her final days. She died on 29 March 1932 and was buried there in the Jewish Cemetery. (**A, AN, G, GB**)

CAHN, DELPHINE, was born on 23 March 1862 in *Strasbourg*, Bas-Rhin, France, to **LÉON CAHN**, a native of *Saverne*, Bas-Rhin, and his wife, FLORETTE/FLORA LEHMANN, born in Landau, Rheinpfalz, Germany. Delphine and her parents immigrated to New York, arriving on 25 January 1866 aboard the ship *Énergie*. Delphine's siblings Rachel and Daniel had both died in Le Havre, Seine-Maritime, France, in October 1865 while awaiting passage to America. The elder Cahns remained in Manhattan, New York, for over thirty years where eight other children were born. Léon worked there as an upholsterer. Delphine was enumerated in the 1880 federal census with her family in Manhattan where she was employed as a dressmaker. She married Louisiana native HENRY SAMUEL on 25 April 1881 in Vidalia,

Concordia Parish, LA. Before his marriage, Henry had been a storekeeper in Pinckneyville, Wilkinson Co., MS. Delphine and Henry were the parents of three children: Jacob B. (b. 1882 in New Orleans), Fannye Isabelle (b. 1883 in MS) and Estelle Bertha "Stella" (b. 1886 in MS). The family moved back to New Orleans in the 1890s where Henry bought a cotton pickery on Terpsichore Street. He died on 11 October 1894 in New Orleans and was buried there in Hebrew Rest Cemetery #1. Delphine Samuel remained in New Orleans where her son, Jacob (aka Jack B.), took over the cotton pickery business. Delphine died in New Orleans on 18 December 1947 and was buried with her husband. Note: Her parents Leon and Florette Cahn moved to Natchez, Adams Co., MS, to be near their daughter Amelia, Mrs. Isaac Schlenker. Leon and Flora Cahn both died in New Orleans, he on 8 February 1915 and she on 29 May 1919. Their remains were returned to Natchez where they were interred together in the Jewish section of the Natchez City Cemetery. (**A, AN, G, GB, TT**)

CAHN, FELIX, was born **FÉLIX KAHN** on 7 December 1824 in *Niederroedern*, Bas-Rhin, France, to **EMANUEL KAHN** and his wife, **NANETTE BAEHR,** both natives of the town. Felix was enumerated with his parents and his sister, Rosalie, in the 1851 census for *Niederroedern*. We believe that he may have been the twenty-nine-year-old "Felix Cahn," a native of France, who arrived in New Orleans, Orleans Parish, LA, on 21 April 1854 from Le Havre, France, aboard the ship *Iowa*. He made his way to Shreveport, Caddo, Parish, LA, where he married **JEANNETTE WEINMANN** on 28 November 1855. Her name on the marriage document was recorded as "Harriet Wagman," which complicated efforts to identify her. Born Jeannette Weinmann, out of wedlock, on 11 September 1824 in *Brumath*, Bas-Rhin, France, to SIMON WEINMANN, a local Hebrew teacher, and NANETTE SAMUEL, both natives of Germany, she had married **ARON LEDERMANN** (See entry) in 1849 and had immigrated to New Orleans, Orleans Parish, LA, with him and their two children, Carl/Jacques and Cérine/Sophia, on 7 November 1853 aboard the ship *Globe*. Felix Cahn, her second husband, and Harriet, as she was often called in Louisiana, appeared together in the 1860 Shreveport census with their first three children: Samuel (b. 1858) and twins Rosa and Carroll (b. 1859). Living with them were Harriet's two children by Aron Ledermann. They were only identified as C. and S. "Littleman" [*sic*], ages ten and eight. Felix was working as a peddler with about $2000 in real estate and personal property. Their last child, Henry, was born in 1862 in Shreveport. The family remained in Shreveport where Felix became a prosperous dry goods merchant. Felix died on 20 March 1898 and was buried there in Hebrew Rest Cemetery #2 (Texas Avenue). His wife died on 25 March 1915 and was buried with him. Note: The spelling of Felix's last name with a "C" instead of a "K" is fairly uniform throughout Louisiana records, starting with his immigration in 1854, and his marriage to Harriet a year later. (**A, AN, B1851, F, G**)

CAHN, LÉON, (*Saverne*) See entry for **DELPHINE CAHN**

CAHN, SOPHIE, was born **SOPHIE KAHN** on 18 July 1823 in *Mommenheim*, Bas-Rhin, France, to **LEBOLD/LEOPOLD KAHN**, a native of the town, and his wife, **LEYEN/LÉA WEILL**, born in *Krautergersheim*, Bas-Rhin. We could find no reliable entry for Sophie's arrival in America, but she first appeared in the 1870 federal census for Vermilionville (now Lafayette), Lafayette Parish, LA, where she was enumerated with ABRAHAM HAAS, a native of Rülzheim, Bavaria, Germany, and a seven-year-old son, FELIX HAAS (b. 1863). In 1866 her husband, Abraham had appeared on the U.S. Internal Revenue Service assessment lists, as having paid taxes in the amount of $20.85 as a liquor dealer in Vermilionville. We believe that Abraham Haas is the same as A. Haas who was enumerated in New Orleans in 1860 as an unmarried thirty-four-year-old man from Baden [*sic*], working in a brewery. The last time the family appeared together was on 2 June 1880, in that year's federal census for the town of Vermilionville Lafayette Parish, LA. Their seventeen-year-old son, Felix, was a clerk in his father's dry goods store. Abraham Haas died at his residence in Lafayette on 24 August 1891, and was buried there in the Jewish Cemetery. According to Felix Haas's obituary, he and his mother moved to New Orleans ca. 1892. Felix had been, for a time, employed by the Southern Pacific Railway as a locomotive engineer in Vermilionville/Lafayette. He subsequently took the civil service exam and passed in order to become a United States customs inspector, which brought him to New Orleans. His eighty-one-year-old widowed mother, Sophie, died on 12 January 1904 in New Orleans, having lived in the city for twelve years. She was buried there in Dispersed of Judah Cemetery. Felix married Alice Fougeret Marchand, a forty-one-year-old widow with three children, on 24 September 1910. He died on 5 January 1914 and was buried in Hebrew Rest Cemetery #1 in New Orleans. Note: According to the 1860 and 1870 census records

Abraham Haas was born in Baden, Germany. His obituary in the *Lafayette Advertiser* recorded his place of birth as Rülzheim, Bavaria. (**A, AN, CA, GB, TT**)

CASPARI, JOSEPH, was born on 23 November 1874 at *Lauterbourg,* Bas-Rhin, France, to **LEOPOLD CASPARI**, a native of the town, and his wife, AMALIA/FANNY LANDAUER, born in Rülzheim, Rheinpfalz, Germany. Joseph emigrated from Antwerp, Belgium, arriving in New York on 30 November 1894 aboard the SS *Westernland*, following his brother, **SAMUEL CASPARI** (See entry), who had come to Louisiana the year before. Joseph settled in Rayville, Richland Parish, LA, where he remained for the rest of his life. He was employed there as a salesman in a dry goods store. Eventually he became the owner and operator of a successful general store in town. He was naturalized at Rayville on 8 December 1897. Joseph never married. He died on 11 March 1947 at Rayville and was buried there in the Masonic Cemetery. Joseph was the first cousin twice removed of **LEOPOLD CASPARI** (See entry). (**A, AN, G**)

CASPARI, LAZA, was born **LAZAR CASPARI** on 31 October 1881 at *Lauterbourg,* Bas-Rhin, France, to **LEOPOLD CASPARI**, a native of the town, and his wife, AMALIA/FANNY LANDAUER, born in Rülzheim, Rheinpfalz, Germany. Lazar departed Hamburg, Germany, for New York, on 8 September 1898, aboard the Hamburg-America Line's SS *Fürst Bismarck*. After his arrival he went to live with his mother's brother Aron L. Landauer in Natchez, Adams Co., MS. He worked there as a clerk in the Landauer store. By 1910 he had moved to Monroe, Ouachita Parish, LA, where his brother **SAMUEL CASPARI** (See entry) had settled. Before Laza married, he lived with Sam's brother-in-law, Marcus Kaliski. According to his own recollection, he was naturalized in 1910 in Louisiana, although we have not been able to find a record of it. Laza married DORRIT MARX, a Louisiana native ca. 1912. The couple had no children. Laza and Dorrit lived in Monroe all their lives. They were enumerated in the 1920 federal census with Dorrit's mother, Dora Marx, and grandmother, Amelia King. Laza was employed as the manager of the Monroe Dry Goods Co., Inc., a position he held through the 1930s. After the company closed, Laza, made a living selling oil and gas leases. Dorrit Caspari died on 10 December 1949 in Monroe and was buried there in Rosena Chapel Jewish Cemetery. Laza continued to work in sales, and was last listed in the Monroe business directory as an oil and gas lease and land salesman in 1959. He died on 17 February of that year and was buried with his wife. Laza was the first cousin twice removed of Natchitoches resident, **LEOPOLD CASPARI**. (A, AN, G)

CASPARI, LEOPOLD, was born on 19 June 1830 in *Lauterbourg*, Bas-Rhin, France, to **DAVID CASPARI (LÖB DAVID** before 1808) and his wife, **HAENÉ LOEVY**, both natives of the town. Leopold's biographers have suggested that he arrived in America ca. 1848, although we have not been able to find a ship's record for him. What is certain is that he appeared in the 1850 federal census for Cloutierville, Natchitoches Parish, LA, where he was enumerated as a twenty-year-old mulatto [*sic*] merchant born in France. Leopold was naturalized at Natchitoches, Natchitoches Parish, LA, on 12 May 1857. He moved to Natchitoches from Cloutierville the following year where he opened a store and did some farming. On 17 May 1861 Leopold enlisted in the Third LA Infantry, Company G, Pelican Rifles #1 at New Orleans, Orleans Parish, LA, an outfit from Natchitoches headed by Winter W. Breazeale. He was discharged from service in May 1862 as a Second Lieutenant to go into state service, where he rose to the rank of Captain. Leopold was paroled at Alexandria, Rapides Parish, LA, on 29 June 1865. He married AMANDA WOODS ca. 1862, a record of which could not be found. A native of Natchitoches Parish, Amanda had been orphaned at an early age and raised on a farm by her godfather, SEVIER LATTIER. Leopold and Amanda were the parents of eleven children, all born in Natchitoches Parish: Henry (b. 1863; died 1863, shares a headstone with his grandfather, Richard Woods at St. John the Baptist Catholic Church Cemetery at Cloutierville), Julie (b. 1864), Richard L. (b. 1866), Samuel (b. 1868), Joseph (b. 1870), David (b. 1872), Emanuel (b. 1873), Charles (b. 1877), Gustave (b. 1879), Dora (b. 1880), and Edward (b. 1881; died 1883). Leopold was a successful merchant and planter at Natchitoches who reported his worth at the time of the 1870 federal census as $10,000 in real estate and $43,400 in personal property, a fortune during the difficult post-Civil War era in the South. Amanda Caspari died on 31 March 1883, nine days after the death of her youngest child, Edward. She was buried in the American Cemetery in Natchitoches. A year later Leopold was elected to the Louisiana State Legislature as a senator from Natchitoches and was instrumental in launching a successful campaign to establish the State Normal School at Natchitoches (now Northwestern Louisiana State University) in 1884. He was also the general manager and president of the Natchitoches and Red River Valley Railway which opened for business on 3 November 1894, as well as a founding member and later President of the People's Bank of Natchitoches. Leopold served as a State Senator for almost thirty years, having lost re-election only once during that period. Louisiana State Senator Leopold Caspari died at his home in Natchitoches on 12 March 1915 and was buried there in the American Cemetery with his wife. (**A, AN, G, GB**)

CASPARI, SAMUEL LANDAUER/ SAM L., was born **SAMUEL CASPARI** on 17 December 1876 at *Lauterbourg,* Bas-Rhin, France, to **LEOPOLD CASPARI**, a native of the town, and his wife, AMALIA/FANNY LANDAUER, born in Rülzheim, Rheinpfalz, Germany. He immigrated to the United States at the age of seventeen from Antwerp, Belgium, arriving in New York on 1 November 1893 aboard the SS *Noordland.* He was enumerated for the first time in Winnsboro, Franklin Parish, LA, in the 1900 federal census where, as yet unmarried, he was working as a salesman in a general merchandise store, probably for his uncle, ARON LANDAUER, who, before relocating his family to Natchez, Adams Co., MS, had been a longtime merchant at Winnsboro. Sam moved on to Monroe, Ouachita Parish, LA, where he was naturalized on 15 May 1901. He married DEBORAH/DEBBIE KALISKI, a Monroe, LA, native ca. 1903. They were the parents of three children: Edmond (b. 1905), Johanna (b. 1909), and Jacques/Jack (b. 1910). The family was enumerated in the 1910 federal census living in Monroe with Jacob Kaliski, Sam's father-in-law, who was a real estate developer. At that time Sam was said to have no occupation. Shortly thereafter, Sam moved his family to Mangham, Richland Parish, LA, to be near his brother **JOSEPH CASPARI** (See entry) who lived in nearby, Rayville. Samuel registered for the World War I draft at Mangham in 1918 where he stated that he was a self-employed merchant. Two years later, he and his family were back in Monroe, where they lived once more with Debbie's father, Jacob Kaliski, and his wife's unmarried brother, Julius, both of whom were still in the real estate business. Sam continued to work as a salesman in a local dry goods store. Debbie Caspari died in New York City on 11 November 1932, where she and her husband had moved the year before. Her remains were brought back to Monroe for interment in Rosena Chapel Jewish Cemetery. Sam moved to Shreveport, Caddo Parish, LA, to live with his son Jacques, who worked as a commercial artist. He died there on 22 February 1947. We have been unable to locate a place of burial for him. Sam, like his brothers, **LAZA** and **JOSEPH CASPARI** (See entries), was the first cousin twice removed of Natchitoches resident, **LEOPOLD CASPARI** (See entry) (**A, AN, G, GB**)

CERF, FANNIE, was born **FANNI CERF** on 3 April 1820 in *Haguenau*, Bas-Rhin, France, to **ALBERT CERF** (**CERF ISAÏAS** before 1808), a native of the town, and his wife **ELIZABETH/LISETTE KOESSLER** (**ETTEL MERLEN** before 1808), born in *Mertzwiller*, Bas-Rhin. Fannie married **DAVID MEYER** who was born on 15 February 1815 in *Schweighouse-sur-Moder*, Bas-Rhin, France, to **JACQUES MEYER**, born in *Froeschwiller*, Bas-Rhin, and his wife, CATHERINE BLOCH, about whom we were able to find nothing. Albert and Fannie were the parents of eleven children, all born in *Schweighouse*: Adelaide (b. 1843), Meyer Jacques (b. 1844; died 1844), Isaac (b. 1845; died 1848), Isaias (b. 1847; died 1848), Marie (b. 1849; See entry), Henriette (b. 1851; died bef. 1861), Sophie (b. 1853; See entry), Emanuel (b. 1855; See entry), Leopold (b. 1857; died 1865), Justine (b. 1859; See entry), Henriette (b. 1861; See entry). The six surviving of the eleven children of David Meyer and Fannie Cerf immigrated to America: Four of them settled in Louisiana: **MARIE, EMANUEL, JUSTINE** (See entries) and Hattie/Henriette. Adelaide and Sophie Meyer lived in Mississippi. Fannie's brother, **ISAÏE CERF** (See entry), had been an earlier immigrant to Pike Co., MS. Fannie Cerf Meyer's husband David, died in *Schweighouse* on 27 December 1876. We believe that Fannie immigrated as "Fanny Meyer," and was accompanied by her youngest daughter, **HENRIETTE MEYER** (See entry), on board the SS *France*, which docked in New York from Le Havre, France, on 9 May 1877. Fanny settled in Canton, Madison Co. Mississippi, with her daughters. She died there on 28 June 1893 and was buried in the Jewish Section of the Canton City Cemetery, as "Fanny Mayer, born at Haguenau, Alsace." (**A, AN, G, TT**)

CERF, FANNY, was born on 26 September 1840 in *Bouxwiller*, Bas-Rhin, France, to LÉON CERF, a native of Nancy, Meurthe, France, and his wife, **RÉGINE WEIL**, born in *Scherwiller*, Bas-Rhin. She followed her brother **SAMSON CERF** (See entry), immigrating to New York from Le Havre on 5 December 1864 aboard the steamship *Washington*. Fanny travelled to New Orleans, Orleans Parish, LA, and was married to SIMON SIESS on 15 November 1865 in the city. Simon was born SIMON SÜSS on 28 November 1830, in Mühlheim, Rheinpfalz, Germany, to MICHAEL SÜSS, a native of Albsheim,

Rheinpfalz, Germany, and his wife **MINDEL/MINETTE LOB/THALSHEIMER**, born at Heiligenmoschel, commune of Niederkirschen, Canton Otterberg, Dept. Mont Tonnerre, France (Germany after 1814). Simon was raised by his step-father, **SALOMON LEHMANN** (See entry), and mother, Minette, in *Lembach*, Bas-Rhin, France. According to his 1890 application for a U.S. passport Simon wrote that he had immigrated to Louisiana from Le Havre, France, on the *William Nelson* which arrived in New Orleans, Orleans Parish, LA, on 30 October 1852. His naturalization papers, filed in October 1874, indicated that he came on the *William Nelson* on 22 December 1852, neither date for which we were able to verify using existing ship's records. Simon settled in Mansura, Avoyelles Parish, LA, with his brothers **DAVID** and **LEOPOLD SIESS** (See entries), and half-brother, **ISAAC LEHMANN** (See entry) where they owned a general merchandise store. Simon defied martial law and left Avoyelles Parish in the summer of 1863 to seek refuge and to work in Union occupied New Orleans. He took a job at Wells Bros. & Co., commission merchants, and met Fanny Cerf, who was working as a nursemaid. Simon and Fanny's first child, Mathilde, was born in New Orleans on 10 September 1866. A year later Simon took Fanny and his daughter back to Mansura where he had been working with his brother David before the war. The two men owned a general store and shared interest in a small cotton plantation complete with a cotton gin and sawmill which David had barely been able to keep going during the war, until he, to, had fled in 1864. Fanny and Simon's second child, Leon, was born in Mansura on 15 February 1872. After ten years in business the brothers had a parting of the ways over financial concerns, which led to a lawsuit, poisoning their relationship forever. Simon and his family moved to nearby Marksville, Avoyelles Parish, LA, where he opened a dry goods store. The couple remained in Marksville, where Simon was a member of the school board and active in local politics. Fanny was a member of the temperance union in town. Nearing retirement, the couple journeyed back to Alsace in 1890, accompanied by their son, Leon. Upon their return, they followed their daughter, Mathilde, out to Florence, Fremont Co., CO, where she and her husband, **ERNEST WEIL** (See entry), were seeking their fortune in the burgeoning silver mining town. With empty pockets, they followed Ernest to Denver, Arapahoe Co., CO, then to Minneapolis, Hennepin Co, MN, before returning to New Orleans in 1910. Fanny died in New Orleans on 3 November 1927 and was buried in Gates of Prayer

Cemetery #2 (Joseph Street) with her husband, Simon, who had passed away on 24 November 1924. (**A, AN, AP, G, GB**)

CERF, ISAÏE, was born on 15 May 1823 in *Haguenau*, Bas-Rhin, France, to **ALBERT CERF**, an itinerant merchant in Haguenau and native of the town, and his wife, **ELIZABETH KOESSLER** born in *Mertzwiller*, Bas-Rhin. Isaïe immigrated to Pike County, Mississippi where he married **ROSINE HILLER,** a native of *Niederroedern*, Bas-Rhin, France, on 22 Jan 1854 in Liberty, Amite County, MS. (Note: This was a double wedding. Julia Cerf, probably Isaie's cousin, married Hertz Hiller, Rosine's cousin at the same time.) Although he lived and died in Pike County, Mississippi, he is mentioned here because he and his first born son, Emanuel, were buried in the Jewish section of the Old German Cemetery in Kirksville, Tangipahoa Parish, Louisiana, scarcely a third of a mile into Louisiana from the Mississippi border. Father and son died eight days apart, Isaïe on 7 October 1878 and Emanuel, his twenty-two year old son, on 15 October 1878, victims of that year's raging yellow fever epidemic. Rosine had died before 1866, but we were unable to locate her grave. Note: Isaïe married a second time ca. 1867 to Estelle Levi, whom we believe to have been a German national. They had one daughter Josephine "Josie" born in 1877 in Kentwood, Tangipahoa Parish, LA. Ninety-year-old Josie, who never married, died in New Orleans, Orleans Parish, LA, on 1 March 1968. She was a longtime resident of New Orleans and a noted historian, in charge of research at the Louisiana State Museum located at the Cabildo. Note: See entry for his sister, **FANNY CERF**(**A, AN, G, GB**)

CERF, SAMSON, was born on 4 July 1836 in *Bouxwiller*, Bas-Rhin, France, to LÉON CERF, a native of Nancy, Meurthe France, and his wife **RÉGINE WEIL**, born in *Scherwiller*, Bas-Rhin. He immigrated to New York from Le Havre, France, arriving on 28 August 1857 on the ship *Globe* He settled in New Orleans, Orleans Parish, LA, and became a shoe merchant in the city. When the Civil War broke out he enlisted in the Frois Co. 3rd Regiment of the European brigade (Garde Française) of the Louisiana Militia. Deeply religious, he followed in the footsteps of his grandfather, Isaac, who was a rabbi, and his father, who was the cantor at *Bouxwiller*. Samson served as cantor and part-time rabbi at the Gates of Prayer synagogue in the city. Samson welcomed his sister, **FANNY CERF** (See entry), to New Orleans in 1864. He married CAROLINE HEIDENHEIM, a native New Orleanian of German extraction, on 20 November 1869. The couple had no children.

Samson died on 9 January 1905 in New Orleans and was buried in Gates of Prayer Cemetery #2 (Joseph Street). Caroline died on 3 July 1913 and was buried with him. (**A, AN, G, GB**)

COHN, HENRY, JR., was born **HENRI KAHN** on 8 December 1854 in *Schirrhoffen*, Bas-Rhin, France, to **ALEXANDRE KAHN** and his wife **JUDITH**, née **KAHN**, both natives of *Schirrhoffen*. He immigrated to the United States, arriving on 20 August 1872 in New York aboard the SS *Stromboli*. He settled in Rodney, Jefferson Co., Mississippi, before making a move to Rosedale, West Baton Rouge Parish, LA, in 1876. "Hy" Kahn, as he was called in the 1880 federal census, was enumerated as a twenty-three-year-old clerk in a store near Brusly Landing. West Baton Rouge Parish, LA. He had lived there since 1877, having been employed at the Cinclare Sugar Plantation and Mill. Cinclare (formerly Marengo Plantation) was operated much like a sawmill town, with its own currency, railway and a plantation store run for the convenience of its workers by a young Henry Cohn. Henry married SOPHIE FARRNBACHER (b. 1862 in Germany) in April 1881 at Brusly Landing. The couple had two sons: Daniel J. (b. 1882) and Isidore (b. 1885). The Cohns moved to Baton Rouge, East Baton Rouge Parish, LA, in 1890. Henry owned and operated the Cohn Flour and Feed Co. with his son Daniel. He was also founder and vice-president of the Bank of West Baton Rouge and organized the Cohn General Merchandise store in Port Allen, West Baton Rouge Parish, LA. He was president and a member of the board of Congregation B'nai Israel in Baton Rouge. Sophie Farrnbacher Cohn died on 10 February 1919 and was buried in the Jewish Cemetery in Baton Rouge. Henry died in Baton Rouge on 11 June 1942 and was interred with his wife. Note: When travelling back to France, Henry Cohn, Jr. used the name **HEYMANN KAHN** on all his passport applications. (**A, AN, GN**)

COHN, HYPOLITE, was born **HYPOLITE KAHN** on 30 September 1846 in *Schirrhoffen*, Bas-Rhin, France, to **LEHMAN CAHN/KAHN** and his wife, **ROSALIE/REINE MEY**, both natives of the town. He immigrated to Louisiana ca.1870, a reliable record for which we were unable to find. and started a dry goods business in West Baton Rouge Parish, LA. Hypolite married FANNIE FARRNBACHER (sister of his cousin Henry Cohn's wife, Sophie) who was a Louisiana native. The couple never had children. He later went in business with his father-in-law, Jacob Farrnbacher, in Baton

Rouge, East Baton Rouge Parish, LA, and rose to the vice-presidency of the Farrnbacher Dry Goods Company. He died on 16 April 1924 and was buried in the Jewish Cemetery in Baton Rouge. His wife died on 26 May 1943 and was interred beside him. (**A, AN, G, GB**)

COHN, JOSEPH, was born **JOSEPH KAHN** on 2 March 1836 in *Schirrhoffen*, Bas-Rhin, France, to **HERMANN KAHN** and his wife, **JEANNETTE/JEANNE BLOCH**, both natives of the town. According to his 1868 naturalization record, Joseph arrived in New Orleans, Orleans Parish, LA, ca. 1851. He may have been the fifteen-year-old Joseph Kahn who arrived in New Orleans on 26 January 1852 from Le Havre, France, aboard the ship *Elizabeth Hamilton*. He may also have been the "J. Cohen" who was enumerated in the 1860 federal census for New Orleans as a twenty-two-year-old merchant from France. He was naturalized in the city on 16 October 1868. Joseph (aka John) Cohn served in the American Civil War as a private in Company A, Confederate States Zouave Battalion, enlisting in New Orleans on 29 March 1861. There are no military records for him after July 1862. He was married to SARA JENNIE/ SARA JANE BADEL ca. 1863. We have not been able to locate a justice of the peace marriage record for this couple, which is not uncommon for those who married during the Union occupation of New Orleans. Joseph and Jennie were the parents of two children: Hiram (b. 1865) and Leon (b. 1869). Joseph was the proprietor of a clothing store on Magazine Street in the city. He died in New Orleans on 27 November 1898 and was buried there in Metairie Lakelawn Cemetery. Jennie Cohn followed her two sons, Hiram and Leon, to Manhattan, New York, where she died on 6 October 1903. Her remains were returned to New Orleans and buried with those of her husband. Note: Joseph was never known by his birth name "Kahn" in Louisiana. (**A, AN, GB**)

COHN, Jr., JOSEPH, was born **JOSEPH CAHN** on 19 December 1856 in *Schirrhoffen*, Bas-Rhin, France, to **LEHMANN CAHN/ KAHN** and his wife **ROSALIE/REINE MAY/MEY**, both natives of the town. According to his naturalization record, he immigrated to America ca. May 1873. A seventeen-year-old German national, "Jos. Cohn," who arrived in New York on 31 May 1873 from Glasgow, Scotland, aboard the SS *India*, is the only likely record we have found for his entry into the United States. Joseph settled in Convent, St. James Parish, LA, where he was naturalized in November 1878 and enumerated in the 1880 federal census as a twenty-two-year-old retail grocer from France. He married CORINNE FEIBLEMAN, a native of Camden, Ouachita Co., AR, on 26 March 1890 in New Orleans, Orleans Parish, LA. Joseph went into business as a wholesale grocer with his father-in-law, Edward Feibleman, in New Orleans, where the Feibleman-Cohn extended family was living together on St. Charles Avenue at the time of the 1900 federal census. Joseph and Corinne were the parents of three daughters: Madeleine Lillian (b. 1890), Ruth Corinne (b. 1895) and Fannie Daisy (b. 1898). Joseph Cohn Jr. died on 25 September 1919 in New Orleans and was buried there at Metairie-Lakelawn Cemetery. Corinne Cohn died on 28 November 1943 and was buried with him. Note: **JOSEPH COHN** (See entry) was Joseph Jr.'s uncle which is probably why the latter used the name suffix "Jr." in New Orleans. (**A, AN, GB**)

COHN, SUZANNE, was born **SUSANNA KAHN** on 22 September 1883 in *Bischwiller*, Bas-Rhin, France, to **HEYMAN/HERMAN KAHN** a native of *Herrlisheim*, Bas-Rhin, France, and his wife, **PALMYRE SOMMER,** born in *Schirrhoffen*, Bas-Rhin, France. Her nephews **SYLVAN** and **LEOPOLD SOMMER** (See entries) immigrated to Louisiana as well. Suzanne first lived in Georgia arriving ca. 1889 with her parents and her siblings Anna (b. 1882), Daniel (b. 1885) and Sylvain (b. 1886), and where a brother, Henry Lehman Kahn was born. We were unable to find a reliable record for the immigration of the family into the United States. They settled in Lorman, Jefferson CO., MS, where **HEYMANN KAHN,** and his two brothers, Joseph and Lehman, opened the COHN Bros. General Store. The COHN/KAHN brothers were considered to be the founders of this small Mississippi town, where Suzanne was raised. Suzanne married **JACQUES WELSCH** (See entry) in 1915, a record for which we have not been able to find. Jacques died, two years later, on 29 December 1917 in Baton Rouge, East Baton Rouge Parish, LA, where the couple had been living and was buried there in the Jewish Cemetery. The couple had had no children. Suzanne married **SELIGMANN "SOL" KAHN** (See entry) on 17 August 1927 in Baton Rouge. Sol died on 7 March 1942 in Natchez, Adams Co., MS. His remains were brought back to the Jewish Cemetery in Baton Rouge, East Baton Rouge Parish, LA, where they were buried with those of his brother, Gus. They share a double tombstone. Susanne died on 8 February 1966 in Vicksburg, Warren Co, MS and was buried alongside her first husband, Jacques Welsch, in the Jewish Cemetery in Baton Rouge, East Baton Rouge Parish, LA. (**A, AN, G, GB, TT**)

DAHLMANN, BABETTE, was born on 29 January 1846 in *Brumath*, Bas-Rhin, France, to **HIRTZ DAHLMANN,** a native of *Surbourg*, Bas-Rhin, France, and his wife, **ELIZABETH/LISETTE GOUDCHAUX,** born in *Brumath*, Bas-Rhin. After the Civil War, Babette followed a number of **GOUDCHAUX** cousins as well as a sister, **PAULINE DAHLMANN** (See entry for **SELIGMAN KAHN**), to Louisiana. We believe her to be the seventeen-year-old "Babette Dahlmann," a native of France, who arrived in New York from Le Havre, France, on 18 January 1865 aboard the ship *Wm. Frothington*. She married JOSEPH "JOE" SCHARFF, a native of Essingen, Germany, on 26 November 1867 in New Orleans, Orleans Parish, LA. The couple settled in Montgomery, Montgomery Co., AL, where their first three children were born: Louis (b. 1869), Morris (b. 1871) and Nora (b. 1873). They relocated ca. 1874 to Cheneyville, Rapides Parish, LA, where Joe was a dry goods merchant and where two of their sons, Henry (b. 1874) and Jules (b. 1876), were born. On 11 December 1878, Joseph almost lost his life in a collision below Donaldsonville, Assumption Parish, LA, between two steamboats, the *Charles Morgan* and the *Cotton Valley*. He was fortunately rescued from the water before he drowned. Babette died on 4 March 1881 in Cheneyville, and was buried in the Jewish Cemetery in Pineville, Rapides Parish, LA. Joseph Scharff married HENRIETTE WEIL, a native of Oberlustadt, Germany, in 1884 in New Orleans. They were the parents of two children: Max (b. 1884) and Beulah (b. 1888). Joseph Scharff died on 6 July 1907 in New Iberia, Iberia Parish, LA, and was buried there in Temple Gates of Prayer Cemetery (the Jewish section of Rosehill Cemetery). (**A, AN, F, G**)

DAHLMANN, ISAAC, was born **ARMAND DAHLMANN** on 10 October 1846 in *Surbourg*, Bas-Rhin, France, to **NOCHEM/NATHAN DAHLMANN/THALMANN,** a native of the town, and his wife, **CAROLINE GUTHSCHO/GOUDCHAUX,** born in *Brumath*, Bas-Rhin. He and his brothers, Aron, Abraham, and Henry, immigrated in the 1860s to Louisiana. Aron, Henry and Abraham settled in Fort Worth, Tarrant Co., TX, where they operated a clothing business. We have not been able to find a reliable ship's record for Armand/Isaac Dahlmann. Isaac married ANNETTE HOLLANDER, a New Orleans native, on 22 October 1871 in New Orleans, Orleans Parish, LA. During most of the 1870s and 1880s the brothers were in the clothing business, selling wholesale and retail clothing, hats, caps, boots and shoes, in Fort Worth, Tarrant Co., TX. Isaac and Annette had three sons: David (b. 1873), Moses (b. 1875) and George (b. 1878). Annette and her children appear in both the Fort Worth and the New Orleans Federal census records for 1880. While David was born in Texas, his two brothers were born in New Orleans, a fact which supports the idea that Annette and the boys travelled back and forth a good deal between the two cities. Before the turn of the twentieth century, Isaac moved back permanently to New Orleans to go into the liquor business which his father-in-law, the late Frederick Hollander, a native of Germany, had started. Isaac died on 25 December 1915 and was buried in Hebrew Rest Cemetery # 1 in New Orleans. His wife, Annette, died on 16 June 1925 and was buried in the same cemetery. Note: he always used the name "Isaac" here in America. In France he was also known as "Auscher." (**A, AN, G, GB, TT**)

DAHLMANN, PAULINE, (*Surbourg*) See entry for **SELIGMAN KAHN**

DALSHEIMER, BRUNETTE, was born **BARBARA DALSHEIMER** on 17 February 1810 in *Struth*, Bas-Rhin, France, to **DANIEL DALSHEIMER (JOCHEL LE JEUNE** before 1808), a native of the town, and his wife, **BEILE/BARBE DAVID**. Brunette arrived in Louisiana before 1854, a reliable record for which we were unable to find. JOHN/JEAN BOTERMAN/BUTTERMAN, a native of Prussia and two years her junior, took out a license to marry "Barbe Daklesheimer," on 27 May 1854 in New Orleans, Orleans Parish, LA. John was the proprietor of a furniture store. He and Brunette, enumerated as "Caroline Butterman" in the 1860 federal census, never had children. John and Caroline were enumerated as "John and Brunette Botermans" in the 1870 federal census. He was still the owner of a furniture store. Ten years later, the elderly couple, now identified as "John and Barbara Botermann," were retired from business. John died on 10 November 1887 in New Orleans. His place of burial is unknown. Brunette died on 6 February 1895 in the city and was buried in Hebrew Rest Cemetery #1. Her burial record identifies her as Brunette "Batterman," the sister of **NATHAN DALSHEIMER** (See entry). (**A, AN, E, TT**)

DALSHEMER, GEORGES was born **GÖTSCHEL/KÖTSCHEL DALSHEIMER** on 4 January 1803 in *Tieffenbach*, Bas-Rhin, France, to **HENRI/HERSCHEL DALSHEIMER**, a native of *Struth*, Bas-Rhin, and his wife **JOHANNA/JEUDEL SALOMON**, born in

Dauendorf, Bas-Rhin. He was enumerated in the 1851 Census of Jews, still living in *Tieffenbach* with his wife, **JEANNETTE KAHN**, a native of *Dossenheim-sur-Zinsel*, Bas-Rhin, and nine children, twins Salomon Leon & Jacques (b.1832; died as children), Joseph (b. 1834; died age 7), Michel (b. 1838), Leopold (b. 1842; died at 15 months), Adèle (b. 1842), Daniel (b. 1845), Nathan (b. 1848; appears as David in 1851, 1856 and 1866 censuses), and Caroline (b. 1851). Georges died on 21 October 1855 in New Orleans, Orleans Parish, LA, , a record of which was filed in the city nine months later on 8 July 1856. The death record stated that he was a forty-eight-year-old peddler from *Tieffenbach*, Bas-Rhin, living in Jefferson City, a suburb of New Orleans. He was married, but the name of his wife was not known to the person reporting his death. Georges' place of burial is unknown. Since 1855 was a particularly bad year for yellow fever, this might explain the delay in filing the death record and the absence of a known place of interment. Jeannette Kahn, his widow, was enumerated in the 1856 census for *Tieffenbach* living with her four children. She died in *Tieffenbach* on 26 July 1866 (**A, AN, B1851, W**)

DALSHEIMER, LEOPOLD, was born **LÄMMLE DALSHEIMER**, (enumerated as **THÉOBALD DALSHEIMER** in 1808), on 29 January 1808 in *Tieffenbach*, Bas-Rhin, France, to **HENRI/ERSCHEL DALSHEIMER**, a native of *Struth*, Bas-Rhin, France, and his wife **JOHANNA/JEUDEL SALOMON,** born in *Dauendorf*, Bas-Rhin. He immigrated to New Orleans, Orleans Parish, LA, as early as 1834, a reliable record for which we were not able to find. He married **ADELE LAMM**, a native of Bavaria, on 29 April 1835 at the home of Rev. Moses S. Reas (See entry for **JEANETTE RIES**). The couple lived in New Orleans, and later in Natchez, Adams Co.,MS, where Leopold was naturalized in 1846. They moved permanently to Baton Rouge, East Baton Rouge Parish, LA, before the 1850 census enumeration, where Leopold became a respected dry goods merchant. Six children were born to them: Sara (b. 1837 in LA), Jeannette (b. 1839 in LA), Alexandre (b. 1843 in MS), Pauline (b. 1844 in MS), Caroline (b. 1848 in MS), and Henry (b. 1850 in LA). Adele Dalsheimer died in Baton Rouge on 26 October 1879 and was buried there in the Jewish Cemetery. Leopold died on 19 June 1886 in Baton Rouge, and was buried there with his wife. (**A, AN, G, GB**)

DALSHEIMER, NATHAN, was born **NADEN LEIB** on 12 June 1816 in *Struth*, Bas-Rhin, France, to **DANIEL DALSHEIMER**

(**JOCHEL LE JEUNE** before 1808), a native of the town and his wife **BEILE/BARBE DAVID**. (Note: The last name "Dalsheimer" does not appear in the margin of the birth record or in the Ten Year Tables for this subject. Daniel was, however, listed with the surname "Dalsheimer" in the text of the original record.) Nathan immigrated to Louisiana ca. 1840, a reliable record for this first arrival which we have not been able to find. Nathan settled in Baton Rouge, East Baton Rouge Parish, LA, where he is said to have married Sarah Carson, a native of South Carolina. Two children were born to the couple: Octavia (b. 1843; married LEOPOLD ROSENFELD and died 15 June 1859 in childbirth), and Céline (b. 1845; married Philip Thalheimer in New Orleans in 1865). Nathan's wife died on 12 May 1854 in East Baton Rouge Parish, LA. Nathan married BABETTE KUHN, a native of Bavaria, on 8 March 1855 in Baton Rouge. They had three children: Daniel (b. 1856), Samuel (b. 1857) and Bertha (b. 1858). Nathan was a prosperous Baton Rouge merchant before the Civil War and the owner of eight slaves. He evidently returned to Europe during the course of the war, arriving back in New York on 23 May 1864 with his wife, Babette, his daughter, Céline (listed as Miss. S. Dalsheimer), and sons, Daniel and Samuel, on the ship *America* out of Bremen, Germany. The couple returned to New Orleans where they were enumerated together in the 1870 federal census with their children: fourteen-year-old Daniel, twelve-year-old Samuel, and eleven-year-old Bertha, his in-laws, Samuel and Caroline Kuhn, as well as several servants. Nathan was in the wholesale fancy goods business reporting $50,000 in real estate and $150,000 in personal property, a fortune for the time. Nathan died on 4 December 1877 and was buried the next day in Hebrew Rest Cemetery # 1 in New Orleans. His wife died on 28 April 1921 in Manhattan, New York, and her remains were returned to New Orleans to be buried with those of her husband. (**A, AN, G, GB**)

DENNERY, CHARLES, was born on 6 April 1869 in *Wissembourg*, Bas-Rhin, France, to THÉODORE DENNERY, a native of Vésoul, Haute-Saône, France, and his second wife, FANNY SALMON, born in Bohl, Rheinpfalz, Germany. Charles' parents took measures to leave France in 1871, and on 7 July of that year, Theodore, a cloth manufacturer in *Wissembourg*, declared his intention to immigrate to America with his wife, Fanny, son Charles, and daughter, **MARGUERITE DENNERY** (See entry), still an infant. On 2 July 1872, Charles, assisted by his father, signed a paper to opt for French nationality at the French Vice-Consul's office in St. Louis City, MO. In a 1918 passport application Charles Dennery indicated that he had arrived via the French Transatlantic Line in August 1871 from Le Havre, France. There is an arrival from Le Havre, France, of a family of four, all natives of France, travelling First Class, who arrived in New York on 15 August 1871 aboard the SS *Pereire*. The given names differ greatly but the ages differ only slightly from those one would expect to find on the manifest. Forty-year-old Auguste Dennery, his thirty-three-year-old wife, Jeanne, and two children, listed separately from their parents on the next page of the manifest, three-year-old Auguste, and two-year-old Marie were passengers on the SS *Pereire*. We believe that this must be the arrival of the Theodore Dennery family, although we are at a loss to explain the choice of names. The Dennerys settled in New Orleans, Orleans Parish, LA, where Theodore and Fanny had six more children: Henry "Harry" (b. 1874), Berthe (b. 1875), Raphael (b. 1877), Julie (b. 1878), Maurice (b. 1879), and Georges Isaac (b. 1883). Theodore worked as an agent for a mercantile house. Charles and his brother, Harry Dennery, founded a bakery and confectionary supply company at 525 Customhouse Street in 1894. Brothers, Ralph, George, and Maurice soon joined the firm which went from simply jobbing to manufacturing in 1901. Charles Dennery married JEANNETTE FRANK, a Natchez, Adams Co., MS, native on 14 May 1907 in Natchez, after which they left on a grand tour of Europe. Charles and Jeannette had one child, Melanie, born in 1909 in New Orleans. Jeannette died on 9 November 1919 and was buried in Hebrew Rest Cemetery #2 in New Orleans. In 1923 the Charles Dennery Co. was expanded and incorporated. It became the largest bakery and confection supply house in the south, with a manufacturing plant in Jefferson Parish and a branch office in Dallas, Dallas Co., TX. Charles Dennery died on 23 February 1939 and was buried in Hebrew Rest Cemetery #2 with his wife. The company he founded outlived him by half a century, staffed by brothers, brothers-in-law, and other trusted employees who stayed with the firm for decades. Note: Charles' great-grandfather, Samuel Dennery, was a native of Ennery, a small town in the Moselle region of France. Samuel d'Ennery (Samuel from Ennery) evolved into the surname the family uses today. (A, AN, GB)

DENNERY, MARGUERITE, was born on 25 June 1871 in *Wissembourg*, Bas-Rhin, France, to THÉODORE DENNERY, a native of Vésoul, Haute-Saône, France, and his second wife, FANNY SALMON, born in Bohl, Rheinpfalz, Germany. On 7 July 1871, Theodore Dennery, a cloth manufacturer in *Wissembourg*, declared his intention to immigrate to America with his wife, Fanny, son **CHARLES DENNERY** (See entry), and daughter Marguerite, still an infant. We believe that Marguerite, who was two months old when she left France, appeared on the passenger manifest of the SS *Pereire*, as two-year-old "Marie Dennery" who arrived with her parents at New York, from Le Havre, France, on 15 August 1871. Marguerite was raised and educated in New Orleans, Orleans Parish, LA, where she married ALBERT SCHWARTZ, a native of the city, on 26 March 1890. The couple never had children. They lived with the Theodore Dennery family, and later with Charles and Jeannette Dennery. Albert Schwartz worked for his brother-in-law at Charles Dennery, Inc. Albert died on 12 February 1935 in New Orleans and was buried there in Hebrew Rest Cemetery #2. Marguerite died on 26 May 1951 and was interred with her husband. (**A, AN, GB**)

DEPRÈS, MAURICE, was born on 24 April 1862 in *Lauterbourg*, Bas-Rhin, France, to **HANEL/HENRI DEPRÈS**, a native of the town, and his wife, REINE MARX, born in Ingenheim, Rheinpfalz, Germany. Maurice immigrated to the United States aboard the steamer *Algeria* from Liverpool, England, arriving in New York on 10 September 1879. According to his 1901 application for a United States passport, he spent the first six years in America in Brownsville, Cameron Co., TX, where he was naturalized in April 1885. Shortly thereafter he settled in Opelousas, St. Landry Parish, LA, where he worked as a clerk in a dry goods store. Although he never married, he was nevertheless, chairman of the Opelousas Social Club for several years beginning in 1891. He applied for and was granted a United States passport to return to France for six months in February 1894. Once abroad, he registered his presence at the *New York Herald* newspaper office in Paris, recording his place of residence as Opelousas. Maurice returned to his job in Opelousas and was enumerated there in the 1900 federal census as a thirty-eight-year-old unmarried dry goods salesman boarding with a private family. He moved to Washington D.C., ca. 1905 where he went into the real estate business. Maurice was the secretary of the Rose-Dale Park Co., located on G Street. By 1910 he had retired and was living in a rooming house on 6th Street, Northwest in Washington D.C. with Mary E. Stack, a widow, and her daughter, Mary, who was married to Isadore Levy, a stock broker. Maurice died on 25 August 1912 at Garfield Memorial Hospital in Washington D.C. He was fifty years of age. His bequests were published in the *Washington Post* in September 1912. He had bought land in Florida which he left to friends in Buffalo, Erie Co., NY and New Orleans, Orleans Parish, LA. He left his jewelry and the residue of his property to his landlady, Mary Stack, and a portfolio of stocks and bonds to her sons. Mary's son-in-law, Isadore Levy, was Maurice's executor. Maurice's death was noted in the report of the Humble Cottage Lodge, Opelousas, St. Landry Parish, LA, Order of Free and Accepted Masons of the State of Louisiana for the year 1913. We were unable to locate his place of burial. (**A, AN, GB, NP**)

DREYFUS, BENJAMIN, was born **BARRACH DREYFUSS** on 7 August 1829 in *Westhouse*, Bas-Rhin, France, to **HERMANN DREYFUS**, a native of the town, and his wife, BABETTE SULZER, born in Grussenheim, Haut-Rhin, France. He arrived in New Orleans, Orleans Parish, LA, as "Barnet Dreyfuss," on 18 May 1848 aboard the ship *James Corner* from Marseilles, France, with his brother, **JOSEPH/BENEDICT DREYFUS** (See entry). They were both enumerated in Iberville Parish, LA, in the 1850 federal census Benjamin was recorded as "Born Drypuse" an eighteen-year-old peddler from France, along with his brother, twenty-six-year-old Joseph, also a peddler. The brothers spent some time in Hinds Co., MS, where Benjamin's first child, Gustave was born in 1858. Although we have not been able to find a record of it, Benjamin had married **MARIE BLOCH** ca. 1857, probably in Mississippi. Marie was born on 11 January 1835 in *Diebolsheim*, Bas-Rhin, France, to **HIRTZ BLOCH**, a native of the town, and his wife, **GERTRUDE MEYER**, born in *Wolfisheim*, Bas-Rhin. Shortly after the birth of Gustave, Benjamin and Marie moved to New Orleans where four more children were born to the couple: Nathalie (b. 1859; died 1862), Rosine (b. 1862), Théophile Georges (b. 1863), and Octavie Hortense (b. 1867). Benjamin and Joseph, who had moved his family to New Orleans ca. 1859, were partners in a prosperous wholesale liquor and dry goods business. The two families went their separate ways ca. 1885. While Joseph relocated to St. Louis, MO, Benjamin took his family to Manhattan, NY, where he opened a cigar store. He was enumerated there in the 1900 federal census with his wife, Mary, and daughter, Rosine. He died on 27 June 1909 and was buried in Mt. Carmel Cemetery in Flushing, Queens, NY. Marie died on 23 November 1917 and was interred with her husband. (**A, AN, G, TT**)

DREYFUS, CLAIRE/CLARA/CLARISSA, was born **CLAIRE DREYFUS** on 20 January 1827 in *Wissembourg*, Bas-Rhin, France, to

AUGUSTE DREYFUS, a native of the town, and his wife **PHILIPPINE HEYMANN**, born in *Soultz-sous-Fôrets*, Bas-Rhin. Claire arrived in New Orleans, Orleans Parish, LA, before 1859, a reliable record for which we were unable to find. She married **BENOÎT (BENJAMIN) SILBERNAGEL**, a native of Niederlustadt, Rheinpfalz, Germany, who had arrived in New Orleans on the ship *Radius* on 27 December 1849. According to the 1850 federal census, he and his brother Joseph, known as "Wolf," were already established near Bastrop, Morehouse Parish, LA, in an area called Prairie Mer Rouge. Benoît (called Benjamin in Louisiana), married Claire Dreyfus on 2 February 1859 in New Orleans, Orleans Parish, LA. The couple returned to Bastrop, where they lived their entire lives. They were the parents of two children: Raymond (b. 1862) and Eugene (b. 1865). Ben was a successful dry goods merchant, land owner, and cotton broker. Claire died on 18 October 1883 in Bastrop and was buried in Rosena Chapel Cemetery in Monroe, Ouachita Parish, LA. Her husband died on 11 May 1899 in Bastrop and was buried with her in Monroe. (**A, AN, G, GB, TT**)

DREYFUS, ÉMILE, was born **ÉMILE DREYFUSS** on 17 August 1848 in *Obernai*, Bas-Rhin, France, to **GOTTLIEB/GEORGE DREYFUS** (See entry), a native of *Westhouse*, Bas-Rhin, France, and his wife, **MARIE/BABETTE SALOMON**, born in *Obernai*, Bas-Rhin. He immigrated with his mother and siblings in the late 1850s, a record for which we were unable to find. He and his family settled in Jackson, Hinds Co., MS. They moved to New Orleans, Orleans Parish, LA, at the end of the Civil War ca. 1865. Emile and his brothers, Samuel, Henry and Simon later took jobs as clerks in Shreveport, Caddo Parish, LA. Émile died on 13 September 1873, a victim of the worst yellow fever epidemic in Shreveport's history. He was the first of the three Dreyfus brothers from *Obernai* to succumb. The town was devastated by this outbreak. Half of its population fled before a quarantine was put in place in late August, which was not lifted until the end of November. Emile was buried in Hebrew Rest Cemetery # 1 (Jewish Section of Oakland Cemetery). His remains were later removed to Hebrew Rest Cemetery # 2 (Texas Ave.) to be with the rest of his family. Only his brother, **SAMUEL GEORGE DREYFUS** (See entry), was spared. (**A, AN, G, TT**)

DREYFUS, EMILIE/EMILY/AMELIA, was born **MARIE EMILIE DREYFUS** on 16 October 1862 in *Sélestat*, Bas-Rhin,

France, to **RAPHAEL DREYFUS**, a native of *Westhouse*, Bas-Rhin, France, and his wife, **JEANNETTE/NANETTE LEVY**, born in *Weiterswiller*, Bas-Rhin. She may have been the twenty-eight-year-old immigrant listed as "Marie Dreyfus" who landed at New York from Le Havre, France, on 16 November 1891 aboard the SS *La Bourgogne*. She lived only a few years in New Orleans, Orleans Parish, LA, where she died on 24 September 1897. She was buried there in Hebrew Rest Cemetery #1 in the same plot as her cousin, Albert Fraenckel, her sister, PALMYRE DREYFUS FRAENCKEL's son, and Albert's wife Carrie Switzer. A notation on the burial record indicates that she was the niece of **GEORGE DREYFUS** (See entry for **GOTTLIEB/ GEORGE DREYFUS**). Her sister, **ANNA DREYFUS**, born on 18 August 1859 at *Sélestat*, Bas-Rhin, France, immigrated to the United States arriving in New York on 17 October 1892 aboard the SS *La Bourgogne*, and lived for many years in Minneapolis, Hennepin Co., MN, where she was a teacher of French. Anna was murdered on 20 December 1942 in Los Angeles, Los Angeles Co., CA. She was cremated and her remains returned to New Orleans to be buried in the same plot with her sister and cousin. (**A, AN, GB, TT**)

DREYFUS, GOTTLIEB/GEORGE, was born on 3 June 1814 in *Westhouse,* Bas-Rhin, France, to **HERMANN DREYFUS**, a native of the town, and his wife, BABETTE SULZER, born in Grussenheim, Haut-Rhin, France. He married **MARIE/BABETTE SALOMON** on 18 July 1844 in *Obernai*, Bas-Rhin, France. Babette was born on 27 February 1814 in *Obernai*, to **ARON SALOMON**, a native of *Krautergersheim*, Bas-Rhin, France, and his wife **ESTHER WEIL**, born in *Obernai*. George and Babette were the parents of six children: Henry T (b. 1846), Raphaël (b. 1846; died 1847), Samuel George (b. 1847), Émile (b. 1848), Simon (b. 1851), and Alphonse (b. 1852; died 1853). Babette and four of their surviving children immigrated to America, records of which we were unable to find. We believe, however, that an entry for a forty-year-old "Gottlieb Dreifuss" who arrived in New York from Le Havre, France alone on 10 August 1854 aboard the ship *Bavaria* is worthy of consideration although Gottlieb was said to have been from "Bade." It was not unusual for the head of the family to precede his wife and children to America. The first indication of the family's presence in the United States was George's declaration of intention, filed in March 1859 in Jackson, Hinds Co., MS, where he settled with Babette, and his four surviving sons, **HENRY, SAMUEL, ÉMILE**, and **SIMON DREYFUS**. (See entries).

The family appeared together in the 1860 census for Jackson, Hinds CO., MS, but, soon thereafter, records for George indicate that the family had moved to New Orleans, probably after the devastation of the Civil War. In 1866 he was listed in a New Orleans Directory as the owner of a clothing business at the corner of Canal and Camp Streets, with his brother, **JOSEPH DREYFUS** (See entry). Both families lived at the same address on Magazine Street. George died on 8 March 1869 in New Orleans and was originally buried in the Hebrew Rest Cemetery # 1 in the city. Babette Dreyfus moved to Shreveport, Caddo Parish, LA, to live with her son, Samuel, and his family. She died on 29 January 1898 in Shreveport and was buried there in Hebrew Rest Cemetery # 2 (Texas Ave.) Her husband George's body was disinterred in 1910 and moved to the same cemetery. (**A, AN, G, TT**)

DREYFUS, HENRY THÉOPHILE, was born **HENRY DREYFUSS** on 20 January 1846 in *Obernai*, Bas-Rhin, France, to **GOTTLIEB/GEORGE DREYFUS**, a native of *Westhouse*, Bas-Rhin, France, and his wife, **MARIE/BABETTE SALOMON**, born in *Obernai*, Bas-Rhin. He immigrated with his mother and siblings in the late 1850s to Jackson, Hinds Co., MS, a record for which we were unable to locate. He and his family moved to New Orleans, Orleans Parish, LA, ca. 1865. Henry and his brothers, **SAMUEL**, **ÉMILE** and **SIMON DREYFUS** (See entries), later took jobs in Shreveport, Caddo Parish, LA, as clerks. Henry died there on 2 October 1873, a victim of the yellow fever epidemic and was buried in Hebrew Rest Cemetery # 1 (Jewish Section of Oakland Cemetery). His remains were later removed to Hebrew Rest Cemetery # 2 (Texas Ave.) to be interred with the rest of his family. (**A, AN, G, TT**)

DREYFUS, JOSEPH, was born **BENEDICT DREYFUSS** on 18 April 1826 in *Westhouse*, Bas-Rhin, France, to **HERMANN DREYFUS,** a native of the town, and his wife, BABETTE SULZER, born in Grussenheim, Haut-Rhin, France. He arrived in New Orleans, Orleans Parish, LA, under the name "Benoît Dreyfuss," on 18 May 1848 aboard the *James Corner* from Marseilles, France, with his brother, **BENJAMIN/BARACH DREYFUS** (See entry). Joseph married **BABETTE GOUDCHAUX** on 16 February 1853 in Plaquemine, Iberville Parish, LA. Babette was born **BABETTE GUTSCHUH** on 8 October 1836 in *Brumath*, Bas-Rhin, France, to **JACQUES GOUDCHAUX/GUTSCHU** and his second wife, **ROSETTE KAHN**, both natives of *Brumath*. Babette immigrated to

New Orleans, from Le Havre with her thirteen year old brother, **HENRY GOUDCHAUX** (See entry), arriving on 2 April 1851 at New Orleans aboard the ship *Old England*. She and Henry went to live with their half-sister, **ESTELLE GOUDCHAUX KAHN,** and her husband, Samuel, in Plaquemine, Iberville Parish, LA, where she was married to Joseph Dreyfus. At the time of their marriage Joseph was a resident of Hinds Co., MS. He had, however, formerly been a peddler, leaving his mark in the 1850 census for Iberville Parish and was probably known to the Kahn family. The couple's first two children, Florence (b. 1857) and Rosa (b. 1858) were born in Mississippi, before Joseph relocated to New Orleans, Orleans Parish, LA, where he became a prosperous wholesale liquor and dry goods merchant in partnership with his brothers, **BENJAMIN** and **GOTTLIEB GEORGE DREYFUS** (See entries). Four more children were born in the Crescent City to Babette and Joseph: Antoinette (b. 1862), Alphonse H. (b. 1864), Emma (b. 1867) and Blanche (b. 1871). In the mid-1880s, the family relocated to St. Louis, MO, where Babette died on 12 February 1886. She was buried there in Mt. Sinai Cemetery. After her death, Joseph moved to Kansas City, Jackson Co., MO, where he worked as a wholesale liquor dealer. Joseph died there on 8 May 1915 and his body was returned to St. Louis for burial with his wife in Mt. Sinai Cemetery. (**A, AN, G, TT**)

DREYFUS, JULIA, was born **JULIE DREYFUS** in *Wissembourg*, Bas-Rhin, France, on 21 October 1815 to **AUGUSTE DREYFUS**, a native of the town, and his wife, **PHILIPPINE HEYMANN**, born in *Soultz-sous-Forêts*, Bas-Rhin. Julie married SOLOMON LEOPOLD, a native of Edenkoben, Rheinpfalz, Germany (about 30 miles from Wissembourg) ca. 1850. Their first two children, twins, Mina and Bertha were born in Germany. The couple immigrated to Ellenville, Ulster Co., New York ca. 1854, where two more children were born: Jennie (b. 1855) and Samuel Augustus (b. 1857). We were unable to find immigration records for this family. The Leopolds were enumerated in the 1860 federal census at Plantersville, outside of Bastrop, Morehouse Parish, LA, where Solomon was a dry goods merchant. Their arrival in Louisiana, was encouraged by the SILBERNAGEL family, immigrants from the same region who had roots both in Wissembourg and in Rhenish Bavarian towns just across the border in Germany. Two of Julie's sisters, **CLAIRE** and **THÉRÈSE DREYFUS** (See entries) had married into the Silbernagel family. At the close of the Civil War, Solomon Leopold was paroled as a private in Company A of the First Louisiana Battalion Reserve Corps. He remained in Morehouse Parish, moving to nearby Bastrop, where he carried on his grocery business. Julie Dreyfus Leopold died in Bastrop on 2 August 1878 and was buried in Rosena Chapel Jewish Cemetery in nearby, Monroe, Ouachita Parish, LA. Solomon followed on 6 April 1879 and was buried there as well. (**A, AN, G**)

DREYFUS, LEHMANN, was born on 12 November 1855 in *Duppigheim*, Bas-Rhin, France, to **ARON DREYFUS**, a native of the town, and his wife, **FANNIE PICARD**, who, judging from her last name, was probably from the Haut-Rhin or Moselle region of France. In the last *Duppigheim* census available to us, taken in 1866, Lehmann was still living with his parents, the sixth of nine children in the family. Seventeen-year-old Lehmann Dreyfus arrived with several other young men from *Duppigheim* on 14 October 1872 at New Orleans, Orleans Parish, LA, from Hamburg, Germany, Le Havre, France, Santander, Spain and Havana, Cuba, aboard the SS *Saxonia*. He died in Louisiana or Mississippi on 23 October 1878, at the age of twenty-two, probably during that year's yellow fever epidemic. He was buried in the Jewish Section of the Old German Cemetery in Kirksville, Tangipahoa Parish, LA. (**A, AN**)

DREYFUS, PALMYRE, (*Sélestat*) See entry for **FÉLIX FRAENCKEL**

DREYFUS, SAMUEL GEORGE, was born **SAMUEL DREYFUSS** on 21 February 1847 in *Obernai*, Bas-Rhin, France, to **GOTTLIEB/GEORGE DREYFUS**, a native of *Westhouse*, Bas-Rhin, France, and his wife, **MARIE/BABETTE SALOMON**, born in *Obernai*, Bas-Rhin. He immigrated with his mother and siblings in the late 1850s to Jackson, Hinds Co., MS, a record for which we were unable to find. The family relocated to New Orleans, Orleans Parish, LA ca. 1866. Samuel and his brothers, **SIMON, HENRY** and **ÉMILE DREYFUS** (See entries), took jobs as clerks in Shreveport, Caddo Parish, LA. The only brother to survive the yellow fever epidemic of 1873, the worst in Shreveport's history, he married **JOHANNAH/ HANNAH SIMON**, a Louisiana native ca. 1876. The couple had two children: Flora (b. 1877), and George T. (b. 1880). Samuel G. Dreyfus was president of S.G. Dreyfus Co., one of the largest wholesale dry goods houses in Shreveport. His vice-president was J.C. Simon, his brother-in-law, and his son, George, eventually became the secretary-treasurer and later headed the company. Sam and Hannah moved to Manhattan ca. 1911 where he died on 16 December 1918. He was buried in Mt. Hope Cemetery in Hastings-on-Hudson, Westchester Co., NY. Hannah died on 5 November 1932 and was buried with him. (**A, AN, G, TT**)

DREYFUS, SARA, was born on 23 May 1835 in *Mertzwiller*, Bas-Rhin, France, to **FERDINAND DREYFUS**, a native of the town, and his wife, **ESTER MANDEL**, born in *Trimbach*, Bas-Rhin, France. Sara married **ABRAHAM KOESSLER**, also a native of *Mertzwiller,* on 11 August 1858 in town. They were the parents of seven children: Emanuel (b. 1858), Samson/Julius (b. 1860), Samuel (b. 1861; See entry), Mathilde (b. 1864;-See entry), Caroline "Carrie" (b. 1868; See entry), Leon (b. 1872; See entry), and Isidore (b. 1877; See entry), all of whom, with the exception of Emanuel, immigrated to America. Samson/Julius settled in St. Louis, MO, but three sons and two daughters came to Louisiana. Sara Koessler, widowed in France, came to join her children after the turn of the twentieth century. She arrived as seventy-three-year-old "Sarah Kessler" at New York on 3 October 1909 from Boulogne-sur-Mer, France, aboard the SS *Graf Waldersee*. Sarah lived with her daughter, Carrie Sternfels, in Belle Rose, Assumption Parish,LA, for a decade, then moved to New Orleans to live with her son, Samuel, and his family on St. Charles Avenue. Sara died on 8 February 1921 and was interred in Bikur Sholim Jewish Cemetery in Donaldsonville, Ascension Parish, LA**. (A, AN, G)**

DREYFUS, SIMON, was born **SIMÉON DREYFUSS** on 12 March 1851 in *Obernai*, Bas-Rhin, France, to **GOTTLIEB/GEORGE DREYFUS**, a native of *Westhouse*, Bas-Rhin, France, and his wife, **MARIE/BABETTE SALOMON**, born in *Obernai,*Bas-Rhin. He immigrated with his mother and siblings in the late 1850s to Jackson, Hinds Co., MS, a record for which we were unable to find. The family relocated to New Orleans, Orleans Parish, LA, ca. 1866. Simon and his brothers, **SAMUEL, HENRY** and **ÉMILE DREYFUS** (See entries) took jobs as clerks in Shreveport, Caddo Parish, LA. Twenty-two-year-old Simon died on 18 September 1873, a victim of the worst yellow fever epidemic in Shreveport's history, and the second of the three Dreyfus brothers from Obernai to succumb. He was buried in Hebrew Rest Cemetery # 1 (Jewish Section of Oakland Cemetery). His remains were later removed to the Hebrew Rest Cemetery # 2 (Texas Ave.) to be interred with the rest of his family. (**A, AN, G, TT**)

DREYFUS, THERESA, was born **THÉRÈSE DREYFUS** on 28 March 1831 in *Wissembourg*, Bas-Rhin, France, to **AUGUSTE DREYFUS**, a native of the town, and his wife, **PHILIPPINE HEYMANN**, born in *Soultz-sous-Fôrets*, Bas-Rhin. She was married to JOSEPH "WOLF" SILBERNAGEL, a thirty year old native of Niederlustadt, Rheinpfalz, Germany, on 18 August 1853 in *Wissembourg*. Wolf, as he was always called in Louisiana, had returned from Morehouse Parish, where he had been living with his brother, Benoît, to marry her. He had originally immigrated at age twenty as "Wolf" Silbernagel arriving in New Orleans on 17 October 1844 aboard the ship *Norman* from Le Havre, France. The couple returned to live in Bastrop, Morehouse Parish, where he and his brother had both prospered as merchants and land owners. Therese and Wolf had one child, Albert M., born on 24 September 1854 in Bastrop. In 1860 the couple was enumerated in Bastrop, where Wolf had real estate valued at $19,200 and personal property worth $37,700. During the Civil War Wolf served as a sutler for Company D, 2nd Louisiana Battery Heavy Artillery in Morehouse Parish. Wolf was murdered on 28 November 1865, shortly after his parole from the army, while returning from a trip north into Arkansas with fellow merchant, DAVID S. LEVY, another Bavraian native. They were several miles from the Arkansas-Louisiana state line when they were waylaid by a band of highwaymen. The pair was suspected of having been in possession of, at least $20,000 in cash. Robbers took everything except $1800 which had been in an envelope in Wolf's breast pocket. Their bodies were returned to Monroe, Ouachita Parish, LA, where they were buried there in Rosena Chapel Cemetery. Theresa did not stay in Morehouse Parish. She remarried in New Orleans on 25 March 1868 to ISAAC L. HAAS, a forty-two year old cotton broker. She appeared as his wife in the 1870 federal census using her name "Theresa", and in the 1880 federal census, using the name "Caroline." Isaac Haas died in New Orleans on 9 June 1882 and was buried there in Hebrew Rest Cemetery #1. Theresa followed her only child, Albert Silbernagel, a jeweler, to Manhattan, New York, where she died on 30 July 1910. We were unable to locate her final resting place, although her son Albert was interred at Union Field Cemetery in Ridgewood, Queens, New York.(**A, AN, GB, N, TT**)

DREYFUS, VICTOIRE/FANNY, (*Westhouse*), See entry for **SAMUEL LEVY** (b. 1823).

DREYFUSS, BRUNETTE/GERTRUD, (*Mertzwiller*) See entry for **MARX BLOCH**.

DREYFUSS, HENRIETTE, was born on 9 March 1856 in *Bouxwiller*, Bas-Rhin, France, to **HENRY DREYFUSS** (See entry), a native of *Woerth-sur-L'Ill* (*Werde*), a hamlet of *Matzenheim*, Bas-Rhin, France, and his wife **SARA AARON**, born in *Bouxwiller*, Bas-Rhin. She immigrated with her mother and brother to join her father, Henry Dreyfuss, before the 1860 federal census, in which she was enumerated as a four-year-old child. She would have been fourteen at the time of the 1870 census, yet she was not enumerated with her family. Henriette may have died before then, but we could find no record of her death or trace of her place of burial (**A, AN, G**)

DREYFUSS, HENRY, was born on 5 June 1818 in *Woerth-sur-L'Ill* (Werde), a hamlet of *Matzenheim*, Bas-Rhin, France, to **DAVID DREYFUSS**, a native of the town, and SARA ULLMANN, born in Eichstetten, Baden-Württemburg, Germany. (Note: His birth record was filed at *Matzenheim*) At the time of his marriage to **SARA AARON,** which took place in *Bouxwiller*, Bas-Rhin, France, on 12 April 1853 he was employed as a police sergeant (constable) in the city of Lyon, France, an unusual occupation for a Jew at the time. His bride, Sara, was born on 7 April 1829 in *Bouxwiller*, Bas-Rhin, to **ISAAC AARON**, a native of *Neuwiller-lès-Saverne*, Bas-Rhin, France, and his wife **ANNETTE** née **AARON**, born in *Bouxwiller*. The couple's first child, **JULES DREYFUSS** (See entry), was born in 1854 in *Matzenheim*. Their second, a daughter, **HENRIETTE DREYFUSS** (See entry), was born in *Bouxwiller* in 1856 after Henry had already left for America. We believe that thirty-year-old [sic] "Henry Dreyfuss" arrived in New Orleans, Orleans Parish, LA, from Le Havre, France, on 12 November 1855 aboard the ship *Johannesburg*. We could find no immigration records for any of the rest of the family. Sara and her children arrived in Louisiana before the 1860 federal census where they joined Henry at Shreveport, Caddo Parish, LA. Henry operated a family grocery store, and was reported to have $700 in real estate and $10,000 in personal property at the time of the 1860 federal census. Three more children were born to the couple in Shreveport: Samuel (b. 1862), Bertha (b. 1866), and Isaac (b. 1872). Henry stayed in Shreveport during the Civil War being one of the founders of the Home Guard, a band of older male residents, who took up arms to protect the city, after it briefly became the capital of the Confederacy following the fall of

Richmond in early 1865. During the war he established the firm of H. Dreyfuss & Sons, which was one of the largest wholesale dry goods establishments in the town. Henry died on 26 January 1886 in Shreveport and was buried in Hebrew Rest Cemetery #1 (the Jewish section of Oakland Cemetery). His remains were later transferred to Hebrew Rest #2 (Texas Ave.), after the death of his wife, Sara on 13 August 1896, where they are both now interred. Note: When searching for an immigration record for Henry Dreyfuss, I found an entry for him having left "Havana, Cuba" on 12 November 1855. Fortunately I checked the first page of the manifest and the ship had come from "Havre." Whomever transcribed these records did not recognize the French city which is occasionally referenced only as "Havre" especially in older records. (**A, AN, G, TT**)

DREYFUSS, JEANNE AGATHE, (*Strasbourg*) See entry for **JOSUÉ DREYFUSS**

DREYFUSS, JOSUÉ, was born on 23 December 1831 in *Mertzwiller*, Bas-Rhin, France, to **ISAAC DREYFUS**, a merchant and native of *Mertzwiller*, and his wife **JEANETTE JOSEPH**. Nineteen-year-old Josué immigrated to New Orleans, Orleans Parish, LA, arriving on 24 Jan 1852 on the ship *Rouennais*. He took out a license to marry **ESTELLE BOMPET** on 3 February 1866 in New Orleans. Estelle was born **ESTHER BOMBET** on 4 November 1841 in *Hochfelden*, Bas-Rhin, France, to **HILAIRE SALOMON POMPET**, a native of *Kuttelsheim*, Bas-Rhin, and his wife, **AGATHE BLUM**, born in *Hochfelden*, Bas-Rhin. She was sent to live with relatives after her mother's death in 1847. At the close of the Civil War, she immigrated to New Orleans to join her brother, **MICHEL BOMPET** (See entry), and sister, **SARAH BOMPET** (See entry). We were unable to find a record of her arrival in America. After their 3 February1866 marriage, Josué and Estelle returned to *Strasbourg*, Bas-Rhin, France, in time for the birth of their first child, **SALOMON CHARLES** on 20 December 1866. A daughter, **JEANNE AGATHE,** was born there on 10 November 1867, after which the couple returned to live in Shreveport, Caddo Parish, LA, where four more children were born: Blanche Sarah (b.1872; lived 3 months), Maurice Isaac (b. 1873), Rosalie (b. 1875), and Mathilde (b. 1876; died at 9 months). By 1880 the couple had moved to Manhattan, New York with their four surviving children. Estelle probably returned to France after her husband died in 1905, as her son Charles indicated in a passport application dated 1916 that he was returning to France to visit his mother and sister. By 1936, Solomon Charles, who had lived in Chicago and New York, had returned to Paris to live. The last record we have for him is a 1936 ship's record. Sixty-nine-year-old Charles was a passenger on the SS *Queen Mary* which landed in New York on 11 November 1936. (**A, AN, B, F, N**)

DREYFUSS, JULES was born on 3 April 1854 in *Matzenheim*, Bas-Rhin, France to **HENRY DREYFUSS** (See entry), a native of the neighboring hamlet of *Woerth-sur-L'Ill* (*Werte*) Bas-Rhin, France, and his wife, **SARA AARON**, born in *Bouxwiller*, Bas-Rhin, France. He immigrated with his mother and sister to join his father, Henry Dreyfuss, before the 1860 federal census, a record for which we were not able to find. He married BELLA LEVI, a Louisiana native, on 3 May 1882 in New Orleans, Orleans Parish, LA. The couple returned to Shreveport where Jules worked with his father at H. Dreyfuss & Sons, dealing in wholesale dry goods. Five children were born to the couple: Henry Levi (b. 1887), Albert M. (b. 1889), Leonard Jules (b. 1891), and twins, Frances and Sadie (b. 1900). Jules died on 2 November 1909 in Shreveport. His wife, Bella, followed on 25 August 1935. They were buried there together in Hebrew Rest Cemetery # 2 (Texas Ave.). (**A, AN, G**)

DREYFUSS, LUCY/LUDMILLA, (*Oberschaeffolsheim*) See entry for **HENRY BRAUN**

DREYFUSS, SOLOMON CHARLES, (*Strasbourg*) See entry for **JOSUÉ DREYFUSS**

EHRLICH, CAROLINE, (*Wissembourg*) See entry for **MARX WEIL**

EHRLICH, CELESTINE, (*Wissembourg*) See entry for **MARX WEIL**

EHRMANN, ADELE, was born **ADÈLE EHRMANN** on 16 December 1841 in *Rothbach*, Bas-Rhin, France, to **NATHAN EHRMANN** (See entry), a native of the town, and his wife, **MARIE HIMMLER,** born in *Gundershoffen*, Bas-Rhin. Sixteen-year-old Adèle immigrated to Louisiana with her mother, Marie Himmler, sisters **CAROLINE, ROSALIE, HENRIETTE** (See entries**)** and brother **URI/FÉLIX** (See entry), arriving in New Orleans, Orleans Parish, LA, on 4 June 1857 aboard the ship *Edmie*. She was enumerated with her parents and siblings in the 1860 federal census at Attakapas, St. Martin Parish, LA, and again in 1870 in New Iberia, Iberia Parish, LA. Adèle was married to **JACQUES EUGÈNE EISENMANN** on 21 October 1874 in New Iberia. **EUGENE EISENMANN** was born on 18 February 1846 in *Haguenau*, Bas-Rhin, France, to **MARX EISENMANN**, a native of the town, and his wife, JUDITH ALTSCHUL, born in Ingenheim, Germany. In his 13 September 1872 naturalization record filed in Iberia Parish, LA, Eugene affirmed that he immigrated to Louisiana in 1866. The arrival of twenty-three-year-old "Jean Isenmann", a native of France who departed from Le Havre, France, and landed at New York on 25 April 1867 aboard the SS *Cella* is definitely worthy of consideration, as there is no other record which is even close to matching his name, date of birth, or ethnicity. At the time of his arrival, Eugene's sister **VALENTINE EISENMANN** (See entry for **MICHEL HEYMANN**), was already settled in New Orleans. Eugene and Adèle were the parents of five children: Nathan (b. 1875), Gustave (b. 1876), Henrietta (b. 1878), Caroline (b. 1881), and Rose (b. 1883). After a decade in the dry goods business in Louisiana, Eugene decided, ca. 1884, to join his brothers-in-law, Henri and Felix Ehrmann in Panama. He established a business in the city of Colon, but it did not go well and he returned to Louisiana within a few years. He died from pneumonia on 4 November 1891 in New Orleans, Orleans Parish, LA, and was buried there in Hebrew Rest Cemetery #1. Adèle lived with her children in New Orleans until her death on 20 February 1906. She was buried with her husband in Hebrew Rest Cemetery #1. Her son, Nathan, a dentist, was the vice-consul-general for Panama at New Orleans for a number of years. (**A, AN, E, G, GB**)

EHRMANN, BERNARD, was born on 6 January 1835 in *Rothbach*, Bas-Rhin, France, to **NATHAN EHRMANN** (See entry), a native of the town, and his wife, **MARIE HIMMLER,** born in *Gundershoffen*, Bas-Rhin. Bernard booked passage on the American sailing ship *Luna*, which left Le Havre, France, on the evening of 16 February 1860, in order to join his parents in Louisiana. He was listed on the passenger manifest as twenty-five-year-old Bernard "Hermann" from Rothbach. The *Luna* was unable to make its way out of the English Channel to the open waters of the Atlantic Ocean, on account of gale winds and a snow storm. She foundered on the rocks, in full sight of horrified witnesses, near Barfleur the next morning. Bernard perished along with more than one hundred other passengers and crew on the morning of 17 February 1860. His body was never found amongst those that eventually washed ashore. Note: Bernard's uncle, **ESAJAS EHRENMANN**, was married to **SAARE LEHMANN**, whose cousin, **SALOMON LEHMANN** (See entry), also perished in the wreck. **(A,GB)**

EHRMANN, CAROLINE, was born **CAROLINE EHRENMANN** on 28 June 1837 in *Rothbach*, Bas-Rhin, France, to **NATHAN EHRMANN** (See entry), a native of the town, and his wife, **MARIE HIMMLER**, born in *Gundershoffen*, Bas-Rhin. Twenty-year-old Caroline immigrated to Louisiana with her mother, Marie Himmler, sisters **ADÈLE, ROSALIE**, and **HENRIETTE**, and brother **URI/FÉLIX EHRMANN** (See entries), arriving in New Orleans, Orleans Parish, LA, on 4 June 1857 aboard the ship *Edmie*. She was enumerated with her parents and siblings in the 1860 federal census at Attakapas, St. Martin Parish, LA. Caroline was married to JOSEPH H. WISE, a Polish immigrant, on 19 October 1865 in New Orleans, Orleans Parish, LA. The couple settled in Vermilionville (now Lafayette), Lafayette Parish, LA, where Joseph ran a general store. Joseph Wise was one of the founders of the Lafayette Jewish Cemetery. He and his wife, who never had children, lived in New Iberia, Iberia Parish, LA, Mobile, AL, and finally Biloxi, Harrison Co., MS, where he was partners in the Wise & Levy general store, with his brother-in-law, DAVID LEVY. He died on 12 November 1902 at Touro Infirmary in New Orleans, where he had gone to seek treatment. His body was returned for burial in the Lafayette Jewish Cemetery in Lafayette, Lafayette Parish, LA. After her husband's death Caroline returned to New Iberia to live with her sister, Henriette Ehrmann Levy. Caroline died on 21 July 1913 and was buried with her husband in the Jewish Cemetery in Lafayette, LA. **(A, AN, E, G, GB)**

EHRMANN, DANIEL LION, was born **LYON EHRENMANN** on 12 November 1831 in *Rothbach*, Bas-Rhin, France, to **NATHAN EHRMANN** (See entry), a native of the town, and his wife, **MARIE HIMMLER**, born in *Gundershoffen*, Bas-Rhin. He married **MADELEINE LEVY**, on 31 August 1852 in *Rothbach*. Madeleine was born in *Bouxwiller*, Bas-Rhin, France, to **LEOPOLD LEVY** and his wife, **ADELAÏDE/BABETTE GRADWOHL,** both natives of *Bouxwiller*. Daniel immigrated to Louisiana, arriving before 1857, a record for which we were unable to find. His wife, Madeleine Levy, was enumerated with her parents in *Bouxwiller*, in both the 1856 and 1861 town censuses, as "Levy, Madeleine, femme (wife of) Ehrman." Madeleine did not appear in the 1866 *Bouxwiller* census and there is no record of her having died there. Daniel Ehrmann married ANAÏSE TRÈGRE, a native of St. John the Baptist Parish, on 24 September 1857 in New Orleans, Orleans Parish, LA. There were no known children from this union. She was enumerated without her husband, in Bonnet Carré (now Lucy), St. John the Baptist Parish, LA, on 19 June 1860, as Anaïse Hermann [*sic*], age 19, living with the family of Zepherin Duhé. Z. Duhé was one of the witnesses to her marriage to Daniel Ehrmann. We could find no date of death or resting place for Anaïse Trègre Ehrmann. Daniel married his third wife, CLEMENTINE VICKNAIR, a native of Reserve, St. John the Baptists Parish, LA, on 20 January 1865 in St. John the Baptist Parish, where he had established himself as a wholesale and retail dealer in dry goods and liquor. By 1880, he was a plantation owner, a justice of the peace, and the clerk of registration in the parish. He and Clementine were the parents of six children: Dina (b. 1867), Estelle Marie (b. 1868; died the same year), Henry (b. 1869), Marie Henriette (b. 1870), Nathan Lucien (b. 1874), and Louis Felix (b. 1877). As the family prospered in St. John the Baptist Parish, Daniel spent more time in Panama with his brothers, **FELIX/URI** and **HENRI EHRMANN** (See entries), working in their various businesses. Daniel moved his family to New Orleans before 1900 to a house on Josephine Street. He died in Panama on 31 December 1904, and was buried in Kol Shearith Israel Cemetery (Cemetery Amador de El Chorillo) in Panama City, Panama. Clementine died on 3 February 1933 in New Orleans. She was interred in St. Mary Catholic Cemetery in the former suburb of Carrollton which was absorbed by the city of New Orleans in 1874. (**A, AN, E, GB, L, N**)

EHRMANN, FELIX, was born **URI EHRMANN** on 27 April 1846, in *Rothbach*, Bas-Rhin, France, to **NATHAN EHRMANN** (See entry), a native the town, and his wife, **MARIE HIMMLER**, born in *Gundershoffen*, Bas-Rhin. Eleven-year-old Felix arrived in Louisiana with his mother, Marie Himmler, and sisters **ADÈLE, ROSALIE, HENRIETTE** and **CAROLINE EHRMANN** (See entries), landing in New Orleans, Orleans Parish, LA, on 4 June 1857 aboard the ship *Edmie*. In 1860 the family, including fourteen-year-old, Uri, now called Felix, was enumerated in Attakapas, St. Martin Parish, LA, where Nathan, his father, was running a boarding house. According to the

1870 federal census, Felix was working as a dry goods merchant in his father's store in New Iberia, Iberia Parish, LA. He was naturalized that same year in New Iberia. He applied for a passport to go to Panama to join his brother **HENRY EHRMANN** (See entry) in November 1877. He, Henry, and later **DANIEL EHRMANN** (See entry), were partners in the Ehrman Banking Co., as well as a building supply business which sold goods to the French and later the Americans for the construction of the Panama Canal. Felix was deeply involved in the negotiations and final expropriation of Panama (originally a part of the country of Colombia), by the United States government. Subsequent to the takeover, Felix was appointed the U.S. ambassador to Panama. He married Henry's daughter, his niece ADELE EHRMAN CONTE, in Panama, where their only child, John Ehrman Ehrmann, was born in 1895. Felix died in Panama on 22 March 1909 and was buried in Kol Shearith Israel Cemetery (Cemetery Amador de El Chorillo) in Panama City, Panama. (**A, AN, E, GB**)

EHRMANN, HENRI, was born **HENRI EHRENMANN** on 2 February 1830 in *Rothbach*, Bas-Rhin, France, to **NATHAN EHRMANN** (See entry), a native of the town, and his wife, **MARIE HIMMLER**, born in *Gundershoffen*, Bas-Rhin. Family lore tells us that Henri was on his way to New Orleans, Orleans Parish, LA, to join his parents when he was shipwrecked off the coast of Cuba. The survivors were taken to Panama, where he stayed, becoming a successful cigar merchant. Other accounts have him living in New York and New Orleans, before settling permanently in Panama. Henri built up the largest banking house in Colombia, located on the Isthmus of Panama with the help of his brothers, **DANIEL** and **FELIX EHRMANN** (See entries), and was the financial agent for the French Canal Company and its successor, the United States Isthmian Canal Commission. He married RAMONA CONTE, a native of Panama, a record for which we were unable to find. They raised five children in Panama City: John (b. 1864), Adele (b. 1865; See entry for **FELIX EHRMANN**), William (b. 1869), Felix (b. 1871 in Paris, France) and Natalio (b. 1875). In later years Henri lived in the family-owned Hotel Central where he died on 2 May 1904. He was buried in Kol Shearith Israel Cemetery (Cemetery Amador de El Chorillo) in Panama City. At his death he was Panama's only millionaire. (**A, AN, GB**)

EHRMANN, HENRIETTE, was born on 7 September 1850 in *Rothbach*, Bas-Rhin, France, to **NATHAN EHRMANN** (See entry), a native of the town and his wife, **MARIE HIMMLER**, born in *Gundershoffen*, Bas-Rhin. Six-year-old Henriette immigrated to Louisiana with her mother, Marie Himmler, sisters, **ADÈLE**, **CAROLINE** and **ROSALIE**, and brother **URI/FELIX EHRMANN** (See entries), arriving in New Orleans, Orleans Parish, LA, on 4 June 1857 aboard the ship *Edmie*. Henriette was enumerated with her parents and siblings in the 1860 federal census at Attakapas, St. Martin Parish, LA, and again in the 1870 federal census taken in New Iberia, Iberia Parish, LA. After her father's death in 1873, she, her sister Adèle, and her mother Marie, moved to New Orleans, Orleans Parish, LA, to live with her sister Rosalie, the wife of DAVID LEVY. Henriette married MAX LEVY, a native of St. James Parish, LA, on 19 January 1881 in New Orleans. The couple returned to New Iberia, where Max was a wood and coal dealer. They were the parents of six children: Nathan (b. 1881), Michel (b. 1883), Bernard Lazard (b. 1886), Mabel (b. 1890), Eugene (b. 1893), and Ruth (b. 1895). Henriette died while on a visit to New York on 5 July 1925. Her remains were returned to New Iberia and were interred there in Temple Gates of Prayer Cemetery (Jewish section of Rosehill Cemetery). Max died on 21 October 1941, and was buried with his wife. (**A, AN, E, G, GB**)

EHRMANN, NATHAN, was born **NADEL HIRZEL (JONATHAN EHRMANN** after 1808) on 13 July 1798 in *Rothbach*, Bas-Rhin, France, to **LEOPOLD EHRENMANN (HIRZEL LEIBEL** before 1808), a native of the town, and his wife, **JUDEL/GERTHRUDE LEVI**, born in *Struth*, Bas-Rhin. He married **MARIE HIMMLER** on 4 February 1829 in *Rothbach*, Marie was born **MIRIAM LEIBEL** (**MARIE HIMMLER** after 1808) on 9 March 1807 in *Gundershoffen*, Bas-Rhin, France, to **LEOPOLD HIMMLER**, a native of the town, and his wife, **JULIE WEIL**, born in *Oberbronn*, Bas-Rhin. Nathan and Marie were the parents of twelve children all born in *Rothbach*: Henri (b. 1830; See entry), Daniel Lion (b. 1831; See entry), Esaijes (b. 1833; died 1839), Bernard (b. 1835; See entry), Caroline (b. 1837; See entry), Samson (b. 1839; died 1839), Fanny (b. 1840; died 1840), Adèle (b. 1841; See entry), Rosalie (b. 1844; See entry), Uri/Félix (b. 1846; See entry), Gustave (b. 1848; died 1852), and Henriette (b. 1850; See entry). Nathan was an iron merchant in *Rothbach*. At the time of his son Daniel's first marriage in *Rothbach* in August 1852, Nathan was incarcerated at a house of detention in *Wissembourg* for an alleged crime unknown to us now. He immigrated to Louisiana, where he appeared in the 1860 federal census for Attakapas, St. Martin Parish,

LA. Marie, his wife, was enumerated as "the widow Ehrmann" in the 1856 *Gundershoffen* town census with her two youngest children, at the home of her aged parents. She immigrated to Louisiana, bringing Caroline (age 28), Adèle (age 14), Rosalie (age 8), Henriette (age 5), and Abraham (in reality, Felix/Uri, age 7), arriving in New Orleans, Orleans Parish, LA, on 4 June 1857 aboard the ship *Edmie*. It is presumed that her husband, Nathan, and sons Henri and Daniel had preceded them to America. In 1860 Nathan was enumerated with his wife, Marie, daughters Caroline, Adele, Rosalie, and Henriette, and son Felix in Attakapas, St. Martin Parish, LA, where he was running a boarding house. By the time of the 1870 federal census, the family had moved to New Iberia, Iberia Parish, LA, where Nathan was the proprietor of a dry goods store. Felix, his son, worked as his clerk. His wife, Marie, and daughters Adèle and Henriette were also enumerated in the household. Nathan died on 29 April 1873 in New Iberia. His remains were transported to Hebrew Rest Cemetery #1 in New Orleans, Orleans Parish, La, where they was interred the next day. After her husband's death Marie went to live in New Orleans with her daughter, Rosalie, the wife of David Levy. She died there on 8 January 1899 and was buried with her husband in Hebrew Rest Cemetery #1. (**A, AN, E, G, GB**)

EHRMANN, ROSALIE, was born on 16 January 1844 in *Rothbach*, Bas-Rhin, France, to **NATHAN EHRMANN** (See entry), a native of the town, and his wife, **MARIE HIMMLER**, born in *Gundershoffen*, Bas-Rhin. Thirteen-year-old Rosalie immigrated to Louisiana with her mother, Marie Himmler, sisters, **ADÈLE, CAROLINE** and **HENRIETTE**, and brother, **URI/FELIX** (See entries), arriving in New Orleans, Orleans Parish, LA, on 4 June 1857 aboard the ship *Edmie*. She was enumerated with her parents and siblings in the 1860 federal census at Attakapas, St. Martin Parish, LA. Rosalie was married to DAVID LEVY, a Polish immigrant ca. 1866, a record for which we were unable to find. They were the parents of three sons: Bernard (b. 1867), Louis M. (b. 1868), and Henry David (b. 1872) The family was living in New Orleans, Orleans Parish, LA in 1880, where David was a merchant. They were enumerated in the 1900 federal census at Biloxi, Harrison Co., MS, where David was in a retail clothing partnership with his brother-in-law, JOSEPH H. WISE. After Joseph's death the couple moved to Pasadena, Los Angeles Co., CA, to be near their son, Louis M. Levy, who was living on the West Coast. David was the proprietor of a men's clothing store in Pasadena, which was probably where he died in 1916. We could find no record of his death. In 1920 the widowed Rosalie was living with her son, Louis, and his wife, Ruby in Los Angeles, where Louis was managing a hotel. Rosalie died on 27 January 1934 and was buried in Hebrew Rest Cemetery # 1 in New Orleans. (**A, AN, E, GB**)

EHRSTEIN, BARUCH/BERNARD, was born on 16 February 1830 in *Weinbourg*, Bas-Rhin, France, to **CHARLES EHRSTEIN,** a native of the town and his wife **SARA/SALOMÉ DALSHEIMER,** born in *Struth*, Bas-Rhin. According to his obituary which was published in the Alexandria *Town Talk,* he immigrated to Alexandria, Rapides Parish, LA in 1853, but we could find no likely record for his arrival. He married **MELANIE WEIL** a year later, the record for which was burned when Union forces torched the town of Alexandria in 1864. Melanie was born **MALAKA WEIL** on 5 September 1820 in *Surbourg*, Bas-Rhin, France to **JOSEPH WEIL** and his wife, **GERTRUDE/CAROLINE GROSS**, both natives of the town. The couple moved to Newton Co., TX, with Baruch's brother-in-law, **DAVID KUHNAGEL** (See entry), where they were all enumerated together in the 1860 federal census They worked under the name of N. Weil & Co. Two children born to the couple, both sons, died in Texas at an early age. The Kuhnagels and Ehrsteins lived in Mexico during the Civil War, returning to Alexandria, Rapides Parish, after the end of the conflict. Ehrstein was a respected merchant in Alexandria, operating the Fashion Bazaar on Second Street. Before Alexandria had any banks he had become a noted loaner of money at interest. He eventually became vice-president of the Rapides Bank. In 1873 Bernard Ehrstein applied for a U.S. passport for himself and his wife, Melanie, to return to France, where they lived for several years before returning to their home in Alexandria. In his passport application he affirmed that he had been born in the state of Pennsylvania on 29 March 1829. We cannot explain a motive behind this deception. He died on 4 December 1902 and was buried in the Jewish Cemetery in Pineville, Rapides Parish, LA. His tombstone inscription reads that he was born in "Weinburg, Alsace, on 16 September 1830," information that is not far off from his actual birth date. His wife, Melanie, died on 4 December 1905 and was buried with him. (**A, AN, FS, G**)

EHRSTEIN, LAZARE, was born on 12 March 1850 in *Ingwiller*, Bas-Rhin, France, to **HAENEL/EMANUEL EHRSTEIN**, a native of *Weinbourg*, Bas-Rhin, and his wife, **DINA/ADÈLE MEIS/MEISS**, born in *Ingwiller*, Bas-Rhin. "Lazard Erstein," as he was usually known in America, wrote in an 1889 United States passport application that he arrived in Louisiana from Bremen, Germany, ca. December 1869. We believe, however, that he is the same person as "Lazarus Erstein" who landed in New Orleans, Orleans Parish, LA, on 25 January 1871 aboard the SS *Koeln* from Bremen, Germany. **ROSALIE STROLITZ** (See entry), a native of *Duppigheim*, Bas-Rhin, was listed just after Lazard on the *Koeln*'s passenger manifest. Both Lazarus and Rosalie were said to have last lived in Baden, Germany, where they may have been working or staying just prior to their departure. Lazard Erstein settled in Alexandria, Rapides Parish, LA, where his uncle **BERNARD EHRSTEIN** (See entry) was a local merchant. Lazard married **DELPHINE KAHN** on 25 October 1876 in Alexandria. Delphine was born on 17 November 1855 in *Schirrhoffen*, Bas-Rhin, France, to **CERF KAHN**, a native of the town, and his wife, **MADEL/MARIE GOUDCHAUX**, born in *Brumath*, Bas-Rhin. Seventeen-year-old Delphine Kahn immigrated to the United States from Le Havre, France, aboard the SS *Ville de Paris* which arrived in New York on 15 March 1873. She was said to be a milliner whose last residence had been Paris. Lazard was naturalized at Alexandria on 24 October 1878. He was a dry goods and grocery merchant in Alexandria, as well as a local dealer in cotton, which he often took in payment for the goods he sold. His store suffered significant damage in an 1879 fire, which also damaged his uncle's brother-in-law, DAVID KUHNAGEL's place of business. Three of Lazard and Delphine's children were born in Alexandria: Leopold (b. 1877), Mathilde (b. 1879), and Henry (b. 1880). Shortly thereafter, the family moved north. The couple's fourth child, Bernard Lazard Erstein, was born in Newark, Essex Co., NJ, ca. 1884. Their last child, Jesse Harry was born in Chicago, Cook Co., IL, ca. 1886, where they would finally settle down. Lazard worked in Chicago as the manager of a millinery company until its bankruptcy in 1889. The 1900 federal census for Chicago listed "furniture dealer" as Lazard's occupation. Lazard died in Chicago on 13 July 1900 and was buried there in Rosehill Cemetery. Delphine died in Chicago on 14 July 1924 and was buried with her husband. Note: Delphine was the half-niece of **LEOPOLD** and **LAZARE GOUDCHAUX** (See entries). (**A, AN, FS, TT**)

EICHEL, CHARLES NATHAN, was born **ISRAËL EICHEL** on 13 February 1877 in *Offwiller*, Bas-Rhin, France, to **NATHAN EICHEL**, a native of the town, and his wife, **ANNE/SARA METZGER**, born in

Ettendorf, Bas-Rhin. He immigrated to America as "Israël Eichel," arriving in New York on 31 July 1893 aboard the SS *La Bourgogne* out of Le Havre, France. He lived for a short time in New York, after which he moved to Evansville, Vanderburgh Co., IN, to work for his paternal uncle, Israël/Charles Eichel, who was an upholsterer by trade. He finally settled in Monroe, Ouachita Parish, LA, to be near his sister Henriette who had immigrated in 1896 with her husband **MOÏSE HIRSCH** (See entry). Charles was naturalized in Monroe, Ouachita Parish, LA, on 13 November 1899. He became the manager of the Hirsch Dry Goods Company, and lived with the Hirsch and Kuhn families in Monroe. After Moïse's death in 1922, he continued to live with his widowed sister Henriette, at least through the 1940 federal census, where he was enumerated as a sixty-three year old unmarried public collector, born in France. He was married, probably after his sister's death, to NEUCIE V. ROGERS, a Louisiana native. Neucie died on 2 February 1954, and Charles followed on 18 October 1958. He and his wife were buried together in Riverview Cemetery in Monroe. **(A, AN, G, TT)**

EICHEL, HENRIETTE/HARRIET, (*Offwiller*) See entry for **MOÏSE HIRSCH**

EISENMANN, JACQUES EUGENE, (*Haguenau*) See entry for **ADÈLE EHRMANN**

EISENMANN, VALENTINE, (*Haguenau*) See entries for **MICHEL HEYMANN**

EPHRAIM, DAVID, was born on 23 January 1861 in *Langensoultzbach*, Bas-Rhin, France, to **JACOB/JACQUES EPHRAIM,** a native of the town, and his wife, **ROSINE/LOUISE WEIL**, born in *Reichshoffen*, Bas-Rhin. According to his 1930 census record, David arrived in America ca. 1878, a record of which we were unable to find. He was first enumerated in Vidalia, Concordia Parish, LA, in 1880, living in the household of Bavarian merchant Morris Wexler. Twenty-five-year-old David Ephraim was employed as a clerk in a store. He was naturalized on 17 October 1882 at Concordia Parish. At that time he was said to have immigrated in 1872. In 1883 David Ephraim and a partner known only as Mr. Schatz opened a small general store in Irishtown, Iberville Parish, LA. Because of Irishtown's proximity to the Mississippi River, cave-ins and floods eventually washed away most of the community. David Ephraim moved his store back into the adjacent town of Plaquemine, first to Seminary Street, then to the corner of Church and Plaquemine where it remained for many years. David married HENRIETTA LEVY, a native of Plaquemine, on 27 February 1883 in Clinton, East Feliciana Parish, LA. Rabbi Simon L. Weil from Woodville, Wilkinson Co., MS, officiated at the ceremony. David and Henrietta were the parents of two children: Maurice J (b. 1884), and Henry Abram (b. 1886). In addition to the successful management of Ephraim's Department Store, David was a director of the Iberville Bank, a longtime member of the Plaquemine Town Council, and mayor pro-tem during the administration of Peter G. Wilbert. David died on 1 October 1930 at his son Maurice Ephraim's home in Plaquemine. He was buried the next day in the local Jewish Cemetery. Henrietta Levy Ephraim and her sons carried on with the business after David's death. Henrietta died on 1 January 1942 in Plaquemine and was buried with her husband. (**A, AN, GB, TT**)

FALK, BENJAMIN, was born on 5 March 1837 in *Duppigheim*, Bas-Rhin, France, to **HEYMANN/HERMANN FALK** and his second wife, **JEANNETTE DRÉYFUS**, both natives of the town. Benjamin was enumerated for the last time in France with his twice-widowed father, Heymann, in the 1851 census for *Duppigheim*. He immigrated to Louisiana, arriving on 1 May 1855 in New Orleans, Orleans Parish, LA, at the age of seventeen, aboard the ship *Radius*. In 1860 the census taker recorded his presence in the home of his half-brother, MARX FALIX [*sic*], in New Orleans. Twenty-three-year-old Benjamin Falix [*sic*] was working as a peddler. He was naturalized on 20 November 1879 using the surname "Felix." He followed his half-brother and family to Kennerville (now Kenner), Jefferson Parish, LA, where he worked in the family business. He was enumerated in the 1880 federal census in the household of his widowed sister-in-law, Mrs."Phélix" (aka Rebecca Kauffmann Felix), in Kenner. He appeared as her forty-two-year-old unmarried brother-in-law from Alsace, employed as a butcher. Benjamin died on 11 September 1899 in Kennerville as Benjamin Felix[*sic*]. His obituary, which appeared in the New Orleans *Daily Picayune* referred to him as "Mr. Felix," a resident of Kennerville for thirty years, who had been the town's mayor for the past twelve years, as well as the treasurer of the local fire department for over a quarter of a century. He was buried as Benjamin "Falk" in what was Tememe Derech Jewish Cemetery, now known as Gates of

Prayer Cemetery #1 (Canal Street). He never married. (**A, AN, B1851, E, G**)

FALK, CAROLINE, was born on 23 October 1828 in *Duppigheim*, Bas-Rhin, France, to **FELIX FALK**, a native of the town, and his wife, **JUDEL LEVY**, born in *Soultz-sous-Fôrets*, Bas-Rhin. Caroline arrived in New Orleans, Orleans Parish, LA, on 9 January 1857, from Le Havre, France, aboard the ship *Mortimer Livingston*. She was accompanied by her cousin, **SARA FALK** (See entry for **AUGUSTE BLOCH)**, and the latter's children, Simon, Charles, Maurice and Cécile Bloch. Caroline Falk married **SAMUEL DREYFUS**, a native of Alsace, whom we have not yet identified, on 2 November 1858 in New Orleans. They were enumerated there in the 1860 census with their young son Felix Dreyfus (b. 1859). Two more children were born to the couple: Estelle/Esther (b. 1861) and Emile (b. 1863; died 1869), before Caroline Falk Dreyfus died on 5 September 1865. She was buried in the old Tememe Derech Jewish Cemetery, now Gates of Prayer Cemetery #1 on Canal Street. We have found no reliable death record for Samuel Dreyfus. His two surviving children, eleven-year-old Felix, and nine-year-old Estelle, were enumerated in the 1870 federal census at the Jewish Widows and Orphans Association in New Orleans. Their presence there does not automatically indicate that Samuel Dreyfus had died before 1870. He might simply have been unable to care for them after the death of his wife. (**A, AN, TT**)

FALK, MARX/MATHIEU, (*Duppigheim*) See **MARX FELIX**

FALK, SARA, (*Duppigheim*) See entry for **AUGUSTE BLOCH**

FALK, SOLOMON FELIX, was born **SALOMON FALK** on 6 June 1840 in *Duppigheim*, Bas-Rhin, France, to **FÉLIX FALK**, a native of the town, and his wife, JULIE/JENDELLE SÉE/SEH, born in Oberbergheim, Haut-Rhin. Solomon immigrated to Louisiana shortly after the American Civil War, a reliable record for which we were unable to find. He settled in Plaquemines Parish, LA. Solomon married **MELANIE BLOCH** on 28 August 1869 in New Orleans, Orleans Parish, LA. Melanie was born on 14 March 1850 in *Duttlenheim*, Bas-Rhin, France, to **MOÏSE BLOCH**, a native of the town, and his wife, **NANETTE DREYFUS**, born in *Duppigheim*, Bas-Rhin. In 1870 Solomon, a grocer, and his wife Melanie, were enumerated in Plaquemines Parish, with their infant son, Felix. Fourteen-year-old

Solomon Felix, son of **MARX** and **REBECCA FELIX/FALK** (See entry for **MARX FELIX**), who was working as a farm laborer, lived in their household. Solomon and Melanie were the parents of eleven children: Felix (b. 1870), Charles (b. 1872), Emma (b. 1875), Julia (b. 1877), Beulah (b. 1878), Morris (b. 1880), twins Bertha and Blanche (b. 1881), Ida (b. 1884), Leon (b. 1888), and Viola (b. 1889). At some time after the birth of their last child the family moved to Houston, Harris Co., Texas, where Solomon was employed as a butcher. In Texas the family consistently used FELIX as their surname. Melanie Bloch, aka Mrs. Sol Felix, died on 1 November 1914 in Houston. She was buried in Beth Israel Cemetery in the city, under a headstone which reads "Felix. Mother," with her dates of birth and death. Only the birth month is incorrect, being 14 April 1850 instead of 14 March 1850. Salomon Falk died as Solomon Felix on 12 November 1930 in Houston and was buried with his wife. The birth date incised on his tombstone is consistent with the birth date from his civil record which is still preserved in *Duttlenheim*. Note: Solomon Felix Falk was a second cousin to Marx/Mathieu Falk, known as Marx Felix in Louisiana. (**A, AN, B1851, E, G**)

FEIST, MARCUS/ ISAAC, was born **MARC FEIST** on 7 September 1837 in *Trimbach*, Bas-Rhin, France, to **MOYSE FEIST**, a native of the town, and his wife, **BEZEL/BABETTE MOOCK**, born in *Oberseebach*, Bas-Rhin, France. We have found no reliable record for his immigration to America. Twenty-two-year-old "M. Feist" was first enumerated in the United States in 1860 in Harrisburg, Poinsett Co., AR, where he was working as a clerk for his uncle **ZADOCK MOOCK**, his mother's younger brother. Thanks to a Confederate pension application filed by Marcus's widow, Henriette, in 1931, we know that he enlisted under the name of "I." Feist as a private in Smith's Co. F, 5th Regiment on 10 June 1861. He served to the end of the war being mustered out as a "musician." His widow's pension application also notes that he and his wife, HENRIETTE KAHN, married in July, 1867 in Magnolia, Pike Co., MS, the record of which burned with all other county records when the Pike County Courthouse went up in flames in 1882. **HENRIETTE KAHN** was born on 7 October 1844 in *Brumath*, Bas-Rhin, France, to **THÉODORE KAHN**, a native of the town, and his wife, **SOPHIE LEVI**, born in *Wingersheim*, Bas-Rhin. Marcus and Henriette's first child, Mose, was born in 1869 in Mississippi. By the time of the 1870 federal census, Marcus, still using the name "Isaac," was enumerated with his wife

"Harriet," and their one-year-old-son, Moses, in New Orleans, Orleans Parish, LA. Their next child, Bettie (b. 1871), according to her 1956 death certificate, was born in Madison Parish where the family settled in the small town of Milliken's Bend. Four more children were born to the couple there: Lazarus (b. 1873), Samuel (b. 1877), Julia (b. 1880), and Marcus (b. 1882). The 1880 federal census for the town of Milliken's Bend finally identified our subject as Marcus Fiest [*sic*], a forty-two-year- old merchant from Germany. Marcus died two years later on 8 November 1882. His body was taken to Vicksburg, Warren Co., MS, where it was interred in Anshe Chesed Jewish Cemetery. Henriette died on 19 February 1934 in Vicksburg, Warren Co., MS, and was buried there with her husband. (**A, AN, F, G, GB, TT**)

FELIX, BENJAMIN, (*Duppigheim*) See entry for **BENJAMIN FALK**

FELIX, MARX, was born **MATHIEU FALK** on 9 July 1821 in *Duppigheim*, Bas-Rhin, France, to **HEYMANN/HERMANN FALK**, a native of the town, and his first wife **JEANNETTE/HANNA LEVI**, born in *Odratzheim*, Bas-Rhin. Although born with the name "Mathieu," the child was enumerated with his father and siblings in the 1836 *Duppigheim* town census as fifteen-year-old **MARX FALK**. He may have been the passenger listed as twenty-eight-year-old "Mathias Felix," who arrived in New Orleans, Orleans Parish, LA, aboard the ship *Flor* on 13 December 1848. Marx married **REBECCA KAUFFMANN**, a record of which we were unable to find. Rebecca was born on 7 January 1832 in *Gundershoffen*, Bas-Rhin, France, to **JACQUES KAUFFMANN**, a native of the town, and his wife, **ELIZABETH/SARA UNGER**, born in *Lembach*, Bas-Rhin. We were unable to find a reliable ship's record for her entry into the United States. Marx was known as MARX/MARK FELIX in Louisiana. Marx and Rebecca were the parents of seven children: Maurice/Moïse/Morris (b. 1854; registered as Maurice Felix), Salomon (b. 1856; registered as Salomon Felix), Alexander "Alex" (b. 1857; registered as Felix Falk), Minette (b. 1860; registered as Minette Fallik), Jannette/Hanna (b. 1861; registered as Jannette Falck), Paul (b. 1866; no registration) and Matile/Matilde (b. 1868; no registration). Marx was enumerated in the 1860 federal census for Orleans Parish as a thirty-nine-year-old tailor. The census taker spelled the family's last name as "Falix." Included with Marx, was his wife, Rebecca, and children, Maurice, Salomon, Mina and Felix. Marx's brother, **BENJAMIN "FALIX"**, a twenty-three year old peddler from France was also living with the family. (See entry for **BENJAMIN FALK**). The family moved to Kennerville (now Kenner) in Jefferson Parish in the 1870s where they opened a grocery. Marx Felix died as "Marx Falk" on 20 September 1876 in Kennerville, and was buried as "Mark Falk" in what was Tememe Derech Jewish Cemetery, now known as Gates of Prayer Cemetery #1 (Canal Street). The widow Felix, as she was always known in Kennerville, opened a large mercantile store there with her sons Salomon and Paul which bore the name Felix & Block. Rebecca died as Rebecca Kaufmann Felix on 5 October 1909 in Kennerville, and was probably buried in Tememe Derech (now Gates of Prayer Cemetery #1 (Canal Street) with her husband. Note: Both Paul and Alexander were mayors of the town of Kenner, Jefferson Parish, LA. Alex and Morris were also associated with the mail order liquor firm of Loeb, Lion & Felix in New Orleans. (**A, AN, B1851, E, G, GB, TT**)

FELIX, SOLOMON, (*Duppigheim*) See **SOLOMON FELIX FALK**

FLEISCHMANN, ISAAC, was born on 3 February 1825 in *Soultz-sous-Fôrets*, Bas-Rhin, France, to **ULRIC FLEISCHMANN**, born in *Bischheim*, Bas-Rhin, France, and his wife **HANNA GROS**, a native of *Soultz-sous-Fôrets*, Bas-Rhin. He probably arrived in Louisiana with or shortly after his sister, **SOPHIE/SUSANNE FLEISCHMANN** (See entry for **JACOB LOEB**) ca. 1850. He took out a license to marry CAROLINE KAUFMANN, a native of Germany, on 4 April 1853 in New Orleans, Orleans Parish, LA. The couple moved to Pine Woods, near Harrisonburg in Catahoula Parish, LA, where Isaac was a merchant. He was naturalized in Harrisonburg on 4 April 1854. The couple was enumerated in Pine Woods in the 1860 federal census. There were no children in the household. Isaac died in Harrisonburg on 27 or 28 December 1861. He was buried in Gates of Mercy Cemetery at Jackson and Saratoga Streets in New Orleans. Note: After the cemetery was razed in the 1950s the remains of those buried there were transferred to Hebrew Rest Cemetery #1. We have found no other information on his widow. (**A, AN, TT**)

FLEISCHMANN, SOPHIE/SUSANNE, (*Soultz-sous-Fôrets*) See entry for **JACOB LOEB**

FRAENCKEL, FÉLIX, was born **BENJAMIN FRAENCKEL** on 30 April 1834 in *Rothbach*, Bas-Rhin, France, to **MARX FRAENCKEL**, a native of the town, and his wife, **JEANNETTE BECKER**, born in *Minversheim*, Bas-Rhin. We believe that Felix arrived in New Orleans, Orleans Parish, LA, as "Benjamin Frenkel," a nineteen-year-old immigrant from France, on 19 October 1853 aboard the ship *R.B. Sumner*. He joined the Confederate cause as a Private in the Third Regiment, Company K, Louisiana Infantry, the *Pelican Rifles* from Baton Rouge, East Baton Rouge Parish, LA. After fighting for the Confederacy in battles in Louisiana and Mississippi, he returned to Baton Rouge where he worked as a dry goods merchant. He took out a license to marry **PALMYRE DREYFUS**, on 2 November 1866 in New Orleans. Palmyre was born on 13 October 1847 in *Sélestat*, Bas-Rhin, France, to **RAPHAEL DREYFUS**, a native of *Westhouse*, Bas-Rhin, and his wife, **JEANNETTE/NANETTE LEVY**, born in *Weiterswiller*, Bas-Rhin. Although civil registrations at *Sélestat* include no record of Palmyre's birth, she does appear there as a three-year-old child in her parents' 1851 household. Seventeen-year-old Mademoiselle "Palmire Breyfus" arrived in New York from Le Havre, France, aboard the steamship *Washington* on 5 December 1864. Her destination was recorded as "New Orleans." After their 1866 marriage, Felix and Palmyre returned to Baton Rouge, East Baton Rouge Parish, LA, ca. 1867, where their seven children were born: Albert (b. 1867), Marx (b. 1869), Herman (b. 1872), Nettie (b. 1875), Maurice/Morris (b. 1877), Nanette (b. 1879), and Sidney (b. 1882). Felix Fraenckel died on 12 February 1888 in Baton Rouge and was buried there in the Jewish Cemetery. After Palmyre died on 18 February 1909 in Shreveport, Caddo Parish, LA, her remains were returned to Baton Rouge for burial next to those of her husband. Note: Two of Palmyre's sisters, **MARIE EMILIE DREYFUS** and **ANNA DREYFUS** (See entry for the former), also immigrated to the United States. (**A, AN, G, GN, TT**)

FRAENCKEL, ROSALIE, (*Rothbach*) See entry for **SAMUEL RAAS**

FRANCK/FRANK, EUGENE/ EUGENE H., was born **EUGENE FRANCK** on 13 October 1856 at *Soultz-sous-Fôrets*, Bas-Rhin, France, to **SALOMON FRANCK**, a native of the town, and his wife **MATHILDE HIRSCH**, born in *Haguenau*, Bas-Rhin. According to information given in the 1900 federal census for New Orleans, Eugene immigrated to Louisiana in 1870. He may have been, however, the nineteen-year-old [sic] "Eugen Frank" who arrived in New Orleans, Orleans Parish, LA, on 31 October 1871 from Bremen, Germany, aboard the SS *Frankfurt*. He married FANNY WOLF (See. entry for **SAMUEL WOLF**), a native of Osyka, Pike County, MS, ca. 1879, a record for which we could not locate. If they were married in the bride's home county, the record would have been destroyed in 1882 when the Pike County Courthouse burned to the ground. Two daughters were born to the couple: Mathilde (b. 1881), and Edith (b. 1882). Eugene worked as a travelling salesman. The family lived in New Orleans, usually boarding with Fanny's sister Delphine and her husband, Sigmund Keiffer, a prosperous shoe manufacturer in the city. Eugene and Fanny died in New Orleans, the former on 18 September 1926 and the latter on 21 August 1940. They were buried there in Metairie-Lakelawn Cemetery. Note: Eugene's father Salomon Franck was the brother of **MICHEL, HANNAH, JACOB/JACQUES** and **MADELEINE FRANCK** (See individual entries), all immigrants to Louisiana. (**A, AN**)

FRANCK/FRANK, HANNAH/HARRIET/HENRIETTE, (*Soultz-sous-Fôrets*) See entry for **JULES/JUDAS WEILL**

FRANCK/FRANK, JACOB, was born **JACQUES FRANCK** on 3 August 1826 in *Soultz-sous-Forêts*, Bas-Rhin, France, to **AUSCHER ELIAS/ DOTTERLÉ FRANCK** and his wife, **ZIBORA WEIL**, both natives of the town. Jacob may have arrived in New Orleans, Orleans Parish, LA on 13 December 1847 as twenty-three-year-old "Jacob Franch" from Le Havre, France, aboard the ship *Tremont*. He may also have been the "Jacob Frank" who was naturalized in St. Helena Parish, LA on 28 May 1855. For purposes of identification, it is significant that this record includes his arrival date as 1847, the same as "Jacob Franch" who arrived on the *Tremont*. Jacob was enumerated in the 1860 federal census at Greensburg, St. Helena Parish, LA as a thirty-two-year-old single merchant. He died on 20 June 1863 in Clinton, East Feliciana Parish, LA, where other members of his family had settled. (See entries for **MICHEL, MATILDA, HANNAH**, and **EUGENE FRANCK**) Jacob was buried at Clinton in the local Jewish Cemetery. (**A, ES, TT**)

FRANCK/FRANK, MADELEINE/MATILDA, was born **MADELAINE FRANCK** on 12 October 1828 in *Soultz-sous-Fôrets*, Bas-Rhin, France, to **AUSCHER ELIAS/ DOTTERLÉ FRANCK** and his wife, **ZIBORA WEIL**, both natives of the town. Sixteen-year-old Madeleine Frank arrived in New Orleans, Orleans Parish, La, on 24

December 1846 from Le Havre, France, aboard the *J.N. Cooper*. (Note: Her immigration year was confirmed to be 1846 at the time of the 1900 federal census where she was recorded as the mother-in-law in the Julius Keiffer household in New Orleans.) Madeleine's brother, **MICHAEL/MICHEL FRANCK** (See entry) had arrived in America three years previously, and had settled in Clinton, East Feliciana Parish, LA. She joined him in Clinton where she was married as "Matilda Frank" to GABRIEL BROWN, a native of Posen, Prussia (now Poland), on 14 September 1849. (Note: From the time of her marriage she used the name "Matilda" in American records.) She returned with Gabriel to Plaquemine, Iberville Parish, LA, where he was employed as a merchant. The couple was enumerated there in the 1860 federal census with their only child, Eugenie (b. 1851). Shortly after the close of the Civil War, Gabriel took his family to live in New Orleans where he went into the shoe business on Canal Street. His firm, later known as the Gabriel Brown Co., Ltd., was eventually moved to Camp Street. Gabriel Brown died in New Orleans on 18 February 1894. He, along with his brother-in-law Michel Franck, had previously purchased a plot of ground for Hebrew burials in Metairie Cemetery in New Orleans where Gabriel was buried the following day. The Gabriel Brown Co., Ltd. continued in business under the direction of JULIUS KEIFFER, his daughter Eugenie's husband. Matilda Frank Brown died on 18 March 1908 and was buried with her husband. (**A, AN, GB, TT**)

FRANCK, MICHAEL, was born **MICHEL FRANCK** on 16 December 1824 in *Soultz-sous-Fôrets*, Bas-Rhin, France, to **AUSCHER ELIAS/ DOTTERLÉ FRANCK** and his wife, **ZIBORA WEIL**, both natives of the town. He immigrated to New Orleans, Orleans Parish, LA, arriving aboard the SS *Deucalion*, on 27 July 1843 from Le Havre, France. Michel married JEANNETTE MOSES, a native of Germany, ca. 1850 in Louisiana and took her back to Clinton, East Feliciana Parish, LA, where he was a merchant. Their only child, REBECCA FRANK, was born there in August 1852. Michael and his family relocated to New Orleans previous to the 1870 federal census where he was a merchant and a banker. Michael Frank was the first president of Temple Sinai which was organized as a reform congregation in 1870. He was also President of Touro Infirmary for several years, and one of three Jewish men, including his sister, Matilda's husband, GABRIEL BROWN (See entry for **MADELEINE/MATILDA FRANCK/FRANK**), who purchased lots in Metairie Cemetery which were consecrated for Jewish burial.

Michael, who died on 4 October 1896, and his wife, who had died on 8 December 1888, were both buried in the Jewish Section of Metairie Cemetery. Note: **EUGENE FRANCK** (See entry), was Michael's nephew, son of his brother, Salomon Franck. (**A, AN, F, G**)

GERST, LOUIS PHILIPPE, was born 1 May 1837 in *Niederbronn-les-Bains*, Bas-Rhin, France, to **CHARLES GERST**, a native of the town, and his wife, MARIE ANNE TOBRINER born in Baden, Germany. Louis immigrated to Louisiana ca. 1859, according to a passport application filed by his only child, Charles Gerst in 1920. We believe, however, that he was probably the nineteen-year-old "Philippe Gerst" who arrived in New York on 12 February 1855 from Le Havre, France, aboard the ship *Olivia*. Louis worked as a merchant in Vermilionville (now Lafayette), Lafayette Parish, LA. He enlisted in the Confederate Army as a private in the 18th LA. Infantry, Co. E (Grays) in May 1862, and was paroled in Alexandria, Rapides Parish, LA in June 1865. He married BABETTE WEIL (b. 1839), a native of Ingenheim, Rheinpfalz, Germany, in Alexandria after the war, a record for which we were unable to find. Gerst was a liquor dealer in town. His only child, CHARLES LOUIS PHILIPPE GERST, was born there on 5 June 1866. Louis Gerst died on 25 September 1866 in Alexandria, and was buried in the Jewish Cemetery in Pineville, Rapides Parish, LA. Babette remained in Alexandria through the 1880 federal census, where she lived with Charles, in the home of SIMON WEIL, her brother. She was employed as a milliner. Eighty-five year-old Babette Gerst died on 20 April 1923 in Manhattan, New York, where she had gone to live with her son, Charles. We were unable to locate her place of burial. (**A, AN, FS, I**)

GOUDCHAUX, BABETTE, (*Brumath*) See entry for **JOSEPH DREYFUS**.

GOUDCHAUX, ESTHER/ESTELLE, (*Brumath*) See entry for **SAMUEL KAHN**.

GOUDCHAUX, FLEURETTE/FLORENCE, (*Brumath*) See entry for **LIPPMAN/LEOPOLD KAHN**

GOUDCHAUX, HENRY, was born **HENRY GUTSCHU** on 29 October 1837 in *Brumath*, Bas-Rhin, France, to **JACQUES GOUDCHAUX/GUTSCHU** and his second wife, **ROSETTE**

KAHN, both natives of *Brumath*. He immigrated to America, from Le Havre, France, with his fifteen year old sister, **BABETTE GOUDCHAUX** (See entry), on board the ship *Old England* which docked in New Orleans, Orleans Parish, LA, on 2 April 1851. Henry and Babette joined their half-sister **ESTELLE GOUDCHAUX KAHN** at her home in Plaquemine, Iberville Parish, LA. (See entry for **SAMUEL KAHN**) During the Civil War, Henry, still unmarried, worked with his brother-in-law, ABRAHAM LEHMANN, his sister **MALINE GOUDCHAUX**'s husband, in a smuggling operation from Matamoros, Mexico to Brownsville, Texas, in order to get supplies into New Orleans, whose port was blockaded by Union ships. His dealings in Mexico and Texas brought him into contact with New York merchants, whom he sought out after the war, seeing no future in the defeated South. He married New York native, PAULINE SCHULTZ in Manhattan on 25 October 1865. They had eight surviving children there: Rose (b. 1866), Sophie (b. 1867), Fanny (b. 1869), Henrietta (b. Feb. 1875; died Aug. 1875), Adele (b. 1877), Jacob Samuel (b. 1879), Mabel (b. 1881), and Irma (b. 1885). Henry owned dry goods stores in Manhattan, and was said to have returned to France to fight with his countrymen during the Franco-Prussian War. He died in Manhattan on 24 August 1891 and was buried in Salem Fields Cemetery in Brooklyn, Kings Co., NY. His wife, Pauline, who died on 11 April 1927 in Manhattan, was buried with him. (**A, AN, G, TT**)

GOUDCHAUX/GODCHAUX, JACQUES, was an immigrant from France, born according to the 1860 federal census ca. 1807, whose life still remains a deep mystery. He may have been from the Bas-Rhin, or perhaps other parts of Alsace, or even the Moselle region of France where "Godchaux" and its variants are a familiar name. According to his naturalization record which was filed in Pointe Coupée Parish, LA, on 24 September 1857, he had come to America in 1847, a reliable record for which we were unable to find. Jacques "Goudchau" was enumerated in the 1860 federal census for Morganza, Pointe Coupée Parish, LA, as a fifty-three-year-old Frenchman with $100 in personal property. Attempts have been made in some on-line genealogies to declare him to be the same person as "Jacques Goudchaux" who lived in San Francisco, with his wife Élise, in the second half of the nineteenth century, and whose children were all born before 1860 in California. This, however, cannot be the case. The "Jacques Goudchaux" who was a peddler in and around Waterloo and New Roads, Pointe Coupée Parish, LA, and who was enumerated at

Morganza, Pointe Coupée Parish in the 1860 federal census, had several children with a free woman of color, MADELEINE OLIVO/OLLIVEAU, born ca. 1826. According to Pointe Coupée historian Brian Costello, the Olivos had been freed ca. 1800. Madeleine was a Catholic, who registered five of her childrens' births, the records for which were preserved at the Diocese of Baton Rouge, East Baton Rouge Parish, LA, where Mr. Costello located them in 2013. Madeleine's first two children, Polite and Julie were the eldest, for whom there were no records found. She bore two daughters by Hypolite Bergeron: Adelaide (b. 1849), and Eudora (b. 1851). Madeleine and her four children were kidnapped and sold as slaves just prior to the Civil War. They were "freed" once more in a lengthy court case based largely on the testimony of the children's godfathers, one of whom was Brian Costello's third-great-grandfather, Gerard Gremillion. Madeleine also bore three children by Jacques Goudchaux: Maximilien (b. 1864), Clement (b. 1867), and Madeleine (b. 1870). Forty-five-year-old Madeleine, a farm laborer, was enumerated with two sons and two daughters in the 1870 federal census for Pointe Coupée Parish: Adelaide and Victoria [*sic*] Bergeron, and six-year-old Max and three-year-old Clement Goudchaux. Max and Clement also used the name "Oliveau" and were enumerated in the 1880 federal census as fifteen-year-old Max and ten-year-old Clement Oliveau, who were living with their half-sister Eudora Bergeron, and her sons, Jacob and Albert. We could not find any other census records for Jacques Goudchaux subsequent to his 1860 enumeration. He may have died before or after the birth of his last child, Madeleine. What we do have is one of those rare photos which, according to the caption, "Mr. Godchaux, peddler of dry goods" captured his likeness for posterity. It appeared in *A History of Pointe Coupée Parish, Louisiana and its Families*, edited by Judy Riffel and published by Le Comité des Archives de la Louisiane, Baton Rouge, East Baton Rouge Parish, LA in 1983. We may never know much more about him. See his photo on page 420.(**AN, BC**)

GOUDCHAUX, LAZARE, was born on 27 September 1849 in *Brumath*, Bas-Rhin, France, to **JACQUES GOUDCHAUX/ GUTSCHU** and his second wife, **ROSETTE KAHN**, both natives of *Brumath*. Seventeen-year-old Lazare emigrated from *Brumath*, after his father's death, arriving in New York on 22 June 1866 aboard the SS *Lafayette*. He joined his brother, **LEOPOLD GOUDCHAUX** (See entry), in Big Cane, St. Landry Parish, LA where he went to work in the plantation store. He also bought and sold horses both in St. Landry

Parish and Evergreen, Avoyelles Parish, LA. Lazare filed his naturalization papers in Marksville, Avoyelles Parish, LA, on 2 October 1874, He married HARRIETT OPPENHEIM, a native of New Orleans, Orleans Parish, LA, on 12 June 1878 and relocated there to go into the wholesale grocery business. The couple's six children were all born in the city: Jacob Oppenheim (1879), Rosa (b. 1880), Bernard (b. 1882), Herbert (b. 1884), Leslie (b. 1887) and May Louisa (b. 1891). Shortly after the birth of their last child, Lazare and his family returned to Evergreen, Avoyelles Parish, LA, where he became one of the several Jewish merchants in town. Harriet died on 27 October 1905 and was buried in New Orleans at Hebrew Rest Cemetery # 1. After her death, Lazare returned to New Orleans where he boarded with his brother-in-law, Charles Oppenheim, and worked as a commission merchant. He died in New Orleans on 22 December 1920 and was interred with his wife in Hebrew Rest Cemetery # 1. (**A, AN, G, GB, TT**)

GOUDCHAUX, LEOPOLD, was born **LÉOPOLD GUTSCHU** on 29 August 29, 1844 in *Brumath*, Bas-Rhin, France, to **JACQUES GOUDCHAUX/GUTSCHU** and his second wife, **ROSETTE KAHN**, both natives of the town. He arrived with his fifteen year old sister, Adèle, in New Orleans, Orleans Parish, LA, on 7 June 1858 from Le Havre, France, aboard the ship *Gulf Stream*. After a few months in New Orleans with another sister, **MALINE GOUDCHAUX** (See entry), and her husband, **ABRAHAM LEHMANN**, he went to live with his half-sister, **ESTELLE GOUDCHAUX KAHN** and her husband, Samuel (See entry for **SAMUEL KAHN**) in Plaquemine, Iberville Parish, LA, where he started working as a clerk in the Kahn's dry goods store. During the Civil War he took to the back roads of Louisiana and worked, when he could, as a peddler. He saved his money and decided to settle in St. Landry Parish. He chose the village of Big Cane as a good place to open a general store. Leopold married a local farmer's daughter, CHARLOTTE EILERT on 22 July 1868 in St. Landry Parish. The couple had eight children: Charles Abraham (b. 1871), Rosa (b. 1872), Caroline (b. 1874), Blanche Matilda (b. 1876), Henry (b. 1878), Adèle (b. 1879) and Leon Eilert (b. 1881). Charlotte died six days after the birth of her last child, and although she was not Jewish, she was interred in Gemiluth Chassodim Cemetery in Opelousas, St. Landry Parish, LA. During the years after the war, Leopold had become very wealthy. His store was the largest around, and he acquired thousands of acres of land from delinquent farmers who owed him money, as well as from tax sales in both St. Landry and Avoyelles Parishes. Like his father before him in *Brumath*, he became one of the largest cattle and horse dealers in the parish. He also was in the lumber business, hiring crews to cut down trees on his vast holdings, which he processed in his own sawmill. Leopold married a second time on 8 May 1883 in New Orleans. The bride was **FLORA MARX** whom he had brought over from Alsace to become his wife. Flora was born **FLORE MARX** on 6 September 1858 in *Surbourg*, Bas-Rhin, France, to **MORTIER/MARX MARX** and his wife **FANNY LEVI**, both natives of *Surbourg*. We were unable to find a reliable record for her entry into the United States. Six children were born to Leopold and Flora: Abraham (b. 1884), Hortense Miriam (b. 1885), Sylvan (b. 1886), Sarah (b. 1891), Julius Joseph (b. 1894), and Elise (b. 1897). Leopold's wealth almost rivaled that of his friend, and fellow Alsatian immigrant to St. Landry Parish, **SAMUEL CERF HAAS** (See entry), with whom many lucrative business deals were struck. Seven years before he died, Leopold bought a logging railroad which ran from the parish line in Avoyelles into Bayou Jack (St. Landry Parish), including all the rolling stock, chain, as well as 12,000 cypress logs and all the cypress sinkers in Bayou Jack. Leopold died on 24 March 1920 while attending to business in Avoyelles Parish. He was buried next to his first wife, Charlotte, in Gemiluth Chassodim Cemetery in Opelousas, St. Landry Parish. LA. His second wife, Flora, died on 26 April 1923 and was buried in the Jewish Cemetery in Pineville, Rapides Parish, LA, near two of her daughters and their husbands. (**A, AN, AP, GB, TT**)

GOUDCHAUX, MALINE, was born **JEANNETTE GUTSCHU** on 16 February 1840 in *Brumath*, Bas-Rhin, France, to **JACQUES GOUDCHAUX/GUTSCHU** and his second wife, **ROSETTE KAHN**, both natives of the town. Fourteen-year-old Maline immigrated to New Orleans, Orleans Parish, LA, on the *Belle Assise*, out of Le Havre, France, with **SARA BOMBET** (See entry), a neighbor from *Brumath*. They arrived on 8 November 1854 in New Orleans. Maline was married to ABRAHAM LEHMANN, a native of Gommersheim, Bavaria in Plaquemine, Iberville Parish, LA, on 29 April 1857. They were the parents of twelve children, all born in New Orleans: Henry (b. 1859), Gustave (b. 1860), Rosa (b. 1861), Clara (b. 1863), Julius (b. 1865), Fanny (b. 1866), Emelie (b. 1867), Henriette (b. 1868), Jacob (b. 1870), Sarah (b. 1874), Isaac (b. 1879) and Juliette (b. 1882). When Abraham Lehmann's dry goods business fell into serious trouble during the Civil War, he partnered with his brother-in-law, **HENRY GOUDCHAUX** (See entry), in a smuggling operation which operated out of Matamoros, Mexico, via Brownsville, Texas. The family did not return to New Orleans until after the 1880 federal census. They moved to Manhattan, New York, following other family members including his old partner Henry Goudchaux, his wife's brother. Abraham Lehmann died in New York on 18 September 1895. His wife followed on 14 January 1911. Their bodies were returned to New Orleans for burial in Hebrew Rest Cemetery #1. (**A, AN, AP, G, GB, TT**)

GOUDCHAUX, SARA, was born **SARA GUTSCHU** on 11 February 1846 in Brumath, Bas-Rhin, France, to **JACQUES GOUDCHAUX/ GUTSCHU** and his second wife, **ROSETTE KAHN**, both natives of *Brumath*. We were unable to find a likely immigration record for her, arrival in America. She married CALMÉ/CHARLES LAZARD, a native of Metz, Moselle, France, on 24 May 1864 in New Orleans, Orleans Parish, LA. Their ten children were all born in the city: Rosa (b. 1865), Florestine (b. 1866), Jacques Calmé (b. 1868), Louis (b. 1869), Corinne (b. 1870), Jules Calmé (b. 1872), Octavie (b. 1874), Leopold Calmé (b. 1876), Henry Calmé (b. 1878) and Edwin Calmé (b. 1882). Lazard was in the clothing and hat business with stores on both Esplanade Ave. and Prytania Street in the city. After his eldest daughter married MAYER ISRAEL, a New Orleans native, the two men opened the Meyer Israel Lazard C. & Co. store on Canal Street, which eventually became one of the largest department stores in the city. Sara Goudchaux Lazard died in New Orleans on 2 January 1886 and was buried in Hebrew Rest Cemetery #1, as was her husband who died on 29 May 1905. (**A, AN, AP, G, GB**)

GOUGENHEIM, FLORESTINE, was born 30 January 1850 in *Obernai*, Bas-Rhin France, to **JYCHAE LOUIS GUGENHEIM**, a native of *Zellwiller*, Bas-Rhin, France (See entry), and his wife, SARA WORMS, born in Boulay, Moselle, France. Five-year-old Florestine immigrated with her mother and three sisters to Louisiana, via New York, arriving on 18 October 1855 aboard the ship *Switzerland*. She was raised in Morgan City, St. Mary Parish, LA where her parents settled down to raise their family. She married ABRAHAM ERMANN, a native of Germany, who was employed as a dry goods merchant in Morgan City. They were wed there on 3 December 1870. The couple had no children. They moved to New Orleans ca. 1892 where Ermann became one of the largest sugar and molasses brokers in Louisiana. Florestine died on 24 November 1893 in New Orleans and was buried there in Hebrew Rest Cemetery # 1. Abraham Ermann, who had remarried, died on 27 Febrary 1903 in New Orleans, and was interred there in Metairie Cemetery. He left a childless widow, the former Pauline Winkler of Cincinnati, Hamilton Co., OH. (**A, AN, F, G, GB**)

GOUGENHEIM, HENRIETTE, (*Obernai*) See entry for **DAVID THEODORE LEHMANN**

GOUGENHEIM, JULIA, (*Obernai*) See entry for **SOLOMON MOCH**

GOUGENHEIM, JYCHAE LOUIS, was born **JYCHEA LOUIS GUGENHEIM** on 9 December 1816 in *Zellwiller*, Bas-Rhin, France, to **SAMUEL GUGENHEIM**, a native of the town, and his wife, NANETTE BERNARD, born in Ribeauville, Haut-Rhin, France. Jychae married SARA WORMS, a native of Boulay, Moselle, France, ca. 1846. The couple had four children in France before immigrating to America: Adèle (b. 1847; See entry for **NATHAN/SOL SOLOMON**), Florestine (b. 1850; See entry), Henriette (b. 1851; See entry for **DAVID THEODORE LEHMANN**), and Julia(b. 1853; See entry for **SOLOMON MOCH**). While we were not able to find a reliable ship's record for Jychae Louis Gougenheim, we know that his twenty-nine-year-old wife, Sara, arrived in New York with her four daughters on 18 October 1855 aboard the ship *Switzerland*. He had probably left ahead of her. Reunited, the family settled in Brashear City (now Morgan City), St. Mary Parish. Five more children were born to them in Louisiana: Raphael (b. 1860), Morris (b. 1863), Felicia (b. 1868), Esther (b. 1869), and Samuel (b. 1871). Louis Gougenheim, as he was known in Louisiana, became a successful grocer and dry goods merchant in Morgan City. His wife, Sara Worms, died in New Orleans on 19 December 1892 and was buried in the Jewish Cemetery in Berwick, St. Mary Parish, LA. Louis followed on 29 November 1900 at Morgan City, and was buried in Berwick with his wife. The inscription on Louis Gougenheim's tombstone gives his date of birth accurately, but indicates erroneously that he was born in *Obernai*. There were no Gougenheims born in Obernai between 1813-1822. He and Sara were enumerated there in the 1851 Obernai town census with two of their children. It was the last place he lived in France before his immigration to Louisiana. (**A, AN, G**)

GRADWOHL, DAVID MOYSE, was born on 1 August 1841 in *Zinswiller*, Bas-Rhin, France, to **DAVID GRADWOHL**, a native of the town, and his wife, **ADÈLE/EDEL MOSSER** (See entry for **DAVID TRAUTMANN**), born in *Surbourg*, Bas-Rhin. He immigrated to New Orleans, Orleans Parish, LA, on the ship *Adelaide Bell*, arriving from Le Havre, France, on 8 March 1861. In the 1870 federal census for New Orleans, he was enumerated as "Morris" Gradwohl, a name by which he would be known in Louisiana records, an unmarried retail clothing dealer. He married HORTENSE KAHN (see entry for **SAMUEL KAHN**), a native of Plaquemine, Iberville Parish, LA, in New Orleans on 15 February 1871. Their first two children, Atty (b. 1871) and Helen (b. 1873) were born in New Orleans. Morris moved his family to Corpus Christi, Nueces Co., TX, ca. 1875, where he owned a boot and shoe store. Two more children were born to the couple in Texas: David Daniel (b. 1878) and Albert Abraham (b. 1880). David moved his family back to Louisiana, ca. 1881, settling in Lake Charles, Calcasieu Parish, LA, where four more children were born: Blanche Bella (b. 1881), Lester Joel (b. 1886), Lionel Edward (b. 1888), and Estelle (b. 1890). Hortense Gradwohl died on 24 January 1900 and was buried in Hebrew Rest Cemetery #1 in New Orleans. Morris died in Beaumont, Jefferson Co., TX, on 26 December 1917. His remains were brought back to New Orleans where they were buried with those of his wife. (**A, N, G, GB, TT**)

HAAS, ALEXANDER MURDOCK, was born **ALEXANDRE HAAS** on 18 August 1838 in *Rothbach*, Bas-Rhin, France, to **SAMUEL HAAS**, a native of the town, and his first wife, **HENRIETTE UHRY,** born in *Ingwiller* Bas-Rhin. Sixteen-year-old Alexandre immigrated on the ship *Baden* from Le Havre, France, arriving in New Orleans, Orleans Parish, LA, on 26 June 1855 to join his brother **SAMUEL HAAS** (See entry), who had arrived two years earlier. The brothers became successful merchants in Opelousas, St. Landry Parish, LA. When the Civil War broke out Alex Haas enlisted in July 1861 as a private in Co. E 10th LA Infantry. He remained with them at Camp Moore until November of that year when he acquired a mount and enrolled as a private in Co. G, First LA Cavalry. He rose to the rank of Lieutenant Colonel in Co. G and served throughout the war. Alex married MARY MACCIE MARSHALL, the Louisiana born daughter of prosperous plantation owner, THOMAS DOUGLAS MARSHALL, on 12 July 1866. The couple made their home near Evergreen, Avoyelles Parish, LA, and later near Eola, Avoyelles

Parish, in an area called Tiger Bend but later renamed Haasville. Through his hard work and his association with a prominent Avoyelles Parish family, Alex acquired thousands of acres of farm land, managed several plantations, and was the owner of a general store He was also the postmaster at Haasville, and a well-known cotton broker. He had a plantation home in Avoyelles Parish and a mansion on St, Charles Avenue in New Orleans, Orleans Parish, LA. Five children were born to the couple: William David (b. 1867), Nannie (b. 1869), Mary Maccie "Bunkie" (b. 1871), Alexander Marshall (b. 1873) and Samuel (b. 1876; died one month later). Mary Marshall Haas died at the birth of her last child on 19 September 1876, and was buried in Thomas Douglas Marshall Cemetery in Evergreen, Avoyelles Parish, LA. Alex remarried on 10 August 1879. The bride was Jewish, this time. HANNAH POKORNY was the New York born daughter of a prosperous New Orleans shoe merchant, MICHAEL POKORNY, an immigrant from the Austro-Hungarian Empire. Hannah never enjoyed life in opulent Oak Hall, the family plantation which spanned parts of three parishes (Avoyelles St. Landry & Evangeline) or in Haasville, at the manor house known as " Grey Gables." After the birth of their only child, ALICE ROSALIND (b. 1882), Alex and Hannah spent more time in New Orleans. That same year Alex and his brother, Sam Haas, donated a parcel of land to the Texas and Pacific Railway under the condition that they could give the town a name. Alex, who had given his little daughter, Mary Maccie, the nickname "Bunkie," because, unable to pronounce "monkey," she had called her favorite toy "Bunkie." As a consequence, Alex christened the station and town "Bunkie" Alex and Hannah Haas also travelled extensively, making several junkets out west to California, where their daughter Alice had settled. Alex Haas was in San Francisco on the day of the great earthquake on 18 April 1906. He immediately took to horseback to begin the rescue of the many victims. He was given charge of one of the relief camps and was cited by the U.S. Army for his actions. Alex Haas died two years later in Bunkie at the home of his son, Dr. William David Haas on 24 February 1908. He was buried beside his first wife, Mary Maccie Marshall, at Thomas Douglas Marshall Cemetery in Evergreen, Avoyelles Parish, LA. Many descendants of the Haas family in Avoyelles Parish were surprised to learn of the families Jewish roots, as none of the children were raised in the Jewish religion. Alex and Sam Haas had given land in Bunkie for the Methodist Church, and later, one of Alex's grandchildren, W.D. Haas, Jr. and his wife gave funds for a new sanctuary for the first Methodist Church of

Bunkie, which was renamed the William David Haas Memorial Methodist Church. Alex's daughter, Nannie, who married her stepmother's brother, David Pokorny, was raised a Methodist. She converted to Judaism before her wedding.(**A, AN, AP, G, GB**)

HAAS, FANNY, (*Ingwiller*) See entry for **ELIE/ELIAS MOCH**.

HAAS, SAMUEL, was born **SAMUEL CERF HAAS** on 29 June 1836 in *Rothbach*, Bas-Rhin, France, to **SAMUEL HAAS**, a native of the town and his first wife, **HENRIETTE UHRY,** born in *Ingwiller* Bas-Rhin. Samuel Cerf Haas was said to have immigrated to Louisiana in 1853 at the age of sixteen. Amongst all the ship's records currently available, there is one for a "Salomon Haas" who arrived on 5 May 1853 at New Orleans, Orleans Parish, LA, from Le Havre, France, aboard the ship *Joseph Holmes* which is worthy of consideration, although the age is off by seven years. Samuel Haas immediately struck out in the remote parishes of Louisiana to begin his life as a peddler. He finally settled in Opelousas, St. Landry Parish, and with the help of his brother, **ALEXANDRE HAAS** (See entry), who arrived two years later, operated a thriving mercantile business. On 27 March 1862, Sam married Martha Ann Cole, the Louisiana born daughter of Kentuckian John Cole and his wife Lavinia Hudson. Sam enlisted as a First Lieutenant in the Third Regiment, Company K, Louisiana Cavalry, also known as the Prairie Rangers or Harrison's Regiment, in August 1862 where he rose to the rank of Captain. His horsemanship and experience as a peddler in the backwoods of Louisiana made him valuable as a scout and guide. His assignments were mostly local, as his regiment was charged with hunting down jayhawkers in the swamps of Central Louisiana. He served with honor until the end of the war. Five children were born to Sam and Martha: John A. (b. 1863), Hattie V. (b. 1868), Charles E. (b. 1873), Alexander Murdock (b. 1876), and Leon Samuel (b. 1878). After the end of hostilities, Sam opened a mercantile business in Bayou Chicot (St. Landry, now Evangeline Parish), LA, where his was the only store for miles around. He also served liquor by the glass or in the bottle, as did many country stores. His wife, Martha, kept the post office. He acquired large parcels of land, and was a noted breeder and seller of horses and mules which was his passion. Sam was, for many years, an elected member of the local police jury (parish council), and active in the democrat party. Martha Cole Haas died on 7 September 1907 in Bayou Chicot and was buried in the nearby Vandenburg Cemetery. After her death Sam spent time living in

Bunkie, Avoyelles Parish, LA, with his daughter Hattie, who had married her first cousin, William David Haas, Alex's eldest son. In 1908 Sam and his oldest son, John, were instrumental in the formation of Evangeline Parish which was carved out of a part of the much larger St. Landry Parish. Sam was, however, always drawn back to Bayou Chicot where he continued to raise his horses and mules, and kept the store for the benefit of the local residents long after it was very profitable. He died on 9 January 1919 at his son Dr. John A. Haas' home in Opelousas, St. Landry Parish, LA. Three of his sons married into local Opelousas Jewish families. His daughter, Hattie, who was married to his nephew, William David, was a Methodist like her mother. Sam was buried alongside Martha in Vandenburg Cemetery in Bayou Chicot. The service, held at his son John's home, was led by a rabbi. The graveside service was read by the local Methodist minister in keeping with the various religious convictions of his large family. **(A, AN, AP, G, GB)**

HAAS, SOLOMON, was born **SALOMON HAAS** on 25 September 1846 in *Ingwiller*, Bas-Rhin, France, to **SAMUEL HAAS**, a native of *Rothbach*, Bas-Rhin, France and his second wife, **ZERLINA WOLFF**, born in *Weinbourg*, Bas-Rhin. He immigrated with his mother's nephew, **LEON WOLFF** (See entry) arriving at New York from Le Havre, France, on 29 August 1871 on the SS *Denmark*, to join his half-brothers, **SAMUEL** and **ALEXANDRE HAAS** (See entries) in Central Louisiana. He stayed for a time in Bayou Chicot, where he learned English. Several years later, with the help of his half-brothers Sam and Alex, who themselves were dealers in livestock, Solomon set himself up in business as a livery stable owner and horse and mule dealer in New Orleans, Orleans Parish, LA. He was later in business as Kuhne & Haas at #92 and #94 Conti Street in the French Quarter selling and boarding horses. He moved his business to a two story brick building with a slate roof at 88 Bourbon Street several years later when the partnership broke up. Solomon married MARIE BLANDIN, the Parisian born widow of ARTHUR MAILLARD, in 1895. Marie was the mother of one child, Angèle Marie Maillard, whom Salomon helped to raise. The couple had no children of their own. Out of gratitude to her step-father, Angèle's only child was named Emile Haas Nikolaus Flauss. Solomon died on 12 January 1935 in New Orleans. His body was taken to the Thomas Douglas Marshall Cemetery in Evergreen, Avoyelles Parish, LA, where he was buried near his half-brother, **ALEXANDRE HAAS** (See entry), and members of the Marshall family, Alex's in-laws. Note: It took several years to find the Haas and Wolff immigration record. Their names were erroneously transcribed as "Jane Wolff" and "Salamona Heuss." (**A, AP, AN, GB**)

HELLER, RACHEL, (*Hoenheim*) See entry for **ISIDORE KLEIN**

HEMMENDINGER, LEON, was born **PANTALÉON HEMMENDINGER** on 3 April 1841 in *Scherwiller*, Bas-Rhin, France, to **LIPPMANN HEMMENDINGER**, a native of the town, and his wife, **HÉLÈNE WEILL**, born in Biesheim, Haut-Rhin, France. (Note: This family had been using the surname HEMMENDINGER in *Scherwiller* at least as early as the 1784 census of Jews in that town.) Pantaléon reported his mother's death in *Scherwiller* on 14 December 1865. According to information given in the 1910 federal census, he immigrated to Louisiana in 1867, a record of which we were unable to find. Leon settled in the Fifth Ward, Lafourche Parish, LA, to tend a general store on the Charles Espenan sugar and rice plantation. He married **MATHILDE KLING**, a native of Lixheim, Moselle, France, on 21 January 1873 in the parish. The couple had two children: Emma, born in 1875 who died at age 22 months, and Adeline, born in 1878. Thirty-year-old Mathilde died on 15 September 1880 and was buried in Bikur Sholim Jewish Cemetery in Donaldsonville, Ascension Parish, LA. Leon never remarried. He and Adeline remained in Lafourche Parish until the turn of the century, when they relocated to Lutcher, St. James Parish, LA. Leon opened a general merchandise store in town. He died in Lutcher on 14 November 1913 and was buried with his wife in Bikur Sholim Jewish Cemetery in Donaldsonville. Note: According to what was engraved on his tombstone, he was born in Schlettstadt (now Sélestat), Alsace, but there were no Hemmendinger births in that town between 1833-1842. Since Scherwiller is only three or so miles from the much larger Sélestat, we can understand why he might have thought he had been born there. (**A, AN, G**)

HESS, SOLOMON, was born **SALOMON HESS** on 20 January 1834 in *Bischheim*, Bas-Rhin, France, to SELIGMANN/ZACHARIE HESS/HESSE, a native of Puttelange-aux-Lacs, Moselle, France, and his wife, **RACHEL/REINE BETTMANN**, born in *Bischheim*, Bas-Rhin. Solomon Hess probably immigrated to America ca. 1852, the date reported in the Hess family's 1910 federal census enumeration in New Orleans, Orleans Parish, LA, and in Solomon's 1913 obituary.

Amongst all the ship's records currently available, there is one for a nineteen-year-old "Salomé Hess" who arrived on 5 March 1852 at New Orleans from Le Havre, France, aboard the ship *Lexington* which is worthy of consideration. Although listed as a female, this could have been a simple error on the part of the person who prepared the manifest. Solomon first appeared in Louisiana records as "S. Hess," a twenty-four-year-old clerk from France who was living alone at the Orleans Hotel in New Orleans at the time of the 1860 federal census. Solomon welcomed his second cousin, SIMON KARPE, who came to New Orleans in 1872 from Puttelange-aux-Lacs, Moselle, France, and whose mother was a member of the Hesse family. By this time Solomon Hess had already established himself in Alexandria, Rapides Parish, LA, where he had opened a grocery business. Simon Karpe followed his cousin to nearby Avoyelles Parish in Central Louisiana, where he settled down at Evergreen to raise his family. Solomon Hess married HARRIET/HENRIETTE HIRSCH, a native of Louisiana, on 10 March 1873 at Alexandria. They were the parents of five children: Celestine (b. 1874), Seligmann/Sidney (b. 1875; See entry for **RACHEL LEVY**), Alexander (b. 1877), Rachel (b. 1880), and Ettie (b. 1882). Solomon, who became a Grand Master in the local Masonic Lodge, remained in Alexandria until 1886 where he continued to operate a grocery, dry goods, and hardware business. Financial problems brought the family back to New Orleans for two years, after which they returned to Alexandria, where they lived until 1891. Solomon and his family then lived briefly in St. James Parish, finally moving back to New Orleans where they were enumerated in the 1900 federal census. Solomon became an insurance salesman and remained in the city until his death on 29 August 1913. He was buried there with full Masonic honors at Gates of Prayer Cemetery #2 (Joseph Street). Harriet Hirsch Hess died on 28 September 1929, just two months after her son Sidney's suicide, and was interred near her husband. (**A, AN, FS, G, GB**)

HEYMAN, ISAAC, was born **VOGEL HEYMAN** on 15 December 1815 at *Schirrhoffen*, Bas-Rhin, France, to **CAÏN/KEIM/ SALOMON HEYMANN,** a native of the town, and his wife, **ROELÉ LEOPOLD** (aka. **ROSALIE VOGEL** or **REHLÉ**), born in *Niederbronn-les-Bains*, Bas-Rhin, France. He married **CLAIRE WELSCH,** born **CLAIRE VELSCH** on 16 July 1817 in *Schirrhoffen*,Bas-Rhin, France, to **SAMUEL WELSCH** and his wife **MERLÉ/ MARIE HEYMANN** both natives of the town. Claire and Vogel were married at *Schirrhoffen* on 24 July 1850 and appeared as a childless couple in the 1851 census for the town. Their daughter, **MARIE HEYMANN** (See entry for **FÉLIX WELSCH**) was born on 27 Aug 1852 at *Schirrhoffen*. The family was not present in either the 1856 or 1861 *Schirrhoffen* censuses. We were unable to find any reliable ship's records for this family. They made their first appearance in Louisiana in 1857 when Isaac registered the birth of his son, Henry Heimann, on 27 Aug 1857 in New Orleans, Orleans Parish, LA, followed by the birth of Herzel/Herman Heimann, born on 31 March 1864. Two children were enumerated with them in the 1870 census for New Orleans: Julius (b. 1861) and Herman (b. 1864), where Vogel, who was enumerated as "Isaac," was a fifty-five year old junk dealer, living with his 52 year old wife, Clara, who took in washing. Isaac/Vogel Heyman died on 6 July 1879 in New Orleans and was buried there in Gates of Prayer Cemetery #2 (Joseph Street). His wife, Claire Welsch Heyman, died on 5 November 1904 in New Orleans and was buried in the same cemetery. **(A, AN, B1851, G, GB, L)**

HEYMAN, JACOB/JACQUES, was born **JACOB HEYMANN** on 12 February 1877 in *Brumath*, Bas-Rhin, France, to **MAXIMILIEN HEYMANN**, a native of the town, and his wife, **ROSALIA/ PAULINE MEYER**, born in *Minversheim*, Bas-Rhin. Jacob immigrated to the United States aboard the SS *L'Acquitaine*, arriving in New York on 10 June 1901. After a short stay in New York he travelled to New Orleans, Orleans Parish, LA. He and fellow Alsatian immigrant **THÉOPHILE HIRSCH** (See entry) founded the Heyman-Hirsch Ribbon Co. located at 528 Canal Street which specialized in silks and fancy goods. The company was the leader in its field for over two decades. Jacques (aka Jac or Jack) married MYRTLE BLUM, a New Orleans native, on 9 October 1912, at the home of her mother, Mrs. Henry Blum, in New Orleans. The couple never had children. They traveled extensively to Europe on business, as well as to and from New York City. In August 1922, Jacques Heyman bought out his partner, Théophile Hirsch, in order to form J. Heyman Co. He adopted a new policy of quick turnover, large volume with a low profit margin. He also hired salesmen to canvas Central America for potential customers. These new ideas seem to have been his undoing. On 2 August 1924 the *New York Sun* newspaper reported that a prominent New Orleans businessman, Jacques Heyman, had been arrested at the Hotel Biltmore in Manhattan, on the authority of the New Orleans Chief of Police, for having obtained $5000 upon presenting a false financial statement at the Whitney Bank and Trust Co. Jacques and Myrtle moved to Manhattan, New York, where they were enumerated there together in the 1930 federal census. Jacques gave his occupation as "silk merchant." Financial troubles drove the couple apart. By 1935 Myrtle was listed in a New Orleans Directory as "Mrs. Myrtle Blum," residing in the Bienville Hotel. Jacques Heyman was reported by the New Orleans *Times-Picayune* to have been sentenced to sixty days in jail in November 1938 for having obtained money under false pretenses. This is the last record we could find for Jacques/Jacob Heyman. Fifty-three-year-old Myrtle was enumerated in the 1940 federal census for New Orleans, living at the Buena Vista Hotel. A divorcee, she was employed by the government as a clerk and public notary. She died in New Orleans on 16 February 1973. Her remains were cremated at the Metairie Cemetery Crematory in the city. Note: Jacques Heyman's grandmother was **LOUISE GOUDCHAUX**, half-sister of **LEOPOLD GOUDCHAUX** (See entry) of Big Cane, St. Landry Parish, LA. Jacques Heyman was also the nephew of **MARX/MAURICE HEYMAN** (See entry) **(A, AN, FPC, GB)**

HEYMANN, ABRAHAM, was born on 13 June 1837 in *Brumath*, Bas-Rhin, France, to **EMANUEL HEYMANN** and his wife **LOUISE GUTSCHU (GOUDCHAUX)** both natives of *Brumath*. As the eldest son in the family, he was the first of three brothers to come to Louisiana. We believe that he immigrated as eighteen-year-old "Abraham Heumann," a native of France, aboard the ship *Shawmut* which arrived in New Orleans, Orleans Parish, LA, on 1 April 1857. He started out as a peddler, and was said to have lived for a time in Plaquemine, Iberville, Parish, LA. He took out a license to marry **DELPHINE BER** in New Orleans in **1862.** Unfortunately there was no month or day recorded on this document. Delphine was born **DAUPHINE BEER** on 18 July 1842 in *Harskirchen*, Bas-Rhin, France, to **SAMUEL HIRSCH BEER** (See entry), a native of the town and his wife, RACHEL LEVY, born in Niedervisse, Moselle, France. Five-year-old Delphine arrived on 7 November 1848 at New Orleans, Orleans Parish, LA, with her mother and two siblings on the ship *Espérance* out of Le Havre, France. We believe her father had gone ahead by several months to prepare for their arrival. After the Civil War, Abraham and Delphine relocated to Alexandria, Rapides Parish, LA. They were the parents of two children: Jennie (b. 1868) and Marx/Maurice (b. 1870). Abraham, whose nickname was "Big" was endowed with the famous Heymann temper and extraordinary strength.

His dry goods business in the 1880s was said to have a capital of $100,000 and he shipped several thousands of bales of cotton from his planting interests each year. Abraham was also the largest handler of sugar and molasses in the town of Alexandria. He was a member of the Police Jury (Parish Council), the local B'nai B'rith, and an honorary member of the Alexandria Fire Department. In 1884, two years before his death, he was involved in an altercation in the Exchange Hotel, where it was alleged that he slapped the wife of another merchant who had demanded money for an outstanding bill. The woman's son was summoned and he commenced to defend his mother with a cowhide whip. Had not several parties intervened the young man would have been severely beaten, as Abraham was not a man to trifle with when outraged. He died on 12 September 1886 in Alexandria, from blood poisoning and was interred in the Jewish Cemetery in Pineville, Rapides Parish, LA. His wife carried on at the Heymann store, with the help of her brother, Adolph Baer, and manager, Daniel Mann. Towards the end of her life she spent several years in the home of her daughter Jennie Heymann Kahn in New Orleans. Delphine died in Alexandria on 22 September 1938 and was buried in the Jewish Cemetery in Pineville, Rapides Parish, LA. (Note in Louisiana her surname is often spelled BER or BAER). (**A, AN, FS, G, N, TT**)

HEYMANN, HENRY, was born on 26 July 1843 in *Brumath*, Bas-Rhin, France, to **EMANUEL HEYMANN** and his wife **LOUISE GUTSCHU (GOUDCHAUX)** both natives of *Brumath*. He joined his brothers, **ABRAHAM** and **MARX HEYMANN** (See entries) in Louisiana after the Franco Prussian War. There is a record for the arrival of a twenty-six-year-old "Henri Heyman," a German citizen, who arrived at New York from Liverpool England on 7 June 1871, which is worthy of consideration. Henry moved back and forth between residences in New Orleans, Orleans Parish, LA, and Alexandria, Rapides Parish, LA where his brothers were residing. He married BERTHA BERNSTEIN, a native of Louisiana, of German extraction, on 29 March 1874 in New Orleans. They had five children: Florence (b. 1876), Delphine (b. 1878), Henriette (b. 1881), Mathilde (b. 1883) and Jacob (b. 1886). In 1880 Henry was enumerated both in New Orleans and in Alexandria, only one day apart, with his wife and three daughters. Nicknamed "the bull" and somewhat of a rogue, he was involved in an altercation in 1884 in Alexandria over money owed him, which resulted in a fistfight, and ultimately a tussle over a loaded gun. Henry was fined $5 which he protested, saying he acted in self-defense.

In 1887, while residing in New Orleans he was confined to the Parish jail for six months for obtaining money and goods under false pretenses. He died in New Orleans on 29 May 1895 and was buried there in Gates of Prayer Cemetery #2 (Joseph Street). We were unable to locate a death record for Bertha Bernstein Heymann. She was enumerated, apparently for the last time, in the 1920 federal census at Alexandria, Rapides Parish, LA, in the home of her daughter Florence Heymann Rosenberg. (**A, AN, FS**)

HEYMANN, MARIE, (*Schirrhofffen*) See entry for **FELIX WELSCH**

HEYMANN, MARX/MAURICE, was born **MARTIN HEYMANN** on 5 December 1842 in *Brumath*, Bas-Rhin, France, to **EMANUEL HEYMANN** and his wife, **LOUISE GUTSCHU/GOUDCHAUX**), both natives of the town. We believe that he immigrated to New Orleans, Orleans Parish, LA, as seventeen-year-old "Martin Heimann," on 18 April 1860 from Le Havre, France, on the ship *Bamberg*.He joined his brother, **ABRAHAM HEYMANN** (See entries), in business in Alexandria, Rapides Parish,, LA He also tended a branch of the store in nearby Cheneyville, Rapides Parish, LA. Marx spent eighteen months in Florida doing business in hides and scrap metal, after which he returned to Alexandria, where he had an office in his brother **HENRY HEYMANN**'s store (See entry). He was a partner with Henry in the late 1870s in the livery stable business. Marx moved to New Orleans in the mid-1890s and married HATTIE BLOCK there on 26 December 1897. Hattie, also a native of *Brumath*, was the widow of **CHARLES BOMBET** (See entry). Marx became a successful life insurance agent in the city. The couple never had children of their own. He died on 18 November 1908 in New Orleans and was buried there in Gates of Prayer Cemetery #2 (Joseph Street). His wife died on 12 March 1923 in Baton Rouge, East Baton Rouge Parish, LA. Her remains were returned to New Orleans where they were buried with those of her second husband. (**A, AN, FS, G, GB**)

HEYMANN, MICHEL, was born on 22 January 1837 in *Schirrhoffen,* Bas-Rhin, France, to **LEOPOLD "Leib" HEYMANN,** a native of the town, and his second wife, **ROSETTE LOEB** (aka **RODSELE LEVI),** born in *Langensoultzbach*, Bas-Rhin. He was trained as a teacher and while still a young man the French government sent him to Algeria to set up a modern education system. Upon return, he taught in *Romanswiller,* Bas-Rhin. Michel journeyed to *Haguenau* to marry **VALENTINE EISENMANN** on 8 December 1864. Valentine was born on 27 April 1840 in *Haguenau*, Bas-Rhin, France, to **MARX EISENMANN**, a native of the town, and his wife JUDITH ALTSCHUL, born in Ingenheim, Germany. Michel's Iberia Parish naturalization record of 31 July 1876 lists his date of immigration as 1866, a record for which we were unable to find. He and Valentine moved briefly to Jeanerette, Iberia Parish, LA, where he tended a general merchandise store. Two children were born to the couple Eugénie (b. 1868), and Leon (b. 1870; died without issue in 1898 while travelling in El Paso, TX.) Michel, his wife, Valentine, and their two children were enumerated in the 1870 federal census as residents of New Orleans, Orleans Parish, LA. Michel had become the Superintendent of the Jewish Widows' and Orphans' Home because of his extensive background in education. His wife, Valentine, worked at his side as the Assistant Director. He held that position for more than three decades, and was much beloved. He was also President of the Prison and Asylums Commission, a director of the Prison Reform Association, and spearheaded the free kindergarten program. He helped to set up the education curriculum at the Isidore Newman Manual Training School, still in its infancy. Michel Heymann died in New Orleans on 28 April, 1909. His wife, Valentine, followed on May 2, 1915. They were both interred there in Hebrew Rest Cemetery # 1.(Note: See entry for Valentine's sister-in-law, **ADÈLE EHRMANN.**) (**A, AN, F, GB**)

HIMMLER, BENJAMIN, was born **WOLF HIMMLER** on 2 April 1852 in *Gundershoffen*, Bas-Rhin, France, to **MICHEL HIMMLER**, a native of the town and his wife, **THERESE/DINA DREYFUS**, born in *Mertzwiller*, Bas-Rhin, France. We were unable to find a reliable record for his immigration. Twenty-one-year-old Benjamin Himmler died on 17 September 1873 in Shreveport, Caddo Parish, LA, a victim of the yellow fever epidemic that swept the town. He was buried in Hebrew Rest Cemetery # 1 (Jewish Section of Oakland Cemetery) in Shreveport. His gravestone, complete with his birth and death date and his town of origin, is the only trace we have of his existence in Louisiana. Note: His sister, **MATHILDE HIMMLER BLOCH** (See entry), immigrated to Louisiana in 1913. (**A, G**)

HIMMLER, MARCEL, was born **MARCELLUS HIMMLER** on 16 December 1888 in *Gundershoffen*, Bas-Rhin, France, to **DANIEL**

HIMMLER, a native of the town, and his wife, **RACHEL BLOCH**, born in *Schirrhoffen*, Bas-Rhin. He immigrated to America, arriving in New York from Bremen, Germany, on 5 September 1906 aboard the SS *Kaiser Wilhelm der Grosse* with his cousin **MARCEL BLOCH** (See entry). He travelled to Louisiana to work for his maternal uncle, **ARNAUD BLOCH** (See entry), who owned a dry goods store in Donaldsonville, Ascension Parish, LA. Marcel married his Uncle Arnaud's daughter, SOPHIE BERTHA BLOCH (b. 1895), a Donaldsonville native, in 1918. Their two daughters, Rachel (b. 1921) and Janis B. (b. 1924) were born in Donaldsonville where Marcel worked as the book keeper in his uncle/ father-in-law's, store. Marcel died on 12 December 1927 in Donaldsonville, and was buried there in Bikur Sholim Jewish Cemetery. His wife, Sophie, died on 23 July 1976 in New Orleans, Orleans Parish, LA. Her remains were returned to Donaldsonville to be buried in Bikur Solim Jewish Cemetery with those of her husband. (**A, AN, G, GB**)

HIMMLER, MARIE/MARIAM, (*Gundershoffen*) – See entry for **NATHAN EHRMANN**

HIMMLER, MATHILDE, (*Gundershoffen*) See entry for **MAURICE BLOCH**

HIRSCH, ALPHONSE, was born on 8 May 1851 in *Niederroedern*, Bas-Rhin, France, to **JACQUES HIRSCH,** a native of the town, and his wife, **SARA NETTER,** born in *Schwindratzheim*, Bas-Rhin. We believe that the immigration record for an eighteen-year-old "Alph. Hersch," who arrived in New Orleans, Orleans Parish, LA, on 19 November 1869 aboard the ship *Bavaria,* is likely his. He had followed his elder siblings, **JOSEPH** and **CHARLOTTE HIRSCH** (See entries), who both settled in East Feliciana Parish, Louisiana. He was naturalized in East Feliciana Parish on 17 July 1876. Twenty-six-year-old Alphonse Hirsch died on 28 September 1877 and was buried in the Jewish Cemetery at Clinton, East Feliciana Parish, LA. We know he was married, although we have no idea to whom or when, only because the words "To my husband" were engraved on his tombstone along with his dates of birth and death. (**A, AN, G**)

HIRSCH, BABETTE, was born on 9 January 1866 in *Rothbach*, Bas-Rhin, France, to **HERMANN HIRSCH,** a native of the town, and his wife, **JEANNETTE LEVY,** born in *Goersdorf*, Bas-Rhin. According to the 1910 federal census, Babette immigrated to Louisiana ca. 1890, a record for which we were unable to find. She joined her brother, **MOÏSE HIRSCH** (See entry), who lived in Monroe, Ouachita Parish, LA. Babette married HERMAN KUHN on 3 March 1894 in Monroe. Herman was a native of Germany and a local merchant. The couple had one child, Harry Julian (b. 1901). Herman Kuhn died on 12 January 1902 and was buried in Rosena Chapel Jewish Cemetery in Monroe. After her husband's death Babette and her son lived with her brother, Moïse, and his family in Monroe. Babette died on 19 December 1945 and was buried with her husband in Rosena Chapel Jewish Cemetery in Monroe. (**A, AN, G**)

HIRSCH, CHARLES, was born on 10 January 1839 in *Batzendorf*, Bas-Rhin, France, to **MOÏSE HIRSCH**, a native of the town, and his second wife, **JUDITH LEVI**, born in *Wingersheim*, Bas-Rhin. Although, according to his naturalization record dated 13 October 1868, he was said to have immigrated in 1857, we believe he was the nineteen-year-old Charles Hirsch who arrived in New Orleans, Orleans Parish, LA, on 9 November 1859 aboard the ship *Wurtemberg* out of Le Havre, France. He settled in New Orleans, Orleans Parish, LA, and became a successful crockery merchant. He took out a license to marry **MINETTE/MINA WEIL** on 14 December 1864. Minette was born on 8 May 1842 at *Dossenheim-sur-Zinsel*, Bas-Rhin, France, to **LOEW/LOEB WEIL** a native of the town, and his wife, **ESTHER BLOCH**, born in *Mertzwiller*, Bas-Rhin. Minette immigrated to America, aboard the ship *Logan*, which arrived in the port of New York on 24 October 1859. She went to St. Louis (Independent City), MO to join her elder brother **RAPHAEL WEIL**, where she was enumerated in the 1860 federal census, working as a servant in the household of Württemberg immigrant, JACOB BLUM. After her marriage to Charles in 1865, she became a permanent resident of New Orleans. Minette and Charles were the parents of four children: Moïse (b. 1866), Estelle (b. 1870), Leon (b. 1875), and Julia (b. 1879). Charles died on 29 May 1912 and was buried in Hebrew Rest Cemetery #2 in New Orleans. Minette died on 5 February 1924, and was buried with him. (Note: Minette's brother, **RAPHAEL WEIL**, never lived in Louisiana.) (**A, AN, G, GB, TT**)

HIRSCH, CHARLOTTE, was born on 25 October 1845 in *Niederroedern*, Bas-Rhin, France, to **JACQUES HIRSCH**, a native of the town, and his wife, **SARA NETTER**, born in *Schwindratzheim*,

Bas-Rhin. Nineteen-year-old Charlotte immigrated to Louisiana via New York, arriving on 7 March 1865 on board the ship *Harpswell*. SOLOMON BLOOM, a native of Laumersheim, Rheinpfalz, Germany, took out a license to marry Charlotte Hirsch on 22 August 1865 in New Orleans, Orleans Parish, LA. Solomon and Charlotte moved to Jackson, East Feliciana Parish, LA, and were enumerated there in 1870 with their three-year-old daughter, Mina, and Solomon's seventeen-year-old sister Fanny. Solomon died on 4 October 1879 and was buried at the Jewish Cemetery in Clinton, East Feliciana Parish, LA. At the time of the 1880 federal census, his widow, C. Bloom, was tending to the store in Jackson. She was living with an older brother, **JOSEPH HIRSCH** (See entry), the latter's wife, **FANNY BLOOM** who was her late husband's sister, and their two children, Carrie and Julius. Charlotte's daughter, Mina Bloom, was not with the family, and we presume that she died before the 1880 federal census, although we could find no burial record for her. Charlotte married JACOB FLONACHER, a widower with no children ca. 1886, a record of which we were unable to find. Jacob had been an itinerant peddler at Port Hudson, East Feliciana Parish, LA, before moving to Clinton, East Feliciana Parish, LA, to open a general merchandise store. His first wife, Matilda, had died on 24 October 1885 and been interred in the Clinton Jewish Cemetery. Jacob and Charlotte had been married less than a decade when she died on 10 February 1893. They had had no children. Charlotte was also buried in the Jewish Cemetery at Clinton, East Feliciana Parish, LA Her tombstone reads "Charlotte Flonacher, née Hirsch, born at Niederroedern, Oct. 25, 1845, died Feb. 11, 1893." (Note: The 11 February 1893 date on the tombstone is the date of interment.) JACOB FLONACHER moved to Natchez, Adams Co. MS, where he married his third wife, **BABETTE BENJAMIN**, a native of *Bouxwiller*, Bas-Rhin, France, in 1899. Jacob died the following year and was buried in Natchez City Cemetery. Note: See entries for Charlotte's brothers, **THÉOPHILE, ALPHONSE,** and **JOSEPH HIRSCH (A, AN, TT)**

HIRSCH, GASTON, was born on 21 February 1909, at *Haguenau*, Bas-Rhin, France, to **SAMUEL HIRSCH** (See entry), a native of *Batzendorf*, Bas-Rhin, France, and **JEANNE/JOHANNA BLOCH**, born in *Saverne*, Bas-Rhin. Gaston Hirsch and his parents, Samuel and Jeanne, followed his sister, **YVONNE HIRSCH** (See entry for **DAVID BLOCH**) to Louisiana, arriving in New York on 15 June 1936 on board the SS *Normandie*. Gaston's parents settled in

Donaldsonville, Ascension Parish, LA, and were enumerated in the 1940 federal census in the David Bloch household. Gaston returned to fight with the Free French forces, and was captured, and sent to an Austrian concentration camp for the duration of the war. After his release he married Olga Leonard in France. He returned with Olga and his son, Michel, to Donaldsonville where Gaston went into business for himself. A second son, Pierre Leonard Hirsch, was born to the couple in Donaldsonville in 1950. When Gaston's brother-in-law, David Bloch, could no longer do the job of caretaker at Bikur Sholim Jewish Cemetery, he stepped in totake over. At the time of his death on 13 July 1994, he was one of only two Jewish residents left in the town. Olga Hirsch died on 6 February 2003, and although not Jewish, was buried in Bikur Sholim Cemetery alongside her husband. (**A, AN, G. GB, GW**)

HIRSCH, HARRIET, was born **HENRIETTE HIRSCH** on 1 February 1841 in *Hatten,* Bas-Rhin, France, to **HERMANN/ HYMAN HIRSCH** (See entry) and his wife **BABETTE MOOCK/MOCK**, both natives of the town. According to the 1900 federal census for New Orleans, Orleans Parish, LA, Harriet immigrated with her parents, brothers **JACOB** and **THÉOPHILE HIRSCH** (See entries), and sisters **NANETTE** and **JULIA HIRSCH** (See entries) to New Orleans ca. 1861, reliable records for which we were not able to find. Four of her siblings, Nanette, Jacob, Théophile and Julie appeared on a list of emigrants preserved at the archives at *Wissembourg* who left France before 1/1/1866. This information was recorded in *The Alsace Immigration Book, Volume 1*, compiled by Cornelia Schrader-Muggenthaler. No record was found there for Henriette. Her father had been a dealer in horses in *Hatten* and took up the same trade in New Orleans, where the family was enumerated together in 1870. After her parents' deaths, Harriet continued to live with her two sisters, Nanette and Julia. She never married. Harriet died on 29 May 1910 and was buried in Hebrew Rest Cemetery #1 in New Orleans in the same plot as her father and sister Nanette. (**A, AL, AN, E, F, GB**)

HIRSCH, HERMANN/HYMAN, was born **HERMANN HIRSCH** on 20 February 1814 in *Hatten*, Bas-Rhin, France, to **JACOB/JACQUES HIRSCH (JACOB ISRAËL** before 1808) and his wife, **JEANNETTE WEIL (JOHANNA JONAS** before 1808), both natives of the town. He married **BABETTE/BARBE MOOCK/MOCK** on 17 June 1839 in *Hatten*. She was born **BARBE**

MOOCK on 24 December 1819 in *Hatten* to **SALOMON MOOCK**, a native of *Froeschwiller*, Bas-Rhin, France, and his wife, **CAROLINE WELSCH**, born in *Schirrhoffen*, Bas-Rhin. (Note: Salomon Moock died at the age of seventy-eight on 19 January 1869, the son of **ZACHARIE MOOCK**. His death record also states that he was a native of *Hatten*. However, Salomon's entry in the 1808 name adoption list of the Jews of *Hatten*, the information for which was provided by his father, gave his date and place of birth as 1791 in *Froeschwiller*.) Hermann and Babette were the parents of five children, all born in *Hatten*: Henriette (b. 1841; See entry), Jacob/Jacques (b. 1843; See entry), Nanette (b. 1844; See entry), Théophile (b. 1846; See entry) and Julie (b. 1856; See entry). Herman worked as a dealer of horses in *Hatten*. According to the 1900 federal census for New Orleans, Orleans Parish, LA, the family immigrated to Louisiana ca. 1861, records for which we were unable to find. Four of their children, Nanette, Jacob, Théophile and Julie, from *Hatten*, appeared on a list of emigrants preserved at the archives at *Wissembourg* who left the canton ca. 1/1/1866. This information was recorded in *The Alsace Immigration Book, Volume 1*, compiled by Cornelia Schrader-Muggenthaler. No corresponding records were found there for Hermann or Babette. The family first appeared in Louisiana in the 1870 federal census living in New Orleans, where Hermann and his two sons Jacob and George (Théophile) were working as dealers in horses. Julie, only thirteen years old at the time, was attending school. Babette, Hermann's wife, and her other daughters, Henriette and Nanette, were keeping house. Babette Moock Hirsch died on 4 February 1883 in New Orleans and was buried there in Hebrew Rest Cemetery #1. Hermann followed on 2 May 1893 and was buried as "Hyman" Hirsch in Hebrew Rest Cemetery #1 as well. His daughters Nanette and Harriet were later buried in the same plot (**A, AL, AN, E, F**)

HIRSCH, JACOB, was born **JACQUES HIRSCH** on 9 May 1824 in *Dehlingen*, Bas-Rhin, France, to **ALEXANDER HIRSCH**, born in Freilingen, Rheinpfalz, Germany, and his wife, **JULIENNE/JUDEL LEVI**, a native of *Dehlingen*, Bas-Rhin. Jacob was a very early immigrant to New Orleans, Orleans Parish, LA, but we have found no reliable ship's record for him. He married ESTELLE/ESTHER CAHN, a native of Frauenberg, Moselle, France, ca. 1843. Civil records this early in the nineteenth century are rarely found. Estelle's 1901 obituary indicated that she had come to Louisiana ca. 1841 and several years later had married Jacob Hirsch, one of the founders of the Gates of

Prayer synagogue at Jackson & Chippewa Streets. The couple was enumerated in the 1850 federal census for New Orleans where twenty-four-year-old Jacob, a rag merchant, was living with his twenty-eight-year-old wife, Estelle, and their children: Jennie/Jane (b. 1844), Levi/Levy/J. Levi (b. 1848) and William (b. 1850). Ten years later, Jacob was still dealing in rags, and the couple had become the parents of three more children: Henriette/Hattie (b. 1852), Julie (b. 1854), and Augusta (b. 1856). Forty-eight-year-old Jacob Hirsch was enumerated for the last time in the 1870 federal census. He was the owner of a junk shop on St. Andrew Street near Dryades. Two more children had been born to the couple: Peter (b. 1860) and John (b. 1865; died1875). There is no record of Jacob's death or his burial. We believe he may have died during one of the yellow fever epidemics in New Orleans and was interred in the old Gates of Mercy Cemetery formerly located at Jackson & Saratoga Streets, which was razed in the 1950s. There is a "Jacob Hirsch" whose name appears on a memorial stone at Hebrew Rest Cemetery #1 for burials which took place at Gates of Mercy, but no additional information about that burial is available. Estelle Hirsch was living with her son, J. Levi Hirsch, at the time of the 1880 federal census. Levi, the father of an eight-year-old boy, Alexander, was the owner of an oyster saloon on Tchoupitoulas Street. Levi Hirsch would become the second husband of **JEANNETTE BLUM** (See entry for **EDOUARD LEVY**) in 1882. Levi Hirsch died in 1889, and his only child, twenty-five-year-old Alexander, committed suicide by shooting himself in the head on the public sidewalk at the corner of Basin and Gravier streets on 26 March 1898. Alexander had been living with his aunt Jennie Hirsch Hochstein at the time. Estelle Cahn Hirsch died on 9 September 1901 in New Orleans and was buried there in Gates of Prayer Cemetery #2 (Joseph Street). Note: Jacob's father, sixty-six-year-old ALEXANDRE HIRSCH, came to New Orleans aboard the ship *Mulhouse* which arrived from Le Havre, France, on 19 October 1854. When Alexandre's wife Judel Levi's died on 26 June 1855 at *Dehlingen*, it was recorded that her husband was a merchant in America. We have unfortunately not been able to find any other records for Alexandre in the United States. (**A, AN, E, G, GB, TT**)

HIRSCH, JACOB, was born **JACQUES HIRSCH** on 19 February 1843 in *Hatten,* Bas-Rhin, France, to **HERMANN/ HYMAN HIRSCH** (See entry) and his wife **BABETTE MOOCK/MOCK**, both natives of the town. According to the 1900 federal census for New Orleans, Orleans Parish, LA, Jacob immigrated with his parents, brother **THÉOPHILE HIRSCH** (See entry), and sisters **HARRIET, NANETTE,** and **JULIA HIRSCH** (See entries) to the city, ca. 1861. While we were unable to find a likely immigration record for Jacob, he and three of his siblings, Nanette, Théophile, and Julie, all from *Hatten*, appeared on a list of emigrants preserved at the archives at *Wissembourg* who left the canton ca. 1/1/1866. This information was recorded in *The Alsace Immigration Book, Volume 1*, compiled by Cornelia Schrader-Muggenthaler. Twenty-six-year-old Jacob was enumerated with his family in the 1870 federal census for New Orleans, working as a horse dealer with his father, Hermann. He died the next year on 4 February 1871 and was interred in New Orleans at Hebrew Rest Cemetery #1. (**A, AL, AN, E, F**)

HIRSCH, JOSEPH, was born on 7 June 1844 in *Niederroedern*, Bas-Rhin, France, to **JACQUES HIRSCH**, a native of the town, and his wife, **SARA NETTER**, born in *Schwindratzheim*, Bas-Rhin. We were unable to find an immigration record for him. Joseph was enumerated in the 1880 federal census for Jackson, East Feliciana Parish, LA, living with his sister **CHARLOTTE HIRSCH** (See entry), the widow of SOLOMON BLOOM. By this time, Joseph had already been married to Solomon's sister, FANNIE BLOOM, since at least 1874, a record for which we were unable to find. They were the parents of two children born in Jackson: Carrie (b. 1875) and Julius (b. 1877). Joseph moved his family briefly to New Orleans, Orleans Parish, LA, in the 1890s, probably after the death of his sister, Charlotte in 1893. Joseph's wife, Fannie Bloom Hirsch, died on 15 February 1896 in New Orleans. Her remains were returned to Clinton, East Feliciana Parish, LA, where they were interred in the Jewish Cemetery. Joseph Hirsch and his daughter, Carrie, moved to Alexandria, Rapides Parish, LA, ca. March 1896 where she was married on 4 November of the same year to SIDNEY SCHMALINSKI, a native of the town. Joseph went into business with **ACHILLE SOLOMON BAUER** (See entry), born in *Romanswiller*, Bas-Rhin, France, who was also his daughter Carrie's brother-in-law. The partnership was dissolved in the spring of 1897. Joseph was last recorded in Alexandria in October 1897 where he was appointed one of the guards to protect Alexandria from that year's yellow fever outbreak. We were unable to trace him any further, or to locate a possible date or place of death. His son Jules moved to San Francisco, CA, where he worked as a painter in a department store. (**A, AN, FS, G,**)

HIRSCH, JULIE, (*Hatten*) See entry for **CHARLES BLOCH**

HIRSCH, LAZARE, was born on 2 January 1848 in *Batzendorf*, Bas-Rhin, France, to **MOÏSE HIRSCH**, a native of the town, and his second wife **JUDITH LEVI**, born in *Wingersheim*, Bas-Rhin. He immigrated to Louisiana ca. 1872 at the conclusion of the Franco-Prussian War, a reliable record for which we were unable to find. Lazare married **CAROLINE LEVY** on 28 February 1875 in New Orleans, Orleans Parish, LA. She was born on 1 January 1850 in *Duppigheim*, Bas-Rhin, France, to **NEPHTALY LEVY**, a native of the town, and his wife **BRENDELE DREYFUS**, born in *Osthoffen*, Bas-Rhin. She immigrated to New Orleans from Le Havre, France, arriving on 4 December 1871 aboard the ship *Hammonia,* ahead of her younger brother, **ABRAHAM LEVY** (See entry). Lazare Hirsch started out as a clerk in New Orleans, for his brother, **CHARLES HIRSCH** (See entry), who owned a crockery business on Decatur Street. Lazare opened up his own crockery business on North Peters Street the following year. Lazare and Caroline's two children, Julia (b. 1880) and Henry (b. 1881), were born while they were still living on Burgundy Street in the French Quarter. The family moved out to Jefferson Parish ca. 1890, where Lazare opened a general store at Rice, a town or plantation, whose location has been lost to time. In 1892 he received a federal appointment as the postmaster at Rice. By 1900 the couple had relocated to Ama, St. Charles Parish, LA, where Lazare owned and operated a general merchandise store until his death there on 12 November 1923. His remains were transported to Hebrew Rest Cemetery #2 in New Orleans for burial. Caroline Levy Hirsch died on 13 April 1940 in New Orleans. She was interred in the same cemetery. **(A, AN, G, GB, TT)**

HIRSCH, MOÏSE, was born on 21 November 1842 in *Niederroedern*, Bas-Rhin, France, to **JACQUES HIRSCH**, a native of the town, and his wife, **SARA NETTER**, born in *Schwindratzheim*, Bas-Rhin. Moïse was the first of five siblings to immigrate to Louisiana. According to his 1868 naturalization record, as well as the 1900 federal census, he came to America in 1858. He may have been the eighteen-year-old [*sic*] "Michel Hirsch," a native of France who arrived in New Orleans, Orleans Parish, LA, on 17 December 1858 from Le Havre, France, aboard the ship *Bethiah Thayer*. Moïse took out a license to marry Hannah Oppenheimer, a Missouri native, on 8 October 1866 in New Orleans, Orleans Parish, LA. They were the parents of two children both born in Louisiana: Henry (b. 1868), and Nora (b. 1871). Moïse was naturalized in West Feliciana Parish, LA, on 2 April 1868. The record indicated that he was born in France in 1843 and had immigrated to the United States in 1858. We were unable to find an entry for him in either the 1860 or 1870 federal census. His presence in West Feliciana Parish in 1868 was not random however, as his wife's parents, Henry Oppenheimer and Mina Wolf, were residents of Jackson, in nearby East Feliciana Parish. Three of his four siblings, **ALPHONSE, CHARLOTTE,** and **JOSEPH HIRSCH** (See entries) also lived in the Felicianas. Both Alphonse and Charlotte were buried in the Jewish Cemetery at Clinton. We finally located Moïse Hirsch and his family in the 1880 federal census for Galveston, Galveston Co., TX, where he was working as a clerk in a store. The couple eventually moved to Corsicana, Navarro Co., TX, where they were enumerated in the home of their daughter, Nora Hirsch Cohen, in both the 1900 and 1910 federal censuses. Moïse died on 25 August 1914 in Corsicana and was interred there in the Hebrew Cemetery. Hannah died on 24 September 1918 and was buried with her husband. Note: See also entry for **THÉOPHILE HIRSCH (A, AN, G, TT)**

HIRSCH, MOÏSE, was born on 29 July 1859 in *Rothbach*, Bas-Rhin, France, to **HERMANN HIRSCH**, a native of the town, and his wife, **JEANNETTE LEVY,** born in *Goersdorf*, Bas-Rhin. He immigrated to America, arriving in New York on 1 September 1883 aboard the SS *Canada.* Moïse settled in Monroe, Ouachita Parish, LA, where he opened up a dry goods store. He married **HENRIETTE/HARRIET EICHEL** on his way back from a visit to Alsace in the summer of 1896. Their banns were published in Paris on 30 August 1896 where they were subsequently wed. Henriette was born on 17 May 1867 in *Offwiller*, Bas-Rhin, France, to **NATHAN EICHEL**, a native of the town, and his wife, **ANNE/SARA METZGER**, born in *Ettendorf*, Bas-Rhin. The newlyweds returned to Monroe, Ouachita Parish, LA where their two children, Jeannette C. (b. 1897) and Martin Herman (b.1903) were born. Moïse Hirsch died on 2 December 1922 in Monroe and was buried there in the Rosena Chapel Jewish Cemetery. Harriet died on 27 October 1951 in Monroe and was buried with her husband. **(A, AN, G, TT)**

HIRSCH, NANETTE, was born on 30 December 1844 in *Hatten*, Bas-Rhin, France, to **HERMANN/ HYMAN HIRSCH** (See entry) and his wife, **BABETTE MOOCK/MOCK**, both natives of the town.

According to the 1900 federal census for New Orleans, Orleans Parish, LA, Nanette immigrated with her parents, and brothers, **JACOB** and **THÉOPHILE HIRSCH** (See entries), and sisters, **HARRIET** and **JULIA HIRSCH** (See entries) ca. 1861. While we were unable to find a likely immigration record for Nanette, she and three of her siblings, Jacob, Théophile, and Julie, all from *Hatten*, appeared on a list of emigrants preserved at the archives at *Wissembourg* who left the canton ca. 1/1/1866. This information was recorded in *The Alsace Immigration Book, Volume 1*, compiled by Cornelia Schrader-Muggenthaler. After her parents' deaths she continued to live with her sisters, Julia and Harriet. She never married. Nanette died on 30 April 1903 in New Orleans and was buried there in Hebrew Rest Cemetery #1 in the same plot as her father. **(A, AL, AN, E, F, GB)**

HIRSCH, SAMUEL, was born on 6 April 1869 in *Batzendorf*, Bas-Rhin, France, to **BAËR HIRSCH**, a native of the town and his wife, **REBECCA CHARLOTTE LEVY**, born in *Minversheim*, Bas-Rhin. He married **JEANNE/JOHANNA BLOCH** on 16 June 1904 in *Saverne*, Bas-Rhin, France. Jeanne/Johanna Bloch was born on 25 August 1880 to **NATHAN BLOCH**, a native of *Lichtenberg*, Bas-Rhin, and his wife **BABETTE POMPET/BOMBET**, born in *Saverne*, Bas-Rhin. Samuel and Jeanne had two children: Yvonne (b. 1905) and Gaston (b. 1909). Samuel, Jeanne and Gaston Hirsch followed Yvonne, to Louisiana. They arrived at New York on 15 June 1936 on board the SS *Normandie*. They settled in Donaldsonville and were enumerated in 1940 federal census in the **DAVID BLOCH** (See entry) household. Samuel Hirsch died on 16 January 1953 in Donaldsonville and was buried there in Bikur Sholim Jewish Cemetery. His wife followed him in death on 9 December 1966 and was buried with him. Note: Johanna Bloch's mother, **BABETTE POMPET/BOMBET,** was the sister of **CLAIRE BOMPET** (See entry), who married LAZARE LEVY and settled in Donaldsonville in the late 1850s. **(A, AN, G, GB)**

HIRSCH, THÉOPHILE, was born on 28 November 1846 in *Hatten*, Bas-Rhin, France, to **HERMANN/ HYMAN HIRSCH** (See entry) and his wife, **BABETTE MOOCK/MOCK**, both natives of the town. Théophile probably immigrated with his parents, brother **JACOB HIRSCH** (See entry) and sisters **HARRIET, NANETTE** and **JULIA HIRSCH** (See entries) to New Orleans, Orleans Parish, LA, ca. 1861. While we were unable to find a likely immigration record for Théophile, he and three of his siblings, Jacob, Nanette, and Julie, all from *Hatten*, appeared on a list of emigrants preserved at the archives at *Wissembourg* who left the canton ca. 1/1/1866. This information was recorded in *The Alsace Immigration Book, Volume 1*, compiled by Cornelia Schrader-Muggenthaler. Twenty-three-year-old Théophile was enumerated as "George" with his family in the 1870 federal census for New Orleans, where he was working as a horse dealer with his father, Hermann. Several of his male Hirsch relatives in *Hatten* also used the name "George." It was not uncommon for Alsatian Jewish men named Théophile to also be known as George or to adopt it as a second name. Efforts to trace him any further using either name have been unsuccessful. He last appeared in a federal census record dated 12 June 1880 in New Orleans where he was enumerated as George Hirch [*sic*]. He may have died on 4 or 5 June 1882, and been buried under the surname "Hirsch," with no first name, in Hebrew Rest Cemetery # 1 in New Orleans. There is, however, no corresponding "Hirsch" entry for that date in the "New Orleans Death Records Index" available at *Ancestry.com* or from the Louisiana Secretary of State's records in Baton Rouge. (**A, AL, AN, E, F, TT**)

HIRSCH, THÉOPHILE, was born on 30 July 1854 in *Niederroedern*, Bas-Rhin, France, to **JACQUES HIRSCH**, a native of the town, and his wife, **SARA NETTER**, born in *Schwindratzheim*, Bas-Rhin. According to his 1909 application for a U.S. passport, he stated that he arrived in Louisiana in December 1871 and was naturalized at Rayville, Richland Parish, LA, in 1878. We have not been able to verify his date of immigration using available ship's records. Théophile was first enumerated in Louisiana in 1880 as an unmarried store clerk in Madison Parish, LA, sharing a house with his first cousin, **SIMON ELIE BLUM** (See entry). Théophile became a successful and respected dry goods merchant in Delhi, Richland Parish, in northeastern Louisiana. Théophile married HANNAH BLOCK, a native of Winnsboro, Franklin Parish, LA, on 1 February 1881 in New Orleans, Orleans Parish, LA. The couple returned to Delhi to start a family. They were the parents of five children, only one of whom lived to adulthood: Theresa/Tessie (b. 1882; died 1887), Sylvan G. (b. 1884; died 1887), Leo Levy (b. 1886), Irma T. (b. 1890; died 1897) and Jules (1893; died 1894). Their four children were buried in Rosena Chapel Jewish Cemetery in Monroe, Ouachita Parish, LA. Théophile, Hannah and their only surviving child, Leo Levy Hirsch remained in Richland Parish through the end of the nineteenth century. Leo, who trained as an electrical engineer, moved to New Orleans to work for a power company. He was enumerated in the 1910 federal census as a single twenty-three year old engineer for an Electric Company living in a boarding house. His parents followed him to the city, having a house built on Dunleith Court ca. 1915 where they were all reunited. Théophile continued to work in New Orleans. He became a wholesale dealer in ribbons and fancy goods in partnership with fellow Alsatian **JACOB/JACQUES HEYMANN** (See entry) at the Heyman-Hirsch Ribbon Company located at 528 Canal Street. He died on 29 March 1932 and was buried in Hebrew Rest Cemetery #2 in New Orleans. Hannah died on 8 February 1956 in New Orleans and was buried with her husband. Note: See entries for his siblings, **CHARLOTTE, ALPHONSE** and **JOSEPH HIRSCH**. (A, AN, F, GB)

HIRSCH, YVONNE, (*Haguenau*) See entry for **DAVID BLOCH**

ISRAEL, BABETTE, (*Romanswiller*) See entry for **SAMSON BLOCH**.

ISRAEL, JACOB, was born on 26 September 1817 in *Oberbronn*, Bas-Rhin, France, to **RAPHAEL ISRAEL**, a native of the town and his wife, CATHERINE FRANCK, born in Pirmasens, Rheinpfalz, Germany. We could not find a likely ship's record for Jacob Israel's arrival into the United States. He became a dry goods merchant in Natchitoches and the neighboring town of Provençal, Natchitoches Parish, LA. Jacob married **NANETTE LEVY** on 1 June 1857 in New Orleans, Orleans Parish, LA. Nanette was born on 8 December 1835 in *Lauterbourg*, Bas-Rhin, France, the daughter of **BENOÎT LEVY**, a native of the town, and **HENRIETTE MENDEL**, born in *Soultz-sous-Fôrets*, Bas-Rhin. Nineteen-year-old Nanette immigrated to New Orleans aboard the ship *Henry Grinnell,* arriving on 19 February 1855. Jacob and Nanette were the parents of six children: Raphael (b. 1859), Gustave (b. 1860), Julia (b. Provençal 1861), Natile, (b. 1862), Rosa (b. 1866), and Bertha (b. 1868). Jacob Israel died on 29 January 1872 at Natchitoches and was buried there in the Jewish Cemetery. After her hurband's death, Nanette moved to Natchez, Adams Co., MS, and subsequently to Vidalia, Concordia Parish, LA. Several years before her death, she settled in Alexandria, Rapides Parish, LA, to be near her nieces and nephews, children of her brother, **ÉDOUARD LEVY** (See entry). She died on 16 November 1902 and was buried in the Jewish Cemetery in Natchitoches, Natchitoches Parish, LA, with her husband, who had been laid to rest there a quarter of a century before. (**A, AN, F, FS**)

ISRAEL, JOSEPH, was born on 21 September 1831 in *Romanswiller*, Bas-Rhin, France, to **SAMUEL ISRAEL**, a native of the town, and his wife **MALGY/MARIE LEVY**, born in *Duttlenheim*, Bas-Rhin. He arrived in Louisiana before 1860, probably before his sister **BABETTE ISRAEL** (See entry for **SAMSON BLOCH**) returned to France after the death of her husband. We have not been able to find a likely ship's record for his immigration to America. In 1860 twenty-eight-year-old Joseph was enumerated in Berwick City, St. Mary Parish, LA, living with Joseph Vigne, the proprietor of a "grog shop." Joseph married MARIE LOUISE GENERES, a New Orleans native, ca. 1861, probably in New Orleans, Orleans Parish, LA, although we were unable to find a record of it. Joseph enlisted in the 4th Company, 3rd Regiment European Brigade (Garde Française) in New Orleans on 2 April 1862. Joseph and Louise were the parents of five children: Ernestine (b. 1862), Josephine (b. 1863), Augustine (b. 1865), Samuel (b. 1868), and Mamie (b. 1872). Joseph was a dry goods merchant in New Orleans. An 1871 directory for the city listed him as a dealer in French, English, German, Swiss, and American dry goods doing business on Canal Street. Joseph died on 26 October 1871 and was buried in New Orleans at Hebrew Rest Cemetery #1. When Joseph's nephews, Marx and Lazare Bloch, his sister Babette Israel Bloch's sons, returned from France (See entry for **SAMSON BLOCH**), they lived with his widow, Louise Generes Israël. In the 1880 federal census Marx Block, a liquor merchant, was enumerated as head of a household that included Louise Israel and her children Ernestine, Augustine, Sam, and Mamie. Lazare Bloch married his cousin Augustine Israel in 1899. In both the 1900 and 1910 federal censuses Louise's nephew, Marx Bloch, who never married, was living with Louise Israel, her children, and grandchildren. Louise Generes Israel died in New Orleans on 15 September 1910 and was buried there in Metairie-Lakelawn Cemetery. (**A, AN, F, G, GB, L**)

JAUDEL, ACHILLE, was born on 6 December 1872 in *Benfeld*, Bas-Rhin, France, to **JUDAS JAUDEL** a native of *Westhouse*, Bas-Rhin, France and his wife, **MARIE REIMS**, born in *Ringendorf*, Bas-Rhin. Thirteen-year-old Achille Jaudel arrived in New York on 13 September 1886 aboard the SS *Normandie* and settled in Lake Charles, Calcasieu Parish, LA, where he boarded with his uncle, David Reims, and worked with him as a butcher. Achille married ESTHER LEHMANN on 20 October 1901 in New Orleans, Orleans Parish, LA. Esther was the daughter of **DAVID THEODORE LEHMANN** (See entry), and his wife, **HENRIETTE GOUGENHEIM**, both immigrants from the Bas-Rhin, living in Morgan City, St. Mary Parish, LA. Achille and Esther raised their two daughters Raie Esther (b. 1902) and Miriam Rae (b. 1921) in New Orleans where Achille gave up butchering and became a sales representative for the Western Meat Company. Achille died on 5 June 1938 in New Orleans and was buried there in Hebrew Rest Cemetery #1. His wife, Esther, followed on 25 January 1960 and was buried there as well (**A, AN, G, GB**)

JAUDEL, ERNEST, was born **ERNESTE JAUDEL** on 28 December 1866 in *Benfeld*, Bas-Rhin, France, to **JUDAS JAUDEL,** a native of *Westhouse*, Bas-Rhin, France, and his wife, **MARIE REIMS**, born in *Ringendorf*, Bas-Rhin. Eighteen-year-old Ernest arrived in New York on 23 December 1884 from Le Havre, France, aboard the SS *St. Simon* He travelled to Louisiana where he joined his uncle, **DAVID REIMS** (See entry), in Lake Charles, Calcasieu Parish, LA. He died there on 17 November 1887 at the age of twenty and his body was sent for burial to New Orleans, Orleans Parish, LA, where it was interred at Hebrew Rest Cemetery #1. Note: His brother, **ACHILLE JAUDEL** (See entry) immigrated to Louisiana in 1886. **(A, AN)**

JOSEPH, MAURICE, was born **MORITZ JOSEPH** on 12 December 1880 in *Buchsweiler*, Germany (*Bouxwiller*, Bas-Rhin, France), to **NATHAN JOSEPH**, a native of the town, and his wife, **SARA/CELESTINE DREYFUS,** born in *Obernai,* Bas-Rhin. He immigrated to Louisiana, arriving in New York on 26 September 1896 aboard the SS *La Bourgogne*. Maurice lived in Napoleonville, Assumption Parish, LA, where he was enumerated in the 1900 federal census. Nineteen-year-old Maurice worked as a clerk for his Alsatian-born cousin, **MAURICE LEVY** (See entry), a storekeeper and boarded with the family. Maurice Joseph moved to Houma, Terrebonne Parish, La, where he and his cousin, Maurice Levy, bought a store ca. 1909 which they renamed The Leader. Maurice Joseph married HANNAH HAGEDORN, an Alabama native, on 17 November 1909 in Lanett, Chambers Co., AL. They were the parents of two sons: William S (b. 1911; lived six days) and Jacques H. (b. 1914). Maurice welcomed his younger brother, **JULIEN JOSEPH** (See entry), to Houma in 1914. Maurice and his wife separated before the 1930 federal census. Maurice remained with the store in Houma and was enumerated in 1930 with his brother Julien and Julien's wife, Alberta. Hannah moved to Lagrange, Troup Co, Georgia, with her son. She was enumerated there in 1930 as a forty-four-year-old widow living alone with her sixteen-year-old son Jack. Ten years later she and Jack were still living there. She was now taking in boarders and her son was employed as a shipping clerk for a wholesale grocery. Maurice Joseph died on 7 October 1956 at Ochsner Hospital in Jefferson Parish, LA. His remains were returned to Houma, where they were interred in Magnolia Cemetery. Hannah Hagedorn Joseph died on 26 December 1967 in West Point, Troup Co., Georgia. She was buried there in Pinewood Cemetery. (**A, AN, G, GB**)

JOSEPH, SAMUEL JULIEN, was born **SAMUEL JULIUS JOSEPH** on 8 September 1895 in *Buchsweiler*, Germany (*Bouxwille*r, Bas-Rhin, France), to **NATHAN JOSEPH**, a native of the town, and his wife, **SARA/CELESTINE DREYFUS,** born in *Obernai*, Bas-Rhin. He immigrated to the United States arriving at New York on 15 June 1914 from Le Havre, France, aboard the SS *Rochambeau*. Julien joined his brother Maurice in Houma, Terrebonne Parish, LA, where he went to work as a clerk for the M. Levy Co., which operated The Leader Store. Twenty-one-year-old Julien registered for the World War I draft in 1918 at Houma as an unmarried alien born in *Buchsweiler*, Alsace, Germany. He married ALBERTA "Bertie" KOHMAN, a native of Terrebonne Parish, Louisiana, on 18 July 1926 in Gretna, Jefferson Parish, LA. Julien and his wife were enumerated in the 1930 federal census for Houma, living with Julien's brother, Maurice. They were both working as sales clerks at The Leader Store. Julien and Alberta had a daughter, Celestine (b. 1932). The two brothers ran The Leader together until Maurice Joseph's death in 1956. Julien remained as the owner and manager of The Leader until it finally closed its doors three years later. Alberta Kohman Joseph died on 15 July 1975 and was buried in Magnolia Cemetery, Houma, Terrebonne Parish, LA. Julien Joseph died on 19 June 1980 in Metairie, Jefferson Parish, LA, and was interred in Magnolia Cemetery in Houma with his wife and brother. (**A, AN, G, GB, GW**)

KAHN, AARON, was born **ARON KAHN** on 22 February 1838 in *Riedseltz*, Bas-Rhin, France, to LAMBERT KAHN, a native of Busenberg, Rheinpfalz, Germany, and his second wife, HANNA HAENCHEN, born in Albersweiler, Rheinpfalz, Germany. According to information given in the 1910 federal census for Shreveport, Caddo

Parish, LA, Aaron immigrated to Louisiana in 1854. His name, date and place of birth appeared on a list of young men who were due to be conscripted in the canton of Wissembourg on 1/1/1858. This information was recorded in *The Alsace Immigration Book, Volume II*, compiled by Cornelia Schrader-Muggenthaler. Many young men who were included on this list had immigrated, either with their parents, or several years before they would have been inducted into the military. An immigration date of 1854 seems likely for Aron, although we were unable to verify it by consulting any reliable ship's record Aaron made his living as a housewares merchant, selling mostly crockery on Texas Avenue in Shreveport. He married JULIA WINTER, a Caddo Parish native, known as JULIA SOUR after her widowed mother's remarriage to ABRAHAM SOUR in 1856. Aaron and Julia were wed on 19 October 1869 in Shreveport. They were the parents of five children: Arthur Lee (b. 1870), Joseph (b. 1874), Hannah (b. 1876), Carrie L. (b. 1881) and Lucille M. (b. 1883). Julia died on 25 August 1899 in Shreveport and was buried there in Hebrew Rest Cemetery #2 (Texas Ave.). Aaron Kahn died on 31 May 1918 in Shreveport and was buried with his wife. (**A, AL2, AN, G**).

KAHN, AARON, was born on 26 July 1849 in *Brumath*, Bas-Rhin, France, to **THÉODORE KAHN**, a native of the town, and his wife, **SOPHIE LEVI**, born in *Wingersheim*, Bas-Rhin. He married **MATHILDE BRAUN** on 5 November 1873 in *Brumath*. Mathilde was born on 13 April 1851 in *Brumath* to **JOSEPH BRAUN**, a native of *Offendorf*, Bas-Rhin, France, and his wife, **CAROLINE KAHN**, born in *Mommenheim*, Bas-Rhin. Their only child, **MARIE KAHN**, was born on 17 January 1879 in *Brumath*. According to the 1900 federal census, Aaron immigrated to Louisiana in 1886, four years after his sister Henriette was widowed by **MARCUS FEIST** (See entry). He joined Henriette and her children in Milliken's Bend, Madison Parish, LA, where he worked as a butcher. While we could not find any reliable ship's record for the arrival of Aaron Kahn, there is a probable arrival for his wife and daughter. A "Mrs. M. Kahn" and a "Miss. M. Kahn" landed in New York on 31 December 1888 aboard the SS *La Bretagne,* although the age of Miss Kahn is off by five years. Mathilde Braun Kahn died on 10 September 1890 not long after her arrival in the U.S. and was buried at Anshe Chesed Jewish Cemetery in Vicksburg, Warren Co., MS. Aaron and his daughter, Marie, remained in Milliken's Bend and were enumerated there in the 1900 federal census, living next to his niece Bettie Feist and her husband Nicholas Kahn.

Aaron Kahn was gunned down by an African-American highwayman in his store on 9 May 1903 and died three days later on 12 May 1903. He was interred the next day in Anshe Chesed Jewish Cemetery in Vicksburg. Marie Kahn never married. She moved to Vicksburg and worked there for many years as a clerk in a railway office. She applied for American citizenship in 1960 and passed away in Vicksburg on 2 January 1980 at the age of 101 years. She was buried there with her parents in Anshe Chesed Jewish Cemetery. (**A, AN, GB, TT**)

KAHN, ARMAND, was born on 1 May 1896 in *Brumath*, Bas-Rhin, France, to **LEOPOLD KAHN** (See entry), a native of *Brumath*, Bas-Rhin, France, and his wife, **FANNY** née **KAHN**, born in *Schirrhoffen*, Bas-Rhin. He was the youngest of the four Kahn Brothers from *Brumath* who made their homes in Baton Rouge, East Baton Rouge Parish, LA. He arrived in New York on 13 March 1921 aboard the SS *France*, accompanied by his father, **LEOPOLD KAHN** (See entry), in time for the wedding of his older brother **JULES KAHN** (See entry) to Marie Levy. He became a naturalized citizen in 1928. Armand worked all his life as a salesman for various family enterprises. He never married. Armand died on 16 January 1973 in Baton Rouge and was buried there in the Jewish Cemetery. (**AN, G, GB**)

KAHN, CAROLINE, was born on 11 August 1831 in *Riedseltz*, Bas-Rhin, France, to ARON KAHN, born in Busenberg, Rheinpfalz, Germany, and his wife, ROSINE KATZ, a native of Dahn, Rheinpfalz, Germany. An immigration record for twenty-three-year-old "Caroline Kenn," a native of France, who arrived on 30 March 1855 from Le Havre, France, aboard the ship *Ashland* is worthy of consideration. Caroline settled in Plaquemine, Iberville Parish, LA, near her paternal uncle, **SAMUEL KAHN** (See entry). Caroline married JACOB BERNSTEIN, a Prussian national who was working as a tailor in Plaquemine. They were wed on 4 November 1857 in Iberville Parish. Their first three children were born in Plaquemine: Michel (b. 1859), Florestine/Florence/Flora (b. 1860), and Julius (b. 1861). Jacob joined the Confederate Guards Response Battalion, Company C (16th Louisiana Battalion), in 1862 and was captured at the Battle of Bisland near Bayou Teche, on 14 April 1863. He was sent to New Orleans to be exchanged. After his release he relocated the family to Baton Rouge, East Baton Rouge Parish, LA. Four more children were born to the couple: Alexander (b. 1864), Lillie (b. 1866), Ernest (b. 1869), and Eddah (b. 1873). By 1880, Jacob, Caroline and the children had moved to Shreveport, Caddo Parish, LA, where Jacob continued to work as a tailor. He died on 22 January 1908 in Shreveport and was buried there in Hebrew Rest Cemetery #2 (Texas Ave.). Caroline died on 26 December 1909 in Shreveport, and was buried with her husband. Note: Two of their daughters, Flora and Eddah, married immigrant brothers, **DAVID** and **FELIX WEILLER**. (See entries) (A, AN, G)

KAHN, CHARLES, was born **JACQUES KAHN** on 19 August 1864 in *Schirrhoffen*, Bas-Rhin, France, to **HERMANN KAHN** and his wife **JULIE LEVY**, both natives of *Schirrhoffen*. His use of the name "Charles" first appeared in the 1866 town census for *Schirrhoffen*. According to information given in the 1900 federal census for White Castle, Iberville Parish, LA, Charles immigrated in 1885. A record for a twenty-year-old German national. "J. Kahn," who arrived at New York from Glasgow, Scotland on 4 March 1884 aboard the SS *State of Indiana* is worthy of consideration. Charles settled in Brusly Landing, West Baton Rouge Parish, LA. He married DELLA FARRNBACHER (sister of Sophie, his first cousin Henry Cohn's wife), about 1890. Two children were born to them: Marion B (b. 1893) and Isadore (b. 1894). After a few decades working in White Castle, Iberville Parish, La, Charles and his wife, Della, spent their later years in Baton Rouge, East Baton Rouge Parish, LA. Charles died on 7 January 1933 and was buried there in the Jewish Cemetery. Della died on 10 July 1946 and was interred with her husband. (See entries for his brothers, **DANIEL** and **GABRIEL KAHN**)(A, AN, F, GB)

KAHN, CHARLES, was born **KARL KAHN** on 20 March 1881 at *Schirrhoffen*, Bas-Rhin, France to **HEYMANN KAHN** and his wife, **MARIE** née **KAHN**, both natives of the town. Sixteen-year-old Charles Kahn arrived in New York from Le Havre, France, on 4 September 1897 aboard the SS *La Touraine*. He and his brothers **GUSTAVE** and **SELIGMANN "SOL" KAHN** (See entries) owned and operated dry goods stores in Rayne, Acadia Parish, LA and in Kahns, West Baton Rouge, Parish, LA. Charles married HATTIE LOEB, a Louisiana native, ca. 1907, a record for which we were not able to find. He maintained a permanent residence in Rayne where his two children: Sigmund (b. 1908) and Dorothy (b. 1914) were raised. Hattie died on 25 May 1928 and was buried in the Jewish Cemetery in Baton Rouge, East Baton Rouge Parish, LA. Charles died on 24 February 1933 and was buried with her.(**A, AN, F, GB**)

KAHN, DANIEL "DAN," was born on 2 November 1862 in *Schirrhoffen*, Bas-Rhin, France, to **HERMANN KAHN** and his wife **JULIE LEVY**, both natives of the town. Daniel arrived in New York on 4 December 1879 from Le Havre, France, aboard the SS *Labrador*. He journeyed to Galveston, Galveston Co., TX where he was employed as a grocery clerk starting at the age of seventeen. Dan moved to Baton Rouge, East Baton Rouge Parish, LA, at the turn of the twentieth century to be near family members. He was naturalized there on 19 March 1902 as "Dan Kohn." Dan was hired as a salesman and manager at Farrnbacher Dry Goods Co, by Jacob Farrnbacher, his brother Charles' father-in-law. Dan never married. He worked for Farrnbacher's Dry Goods until he died of heart failure on 4 December 1930. He was buried next to Charles in the Jewish Cemetery in Baton Rouge. Note: See entries for **CHARLES** and **GABRIEL KAHN**. (A, AN, G, GB)

KAHN, DANIEL, was born on 21 February 1889 in *Brumath*, Bas-Rhin, France, to **LEOPOLD KAHN** (See entry), a native of *Brumath*, Bas-Rhin, France, and his wife, **FANNY** née **KAHN**, born in *Schirrhoffen*, Bas-Rhin. According to his 1914 application for a U.S. passport, Daniel indicated that he had immigrated to America in August 1904 aboard the SS *Kaiser Wilhelm II*. We were unable to verify this using available ship's records. Daniel started out working for his uncle, **GABRIEL KAHN** (See entry), in Brusly, West Baton Rouge Parish, LA. He accompanied fellow Alsatian, **EMANUEL LEVY** (See entry), on a trip to Alsace in 1914 to visit relatives, just in time to get caught up in the furor of the start of World War I. In 1915 he and his brother, **JULES KAHN** (See entry) opened their first store in Baton Rouge, East Baton Rouge Parish, LA, Kahn Dry Goods, (with Gents' furnishings and shoes) on Third and North Blvd. In 1918 their brother, **PAUL KAHN** (See entry), who had been working in New Orleans, Orleans Parish, LA, joined them. In 1920 the three brothers were all still unmarried. They roomed together in Baton Rouge. Eventually Daniel went to work for Weill Wholesale Dry Goods, then the Bart-Well Company. At the age of fifty-nine he married Fanny Kaufmann, a fifty year old Baton Rouge native, the widow of GUSTAV BRAUN, a Swiss physician and Baton Rouge shoe entrepreneur. Dan and Fannie were wed on 3 April 1948. Dan died on 7 January 1957 in Baton Rouge and was buried there in the Jewish Cemetery. Engraved on his tombstone is the information that he served as a Corporal in the 64th Field Artillery, World War I. Fannie Braun Kahn died on 26 November

1976 in Baton Rouge and was buried there in the Jewish Cemetery with her first husband. **(A, AN, G, GB)**

KAHN, DELPHINE, (*Schirrhoffen*) See entry for **LAZARE EHRSTEIN**

KAHN, EMANUEL, was born **EMMANUEL KAHN** on 6 July 1858 in *Romanswiller*, Bas-Rhin, France, to **SAMUEL KAHN** and his wife, **FANNY ROOS**, both natives of the town. Emanuel immigrated to America either in 1875 or in 1878, dates reported in two successive federal census enumerations. We were not able to find a reliable ship's record for his arrival in the United States. He joined his brother, **SOLOMON KAHN** (See entry), in St. James Parish, LA, where he remained for the rest of his life. Emmanuel married MINNIE LEVY, a native of Louisiana, on 12 July 1882 at Minerva Hall in New Orleans, Orleans Parish, LA. He and his bride travelled to Belmont (Plantation) St. James Parish, LA, where he operated a general merchandise store. Since the 1850s Belmont, originally owned by the Louis LeBourgeois family, had been a large sugar plantation on the Mississippi River. Emmanuel and Minnie were the parents of eight children: Samuel (b. 1883) Emilie (b. 1884), Benjamin (b. 1886), Moïse (b. 1889), Edna (b. 1890), Hester (b. 1891), Gertrude (b. 1895), and Alvin (b. 1896). The 1910 federal census for St. James Parish reported Emmanuel's occupation as "farmer," and that of his three sons as clerks in a general store. Emanuel died at Belmont on 12 January 1918. He was interred at Hebrew Rest Cemetery #2 in New Orleans. After his death, Minnie moved to New Orleans, where she was enumerated in the 1920 federal census with three of her children: Alvin, a "cotton farmer," Benjamin, who worked as a dry goods merchant, and Edna. Minnie Levy Kahn died on 7 July 1925 and was buried in Hebrew Rest Cemetery # 2 with her husband. Note: Emmanuel Kahn was the nephew of **MARY ROOS STRAUSS** (See entry for **BERNARD STRAUSS**) **(A, AN, GB, TT)**

KAHN, FANNIE was born on 17 January 1857 in *Schirrhoffen*, Bas-Rhin, France, to **ALEXANDRE KAHN** and his wife **JUDITH**, née **KAHN**, both natives of the town. Fannie, who had never married, immigrated to Baton Rouge, East Baton Rouge Parish, LA, to live with her widowed brother, **HENRY COHN** (See entry), ca. 1920, a record for which we were unable to locate. She died on 25 March 1948 and was buried in the Jewish Cemetery in Baton Rouge. **(A, AN, G)**

KAHN, FANNY, was born on 27 January 1874 in *Hatten*, Bas-Rhin, France, to CHARLES KAHN, a native of Heidelberg, Baden, Germany, and his wife, **HANNAH/HENRIETTE WELSCH** (See entry), born in *Schirrhoffen*, Bas-Rhin. Fanny probably came to Louisiana with her mother ca. 1893, a date which was given for their immigration in the 1910 federal census for Algiers, Orleans Parish, La. We were unable, however, to find a reliable record for their arrival. Fanny married JULIUS BODENGER, a native of Austria, in New Orleans, Orleans Parish, LA, on 30 January 1899. Julius was a tinsmith and master plumber who lived and worked in Algiers, Orleans Parish, LA. The couple had two children: Charles (b. 1899) and Harry (b. 1909). In 1931 the citizens of Algiers paid tribute to Julius Bodenger for having bought and developed the subdivision of Elmwood, which once had been a water-soaked jungle. Fanny's mother **HANNAH/ HENRIETTE WELSCH** (See entry) lived with the couple in Algiers. Fanny died on 23 November 1932 and was buried near her mother in Gates of Prayer Cemetery # 2 (Joseph Street) in New Orleans. Her husband, JULIUS BODENGER, who died on 22 November 1937 in Algiers, was buried there as well. (See entries for Fanny's brothers, **HENRY**, **LEON** and **LOUIS KAHN**) **(A, AN, G)**

KAHN, FÉLIX, (*Niederroedern*), See entry for **FELIX CAHN**.

KAHN, FÉLIX, was born on 21 November 1858 in *Schweighouse-sur-Moder*, Bas-Rhin, France, to **JACQUES SCHILLEN/SIMON KAHN**, a native of the town, and his wife **GIDEL/GERTRUDE HIRSCH**, born in *Batzendorf*, Bas-Rhin. He emigrated from Le Havre, France, to New York, aboard the SS *Amérique*, arriving on 4 October 1880. Felix settled in Plaquemine, Iberville Parish, LA, where he worked as a clerk in a dry goods store. He married HENRIETTA LEVY, a native of Louisiana, on 14 July 1886 in Donaldsonville, Ascension Parish, LA. They were the parents of one son and two daughters: Simon (b. 1887), Miriam (b. 1889) and Ray (b.1893). After the couple moved to Donaldsonville ca. 1890, Félix worked as a commercial traveler. At the time of the 1910 federal census, Félix and his family were still living together in Donaldsonville. The head of household was employed as a salesman in a local hat store. Henriette died on 23 February 1913 and was buried in Hebrew Rest Cemetery #2 in New Orleans, Orleans Parish, La. Felix moved permanently to New Orleans after his wife's death. He lived on Cadiz Street with his two unmarried daughters for the rest of his life. Felix found work as a salesman for a wholesale millinery house He died on 27 September 1937 and was interred next to his wife in Hebrew Rest Cemetery #2 in New Orleans. Note: Two of his applications for a U.S. passport to travel to France show his birthplace incorrectly as Lunéville, France. Fortunately his 1900 passport application gave his correct place of birth.(**A, AN, G, GB**)

KAHN, GABRIEL, was born on 27 December 1868 at *Schirrhoffen*, Bas-Rhin, France, to **HERMANN KAHN** and his wife **JULIE LEVY**, both natives of the town. According to his naturalization record, he immigrated to Louisiana in 1888. There is an entry for a Gabriel Kahn, who arrived on 16 July 1888 in New York from Le Havre, France, aboard the SS *La Champagne* which may be his record, although his destination was listed as "Kentucky." He joined his brother, **CHARLES KAHN** (See entry), at Brusly Landing, West Baton Rouge Parish, LA. where he was naturalized on 27 September 1899. Gabriel married JEANNE MOYSE in 1903, the sister of HENRIETTE MOYSE who had married **LEOPOLD SOMMER** (See entry), another *Schirrhoffen* native, the previous year. Two children were born to the couple: Armand (b. 1905) and Lucille Fay (1908) at Brusly Landing. Gabe and his family moved to Baton Rouge, East Baton Rouge Parish, LA, before 1920 where he worked as a dry goods merchant and became the manager of the Dixie Mercantile Co. Towards the end of his life he was employed as a salesman for Welsh & Levy. His wife, Jeanne, died on 15 June 1938 in Baton Rouge and was buried there in the Jewish Cemetery. Gabriel Kahn died on 23 May 1939 at Baton Rouge and was buried beside her. (**A, AN, G, GB**)

KAHN, GUSTAVE "Gus," was born **GUSTAV KAHN** on 8 March 1877 at *Schirrhoffen*, Bas-Rhin, France, to **HEYMANN KAHN** and his wife, **MARIE** née **KAHN**, both natives of the town. He followed his younger brother, **CHARLES KAHN** (See entry), to Louisiana in 1892 according to information he gave at the time of the 1920 federal census. An entry for a nineteen-year-old [sic] Gustave Kahn who arrived in New York from Le Havre, France, on 27 November 1893 on board the SS *La Bretagne*, and whose destination was New Orleans, is likely his record. Gustave and Charles Kahn were partners in dry goods stores in both Acadia and West Baton Rouge Parishes. Gus travelled for their establishment, but could usually be found at Kahns, West Baton Rouge Parish, living with relatives. In 1900 he lived alone and managed the general store at Kahns. In 1910 he was a salesman for the store, staying with his cousin, **LEOPOLD KAHN** (See entry), at Kahns. In 1920 he was living with another cousin, **SIMON LEVY** (See Entry), next door to his half-sister **MARGUERITE KAHN SOMMER** (See Entry), still at Kahns. He was naturalized in June of that year at East Baton Rouge Parish, LA. Gus was enumerated in the 1930 federal census at Rayne, Acadia Parish, LA, while on a selling trip. He was staying at the Commercial Hotel. Gus never married. He died after a week's illness at Rayne, Acadia Parish, LA, on 3 November 1940. He and his brother, **SELIGMANN "SOL" KAHN** (See entry), share a double headstone in the Jewish Cemetery in Baton Rouge, East Baton Rouge Parish, LA. **(A, AN, G, GB)**

KAHN, HENRI, *(Schirrhoffen)* See entry for **HENRY COHN, JR**.

KAHN, HENRIETTE, *(Brumath)* See entry for **MARCUS FEIST**

KAHN, HENRY, was born **HEINRICH CAHN** on 21 August 1870 in *Hatten*, Bas-Rhin, France, to **CHARLES KAHN**, a native of Heidelberg, Baden, Germany, and his wife, **HANNAH/HENRIETTE WELSCH** (See entry), born in *Schirrhoffen*, Bas-Rhin, France. He and his brothers, **LOUIS** and **LEON KAHN** (See entries), arrived in Louisiana, ca. 1890. We could not find a likely record for his arrival in the United States. Henry worked as a clerk and peddler in the lower parishes south of New Orleans, Orleans Parish, LA, for a decade before settling down. In 1900 Henry, still unmarried, was living with his brother, Louis, in Labadieville, Assumption Parish, LA, where they were both merchants. They joined their brother, Leon, in Morgan City, St. Mary Parish, LA, ca. 1903 where they all worked in the dry goods business. Henry married **BERTHA LEVY** in New Orleans, on 17 September 1902. She was a native of Grand Coteau, St. Landry Parish, LA. They were the parents of three children: Charles (b. 1904), Hannah (b. 1908) and Mose Dave (b. 1912). Henry was a dry goods merchant in Morgan City for the rest of his life. He died on 1 February 1937 at his home in Morgan City. He was buried the next day in the Morgan City Cemetery and Mausoleum. His wife, Bertha, died on 5 October 1937 at Touro Infirmary in New Orleans. Her remains were brought back to Morgan City, where they were interred with those of her husband. **(A, AN, G, GB)**

KAHN, HERMAN HENRY, was born on 4 April 1887 in *La Walck*, Bas-Rhin, France, to **SIMON KAHN**, a native of the town and

VALERIE KAHN (See entry), born in *Schirrhoffen*, Bas-Rhin. Herman immigrated to New York aboard the SS *La Savoie* from Le Havre, France, on 19 March 1904 and came to Louisiana where he settled in Clayton, Concordia Parish, LA. He became a successful merchant and planter in the parish. He married twenty-two year old LOIS EASTIN MORRIS, a native of Sicily Island, Catahoula Parish, LA, in an Episcopal ceremony in Baton Rouge, East Baton Rouge Parish, LA, on 14 August 1938. The couple had one child, Miriam, born in 1940. Herman was naturalized at Monroe, Ouachita Parish, LA on 20 April 1939. He died on 6 July 1961 in Concordia Parish, LA, and was buried in Natchez City Cemetery, Natchez, Adams Co., MS, near his mother, VALERIE KAHN KAHN and other members of his family. **(A, AN, G, GB, TT)**

KAHN, HYPOLITE, (*Schirrhoffen*) See entry for **HYPOLITE COHN**

KAHN, ISAAC, was born on 22 October 1839 in *Waltenheim-sur-Zorn*, Bas-Rhin, France, to **LÉON/LION/LOEWEL KAHN**, a native of the town, and his wife HANNA LEVI, born in Biesheim, Haut-Rhin, France. Isaac was last enumerated with his family in *Waltenheim-sur-Zorn* in the 1856 town census. He may have been the eighteen-year-old [*sic*] Isaac Kahn, a French immigrant, who arrived in New York from Le Havre, France, on 18 July 1859 aboard the ship *Zurich*. Sources report that he and his brothers, **RAPHAEL** and **JULIUS KAHN** (See entries), were in business in Savannah, GA, before coming to Shreveport, Caddo Parish, LA, shortly before the start of the Civil War. Isaac served as a Sergeant in Co. K, 24th LA Infantry, Crescent Regiment (Sumter Rifles) throughout the War and was paroled at Natchitoches, Natchitoches Parish, LA, in June 1865. He returned to Shreveport to marry FANNIE CAHN, a native of Chicot Co., AR, ca. 1865, a record for which we were unable to find. Their first child, Bernard Benjamin was born in 1866. Isaac and his brothers operated Kahn & Bros., a very successfully mercantile business in Shreveport. Three more children were born to Isaac and Fannie: Cécile (b. 1868), Léon (b. 1870), and Arthur T. (b. 1872), before Isaac died in a yellow fever epidemic on 24 October 1873. He was buried at Shreveport in Hebrew Rest Cemetery # 1 (Jewish Section of Oakland Cemetery), along with his first born son, Bernard, who had succumbed on 19 September 1873 to the same disease which had swept Shreveport that year. Fannie Cahn Kahn remained in Shreveport to raise her children.

She was joined by her brother, Adolph, also an Arkansas native, who became a successful cotton broker in town. Fannie died on 11 Nov 1890 and was buried in Hebrew Rest Cemetery # 2 (Texas Ave.) in Shreveport. (**A, AN, G**)

KAHN, JOSEPH, (*Schirrhoffe*n) See entry for **JOSEPH COHN**

KAHN, JULES, was born **JULIUS KAHN** on 14 August 1887 in *Brumath*, Bas-Rhin, France, to **LEOPOLD KAHN** (See entry), a native of *Brumath*, Bas-Rhin, France, and his wife, **FANNY** née **KAHN**, born in *Schirrhoffen*, Bas-Rhin. Fifteen-year-old Jules Kahn immigrated to America, arriving in New York on 2 September 1902 aboard the SS *Kaiser Wilhelm der Grosse*. He went to work for his uncle, **GABRIEL KAHN** (See entry), as a clerk, and lived with the family in Brusly Landing, West Baton Rouge Parish, LA. He enlisted and served in the American Army during World War I. Upon return he joined his brothers, **DANIEL** and **PAUL KAHN** (See entries) in Baton Rouge, East Baton Rouge Parish, LA, where they roomed together and worked as dry goods merchants in their own establishment, Kahn Dry Goods Co. He married MARIE LEVY, a Mississippi native, on 20 September 1921 at her parents' home in Port Gibson, Claiborne Co. MS. By the time of the 1930 federal census he was enumerated as having been confined to the United States Veteran's Hospital in Gulfport, Harrison Co., MS, where he died on 9 February 1944. His body was returned to Baton Rouge, where it was interred there in the Jewish Cemetery. (**A, AN, G, GB**).

KAHN, JULIUS, was born **DAVID KAHN** on 10 April 1835 in *Waltenheim-sur-Zorn,* Bas-Rhin, France, to **LÉON/LION/LOEWEL KAHN**, a native of the town, and his wife HANNA LEVI, born in Biesheim, Haut-Rhin, France. Although he is consistently listed as David in the 1836, 1841 and 1851 censuses for *Waltenheim*, he is the only age appropriate person who could be Julius from that town, and a brother to both **ISAAC** and **RAPHAEL KAHN** (See entries). Since he, of the four brothers who came to America, was the only one absent from the family at the time of the 1856 town census taken at *Waltenheim*, we assume that he had already immigrated in preparation for the arrival of his younger brothers. We could find no reliable record for his arrival.Sources report that he and his brothers were in business in Savannah, GA before coming to Shreveport, Caddo Parish, Louisiana, before the Civil War in which Julius served as a Private in

Co. G, 3rd (Harrison's) LA Cavalry, the "Red River Rangers." He was paroled in Shreveport at the end of the war in 1865. Julius married CAROLINE/CARRIE MAYER/MEYER, in New Orleans, Orleans Parish, LA, on 5 October 1866 Carrie was born in Harrisonburg, Catahoula Parish, LA on 21 January 1848. Julius returned to Shreveport to work at the Kahn & Bros. mercantile business. Four children were born to the couple: Lazare (b. 1867), Raphael (b. 1869), Celestine (b. 1871; died 1872), and Leon B. (b. 1873), before Julius died on 11 September 1873 of yellow fever. He was buried in Hebrew Rest Cemetery # 1 (Jewish Section of Oakland Cemetery), near his baby daughter, Celestine. His widow, Caroline, married EMANUEL J. LEMAN, a native of Lyon, France, on 18 May 1880, had four more children, and continued to live in Shreveport. She died on 26 Jan 1907 and was buried there with her second husband in Hebrew Rest Cemetery # 2 (Texas Ave.). **(A, AN, G.)**

KAHN, LEHMAN, was born **LEHMANN KAHN** on 1 July 1879 in *Schirrhoffen*, Bas-Rhin, France, to **DANIEL KAHN** and his wife, **FANNY HIRSCH**, both natives of the town. He immigrated to the United States with his brother **LUCIEN LIPPMAN KAHN**, born **LUCIAN KAHN**, on 20 March 1877. They arrived in New York on 11 May 1895 aboard the SS *La Touraine*. The brothers were enumerated in the same Manhattan, New York household, in the 1900 federal census. Lucien's name was erroneously reported as "Lucille." Twenty-one-year-old Lehman was a dry goods clerk and twenty-three-year-old "Lucille" was a clerk for a wholesale clothing company. According to Lehman's 1922 application for a United States passport he spent at least six years in New York and was naturalized there on 3 August 1901. Shortly thereafter he and his brother headed south to Louisiana. Lehman and Lucien were the nephews of **JOSEPH COHN, JR**. (See entry) who had settled in Convent, St. James Parish, LA, and later in New Orleans, Orleans Parish, LA. According to Lucien's 1920 application for a United States passport, he spent time in Louisiana, although there are no civil records to document it. Lucien moved on to Fort Smith, Sebastian Co., AR, and was naturalized there on 7 December 1908. Lehman stayed in Louisiana, at least through World War I. When he signed for the draft in 1918, he was working in Houma, Terrebonne Parish, LA, as a clerk at **JULIEN** and **MAURICE JOSEPH**'s Leader Store. (See entries). When Lehman applied for his U.S. passport in 1922, he was living in Baton Rouge, East Baton Rouge Parish, LA. Another cousin from *Schirrhoffen*, **DANIEL KAHN** (See entry), signed his passport application as a witness. Daniel Kahn worked as a clerk for the Farrnbacher Dry Goods Co. It is presumed that Lehman was working there as a clerk as well. Not long after that Lehman reunited with his brother in Fort Smith, AR. Lehman died on 2 February 1927 in Pulaski Co., AR, and was interred in the Jewish Cemetery at Fort Smith. Lucien died just over a year later on 8 August 1928 and was buried there as well. Neither brother ever married. Note: Entries for Lucien and Lehman at *Findagrave.com* show them erroneously as husband and wife. (**A, AN, G**)

KAHN, LEON, was born **LEOPOLD KAHN** on 31 March 1867 in *Hatten*, Bas-Rhin, France, to **CHARLES KAHN**, a native of Baden, Germany, and his wife, **HANNAH/HENRIETTE WELSCH** (See entry), born in *Schirrhoffen*, Bas-Rhin France. He immigrated to Louisiana, ca. 1886, and worked as a clerk and peddler in and around New Orleans, Orleans Parish, LA, and the lower parishes, with his brothers, **LOUIS** and **HENRY KAHN** (See entries). We believe that the record for a twenty-year-old Leon Kahn, a native of Germany, who immigrated to America from Liverpool, England, arriving in New York on 26 November 1887 is worthy of consideration. Leon married MATHILDE/TILLIE LOEB, a Louisiana native, on 29 October 1899 in Lafourche Parish, LA. The couple settled near Live Oak Plantation in the parish where Leon worked as a grocer. By 1903 the couple had moved with their only child, Charles (b. 1902), to Morgan City, St. Mary Parish, LA, where Leon was a dry goods merchant and where he was naturalized on 22 September of that year. Leon died on 23 February 1922 in Morgan City and was buried in the Morgan City Cemetery and Mausoleum. His wife, who continued to live in Morgan City and to run the family business, died there on 18 July 1958. She was buried with her husband in the local cemetery. (**A, N, G, GB**)

KAHN, LEOPOLD, was born on 13 April 1860 in *Brumath*, Bas-Rhin, France, to **ARON ISAAC KAHN,** born in *Mommenheim*, Bas-Rhin, and his wife**, RACHEL BLUM**, a native of *Hatten*, Bas-Rhin. He married **FANNY KAHN** on 18 August 1886 in *Brumath.* Fanny was born on 9 August 1859 in *Schirrhoffen*, Bas-Rhin, France, to **HERMANN KAHN** and his wife, **JULIE LEVY**, both natives of *Schirrhoffen*, Bas-Rhin. Leopold's bride, Fanny, was the sister of **DANIEL, CHARLES** and **GABRIEL KAHN**, all eventually residents of Baton Rouge, East Baton Rouge Parish, LA. Leopold and Fanny's four sons, **JULES, DANIEL, PAUL,** and **ARMAND KAHN** (See individual entries) all immigrated to Louisiana. Sixty-year-old Leopold Kahn arrived in New York on 13 March 1921, from Le Havre, France, aboard the SS *France*, accompanied by his son, Armand, in time for the wedding of another son, Jules, to Marie Levy. Leopold appeared in the 1930 federal census, living as a roomer in the MAAS household in Baton Rouge, East Baton Rouge Parish, LA. His occupation was listed as retired real estate salesman. He died on 23 May 1937 in Baton Rouge and was buried there in the Jewish Cemetery. (**A, AN, G, GB**)

KAHN, LIPPMAN/LEOPOLD, was born **LEMANN KAHN** on 16 November 1812 in *Riedseltz*, Bas-Rhin, France, to **ABRAHAM ARYEH KAHN** a native of the town, and his wife HANNE TRAUTMANN, born in Busenberg, Germany. Leopold immigrated to New Orleans, Orleans Parish, LA, ca. 1845, a reliable record for which we were unable to find. He married **FLEURETTE/FLORENCE GOUDCHAUX** there on 31 July 1849. Fleurette was born **PHILIPPINE GUTSCHO** on 13 February 1830 in *Brumath*, Bas-Rhin, France, to **JACQUES GOUDCHAUX/GUTSCHO**, a native of *Brumath*, Bas-Rhin, and his wife, **BARBE LEVI**, born in *Niederbronn-les-Bains*, Bas-Rhin. Fleurette's sister, Esther, was married to Lippman's brother **SAMUEL KAHN** (See entry). Fleurette arrived in New Orleans, Orleans Parish, LA, just a month before her marriage, as "Philippina Couchout"on 25 June 1849 aboard the ship *J.H. Glidden* out of Le Havre, France. The couple were the parents of seven children: Henriette (b. 1853), Mervine (b. 1855), Belle (b. 1860), Médar (b. 1862), Abraham (b. 1864; died 1866), Jacob (b. 1866), and Alfred (b. 1867). Originally in partnership with his brother, Samuel Kahn, in Plaquemine, Iberville Parish, LA, Leopold remained there with his family after Samuel's departure to New Orleans. In the 1880s he moved his family to Rayne, Acadia Parish, LA where he opened up a business which was eventually taken over by his sons, Mervine and Alfred. Fleurette Kahn died in Rayne on 30 March 1887 and was buried in the Jewish Cemetery at Plaquemine, Iberville Parish, LA. Lippman died on 11 August 1894. He was interred at the Jewish Cemetery in Lafayette, Lafayette Parish, LA. (**A, AN, G, TT**)

KAHN, LOUIS, was born on 31 December 1868 in *Hatten*, Bas-Rhin, France, to CHARLES KAHN, a native of Heidelberg, Baden, Germany, and his wife, **HANNAH/HENRIETTE WELSCH** (See entry), born in *Schirrhoffen*, Bas-Rhin France. He and his brothers, **HENRY** and **LEON KAHN**(See entries), arrived in Louisiana in the mid-1880s. We believe that eighteen-year-old Louis Kahn, a male butcher, whose destination was New Orleans, Orleans Parish, LA, arrived in New York on 24 January 1887 aboard the SS *La Bourgogne*. He worked with his brothers as a clerk and peddler in the lower parishes south of New Orleans for a decade before settling down. In 1900 Louis, still unmarried, was living with his brother, Henry, in Labadieville, Assumption Parish, LA, where they were both merchants. They joined their brother, Leon, in Morgan City, St. Mary Parish, LA, ca. 1903 where they all worked in the dry goods business. Louis married AGNES LEBLANC, a non-Jewish Louisiana native, on 21 November 1910 in Morgan City. They had one child, Selma Rae (b. 1912). Louis died two years later on 6 December 1914 and was buried in the Morgan City Cemetery and Mausoleum. His wife and daughter continued to live in Morgan City, with the exception of several years when Agnes accompanied Selma Rae to Natchitoches, Natchitoches Parish, LA, where the latter attended the Natchitoches Normal School to train as a teacher. The two women then returned to Morgan City, where Selma was worked in the local school district for forty-three years. We were unable to find a date of death or place of burial for Agnes LeBlanc Kahn. (**A, AN, G, GB**)

KAHN, LUCIEN LIPPMAN, (*Schirrhoffen*) See entry for **LEHMAN KAHN**

KAHN, MARGUERITE, (*Schirrhoffen*) See entry for **SYLVAN SOMMER**

KAHN, MARIE, *(Brumath)* See entry for **AARON KAHN**

KAHN, MATHIAS, was born **MATZ KAHN** on 28 June 1805 in *Osthoffen*, Bas-Rhin, France, to HIRSCH KAHN, born in Bodersweier, Baden, Germany and his wife **BESSEL DREYFUS**, a native of *Osthoffen*, Bas-Rhin. He immigrated to America, arriving in New Orleans, Orleans Parish, LA, on 30 October 1845 from Le Havre, France, aboard the ship *Viola*. Mathias started out in St. James Parish, working as a dry goods merchant. He married AMALIA/EMMA SALOMON ca. 1855, a record for which we were unable to find. Amelia was born on 27 June 1835 in Kurweiler, Rheinpfalz, Germany. Matz and Amalia were enumerated in Brashear City (now Morgan City), St. Mary Parish, LA in the 1860 federal census with two children: Mathilde (b. 1859) and Eugene (b. 1860). Isaac Solomon, who may have been Emma's brother, born about 1830 was also enumerated in the household. Mathias and Emma were enumerated in the 1870 federal census for Brashear City with two more children: Simon (b. 1863) and Blanche (b. 1868; See entry for **LEON LEMMEL**). Amalia died on 1 September 1877 and was buried in the Hebrew Cemetery in Berwick, St. Mary Parish, LA. Mathias died two years later on 20 April 1879 and was buried in the same cemetery. The couple's twenty-two-year-old son Eugene died on 16 June 1882 and was buried there as well. (**A, AN, G**)

KAHN. MOÏSE, was born on 28 February 1848 in *Waltenheim-sur-Zorn*, Bas-Rhin, France, to **LÉON/LION/LOEWEL KAHN**, a native of the town, and his wife HANNA LEVI, born in Biesheim, Haut-Rhin, France. According to his naturalization record filed at Shreveport, Caddo Parish, LA, on 4 October 1872, he immigrated to Louisiana in 1865, a likely record for which we were unable to find. He joined his brothers, **ISAAC**, **RAPHAEL** and **JULIUS KAHN** (See entries), and his uncle **SIMON KAHN** (See entry), in Shreveport where he was a clerk in Kahn & Bros. Moïse was one of two family members to survive the 1873 yellow fever epidemic which laid waste to the residents of that city. He left Shreveport to marry SARAH HOLLANDER, a native of New Orleans, Orleans Parish, LA, in the city on 20 October 1875. They had two children: Naomi (b. 1877) and Ruth (b. 1879), the latter of whom was born in Texas where the couple had relocated. The marriage fell apart and Sarah returned from Texas to New Orleans with her children to live with her sister Annette and her husband, **ISAAC DAHLMANN** (See entry). Moïse moved to San Francisco, San Francisco Co., CA, where he worked in real estate, later becoming an insurance agent. He married a second time, to SARAH GOLDSTEIN in 1890, about whom nothing is known. He was arrested on 31 December of the same year, for embezzling from his employer, the Northwestern Life Insurance Co., where he had been a travelling agent for them. On 27 January 1891 he attempted suicide by asphyxiation in a rented hotel room. He stuffed all the cracks in the windows and under the doors, turned on the gas jets, and waited to die. He was found unconscious and taken to the hospital but not expected to live. Moïse was traced to California, and sorted out from another Moïse Kahn living in the area, by the San Francisco voter registration rolls for 1888 and 1890 which listed his place of naturalization as Shreveport, LA. He died on 29 January 1891 in San Francisco and was buried at Home of Peace Cemetery in Colma, San Mateo Co., CA. Sarah

Hollander Kahn was killed on 10 October 1907 in New Orleans when she was thrown from the horse-drawn buggy she was driving after the animal bolted and ran wildly through the streets. She was buried at Hebrew Rest Cemetery #2 in the city. (**A, AN, GB, TT**)

KAHN, PAUL, was born on 5 January 1891 in *Brumath*, Bas-Rhin, France, to **LEOPOLD KAHN** (See entry), a native of *Brumath*, Bas-Rhin, France, and his wife, **FANNY** née **KAHN**, born in *Schirrhoffen*, Bas-Rhin. Seventeen-year-old Paul Kahn emigrated from Cherbourg, France, to New York, arriving on 7 July 1908 aboard the SS *Kronprinz Wilhelm*. He worked as a travelling salesman and ultimately a clerk for Louis Goldstein & Co., in New Orleans, Orleans Parish, LA. In 1918 he joined his brothers, **JULES** and **DANIEL KAHN** (See entries) at Kahn Bros. and Kahn Dry Goods Co. in Baton Rouge, East Baton Rouge Parish, LA. He married GOLDIE TOBIAS, a Baton Rouge native, on 14 March 1920 at the Hotel Gruenwald (now Hotel Roosevelt), in New Orleans. Their marriage was short and without issue. She died suddenly on 15 September 1926 while on vacation in Memphis, Shelby Co., TN. Paul died three years later on 2 November 1929 in Baton Rouge. He and Goldie were buried there in the Jewish Cemetery. (**A, AN, G, GB**)

KAHN, RAPHAEL, was born on 8 May 1843 in *Waltenheim-sur-Zorn*, Bas-Rhin, France, to **LÉON/LION/LOEWEL KAHN**, a native of the town, and his wife HANNA LEVI, born in Biesheim, Haut-Rhin, France. Raphaël last appeared in a *Waltenheim-sur-Zorn* town census with his family in 1856. We believe that seventeen-year-old Raphael Kahn (transcribed in error as Raphael "Fahn") arrived at New Orleans, Orleans Parish, LA, from Le Havre, France, on 21 December 1860 aboard the ship *Lemuel Dyer*. Raphaël served in the Civil War on the state level with Bickham's Company, the Caddo Militia, while working for his brothers, **ISAAC** and **JULIUS** KAHN (See entries) in the Kahn & Bros. firm in Shreveport, Caddo Parish, LA. In 1870 he was enumerated with his younger brother, **MOÏSE KAHN** (See entry), who had arrived just after the Civil War, to work as a clerk for Kahn & Bros. After the deaths of his brothers, Isaac and Julius, and his uncle, **SIMON KAHN** (See entry), Raphael applied for a passport to return to France in April 1877. Upon his return from Europe he moved to New York. He married ANNIE HIRSCHHORN, a native of the state, on 21 June 1881. Their daughter, Frances C. Kahn, was born the next year. Raphael died in New York on 19 May 1911. He was buried in Beth

Olam Jewish Cemetery in Ridgewood, Queens Co., NY. **(A, AN, E, I, TT)**

KAHN, REINE, was born **REGINA KAHN** on 6 March 1888 at *Schirrhoffen*, Bas-Rhin, France, to **HEYMANN KAHN,** a native of the town, and his second wife, **RACHEL DREYFUSS**. We have found no reliable record of her entry into the United States. She may have followed her sister, **MARGUERITE KAHN** (See entry), who settled in Louisiana in 1905. Twenty-year-old Reine Kahn died very soon after her arrival in Baton Rouge, East Baton Rouge Parish, LA, on 29 August 1908 and was buried there with other family members in the Jewish Cemetery. **(A, G)**

KAHN, SAMUEL, was born **SCHMULEN KAHN** on 21 July 1815 to **ABRAHAM ARYEH KAHN,** a native of *Riedseltz*, Bas-Rhin, France, and his wife HANNE TRAUTMANN, born in Busenberg, Germany. Samuel immigrated to New Orleans, Orleans Parish, LA, ca. 1839, according to his 1851 naturalization document. We could not find a likely record for this early immigration. He married **ESTHER GOUDCHAUX** on 20 March 1848 in New Orleans. Esther was born **ESTHER GUTSCHOU** on 22 September 1825 in *Brumath*, Bas-Rhin, France to **JACQUES GOUDCHAUX/GUTSCHOU**, a native of the town, and his first wife **BARBE LEVI**, born in *Niederbronn-les-Bains*, Bas-Rhin, France. We could not find a likely immigration for Esther into the United States. Samuel settled with his wife Esther, their first child, Emile Jean (b. 1848), and his brother **LIPPMAN/LEOPOLD KAHN,** in Plaquemine, Iberville Parish, LA, where they opened up a thriving dry goods business. Seven more children were born to Samuel and Esther: Palmyra (b. 1850), Max (b. 1851), Hortense (b. 1853), Helvena (b. 1857), Henry (b. 1859),and Aaron (b. 1860). Their last child, Avery Sylvester, was born back in New Orleans in 1865 where the family had relocated during the Civil War. Samuel worked in New Orleans for almost forty years, first in the dry goods business, later as a dealer of wholesale shoes. Esther died on 10 October 1887 in New Orleans and Samuel followed on 1 July 1898. They were both buried there in Hebrew Rest Cemetery # 1. **(A, AN, G, GB, TT)**

KAHN, SELIGMAN, was born **LEMANN KAHN** on 21 November 1834 in *Riedseltz*, Bas-Rhin, France, to LAMBERT KAHN, a native of Busenberg, Rheinpfalz, Germany, and his second wife, HANNA HAENCHEN, born in Albersweiler, Rheinpfalz. Seligman Kahn immigrated between 1851, when he was enumerated with his family in *Riedseltz*, and 1856, when the census that year showed that he was no longer living there. We were unable to find a reliable record for his arrival into the United States. Upon his death in 1888, an obituary which appeared in the New Orleans *Daily Picayune* indicated that he had been a resident of Louisiana for 33 years, putting his arrival ca. 1855.He may have been the "Solomon" Kahn enumerated in the 1860 federal census for Plaquemine, Iberville Parish, LA, who was a twenty-five-year-old butcher from France. His participation as a private in the 3rd Regiment, Louisiana Infantry, Company "A," the Iberville Greys, during the American Civil War, however, is incontrovertible. Recorded variously as S. Kohn, S. Kahn, and Selamon Kahn, he enlisted on 17 May 1861 in New Orleans, Orleans Parish, LA. He fought with his unit and was wounded on 14 June 1863 while in the trenches during the siege at Vicksburg, Warren Co., MS. He was captured after the Union Army took control of the town on 4 July 1863 and was paroled and sent back to Louisiana on 16 July 1863. He took out a license to marry **PAULINE DAHLMANN,** the widow of Aaron Seligman**,** on 12 December 1864 in New Orleans. Pauline was born on 28 February 1840 in *Surbourg*, Bas-Rhin, France, to **HIRTZ DALHMANN**, a native of the town, and his wife **ELIZABETH/LISETTE GOUDCHAUX**, born in *Brumath*, Bas-Rhin. Eighteen-year-old Pauline Dahlmann immigrated to Louisiana on board the ship *Gulf Stream* which arrived in New Orleans on 7 June 1858, accompanied by her much younger thirteen-year-old half-uncle **LEOPOLD GOUDCHAUX** (See entry), and half-aunt, Adèle Goudchaux. (Note: Adèle married JACOB FIES, a native of *Trimbach*, Bas-Rhin-France, at New Orleans on 24 May 1859, but the couple always lived in Arkansas or Tennessee.) Seligman and Pauline Kahn settled in the town of Plaquemine where they raised eleven children: Leontine (b. 1866), Alphonse (b. 1867), David (b. 1868), Hortense (b. 1869), Julius (b. 1870), Corinne (b. 1872), Helvina (b. 1873), Ernest (b. 1876), Marx (b. 1879), Dora (b. 1880; See entry for **HIPPOLYTE UHRY**) and Belle B. (b. 1883). Seligman was a successful dry goods merchant, providing clothing, hats, shoes, and sundries to his customers. His wife, Pauline, died on 15 August 1887 in Plaquemine and was interred in the town's Jewish Cemetery. Seligman died just over a year later on 7 October 1888, leaving a small estate for the support of his younger children. He was buried with his wife in his adopted town of Plaquemine. (**A, AN, B1851, E, G, GB, TT**)

KAHN, SELIGMANN "SOL," was born on 24 August 1875 at *Schirrhoffen*, Bas-Rhin, France, to **HEYMANN KAHN** and his wife **MARIE** née **KAHN**, natives of *Schirrhoffen*, Bas-Rhin. He followed his brothers, **GUSTAVE** and **CHARLES KAHN** (See entries), to Louisiana. In a 1909 application for a U.S. passport to return to France for a visit, he wrote that he had immigrated to New York from Le Havre aboard the SS *La Champagne*, on 21 February 1891. Seligmann Kahn actually arrived, on the SS *La Champagne* in New York from Le Havre, France, on 2 March 1891. He travelled to Kahns, West Baton Rouge Parish, La, to work in his brothers' general store. Still unmarried in 1910 he lived at Kahns with his sister Marguerite's mother-in-law, **VALERIE BRAUN SOMMER** (See entry). By 1920 he had moved to Rayne, Acadia Parish, LA, and was living and working with his brother Charles. He married **SUZANNE COHN** (See entry), the widow of **JACQUES "JACOB" WELSCH** (See entry), on 17 August 1927 at Baton Rouge, East Baton Rouge Parish, LA. Suzanne had immigrated with her parents from *Bischwiller*, Bas-Rhin, France, at the age of six and was raised in Lorman, Jefferson Co., MS. Sol and Suzanne lived in Rayne where Sol tended to the family store. The couple had no children. Sol died on 7 March 1942 in Natchez, Adams Co., MS. His body was brought back to the Jewish Cemetery in Baton Rouge, East Baton Rouge Parish, LA, where he was buried under a double headstone with his brother, Gus. Suzanne Welsch Kahn died on 8 February 1966 in Vicksburg, Warren Co., MS. Her remains were returned to Baton Rouge where she was interred with her first husband, Jacques Welsch. (**A, AN, GB**)

KAHN, SIMON, was born on 6 March 1818 in *Waltenheim-sur-Zorn*, Bas-Rhin, France, to **LAZARE/LEYSER K**AHN, a native of the town and his wife, **FEILE/FANNY WEIL**, born in *Bischheim*, Bas-Rhin. In 1851 he was enumerated with his parents in *Waltenheim.* Still unmarried at the age of thirty-three, he worked as a horse trader with his thirty-six-year-old bachelor brother, Michel. Simon immigrated to Louisiana on the ship *George Hurlburt* out of Le Havre, France, arriving in New Orleans on 1 March 1853. He did not appear again in Louisiana records until 1870 when he was enumerated as a resident of Shreveport, Caddo Parish, LA, living near his nephews, **ISAAC**, **RAPHAEL** and **JULIUS KAHN** (See entries) who had also immigrated to Louisiana. Simon was a stable keeper in town with $15,000 in real estate and personal property. Fifty-four-year-old Simon Kahn married twenty-four-year-old **BABETTE LEVY**, a native of

Alsace, whom we have not been able to identify, on 27 February 1872. He died on 2 September, 1873, a victim of the yellow fever epidemic that decimated Shreveport that year. Simon was buried in Hebrew Rest Cemetery # 1 (Jewish Section of Oakland Cemetery) the next day. Babette married German native, **BENJAMIN LANDMAN**, on 11 September 1876. They had no children. Ben died in 1910 and Babette on 12 June 1925. They were both buried in Hebrew Rest Cemetery # 2 (Texas Ave.) in Shreveport. (**A, AN, B1851, G**)

KAHN, SOLOMON, was born **SYLVAIN KAHN** on 17 July 1857 in *Schirrhoffen*, Bas-Rhin, France, to **BERNARD/BARUCH KAHN** and his second wife, **GOTHON/CAROLINE SOMMER**, both natives of the town. According to his naturalization petition witnessed by **JOSEPH COHN Jr.** (See entry), he immigrated to Louisiana in 1872 at the age of sixteen, a reliable record for which we were unable to find. In the 1880 federal census for New Orleans, Orleans Parish, LA, Solomon was enumerated as Solomon "Cohn," living in the household of **JOSEPH COHN** (See entry), Joseph Cohn Jr.'s uncle. He was a twenty-four-years-old immigrant from France, working as "a helper in a country store," and said to be the nephew of the head of household. We were unable trace this immigrant any further. (**A, AN**)

KAHN, SOLOMON, was born **SALOMON KAHN** on 10 August 1856 in *Romanswiller*, Bas-Rhin, France, to **SAMUEL KAHN** and his wife, **FANNY ROOS**, both natives of the town. In the 1910 federal census Solomon indicated that he had immigrated to America in 1873. We have not been able to find a reliable ship's record for his arrival. Twenty-four-year-old Solomon Kahn, an unmarried immigrant from Alsace, France, was enumerated in the 1880 federal census working as a dry goods and grocery merchant in the Fourth Ward of St. James Parish. He married HANNAH FELIX/FALK, daughter of **MARX FELIX** (See entry), ca. 1883, a record for which we were unable to find. Solomon Kahn became a wood and coal merchant in New Orleans, Orleans Parish, LA. He and Hannah were the parents of five children: Ella (b. 1884), Mina Valentine (b. 1886; died 1886), Gertrude (b. 1887; died 1887), Seraphine (b. 1888) and Sylvan Bernard (b. 1890). Although an April 1893 bankruptcy forced him out of the wood and coal business, and his property, including one horse, two mules, three carts, and a wagon, were sold at auction several months later Solomon and Hannah stuck it out in New Orleans before finally moving to Abita Springs, St. Tammany Parish, LA, ca. 1905, where he opened a country store. That business also failed, and he filed for bankruptcy in November 1909. He and Hannah appeared together for the last time in the 1910 federal census for Abita Springs at which time he was working in a local livery stable. Solomon Kahn died on 29 April 1911 at Abita Springs. He was buried in Hebrew Rest Cemetery #1 in New Orleans. Hannah Felix Kahn died on 13 September 1942 in Houston, Harris Co., TX. Her remains were returned to New Orleans where they were interred with those of her husband. Note: Solomon Kahn was the nephew of **MARY ROOS STRAUSS** (See entry for **BERNARD STRAUSS**), and the brother of **EMANUEL KAHN** (See entry). (**A, AN, E, G, GB, TT**)

KAHN, SUSANNA, (*Bischwiller*) See entry for **SUZANNE COHN**

KAHN, THEODORE, was born **THEODORE KAEN** on 16 September 1869 in *Bischwiller*, Bas-Rhin, France, to **JOACHIM KAEN**, born in *Schweighouse-sur-Moder*, Bas-Rhin, and his wife **SARA EISEMANN/EISENMANN**, a native of *Wittersheim*, Bas-Rhin. Theodore Kahn indicated in a 1908 United States passport application that he sailed on board the SS *Havre* from Bordeaux, France on 15 September 1888. The record shows that nineteen-year-old Théodore Kahn (transcribed in error as "Cheodore Kaky," age "10," but it is clearly "19") arrived in New Orleans, Orleans Parish, LA, from Bordeaux, France, on 29 October 1888 aboard the SS *Havre*. He was naturalized at Lake Charles, Calcasieu Parish, LA, on 30 November 1907. Theodore settled in Jennings, Jefferson Davis Parish, LA, where he became the manager of a general merchandise store. He married JULIA BLOCK, a Louisiana native, on 19 June 1906 in New Orleans, Orleans Parish, LA. They were the parents of four children: Ray (b. 1907), Jules (b. 1909), Sarah (b. 1913) and Arthur (b. 1916). Julia Kahn died in Jennings on 26 July 1944 and was buried in Graceland, the Jewish section of Orange Grove Cemetery in Lake Charles, Calcasieu Parish, LA. Theodore Kahn died on 17 July 1948 and was buried in Orange Grove Cemetery with his wife. (**A, AN, G**)

KATZ, JACOB/JACQUES, was born on 6 June 1835 in "Alsace" according to an inscription on his tombstone. A search of over 100 towns in the Bas-Rhin and Haut-Rhin has turned up no birth record for him. Jacob was born to **MEYER/MAYER KATZ**, a native of Landau, Waldeck, Germany, and his wife **JEANNETTE LEVY**, said to have been born in Switzerland. Jacob's sister, **CAROLINE/GOTHON KATZ**, was born in *Rosheim*, Bas-Rhin, France, on 24 February 1837. A notation in Caroline's birth record identified her father as a peddler (marchand ambulant), and her mother as Jeannette Levy, who were just passing through town. The family's last place of residence was given as Seppois-le-Haut, a commune in the Haut-Rhin, about eighty-five miles from *Rosheim*. Another child, Ester Katz, whose 30 December 1849 death was registered at *Struth*, affirmed that she had been born in the town ten years previously. The family was enumerated in the 1841 *Struth* town census. Meyer, a tailor, was living with his wife, Jeannette Levy, son Jacques (Jacob) Katz, and daughters, Gothon (Caroline) and Blume (Ester). No ages were given. Although the 1846 census for *Struth* was, unfortunately not preserved, the family was enumerated in *Struth* again in 1851. Forty-seven-year-old Meyer Katz, a dealer from the principality of Waldeck, his forty-two-year-old wife, Jeannette Levy, a native of Switzerland, and their sixteen-year-old son Jacques, a dealer as well, appeared together with another son, eight-year-old Moïse for whom there was no birth record in *Struth*. Nineteen-year-old Jacob Katz arrived in New Orleans, Orleans Parish, LA, on 15 February 1854 aboard the ship *Great Britain* from Le Havre, France. Fifty-one year old Meyer Katz, his forty-seven-year-old wife, Jeannette Levy, his ten- year-old son, Moses, and two young nieces, nine-year-old Sara and eight-year-old Babette Levy, arrived in New Orleans ten months later, on 15 December 1854, from Le Havre, France, aboard the ship *Plymouth*. Jeannette Levy Katz died shortly after her arrival in New Orleans, probably in the 1855 yellow fever epidemic, although there are no records of her death, hospitalization or burial. Her husband Meyer remarried in New Orleans, taking out a license to wed, German born, Barbara/Babette Meyer, on 16 November 1855. Their son, Leopold, born in 1857, died in Big Rock, Pulaski Co, AR in 1880 at the age of twenty-four from typhoid/pneumonia. Meyer's son, Jacob Katz, took out a license to marry **BABETTE/BARBARA LOEB** on 26 January 1856 in New Orleans. Babette was born on 11 April 1827 in *Dettwiller*, Bas-Rhin, France, to **MICHEL LOEB (MEYER LOEW** before 1808) and his wife, **NANETTE/JEANNETTE HIRSCH (LÉA/NANETTE ABRAHAM** before 1808), both natives of the town. Babette did not appear with her family at the time of the 1851 census for *Dettwiller*. She may have been the "Babette Loeb" who was listed as a passenger on the ship *Ferrière* which arrived in New Orleans on 27 November 1849 from Le Havre, France. Unfortunately no Babette/Barbe/Barbara Loeb could be found in the 1850 federal census for Louisiana. Jacob and Babette's first child, Abraham Katz, was born in 1857 in New Orleans. Their second child, Gabriel/Gabe Katz, was born in Memphis, Shelby Co., TN, ca. November 1858. Unusual as it may seem, all census records show this to be the case. His 1909 obituary reported his place of birth as Memphis, TN, adding that he had been a resident of New Orleans for forty-eight of the forty-nine years of his life. Three more children were born to Jacob and Babette in New Orleans: Jeannette/Jennie (b. 1862), Ester, (b. 1865), and Emanuel/Manuel (b. 1868). There is a record for Jacob Katz having served in the American Civil War in the Third Regiment European Brigade (Garde Française) headed by Captain Theodore Frois. Whatever service he had rendered would have been brief, and after the fall of New Orleans to Union forces on 29 April 1862 the militia would have been disbanded. Jacob worked as a peddler and dry goods merchant in the Tenth Ward of New Orleans. He lived near his father Meyer Katz, who was listed in various New Orleans directories of the 1860s and 1870s, working as a rag dealer/picker. Meyer Katz died at Touro Infirmary on 8 December 1879. Forty-five year old Jacob, his wife, Barbara and two children, seventeen-year-old Jennie and twelve-year-old Manuel were enumerated in 1880 in New Orleans, where the head of household was working as a jeweler. Jacob was listed as late as 1893 in the *New Orleans, Louisiana, City Directory* as a jeweler at 802 Magazine Street. Jacob's wife, Barbara, died on 13 August 1883 in New Orleans and was interred there in Gates of Prayer Cemetery #2 (Joseph Street.) Her tombstone lies on the ground broken in half. Jacob died in New Orleans on 19 August 1896, and was buried near his wife. **(A, AN, B1851, E, G, GB, GN, TT)**

KAUFMAN, JOSEPH, was born **JOSEPH KAUFFMANN** on 11 September 1844 in *Gundershoffen*, Bas-Rhin, France, to **CHARLES KAUFMANN** and his wife, **MADELEINE/JULIE BLUM**, both natives of the town. Joseph Kauffmann was listed as an immigrant to New Orleans, Orleans Parish, LA, from *Gundershoffen*, who left prior to 1 January 1864. This record was included in *The Alsace Immigration Book, Volume II*, compiled by Cornelia Schrader-Muggenthaler. Many young men who appeared on a list of conscriptees, used, in part, to compile this book, had immigrated, several years before they would have been inducted into the military. Joseph's year and place of birth were included in this record. We believe that he was the sixteen-year-old Joseph Kauffman, a native of France, who arrived at New Orleans from Le Havre, France, on 21 December 1860 aboard the ship *Lemuel*

Dyer. Joseph was enumerated only once in Louisiana, in the 1870 federal census for Washington, St. Landry Parish, LA, living with his younger brother, **SAMUEL KAUFMAN** (See entry). Joseph's occupation was given as "merchant," and his brother's as "clerk.."Joseph died on 22 June 1878, presumably at Washington, and was buried at Gemiluth Chassodim Jewish Cemetery in Opelousas, St. Landry Parish, LA. (**A, AL2, AN, G**)

KAUFMAN, JOSEPH, was born **LAZARE KAUFFMANN** on 19 February 1846 in *Gundershoffen*, Bas-Rhin, France, to **JACQUES/ JACOB KAUFFMANN** and his wife **JEANNETTE LEVI.** Although born as Lazare Kauffmann, he was enumerated as ten-year-old "Joseph Kauffmann" with his parents in the 1856 *Gundershoffen* town census. A three-year-old sister, Julie, was also enumerated with the family. We were unable to find a reliable immigration record for Joseph. He was first enumerated in Louisiana with his sister, **JULIE KAUFFMANN** (See entry for **ISIDORE MÜLLER**) in June 1870 in the federal census for Convent, St. James Parish, LA. Joseph and Julie were living next to **ROSALIE FRAENCKEL** the widow of **SAMUEL RAAS** (See entry). Joseph was working as a clerk in the Widow Raas' store. Thirty-year-old Joseph Kaufman died on 13 July 1876 in Bayou Lafourche, Lafourche Parish, La, and was buried in Hebrew Rest Cemetery #1 in New Orleans. His death certificate indicates that he died from a lung disease. (**A, AN, E, G, L**)

KAUFMAN, JULIE, (*Gundershoffen*) See entry for **ISIDORE MÜLLER**

KAUFMAN, LEOPOLD, was born **LEOPOLD KAUFMANN** on 16 September 1851 in *Gundershoffen*, Bas-Rhin, France, to **ISRAEL KAUFFMANN**, a native of the town, and **BABETTE GRADWOHL**, born in *Zinswiller*, Bas-Rhin. We believe that the arrival record for twenty-year-old "Leop. Kaufmann" who arrived at New York from Hamburg, Germany, on 24 July 1871 aboard the SS *Westphalia* is a likey record for our immigrant. His 1917 obituary had given his correct date and place of birth, as well as an indication that he had arrived after the Franco-Prussian War, which ended on 10 May 1871 with the Treaty of Frankfort. Leopold was following in the footsteps of his cousin, **SAMUEL KAUFMAN** (See entry) who had left several years earlier. He joined Samuel to work for several years in Washington, St. Landry Parish, La, and then followed him to Lake Charles, Calcasieu Parish,

LA, ca. 1879. Leopold went into business there with **DAVID BLOCH**, an immigrant from *Riedseltz*, Bas-Rhin, with whom he was enumerated in the 1880 federal census for Lake Charles. Leopold married his half first-cousin, PAULINE RAAS (See entry for **ISAAC RAS**) on 21 March 1882 in New Orleans. Two children were born to them: Bessie (b. 1883) and Elias Raas (b. 1889) in Lake Charles. Leopold Kauffmann worked with others to get the deep water channel built at Lake Charles, which facilitated the shipments of oil from the surrounding parishes after it was discovered at the turn of the 20th Century. He was also president of the First National Bank of Lake Charles. His wife, Pauline, died on 22 June 1929 in Lake Charles, and was buried there in Graceland, the Jewish section of Orange Grove Cemetery. Leopold died on 29 March 1937 in Lake Charles, and was buried with her. (**A, AN, F, G**)

KAUFMAN, SAMUEL, was born **SAMUEL KAUFMANN** on 1 March 1849 in *Gundershoffen*, Bas-Rhin, France, to **CHARLES KAUFMANN** and his wife, **MADELEINE/JULIE BLUM**, both natives of the town. Nineteen-year-old Samuel immigrated to the United States aboard the ship *Teutonia* which arrived in New Orleans, Orleans Parish, LA, on 31 December 1868. He travelled to Washington, St. Landry Parish, LA, where he found employment as a clerk in a local dry goods store. He was enumerated at Washington in the 1870 federal census with his elder brother **JOSEPH KAUFMAN** (See entry b. 1844), a twenty-five-year-old unmarried merchant from France. A cousin, **LEOPOLD KAUFMAN** (See entry), joined him there in 1871. Sam married SOPHIE GERNSBACHER, a New Orleans native, on 22 March 1876 in New Orleans, Orleans Parish, LA. The couple returned to Washington, LA, where Sam and Leopold were employed as dry goods salesmen. Searching for greener pastures, the brothers moved to Lake Charles, Calcasieu Parish, LA, ca. 1882. Sam went into the hardware business. He and Sophie were the parents of seven children: Max J. (b. 1878), William C. (b. 1880), Sidney Albert (b. 1886), Mathilde (b. 1889), May Barbara (b. 1892) and Lillie (b. 1894). Sam made a fortune in Lake Charles dealing in farm implements, carriages, bicycles, delivery wagons, as well as standard hardware building supplies. It was said that he had once received fifty buggies at one time. He later went into the motor car business. Sam, or "Uncle Sam" as he was affectionately called, was vice-president of both the Louisiana Retail Hardware Association and the Rice Belt Retail Implement Dealers Association. Sophie died on 4 July 1920 in

Lake Charles and was buried there in Graceland, the Jewish section of Orange Grove Cemetery. Sam followed on 20 October 1926, also in Lake Charles, and was buried with his wife. (**A, AN, G, GB**)

KAUFMAN, SARA, (*Gundershoffen*) See entry for **ISAAC RAAS**

KELLER, ISAAC, was born on 26 February 1849 in *Hoenheim*, Bas-Rhin, France, to **JACQUES KELLER**, a native of the town, and his wife, **BABETTE WEIL**, born in *Haguenau*, Bas-Rhin. Written in faint pencil next to his birth record was the following notation: "en Amérique – Cincinatty – fils de Babette Weil, décédée à Hoenheim 19 mars 1855." [in America - Cincinnati – son of Babette Weil who died in Hoenheim 19 Mars 1855] The notation about his mother's death was added because her name was inadvertently left off the birth record. It is unlikely that Isaac spent much time, if any, in Cincinnati, Hamilton Co. Ohio. Isaac immigrated to America aboard the SS *Westphalia*, a ship of the German-American Line, which arrived in New York on 28 July 1869. Although the steamer originally left Hamburg, Germany, Isaac was recorded as one of the nine passengers who boarded at Le Havre, France. He was enumerated at Bayou Chicot, St. Landry (now Evangeline) Parish, LA, in the 1870 federal census as a nineteen-year-old unmarried horse trader from France. Isaac was most likely doing business with a young **SAMUEL HAAS** (See entry), an immigrant from *Rothbach*, Bas-Rhin, France, who amongst other commercial interests at Bayou Chicot, specialized in the trading of horses and mules. Isaac Keller married SARAH LANG, a New Orleans native, on 21 March 1876 at New Orleans Orleans Parish, LA. The couple made their first home in Assumption Parish where Isaac became a retail grocer. They were the parents of two children: Bertha (b. 1878) and Sidney Garfield (b. 1880). Changing course one more time, Isaac moved his family to New Orleans before the 1900 federal census enumeration. Isaac became a drummer (commercial traveler), and his son, Sidney, worked as a clerk. The 1900 and 1910, census enumerations for the Keller family indicate that they were prosperous enough to have live-in household help. Isaac died in New Orleans on 16 August 1920 and was buried there in Hebrew Rest Cemetery #2. Sarah died three years later on 5 December 1923 and was interred with him. (**A, AN, G, GB**)

KERN, NATHAN, was born on 19 March 1827 in *Struth*, Bas-Rhin France, to **LEONARD KERN (LE JEUNE)**, a native of *Struth* and his wife **SARA/SERETTE EMANUEL KAHN**, born in *Neuwiller-lès-Saverne*, Bas-Rhin, France. Nineteen-year-old Nathan immigrated to New Orleans, Orleans Parish, LA, from Le Havre, France, arriving on 3 August 1847 aboard the ship *Viola*. He married **ROSINE MICHEL**, a native of *Struth*, on 14 October 1851 in Pointe Coupée Parish, Louisiana. The couple had grown up together in *Struth* before their immigration. Rosine was born on 16 January 1827 in *Struth*, Bas-Rhin, France, to ABRAHAM MICHEL, a native of Metz, Moselle, France, and his wife, **JEANNETTE/CHRISTINE NEUBURGER,** born in *Struth*. We believe that Rosine, listed as "Rosin Michel," arrived on 18 May 1849 at New Orleans, from Le Havre, France, aboard the ship *Charlemagne.* Nathan and Rosine settled in Pointe Coupée Parish, LA, at a location across the Mississippi River from Bayou Sara, West Feliciana Parish, LA, where Rosine's brother, **JACOB MICHEL** (See entry) and his family would later live. Nathan Kern started out as a peddler of general merchandise based in New Roads (False River). He subsequently opened a general merchandise store at Waterloo, Pointe Coupée Parish, LA. Nathan and Rosine were the parents of six children: Abraham (b. 1853), Solomon (b. 1856), Meyer (b. 1860), Lazard (b. 1862), David (b. 1865), and Leopold (b. 1868). Nathan Kern died on 28 March 1869. He was interred in Hebrew Rest Cemetery # 1 in New Orleans. Rosine Kern stayed on in Pointe Coupée parish through 1880 to run the store with the help of her six sons. Shortly after the 1880 federal census, she relocated to the town of Plaquemine, Iberville Parish, LA, where two of her children, Lazard and David, had opened up a dry goods store. She died on 23 April 1888 in Plaquemine, and was buried near her husband in Hebrew Rest Cemetery # 1, in New Orleans. **(A, AN, BC, E, G, GB, TT)**

KERN, NATHAN, was born on 31 December 1848 in *Struth*, Bas-Rhin, France, to **GERSCHEL KERN** and his wife **BEYERLE/ BABETTE** née **KERN**, both natives of the town. Nathan was probably the "N. Kerne" who immigrated to America, arriving in New Orleans, Orleans Parish, LA, from Le Havre, France, on 23 December 1865 aboard the ship *James Allen* He went to Pointe Coupée Parish where he was employed by his uncle/first cousin once removed, **NATHAN KERN** (See entry). He worked as a peddler in the parish until the mid-1870s, then left Louisiana and headed for Chicago, Cook Co, IL, where he married JULIA FALK a native of Baden, Germany, in 1884. Nathan was the proprietor of a furniture store in Chicago. The couple had one child, Albert (b. 1891). Nathan died on 5 January 1925 in Chicago, and was buried there in Waldheim Cemetery. Note: His first cousin, **JULIE KERN**, (b. 1863 in *Struth*) married **ABRAHAM/ALBERT LEVY** (b. Belfort, Haut-Rhin, France), brother of **ADELE AND CÉCILE LEVY**, both wives of **JACOB MICHEL** (See entry) **(A, AN, TT)**

KERN, SALOMON, was born on 14 December 1835 in *Struth*, Bas-Rhin, France, to **GERSHEL KERN** and his wife **BEYERLE/ BABETTE** née **KERN,** both natives of *Struth*. Eighteen-year-old Salomon Kern sailed on the ship *Plymouth* from Le Havre, France, arriving on 15 December 1854 in New Orleans, Orleans Parish, LA. This is probably the same as the "Solomon Kern" buried in the Jewish Cemetery, Clinton, East Feliciana Parish, LA, said to be from "Stru-Alsace" b. 1845, died 1858". "Kern" is a name common only to *Struth*, taken by one family in 1808. Gershon and Beyerle Kern were first cousins. The census enumerator for *Struth* wrote at the end of the 1856 census that the town had lost fifty-two inhabitants since 1851 due mostly to immigration to America. There were several Salomon Kerns listed in the 1856 *Struth* town census, but no one his age. The "1845" date on the tombstone is probably, or should be, "1835" as the stone is half buried and very degraded with time. **(A, AN, E, ES)**

KESSLER, CAROLINE "CARRIE," was born **CAROLINE KOESSLER** on 3 September 1868 in *Mertzwiller*, Bas-Rhin, France, to **ABRAHAM KOESSLER** and his wife **SARE/SARAH DREYFUS**, both natives of the town. According to information given in the 1910 federal census, Carrie immigrated to Louisiana in 1888, but we have found no record to be able to substantiate it. She married **JULIUS STERNFELS** a native of Erfelden, Germany, ca. 1891, a record for which we were unable to find. Eleven children were born to the couple, of whom seven survived to adulthood: Isidore (b. 1892), Emile (b. 1894), Hilda (b. 1897), Maud (b. 1900), Alfred (b. 1904), Roy (b. 1908) and Mabel (b. 1911). Sternfels started his career as a clerk at the Belle Rose Plantation store of Samuel and Leon Kessler in Assumption Parish, LA. He handled the retail end of the grocery business until his death on 16 October 1923. He was buried in Bikur Sholim Jewish Cemetery in Donaldsonville, Ascension Parish, LA. Carrie stayed on in the parish, living with her son, Emile, and his wife, Eunice, who were sugar cane farmers. Carrie was enumerated in the 1940 federal census in her son Alfred's household. He was the proprietor of a wholesale grocery business, a few miles down the road, in Klotzville, Assumption Parish,LA, Her daughter Mabel Sternfels

Landry, whose husband, Louis, worked as a salesman for his brother-in-law, also lived with the Alfred Sternfels family. Carrie died in Klotzville on 18 July 1943 and was buried in Bikur Sholim Jewish Cemetery in Donaldsonville, Ascension Parish, LA with her husband. **(A, AN, G, GB)**

KESSLER, EMANUEL, was born **EMANUEL KOESLER** on 14 September 1858 in *Mertzwiller*, Bas-Rhin, France, to **ABRAHAM KOESSLER** and his wife **SARE/ SARAH DREYFUS**, both natives of the town. Emanuel was the first of six brothers and sisters to immigrate to Louisiana, and the only one who returned to France to live permanently. According to his 1890 application for a U.S. passport, he arrived in the United States on 1 May 1875, a record of which we were unable to find. He spent a few years in Mississippi, then came to Louisiana, where he was enumerated in the 1880 federal census living and working in Raceland, LaFourche Parish, LA. Several years later he joined with his brothers to open a store in Belle Rose, Assumption Parish, LA, near Klotzville. He was naturalized at Napoleonville, Assumption Parish, LA, on 12 March 1890, and several months later applied for a passport to return to France for a visit. He remained in Paris. Banns for his marriage to MARGUERITE WEYLER were published in Paris on 8 April 1894. At the time of his brother Isidore's death in New Orleans, Orleans Parish, LA, on 11 June 1909, he was mentioned in an obituary carried in the New Orleans *Daily Picayune* as still living in Paris. Note: "Koesler" was the preferred spelling for Emanuel's surname in both U.S. and French records. **(A, AN, GB, TT)**

KESSLER, ISIDORE, was born **ISIDORE KOESSLER** on 18 May 1877 in *Mertzwiller*, Bas-Rhin, France, to **ABRAHAM KOESSLER** and his wife **SARE/ SARAH DREYFUS**, both natives of the town. He immigrated to Louisiana, following his brothers, Samuel and Leon, arriving in New York, from Le Havre, France, on board the SS *La Champagne* on 12 June 1893. He operated a plantation store at Belle Rose, Assumption Parish with his two brothers, and was naturalized at Napoleonville, Assumption Parish on 29 July 1903. Isidore was hospitalized at Touro Infirmary in New Orleans, Orleans Parish, La, for nineteen weeks in 1909. He was operated on but never regained his health. He died at Touro Infirmary on 11 June 1909. His body was returned to Donaldsonville, where it was buried in Bikur Sholim Jewish Cemetery. He never married. **(A, AN, G, GB)**

KESSLER, LEON, was born **LEON KOESSLER** on 4 April 1872 in *Mertzwiller*, Bas-Rhin, France, to **ABRAHAM KOESSLER** and his wife **SARE/ SARAH DREYFUS**, both natives of the town. According to his naturalization record he arrived in the United States in 1887. A record for seventeen-year-old "Ludwig Kessler," a German national, who arrived at New York from Amsterdam, Netherlands, on 18 July 1887 aboard the SS *Zaandam*, is worthy of consideration. He became a U.S. citizen on 8 April 1903 in Assumption Parish, LA. He and his brother, Isidore, were enumerated in the 1900 federal census with their sister, **MATHILDE KESSLER** (See entry), the wife of EUGENE KAHN in Assumption Parish. They were employed as merchants. Leon married EDAH SCHWARTZ ca. 1915, a record for which we were unable to find. Edah was a Louisiana native whose sister, Selma, was married to Leon Kessler's brother, **SAMUEL KESSLER** (See entry). Leon and Edah were the parents of two children: Elaine (b. 1916) and Paul (b. 1919). A successful merchant, he soon began buying up land. He moved to Iberville Parish where he became a sugar planter. Leon resided at Cora Plantation, one of his holdings near White Castle. He was also president of a Sugar Refinery in Iberville Parish. He died on 20 July 1948 at his home on Cora Plantation, and was buried at Bikur Sholim Jewish Cemetery in Donaldsonville, Ascension Parish, LA. His wife, Edah, passed away on 31 August 1957 in Baton Rouge, East Baton Rouge Parish, LA . Her remains were returned to Donaldsonville where they were interred there with those of her husband. **(AN, G, GB)**

KESSLER, MATHILDE was born **MATHILDE KOESSLER** on 1 April 1864 in *Mertzwiller*, Bas-Rhin, France to **ABRAHAM KOESSLER** and his wife **SARE/ SARAH DREYFUS**, both natives of the town. According to 1900 and 1910 federal census records, Mathilde immigrated to Assumption Parish, Louisiana in 1893 where her brothers, Sam, Leon and Isidore had settled. We were unable to find a reliable immigration record for her. Mathilde was married to EUGENE KAHN, a native of Imlingen, Lorraine, France ca. 1896. The couple had six children, four of whom survived to adulthood: Helen (b. 1896), Aline (b. 1900), and twins Herbert and Walter (b. 1903). Eugene worked all his life in Belle Rose, Assumption Parish, LA, at the Kessler enterprises. He managed the plantation store with his brother-in-law Julius Sternfels. Eugene died at Belle Rose on 2 June 1940 and was buried at Bikur Sholim Jewish Cemetery in Donaldsonville, Ascension Parish, LA. Mathilde died at the family home in Belle Rose on 2

September 1945 and was buried at Bikur Sholim as well. (A, AN G, GB)

KESSLER, SAMUEL, was born **SAMUEL KOESSLER** on 30 July 1861 in *Mertzwiller*, Bas-Rhin, France, to **ABRAHAM KOESSLER** and his wife **SARE/ SARAH DREYFUS**, both natives of the town. According to the 1910 federal census Samuel immigrated to Louisiana in 1878, a reliable record of which we were unable to find. He started working at the plantation store of Gabriel Kling, another immigrant from France, in Assumption Parish. Samuel was naturalized on 11 November 1886 in the parish. He married SELMA SCHWARTZ on 15 September 1897 at New Orleans, Orleans Parish, LA. Selma, a Louisiana native, was his brother Leon's wife's sister. Sam and Selma were the parents of three children: Lillian (b. 1899), Samuel, Jr. (b. 1901), and Marion (b. 1907). Although a successful merchant, he began buying up sugar plantations near Belle Rose, Assumption Parish, LA, where he and his family made their home. The little town of Kessler, LA, halfway between Belle Rose and Klotzville on State Highway #1, marks the location of the Kessler family sugar interests. Samuel retired to New Orleans ca. 1915 to a comfortable mansion on St. Charles Avenue. His wife, Selma, died on 26 November 1944 and was buried in Hebrew Rest Cemetery #2. Samuel passed away on 28 November 1950 and was buried with her. (**A, AN, G, GB**)

KIRSCH, ABRAHAM, was born on 2 January 1864 in *Mertzwiller*, Bas-Rhin, France, to **HENRI/HERMANN KIRSCH**, a native of the town, and his wife, **ROSALIE SIMON**, born in *Ettendorf*, Bas-Rhin. In his 1900 application for a U.S. passport, Abe stated that he had immigrated at the age of seventeen, arriving on the ship *St. Germain* on 15 October 1881. While the SS *St. Germain* docked at New York, from Le Havre, France, on 7 September 1881, Abraham Kirsch was not on the passenger list, nor was he aboard any other landings for this ship at New York between 1880 and 1889. Abraham settled in Shreveport, Caddo Parish, LA, where he went into the general merchandise business. He married BEULAH KAUFMAN, a Louisiana native, on 7 January 1891 in Shreveport. Abe was naturalized on 26 April 1900 at Shreveport. He and Beulah were the parents of five children: Moïse Kaufman (b. 1892; died 1915), Estelle (b. 1894), Martin G. (b. 1895), Gertrude B. (b. 1898), and Henry Abe (b. 1905). Abe was the manager of Kirsch Bros. & Co, in partnership with his brother, **MARTIN KIRSCH** (See entry), and a brother-in-law, J. M. Kaufman. The Kirsch brothers were also partners with I.J. Schnitt in Kirsch Bros., Schnitt & Co, a large hardware store. Abe died on 12 August 1907 in Shreveport and was buried there in Hebrew Rest Cemetery #2 (Texas Ave.). Beulah stayed on in Shreveport with her children, living there in the 1930s and 1940s with her son, Henry, and his wife. She died on 25 September 1944 and was buried with her husband. (**A, AN, G**)

KIRSCH, MARTIN, was born on 18 September 1872 in *Mertzwiller*, Bas-Rhin, France, to **HENRI/HERMANN KIRSCH**, a native of the town, and his wife, **ROSALIE SIMON**, born in *Ettendorf*, Bas-Rhin. Sixteen-year-old Martin Kirsch immigrated to America aboard the SS *La Bourgogne* arriving in New York, from Le Havre, France, on 29 July 1889. He joined his brother, **ABRAHAM KIRSCH** (See entry) in Shreveport, Caddo Parish, LA. Martin worked for him as a clerk in the Kirsch general merchandise store. He was naturalized in Shreveport on 5 April 1894. Martin married ANITA PHELPS, a Louisiana native, ca. 1904, a record of which we were unable to find. Martin and Anita were the parents of four children: Rosalyn (b. 1905), Julia Bertha (b. 1907), Martin, Jr. (b. 1913), and Phelps Emanuel (b. 1918; name changed to Jean-Pierre Piqué). After his brother Abe's death in 1907, Martin worked as a clerk in his father-in-law EMANUEL PHELPS' shoe business. He remained with the Phelps' Shoe Co., becoming the manager after his father-in-law's retirement. Martin died on 24 February 1952 in Shreveport, the same year that Anita and her son, Martin, Jr., applied for an FCC license to operate a television station, KAPK, out of Shreveport. Anita died in April 1966 and was probably buried in Shreveport, although we have failed to find the location for grave sites for either Martin or Anita. (**A, AN**)

KLEIN, BERNARD, was born **BENOÎT KLEIN** on 1 July 1876 in *Haguenau*, Bas-Rhin, France, to **SAMUEL KLEIN**, a native of *Dauendorf*, Bas-Rhin, and his wife, **MARIE LEVY**, born in *Rosheim*, Bas-Rhin. Bernard immigrated to the United States, arriving in New York on 10 July 1893 from Le Havre, France, aboard the SS *La Champagne*. He travelled to Shreveport, Caddo Parish, LA, where he joined his brother, **GUSTAVE "GUS" KLEIN** (See entry). Bernard was naturalized in Caddo Parish on 5 September 1899. He worked for most of his life as a salesman for S.G. Dreyfus Co. He never married. Bernard lived in a series of rented rooms around town. After his brother's death in 1930, Bernard lived with his sister-in-law Annie Moch Klein, her mother Dina Moch, and Annie's son, Edward S.

Klein, a Shreveport attorney. After Annie's death Bernard lived with his nephew Edward. Bernard was last enumerated in the 1940 federal census for Shreveport in the home of Edward Klein, Edward's wife, Bertha and their daughter Annie. Sixty-four-year-old Bernard was working as a salesman for a wholesale liquor company. He died on 7 August 1947 and was interred with his brother Gus and sister-in-law Annie at Hebrew Rest Cemetery #2 (Texas Ave.) in Shreveport. (**A, AN, G**)

KLEIN, GUSTAVE "GUS," was born **GUSTAV KLEIN** on 1 August 1872 in *Daudendorf*, Bas-Rhin, France, to **SAMUEL KLEIN**, a native of the town, and his wife, **MARIE LEVY**, born in *Rosheim*, Bas-Rhin. According to his 1895 application for a U.S. passport to return to France for four months, Gustave Klein wrote that he had immigrated on 17 August 1889 from Le Havre, France, to New York aboard the SS *La Gascogne*. A check of the passenger manifest for that ship which arrived on 24 August 1889 failed to identify him as a passenger, nor was there a Gustav Klein on any other arrival for the SS *La Gascogne*. He may actually have been the seventeen-year-old "Gustav Klein, a German national, who arrived at New York from Hamburg, Germany, on 2 November 1889 aboard the SS *Rhaetia*. Gustave settled in Shreveport, Caddo Parish, LA, where he was naturalized on 24 August 1894. He married ANNIE MOCH (See entry for **MARX MOCH**) on 30 December 1896 in Shreveport, the same year his brother, **BERNARD KLEIN** (See entry), came over from France to join him. Gus and Annie were the parents of two children: Fannie (b. 1899) and Edward S. (b. 1906). Gus worked variously as a salesman, a book keeper for Kaufman & Meyer and even a music teacher in Shreveport where he spent the rest of his life. He died on 7 March 1930 in Shreveport and was buried there in Hebrew Rest Cemetery #2 (Texas Ave.). Annie Moch Klein died on 4 September 1934 in Shreveport and was buried with her husband. (**A, AN, G**).

KLEIN, ISAAC, was born **ISAC KLEIN** on 20 November 1822 in *Osthouse*, Bas-Rhin, France, to **DAVID KLEIN (HIRTZEL DAVID** before 1808), a native of the town and his wife, **JEANNETTE GROSS,** born in *Westhouse*, Bas-Rhin. Twenty-eight-year-old Isaac last appeared in *Osthouse* in the 1851 town census living with his widowed father and three siblings. We believe him to be the thirty-six-year-old Isaac Klein who arrived in New York on 23 March 1858 from Le Havre, France, aboard the ship *Key Stone*. Isaac settled in New

Orleans, Orleans Parish, LA, where he took out a license to marry Mary Welsh [*sic*] on 19 March 1860. **MARIE/MARY WELSCH** was born **MARIE ANNE WELSCH** on 30 November 1824 in *Schirrhoffen*, Bas-Rhin, France, to **SAMUEL WELSCH** and his wife, **MERLÉ/MARYANNE HEYMANN,** both natives of *Schirrhoffen*. Marie probably accompanied her elderly father, Samuel Welsch, to America at some time after their appearance together in the 1851 *Schirrhoffen* census and before their 1860 enumeration as next door neighbors in New Orleans, Orleans Parish, LA. We were unable to find immigration records for either of them. Isaac Klein was enumerated in New Orleans with his wife, Mary, in the 1860 federal census at which time their surname was mistakenly recorded as "Lynn." The couple lived next door to **VOGEL/ISAAC HEYMAN** (See entry) and the latter's wife, **CLAIRE WELSCH**, Mary's sister. Seventy-five-year-old **SAMUEL WELSCH** (See entry), Claire and Mary's father, was living alone in the next house over. The Heymans and Kleins were both in the rag business. Isaac and Marie Welsch Klein were the parents of four children: Fanny (b. 1860), Herman (b. 1862), Julius (b. 1863), and Mary/Melanie (b. 1868). Isaac Klein served in the Civil War as a Corporal in the Third Regiment European Brigade (Garde Française) headed by Captain Theodore Frois. Whatever service he rendered would have been brief, and after the fall of New Orleans to Union forces on 29 April 1862, the militia would have been disbanded. The family was enumerated together for the last time in the 1870 federal census in New Orleans. Marie Welsch Klein died there from consumption on 10 August 1874. She was buried in Gates of Prayer Cemetery #2 (Joseph Street). Isaac followed on 14 October 1882 and was buried in the same cemetery. (**A, AN, B1851, F, G, GB, L, TT**)

KLEIN, ISIDORE, was born on 27 September 1847 in *Bischheim*, Bas-Rhin, France, to **BENJAMIN KLEIN**, a native of the town, and his wife **MARIE HOFFMANN**, born in *Mutzig*, Bas-Rhin. He married **RACHEL HELLER,** born on 7 August 1849 in *Hoenheim*, Bas-Rhin, France, to **LEOPOLD HELLER,** a native of *Ettendorf*, Bas-Rhin, who was working as a bookbinder, and his wife **SARA LEVY,** born in *Niederbronn-les-Bains*, Bas-Rhin. Isidore and Rachel were married on 5 August 1874 in the bride's hometown. A daughter, **JEANNE** (Johanna), was born in *Bischheim* on 12 June 1881. Seventy-one-year-old Isidore Klein and his elderly wife Rachel left the home of another daughter, Mrs. S. WOLFF, living at Nancy, France at the close of World War I. They arrived in New York on 5 August 1918 from

Bordeaux, France, aboard the SS *Rochambeau* to join their daughter, Jeanne Klein Lehman, and her two children, Ben and Albert, who were living in Alexandria, Rapides Parish, Louisiana.(See entry for **CHARLES LEHMAN**). Isidore Klein died on 19 August 1923, and Rachel followed on 12 Feb 1931. They were both interred in the Jewish Cemetery in Pineville, Rapides Parish, LA. (**A, AN**)

KLEIN, JEANNE/JOHANNA, (*Bischheim*) See entry for **CHARLES LEHMAN**

KLEIN, LEOPOLD, was born on 9 May 1859 in *Ingwiller*, Bas-Rhin, France, to **ISAAC KLEIN**, a native of the town, and his wife, **HENRIETTE/ADÈLE LEVI**, born in *Bouxwiller*, Bas-Rhin, France. Seventeen-year-old Leopold Klein emigrated from Le Havre, France to New York, arriving on 7 September 1876 aboard the SS *France*. New Orleans was listed as his destination. He appeared for the first time in American records in the 1880 federal census for Lafourche Parish at the home of Samuel Karger, a Russian-born store keeper. Twenty-one year-old Leopold was enumerated there as an unmarried immigrant from France who was working as a store clerk. Several years later he moved to New Orleans, Orleans Parish, LA, where he was hired by his first cousin, **LEON LEVY** (See entry), a native of *Ingwiller*, Bas-Rhin. Leon, a prosperous general merchant in the city, had expanded his business to include branches in the developing markets of Central America, specifically in Livingston, Guatemala, and Belize, British Honduras. Since 1881 the French government, fresh on the heels of its triumphant completion of the Suez Canal, had been struggling in its efforts to construct a canal across the isthmus of Panama, then a part of the country of Colombia. The French Canal Company flooded the area with laborers and managers to complete the task. This new activity in the jungles of Central America spilled over into the neighboring countries of British Honduras and Guatemala. Many New Orleans merchants took the opportunity to join the exploitation of these new markets. None was more enthusiastic than Leon Levy and his family. Leopold Klein started to work for Leon Levy as a commercial traveler, and met the latter's family including his wife, Felicie Levy, a native of New Orleans, and her daughters, Ella and Ernestine. Ship's records reveal that Leon's wife and daughters travelled back and forth frequently to Central America to support Leon in his commercial efforts. Leopold Klein was soon engaged to Leon's youngest daughter, Ernestine "Tinie" Levy, his first cousin once removed. On 1 May 1888,

Leon, his wife Felicie, daughter Tinie, and fiancé Leopold Klein, returned to New Orleans from Belize on the SS *City of Dallas*. Leopold and Tinie were married in New Orleans, just eight days later, on 9 May 1888. Tinie's sister, Ella, had married another Levy employee, Isidore Rich, a Polish immigrant, who would go on to make and lose a fortune in Central America. The two young wives were often passengers on United Fruit Company vessels that made regular trips from Central American ports to New Orleans, bringing in thousands of pounds of bananas and a handful of passengers at a time. As profitable as the Central American trade was, it was not without its risks, especially for recent Alsatian immigrants. Many of them had already succumbed to yellow fever, typhoid, and cholera in the semi-tropical climate of New Orleans. Many more would find the tropical climate of Central America equally inhospitable. Thirty-five-year-old Leopold Klein died in Livingston, Guatemala, on 14 September 1894. He was likely buried there in the local Jewish Cemetery, near his father-in-law, Leon Levy, who had succumbed at Livingston in 1889. A three-line obituary in the New Orleans *Daily Picayune* was Leopold Klein's only memorial. His pregnant wife, Tinie, gave birth to his namesake, Leopold, on 26 November 1894 in New Orleans. She and the baby lived with her widowed mother until her remarriage to Joseph Brooks Joseph Hyams in Manila, Philippine Islands, on 2 March 1904. Tinie had no other children. She died in Burlingame, San Mateo Co., CA, on 24 April 1957 and was buried in San Francisco National Cemetery, San Francisco Co., CA, with her second husband who had died in 1939. Note: See entry for Tinie Levy's grandmother, **MINETTE RIES**, a native of *Obernai*, Bas-Rhin. (**A, AN, AP, GB, TT**)

KLEIN, LUCIEN, was born on 20 January 1863 in *Surbourg*, Bas-Rhin, France, to **CALMEN KLEIN**, a native of the town, and his wife, JULIE MEYER, born in Gougenheim, Rheinpfalz, Germany. Eighteen-year-old Lucien immigrated to America, arriving in New York, from Le Havre, France, on 21 February 1881 aboard the SS *Ville de Marseille*. (Note: There is no final "s" on this ship's name, unlike the city in France) He stayed briefly in New York, and then spent a few years in Alexandria, Rapides Parish, La. By 1884, when he applied for American citizenship, he was living in Houma, Terrebonne Parish, LA. He was enumerated in New Orleans, Orleans Parish, LA, in the 1900 federal census where he boarded with the Samuel and Sara Strauss Plonsky family. Thirty-six-year-old Lucien was a travelling salesman, and still unmarried. ESTHER STRAUSS, Sara Plonsky's sister, was, however, living in the same household. Twenty-three-year-old Esther, a Louisiana native, was employed as a stenographer. Lucien and Esther married in New Orleans on 2 August 1904. The couple lived in a series of boarding houses before moving to their own apartment on St. Charles Avenue ca. 1920. They never had children. Esther "Essie" Strauss Klein died on 25 May 1922 in New Orleans and was buried in Gates of Prayer Cemetery # 1 (Canal Street). Lucien died on 22 June 1927 and was buried in the same cemetery. (**A, AN, G**)

KLEIN, MARX, was born on 2 February 1853 in *Hatten*, Bas-Rhin, France, the last of eight children, to **FRÉDÉRIC KLEIN**, a native of *Surbourg*, Bas-Rhin, France, and his wife **ROSINE MOOCK/MOCK**, born in *Hatten* Bas-Rhin. Marx was educated in Landau and Ingenheim, Rheinpfalz, Germany as a rabbi. According to his 1900 U.S. passport application, he immigrated ca. 12 September 1872 aboard the SS *St. Laurent* from Le Havre, France to NewYork. We could not find his name on the passenger manifests for any arrival for the SS *St. Laurent*. We believe that the record for the arrival of twenty-year-old Marx Klein, a German clerk , who arrived at New York from Bremen, Germany, aboard the SS *Holsatia* on 2 August 1871 is worthy of consideration. His first assignment was in Alexandria, Rapides Parish, LA, at the Temple Gemiluth Chassodim, where due to his youth, and his part-time employment, he was given the title of "chazan" or "cantor." He did, however, perform all the duties of a rabbi. He also worked as a merchant in town. Marx Klein's name first appeared in synagogue records on 28 January 1873 as the officiant at the marriage of Simon Weil to Josephine Levy. Marx was naturalized on 1 December 1879 at Alexandria. He left in the 1880s to become a traveling salesman for a liquor and cigar company. He resumed his duties as a rabbi at B'nai Israel in Baton Rouge, East Baton Rouge Parish, LA, ca. 1886 where he stayed for fourteen years. In 1900 he returned to France to be with his aged mother. After her death in December 1902, he came back to Louisiana to become the rabbi of the congregation at Donaldsonville, Ascension Parish, LA. He died there on 15 May 1908 and was buried in Bikur Sholim Jewish Cemetery in town. Marx never married. (**A, AN, FS, G, GB**)

KLING, DAVID, was born **KAUFFMANN KLING** on 21 October 1841 in *Dauendorf*, Bas-Rhin, France, to **GERSTEL KLING**, a native of *Uhlwiller*, Bas-Rhin, France, and his wife, **LOUISE KLING**, born in *Dauendorf*, Bas-Rhin. He immigrated to New Orleans, Orleans

Parish, LA, from Le Havre, France, as "Kaufmann Kling," aboard the ship *Nuremberg* with fellow townsman, **LEHMANN MEYER** (See entry), arriving on 23 March 1861, less than a month before the start of the Civil War. Kauffmann, usually called David in Louisiana, settled in Thibodaux, Lafourche Parish, LA. He married MATHILDE KAHN, the daughter of **MATHIAS KAHN** (See entry), a native of *Osthoffen*, Bas-Rhin, France. Mathilde was born at Brashear City (now Morgan City), St. Mary Parish, LA, ca. 1858. David and Mathilde were married on 30 December 1875 in Lafourche Parish, LA. David operated a dry goods store in Thibodaux, Lafourche Parish, where his four children: Pauline (b. 1876), Amelia (b. 1877), Lillian (b. 1879), and Maurice (b. 1881) were born. David filed a claim with the "French & American Claims Commission," which took testimony during the early 1880s from French citizens who sought reparations for goods seized by the Union Army during the Civil War. David petitioned for payment account of horses and mules taken by Major General Godfrey Weitzel on 2 November 1862, a claim which was eventually disallowed for want of jurisdiction. David died in Donaldsonville, Ascension Parish, LA, on 7 April 1883 and was buried there in Bikur Sholim Jewish Cemetery. His wife, Mathilde, died on 31 December 1892 at Hôtel Dieu in New Orleans, Orleans Parish, LA. Her remains were returned to Donaldsonville where they were interred in Bikur Sholim Jewish Cemetery with those of her husband. Note: The 11 April 1883 edition of the New Orleans *Daily Picayune* reported that David Kling, a native of *Dauendorf*, Alsace, had died on 7 April 1883 at Donaldsonville, at the age of thirty-nine years and five months. (**A, AN, G, GB, TL, TT**)

KLING, DAVID, was born on 24 August 1881 in *Mommenheim*, Bas-Rhin, France, to **JACQUES/JACOB KLING**, a native of *Wittersheim*, Bas-Rhin, and his wife, **MATILDA/MAGDALENA DREYFUS**, born in *Reichshoffen*, Bas-Rhin. In a 1910 application for a U.S. passport David stated that he arrived in New York on 3 November 1900 aboard the SS *La Champagne*, a reliable record of which we were not able to find. He settled in New Orleans, Orleans Parish, LA, where he was a clerk for H. & C. Newman, and later Silvan Newburger & Co., cotton brokers. He was naturalized at New Orleans, on 31 December 1909. David never married. Throughout the years he lived in a series of boarding houses in New Orleans. After the cotton market slowed down, he became a bookkeeper for a wholesale liquor company. David died on 26 November 1953 and was interred in the nonsectarian Hope Mausoleum on Canal Street in New Orleans. (**A, AN, GB**)

KLING, JULES, was born on 1 December 1879 in *Mommenheim*, Bas-Rhin, France, to **MOSES/MICHEL KLING**, a native of *Wittersheim*, Bas-Rhin, and his wife ROSALIE GOERSTEL/ GERSTEL, born in Lixheim, Moselle, France. Eighteen-year-old Jules Kling died in Louisiana on 7 March 1898 and was interred in the Hebrew Cemetery in Berwick, St. Mary Parish, LA. We were unable to find a reliable ship's record for Jules, who could not have been in Louisiana for more than a few years, if that, before his death. Note: An entry at *Findagrave.com* has incorrectly identified his parents as Gabriel and Julie Kling. (Note: His date of birth on the tombstone shows 4 December 1879 at Mommenheim, Alsace) (**A, AN, G, TT**)

KLOTZ, ABRAHAM, was born on 10 May 1812 in *Lauterbourg*, Bas-Rhin, France, to **JOACHIM KLOTZ** of Gross-Gerau, Darmstadt, Germany, and his wife, **THERESE DOMASIS**, a native of *Lauterbourg*, Bas-Rhin. We believe that the ship's record for an eighteen-year-old [sic] Abraham Klotz who arrived in New York City from Le Havre, France, on 10 August 1833 aboard the ship *Marengo* is worthy of consideration. Abraham worked as a dry goods merchant in New Orleans, Orleans Parish, LA, and later in Alexandria, Rapides Parish, LA. He married SARAH BEER on 16 February 1848 in St. Tammany Parish, LA. She was born in 1826 in Ingenheim, Rheinpfalz, Germany, Abraham died on 5 July 1848 in New Orleans, five months after his marriage. He was buried in Gates of Mercy Cemetery formerly located at Jackson & Saratoga Streets, which was razed in the 1950s. The couple had no children. In the 1850 slave schedule for Alexandria, Rapides Parish, the estate of A. Klotz was listed as owning three slaves. Three years after Abe's death, his widow Sarah, married her late husband's nephew, **HENRI KLOTZ**. (See entry) (**A, AN, F, TT**).

KLOTZ, ABRAHAM, was born **ABRAHAM GLOTZ** on 8 April 1836 in *Uhrwiller*, Bas-Rhin, France, to **SALOMON GLOTZ**, a native of the town, and **DOROTHÉE MOCH**, born in *Mertzwiller*, Bas-Rhin. Abraham immigrated to New Orleans, Orleans Parish, LA, arriving on 15 January 1855 aboard the ship *Gosport* from Le Havre, France, with his sister, **MINA/MINETTE/GUILLEMETTE KLOTZ** (See entry). He fought for the South during the Civil War as a private in Landry's Company, Donaldsonville Light Artillery. He was paroled in the state of Virginia in June 1865 and returned to Louisiana. Abraham married **JULIA ABRAHAM**, a native of *Reichshoffen*, Bas-Rhin, France, on 5 March 1868 in New Orleans. Julia was born on 11

February 1845 in *Reichshoffen*, Bas-Rhin, France, to **DAVID ABRAHAM**, a native of the town, and his wife, **ÈVE LEVY**, born in *Wingersheim*, Bas-Rhin. Abraham and Julia settled permanently in Assumption Parish, Louisiana in an area just north of Napoleonville, which, twenty years later, would be called Klotzville, after its founder and most important resident. Two children were born to them: Delia (b. 1869) and Florence (b. 1871). Julia died on 15 August 1871 and was buried in Bikur Sholim Jewish Cemetery in Donaldsonville, Ascension Parish, LA. Abraham married Julia's sister, **PAULINE ABRAHAM**, who was born on 12 July 1853 in *Reichshoffen*, Bas-Rhin, France, to **DAVID ABRAHAM**, a native of the town and his wife, **ÈVE LEVY**, born in *Wingersheim*, Bas-Rhin. According to information in the 1900 federal census, Pauline emigrated from *Reichshoffen* ca. 1872, and may have been the twenty-year-old "Caroline Abraham" who arrived at New York, from Hamburg, Germany, on 15 June 1872 aboard the SS *Allemannia*. The names "Caroline" and "Pauline" are, oftentimes used interchangeably by our Jewish ancestors. Abraham and Pauline were wed on 18 November 1874 in New Orleans. Five children were born to them: Jeanne (b. 1875), Rachel (b. 1877), Solomon Paul (b. 1880), and twins Edmond and Denise (b. 1882). Over the course of the years, Abraham Klotz developed a huge plantation store, bought land and became a sugar planter. His store and surrounding farmland became the town of Klotzville (la ville de Klotz). His wife's brothers, **SIMON, RAPHAEL** and **EUGENE ABRAHAM** (See entries) immigrated one by one to work at the family enterprise. Shortly before Abraham's death, he transformed his small empire into a stock company, becoming president of the Abraham Klotz Planting and Mercantile Co., Ltd. His son-in-law, Philip Bodenheimer, Florence's husband, was the vice-president, **ALPHONSE B. WEIL** (See entry), the secretary, and his son, Edmond, the treasurer. Abraham died, while seeking relief from his infirmities on 27 March 1907 in Asheville, Buncombe Co., NC. His body was brought back, and consistent with his wishes, was interred in Metairie Cemetery in the Tomb of the Army of Northern Virginia. His second wife, Pauline, who died on 7 March 1916, was buried with her sister, Julia, in Bikur Sholim Jewish Cemetery in Donaldsonville. (**A, AN, G, GB**)

KLOTZ, ADOLPHE, was born on 7 July 1836 in *Lauterbourg*, Bas-Rhin, France, to **JOSEPH KLOTZ (GOETSCHE JOACHIL** before 1808), a native of the town, and his wife, **THÉRÈSE KAHN**, born in *Balbronn*, Bas-Rhin. Adolphe was the first of ten children born to the couple. Fifteen-year-old Adolphe was enumerated with them in the 1851 *Lauterbourg* town census, but was absent from the next census, taken in 1856. Adolphe Klotz, born in 1836 in *Lauterbourg*, was listed as an immigrant to America who left prior to 1 January 1856. This record was included in *The Alsace Immigration Book, Volume II*, compiled by Cornelia Schrader-Muggenthaler. Many young men who appeared on a list of conscripts, used in part to compile this book, had immigrated, several years before they would have been inducted into the military. We believe that the arrival of a twenty-three-year-old [*sic*] Adolph Klotz, said mistakenly to be from Wurtemberg, arrived in New Orleans, Orleans Parish, LA, from Le Havre, France, on 11 December 1854 aboard the ship *Saxon*. A notation on his burial record indicated that he had lived in Mississippi. We were, however, unable to find him in either the 1860 or 1870 federal censuses for Mississippi or Louisiana. Two clues to his existence in America surfaced in two different New Orleans newspapers. The 20 November 1874 edition of the *New Orleans Times* documented his arrival on the previous day at the St. Charles Hotel, listing "A. Klotz, Miss." as a guest. The information that "A. Klotz, Miss." was staying at Cassidy's Hotel was reported in the New Orleans *Daily Picayune* dated 9 March 1876. Adolphe died at Touro Infirmary on 22 April 1876, and was interred at Hebrew Rest Cemetery #1 in New Orleans. His tombstone, which has toppled over, reads "In Memory of Adolph Klotz born in Louderburg Alces [*sic*]. Died April 22, 1876. Aged 39 years." Adolphe was the nephew of **ABRAHAM KLOTZ** (b. 1812; See entry) who died in New Orleans in 1848, and the cousin of **HENRI KLOTZ** (See entry), who married Abraham Klotz's widow, SARAH BEER. Two of Henri's sisters, **CAROLINE/CELESTINE** and **SOPHIE KLOTZ** (See entries), were residents of New Orleans at the time of their cousin Adolphe's death. (**A, AL2, AN, B1851, GB, TT**)

KLOTZ, CAROLINE, was born **DOROTHÉE GLOTZ** on 25 December 1830 in *Uhrwiller,* Bas-Rhin, France, to **SALOMON GLOTZ**, a native of the town, and **DOROTHÉE MOCH**, born in *Mertzwiller*, Bas-Rhin. In census records for *Uhrwiller*, Bas-Rhin, France taken in 1836, 1841, and 1846, she was enumerated under the name "Guttel." (Note: Although she had an older sister who was born Caroline Glotz on 6 April 1824, who was known in census records as "Gellen," given ages used in subsequent records, including her obituary notice, we have concluded that the girl born Dorothée, called "Guttel," is the person who immigrated to Louisiana.) According to information

Caroline gave at the time of the 1900 federal census at Napoleonville, Assumption Parish, LA, she immigrated to Louisiana ca. 1855. We have not been able to locate an appropriate ship's record for her arrival. Caroline married HERMANN WEILL on 11 September 1856 in Iberville Parish, LA. Hermann Weill was a native of Baden, Germany. Hermann's brother, Louis, married Caroline's sister, **MINA/ GUILLEMETTE KLOTZ** (See entry), several years later. Hermann and Caroline were enumerated in the 1860 federal census for New River near Donaldsonville, Ascension Parish, LA, with their two children: Henry (b. 1858) and Adele (b. 1860). He and his brother, Louis Weil, were horse traders in the town. The couple's only son, Henry, died on 3 January 1873 and was buried in Bikur Sholim Jewish Cemetery at Donaldsonville. Hermann and his family moved shortly thereafter to Napoleonville, Assumption Parish, LA, where he opened a retail store. Hermann Weill died in Napoleonville in 1882 and was buried in Bikur Sholim Jewish Cemetery in Donaldsonville. His widow, Caroline, lived with her daughter, Adele, son-in-law, Adolph Weil, and their children in Napoleonville where she added to the family income by working as a dressmaker. Eighty-five year old Caroline Klotz Weil died on 14 September 1914 at Napoleonville. She was buried in Donaldsonville at Bikur Sholim Jewish Cemetery near her husband and son, Henry. (**A, AN, E, G, GB, TT**)

KLOTZ, CELESTINE, was born **CAROLINE KLOTZ** on 3 September 1832 in *Lauterbourg*, Bas-Rhin, France, to **EMANUEL KLOTZ**, a native of the town, and his wife, SALOMÉ BEHR, born in Leimersheim, Rheinpfalz, Germany. She was probably the Celestine Klotz said to be from Bavaria who arrived in New Orleans, Orleans Parish, LA, on 7 May 1852 aboard the ship *Jersey* from Le Havre, France. Since she was an orphan by the age of three, it is likely that she and her siblings were raised by Behr relatives in Bavaria and probably had emigrated from there. MEYER LEHMAN, a dry goods merchant and native of Böchingen, Rheinpfalz, Germany, took out a license on 30 March 1853 in New Orleans to marry Celestine Klotz. The couple returned to Woodville, Wilkinson Co., MS, to start their family.Two sons were born to them in Mississippi: Moses (b. 1854) and Marcus (b. 1856). They moved to New Orleans in 1857, where Meyer was a dry goods merchant on Dryades Street. Six more children were born to the couple in New Orleans: Louis (b. 1857), Henry (b. 1860), Rosa (b. 1863), Julius (b. 1865), Bertha (b. 1867), and Jonas (b. 1870). Meyer started out in a small way, but his store, eventually called M. Lehman

& Co., grew threefold, employing him as the senior partner, with five of his sons working in the business. Meyer died of heart failure on 23 November 1897 in the city and was buried in Hebrew Rest Cemetery #1. Celestine died on 16 October 1916 in New Orleans and was buried with her husband. Note: In the 1880 federal census she was enumerated as Caroline Lehman. She was the sister of **SOPHIE** and **HENRI KLOTZ** (See entries). (**A, AN, GB, TT**)

KLOTZ, DAVID was born **DAVID GLOTZ** on 15 April 1826 at *Uhrwiller*, Bas-Rhin, France, to **SALOMON GLOTZ,** a native of the town and **DOROTHÉE MOCH,** born in *Mertzwiller*, Bas-Rhin, France. He married **RACHEL/ ROSINE MEYER** on 20 June 1853 in *Uhrwiller*. Rachel was born on 1 March 1814 in *Wolfisheim*, Bas-Rhin, France, to **MATHIAS MEYER**, a native of the town, and his wife, **FROMET/ROSETTE KAHN,** born in *Krautergersheim*, Bas-Rhin, France. David and Rachel had one child, **SALOMON GLOTZ** (See entry), born on 15 June 1854 in *Uhrwiller*. The family immigrated to Louisiana at the conclusion of the Franco-Prussian War in 1871. Eighteen-year-old Salomon Glotz arrived alone in New Orleans, Orleans Parish, LA, from Le Havre, France, aboard the SS *Saxonia* on 14 October 1872. His parents were probably not far behind, but we were unable to find a reliable record for their entry. David was following in the footsteps of a younger brother, **ABRAHAM KLOTZ** (b. 1824; See entry), who had immigrated two decades earlier. David opened a store in Plattenville, Assumption Parish, LA, and ran it with the help of his son, Salomon. Rachel Klotz died in Plattenville on 15 September 1881 and was buried in Bikur Sholim Jewish Cemetery in Donaldsonville, Ascension Parish, LA. David died on 21 December 1890 and was buried in Bikur Sholim Jewish Cemetery with his wife. Note: The spelling "Glotz" was never used in Louisiana (**A, AN, G, GB**)

KLOTZ, HENRY, was born **HENRI KLOTZ** on 10 August 1828 in *Lauterbourg*, Bas-Rhin, France, to **EMMANUEL KLOTZ,** a native of the town, and his wife, SALOMÉ/SARAH BEHR/BEER, born in Leimersheim, Rheinpfalz, Germany. Eighteen-year-old Henry immigrated to New Orleans, Orleans Parish, LA, arriving on 31 December 1846, aboard the ship *Maria Cleaves*. He was enumerated in the 1850 federal census for Alexandria, Rapides Parish LA, living in the same household as Sarah Beer, his uncle Abraham Klotz's widow, whom he married on 27 March 1851 in New Orleans. Henry owned a dry goods store in Alexandria. He also opened a bar room and billiard "saloon" called "Our House," ca. 1859. Henry was one of the three founding members and contributors to the establishment of the Jewish Cemetery in Pineville, Rapides Parish, as well as a charter member of Temple Gemiluth Chassodim in Alexandria. Henry and Sarah had five children: Bertha (b. 1852), Edward (b. 1854), Rosannah (b. 1856; died 1863), Leon (b. 1859) and Sidney (b. 1863). Henry died on 27 November 1863 only one month after his last child was born. Henry and his daughter, Rosannah, who died the same year, were buried in the Jewish Cemetery in Pineville, Rapides Parish, LA. Sarah Beer Klotz died on 21 October 1909 in New Orleans, Orleans Parish, LA, and was buried there in Hebrew Rest Cemetery #1. Note: Two of his sisters, **SOPHIE** and **CELESTINE/CAROLINE KLOTZ** (See entries) immigrated to New Orleans as well. (**A, AN, F. FS, TT**)

KLOTZ, MINA/MINETTE, was born **GUILLEMETTE KLOTZ** on 3 December 1833 in *Uhrwiller*, Bas-Rhin, France, to **SALOMON GLOTZ,** a native of the town and **DOROTHÉE MOCH,** born in *Mertzwiller*, Bas-Rhin. (Note: In 1836 she appeared in the *Uhrwiller* census as "Munchel," in 1841 as "Moennig," and in 1846 as "Monnig." Her paternal grandmother, Salomé Blühme, who died eight months before she was born, was mysteriously registered at death as "Minette Klein," leading to the conclusion that, according to custom, Guillemette was called by the name of a recently deceased relative. Twenty-year-old Minette immigrated to New Orleans, Orleans Parish, LA, with her brother, **ABRAHAM KLOTZ** (See entry), aboard the ship *Gosport* which arrived from Le Havre, France, on 15 January 1855. (Abraham's age was recorded mistakenly as twenty-eight, instead of eighteen.) She married, LOUIS WEILL, a native of Baden, Germany, on 18 July 1861 in Donaldsonville, Ascension Parish, LA. They made their home in Paincourtville, Assumption Parish, LA, where Louis, a dry goods merchant, was appointed postmaster in 1869. They were the parents of six children: Adele (b. 1861) Sarah (b. 1862), Henry (b. 1863), Marx G. (b. 1870), Bella (b. 1871), and Ida (b. 1876). Louis Weill died on 28 May 1893 and was buried in Bikur Sholim Jewish Cemetery in nearby Donaldsonville. Mina continued in business through 1900, with her son, Marx, acting as salesman. After her son's marriage to Lillian Kling, daughter of *Dauendorf*, Bas-Rhin native, **DAVID KLING** (See entry), the family moved to New Orleans, where Mina lived with Marx, Lillian, their daughter, Mathilde, and Marx's sister, Ida. Mina died on 17 October 1924 and was buried in Metairie Cemetery in New Orleans.

She shares a double stone with her daughter IDA WEILL MCLENDON. (**A, AN, G, GB**)

KLOTZ, SALOMON, was born **SALOMON GLOTZ** on 11 March 1849 in *Herrlisheim*, Bas-Rhin, France, to **HENRI GLOTZ**, a native of *Uhrwiller*, Bas-Rhin, and his wife **MARGUERITE LEVY**, born in *Herrlisheim*, Bas-Rhin. Seventeen-year-old Salomon emigrated from Le Havre, France, on board the ship *Marcia C. Day*, arriving in New Orleans on 2 March 1867. He started his career as a merchant in Napoleonville, Assumption Parish, LA, appearing in the 1870 census as a twenty year old single storekeeper with $500 in personal property. He married RENÉ (sic) CAHEEN, a Morgan City, St. Mary Parish, LA native, on 1 January 1879 in St. Mary Parish. Renée was the daughter of HENRY CAHEEN, born in Metz, Moselle France. Solomon took his bride to Monroe, Ouachita Parish, in northern Louisiana to live. They had one child, Marcelle, born in October 1879. Solomon Klotz died at Monroe on 23 October 1880 and was buried there in Rosena Chapel Jewish Cemetery. His daughter, Marcelle died on 10 February 1882 and was buried in the Hebrew Cemetery at Berwick, St. Mary Parish, LA. After the death of her child, Renée Caheen Klotz followed her brothers, Fernand and Salvador Caheen to Birmingham, Jefferson Co., AL, where they had opened up a business. She never remarried. Note: Salomon Klotz of *Herrlisheim* was the nephew of **DAVID, ABRAHAM, GUILLEMETTE** and **CAROLINE KLOTZ,** all from *Uhrwiller*, Bas-Rhin. (See entries). (**A, AN, G, TL**)

KLOTZ, SALOMON/SOLOMON, was born **SALOMON GLOTZ** on 15 June 1854 in *Uhrwiller*, Bas-Rhin, France, to **DAVID GLOTZ**, a native of the town, and his wife **RACHEL/ROSINE MEYER**, born in *Wolfisheim*, Bas-Rhin, France. A 1976 article about those buried in the Donaldsonville Jewish Cemetery recalls that Salomon had witnessed a battle of the Franco-Prussian war at the age of sixteen, atop a hill at *Uhrwiller*. Salomon Glotz arrived in New Orleans, Orleans Parish, LA, from Le Havre, France, aboard the SS *Saxonia* on 14 October 1872. (See entry for his father, **DAVID KLOTZ**). He worked as a clerk in the family store in Plattenville, Assumption Parish, LA. Salomon married FANNIE WOLF, a native New Orleanian of Alsatian and German extraction (See entry for **SARAH WEIL**) on 12 April 1883 in New Orleans. The couple had seven children: Regina (b. 1883; died as a child), Lizette (b. 1885), Maurice (b. 1887), Carrie (b. 1889), David (b. & d. 1893), and Samuel (b. 1897). In 1900 the family relocated to Napoleonville, Assumption Parish, LA, where Salomon became an insurance agent. Salomon served as the postmaster at Donaldsonville, the Mayor of Napoleonville and was a member of the Police Jury (Parish Council) and the school board in Assumption Parish. Fannie Wolf Klotz died in Napoleonville on 19 January 1922 and was buried in Bikur Sholim Jewish Cemetery in Donaldsonville, Ascension Parish, LA. Salomon died on 10 May 1931 in Napoleonville and was buried with his wife. (**A, AN, G, GB, USGW**)

KLOTZ, SOPHIE, was born on 21 September 1834 in *Lauterbourg*, Bas-Rhin, France, to **EMANUEL KLOTZ**, a native of the town, and his wife, SALOMÉ BEHR, born in Leimersheim, Rheinpfalz, Germany. According to her obituary, she arrived in New Orleans, Orleans Parish, LA, ca. 1866, an appropriate record for which we were unable to find. Sophie was enumerated in the 1870 federal census for New Orleans as a domestic servant in the household of FERDINAND BEHR, who may have been one of her mother's relatives from Leimersheim. Ten years later, still unmarried, she was enumerated as a sister-in-law in the household of MEYER LEHMAN, who had married her sister, **CAROLINE/CELESTINE KLOTZ** (See entry). Sixty-one-year-old Sophie died on 7 April 1896 in New Orleans and was interred there in Hebrew Rest Cemetery #1. Note: She was also the sister of **HENRI/HENRY KLOTZ** (See entry). (**A, AN, GB, TT**)

KUHNAGEL, BENJAMIN, was born on 16 March 1831 in *Ringendorf*, Bas-Rhin, France, to **MEYER KUHNAGEL**, a native of *Ettendorf*, Bas-Rhin, and his wife, **CAROLINE LEVI**, born in *Surbourg*, Bas-Rhin. Caroline Levi was more commonly known as **CAROLINE/GERTRUDE GROSS**, a name which appeared on the birth records of all her children, except those of Benjamin and his brother, **DAVID KUHNAGEL** (See entry), as well as on her 1846 death record in *Ringendorf*. Benjamin arrived on 4 November 1859 at New Orleans, Orleans Parish, LA, from Le Havre, France, aboard the ship *Wurtemberg*. (Note: His surname was transcribed on *Ancestry.com* as "Ruhnagel.") He was briefly mentioned in "Confederate Papers relating to Citizens or Business firms (1861-65)" as a witness, with no further information given about his Civil War activities. We believe that he engaged in a smuggling business with his brother, David, and brothers-in-law, **BERNARD EHRSTEIN** and **NOCHIM WEIL** (See entries), bringing essential goods into the Confederacy and facilitating the shipping of cotton outbound through Mexico to England. Benjamin remained in Texas and/or Mexico after the end of the war. In August 1870 an article in a Brownsville, Cameron Co., TX, newspaper, *The Daily Ranchero*, listed B. Kuhnagel as the treasurer of the local chapter of the International Order of Odd Fellows. Birth and christening records in Texas and Mexico suggest that Benjamin had at least two children. **CAROLINA KOLL** [*sic*] was born to **BENJAMIN KOLL** [*sic*] of France and **PETRA GARCIA** in Brownsville in June 1874, and baptized in Matamoros, Tamaulipas, Mexico, on 23 March 1878. **HORTENCIA KUNANGEL** [*sic*] was born to **BENJAMIN KUNANGEL** [*sic*], a native of France, and **PETRA GARCIA** on 15 June 1884 in Matamoros, and baptized there on 6 June 1885. The children's maternal grandparents, Crescencio Garcia and Juana Flores were included in both records. In addition, Hortencia's paternal grandparents, **ROQUE KUNANGEL** [*sic*] and **CAROLINA CROS** [*sic*] were noted on her birth record. A burial card for Benjamin Kuhnagel at the Old City Cemetery in Brownsville, Cameron Co., TX, recorded his interment there in its Jewish Section on 2 July 1888, but no marker was ever erected. Although Kuhnagel is very unusual name, there are a surprising number of Kuhnagel descendants living in the Brownsville, Cameron Co., TX-Matamoros, Tamaulipas, Mexico metropolitan area. (**A, AN, F, F3, G, GB, TT**)

KUHNAGEL, DAVID, was born on 10 October 1833 in *Ringendorf*, Bas-Rhin, France, to **MEYER KUHNAGEL**, a native of *Ettendorf*, Bas-Rhin, and his wife, **CAROLINE LEVI**, born in *Surbourg*, Bas-Rhin. (Note: Caroline Levi was more commonly known as **CAROLINE/GERTRUDE GROSS**, a name which appeared on the birth records of all her children, except those of David and his brother, **BENJAMIN KUHNAGEL** (See entry), as well as on her 1846 death record in *Ringendorf*.) David was a merchant in Alexandria, Rapides Parish, LA, for over forty years. He arrived in New Orleans, Orleans Parish, LA, on 9 June 1855 aboard the ship *Guttenberg* out of Le Havre, France. He became the second husband of **MIRIAM WEIL** in July 1858 in Rapides Parish, the record of which was destroyed in the Parish courthouse when the Union army burned most of the town of Alexandria as they retreated towards New Orleans on 13 May 1864. Miriam Weil was born on 28 November 1823 in *Surbourg*, Bas-Rhin, France, to **JOSEPH WEIL** and his wife, **CAROLINE/GERTRUDE GROSS**, both natives of *Surbourg*. Miriam immigrated to Louisiana ca. 1851 an appropriate record of which we were unable to find. Miriam Weil Kuhnagel had one son, JACOB LEVY, born on 3 January

1854 from a previous marriage, about whom we could find little information. He was probably enumerated as six-year-old "Jacob L. W. Kuhnagel" in the 1860 federal census for Newton, Newton Co., TX, living with his mother, Miriam, step-father, David Kuhnagel, and his mother's extended Weil family. He was also mentioned as Carrie Kuhnagel's half-brother at her 1887 wedding to Joseph Greenwald, and listed as one of Miriam Kuhnagel's children in her 1901 obituary. Miriam's first husband may have been **JACOB LEVY** (See entry) of *Lauterbourg*, Bas-Rhin, France, who died in Alexandria from yellow fever in September 1853. It was quite common for a son born posthumously to bear his deceased father's name. David and Miriam Kuhnagel were the parents of three children, a son, Joseph, born ca. April 1860 in Texas, who probably died as a child, and two daughters: Caroline/Carrie (b. 1861) and Augusta (b. 1864). During the Civil War David was associated with his brother, Bernard, and brothers-in-law, **NOCHIM WEIL** and **BERNARD EHRSTEIN** (See entries), as merchants in Newton, Newton County, Texas, and then in Mexico where they were engaged in bringing essential goods into the Confederacy and facilitating the export of cotton through Mexico to England. On 27 May 1863, David Kuhnagel was conscripted at Alexandria as a private in Co. B, 16th Battalion, Louisiana Infantry (Confederate Guards Response Battn.), and may have served until 30 August of that year, although there are no surviving records to show that he was ever paid for his service. After this brief interlude, he continued his smuggling operation only returning to Alexandria with the Weil and Ehrstein families at the close of hostilities. Kuhnagel later sued through the French and American Claims Commission for property seized and later destroyed by Union General Nathaniel Banks in May 1864. His claim was for $4538 and he was awarded $360 in 1882. Miriam Kuhnagel died on 9 June 1901 in Alexandria and was buried the next day at the Jewish Cemetery in Pineville, Rapides Parish, LA. After his wife's death, David moved to Baton Rouge to live with his daughter Augusta, Mrs. Jonas Tobias. He died there on 19 November 1904 and was brought back to Pineville to be interred with his wife. (**A, AN, F, FS, G, TT**)

LEADMAN, CHARLES/CARL, was born as **JACQUES LEDERMANN** on 13 August 1850 in *Fegersheim*, Bas-Rhin, France, to **ARON LEDERMANN**, a native of the town, and his wife **JEANNETTE/HENRIETTE WEINMANN**, born in *Brumath*, Bas-Rhin. "Carl", his parents, and his sister, "Cérillie Lederman," immigrated to New Orleans, Orleans Parish, LA, arriving on 7 November 1853, from Le Havre, France, aboard the ship *Globe*. Aron Ledermann died sometime after the family's arrival in Louisiana in November 1853 and before his widow's remarriage in November 1855 to FELIX CAHN (See entry). At the time of the 1860 federal census Charles and Sophie were living in Shreveport, Caddo Parish, LA, with their mother, Jeannette, their stepfather Felix Cahn, and their half-siblings, Samuel Cahn and twins Rosa and Carroll Cahn. Jacques/Charles Ledermann's sister Sophie/Cérine married **ALEX B. WEIL** (See entry) in January 1870. Jacques/Charles reappeared in the 1880 federal census for Shreveport as "Chas. LEADMAN." He remained in Shreveport all his life. Charles married HELEN LEVY, a New Orleans native, on 12 October 1880 in Caddo Parish. They were the parents of two sons: Gabriel M. (b. 1882) and Sidney Seymour (b. 1884). Charles was a merchant in town and was enumerated in the 1900 federal census as the owner of a cigar stand. He died on 15 June 1904 and was buried in Hebrew Rest Cemetery #2 (Texas Ave.) in the city. Helen died on 25 September 1948 and was buried with him. (**A, AN, G, TT**)

LEDERMANN, ARON, was born on 14 May 1823 in *Fegersheim*, Bas-Rhin, France, to **LAZARE LEDERMANN**, a native of the town, and his wife, **CIBORE/ZIBORA WEIL**, born in *Osthouse*, Bas-Rhin. Aron, a local grocer, married **JEANNETTE/HENRIETTE WEINMANN** on 30 October 1849 in *Fegersheim*. Jeannette was born out of wedlock on 11 September 1824 in *Brumath*, Bas-Rhin, France, to SIMON WEINMANN, a Hebrew teacher, and NANETTE SAMUEL, both natives of Germany. Aron and Henriette were the parents of three children: twins Joseph and Jacques, born 13 August 1850, and Cérine, born 30 March 1852. Joseph died in *Fegersheim* on 28 April 1851. The family immigrated to New Orleans, Orleans Parish, LA, arriving on 7 November 1853, from Le Havre aboard the SS *Globe*. Aron Ledermann, who left no record in the U.S. other than the 1853 *Globe* passenger list, died between November 1853 and November 1855. His final resting place is unknown. His widow, Jeannette/Henriette married **FELIX CAHN** (See entry) on 28 November 1855 in Shreveport, Caddo Parish, LA. Her name appears on her marriage record as HARRIET WAGMAN, which caused some difficulty in being able to discover her true identity. She and Felix raised their blended family in Shreveport. (**A, AN, G, GN, TT**)

LEDERMANN, CÉRINE/ SOPHIA, (*Fegersheim*) See entry for **ALEX B. WEIL**

LEDERMANN, JACQUES, (*Fegersheim*) See entry for **CHARLES LEADMAN.**

LEHMAN, ADÈLE, was born **ADÈLE LEHMANN** on 29 July 1836 in *Ingwiller*, Bas-Rhin, France, to **ISRAËL LEHMANN**, a native of *Schwenheim*, Bas-Rhin, France, and his wife, **MARIE BAER**, born in *Ingwiller*, Bas-Rhin. She immigrated to New Orleans, Orleans Parish, LA, ca. 1859, an appropriate record for which we were unable to find. SAMUEL/SOLOMON HAYEM, a native of Metz, France, took out a license to marry her in New Orleans on 14 January 1860. Adele and Samuel were the parents of eight children: Salomon (b. 1860; died 1871), Edward (b. 1862), Isidore (b. 1865), Ester/Gertrude (b. 1866; died 1881), Clémence (b. 1867), Leon (b. 1874; died at ten days), Coralie (b. 1870) and Lazard (b. 1872). Samuel was a butcher in New Orleans until his death on 25 April 1879. He was buried in Hebrew Rest Cemetery #1 in the city. Adele was enumerated as a widow in the 1880 federal census living with four of her children: fifteen-year-old Isadore, who was working at a market, thirteen-year-old Gertrude, who was paralyzed, nine-year-old Cora, and eight-year-old Lazard, Adèle was said to have married F.S. Lyons in Jefferson Parish on 28 May 1882. She died on 20 March 1892 and was buried in Hebrew Rest Cemetery #1 in New Orleans under the name of "Mrs. F.S. Lyons." Solomon Hayem was listed on the burial card as her husband. Adele's sister, **SOPHIE LEHMAN** (See entry), who lived in New Orleans, was married to ABRAHAM HAYEM, also a butcher. Abraham was probably SAMUEL/SOLOMON HAYEM's brother. Two of Adèle's brothers, **ISIDORE** and **LEON LEHMANN** (See entries) immigrated to Louisiana as well. (**A, AN, G. GB, TT**)

LEHMAN, ALBERT, was born **ALBERT LEOPOLD LEHMANN** on 11 March 1909 in *Strasbourg*, Bas-Rhin, France, to **CHARLES LEHMAN** (See entry), a native of the town, and his wife, **JEANNE/JOHANNA KLEIN**, born in *Bischheim*, Bas-Rhin. Twenty-four-year-old Charles Lehman immigrated to the United States, arriving on 15 August 1903 in New York, aboard the SS *La Savoie*. He was accompanied by his bride-to-be, twenty-two-year-old **JEANNE KLEIN**. The couple was married ca. August 1903 in Alexandria, Rapides Parish, LA. After Charles and Jeanne were married they returned to *Strasbourg*, Bas-Rhin, France, where Charles worked as a merchant, and where their two sons, Albert and **BENJAMIN LEHMAN** (See entry) were born. Charles Lehman arrived back in New York on 3 October 1909 from Le Havre, France, aboard the SS *La Touraine*. Jeanne Lehman and her two children followed him back on 18 December 1909, arriving in New York from Le Havre, France, aboard the SS *Provence*. The 1910 Federal Census for Alexandria, Rapides Parish, LA found Charles, Jeanne, and their two sons, Benjamin and Albert, living with his brother, **LÉON LEHMAN** (See entry), who owned and operated a retail grocery in Alexandria, Rapides Parish, LA. After both Charles and his brother, Léon Lehman, died in Alexandria, Benjamin and Albert stayed with their mother to help her make a living. They were enumerated in the 1910 and 1920 federal censuses for Alexandria, where it was recorded that they had been born in Germany. Yet in the 1930 census, Benjamin, who was using the name "Benjamin J. Lehman," and his brother, Albert L. Lehman were said to have been born in New York. Albert remained in Alexandria to work in the retail dry goods business in his mother's store. He died on 28 September 1965 and was interred in the Jewish Cemetery at Pineville, Rapides Parish, LA, near his mother and maternal grandparents. (**A, AN, G**)

LEHMAN, BENJAMIN, was born **BENJAMIN SIMON LEHMANN** on 14 August 1904 in *Strasbourg*, Bas-Rhin, France, to **CHARLES LEHMAN** (See entry), a native of the town, and his wife, **JEANNE/JOHANNA KLEIN**, born in *Bischheim*, Bas-Rhin. Twenty-four-year-old Charles Lehman immigrated to the United States, arriving on 15 August 1903 in New York, aboard the SS *La Savoie*. He was accompanied by his bride-to-be, twenty-two-year-old **JEANNE KLEIN**. The couple was married ca. August 1903 in Alexandria, Rapides Parish, LA. After Charles and Jeanne were married they returned to *Strasbourg*, Bas-Rhin, France, where Charles worked as a merchant, and where their two sons, Benjamin and **ALBERT LEHMAN** (See entry) were born. Charles Lehman arrived back in New York on 3 October 1909 from Le Havre, France, aboard the SS *La Touraine*. Jeanne Lehman and her two children followed him back on 18 December 1909, arriving in New York from Le Havre, France, aboard the SS *Provence*. The 1910 Federal Census for Alexandria, Rapides Parish, LA found Charles, Jeanne, and their two sons, Benjamin and Albert, living with his brother, **LÉON LEHMAN** (See entry), who owned and operated a retail grocery in Alexandria, Rapides

Parish, LA. After both Charles and his brother, Léon Lehman, died in Alexandria, Benjamin and Albert stayed with their mother to tend to the grocery store. They were enumerated in the 1910 and 1920 federal censuses for Alexandria, where it was recorded that they had been born in Germany. Yet in the 1930 census, Benjamin, who was using the name "Benjamin J. Lehman," and his brother, Albert L. Lehman were said to have been born in New York. Benjamin was not enumerated in the 1940 census at Alexandria, LA, with his family. Jeanne Lehman, however, was still living there with her other son, Albert. She was the co-owner and Albert was the salesman at a dry goods store in town. Benjamin Lehman, born in "New York," was living in New Orleans, Orleans Parish, LA, where he was a thirty-six-year old intern at Charity Hospital with a specialty in obstetrics. He had graduated with a Bachelor of Medicine from Louisiana State University at Baton Rouge in 1938, the same year that his photo had appeared in the LSU Yearbook, *The Gumbo*, listing him as "Ben Lehman from Alexandria." An article in the 23 June 1940 edition of the New Orleans *Times Picayune* listed all the interns at Charity Hospital, where Benjamin Joseph Lehman was a second year intern in Obstetrics and Gynecology. There was a Dr. Benjamin J. Lehman, a graduate of Louisiana State Medical School, who practiced obstetrics and gynecology in Hamilton Co., OH, which is worthy of consideration, but no further information was available. We were not able to trace him any further. (**A, AN, GB**)

LEHMAN, CHARLES, was born **ALPHONSE CARL LEHMANN** in *Strasbourg*, Bas-Rhin, France, on 24 May 1879 to **GUILLAUME LEHMANN,** a native of *Illkirch-Graffenstaden*, Bas-Rhin, and his wife **RACHEL KAHN,** born in *Mommenheim*, Bas-Rhin. Twenty-four-year-old Charles Lehman immigrated to the United States, arriving on 15 August 1903 in New York, aboard the SS *La Savoie.* He was accompanied by his bride-to-be, twenty-two-year-old **JEANNE KLEIN.** The couple was married ca. August 1903 in Alexandria, Rapides Parish, LA. Jeanne Klein was born **JOHANNA KLEIN** on 12 June 1881 in *Bischheim*, Bas-Rhin, France, to **ISIDORE KLEIN** (See entry), a native of the town, and his wife, **RACHEL HELLER**, born in *Hoenheim*, Bas-Rhin. After Charles and Jeanne were married in Alexandria, they returned to *Strasbourg*, Bas-Rhin, France, where their two sons **BENJAMIN** and **ALBERT LEHMAN** (See entries) were born in 1904 and 1909 respectively. Charles Lehman arrived back in New York on 3 October 1909 from Le Havre, France, aboard the SS *La Touraine*. Jeanne Lehman and her two children followed him back on

18 December 1909, arriving in New York from Le Havre, France, aboard the SS *Provence*. The 1910 Federal Census for Alexandria, Rapides Parish, LA found Charles, Jeanne, and their two children living with his brother, **LÉON LEHMAN** (See entry), who owned and operated a retail grocery in Alexandria, Rapides Parish, LA. After the Lehman brothers' deaths, Jeanne remained with her two sons in Alexandria to run the store. Jeanne died on 26 September 1959 and was buried with her parents, Isidore and Rachel Klein, in the Jewish Cemetery in Pineville, Rapides Parish, LA. It is known that Charles Lehman was living in Alexandria at the time of his brother Leon's death in 1911, according to the latter's obituary which appeared in the 14 June 1911 edition of the New Orleans *Daily Picayune*. His wife, Jeanne, was enumerated as a widow in the 1920 federal census for Alexandria. When or where Charles died between 1911and1920 is still a mystery, as he was not interred with his family in the Jewish Cemetery at Pineville, Rapides Parish, LA. (**A, AN, FS, GB**)

LEHMAN DAVID, was born on 2 November 1833 in *Illkirch-Graffenstaden*, Bas-Rhin, France, to **JOSEPH LEHMANN**, a clockmaker and native of *Bischheim*, Bas-Rhin, France, and his wife ROSA/ROSINE BERNHEIM, born in Pfastatt, Haut-Rhin. The couple moved to *Strasbourg*, Bas-Rhin, in 1836 with their children. According to the 1900 federal census record, David Lehman was said to have immigrated to Louisiana in 1855. There is a record for a sixteen-year-old [sic] David Lehmann, a French citizen, who arrived from Le Havre, France at New York on 13 October 1851 aboard the ship *Republic* which is worthy of consideration. David settled in Alexandria, Rapides Parish where he started out as a peddler. He married Polish immigrant CECELIA MALACHOWSKY ca. 1858. (Note: No pre-Civil War vital records are available in Rapides Parish, because Union soldiers burned down the courthouse on 13 May 1864.) Nine children were born to the couple: Hannah (b. 1859), Bessie (b. 1864), Lippman (b. 1867), Augusta (b. 1869), Rosa (b. 1870), Joseph (b. 1873), Flora (b. 1875), Charles A. (b. 1877), and Leon (b. 1879). David and Cecelia were lifelong residents of Alexandria where David was a retail merchant. His brother Guillaume's sons, **LEON** and **CHARLES LEHMAN** (See entries), and their families eventually came to Alexandria to live as well. David, who died on 30 October 1909, at the home of his son Charles A. Lehman in Los Angeles, CA, and his wife Cecelia, who died on 14 April 1925 were both buried in the Jewish Cemetery in Pineville, Rapides Parish, LA. (**A, AN, E, FS, GN**)

LEHMAN, ISIDORE, was born on 7 July 1844 in *Ingwiller*, Bas-Rhin, France, to **ISRAËL LEHMANN**, a native of *Schwenheim*, Bas-Rhin, and his wife, **MARIE BAER**, born in *Ingwiller*, Bas-Rhin. Isidore was enumerated with his parents and eight brothers and sisters in the 1851 census for the town of *Ingwiller*. His father died in 1854, leaving children ranging in age from three to twenty-four years. Isidore, along with another brother **LEON LEHMAN** (See entry), and two sisters, **ADELE** and **SOPHIE LEHMAN** (See entries) immigrated to Louisiana. According to information given in the 1900 federal census Isidore immigrated ca. 1872, a reliable record for which we were unable to find. He started out working as a clerk while living with his brother, Leon, in New Orleans, Orleans Parish, LA, where he was enumerated in the 1870 federal census. After Leon's death, Isidore worked for a time in Pointe Coupée Parish, where he was enumerated in the 1880 federal census. He married REGINA/LENA/SENA MANN, a Louisiana native, in Bayou Sara, West Feliciana Parish, LA, on 2 January 1887. The couple settled down in Rayne, Acadia Parish, LA, to raise their five children: Theresa (b. 1889), Mabel (b. 1892), Leona (b. 1894), Maude (b. 1896) and Alphonse (b. 1898). Isidore was a dry goods merchant in the town for more than twenty years. Sena Mann Lehman died on 28 November 1920 in Rayne and was buried in the Jewish Cemetery in Lafayette, Lafayette Parish, LA. Isidore died on 22 August 1927 in Austin, Travis Co., TX, where he had gone to live with his son, Alphonse. His remains were returned to Lafayette, Louisiana, where they were interred with those of his wife. Note: Isidore used the name Isaac in many Louisiana records. (**A, AN, B1851, F, G**)

LEHMAN, LÉON, was born **JUDAS LEHMANN** on 9 November 1832 in *Ingwiller*, Bas-Rhin, France, to **ISRAËL LEHMANN**, a native of *Schwenheim*, Bas-Rhin, and his wife, **MARIE BAER**, born in *Ingwiller*, Bas-Rhin. Leon was enumerated with his parents and eight brothers and sisters in the 1851 census for *Ingwiller*. His father died in 1854, leaving children ranging in age from three to twenty-four years. Leon, along with another brother **ISIDORE LEHMAN** (See entry), and two sisters, **ADELE** and **SOPHIE LEHMAN** (See entries) immigrated to Louisiana. We could find no likely immigration record for Leon who married HENRIETTA FEITEL, a native of Hesse-Darmstadt, Germany, in New Orleans, Orleans Parish, LA, on 28 October 1864. Leon worked as a retail grocer in New Orleans where the couple raised five children: Isidore (b. 1865; died 1877), Sarah (b.

1866), Joseph (b. 1868), Jules (b. 1871) and Lena/Lilly (b. 1872). Leon Lehman died in New Orleans on 16 September 1873 and was buried there in Gates of Prayer Cemetery #2 (Joseph St.). Henrietta married MAYER LEVY, a native of Prussia, on 29 December 1874, and had two more children: Edward Levy (b. 1875) and Ernest Levy, (b. 1878). Henrietta died on 14 July 1915 in New Orleans and was buried there in Gates of Prayer Cemetery #2 (Joseph St.). Mayer Levy died on 26 February 1919 and was buried with her. (**A, AN, B1851, G, GB**)

LEHMAN, LÉON was born **LÉON LÉONARD LEHMANN** on 27 September 1859 in *Strasbourg*, Bas-Rhin, France, to **GUILLAUME LEHMANN,** a native of *Illkirch-Graffenstaden*, Bas-Rhin, working as a merchant, and his wife **RACHEL KAHN,** born in *Mommenheim*, Bas-Rhin. He immigrated to America, arriving at New York as "L. Lehmann" on 21 May 1878 from Le Havre aboard the ship *Pereire*. He settled in Alexandria, Rapides Parish, LA, where he operated a retail grocery on Lee Street. Leon was naturalized on 19 April 1900 in Rapides Parish, LA. He never married. Leon died on 12 June 1911 and was buried in the Jewish Cemetery in Pineville, Rapides Parish, LA. (Note: See entry for his brother, **CHARLES LEHMAN**) (**A, AN, FS**)

LEHMAN, SOPHIE, was born **SOPHIE LEHMANN** on 20 August 1840 in *Ingwiller*, Bas-Rhin, France, to **ISRAËL LEHMANN**, a native of *Schwenheim*, Bas-Rhin, and his wife, **MARIE BAER**, born in *Ingwiller*, Bas-Rhin. According to the 1900 federal census, Sophie immigrated to Louisiana ca. 1866, although we were unable to find a likely record for her arrival in the United States. ABRAHAM HAYEM, a native of Metz, France, took out a license to marry her in New Orleans, Orleans Parish, LA, on October 8, 1866. Abraham operated butchering concessions at the Magazine Street Public Market, as well as at several other locations for many years. Sophie and Abraham were the parents of eight children: Clémence (b. 1867), Édouard (b. 1869), Eugénie/Fannie (b. 1871), Flora (b. 1874; died 1880), Camille/Hermina (b. 1876), Blanche (b. 1878), Léontine (b. 1880), and Juliette (b. 1882). Abraham died on 2 March 1891 and was buried in Gates of Prayer Cemetery #2 (Joseph Street) in New Orleans. After his death Sophie lived with one or another of her married daughters on Magazine Street in the city. She died on 12 August 1926 and was buried with her husband. Sophie's sister, **ADÈLE LEHMAN** (See entry), who lived in New Orleans, was married to SAMUEL/SOLOMON HAYEM, also a butcher, who was believed to be Abraham Hayem's brother. Sophie's brother, **LÉON LEHMAN** (See entry) died in New Orleans in 1873. (**A, AN, G, TT**)

LEHMANN, AARON, was born **ARON HANNEL**, ca. 1783 in *Lembach*, Bas-Rhin, France, to **ISAAC LÖW**, a native of *Wissembourg*, Bas-Rhin, France, and his wife, **MÖRLE LEIBEL**, born in *Ingwiller*, Bas-Rhin. He married **SOPHIE JACOB** on 2 December 1807 in *Lembach*. Sophie was born ca. 1784 in *Romanswiller*, Bas-Rhin, France, to **JACQUES JACOB** and his wife, **FEYLÉ SCHMULÉ**, about whom nothing further is known. Aron and Sophie were the parents of ten children: Saare (b. 1809; died 1809), Jacques (b. 1810), Julie (b. 1811), Samuel (b. 1813; See entry), Charlotte (b. 1815), Ève (b. 1818), Isaac (b. 1819; died 1820), Elizabeth (b. 1821), Léobold (b. 1823), and Philippine (b. 1825). Sophie died on 3 July 1834 in *Lembach*. Aaron was last enumerated in *Lembach* in 1846 where he lived with his son Samuel and two daughters, Ève and Philippine. The absence of a death record for him in *Lembach* suggests he is likely the sixty-five-year-old "Aron Lehmann" who arrived in New Orleans, Orleans Parish, LA, on 2 December 1848 aboard the ship *Ferrière*. He was accompanied by his twenty-six year old daughter, **ELISA /ELIZABETH LEHMANN.** Aaron was enumerated in the 1850 federal census in New Orleans, living with his daughter Eliza, and her husband LITTMANN/ LIPPMANN LEVY, said to be a native of Germany. Littmann Levy had married Elise Lehmann on 11 November 1850 in New Orleans, Their first child, Mathilde, was born in December 1851. Littmann moved his family to Lauderdale Co., MS, ca. 1853 to be near his wife's brother, **SAMUEL LEHMANN** (See entry) Two more daughters, Sophie (b. 1853) and Fanny (b. 1856) were born to Littmann and Elisa in Mississippi. We have been unable to find a date or place of death for Aaron Lehmann. He was not enumerated with the Littmann Levy family in the 1860 federal census for Lauderdale Co., MS, so it is presumed that he had died before that date. By 1870 Littman Levy and his family had moved to Manhattan, New York. Note: Aaron Lehmann was the uncle of **SALOMON LEHMANN** (See entry), who died in the wreck of the ship *Luna* in 1860. (**A, AN, E, TT**)

LEHMANN, CÉLINE/ESTHER, was born **CÉLINE LEHMANN** on 3 April 1868 in *Obernai*, Bas-Rhin, France, to **JACQUES LEHMANN**, a native of *Zellwiller*, Bas-Rhin, and his wife **ELIZABETH LEVY**, born in *Obernai*, Bas-Rhin. Two-year-old

Céline immigrated with her parents and two other siblings, arriving in New York from Hamburg, Germany and Le Havre, France, on 16 March 1870 aboard the SS *Cimbria*. The family settled in Morgan City, St. Mary Parish, LA. Céline married **EMANUEL BLUMENTHAL**, a native of Cincinnati, Hamilton Co., OH, on 16 April 1893. The couple had two children, both born in Morgan City: Myrtle (b. 1894) and Jacqueline (b. 1897). Emanuel was the manager of a local dry goods store. In 1904 Emanuel Blumenthal moved his family to New Orleans, where he worked his way up from salesman to floor manager in a department store. He died in New Orleans on 7 April 1928 and his body was returned to the Morgan City Cemetery and Mausoleum for burial. Céline died on 6 January 1953 in New Orleans and she was laid to rest near her husband in the Morgan City Cemetery. **(A, AN, G, GB)**

LEHMANN, CHARLES, was born on 1 August 1851 in *Zellwiller*, Bas-Rhin, France, to **ABRAHAM JUDAH LEHMANN** and his wife **ESTER ADELE GOUGENHEIM** (sister of **JYCHAE LOUIS GOUGENHEIM**), both natives of the town. He immigrated to the United States with his brother, **DAVID THEODORE LEHMANN** (See entry), arriving in New York from Le Havre, France, on 29 August 1871 aboard the SS *Denmark*. Charles settled in Morgan City, St. Mary Parish, LA to be near his brother, **JACQUES LEHMANN**, who had come there the year before with his family. Charles was a victim of the 1878 yellow fever epidemic. Twenty-seven-year-old Charles Lehmann died on 27 September 1878. He was buried in the Morgan City Cemetery and Mausoleum with other members of his family. **(A, AN, G)**

LEHMANN, DAVID THEODORE, was born **DAVID LEHMANN** on 6 March 1850 in *Zellwiller*, Bas-Rhin, France, to **ABRAHAM JUDAH LEHMANN** and his wife **ESTER ADELE GOUGENHEIM** (sister of **JYCHAE LOUIS GOUGENHEIM**), both natives of the town. He immigrated to the United States with his brother, **CHARLES LEHMANN** (See entry), arriving in New York from Le Havre, France, on 29 August 1871 aboard the SS *Denmark*. He and Charles joined their brother, **JACQUES LEHMANN** (See entry) and his family in Morgan City, St. Mary Parish, LA. David married his first cousin, **HENRIETTE GOUGENHEIM** on 14 May 1875 in St. Mary Parish. Henriette was born on 21 December 1851 in *Obernai*, Bas-Rhin, France, to **JYCHAE LOUIS GUGENHEIM** (See entry), a native of *Zellwiller*, Bas-Rhin, France, and his wife, SARA WORMS, born in

Boulay, Moselle, France. Three-year-old Henriette immigrated with her mother and three sisters to Louisiana, via New York, arriving on 18 October 1855 from Le Havre, France, aboard the ship *Switzerland*. She was raised in Morgan City, St. Mary Parish, LA, where her parents settled down. David and Henriette Lehmann's six children were born in Morgan City: Leon D. (b. 1876), Esther (b. 1878), Antoinette (b. 1879), Ruth (b. 1884), Cécile (b. 1886), and Mervin (b. 1890). David, or Theodore as he was more commonly known in Louisiana, spent over a quarter of a century as a grocer and dry goods dealer in Morgan City, St. Mary Parish. He and his wife retired to New Orleans just before 1910 where they lived out the rest of their lives. Theodore died on 12 June 1916 in New Orleans and was buried there in Hebrew Rest Cemetery # 2. Henriette died on 4 July 1933 and was interred in the same cemetery. **(A, AN, G)**

LEHMANN, ELIZA/ELIZABETH, (*Lembach*) See entry for her father, **AARON LEHMANN**

LEHMANN, ISAAC, was born ca. 1839 to **SALOMON LEHMANN**, a native of *Lembach*, Bas-Rhin, France, and **MINDEL/MINETTE LOB/THALSHEIMER**, the widow of MICHAEL SÜSS. Minette was born on 11 June 1806 as MINDEL LÖB, at Heiligenmoschel, commune of Niederkirschen, Canton Otterberg, Dept. Mont Tonnerre, France (Germany after 1814). We have not been able to locate a birth record for Isaac. He was born three years before his parents were able to marry so he may have been registered in another town. Salomon and Minette married in *Lembach* on 14 January 1842. Isaac appeared as the only child in his parents' household in the 1856 *Lembach* town census. His half-brothers **SIMON, LEOPOLD,** and **DAVID SÜSS/SIESS** (See entries) had already left for America. Isaac joined them in Louisiana ca. 1858, a record of which we have been unable to find. Isaac was enumerated with Simon and David in the 1860 federal census for Mansura, Avoyelles Parish, LA. He was employed as a clerk in their general store. As a non-citizen at the time the Civil War broke out, he was not conscripted to fight for the Confederacy. He remained in Mansura during its course. He fathered one child, Paul Marius Lehman, born in March 1864 to MARIE CHARLOT, a recently freed slave. On 16 April 1864, Leopold Siess, who had deserted the Confederate Army, and subsequently joined the "Home Guard," a band of Union sympathizers, came out of hiding with his men and met with his half-brother, Isaac. Several hours later, they were all captured by a band of Confederates. Some were let go, others, including Leopold, managed to fight their way free. Isaac, however, was left behind. He was taken the next day, along with eleven other men, to an isolated spot near Holmesville, Avoyelles Parish, LA, stripped naked and shot as a traitor. His body was never recovered. (**A, AN, AP, B1851**)

LEHMANN, JACQUES, was born on 29 October 1840 in *Zellwiller*, Bas-Rhin, France, to **ABRAHAM JUDAH LEHMANN** and his wife **ESTER ADELE GOUGENHEIM** (sister of **JYCHAE LOUIS GOUGENHEIM**), both natives of the town. He married **ELIZABETH LEVY** on 16 April 1866 in *Obernai*, Bas-Rhin. Elizabeth was born **ÉLISE LEVY** on 22 May 1841 in *Obernai*, Bas-Rhin, France, to **MARC LEVY**, a native of *Bouxwiller*, Bas-Rhin, France, and his wife, **ESTHER SCHEYEN**, born in *Obernai*, Bas-Rhin. The couple had three children, before immigrating to the United States: Lucien (b. 1867; See entry), Céline (b. 1868; See entry) and Octavie (b. 1869; See entry), all born in *Obernai,* where Jacques Lehmann was an innkeeper. Twenty-nine year-old Jacques Lehmann immigrated with his wife and three children, arriving in New York from Le Havre, France, on 16 March 1870 aboard the SS *Cimbria.* The family settled in Morgan City, St. Mary Parish, LA, near Jacques' brother **DAVID THEODORE LEHMANN** (See entry), where the couple had four more children: Meyer (b. 1872), Albertine (b. 1874), Clara (b. 1877), and Melanie (b. 1881). Jacques was the keeper of a coffee house in town, and served for a time as the postmaster of Morgan City in the 1880s. He was also a town councilman, and ran a thriving oyster packing business. Jacques died on 16 September 1896 in New Orleans, Orleans Parish, LA. His body was returned to Morgan City for burial in the Morgan City Cemetery and Mausoleum. After Jacques' death in 1896, Elizabeth stayed on with her children in Morgan City, where she saw to her various land holdings. Her son, Meyer, continued in the oyster business. She died on 25 April 1923 in Morgan City, and was buried in the Morgan City Cemetery and Mausoleum with her husband. (**A, AN, G**)

LEHMANN, LUCIEN, was born on 6 February 1867 in *Obernai*, Bas-Rhin, France, to **JACQUES LEHMANN** (See entry), a native of *Zellwiller*, Bas-Rhin, France, and his wife **ELIZABETH LEVY**, born in *Obernai*, Bas-Rhin. Three-year-old Lucien immigrated with his parents and two other siblings, arriving in New York from Le Havre, France, on 16 March 1870 aboard the SS *Cimbria*. The family settled in Morgan City, St. Mary Parish, LA. Lucien married HANNAH HALFF, a Texas native of Alsatian and German extraction, in Houston, Harris Co., TX, on 8 April 1894. The couple had three children, all born in Morgan City: Bernice (b. 1895), Jacques (b. 1898), and Valerie (b. 1899). Lucien was an oyster and fish packer for the family business. The family eventually moved back to Houston, his wife's home town, where Lucien became a travelling salesman for a shoe company. Hannah died on 16 December 1943 and Lucien followed on 8 February 1948. They were both buried in the Beth Israel Cemetery in Houston. **(A, AN, F)**

LEHMANN, OCTAVIE, "TAVIE," was born on 8 November 1869 in *Obernai*, Bas-Rhin, France, to **JACQUES LEHMANN** (See entry), a native of *Zellwiller*, Bas-Rhin, France, and his wife **ELIZABETH LEVY**, born in *Obernai*, Bas-Rhin. She immigrated with her parents as a four-month-old infant, arriving in New York from Le Havre, France, on 16 March 1870 aboard the SS *Cimbria*. The family settled in Morgan City, St. Mary Parish, LA. She was a lifelong resident there. After her parents' death she lived with her brother, Meyer, and his family, and her widowed sister, Clara. She never married. She was employed in a local printing plant as a reporter and collector. "Tavie" died in Morgan City on 7 June 1946 and was buried with family in the Morgan City Cemetery and Mausoleum. **(A, AN, G)**

LEHMANN, PHILIPPINE/FANNY, was born **PHILIPPINE LEHMANN** on 27 December 1825 in *Lembach*, Bas-Rhin, France, to **ARON LEHMANN**, a native of the town, and his wife, **SOPHIE JACOB**, born in *Romanswiller*, Bas-Rhin. She probably followed closely behind her brother, **SAMUEL LEHMANN** (See entry) who had immigrated to New Orleans, Orleans Parish, LA, in 1847, although we could find no likely immigration record for her. Philippine wed LEON DENNERY, a native of Metz, Moselle, France, who took out a license to marry her on 8 February 1848 in New Orleans. Their only child, Isidore Isaac, was born on 17 August 1851. The family moved to San Francisco, San Francisco, Ca, where Leon died on 4 March 1853. Fanny married **MARX WORMSER** in California ca. 1854. Marx was a native of *Marmoutier*, Bas-Rhin, France, with whom she had eight children: Eugene (b. 1855), Isaac (b. 1856), Jeannette (b. 1858, Sophie (b. 1860), Pauline (b. 1861), Melanie (b. 1863), Benjamin (b. 1865), and Julius (b. 1869). Philippine/Fanny Lehmann died in San Francisco on 28 December 1885. She was interred at the old 18th Street Cemetery at what is now Dolores Park in San Francisco. The bodies of those buried there were moved to Colma, San Mateo Co., CA, when burial within the San Francisco city limits was no longer permitted. She was reinterred on 13 July 1893 with her second husband, Marx Wormser, who had died on 2 April 1892, at Home of Peace Jewish Cemetery in Colma, San Mateo Co., CA. (**A, AN, G, GB, TT**)

LEHMANN, SALOMON, was born on 15 November 1801 in *Lembach*, Bas-Rhin, France, to **ISAAC LEHMANN**, a native of the town, and his wife DÉYE LEVY, born in Ottersheim, Haut-Rhin, France. He married **MINDEL/MINETTE LOB/THALSHEIMER**, the widow of MICHAEL SÜSS, on 14 January 1842 in *Lembach*. Minette was a native of Heiligenmoschel, commune of Niederkirschen, Canton Otterberg, Dept. Mont Tonnerre, France (Germany after 1814). Three children were born to the couple: Isaac (b. 1839), Abraham (b. 1841; died at nine months), and Michel (b. 1846; died nine days later). Salomon and Minette raised her sons, **SIMON, LEOPOLD,** and **DAVID SÜSS/SIESS** (See entries) and their surviving child, **ISAAC LEHMANN** (See entry) together in Lembach, sending them to school, and taking them into the family business. Their children immigrated to Louisiana one by one, until, by 1858, the household was empty. The couple decided to follow their sons to Louisiana. They booked passage on the American sailing ship *Luna*, which left Le Havre, France, on the evening of 16 February 1860. Unable to make its way out of the English Channel to the open waters of the Atlantic Ocean, on account of gale winds and a snow storm, the ship foundered on the rocks, in full sight of horrified witnesses near Barfleur the next day. Salomon and Minette perished along with 102 other immigrants and crew on the morning of 17 February 1860. Their bodies were never found amongst those that eventually washed ashore. (**A, AP, E**)

LEHMANN, SAMUEL, was born on 12 August 1813 in *Lembach*, Bas-Rhin, France, to **AARON LEHMANN** (See entry), a native of the town, and his wife, **SOPHIE JACOB**, born in *Romanswiller*, Bas-Rhin. Samuel's last appearance in a *Lembach* town census was in 1846, when he was enumerated with his father, **AARON LEHMANN** (See entry), and two sisters, Ève and Philippine. He immigrated to New Orleans, Orleans Parish, LA, arriving on the ship *Oxnard* from Le Havre, France, on 4 October 1847. He may have spent a few years in

New Orleans, or was, perhaps, on the road as a peddler. He settled in Lauderdale Co., MS, where he was naturalized on 23 August 1855. He married Ann, a native of North Carolina, whose maiden name is unknown. Four children were born to them: Henry (b. 1857), Simon (b. 1858), Joseph S. (b. 1861), and Isaac (b. 1865). Samuel, Ann, Henry and Simon were enumerated in the 1860 Federal census for Marion, Lauderdale, Co., MS. After his wife's death, Samuel married LUCINDA EMALINE TRUSSELL on 28 February 1870 in Lauderdale Co., MS. They were the parents of six children: Mary (b. 1871), Abraham William (b. 1874), Sophie (b. 1876), Ella (b. 1878), Benjamin (b. 1880), and John S. (b. 1883). At the time of the 1880 federal census, the family was living in Meridian, Lauderdale Co., MS. Samuel died at Touro Infirmary in New Orleans on 26 January 1893. His death certificate, which identified him erroneously as Solomon Lehmann, reported that he was a widower who had lived in New Orleans for four years and ten months. He was buried in Gates of Prayer Cemetery #2(Joseph Street). His tombstone reads "Samuel Lehmann, A native of Lembach, Alsace, Died at New Orleans, Jan. 26, 1893, Aged 75 years." Note: See entry for his sister, **PHILIPPINE/FANNY LEHMANN. (A, AN, E, G, L, TT)**

LEMMEL, LEON, was born **LÉONARD LEMMEL** on 8 November 1853 at *Struth*, Bas-Rhin, France, to **SELIGMANN LEMMEL,** a native of the town, and his wife, **HENRIETTE SALOMON,** born in *Tieffenbach*, Bas-Rhin. According to his 1889 application for a United States passport, he immigrated to America aboard the SS *Saxonia* arriving ca. 12 September 1872. We found a ship's record for a twenty-one-year-old Leon Lemmel arriving on the *Saxonia* at New Orleans, Orleans Parish, LA, on 12 October 1872, which, despite a few discrepancies, may very well document his arrival. Leon settled in Napoleonville, Assumption Parish, LA, where he was naturalized on 25 November 1879. He was enumerated in the 1880 federal census for Napoleonville as a twenty-five-year-old unmarried immigrant from France who worked as a clerk in a local dry goods store. The 20 June 1891 edition of the Asumption Parish newspaper, *The Pioneer*, reported that Leon Lemmel had married BLANCHE KAHN at the home of her sister Mathilde Kahn Kling (See entry for **DAVID KLING**) at Thibodaux, Lafourche Parish, LA. Blanche was the daughter of **MATHIAS KAHN** (See entry), originally from *Osthoffen,* Bas-Rhin, France, who was an early settler in Brashear City (now Morgan City), St. Mary Parish, LA. Leon and Blanche had one child, a daughter,

Alma, born ca. 1894. Leon and Blanche lived the rest of their lives in Napoleonville, where Leon was the proprietor of the Lemmel Dry Goods Store. Although the building was heavily damaged in the hurricane of 21 September 1909, its roof being blown off, and all its glass showcases shattered, Leon restocked his merchandise, and the David Levy estate, which owned the building, made the necessary repairs. Blanche Kahn Lemmel died on 10 June 1930 at Napoleonville and was interred at Bikur Sholim Jewish Cemetery in Donaldsonville, Ascension Parish, LA. Leon Lemmel died at Napoleonville on 31 May 1943, six months shy of his ninetieth birthday. His remains were transported to Donaldsonville where they were interred next to those of his wife. (**A, AN, G, GB**)

LEVY, AARON, was born **ARON LEVY** on 11 August 1872 in *Schirrhoffen*, Bas-Rhin, France, to **JACQUES LEVY** and his wife, **SARA WELSCH,** both natives of the town. Seventeen-year-old Aron Levy emigrated from Le Havre, France, to New York aboard the SS *La Champagne,* arriving on 10 August 1889 with his first cousin, **KAUFFMAN WELSCH** (See entry for **EMANUEL/MANNIE WELSCH**). He spent the first two decades in Louisiana near Port Allen, West Baton Rouge Parish, LA at Chamberlain, situated in the midst of the Orange Grove, Cypress Hall and Seidenbach sugar plantations, as a retail dealer in general merchandise. His brothers, **EMANUEL, GABRIEL** and **SIMON LEVY** (See entries) operated a retail dry goods business in nearby Port Allen, West Baton Rouge Parish, LA. Aaron married FANNIE DIEFENTHAL, a Louisiana native, on 19 August 1903 at New Orleans, Orleans Parish, LA. They had three children: Sadie (b. 1905), Bertha Clementine (b. 1907), and Edward D. (b. 1911). Aaron moved his family to New Orleans after freezing weather destroyed the sugar cane crops in 1911, causing a downturn in the local economy in West Baton Rouge Parish. He took a job as a clerk at the Southern Scrap Co., an enterprise owned by his brother-in-law, Adolph Diefenthal, where he rose to the position of manager, and finally to a co-ownership. Aaron died on 22 December 1950 and was buried in Hebrew Rest Cemetery #2 in New Orleans. His wife, Fannie, died on 22 June 1956 and was buried with him. Note: Aron Levy erroneously reported, in a 1908 application for a U.S. passport, that he had arrived from Le Havre aboard the SS *La Bourgogne* on 10 July 1889.(**A, AN, G, GB**)

LEVY, ABRAHAM, was born on 23 November 1854 in *Duppigheim*, Bas-Rhin, France, to **NEPHTALY LEVY**, a native of the town, and his wife, **BRENDELE DREYFUS**, born in *Osthoffen*, Bas-Rhin. Eighteen-year-old Abraham Levy arrived in New Orleans, Orleans Parish, LA, on 14 October 1872 from Le Havre, France, aboard the SS *Saxonia*. He worked as a dry goods clerk in Rosedale, Iberville Parish, LA, for Max Fraenckel, then at Port Allen, West Baton Rouge Parish, LA, and finally at Elkinsville and St. Rose, St. Charles Parish, LA. Abe married EMMA MORITZ, a native of Germany, on 18 April 1883 in Baton Rouge, East Baton Rouge Parish, LA. They were the parents of six children, all born in St. Charles Parish: Flora (b. 1884), Salomon (b. 1885), Sadie (b. 1887), Harry (b. 1888), Beatrice (b. 1890), and Beulah (b. 1894). Abe was both a merchant and a planter in St. Charles Parish for many years, having been naturalized at the parish seat, Hahnville, on 7 May 1886. The couple moved to Lowerline Avenue in New Orleans, Orleans Parish, LA, before the 1920 federal census. Emma died in New Orleans on 24 June 1932 and was buried in Hebrew Rest Cemetery #2 in the city. Abe died on 18 January 1935 in New Orleans and was buried with his wife. Their daughter, Beulah Levy Ledner, was a renowned baker in New Orleans. She created the doberge cake, a variation on the Hungarian dobos torte, which has been a New Orleans favorite for over half a century. (**A, AN, E, G, GB**)

LEVY, ABRAHAM, was born on 2 July 1864 in *Duppigheim*, Bas-Rhin, France, to **RAPHAEL LEVY (See entry)**, a native of the town, and his wife, THÉRÈSE DOROTHÉE KOCH/KOCK, born in Germany. After living almost a decade in Louisiana, Raphael, Thérèse, and their four children sought temporary refuge back in *Duppigheim* during the American Civil War. The Levy family, including two year old Abraham, sailed aboard the SS *Sorrento* out of Le Havre, France, arriving back at New Orleans, Orleans Parish, LA, on 1 December 1866. He was enumerated with his parents in the 1870 federal census for Convent, St. James Parish, LA, as six-year-old "Abram Levy," a native of France. He was enumerated again in the 1880 federal census as sixteen-year-old "Abrom Levy," the eldest of seven children, living with his widowed mother "Rafile" Levy (the widow of Raphael Levy). There was a feeble attempt to write "Duppigheim" as his place of birth, which was spelled "Dupichan" and had led someone to write "Russia" over it. Abraham was not mentioned in the 1903 New Orleans *Daily Picayune* newspaper article which reported his brother, **LAZARE LEVY**'s murder (See entry). However in the 20 January 1933 obituary for his Louisiana born brother, Marcus M. Levy, Abraham was said to have been living in Georgia. We were unable to ascertain any further information about him. (**A, AN, GB**)

LEVY, ACHILLE, was born on 13 May 1849 in *Marmoutier*, Bas-Rhin, France, to **MICHEL LEVY** and his wife, **LÉA/AGATHE DREYFUSS**, both natives of the town. Achille may have been the twenty-two-year-old "A. Levy" who arrived in New York on 8 September 1871 aboard the SS *Erin*. He came to Louisiana and worked in various small country stores as a clerk, first in St. Charles Parish, then at Campti, Morehouse Parish, LA, to be near his brothers **MATHIEU** and **JACQUES M. LEVY** (See entries). Achille found employment at Campti in a dry goods store. In 1910 he could be still be found in Campti, living with his sister **HELENE JEANNE LEVY** (See entry) on Hickory Street. Achille never married. He died on 16 November 1917 and was buried in B'nai Sholom Jewish Cemetery in Bastrop, Morehouse Parish, LA. (**A, AN**)

LEVY, ACHILLE, was born on 14 July 1869 in *Neuwiller-lès-Saverne,* Bas-Rhin, France, to **MICHEL LEVY**, a native of *Langensoultzbach*, Bas-Rhin, France, and his wife, **SARA LEVY**, born in *Ingwiller*, Bas-Rhin. Achille stated in a May 1908 application for a U.S. passport that he had immigrated to America in September 1890 aboard the SS *La Bretagne*. A search of that ship's record did not, however, turn up a suitable candidate. There is a record for an "A. Levy" who was on board the SS *La Gascogne* which arrived in New York on 10 November 1890 from Le Havre, France, which is worthy of consideration, although the age is incorrect by three years. Achille joined his brother, **ISIDORE LEVY** (See entry), who was a merchant in Napoleonville, Assumption Parish, La. They were enumerated there together in the 1900 federal census. Achille was a thirty-year-old unmarried immigrant from Germany working as a salesman in his brother's general merchandise store. Achille was naturalized on 10 December 1901 in Napoleonville. In his 1908 application for a U.S. passport, Achille wrote that he had lived in America since 1890 at Napoleonville, then in Orange, Orange Co., TX, and was currently living in Belzoni, Humphreys Co., MS, where he worked as a salesman. His brother, Isidore ,applied for a passport at the same time to return to France. We failed to find Achille listed in any census record for 1910. He died at the age of forty-four on 23 October 1913 in Ponchatoula, Tangipahoa Parish, LA. A brief obituary in the New

Orleans *Daily Picayune* contained the information that he worked for Levy Bros. and had dropped dead at breakfast presumably from a heart attack. He was buried the next day in Hebrew Rest Cemetery #1 in New Orleans, Orleans Parish, LA. He had never married. (**A, AN, GB**)

LEVY, ACHILLE ALPHONSE, was born on 11 February 1852 in *Oberschaeffolsheim*, Bas-Rhin, France, to **JOSEPH LEVY**, a native of the town, and his wife, **JUDITH/JULIE BLUM**, born in *Gundershoffen*, Bas-Rhin. He may have been the eighteen-year-old "Achille Levy" who arrived at New York on 18 July 1871 aboard the SS *Harmonia*. At the conclusion of the Franco-Prussian War, residents of Alsace, and certain areas of Lorraine, which had been ceded to the German Empire, were forced to decide whether or not to accept German citizenship, or move into an area that was still controlled by France. Many Alsatian expatriates in the United Stated filed the necessary papers at a French embassy declaring their wish to remain French citizens. Achille Alphonse Levy was one of them. He declared his preference for French citizenship on 11 August 1873 in New Orleans, Orleans Parish, LA. Several years later he moved to Opelousas, St. Landry Parish, LA, where he was a retail dry goods merchant. His younger brother, **LAZARE LEVY** (See entry), joined him in St. Landry Parish before the 1880 federal census. Alphonse died, at the age of forty-four, on 25 February 1896 in Opelousas. His remains were sent to New Orleans where they were interred in Hebrew Rest Cemetery #1 in the city. He was never married. (**A, AN, G, TT**)

LEVY, ALEXANDER, was born **ELIE LEVI** on 15 December 1834 in *Ingwiller*, Bas-Rhin, France, to **HENRI/HIRTZEL ELIE LEVY** (See entry) and his wife, **SARA KLEIN**, both natives of the town. Thirty-nine-year-old Sara, her two children ELIE/ALEXANDER, age sixteen and **LAZARE/LÉON LEVY**, age fifteen (See entry), were enumerated in the 1851 French census for *Ingwiller,* living with her seventy-three-year-old father, Moïse Klein, and her thirty-four-year-old sister, Élise Klein. Sara's husband, Henri, had already gone to America to establish himself in order to bring his family over at a later time. Henry returned to France ca. 1852 to accompany his family back to New Orleans, Orleans Parish, LA. Henry, Sara, Lazare, and Elie were recorded as passengers arriving at New Orleans from Le Havre, France, on 5 April 1852 aboard the SS *Edward Everett*. On 17 October 1856, twenty-two year old Alexander Levy, as he was always called in Louisiana, took out a license to marry seventeen-year-old BERTHA

KRATZENSTEIN in New Orleans. Bertha was a native of Hesse-Darmstadt, Germany. Alexander worked as a dry goods clerk and, after his father's departure back to France, as an independent dry goods merchant. He left that business to become a full-time auctioneer in New Orleans, and according to his *Daily Picayune* obituary, one of the best and most successful in the south. At the outset, he worked for Hogan, Marks & Co, which was succeeded by A. Marks, Levy & Co. In May 1878, after Alex Marks bowed out of the firm it was renamed A. & L. Levy, when his brother, Leon, invested in the auction house. Bertha and Alexander were the parents of five children: Adeline (b. 1859), Jacob K (b. 1860), Dina (b. 1862; died 1864), Hermann (b. 1864) and Moses (b. 1865). Bertha died on 7 January 1869 in the city. Her place of burial is not known. She may have been interred in the now defunct Gates of Mercy Cemetery at Jackson & Saratoga Streets which was razed in 1957. Alexander never remarried. During the last eight years of his life, he was a partner in the auction firm of W.G. Vincent & Co. He died in New Orleans on 18 August 1889, only two weeks after his younger brother, Leon, died in Livingston, Guatemala. Alexander was buried in Gates of Prayer Cemetery #2 (Joseph Street) in New Orleans. (**A, AN, B1851, E, G, GB, TT**)

LEVY, ANNETTE, was born **NANETTE LEVY** on 27 July 1848 in *Romanswiller*, Bas-Rhin, France, to **ARON LEVY**, a native of the town, and his wife **MINDEL/MADELEINE MARX**, born in *Kuttolsheim*, Bas-Rhin. According to information in the 1900 Federal Census, Annette immigrated to Louisiana in 1869, a record for which we were unable to find. She married MOÏSE BLOCH, a native of Fénétrange, Moselle, France, on 15 November 1871 in New Orleans, Orleans Parish, LA. Moïse Bloch, who had settled in Franklin, St. Mary Parish, LA, ca. 1870, took his bride back there to live. They were the parents of eight children: Isaac (b. 1872), Clara (b. 1874), Jules (b. 1876), Herman (b. 1880), Henry Garfield (b. 1881), Fannye (b. 1883), Edward Cleveland (b. 1884), and Alexander (b. 1888). At the time of his death on 9 November 1902, Moïse had been a respected dry goods merchant in Franklin for over thirty-two years. He was buried in the local Franklin Cemetery. Two years later his widow relocated to New Orleans to live with her children, Edward, Henry and Fannye. She died there on 28 August 1931 and was buried in Hebrew Rest Cemetery # 2 in the city. Note: See also entry for her brother, **LOUIS LEVY**. (**A, AN, G, GB**)

LEVY, ARTHUR, was born on 31 January 1854 in *Marmoutier*, Bas-Rhin, France, to **MICHEL LEVY** and his wife **LÉA/AGATHE DREYFUS,** both natives of the town. He was probably the eighteen-year-old Arthur Levy who immigrated to New Orleans, Orleans Parish, LA, arriving on 19 February 1872 aboard the SS *Saxonia* from Le Havre, France. Arthur joined his brother, **MATHIEU LEVY** (See entry), in Bastrop, Morehouse Parish, LA, where he was naturalized on 12 September 1876. According to the 1880 federal census he was living in Monroe, Ouachita Parish, LA, where he worked as a clerk for Bavarian native, SAMUEL KUHN, a retail liquor dealer. Arthur died on 11 August 1883 in Monroe and was buried there in Rosena Chapel Jewish Cemetery. He was only twenty-nine years of age. Note: His brothers, **ACHILLE** and **JACQUES M. LEVY** (See entries), and a sister, **HELEN JEANNE LEVY** (See entry), also settled in northern Louisiana. (**A, AN, G, TT**)

LEVY, BABETTE, (*Bouxwiller*) See entry for **LAZARD BENJAMIN**

LEVY, BABETTE, (*Niederbronn-les-Bains*) See entry for **SAMUEL WOLFF**

LEVY, BERNARD/BEN, was born on 18 May 1844 in *Schleithal*, Bas-Rhin, France, to **MARX LEVY**, a native of *Niederseebach*, Bas-Rhin, and his second wife, **FROMET WEILLER,** born in *Dauendorf*, Bas-Rhin. Bernard appeared in the 1870 federal census for Shreveport, Caddo Parish, as a clerk employed by his brother, **CAPT. SIMON LEVY, JR.** (See entry). Ben died on 15 October 1893 and was buried in Hebrew Rest Cemetery # 1, (the Jewish section of Oakland Cemetery) in Shreveport, LA. He was never married. (**A, F**)

LEVY, BERNARD, was born on 20 December 1867 in *Kuttolsheim*, Bas-Rhin, France, to **NATHAN LEVY**, a native of *Wintzenheim*, Bas-Rhin, and his wife, **LEAH/LISETTE PIOSO**, born in *Kuttolsheim*. We believe that the "B and R. Levy" who arrived 14 November 1884 in New York City from Antwerp, Belgium, on board the SS *Noordland* were Bernard and his older sister, **RACHEL LEVY** (See entry). Bernard and Rachel were enumerated together in the 1900 federal census at St. Mary Parish, LA, with eight-year-old Regina Levy, daughter of their brother **HENRY LEVY** (See entry). Bernard operated a general store there in Ward 2, either at the Cote Blanche or Azima plantations in the area of Glencoe. He married MAY MARGUERITE THERIOT, a Louisiana native, on 25 August 1903 at New Orleans, Orleans Parish, LA. Bernard and May were the parents of five children: Nathan (b. 1906), May Margaret (b. 1908), Nell (b. 1911), Ruth (b. 1913), and Bernice (b. 1919). Bernard and May remained in St. Mary Parish their entire lives where he continued to operate his general merchandise store. Bernard was elected Justice of the Peace for Ward 2 in 1935. After his retirement from business, the couple made their home in nearby Franklin, St. Mary Parish, where Judge Bernard Levy died on 22 November 1951. His remains were transported to New Orleans, where they were interred in Masonic Cemetery #1 at City Park Avenue. May Theriot Levy died on 30 October 1973 at Franklin. Her remains were brought to New Orleans to be buried with those of her husband. (**A, AN, G, GB**)

LEVY, BERTHA, (*Marckolsheim*) See entry for **JULIUS WEILL**

LEVY, BERTHA, (*Sélestat*) See entry for **SAMUEL LEVY** (b. 1823 in *Weiterswiller*)

LEVY, CHARLES, was born **KARL LEVY** on 19 July 1874 in *Brumath*, Bas-Rhin, France, to **MAXIMILIEN/MARX LEVY**, a native of the town, and his wife, **JEANNETTE LOEB**, born in *Reichshoffen*, Bas-Rhin. He immigrated to the United States, arriving in New York on 3 February 1891, aboard the SS *La Champagne*. Charles was in the dry goods business with his brother, **FELIX LEVY**, (See entry), for over a decade in Jeanerette, Iberia Parish, LA. He was naturalized in New Iberia, Iberia Parish, LA, in 1899. Charles left the partnership and moved to New Orleans ca. 1904. He married CELESTE/CELESTINE WILDENSTEIN, a Louisiana native, in the city on 6 June 1905. They were the parents of a son, Leonard, born the next year. Charles went into the wholesale liquor business with his father-in-law, **JACQUES WILDENSTEIN** (See entry). He became president of the company after his father-in-law's death. In his later years he also headed a silk cloth manufacturing firm. Charles died on 10 May 1932 in New Orleans. Celestine died on 15 June 1959. They were both buried in Gates of Prayer Cemetery #1 (Canal Street) in New Orleans. (**A, AN, G, GB**)

LEVY, DINA/THÉRÈSE, (*Schleithal*) See entry for **MARX MOCH**

LEVY, EDOUARD, was born on 18 October 1817 in Frankfort-am-Main, Germany, to **BENOÎT LEVY** a native of *Lauterbourg,* Bas-Rhin, France, and to **HENRIETTE MENDEL**, born in *Soultz-sous-Forets*, Bas-Rhin. At the couple's 1820 marriage in *Lauterbourg*, Édouard was legitimized as their son and his place of birth was recorded in the entry. He may have been the passenger listed as "Edouard Levi" on the Barque *Clement* which arrived in New Orleans, Orleans Parish, LA, on 4 January 1841. Édouard married ADILIE (ATHALIE) HERNANDEZ ca. 1849, for which we have no record. She was born to JEROME EMMANUEL HERNANDEZ and MARIE AGATHE NOLASCO de PORCUNA, ca. 1833 in Natchitoches Parish, LA. Édouard and Adilie had four children: Félonise Celine (b. 1850 in Colfax, Grant Parish, LA), Josephine (b. 1855 in Marco, Natchitoches, Parish), Jérome (b. 1858), and Athalie (b. 1865, Rapides Parish, LA). The couple settled in Alexandria, Rapides Parish, LA, before the 1860 census, where Adilie died after giving birth to their last child. Her final resting place is not known. Edouard married **JEANNETTE/SCHANNET BLUM** on 30 April 1866 in New Orleans, Orleans Parish, LA. She was born on 5 June 1842 in *Dettwiller*, Bas-Rhin, France, to **MARX/MARC BLUM**, a native of the town, and his second wife, **MADELEINE WEIL**, born in *Schwenheim*, Bas-Rhin. One of five Blum sisters to come to Louisiana from *Dettwiller*, she was enumerated in the 1900 federal census for Berwick, St. Mary Parish, LA, at which time she stated that she had immigrated to the United States in 1865. There is, however, the arrival of an eighteen-year-old Jeannette Blum who landed on 31 December 1859 at New Orleans from Le Havre, France, aboard the ship *Lemuel Dyer*, which is worthy of consideration. .Edouard took Jeannette back to Alexandria where he continued to work as a merchant. The couple had no children of their own. Edouard died on 3 May 1881 in Alexandria and was buried in the Jewish Cemetery in Pineville, Rapides Parish, LA. Jeannette filed for probate of her late husband's will on 15 October 1881. She married J. LEVI HIRSCH, a native of Louisiana and owner of an oyster saloon, on 20 November 1882 in New Orleans, but was widowed seven years later when he expired on 27 April 1889. He was interred at Gates of Prayer Cemetery #2 (Joseph Street) in New Orleans. His tombstone lies broken on the ground in three pieces. Jeannette moved to Berwick, St. Mary Parish, LA, to live near her sisters **ADELE, MARIE, PAULINE** and **SARA BLUM** (See individual entries). According to the 1900 federal census for Berwick, fifty-eight-year-old widow Jeannette Hirsh [*sic*], a native of France, was living alone on Pacific Avenue West not far from her older siblings. Jeannette died on 1 August 1903 in Berwick and was buried there in the Hebrew Cemetery. Her date of death was taken from her tombstone, as we have not been able to find a civil death record for her. (**A, AN, FS, L, N, TT**)

LEVY, ELIZA, was born on 16 September 1847 in *Marmoutier*, Bas-Rhin, France, to **JONAS LEVY**, born in *Birkenwald*, Bas-Rhin, France and his wife, **JEANNETTE MICHEL**, a native of S*chwenheim*, Bas-Rhin. We have been able to find no reliable ship's record for her arrival in America. She appeared in one census in Bastrop, Morehouse Parish, LA, with her brother, **JOSEPH**, and uncle, **MICHEL LEVY** (See entries) in the 1870 census, at age 21, as an immigrant from France. No other trace of her has been found. (**A, AN**)

LEVY, ELIZABETH, (*Obernai*) See entry for **JACQUES LEHMANN**

LEVY, EMANUEL, was born on 16 April 1846, in *Schleithal*, Bas-Rhin, France, to **MARX LEVY**, a native of in *Niederseebach*, Bas-Rhin, and his second wife, **FROMMIT WEILLER,** born in *Dauendorf*, Bas-Rhin. Emanuel worked as a butcher in Shreveport, Caddo Parish, LA, after immigrating to America to join brothers, **CAPT. SIMON, SAMUEL** and **SOLOMON LEVY** (See entries). We have not been able to find a reliable ship's record for his arrival in America. He was committed to the State Insane Asylum at Jackson, East Feliciana Parish, LA in July 1877 by his brother, Capt. Simon Levy, Jr., who had tried for several years to get him the best medical help available at the time. Emanuel Levy died at the asylum on 2 March 1884. He was never married. We have not been able to find his place of burial. (**A, AN**)

LEVY, EMANUEL, was born **KAUFFMANN LEVI** on 8 August 1870 in *Schirrhoffen*, Bas-Rhin, France, to **JACQUES "JACOB" LEVI** and his wife, **SARA WELSCH,** both natives of the town. In a 1901 application for a U.S. passport, Emanuel stated that he immigrated to America ca. May 1887, but did not remember the name of the ship. We were not able to find a reliable record for his arrival in America. He went to Galveston, Galveston CO, TX, where he worked for several years as a clerk in a dry goods store. He joined forces with his cousin, **JACQUES WELSCH** (See entry), to open Welsh & Levy, a clothing store in Port Allen, West Baton Rouge Parish, LA, just before the turn of the twentieth century. In 1914 he journeyed back to Alsace to visit family. He was accompanied by another first cousin, **DANIEL KAHN** (See entry). They barely missing involvement in World War I. Emanuel enlisted in the American Army at the close of the war, but was never sent overseas. After Welsh & Levy closed its doors in Port Allen ca. 1915, he moved to Baton Rouge, East Baton Rouge Parish, LA. Emanuel took over the reins of the Baton Rouge store after Jacques Welsch's premature death in 1917. He never married. Emanuel died on 30 March 1948 and was buried in the Jewish Cemetery in Baton Rouge. He shares a double headstone with his brother, **SIMON LEVY** (See entry), who died the same year. Note: See also entry for his brother, **GABRIEL LEVY**. (A, AN, G, GB)

LEVY, EMANUEL, was born **LIPPMANN LEVY** on 31 March 1861 in *Duppigheim*, Bas-Rhin, France, to **MARX LEVY**, a native of the town, and his wife, **PAULINE/ROSINE RECHT**, born in *Schaffhouse-sur-Zorn*, Bas-Rhin. In a 1903 application for a U.S. passport, Emanuel stated that he immigrated on the SS *La Normandie* in August 1878. While there were no landings at New York or New Orleans for the SS *La Normandie* in 1878, we did find the arrival of a twenty-year-old "E. Levy," a native of "Alsatia, Germany," who arrived in New York on 6 November 1879 aboard the SS *France*, which is worthy of consideration. Emanuel joined his half-brother **GABRIEL BLUM** (See entry) in St. Joseph, Tensas Parish, LA, where they both worked as a dry goods merchants. Emanuel left St. Joseph in 1890 to move to New Orleans, Orleans Parish, LA where he married SELMA HEIDENHEIM, a native of the city, whose parents hailed from Hesse-Darmstadt, Germany. He went into business with his brothers-in-law, Simon and Emanuel Heidenheim, and brother, **NATHAN LEVY** (See entry), as Heidenheim, Levy & Weiss, manufacturers of shirts and overalls. Emanuel and Selma were the parents of three children: Neville (b. 1892), Irvine (b. 1894) and Beatrice (b. 1904). In 1914 Selma was hospitalized for depression at a sanitarium in Cincinnati, Hamilton Co. OH. She hanged herself there on 26 July 1916. Her remains were returned to New Orleans, where they were interred in Gates of Prayer Cemetery #2 (Joseph Street). Emanuel Levy died on 1 July 1936 in New Orleans and was buried with his wife. Note: The couple's son, Captain Neville Levy, a graduate mechanical and electrical engineer, became chairman of the Mississippi River Bridge Commission. He was instrumental in the planning and construction of the bridge from New Orleans to the West Bank known as the Crescent City Connection. Note: The *La Normandie*, a British built ocean liner, was launched in 1882 and scrapped in 1911. (**A, AN, G, GB**)

LEVY, EMILE, was born on 23 April 1863 in *Sélestat*, Bas-Rhin, France, to **SAMUEL LEVY** (See entry), a native of *Weiterswiller*, Bas-Rhin, and his wife, **VICTOIRE/FANNY DREYFUS**, born in *Westhouse*, Bas-Rhin. He immigrated with his family ca. 1865 to New Orleans, Orleans Parish, LA, a record of which we were unable to find. Emile was enumerated in the 1900 federal census in Bastrop, Morehouse Parish, LA, where he was working as a dry goods salesman. He informed the census taker that he had emigrated from Germany (Alsace) in 1865, and was still single. He married MELANIE GUGENHEIM on 8 August 1900 in Houma, Terrebonne Parish, LA. Melanie was born in 1875 in Galveston, Galveston Co., TX, and was living with her married sister in Houma at the time of her marriage. Emile and Melanie moved to New Orleans where he became a clerk in a retail dry goods firm, then a salesman for a dry goods company, and finally a grocery clerk in the city. Emile and Melanie were the parents of one son, Samuel Sanford Levy (b. 1903). Emile died on 23 May 1938 in New Orleans and was buried there in Metairie Cemetery. Melanie died on 11 June 1946 and was buried with him. (**A, AN, G, GB, TT**)

LEVY, FANNY/MINETTE, (*Duppigheim*) See entry for **LEHMANN LEVY**

LEVY, FELIX, was born on 8 April 1876 in *Brumath*, Bas-Rhin, France, to **MAXIMILIEN/MARX LEVY**, a native of the town, and his wife, **JEANNETTE LOEB**, born in *Reichshoffen*, Bas-Rhin. He immigrated to America, arriving in New York on 19 August 1893, aboard the SS *La Touraine* from Le Havre, France. Felix was in the dry goods business with his brother, **CHARLES LEVY** (See entry), in Jeanerette, Iberia Parish, LA. He was naturalized in New Iberia, Iberia Parish, LA in 1902. Thirty-five-year-old Felix Levy died in New Orleans, Orleans Parish, LA, on 19 February 1912, and was buried there in Gates of Prayer Cemetery #2 (Joseph Street). He never married. (**A, AN, G, GB**)

LEVY, GABRIEL, was born **GABRIEL LEVI** on 25 April 1881 in *Schirrhoffen*, Bas-Rhin, France, to **JACQUES "JACOB" LEVI** and his wife, **SARA WELSCH**, both natives of the town. Sixteen-year-old Gabriel Levy arrived in New York on 4 September 1897 from Le Havre, France, aboard the SS *La Touraine*. His destination was listed as Port Allen, West Baton Rouge Parish, LA, to join his brother. He worked for 37 years for his brother **EMANUEL LEVY** (See entry) at the latter's clothing store, Welsh & Levy, both in Port Allen and later in Baton Rouge, East Baton Rouge Parish, LA. He lived on and off with various relatives from *Schirrhoffen*. In 1920 he roomed in Baton Rouge with **CLEMENTINE BENJAMIN**, née **WELSCH** (See entry), his first cousin, and sister of the co-owner of the Welsh & Levy Clothing store. Ten years later he was living with his brother Emanuel Levy, co-owner of Welsh & Levy. After his brothers, Emanuel and **SIMON LEVY** (See entry), died in 1948, he married a long-time acquaintance, MYRTLE ALBRITTON NURDIN (b. 1907 at Baton Rouge), a divorcee, who had owned the Ritz Beauty Salon in Baton Rouge. They were wed at the Roosevelt Hotel in New Orleans by a Baptist Minister on 19 June 1948. Gabe died three years later on 23 June 1951 and was buried in the Earl Albritton plot at Roselawn Memorial Park in Baton Rouge. Myrtle Levy died on 1 June 1979 and was buried with him. (**A, AN, G, GB**)

LEVY, GUSTAVE, was born on 15 September 1863 in *Niederroedern*, Bas-Rhin, France, to **MOISE LEVY** (See entry), a native of *Niederbronn-les-Bains*, Bas-Rhin, and his wife **ROSALIE/ ROSETTE MEYER**, born in *Niederroedern*, Bas-Rhin. He immigrated with his parents and siblings, arriving in New York on 8 December 1868 from Hamburg, Germany, aboard the SS *Holsatia*. The family originally settled in Forest, Scott Co, MS, but moved to Evergreen, Avoyelles Parish, LA, before the 1880 federal census. Gustave married OMEGA WEIL, a native of Homer, Claiborne Parish, LA, on 30 April 1895 in New Orleans, Orleans Parish, LA. Omega was his brother Sol's wife's sister. Gus stayed on in Evergreen, Avoyelles Parish, LA, to run his late father Moïse Levy's large mercantile business until World War I. The couple had three daughters all born in Evergreen, Lucille (b. 1896), Lillian (b. 1898), and Helen (b. 1901). The family relocated to New Orleans ca. 1915 where Gus died on 20 May 1918. He was buried in Hebrew Rest Cemetery # 2 in New Orleans. Omega died on 14 May 1938 in Shreveport, Caddo Parish,

LA. Her remains were returned to New Orleans where they were interred with those of her husband. (**A, AN, AP, F**)

LEVY, HELENE JEANNE, was born on 29 August 1860 at *Marmoutier*, Bas-Rhin, France, to **MICHEL LEVY** and his wife, **LÉA/AGATHE DREYFUSS**, both natives of the town. She immigrated to Louisiana to join her brother, **ACHILLE LEVY**, in Bastrop, Morehouse Parish, LA, arriving in New York on 19 September 1905 aboard the SS *L'Aquitaine*. She never married. Hélène died on 15 February 1931 in Shreveport, Caddo Parish, LA, and was buried in B'nai Sholom Jewish Cemetery in Bastrop. (**A, AN, L**)

LEVY, HENRY/HENRI, was born **HIRTZEL ELIE LEVI** on 2 January 1807 in *Ingwiller*, Bas-Rhin, France, to **ELIE LEVI**, born in *Mulhausen*, Bas-Rhin, France, and his wife, **REBECQUE BLUM** (**EDEL RIFGÉ DAVID** before 1808), a native of *Ingwiller*, Bas-Rhin. Henri married **SARA KLEIN** on 2 January 1833 in *Ingwiller*. Sara was born on 10 October 1810 in *Ingwiller*, Bas-Rhin, France, to **MOÏSE KLEIN** and **DINA/ANNE NETTER**, both natives of the town. We believe that thirty-seven-year-old Henri left for America, arriving in New Orleans, Orleans Parish, LA, on 27 March 1848 aboard the SS *Rome,* leaving his wife and two children behind in *Ingwiller*. Thirty-nine-year-old Sara, her children ELIE/ALEXANDER, age sixteen and LAZARE/LÉON, age fifteen, were enumerated in the 1851 town census for *Ingwiller,* living with her seventy-three-year-old father, Moïse Klein, and her thirty-four-year-old sister, Élise. A notation after Sara's name and age recorded that her husband was "en amérique" [in America]. Henry apparently returned from Louisiana to France ca. 1852 to accompany his family back to New Orleans. Henry, Sara, Lazare and Elie were recorded as passengers arriving in New Orleans on 5 April 1852 aboard the SS *Edward Everett.* The family settled down in the city where Henri was a dry goods merchant. They last appeared together as a family in the 1860 federal census for New Orleans, where Henry was still working as a dry goods merchant with his son **LEON LEVY** (See entry) employed as a clerk. **ALEXANDER LEVY** (See entry), also working as a clerk, had already married and was living with his wife and daughter in the same household. Neither Henry nor his wife appeared in 1870 federal census records in the United States. It is not certain when they left to go back to France, but Henry died in his hometown of *Ingwiller* on 8 March 1876. His death was reported in the New Orleans *Daily Picayune* dated 31 March 1876.

It was said that he was the father of Alexander and Leon Levy and had formerly been a resident of the city. His widow, Sara Klein Levy, returned to New Orleans after Henry's death. Her son, **LEON LEVY** (See entry), sailed for France to bring her back to Louisiana. Thirty-nine-year-old Leon and his fifty-seven-year-old mother, Sara, left from Hamburg, Germany aboard the SS *Wieland*. They landed in New Orleans on 11 May 1876. Sara died in New Orleans on 24 February 1894, surviving both of her children. She was interred there in Gates of Prayer Cemetery # 2 (Joseph Street) near her son, Alexander. (**A, AN, E, GB, TT**)

LEVY, HENRY, was born on 11 April 1862 in *Kuttolsheim*, Bas-Rhin, France, to **NATHAN LEVY**, a native of *Wintzenheim*, Bas-Rhin, and his wife, **LEAH/LISETTE PIOSO**, born in *Kuttolsheim*, Bas-Rhin. According to the 1900 and 1910 federal censuses, Henry immigrated to Louisiana between 1882 and 1885. We believe that the twenty-year-old "H. Levy," a German national, who arrived at New York on 25 July 1883 from London, England, aboard the SS *Persian Monarch* is a likely candidate. Henry was naturalized on 20 February 1890 in St. Mary Parish, LA, where he was working as a merchant. He married SARAH GOLDSTICKER (See entry for **JEANNETTE LEVY**) in New Orleans, Orleans Parish, LA, on 2 April 1890. The couple returned to St. Mary Parish to start their family. They were the parents of seven children: Regina (b. 1892), Rosa (b. 1894), Delphine (b. 1896), Leah (b. 1898), Nathan (b. 1903), Hermina (b. 1907), and Natalie (b. 1909) Henry, Sarah, and their children were enumerated together in the 1910 federal census in Houma, Terrebonne Parish, LA, where they had relocated several years before. Henry was working as a butcher in a slaughter house. His unmarried brother, **SOLOMON LEVY** (See entry), who lived with the family, was working as a laborer in a local market. Henry died on 6 July 1917 at Hotel Dieu Hospital in New Orleans. He was interred at Gates of Prayer Cemetery #2 (Joseph Street). After his death, Sarah Levy moved her family to Youngstown, Mahoning Co., OH, to be near her married daughter, Rosa, the wife of CHARLES SHORR. Sarah was the proprietor of a lodging house there, which according to the 1920 federal census, housed five of her unmarried children, her daughter Rosa Shorr, son-in-law, Charles, grandson, Henry, and nephew Maurice Goldman, as well as seven boarders. Sarah died on 27 September 1924 in Youngstown. Her remains were returned to New Orleans to be buried beside those of her husband at Gates of Prayer Cemetery #2 (Joseph Street). (**A, AN, G, GB, TT**)

LEVY, ISAAC, was born **ISAAC LEVI** on 11 January 1823 in *Marmoutier*, Bas-Rhin, France, to **EMANUEL LEVI**, a native of the town, and his wife, **JEANNETTE/HANNAH BLUM**, born in *Ingwiller*, Bas-Rhin. We believe that twenty-five-year-old Isaac Levy, accompanied by a thirty-year-old cousin, MAX LEVY, arrived in New Orleans, Orleans Parish, LA, on 13 June 1847 from Le Havre, France, aboard the ship *Leonidas*. Isaac started out his career in America as a peddler and settled down in the 1850s with his brother, **JACOB LEVY** (See entry) in Alexandria, Rapides Parish, LA. He was joined by **BENJAMIN WEIL** (See entry), a native of *Bouxwiller*, Bas-Rhin, who would become his business partner and, eventually, his brother-in-law. The Levy brothers and Benjamin Weil formed a warehousing business in Alexandria, which was in operation, according to newspaper accounts, as early as 1859. That same year Isaac became the first president of the Hebrew Benevolent Society of Rapides which was formed in order to dispense funds for the sick and needy Jewish inhabitants in the parish. The society was the forerunner of the Congregation Gemiluth Chassodim, and Isaac, who served until 1861, was, therefore, considered to be the first president of the first Alexandria Jewish Congregation. Thirty-six-year-old Isaac was enumerated, with his mercantile partner, Benjamin Weil, in the 1860 federal census at Alexandria. The two men, working as merchants, were in possession of $10,000 in personal property. After his brother Jacob returned to France in 1862, Isaac enrolled in the First Louisiana Cavalry, Company D, the Rapides Rangers, for service in the War Between the States. Nothing is known of his service, but from other records we have gathered, we know that he continued to engage in the mercantile business in Alexandria, Rapides Parish, Opelousas, St. Landry Parish, and Texas. In March 1863 Isaac Levy & Co. joined with Bloch, Firnberg & Co. of Opelousas, under the name of Levy Bloch & Co. This new partnership had a contract with the Confederate State of Louisiana to import arms and ammunition from Europe via Mexico, and to export cotton back in payment. We know that Isaac was constantly on the move from Louisiana through Texas and into Mexico in order to facilitate cotton and arms shipments. On 17 June 1863, for example, Isaac Levy was reported aboard the British Schooner *Tip Top* which arrived in New Orleans from Matamoros, Mexico. There was much money to be made during this period when the only avenue of trade for the South was the transportation of essential goods and armaments from Europe to Mexico, via ship, and from Mexico through Texas into Louisiana via wagon train. It is not known if Isaac was in Alexandria in April and May of 1864 to witness the destruction of the town by Union troops. However, 1866 tax records show that Isaac, a commission merchant, was doing a brisk trade in sugar, molasses, cotton and leather. He also paid taxes on a carriage, a gold watch and a gold plate. Isaac's partner, Benjamin Weil, returned to France in early 1866 where he was married. Ben returned on 22 June 1866 from Le Havre to New York aboard the SS *Lafayette*. Accompanying him on the voyage were his eighteen-year-old bride, ALICE BLOCH, an eleven-year-old relative, Camille Weil, both natives of Meurthe, Lorraine, France, and his twenty-eight-year-old sister, **SARA WEIL**. Isaac Levy took out a license to marry his partner's sister on 10 July 1866 at New Orleans. His bride was born **SARA WEYL** on 7 June 1834 in *Bouxwiller*, Bas-Rhin, France, to **MARX/MARC WEIL**, a native of *Uhrwiller*, Bas-Rhin, and his wife, **JUDITH REICHSHOFFER**, a native of *Bouxwiller*. Isaac and Sara returned to Alexandria to live. Isaac Levy was naturalized in Rapides Parish on 10 May 1867. Less than seven months later, Isaac, who had returned to New Orleans to seek medical treatment, died on 11 January 1868. The cause of death was consumption. He was interred at Hebrew Rest Cemetery #1 in the city. It is believed that Sara, who had borne one child before her husband's death, returned to France to live as she could not be found in any other American records. (A, AN, FS, G, TT)

LEVY, ISAAC, was born **ISAAC LEVI** on 12 August 1828 in *Riedseltz*, Bas-Rhin, France, to SAMSON LEVI, a native of Heuchelheim, Rheinpfalz, Germany, and his wife ROSETTE LOEB, born in Pleisweiler, Rheinpfalz, Germany. According to the 1900 federal census, Isaac immigrated to New York in 1849. We were unable to find a reliable ship's record for his entry into the United States. His obituary stated that he lived in New York, then in Nebraska, before heading south to Louisiana, where he was enumerated in the 1860 federal census for Pointe Coupée Parish, LA, as a peddler owning $500 worth of merchandise. He served the Confederacy in the Pointe Coupée Artillery, Battery A, enlisting on 29 June 1861. He was assigned to the commissary and acted as a sutler for his company. Wounded at Vicksburg, he returned to his regiment and served at least through 1864. He married SARAH "SETTIE" GUMBEL on 11 June 1867 in New Orleans, Orleans Parish, LA. Settie, born in Rheinpfalz,

Germany, was the sister of SIMON and CORNELIUS GUMBEL, who started out as a merchants in Pointe Coupée Parish, only to become millionaires in New Orleans. Six children were born to Isaac and Settie, three of whom predeceased their parents: Helen (b. 1868), Henry (b. 1872; died 1903), Caroline (b. 1876), Samuel (b. 1878; drowned 1898 in Lake Ponchartrain), Irma H. (b. 1881; died 1898), and Jacob (b. 1882). Isaac Levy, doing business as I. Levi & Co. in partnership with his brother-in-law, Cornelius Gumbel, and Pointe Coupée resident, J.A. St. Germain, owned a general merchandise store at Bayou Fordoche, known as the Eliska Store, and later the Argyle Store. Although a successful merchant in the parish, Isaac moved his family to New Orleans in 1873 where he conducted a wholesale grocery business. Attracted by the rice industry, he opened up the Levy Rice Mill, which he operated until his death on 21 February 1914. He was buried in Hebrew Rest Cemetery # 1 in the city. His wife, Settie, followed on 17 February 1937 and was buried there as well. (**A, AN, BC, G, GB, TT**)

LEVY, ISAAC, died on 6 January 1886 in Clinton, East Feliciana Parish, LA, Engraved on his tombstone were the words "Born at Diefenbach, Alsace. Died Jan. 6, 1886. Age 30 years." We have identified him as Isaac Levy from *Tieffenbach*, Bas-Rhin, as there were no Levy births between 1843-1862 in either *Dieffenbach-lès-Woerth* or *Dieffenbach-au-Val*, two small towns located in the Bas-Rhin. An ISAAC LEVY, however, was born in *Tieffenbach*, Bas-Rhin, France, on 5 September 1850 to JEAN LEVY, a native of Gosselming, Moselle France and his wife **JÜDEL/CAROLINE DALSHEIMER**, born in *Tieffenbach*. Isaac was living there as late as 1866 with his parents. Since two of Caroline Dalsheimer's brothers, **GEORGES** and **LEOPOLD DALSHEIMER** (See entries) had immigrated to Louisiana, it is likely that Isaac Levy from "Diefenbach" was their young nephew. We believe that "Isaac Levy," a twenty-year-old French merchant, who arrived in New York on 19 July 1872, from Brest and Le Havre, France, aboard the SS *St. Laurent*, is likely his record of entry. We also believe that he may have been enumerated in the 1880 federal census as twenty-eight-year-old Isaac Levy, a French retail merchant, who was doing business in St. Charles Parish, LA. (**A, AN, E, ES**)

LEVY, ISIDORE, was born on 20 November 1865 in *Neuwiller-lès-Saverne*, Bas-Rhin, France, to **MICHEL LEVY**, a native of *Langensoultzbach*, Bas-Rhin, France, and his wife, **SARA LEVY**, born in *Ingwiller*, Bas-Rhin. In a 1908 application for a U.S. passport, Isidore stated that he arrived in New York from Le Havre, France, on 12 October 1889 aboard the SS *La Gascogne*. The SS *La Gascogne* docked at New York on 21 October 1889, with but one passenger using a similar name: twenty-one-year-old "Arth. Levy," who may or may not be our immigrant. Isidore made his way to Louisiana just one year ahead of his brother, **ACHILLE LEVY** (See entry), and settled in Napoleonville, Assumption Parish, LA. Isidore was naturalized in Assumption Parish on 3 April 1899. According to the 1900 federal census taken at Napoleonville he and his brother were living together in the town. Thirty-four-year-old Isidore and his thirty-year-old brother Achille were both immigrants from Germany. Isidore was working as a general merchant while Achille was a salesman. By the spring of 1908 when Isidore applied for a U.S. passport to return to France for a few months, he was living in St. Francisville, West Feliciana Parish, LA, where he worked as a salesman. His brother, Achille, who applied for a passport at the same time from Belzoni, Humphreys, Co., MS, probably accompanied Isidore back to France. Forty-four-year-old Isidore was enumerated in the 1910 federal census living in St. Francisville. He was still unmarried and worked as a salesman. Isidore Levy died on 6 April 1916 at Ponchatoula, Tangipahoa Parish, LA. He was interred in Hebrew Rest Cemetery # 1 in New Orleans, Orleans Parish, LA, near his brother. (**A, AN**)

LEVY, ISRAËL, was born **ISRAËL LEVI** on 5 December 1795 in *Bouxwiller*, Bas-Rhin, France, to **MICHEL/MACHOLE LEVI**, a native of *Dettwiller*, Bas-Rhin, France, and his wife **KAILE/SARA JACOB,** born in *Reichshoffen*, Bas-Rhin. Israël married **ESTHER WOLF,** a native of *Büswiller*, Bas-Rhin, France, on 5 March 1818 in *Bouxwiller.* They were the parents of six children: Caroline (b. 1819), Emmanuel (b. 1826), Jeannette (b. 1827) Babette (b. 1829), Heimann (b. 1831) and Sara (b. 1832). Their two sons died in infancy. Israël's wife, Esther, died in Bouxwiller on 19 January 1850. Israel was enumerated with his daughter, Sara, in the 1851 census. A notation next to his name indicated that he was under "high" police surveillance. Israël left France soon afterwards and was enumerated in New Orleans, Orleans Parish, LA, in the 1860 federal census at the home of his daughter, Babette, her husband, **LAZARD BENJAMIN** (see entry), and their son, Charles. We could find no reliable record for his entry into the United States. Israël was engaged in business with his son-in-law. He always lived with or next to Babette while in New Orleans. He followed the family when they moved briefly to Opelousas, St. Landry Parish, LA, where Lazard Benjamin went into business with his son, Charles. Israël died in Opelousas on 19 July 1881 and was buried there in Gemiluth Chassodim Cemetery. (**A, AN, B1851, E, G**)

LEVY, JACOB, was born on 9 January 1819 in *Lauterbourg*, Bas-Rhin, France, to **JOSEPH** LEVY, a native of the town and his wife VOGEL/FANNY ETLINGER, born in Karlsruhe, Baden-Württemberg, Germany. We believe that Jacob was the same as the twenty-nine-year-old "Jacque Levy" who arrived in New Orleans, Orleans Parish, LA, on 7 February 1849 from Le Havre, France aboard the ship *Gironde*. "Jacque" was accompanied by twenty-two-year-old **ROSALIE LEVY** (See entry) and twenty-one-year-old **JACOB LEVY** (See entry) both also natives of *Lauterbourg*. Jacob, who lived only three years in Lousiana, died in Rapides Parish, LA, on 20 September 1853 during one of the worst epidemics of yellow fever that ever plagued the state. He was buried in the Jewish Cemetery in Pineville, Rapides Parish, LA under a marker that gave his correct birth date, his date of death, and his town of origin. He was probably the first husband of MIRIAM WEIL (See entry for **DAVID KUHNAGEL**). Miriam gave birth to a son, Jacob Levy, in 1854, named for his father who had died only months before the baby's birth. Unfortunately, all marriage records for Rapides Parish were lost in May 1864 when the Union Army destroyed most of Alexandria by fire.(**A, AN, G**)

LEVY, JACOB, was born **JACQUES LEVY** on 27 September 1827 in *Lauterbourg*, Bas-Rhin, France, to **BENOÎT LEVY**, a native of the town, and **HENRIETTE MENDEL**, born in *Soultz-sous-Forêts*, Bas-Rhin. We believe that Jacob was the same as the twenty-one-year-old "Jacque Levy" who arrived in New Orleans, Orleans Parish, LA, on 7 February 1849 from Le Havre, France aboard the ship *Gironde*. "Jacque" was accompanied by twenty-two-year-old **ROSALIE LEVY** (See entry), and twenty-nine-year-old "Jacque Levy" (See entry for **JACOB LEVY**. b. 1819), also young immigrants from *Lauterbourg*. We know from the civil records at *Lauterbourg* that Jacob (b. 1827) had a sister, Rosalie, one year his senior. We also know that she had immigrated to Louisiana before 1850, and feel it is highly likely that these two siblings came together to New Orleans. Their elder brother, **ÉDOUARD LEVY** (See entry), who had preceded them in 1842, had married and moved from Colfax, Grant Parish, LA, to Marco, Natchitoches Parish, LA, before finally settling in Alexandria, Rapides

Parish, LA. Rosalie and Jacob settled in Rapides Parish as well. Because there were two Jacob Levys in the Rapides Parish area in the early 1850s, both of them born ca. 1827, one the brother of ÉDOUARD LEVY (See entry), the other, a brother of ISAAC LEVY (See entry) of *Marmoutier* we cannot tell which one of them was enumerated in the 1850 federal census in Rapides Parish, LA, as "Jacob Levy" a twenty-two-year-old peddler from France. We do know that, Edouard's brother, Jacob Levy from *Lauterbourg*, the subject of this entry, took out a license to marry HENRIETTA/LEHDA BROWN, a native of Prussia, on 4 February 1855 in New Orleans. The couple settled in Natchitoches, Natchitoches Parish, LA, where they were enumerated in the 1860 federal census. Jacob owned a retail merchandise store in town. They were the parents of four children: Julia (b. 1856), Coleman (b. 1857), Benjamin (b. 1859), and Daniel (b. 1862). Henrietta died on 11 March 1897 at Natchitoches and was buried there in the Jewish Cemetery. After her death, Jacob stayed in Natchitoches and lived with his daughter Julia, her husband, HARRIS KAFFIE, and their ten children. Jacob died on 22 January 1906 in Natchitoches and was interred with his wife. Note: We know that this "Jacob Levy, " who died in Natchitoches, was Edouard Levy's brother because Jacob's 1906 obituary listed him as the uncle of Mrs. C[elina] Geiger, Edouard Levy's daughter. (**A, AN, FS, G**)

LEVY, JACOB, was born **JACQUES LEVI** on 28 March 1828 in *Ingwiller*, Bas-Rhin, France, to **EMANUEL LEVI**, a native *Marmoutier*, Bas-Rhin, and his wife, **JEANNETTE/HANNAH BLUM**, born in *Ingwiller*, Bas-Rhin. He may have immigrated to Louisiana from Le Havre, France, arriving in New Orleans, Orleans Parish, LA, on 13 December 1847 aboard the ship *Francis Depau*. We were unable to find any other reliable ship's record for his entry. His brother, **ISAAC LEVY** (See entry), born in 1823 in *Marmoutier*, Bas-Rhin, had arrived in June of 1847 aboard the ship *Leonidas*. Because there were two Jacob Levys in the Rapides Parish area ca. 1850, one the brother of **ÉDOUARD LEVY** (See entry), the other, a brother of **ISAAC LEVY** (See entry) of *Marmoutier*, Bas-Rhin, we do not know which one of them was enumerated in the 1850 federal census in Rapides Parish, LA, as "Jacob Levy" a twenty-two-year-old peddler from France. Jacob from *Ingwiller*, the subject of this entry, joined forces with his brother, Isaac, and Isaac's partner, **BENJAMIN WEIL** (See entry), and a cousin, MARX/MAX LEVY, about whom we could find no more credible information, at the firm of Isaac Levy & Co., working as a commission merchant in Alexandria, Rapides Parish. Before long, a branch office was opened in St. Landry Parish, with Jacob as its manager. Jacob was enumerated in the 1860 federal census at Opelousas as a thirty-two-year-old merchant from France with $4200 in real estate and $6300 in personal property. Jacob did not remain in the United States for much longer, although he remained a named partner in Isaac Levy & Co until its dissolution in 1865. Upon returning to France, ca. 1861, Jacob, always called "Jacques" in France, married **HENRIETTE LEVI**, his first cousin, on 18 July 1861 in *Strasbourg*, Bas-Rhin. Henriette was born on 27 October 1833 at *Marmoutier*, Bas-Rhin, France, to **ISAAC LEVI** and **SARA**, née **LEVI**, both natives of the town. Jacques and Henriette were the parents of six children, all born at *Strasbourg*: Anna (b. 1862), Emanuel (b. 1863), Myria (b. 1865), Arthur (b. 1867), Jules (b. 1868), and Rosa (b. 1870). Jacques Levi died at *Strasbourg* on 1 March 1871. His widow, Henriette Levi, pursued a claim with the "French & American Claims Commission," which started taking testimony in 1880 from French citizens who sought reparations for goods seized by the Union Army during the Civil War. Henriette alleged that her deceased husband was, during his life, a member of the firm of Isaac Levy & Co., consisting of Jacob Levy, deceased, Isaac Levy, deceased, Benjamin Weil, deceased, and Marx Levy, a resident of New Orleans. Isaac Levy & Co. had been in business in Alexandria, Rapides Parish, LA, during the Civil War. Henriette was seeking remuneration in the amount of one-fourth of the monies due on account of the seizure of 253 bales of cotton taken by Union Captain F. G. Pope, Company D, Forty-First Regiment Massachusetts Volunteers in April 1863. She also claimed Benjamin Weil's share of any settlement made because her late husband had purchased his share of the business in March 1866. Henriette Levy's claim was disallowed on 25 June 1881. According to the agreement between the governments of France and the United States, the claimant (in this case, the widow, on behalf of herself and her minor children) had to be a citizen of France to have any standing before the Commission. Henriette and her children had become citizens of Germany when Alsace was ceded to Germany on 10 May 1871 at the close of the Franco-Prussian War. Although the people of Alsace had had the opportunity to opt for French citizenship until 1 October 1872, Henriette had not elected to do so. Therefore she had no standing before the Commission. Moreover, since Benjamin Weil was a citizen of the United States at the time of the alleged seizure of the firm's cotton, Henriette Levy was not entitled to collect from the share her late husband had purchased from him. (**A, AN, CA, GB, TT**)

LEVY, JACQUES M., was born **JACQUES LEVI** on 16 January 1845 in *Marmoutier*, Bas-Rhin, France, to **MICHEL LEVY** and his wife, **LÉA/AGATHE DREYFUSS**, both natives of the town. According to his own recollection in an 1890 U.S. passport application, he immigrated to Louisiana from Le Havre in October 1859 aboard the ship *Lemuel Dyer*, an assertion which could not be proven given the records available to us at present. He was the first of four siblings to immigrate to Louisiana. Jacques settled in Bastrop, Morehouse Parish, LA where he was enumerated with his brother, **MATHIEU LEVY** (See entry) in 1870. Jacques, a dry goods merchant, was a single twenty-six-year old immigrant from France who owned $7000 in real estate and $7000 in personal property, quite a large sum for the time. He married MARY E. R. MCLEOD in New Orleans on 1 April 1873 at the bride's mother's home. Mary was a New Orleans native whose parents were of Scottish origin. He and his wife remained in New Orleans where he worked as a clothing clerk. Jacques and Mary were the parents of two children: Jacqueline (b. 1874) and William (b. 1876). Jacques later became a traveling salesman for a New Orleans dry goods firm. The couple's son, William McLeod Levy, drowned in New Orleans on 1 June 1883 at the age of seven years, five months and five days. Jacques' wife, Mary, died in New Orleans on 17 July 1887. On December 30 1896, Jacques who was still working as a travelling salesman almost lost his life in a fire which destroyed the Exchange Hotel in Alexandria, Rapides Parish, LA. He was brought out unconscious but survived with only the loss of his clothing. Jacques died in Little Rock, Pulaski Co., AR, on 14 February 1900, while on a business trip. According to a report in the New Orleans *Daily Picayune*, Jacques' remains were returned to New Orleans where they were interred next to his wife. We have not been able to locate a place of burial for Jacques, his wife, or his son William, although we know that Mary's father, William McLeod, a New Orleans fireman, who was killed in the line of duty, on 17 March 1854, while fighting a blaze at the corner of Magazine and Natchez Streets,was buried in Greenwood Cemetery in New Orleans. (**A, AN, E, G, GB**)

LEVY, JEANNETTE, was born on 12 December 1834 in *Niederbronn-les-Bains*, Bas-Rhin, France, to **ELIE/ELIAS LEVI/ LEVY**, a native of the town, and his wife, RÉGINE/REINE

EBERHARDT, born in Burrweiler, Rheinpfalz, Germany. The marriage banns between NATHAN HIRSCH GOLDSTICKER and Jeannette Levy were posted in Paris, Ile-de-France, France on 23 August 1860. Nathan may have been born in Pirmasens, Rheinpfalz, Germany, the birth place inscribed on his elder sister FANNY GOLDSTICKER JOSEY's tombstone at Beth-El Cemetery in San Antonio, Bexar Co., TX. Jeannette and Nathan remained in Paris during the course of the American Civil War where four of their children were born: Herman (b. 1861), Rosalie (b. 1863), Morris (b. 1865), and Bertha (b. 1867). Nathan, as was the case with many immigrant families, left for America ahead of his wife, a record of which we have been unable to find. Jeannette set out with her four children from Le Havre aboard the SS *Cordova*, which arrived in New York on 17 April 1868. It is possible that the family remained in New York for a time. Their last child, Sarah, according to several census records, was born there in 1870, no record of which has been located. The family did not appear in the 1870 federal census for New York or for Louisiana. It is possible that they were en route during the time the censuses were taken. What is clear is that the family settled in Monroe, Ouachita Parish, Louisiana, where Nathan Hirsch Goldsticker worked as a butcher. He was set upon at his place of business by an African-American assailant who struck him on the side of the head with a tree limb on 16 October 1874. Nathan was carried home to his wife and five children and succumbed there twelve hours later on Saturday, 17 October 1874. A member of the local chapters of the Odd Fellows and B'nai B'rith, as well as a firefighter with the Ouachita Steam Fire Company, he was laid to rest with honors at Rosena Chapel Jewish Cemetery in Monroe. His widow and children moved to New Orleans, Orleans Parish, LA. Because Jeannette was unable to take care of all of her children, the family had split up by the time of the 1880 federal census. The two youngest children, thirteen-year-old Bertha and nine-year-old Sarah, had been placed in the Home for Jewish Widows and Orphans in New Orleans. Jeannette and her fifteen-year-old son, Morris, said to be a jeweler, and fifteen-year-old daughter, Rosalie, lived on Dryades Street where Jeannette was working as a peddler. Her eldest son, Herman, had been sent to Luling, Caldwell Co., TX, where he was enumerated in the household of his uncle and aunt, Joseph and Fanny Goldsticker Josey. Joseph Josey owned a grocery where Herman worked as a clerk. Morris Goldsticker moved to Louisville, Jefferson Co. KY ca. 1884. Nineteen-year-old Morris died from an "abscess of the ear" on 1 January 1885 at City Hospital in Louisville. He was alleged to have been buried in Potter's Field because no relatives could be located. After his employer learned of his death a committee of Jewish citizens took steps to find his body. When the wooden casket was located and brought up, there was no corpse contained within. This same committee instituted a search warrant for the body, which was located on 9 January 1885 at the Louisville University of Medicine on a dissecting table surrounded by medical students. He was reinterred as "Morris Goldstick" at Schardein Cemetery in Louisville. Rosalie Goldsticker married Raphael Goldman on 7 November 1883 in New Orleans. The couple moved to Ohio, where twenty-nine-year-old Rosalie, a mother of four, died from an "abscess" in March 1893. Thirty-three-year-old Herman Goldsticker died a year later on 12 August 1894 in New Orleans and was interred there in Gates of Prayer Cemetery # 2 (Joseph Street). Only two of her children, Bertha and Sarah, survived Jeannette Levy Goldsticker who died on 25 October 1916 in New Orleans. She was buried there in Gates of Prayer Cemetery #2 (Joseph Street). Sarah married **HENRY LEVY** (See entry) and had a large family in Houma, Terrebonne Parish, LA. Bertha never married. She was interred near her mother on 3 January 1959. Note: Jeannette was the sister of **LEON LEVY** (See entry), and **BABETTE LEVY** (See entry for **SAMUEL WOLF**). (**A, AN, G, GB, NP, TT**)

LEVY, JOSEPH, was born on 15 May 1843 at *Lauterbourg*, Bas-Rhin, France, to **BENOÎT LEVY**, a native of the town, and his second wife, **JEANNETTE KAHN**, born in *Odratzheim*, Bas-Rhin. He immigrated to Louisiana, following four half-siblings, and settled in Natchitoches Parish, LA, after the Civil War. According to the 1920 federal census for Alexandria, Rapides Parish, LA, seventy-four-year-old Joseph Levy, a widower had immigrated to Louisiana in 1866, a reliable record for which we were not able to find. Joseph married JULIA BLOOM, born in 1846 in Ingenheim, Rhinepfalz, Germany, on 11 January 1875 in Alexandria, Rapides Parish, LA. The couple had no children. Joseph Levy retired from his business in Provençal, Natchitoches Parish, LA, in 1908 and he and his wife moved back to Alexandria. Julia Bloom Levy died in Alexandria on 20 October 1913 and was buried in the Jewish Cemetery in Pineville, Rapides Parish, LA. Joseph died on 25 September 1929 and was interred near his wife. Note: See entries for **EDOUARD LEVY**, **JACOB LEVY** born 1827, **ROSALIE LEVY**, and **JACOB ISRAEL**, husband of **NANETTE LEVY**)(**A, AN, FS, G**)

LEVY, JOSEPH, was born on 6 December 1849 in *Marmoutier*, Bas-Rhin, France, to **JONAS LEVY**, born in 1818 at *Birkenwald*, Bas-Rhin, France and his wife, **JEANNETTE MICHEL**, a native of *Schwenheim*, Bas-Rhin. He may have been the nineteen-year-old "Joseph Levi, a French citizen, who arrived at New York from Liverpool, England, on 15 June 1868 aboard the ship *Isaac Webb*. He first appeared in the 1870 federal census for Bastrop, Morehouse, Parish, LA, working as a clerk in his Uncle **MICHEL LEVY**'s store. (See entry) Ten years later he was still employed by his uncle at Bastrop. Joseph never married. He died in Bastrop on 6 March 1889 and was buried there in B'nai Sholom Jewish Cemetery. (**A, AN, G**)

LEVY, JOSEPH, was born on 5 November 1872 in *Duppigheim*, Bas-Rhin, France, to **HENRI LEVY**, a native of *Duppigheim*, Bas-Rhin, France, and his wife, **CAROLINE KLOTZ**, born in *Bischheim*, Bas-Rhin. In his 1907 application for a U.S. passport, Joseph wrote that he arrived in America aboard the SS *Gascogne* on 16 July 1893. Nineteen-year-old Joseph Levy, whose destination was New Orleans, Orleans Parish, LA, did, in fact, arrive on 25 July 1892 at New York from Le Havre, France, aboard the SS *La Gascogne*. Joseph worked as a merchant with his first cousin, **OSCAR LEVY** (See entry), in both Franklin, St. Mary Parish, LA, and later St. Joseph, Tensas Parish, LA. He married FABIOLA LOWENSTEIN MOORE in 1912 in New Orleans. They had one child, Joseph N., born in 1913 in New Orleans. Shortly thereafter the family moved to Oklahoma, where Joseph was a shoe merchant. Joseph Levy died on 10 May 1954 in Tulsa City, Tulsa Co., OK. He was buried in the Jewish section of Rose Hill Cemetery in Tulsa. Fabiola died four years later on 23 September 1958 and was interred with her husband.(**A, AN, G**)

LEVY, LAZARD, was born **LAZARE LEVY** on 16 March 1866 in *Duppigheim*, Bas-Rhin, France, to **RAPHAEL LEVY** (See entry), a native of the town, and his wife, THÉRÈSE DOROTHÉE KOCH/KOCK, born in Germany. After living almost a decade in Louisiana, Raphael, Thérèse, and their four children had sought temporary refuge back in *Duppigheim* during the American Civil War. The Levy family, including five-month-old Lazard, sailed aboard the SS *Sorrento* out of Le Havre, France, arriving back at New Orleans, Orleans Parish, LA, on 1 December 1866. They settled in St. James Parish, Louisiana. Lazard and several of his brothers went on to develop their father's sugar interests. Lazard expanded the family's holdings, buying the Cote Blanche sugar plantation in Franklin, St. Mary Parish, LA, which he developed and then sold to a Kansas City Consortium in 1903 for a large profit. He retained the presidency of this new corporation for himself. Lazard's life, however, ended tragically. On 30 June 1903, while he stood at the Cote Blanche crossing of the Morgan Railway where sugar was shipped out to nearby refineries, he was fatally shot by Benjamin Johnson, a local resident. Lazard was taken to the Franklin Sanitarium where, with his brother, Marcus, at his side, he died several hours later. Conscious until the end, he refused to explain why he had been shot. Johnson, speaking from his jail cell, would only say that he had done it to preserve his family's honor. Days later, friends of the accused came forward to say that Johnson believed that Levy had sullied his daughter's reputation and demanded that he marry her. The situation came to a head when, according to these same friends, Johnson learned that Levy intended to return to Alsace for a time. On the morning of Levy's departure, Johnson and his son provoked a confrontation at the Morgan crossing which led to the fatal shooting. On 1 July 1903, Lazard's remains were taken to Hebrew Rest Cemetery #2 in New Orleans, Orleans Parish, LA, where they were interred. He was only thirty-seven years of age and had never married. (**A, AN, E, GB, TT**).

LEVY, LAZARE, was born on 5 April 1858 in *Strasbourg*, Bas-Rhin, France, to **JOSEPH LEVY**, born in *Oberschaeffolsheim*, Bas-Rhin, and his wife, **JUDITH BLUM**, a native of *Gundershoffen*, Bas-Rhin. We believe that he was likely the sixteen-year-old "Lazarus Levy" who arrived from Le Havre, France, at New York on 18 May 1874 aboard the SS *Holland*. He was enumerated in Opelousas, St. Landry Parish, LA, in the 1880 federal census where he was working as a clerk in a store. He boarded with several fellow Frenchmen, including his brother, **ACHILLE ALPHONSE LEVY** (See entry), and Joseph L. Cain, his future brother-in-law. Lazare moved to New Orleans, Orleans Parish, LA, ca. 1888, where he married JEANNETTE/JENNIE CAIN, the Louisiana born, daughter, of LAMBERT BERNARD CAIN, a native of Thiaucourt, Meurthe-et-Moselle, France, who became the first president of Touro Infirmary. Lazare and Jennie were married on 14 June 1888 in New Orleans. Twenty-five-year-old Jennie died on 2 May 1891 and was buried in Hebrew Rest Cemetery #1 in New Orleans. Lazare married Jennie's sister, Isabella, on 27 December 1892. The couple raised their seven children in New Orleans: Jeannette (b. 1895), Caroline Cain (b. 1898), Alphonse (b. 1901), Milton (b. 1903), Edwin

(b. 1905), Gladys (b. 1908) and Lazare (b. 1910). Lazare opened a wholesale grocery business, Lazare Levy & Co., in partnership with his brother-in-law, Joseph L. Cain. Lazare was following in the footsteps of his father, Joseph, who had been in the same business in *Strasbourg*. Lazare died on 19 September 1941 in New Orleans and was buried in Hebrew Rest Cemetery #2 in the city. Isabella died on 4 November 1943, and was buried with him. (**A, AN, G, GB, HJL**)

LEVY, LEHMANN, was born **LEHMANN LEVI** on 3 November 1829 in *Dehlingen*, Bas-Rhin, France, to **JOSEPH LEVI**, a native of *Neuwiller-lès-Saverne*, Bas-Rhin, and his wife, **ROSINE/REINE LEVI**, born in *Dehlingen*, Bas-Rhin. At the time of the 1851 census of *Dehlingen*, twenty-one-year-old Lehmann Levy was living with his parents and working as a merchant. Lehmann immigrated to Louisiana before 1854, a reliable record for which we have not been able to find. He was first recorded in New Orleans, Orleans Parish, LA, on 26 April 1854, when he took out a license to marry **FANNY LEVY**. Fanny was born **MINETTE LEVI** on 13 December 1824 in *Duppigheim*, Bas-Rhin, France, to **LIPPMAN LEVI** and his wife, **ZIBORE** née **LEVI**, both natives of the town. Minette was enumerated as "Fanny" Levy, a twenty-six-year-old single woman living in her widowed mother's *Duppigheim* household, in the 1851 census for *Duppigheim*. We were unable to locate an immigration record for her. Lehmann and Fanny settled in New Orleans where he worked as a peddler in the city. He and Fanny had four children before the start of the Civil War: Goton (b. 1855; died before 1860), Liebmann/Leon (b. 1856), Pauline (b. 1858) and Joseph (b. 1860). The family returned to France after the beginning of hostilities between the North and the South. Their daughter Julia was born there in 1865. We have not been able to find her birth record as we could not ascertain where they settled when they returned to their native land. They did not go back to *Duppigheim* as had Fanny's brother, **RAPHAEL LEVY** (See entry), nor to Lehmann Levy's home town of *Dehlingen*. Thirty-six-year-old Lehmann, thirty-nine-year-old Fanny and their children Leon (7y), Pauline (6y), Joseph (4y), and four-month-old Julia returned to New Orleans on 6 December 1865 from Le Havre aboard the SS *Maria Luck*. Lehmann resumed his work as a peddler and the couple had one more child, Salomon, born on 29 September 1868. Lehmann eventually made enough money to open up a small dry goods store. Fanny died in New Orleans on 3 April 1908 and was buried there in Gates of Prayer Cemetery #2 (Joseph Street). Lehmann followed on 9 February 1913 and was buried with her. Their daughter Julia never married. She died on 19 January 1919 and was buried near her parents. (**A, AN, B1851, E, G, GB**)

LEVY, LÉON, was born on 13 July 1838 in *Niederbronn-les-Bains*, Bas-Rhin, France, to **ELIE/ELIAS LEVI/LEVY**, a native of the town, and his wife, **RÉGINE/REINE EBERHARDT**, born in Burrweiler, Rheinpfalz, Germany. Nineteen-year-old Leon Levy arrived in New Orleans, Orleans Parish, LA, with an older sister, **BABETTE LEVY** (See entry), from Le Havre, France, on 7 December 1857 aboard the ship *Nuremberg*. Twenty-one-year-old Leon was enumerated for the first time in Louisiana, in the 1860 federal census as the next door neighbor of his sister, Babette Levy Wolf, at Waterloo, Pointe Coupée Parish, LA. He took out a license to marry Wilhelmina/Mina Gerken, the widow of Louis Seitz, in New Orleans on 24 June 1864. Leon opened his own tobacco shop in New Orleans where he and Mina raised her daughter, Amelia/Emelia Seitz, as well as three children of their own: Leontine (b. 1865), Savina (b. 1866), and Isidore (b. 1869). Mina, who was not Jewish, died on 6 December 1892 in New Orleans and was buried there in Greenwood Cemetery. Leon followed on 23 May 1912 and was buried with her. (**A, AN, GB, TT**)

LEVY, LÉON, was born **LAZARD LEVI** on 8 May 1837 in *Ingwiller*, Bas-Rhin, France, to **HENRI/HIRTZEL ELIE LEVY** (See entry) and his wife, **SARA KLEIN**, both natives of the town. Thirty-nine-year-old Sara, her two children, sixteen-year-old Elie, and fifteen-year-old Lazare, were enumerated in the 1851 Bas-Rhin census for *Ingwiller,* living with her seventy-three-year-old father, Moïse Klein, and thirty-four-year-old sister, Élise Klein. Sara's husband, Henri, had already gone to America to establish himself in order to bring his family over at a later time. Henry returned to France ca. 1852 to accompany his family back to New Orleans, Orleans Parish, LA. Henry, Sara, Lazare and Elie were recorded as passengers arriving at New Orleans on 5 April 1852 aboard the SS *Edward Everett.* According to the 1860 federal census for New Orleans, twenty-three-year-old Leon Levy was living with his parents, Henri and Sara Levy, and working as a clerk. Leon took out a license to marry FELICIE LEVY, a twenty-one-year-old native of New Orleans, on 23 February 1865. Felicie was the daughter of **MINETTE RIES** (See entry) of *Oberna*i, Bas-Rhin, and her husband, BINELL LEVY, a native of Lixheim, Meurthe, France. Leon and Felicie were the parents of three daughters: Ada (b. 1866; died 1871), Ella (b. 1867) and Ernestine

"Tinie" (b. 1869; See entry for **LEOPOLD KLEIN**). Leon was originally a dry goods merchant. He had probably taken over his father's store after the latter retired to France. In May 1876 Leon returned to France to bring his newly-widowed mother, **SARA KLEIN** (See entry for **HENRY LEVY**), back to New Orleans to live. Several years later, ca. 1878, he joined his brother **ALEXANDER LEVY** (See entry) in partnership in the auction house, A. & L. Levy. Forty-five-year-old Leon Levy, his thirty-five-year-old wife, "Felice," and their two daughters, thirteen-year-old Ella and eleven-year-old "Dina, [sic]" were enumerated in the 1880 federal census as boarders living at #13 Royal Street in the French Quarter. Leon was employed as an "auctioneer." Not long after that, Leon abandoned the business to go into the Central American trade. As early as January 1883 his passage from Colon, Panama to New Orleans aboard the *Lucy P. Miller* was recorded in the New Orleans *Daily Picayune*. He was one of seven passengers returning to the city along with 2950 bunches of bananas. From that date until his death in 1889 there were numerous ship's records for him, his wife Félicie, his two sons-in-law: Tinie's husband, Leopold Klein, and Ella's husband, Isidore Rich, as well as Isidore's brother Abe Rich. The families traveled back and forth between Panama, British Honduras, Livingston, Guatemala and New Orleans, taking advantage of the trade opportunities that had opened up in Central America due to the efforts of the French government to construct the Panama Canal. Leon's new career was short-lived. He died in Livingston, Guatemala on 3 August 1889. Since there is no burial record for him in New Orleans, it is presumed that he was buried in Livingston at the local Jewish cemetery. His son-in-law, Leopold Klein, who continued to work in Central America, died in Livingston five years later at the age of thirty-five and was also buried in Central America. Leon's wife, Felicie Levy died on 4 February 1916 in New Orleans and was buried there at Hebrew Rest Cemetery # 1. (**A, AN, AP, B1851, GB, TT**)

LEVY, LOUIS, was born **NEPHTALI LEVY** on 17 January 1854 in *Romanswiller*, Bas-Rhin, France, to **ARON LEVY**, a native of the town, and his wife **MINDEL/MADELEINE MARX**, born in *Kuttolsheim*, Bas-Rhin. He immigrated after the Franco-Prussian War to join his sister, **ANNETTE LEVY** (See entry), in Franklin, St. Mary Parish, LA. He may have been the twenty-four-year-old grocer "L. Levy" who emigrated from Le Havre, France, arriving at New York on 9 October 1878 aboard the SS *Labrador*. Louis became a storekeeper for Edward Kissack, an English planter, in Calumet, near Franklin, St. Mary Parish, LA. He married PAULINE MAYER, a Louisiana native, on 19 February 1884, in the parish. Pauline was the twenty year old daughter of Reine Bloch Mayer, who was a sister-in-law of Louis's sister Annette. Louis and Pauline had eight children, all born in Calumet, St. Mary Parish: Edna (b. 1885), Harcourt Nathaniel (b. 1886), Norma Reine (b. 1889), Florence Clara (b. 1891), Gertrude Miriam (b. 1892) Edwin Mayer (b. 1894), Clarice Fannie (b. 1897), and Ida Emily (b. 1900). The family moved into the town of Franklin after the First World War, where Louis was a dry goods merchant, and then from there, ca. 1920, to New Orleans, Orleans Parish, LA, where Louis was the president of his own mattress factory. He died on 7 June 1926 and was buried in Hebrew Rest Cemetery # 2 in the city. Pauline died on 9 February 1941, and was buried in the same cemetery (**A, AN, G, GB**)

LEVY, LUCIEN, was born **LEHMANN LEVY** on 24 February 1869 in *Duppigheim*, Bas-Rhin, France, to **LIPPMANN LEVY** and his wife **JEANNETTE DRÉYFUS**, both natives of the town. Lucien, as he was always called in the United States, emigrated from Le Havre, France, arriving at New York on 22 July 1889 aboard the SS *Normandie*. He settled in Louisiana where he worked as a clerk and salesman in various dry goods establishments. He filed his declaration of intention to become a U.S. citizen at Crowley, Acadia Parish, LA, on March 25, 1896. By the time citizenship was granted to him on 11 December 1907, Lucien was a resident of New Orleans, Orleans Parish, LA. He sailed to France in September 1919 where he visited a brother, Alfred Aaron Levy, who worked there as an engraver at a printing company. He returned to the states via New York in May 1920. Lucien applied for a U.S. passport in June 1921 to return to France to visit his parents. He gave his address as 225 Bourbon Street. He sailed home from France in October 1921 landing once again in New York. This was just one of many trips he would make back and forth. Between these voyages he lived variously at 1200 Lowerline Street and 221 Bourbon Street in New Orleans and continued to worked as a clerk and salesman in the city. The last record we have for him was his return passage from France to New York on 17 September 1929. He had given his address as 221 Bourbon Street, New Orleans. Lucien died on 12 March 1953 at Créteil, Val-de-Marne, France. Créteil is a suburb of Paris, southeast of the city. A notation of his date and place of death was affixed to his *Duppigheim* birth record. (**A, AN**)

LEVY, MARX MEYER, was born **MARC LEVY** on 19 July 1866 in *Niederroedern*, Bas-Rhin , France , to **MOISE LEVY** (See entry), a native of *Niederbronn-les-Bains*, Bas-Rhin, France, and his wife, **ROSALIE MEYER**, born in *Niederroedern*, Bas-Rhin. He immigrated with his parents and siblings, arriving in New York on 8 December 1868 from Hamburg, Germany, aboard the SS *Holsatia*. The family settled in Forest, Scott Co, MS, then moved to Evergreen, Avoyelles Parish, LA before the 1880 federal census. Marx worked in his father's general store. He married BLANCHE MATILDA "BONNIE" GOUDCHAUX on 29 January 1899 in Opelousas, St. Landry Parish, LA. She was born on 13 May 1876 at Big Cane, St. Landry Parish, LA, to **LEOPOLD GOUDCHAUX** (See entry) and his wife, CHARLOTTE EILERT. Marx and Bonnie lived in Provençal, Natchitoches Parish, LA, where Marx was a merchant. They moved to Alexandria, Rapides Parish, LA, before the 1910 federal census where Marx worked as a travelling salesman for over 20 years. Three sons, Marion G. (b. 1900), Victor L. (b. 1904), Donald Eilert (b. 1905), and a daughter, Lottie Rhoda (b.1901) were born to the couple. After a few years out west in the 1930s, in San Francisco, San Francisco Co., CA, where they had joined their son,Victor, who was employed as a window trimmer in a department store, they returned to Louisiana. They lived with their daughter, Lottie, and her husband, Sol Riff, in Lake Charles, Calcasieu Parish, LA. Marx died on 7 October 1937 in Lake Charles, and was buried there in Graceland, the Jewish section of Orange Grove Cemetery. His wife, Blanche died on 25 July 1962 and was buried with him. (**A, AN, AP, FS, G**)

LEVY, MARY, was born **MARIE LEVY** on 30 August 1845 in *Duppigheim*, Bas-Rhin, France, to **ABRAHAM LEVY**, a native of the town, and his wife, **SARA LANG**, born in *Dambach-la-Ville*, Bas-Rhin. Twenty-one-year-old Marie Levy was enumerated in the 1866 *Duppigheim* town census, living with her father, Abraham Levy, step-mother, **ROSETTE BLUM**, and six siblings. We were unable to find a reliable ship's record for her arrival in the United States. Mary died in New Orleans, Orleans Parish,LA, on 9 September 1878 during one of the worst yellow fever epidemics in the city after the end of the Civil War. She was interred in the Gates of Mercy Cemetery at Jackson and Saratoga Streets, which was razed in the 1950s. Her tombstone, with her correct date and place of birth "*Duppigheim*, Elsas," clearly visible, is in Gates of Prayer Cemetery #2 (Joseph Street), where the stone, and, perhaps, her remains were moved subsequent to the closing of Gates of

Mercy Cemetery. We ordered the death record for a "Mary Levy" who died on 9 September 1878 in New Orleans. Unfortunately this record listed her age as "seven years" and that she died in Touro Infirmary from yellow fever on 8 September 1878. Although the 9 September date of death on the tombstone may have been the date of burial, during a year such as 1878 when there was high mortality, there was probably much confusion with record keeping. For that reason we cannot be sure that the thirty-three-year-old Mary Levy from *Duppigheim* who died on 9 September 1878 is the same as the Mary Levy who died at Touro Infirmary from yellow fever. (**A, AN, E, L, TT**)

LEVY, MATHIEU, was born on 25 June 1846 in *Marmoutier*, Bas-Rhin, France, to **MICHEL LEVY** and his wife, **LÉA/AGATHE DREYFUSS**, both natives of the town. According to his naturalization papers, dated 4 May 1875, issued in Bastrop, Morehouse Parish, LA, he immigrated to America in 1866. We believe he may have been the "Mathu Levy" who arrived in New York from Le Havre, France, on 28 February 1867 aboard the SS *Harvest Home*. Mathieu joined his brother, **JACQUES M. LEVY** (See entry), who had settled in Bastrop six years previously. Mathieu was married in Morehouse Parish on 26 February 1873 to HERMINA LEOPOLD, a native of Germany. Mathieu and his family lived in Bastrop for fifteen years, being joined by a brother **ACHILLE LEVY** (See entry), who came over in 1871 and who settled in nearby Campti, Morehouse Parish, LA. Three of Mathieu's six children were born in Bastrop: Jeannette (b. 1873), Alphonse Samuel (b. 1876), and Julia (b. 1880). Shortly after Julia's birth Mathieu and Mina relocated to Hot Springs, Garland Co., AR, where he opened up a dry goods store. Two more sons were born to the couple in Hot Springs: Sylvan (b. 1881) and Arthur Aaron (b. 1884). The family moved permanently to New Orleans, Orleans Parish, LA, before the birth of their last child, William Salomon, in August 1886. Mathieu died on 16 October 1897 of yellow fever and was buried in Dispersed of Judah Cemetery in the city. His wife, Mina Leopold, died on 7 September 1941 in New Orleans, and was buried with him. (**A, AN, G, GB**)

LEVY, MAURICE, was born on 5 December 1864 in *Ingwiller*, Bas-Rhin, France, to **JACQUES LEVY**, a native of the town, and his wife, **FRÉDÉRIQUE/FANNY LEVY**, born in *Niederbronn-les-Bains*, Bas-Rhin. According to information he supplied in his 1890 application for a U.S. passport, he arrived in America in March 1880 aboard the SS

Gascogne from Le Havre, France. Five years later in another passport application he stated that he had arrived in 1880 on the SS *Normandie*, neither assertion we were able to verify using the records available to us. We did find the arrival of a sixteen-year-old "M. Levy," a native of "Alsatia, Germany," who arrived in New York from Le Havre, France, on 6 November 1879 aboard the SS *France*, which is worthy of consideration. Maurice went to work in Assumption Parish, first in Hohen Solms, probably as a store keeper at the Germania-Elise Plantation, a 1700 acre sugar cane farm complete with its own sugar refinery. Maurice was married to DELPHINE FARRNBACHER on 6 June 1899 at the bride's home in Baton Rouge, East Baton Rouge Parish, LA, by Rabbi **MARX KLEIN** (See entry), a native of *Hatten*, Bas-Rhin. Delphine, a Louisiana native, was the daughter of **PAULINE BLOCH** (See entry) and her husband JACOB FARRNBACHER. Maurice and Delphine settled at Elm Hall, the largest sugar plantation in Assumption Parish, two miles from Napoleonville, where Maurice had accepted a position as manager of the general store. Their only son Jacques/Jack Farrenbacher Levy was born there in 1908. By the time of the 1910 federal census the Levy family had settled in New Orleans, Orleans Parish, LA, where Maurice worked as a dry goods merchant. Maurice died on 18 July 1925 in the city and was buried at Hebrew Rest Cemetery #2. Ninety-five-year-old Delphine died on 14 December 1968 in New Orleans. She was buried with her husband. (**A, AN, GB**)

LEVY, MICHEL, was born on 17 July 1824 to **SAMSON LEVY**, a native of *Birkenwald*, Bas-Rhin, France, and his wife, **CAROLINE KAHN,** born in *Balbronn*, Bas-Rhin. He arrived in New Orleans on 20 July 1846 from Le Havre, France, aboard the ship *J.H. Cooper*. Michel worked as an itinerant merchant, and was enumerated in the 1850 federal census in Avoyelles Parish with Bavarian native, Solomon Zucker (later Solomon Sugar), both of whom would eventually settle in Bastrop, Morehouse Parish, LA. Michel married ELIZA FRIEDHEIM ca. 1853, a record of which we were unable to find. Eliza was a native of Lamsheim, Bavaria, Germany. Michel and Eliza were the parents of four children: Rosalie (b. 1854), Samson (b. 1856), Julia (b. 1859), and Joseph (b. 1866), all born in Bastrop, where Michel had opened a very successful dry goods store. Michel died on 1 June 1895 in Bastrop and was buried there in B'nai Sholom Jewish Cemetery. Eliza died six months later, on 4 December 1895 and was buried next to him. (**A, AN, G**)

LEVY, MOÏSE, was born on 12 October 1808 in *Obernai* (*Obereinheim*), Bas-Rhin, France, to **LAZARE LEVY** and his wife, **ZIPPORE/ZIBORA/SARA GOMBRICH**. Both Lazare and Zippore were enumerated with their respective families in the 1784 Census of Jews for *Obereinheim*, so there is a high probability that they were born in the town. Moïse was their seventh child, their first, Ève, having been born in *Obereinheim* in 1788. Forty-six-year-old Moïse Levy immigrated to New Orleans, Orleans Parish, LA, on 2 July 1855 aboard the ship *Wurtemberg* from Le Havre, France. He took out a license to marry **HENRIETTE/HARRIET UHRY** on 5 February 1856 in New Orleans. Henriette was probably born **ESTER UHRY** on 2 September 1828 in *Ingwiller*, Bas-Rhin, France, to **ISAAC UHRY**, a native of the town, and his wife **AGATHE WOLFF**, born in *Büswiller*, Bas-Rhin. The couple had another daughter HANNETTE/HENRIETTE UHRY born in 1834. Hannette died on 22 August 1851 in *Ingwiller* at the age of seventeen. We believe that Ester, called Sara, in the 1836 town census for *Ingwiller,* adopted her late sister's name after her death. Twenty-four-year-old "Henriette Uri" arrived in New Orleans on 26 January 1852 aboard the ship *Elizabeth Hamilton*, from Le Havre, France. Moïse and Henriette were the parents of four children: Lazare (b. 1856) Sara (b. 1859), Fanny (b. 1861) and Samuel (b. 1865), all of whom were born in New Orleans. Moïse was the proprietor of a dry goods store on Magazine Street in the city. He died in New Orleans on 19 March 1897 and was buried in Gates of Prayer Cemetery #2 (Joseph Street), where a date of birth (8 October 1808) and town of origin ("Oberne," barely legible) helped in our being able to locate his birth record. His wife, Henriette, died on 15 January 1907. She was also buried in Gates of Prayer #2. Although her tombstone does not give her date of birth, her age (79), and place of birth (*Ingwiller*) are clearly visible. (**A, AN, G, GB, TT**)

LEVY, MOÏSE, was born on 27 February 1823 in *Niederbronn-les-Bains*, Bas-Rhin, France, to **SAMUEL LEVY**, a native of the town, and his wife, **ESTHER MOSES**, born in *Bouxwille*r, Bas-Rhin. He married **ROSALIE MEYER/MYERS** ca. 1861 in Alsace. She was born. **ROSETTE MEYER** on 30 August 1837, in *Niederoedern*, Bas-Rhin, France, to **SAMUEL MEYER**, le jeune, a native of the town and **AMALIE/MADELEINE AUSCHER**, born in *Oberlauterbach*, Bas-Rhin. Moïse and Rosalie immigrated to Louisiana with their three children, **SOLOMON LEVY** (b.1862; See entry), **GUSTAVE LEVY** (b.1863; See entry), and **MARX MEYER LEVY** (b. 1866; See entry), obtaining a "laisser passer" (passport) from the French government in *Wissembourg*, Bas-Rhin, France, in October 1868, which also included his sister-in-law, **GERTRUDE/MARY MEYER** (See entry). Moise, his wife, Rosette, and three children arrived in New York on 8 December 1868 from Hamburg, Germany, aboard the SS *Holsatia*. On 22 December 1868, Rosalie Levy gave birth to twins, Estelle and Jacob Levy in Louisiana. The couple moved to Scott Co., MS, where their son Benjamin Franklin Levy was born on 26 July 1872. By 1874 they had returned to Louisiana, and had settled in Evergreen, Avoyelles Parish, where they spent the rest of their lives. Four more children were born in Evergreen: Ernest Aaron (b. 2 September 1874), Matilda (b. 26 June 1876), Julius Meyer (b. 20 September 1878), and Mary (b. Mar. 1880). Moïse Levy owned a large general merchandise store in Evergreen, which his sons carried on after his death there on 20 July 1885. Moïse was buried in the Jewish Cemetery in Pineville, Rapides Parish, LA. His wife, Rosalie died on 30 August 1886 in Evergreen, and was buried alongside of him. Two of Rosalie's brothers, **ARON/JOHN MEYER/MYERS** and **JACOB/JACQUES MEYER/MYERS** (See entries), also settled in Louisiana. Note: The family always spelled their last name "Myers" in Louisiana. (**A, AN, AP, FS**)

LEVY, MOÏSE, was born on 30 January 1828 at *Niederseebach*, Bas-Rhin, France, to **MARX LEVY**, a native of the town and his first wife, **EVE LEVY**, born in *Niederbronn-les-Bains*, Bas-Rhin. He followed his brother, **SAMUEL LEVY** (See entry), to Shreveport, Caddo Parish, LA. We were unable to find an immigration record for him. Moïse married **REBECCA/ROSALIE BOMPET** in New Orleans, Orleans Parish, LA, on 29 March 1870. Rosalie was born **REBECCA POMBET** on 18 June 1839 at *Hochfelden*, Bas-Rhin, France, to **HILAIRE SALOMON POMBET,** a native of *Kuttolsheim*, Bas-Rhin, France, and his wife, **AGATHE BLUM**, a native of *Hochfelden,* Bas-Rhin. We were not able to find a record of her arrival in America. Moïse and Rosalie settled in Shreveport, Caddo Parish, LA, where she died there six months later on September 24, 1870. She was buried in Hebrew Rest Cemetery # 1 (the Jewish section of Oakland Cemetery) in Shreveport, near her brother, Michel Bompet. Her husband, Moïse, sold his business and retired to *Wissembourg*, Bas-Rhin, France, where he died ca. 1896. He was the only one of the six Levy siblings who settled in Shreveport to return to France permanently to live. (**A, AN, G, J, N**)

LEVY, NANETTE, (*Lauterbourg*) See entry for **JACOB ISRAEL**

LEVY, NATHAN, was born on 23 March 1864 in *Duppigheim*, Bas-Rhin, France, to **MARX LEVY**, a native of the town and his wife, **PAULINE/ROSINE RECHT**, born in *Schaffhouse-sur-Zorn*, Bas-Rhin. According to his own recollection in a 1900 U.S. passport application, he immigrated to Louisiana in September 1881. We believe he may have been the eighteen-year-old "Mr. N. Levy" who arrived in New York on 1 September 1882 from Le Havre, France, on the SS *St. Germain*, whose destination was "Louisiana." He joined his half-brother, **GABRIEL BLUM** and brother, **EMANUEL LEVY** (See entries) in St. Joseph, Tensas Parish, LA, where he was naturalized in November 1888. By 1890 he was living and working in nearby Goldman (north of Waterproof) in Tensas Parish. Shortly before the turn of the twentieth century he followed his brother Emanuel to New Orleans, Orleans Parish, LA, where he opened up a men's furnishing store at the corner of Canal Street and Exchange Place. He was enumerated in the 1900 federal census living with his brother Emanuel, sister-in-law Selma Heidenheim, their children, as well as two of Selma's brothers, Emanuel and Simon, and a nephew, Arthur Katten. Nathan began working as a traveling salesman for his brother, Emanuel, and the latter's brothers-in-law, Emanuel and Simon Heidenheim, at Heidenheim, Levy & Weiss, manufacturers of shirts and overalls. Nathan Levy never married. After his brother's wife died in 1916, he lived in boarding houses in the city. He divided his time between New York and New Orleans. During the 1930s Nathan was also somewhat of an art collector. His efforts to sell a painting he had bought entitled *Andromaque at the Siege of Troy* by Georges Marie Rochegrosse, a six foot by eight foot artists replica of a much larger work that hung in a museum in Rouen, France, caused a local sensation here in the Crescent City. He spent his last years in New Orleans living in yet another boarding house and working as a life insurance agent. Eighty-year-old Nathan died at Touro Infirmary in the city. He was buried in Gates of Prayer Cemetery #2 (Joseph Street). (**A, AN, GB**)

LEVY, OSCAR, was born on 14 February 1873 in *Duppigheim*, Bas-Rhin, France, to **MARX LEVY**, a native of that town and his wife, **PAULINE/ROSINE RECHT**, born in *Schaffhouse-sur-Zorn*, Bas-Rhin. Oscar may have emigrated from Le Havre, France, aboard the SS *La Normandie* that landed in New York on 9 December 1889. Although the passenger manifest showed his age as "forty-one," two passport applications that he made in 1903 and 1908 repeated the information that he arrived in America in December 1889. Oscar joined his half-brother **GABRIEL BLUM** (See entry) and brother, **EMANUEL LEVY** (See entry) in St. Joseph, Tensas Parish, LA, working as a dry-goods merchant. He married Henrietta Katten, a Texas native, on 27 May 1908 in New Orleans, Orleans Parish, LA. Henrietta's mother, Celestine Heidenheim, was Oscar's brother Emanuel's sister-in-law. Oscar and Henrietta were the parents of three children, all born in St. Joseph: Loris Katten (b. 1909), Elaine (b. 1916) and Janet (b. 1921). Oscar was the first vice-president of the Bank of St. Joseph and Trust Co., and in later life was the treasurer of the town of St. Joseph. He died there on 26 April 1938, and was buried in Hebrew Rest Cemetery # 2 in New Orleans. Henrietta Katten Levy died on 12 October 1947 in New Orleans and was buried with her husband. (**A, AN, GB**)

LEVY, RACHEL, was born on 31 May 1864 in *Kuttolsheim*, Bas-Rhin, France, to **NATHAN LEVY**, a native of *Wintzenheim*, Bas-Rhin, and his wife, **LEAH/LISETTE PIOSO**, born in *Kuttolsheim*, Bas-Rhin. We believe that the "B and R. Levy" who arrived 14 November 1884 in New York City from Antwerp, Belgium, on board the SS *Noordland* were Rachel and her younger brother, **BERNARD LEVY** (See entry). Rachel and Bernard were enumerated together in the 1900 federal census in St. Mary Parish, LA, with eight-year-old Regina Levy, daughter of their brother **HENRY LEVY** (See entry). Forty-five-year-old Rachel Levy married thirty-four-year-old SIDNEY HESS on 10 November 1909 in New Orleans, Orleans Parish, LA. Sidney, the son of **SALOMON HESS** (See entry), was a native of Alexandria, Rapides Parish, LA. Sidney and Rachel never had children. They lived in New Orleans where Sidney worked as a postal clerk and Rachel ran their small city accommodations as a boarding house. In 1928 Sidney Hess pleaded guilty to charges of having misappropriated more than $900 in cash from the post office. He served one year in jail. Rachel filed for divorce in April 1929. On 18 July 1929, shortly after his release from prison, Sidney, who faced more charges, walked down to the end of Dumaine Street in New Orleans and ended his life in the waters of the Mississippi River. He was interred on 21 July 1929 in New Orleans at Cypress Grove Cemetery. Rachel died on 10 July 1933 in New Orleans and was buried there in Gates of Prayer Cemetery #2 (Joseph Street). (**A, AN, G, GB, TT**)

LEVY, RAPHAEL, was born on 7 December 1826 at *Duppigheim*, Bas-Rhin, France, to **LIPPMANN LEVI** and his wife, **ZIBORE LEVI**, both natives of the town. He married THÉRÈSE DOROTHÉE KOCH/KOCK, a native of Germany on 13 March 1856 in *Duppigheim*. (We have had to rely on an on-line genealogy for this information as the civil records for *Duppigheim,* 1853-62, are not available at the Bas-Rhin archives.)We were not able to locate an immigration record for this couple. They were enumerated in the United States for the first time in the 1860 federal census at Grande Pointe, St. James Parish, LA, where twenty-seven-year-old Raphael was operating a dry goods store. His wife, "Dorothea," was keeping house. The couple had four children in St. James Parish before they returned to France to escape the ravages of the Civil War: Josephine (b. 1858), Julia (b. 1860), Leon (b. 1861) and Rosa (b. 1862). They returned to Raphael's home town, *Duppigheim*, ca. 1862, where he worked as a merchant to support his growing family. Two children were born to them in *Duppigheim*: **ABRAHAM** (b. 2 July 1864; See entry) and **LAZARE/LAZARUS** (b. 16 March 1866; See entry). The family was enumerated in the 1866 *Duppigheim* town census several months before their return to Louisiana: thirty-seven-year-old Raphael and his wife, Dorothée, a year younger, along with Josephine (9y), Julie (7y), Leon (5y), Rosa (4y), Abraham (2y) and two-month-old Lazare. Raphael's sister **FANNY LEVY** and her husband, **LEHMANN LEVY** (See entry), and their children had returned to New Orleans, Orleans Parish, LA, from their refuge in France in December 1865. Raphael, Dorothée and their six children followed, arriving back in New Orleans on 1 December 1866 aboard the SS *Sorrento*. They rebuilt their store and developed a small parcel of farmland near Convent, St. James Parish, where they had previously gone into the very lucrative sugar cane business. Five more children were born to them after their return: Marcus M.(b. 1868), Flora (b. 1870), Selma (b. 1871), Morris (b. 1873), and Raphaella (b. 1877). Raphael Levy died on 11 January 1877 at Longview (near Lutcher) St. James Parish, LA and was buried in New Orleans, Orleans Parish, LA, at Gates of Mercy Cemetery, formerly at Jackson and Saratoga Streets, until it was razed in the 1950s. Dorothée died on 30 May 1898 and was buried in New Orleans in Gates of Prayer Cemetery #2 (Joseph Street). Note: Grande Pointe, which no longer appears on maps was on the left descending bank of the Mississippi River in St. James Parish, west of Gramercy. (**A, AN, E, G, GB**)

LEVY, ROSALIE, was born **JEANNETTE LEVY** on 10 June 1826 in *Lauterbourg*, Bas-Rhin, France, to **BENOÎT LEVY**, a native of the town, and his wife, **HENRIETTE MENDEL**, born in *Soultz-sous-Fôrets*, Bas-Rhin. We believe that Rosalie and her brother, **JACOB/JACQUES LEVY** (See entry), were following an elder brother, **EDOUARD LEVY** (See entry), who arrived in Louisiana in 1841 and settled in Rapides Parish. We have concluded that Rosalie was the same as the twenty-two-year-old "Rosalie Levy" who arrived in New Orleans, Orleans Parish, LA, on 7 February 1849 from Le Havre, France, aboard the ship *Gironde*. Rosalie was listed on the passenger manifest of the *Gironde* next to twenty-one-year-old "Jacque" Levy, her brother. Rosalie was married on 28 January 1854 in New Orleans, Orleans Parish, LA, to LOUIS LEMLE, a native of Ingenheim, Germany. They were the parents of six children. Isadore (b. 1854), Julia (b. 1855), and Bertha (b. 1857) were born while the couple was still living in New Orleans. Gustave was born in 1862 at Alexandria, Rapides Parish, LA, where the family was enumerated in the 1860 federal census. At that time, Louis was working as a shoemaker. The couple's son Emanuel was born either at Alexandria or in New Orleans in 1863. On 26 June 1862 martial law had been declared in the parishes of Avoyelles, Rapides, and Natchitoches, and travel was prohibited to New Orleans, which, at that time, was in the hands of the Union army. Although Emmanuel's death record at Natchez showed his birth place as New Orleans, absent an actual record, we cannot be sure. Louis and Rosalie's last child, Sophie, was born just before the end of the Civil War in February 1865 at New Orleans. They relocated soon after to Natchez, Adams Co., MS, to be near other members of the Lemle family. Louis worked as a storekeeper in Natchez until his death on 29 January 1871. He was buried in the Jewish section of the Natchez City Cemetery. Rosalie Lemle and her children moved across the Mississippi River to Vidalia, Concordia Parish, LA, where they lived for some years. Rosalie and her five children were enumerated there in the 1880 federal census. Isadore, Gustave (who later became a prominent lawyer in New Orleans), and Emanuel worked as clerks in a dry goods store to support the family. Rosalie died on 9 July 1899 in Natchez at the home of her daughter Mrs. Bertha Lemle Hart and was buried in the Lemle family plot on Jewish Hill in the Natchez City Cemetery. (**A, AN, G, TT**)

LEVY, SAMUEL, was born on 20 February 1823 in *Weiterswiller*, Bas-Rhin, France, to **ISAAC LEVY**, a native of the town, and his wife,

JEANNETTE KATZ, born in Cernay, Haut-Rhin. He married **VICTOIRE/FANNY DREYFUS** on 16 February 1852 in *Sélestat*, Bas-Rhin. She was born on 26 February 1823 in *Westhouse*, Bas-Rhin, France, to **HERMANN DREYFUS**, a native of the town, and his wife, BABETTE SULZER, born in Grussenheim, Haut-Rhin. The couple were the parents of three children born in *Sélestat*, Bas-Rhin: Alphonse (b. 1857), Berthe (b. 11 September 1858) and Émile (b. 1863; See entry).We believe they immigrated as a family to America at the close of the Civil War, ca. 1865, but have been unable to find a reliable immigration record for them. Samuel worked as a retail dry goods merchant in New Orleans, Orleans Parish, LA. Bertha Levy, their seven-year-old daughter, died on 3 September 1866 in New Orleans. Her death certificate recorded that she was a native of Schlettstadt (now Sélestat), France. Bertha was buried in Hebrew Rest Cemetery #1 in the city. Victoire/Fanny Levy died on 14 September 1867 of yellow fever and was buried in Hebrew Rest Cemetery #1 as well. Samuel took out a license to marry **ROSALIE REBLAUB** on 5 January 1868 in New Orleans. Rosalie was born **ROSINA REBLAUB** on 10 April 1830 in *Weinbourg*, Bas-Rhin, France, to **JACOB/JACQUES REBLAUB**, a native of the town, and his wife, **RACHEL DREYFUS**, born in *Schirrhoffen*, Bas-Rhin. According to her obituary, Rosalie immigrated to New Orleans ca. 1861. We believe that she appeared on the passenger manifest of the ship *Kate Dyer* as the thirty-year-old "Rosalie Beblaut" who arrived in New Orleans on 4 February 1861 from Le Havre, France. Samuel and Rosalie were the parents of two daughters: Jennie (b. 1869) and Rachel (b. 1872). Samuel died in New Orleans on 14 August 1892 and was buried in Gates of Prayer Cemetery #2 (Joseph Street). Rosalie died on 27 February 1896 and was buried with him. We have found no reliable records to be able to trace Samuel's eldest son, Alphonse. (**A, AN, G, GB, L, TT**)

LEVY, SAMUEL, was born on 29 April 1825 at *Lauterbourg*, Bas-Rhin, France, to **SIMON LEVY**, a native of the town, and his wife, **ROSINE WEIL**, whom we were not able to trace. He followed several other Levy cousins who emigrated from *Lauterbourg* to Rapides Parish, LA, where he worked as a peddler in the back country of Louisiana. We were unable to find a reliable immigration record for him. Samuel died on 23 September 1853, a victim of the yellow fever epidemic which decimated Louisiana that year. He was buried alongside two brothers, **SIMON** and **JACOB LEVY** (See entries),also from *Lauterbourg*, in the Jewish Cemetery in Pineville, Rapides Parish,

LA. Judging from their dates of death in the summer and fall of 1853, they were all struck down by yellow fever. (**A, AN, G**)

LEVY, SAMUEL, was born on 26 April 1836, in *Niederseebach*, Bas-Rhin, France, to **MARX LEVY**, a native of the town and his first wife **EVE LEVY,** born in *Niederbronn-les-Bains*, Bas-Rhin. Eighteen-year-old Samuel Levy arrived in New Orleans, Orleans Parish, LA, on 25 May 1854 from Le Havre, France, aboard the ship *Charlemagne* with his fifteen-year-old half- brother, **SIMON LEVY** (See entry) He worked as a merchant and butcher in Shreveport, Caddo Parish, LA, after starting his career as a peddler with his brothers, Simon and Moise Levy, all of whom appear in the 1860 Census for Rusk County, Texas. Samuel became the first Jewish Mayor of Shreveport. He married **LOUISA STEIGLEMAN**, the widow of **GEORGE SHOBER,** during the Civil War, for which there is no surviving record. Seven children were born to Samuel and Louisa, all in Shreveport: Fanny (1864), Julia (1866; died 1881), Moses (1869; died 1869), Simon (1871), John Emmanuel (1873), Sidney (1875), and Marx (1878). Samuel died on 4 March 1883 and was buried in Hebrew Rest Cemetery #1 (Jewish section of Oakland Cemetery) in Shreveport, LA. His wife, Louisa, died on 21 August 1895 in Shreveport and was buried in the same cemetery. Her grave is unmarked. (**A, AC, G**)

LEVY, SIMON (aka. **CAPT. SIMON LEVY, JR.)**, was born on 8 April 1841 in *Niederseebach*, Bas-Rhin, France, to **MARX LEVY**, a native of the town, and his second wife **FROMMIT WEILLER,** born in *Dauendorf,* Bas-Rhin. Fifteen-year-old Simon Levy arrived in New Orleans, Orleans Parish, LA, on 25 May 1854 from Le Havre, France, aboard the ship *Charlemagne* with his eighteen-year-old half-brother, **SAMUEL LEVY** (See entry). Simon and his siblings, **SAMUEL** and **MOÏSE LEVY**, went to Texas where they worked as peddlers. According to Simon's application for a U.S. passport in 1897, he was naturalized at Henderson, Rusk Co., TX, on 27 June 1860. He and his brothers finally settled down in Shreveport, Caddo Parish, LA. Simon fought for the Confederacy, serving as Captain of the Caddo Greys, as well as with the First Battalion Co. D, 5th Washington Artillery. He married HARRIETT BODENHEIMER, a Louisiana native on July 11, 1866. Three children were born to them: Juliette (1871), Jake Myron (1874) and Frances Hattie (1877). Harriett died on 12 February 1878 and was buried in Hebrew Rest Cemetery #1 (the Jewish section of Oakland Cemetery). Simon never remarried. He remained in

Shreveport his entire life, and was a founding member of the B'nai Zion Congregation, as well as its first President. He was also a cofounder of the Commercial National Bank, and heavily invested in the Kansas City Southern Railway. In 1897 he took his children on a grand tour of Europe. Simon died shortly after his return on 27 March 1898, and was buried with his wife. His ornate monument is the largest one in Oakland Cemetery. (**A, AC, G**)

LEVY, SIMON, was born on 2 January 1834 in *Lauterbourg*, Bas-Rhin, France, to **JOSEPH LEVY**, a native of the town, and his wife, VOGEL/FANNY ETLINGER, born in Karlsruhe, Baden-Württemberg, Germany. Seventeen-year-old Simon had been last enumerated in *Lauterbourg* in the 1851 town census living with his widowed mother and two younger brothers. He followed his brother, **JACOB LEVY** (See entry), to Louisiana to work as a peddler in Rapides Parish. We believe that he may have been the seventeen-year-old Simon Levy who landed in New Orleans, Orleans Parish, LA, on 4 November 1851 aboard the ship *Isaac Bell*. Although he was listed as being a shoemaker from Bavaria, two other immigrants from *Lauterbourg*, seventeen-year-old-Salomon and Samuel Halff, arrived in New Orleans on the same ship. Simon Levy died in Alexandria, Rapides Parish, LA, two weeks after his brother, on October 3, 1853 and was buried in the Jewish Cemetery at Pineville, Rapides Parish, LA, another victim of the deadly yellow fever epidemic of 1853 (**A, AN, B1851, G**)

LEVY, SIMON, was born **SIMON LEVI** on 14 March 1876 in *Schirrhoffen*, Bas-Rhin, France, to **JACQUES LEVY** and his wife **SARA WELSCH**, both natives of the town. He followed his brothers, **EMANUEL** and **AARON LEVY** (See entries) to Louisiana. In 1911 he applied for a U.S. passport to return to France for a visit. In it he stated that he had immigrated to America ca. June 1893 aboard the SS *La Touraine*. It appears that he did arrive in New York from Le Havre, France, on 17 June 1893 aboard the SS *La Touraine*. His age was, however, mistakenly recorded as "42" instead of "17." However, his place of origin was correctly entered as "*Schirrhoffen*." In that same 1911 passport application, Simon also stated that he had been a resident of Chamberlin, West Baton Rouge Parish, LA, for eighteen years, and had been naturalized in East Baton Rouge Parish on 25 September 1906. He eventually moved to Baton Rouge, East Baton Rouge Parish, LA. He was employed at various retail stores, including Welsh & Levy. He was married briefly to LIVIA BURGESS, a record for which we were unable to find. Fifty-three-year-old Simon Levy was enumerated in the 1930 federal census for Baton Rouge with twenty-four-year-old Livia, her sister, Juanita, and mother, Sara. He was employed for many years at The Fair, Inc., a retail clothing outlet. Simon died on 25 May 1948 in Baton Rouge and was buried there in the Jewish Cemetery. He shares a stone with his brother, **EMANUEL LEVY** (See entry), who died three months before him. There was no mention of his wife as one of his survivors in the local newspaper, the *Baton Rouge Advocate,* so it is assumed that the marriage ended in divorce. There were no children. Note: See also the entry for **GABRIEL LEVY**, another brother. Also note: Chamberlin was the site of the homestead plantation of William Benjamin Chamberlin, born in Jamestown, NY, who was a prominent lawyer in West Baton Rouge Parish. **(AN, G, GB)**

LEVY, SOLOMON, was born **SALOMON LEVY** on 26 July 1862 in *Niederroedern*, Bas-Rhin, France, to **MOISE LEVY** (See entry), a native of *Niederbronn-les-Bains*, Bas-Rhin, and his wife, **ROSALIE/ ROSETTE MEYER**, born in *Niederroedern*, Bas-Rhin. He immigrated with parents and siblings, arriving in New York on 8 December 1868 from Hamburg, Germany, on board the SS *Holsatia*. The family initially lived in Forest, Scott Co, MS but moved to Evergreen, Avoyelles Parish, LA before the 1880 federal census. Solomon married CARRIE JUSTINE WEIL, a native of Homer, Claiborne Parish, LA, on 1 October 1890 in New Orleans, Orleans Parish, LA. They had one child, Rosalie Weil Levy (b.1891). Sol Levy was a general merchant in Evergreen, where he and his brothers had taken over his late father's holdings. He moved his family to New Orleans, Orleans Parish, LA before the 1920 federal census, where he was enumerated with his wife, his daughter Rosalie, her husband, Arthur Katten, and his grandchildren. Solomon died on 21 December 1928 in New Orleans. He was buried there in Hebrew Rest Cemetery #2. His wife died on 22 June 1944 and was buried with him. **(A, AN, AP, F)**

LEVY, SOLOMON, was born on 14 March 1839 in *Niederseebach*, Bas-Rhin, France, to **MARX LEVY**, a native of the town, and his second wife, **FROMMIT WEILLER**, born in *Dauendorf*, Bas-Rhin. He was enumerated in the 1846 Census for *Schleithal*, Bas-Rhin, as Salomon Levy, age 6. Solomon came to Shreveport, Caddo Parish, LA to join his brothers, Capt. **SIMON LEVY**, **BERNARD LEVY**, and a half-brother, **SAMUEL LEVY** (See entries) before 1860. His name, year and place of birth, 1839 in *Niederseebach*, as well as his occupation, butcher, appeared on a list of young men who were due to be conscripted in the canton of Wissembourg on 1/1/1859. Men whose names appeared on this list often had immigrated several months or even years before the given date of possible conscription. This information was recorded in *The Alsace Immigration Book, Volume 2*, compiled by Cornelia Schrader-Muggenthaler. We believe he may have been the Salomon Levy who emigrated from Le Havre, France, to New Orleans on 30 December 1854 aboard the *John Hancock*, although his age was off by three years. He never married. Solomon worked as a butcher, and died on 24 November 1905 in Shreveport. He was buried in Hebrew Rest Cemetery #1 (the Jewish section of Oakland Cemetery). **(A, AL2, E, G)**

LEVY, SOLOMON, was born **SALOMON LEVY** on 26 September 1871 in *Kuttolsheim*, Bas-Rhin, France, to **NATHAN LEVY**, a native of *Wintzenheim*, Bas-Rhin, and his wife, **LEAH/LISETTE PIOSO**, born in *Kuttolsheim*. "Salomon Lévy" arrived in New York from Le Havre, France, on 30 January 1893 aboard the SS *La Gascogne*. He was enumerated for the first time in the United States at Houma, Terrebonne Parish, LA, in the 1900 federal census, where he was boarding with a family and working as a grocery clerk in a local store. Three siblings, **BERNARD, HENRY,** and **RACHEL LEVY** (See entries) had come to Louisiana in the 1880s and settled in nearby parishes. After the Henry Levy family moved to Houma, Solomon took up residence with his brother, sister-in-law, and their seven children. They were all enumerated together at Houma in the 1910 federal census. Thirty-seven-year-old unmarried Solomon, no longer a grocery clerk, was working in town as a laborer in a local market. Solomon Levy died on 20 October 1924 at Presbyterian Hospital in New Orleans, Orleans Parish, LA, and was interred with other family members in Gates of Prayer Cemetery #2 (Joseph Street) in New Orleans. **(A, AN, G, GB)**

LOEB, BABETTE/BARBARA, (*Dettwiller*) See entry for **JACOB KATZ**

LOEB, FÉLIX VALENTIN, was born **VALENTIN LOEB** on 9 April 1852 in *Niederbronn-les-Bains*, Bas-Rhin, France, to **CHARLES LOEB**, a native of *Reichshoffen*, Bas-Rhin, and his wife **JULIE KAUFFMANN**, born in *Bouxwiller*, Bas-Rhin. Félix indicated on three different U.S. passport applications that he had immigrated to Louisiana in 1867, and in one document wrote that he arrived on the SS *Oregon* ca. 1 April 1867, an assertion that we were unable to prove using existing available ship's records. Felix was enumerated in the 1870 federal census for Homer, Claiborne Parish, LA, where he worked in a general store. He was naturalized in Shreveport, Caddo Parish, LA, on 3 September 1874. Felix relocated to New Orleans ca. 1880, where he joined his two brothers, **ISAAC** and **SOLOMON LOEB** (See entries), becoming the senior member of Felix Loeb & Bros., wholesale liquor merchants. He married SARAH ROSENTHAL, a native of New Orleans, on 30 October 1884 in the city. They were the parents of one child: Charles Gerson (b. 1885). Except for a few years spent in San Francisco, where Felix and his family experienced the great earthquake of 18 April 1906, he lived in New Orleans. Felix Loeb & Bros. was dissolved ca. 1907 with Isaac Loeb's departure for Europe for health reasons. Felix and his family followed in 1909, settling in Paris. Sarah Loeb died there on 18 January 1913. Felix remained in Paris with his son, Charles, who became a renowned international lawyer, receiving many awards including the French Legion of Honor. Charles married Clémence VanSteenberghe while in Paris. Felix, Isaac, and Charles Loeb fled Paris after the Nazi occupation in June 1940. They escaped via Portugal, on the SS *Excalibur*, which arrived in New York on 30 October 1940. Charles' wife, Clémence, and her mother, Georgette VanSteenberghe, received exit visas in January 1941, and left on 5 April 1941 via Lisbon on the SS *Excambion*. The family reunited in Manhattan, New York. Felix died there on 19 March 1944, at the age of ninety-two. He had taken his own life several hours after finding that his only son, Charles, had hanged himself in his suite at the Hotel Dorset. Clémence Loeb died in Manhattan, New York, on 18 January 2005. She was 104 years old. We were unable to locate their places of burial. (**A, AN, G. GB, TT**)

LOEB, ISAAC, was born on 11 March 1854 in *Niederbronn-les-Bains*, Bas-Rhin, France, to **CHARLES LOEB**, a native of *Reichshoffen*, Bas-Rhin, and his wife **JULIE KAUFFMANN**, born in *Bouxwiller*, Bas-Rhin. In an 1896 U.S. passport application, Isaac Loeb stated that he had immigrated to Louisiana, at the age of seventeen, aboard the SS *Vandalia* out of Hamburg, Germany, arriving in October 1871. The SS *Vandalia* landed at New York on 25 October 1871 from Hamburg, Germany, but a person by person search for Isaac Loeb turned up no such entry. Isaac joined his brother, **FÉLIX VALENTIN**

LOEB (See entry), in Homer, Claiborne Parish, LA, where they worked as clerks in a store. Isaac was naturalized in October 1876 in Shreveport, Caddo Parish, LA. He relocated to New Orleans, Orleans Parish, LA, ca. 1880, where he joined his two brothers, Félix and **SOLOMON LOEB** (See entry) as part of the firm of Felix Loeb & Bros., wholesale liquor merchants. He sold his share of the business in 1907, and returned to live in Europe for health reasons, residing in Paris, Switzerland, Nice, France, before finally returning to Paris to be near his brother Félix and nephew Charles. Isaac fled Paris with them, after the Nazi occupation in June 1940. They escaped via Portugal, on the SS *Excalibur*, which arrived in New York on 30 October 1940. Isaac never married. He died in Manhattan, New York on 7 June 1944. We were unable to locate his place of burial (**A, AN, G, GB, TT**)

LOEB, JACOB, was born **JACQUES LOEW** on 25 November 1822 in *Ingwiller*, Bas-Rhin, France, to **ABRAHAM LOEW**, a native of the town, and his first wife, **GOTON/COTON LEVI**, born in *Bischheim*, Bas-Rhin. Jacob immigrated to New Orleans, Orleans Parish, LA, ca. 1849, a reliable ship's record for which we were unable to find. He married **SOPHIE/SUSANNE FLEISCHMANN** on 3 February 1851 in the city. Sophie was born **SUSANNE FLEISCHMANN** on 3 November 1827 in *Soultz-sous-Fôrets*, Bas-Rhin, France, to **ULRIC FLEISCHMANN**, born in *Bischheim*, Bas-Rhin-France, and his wife, **HANNA GROS**, a native of *Soultz-sous-Fôrets*. We were unable to find a reliable ship's record for her entry into the United States either. Jacob and Sophie were the parents of four children: Gotton Jacques (b. 1852), Caroline (b. 1853), Leon (b. 1853), and Jacob (b. 1865). Only Caroline and Leon survived to adulthood. Jacob was a retail dry goods dealer and a huckster (travelling salesman) for fifty-five years in New Orleans. Sophie died on 22 March 1905, and was buried in Gates of Prayer Cemetery #1 (Canal Street) in New Orleans. Jacob died on 25 March 1906, and was buried with her. Their obituaries, their shared tombstone, as well as obituaries of their daughter Caroline, all used the spelling "Loab" instead of the more conventional "Loeb." (**A, AN, E, G, GB, TT**)

LOEB, JOSEPH, was born on 9 August 1836 in *Lembach*, Bas-Rhin, France, to **ELIE LOEB** and **ROSALIE BLOCH**, both natives of the town. Twenty-four-year-old Joseph booked passage on the American sailing ship *Luna*, which left Le Havre on the evening of 16 February 1860. He was leaving France to join his brother, **SAMUEL LOEB**

(See entry), who had already settled in New Orleans, Orleans Parish, LA. Unable to make its way out of the English Channel to the open waters of the Atlantic Ocean, on account of gale winds and a snow storm, the *Luna* foundered on the rocks, in full sight of horrified witnesses near Barfleur the next day. Joseph perished along with six other residents from *Lembach* and one hundred other immigrants and crew on the morning of 17 February 1860. Their bodies were never found amongst those that eventually washed ashore. (**A, AP**)

LOEB, SAMUEL, was born on 4 March 1833 in *Lembach*, Bas-Rhin, France, to **ELIE LOEB** and **ROSALIE BLOCH**, both natives of the town. According to his naturalization record dated 16 October 1874, he immigrated to Louisiana ca. 1851. We have found only one likely candidate for our subject. Twenty-two-year-old Samuel Loeb arrived at New Orleans, Orleans Parish, LA, from Le Havre, France, on 26 January 1855 aboard the ship *Judith*. Although he was said to have been from "Hesse," there were quite a few people on the same ship who were from France. Samuel settled in New Orleans, Orleans Parish, LA, where he remained during the Civil War. He was cited in Union records as one of the men who had committed treason against the United States by contributing funds ($100) for the defense of the city of New Orleans against Union troops. He was fined $25 for his treachery. Samuel married CECILE REBECCA DREYFOUS, a Louisiana native, on 3 April 1866 in the city. Cecile was the eldest daughter of the renowned New Orleans notary, ABEL ABRAHAM DREYFOUS, and his first wife, CECILE BRUNSCHWICK, both born in Belfort, Haut-Rhin, France. Samuel moved his wife to Houston, Harris Co., TX, where their first child, Ernest Manuel Loeb was born in 1867. Five more children were born to the couple. Bella and Edgar were born in 1868 and 1874 respectively in Galveston, Galveston Co. TX, where Samuel worked as an office clerk. The family returned to New Orleans before the birth of their daughter Alice in 1875. By this time Samuel was listed in the New Orleans City Directory as the President of the American Mutual Insurance Assn. Only a year later, he was employed as an agent for a stove company, then a travelling salesman. The couple's last two children Harry B. (b. 1878) and Rhea (b. 1886) were born in the city as well. Samuel continued to work as a travelling salesman, then a gauger (a customs inspector for goods shipped in bulk), and finally a commission merchant and broker with offices on Bourbon Street. Samuel and Cecile may have separated before the turn of the twentieth century. Cecile was enumerated as a widow living with her three youngest children at 1522 Felicity St. in New Orleans in the 1900 federal census. Samuel, although appearing before and after 1900 in various New Orleans City Directories could not be located in that census. Samuel died on 28 November 1905 in Pearl River, St. Tammany Parish, LA. He was buried in Metairie-Lakelawn Cemetery in New Orleans. Cecile died on 7 August 1907 in Pass Christian, Harrison CO., MS. Her remains were returned to New Orleans where they were also interred in Metairie-Lakelawn Cemetery. (**A, AN, G, GB, TT**)

LOEB, SOLOMON, was born on 5 March 1856 in *Niederbronn-les-Bains*, Bas-Rhin, France, to **CHARLES LOEB**, a native of *Reichshoffen*, Bas-Rhin, and his wife, **JULIE, KAUFFMANN**, born in *Bouxwiller*, Bas-Rhin. According to two different U.S. passport applications, Solomon stated that he immigrated to America in 1872, arriving on the SS *Helvetia* in September of that year. We were unable to verify his assertion using any available ship's records. He started his career as a merchant in Pointe Coupée Parish, where he was naturalized in New Roads on 16 April 1878. He remained there through 1880, working as a clerk in a dry goods store. He joined his brothers, Félix and Isaac, in New Orleans, Orleans Parish, LA, a few years later, to become a partner in Felix Loeb & Bros., wholesale liquor merchants. He left Louisiana, ca. 1895 to try his luck out west, moving to San Francisco, San Francisco Co., CA, where he married DAHLIA LEVY, a California native, in 1897. The couple had two children: Gerald Martin (b. 1899), and Sidney S. (b. 1904). Solomon worked as a wholesale liquor merchant, branching out later to try his hand at real estate. He died on 4 July 1908 near San Francisco in a train wreck that took the lives of six other people. He was buried in Cypress Lawn Cemetery in Colma, San Mateo Co., CA. His widow took her sons to live in Manhattan, New York, ca. 1921, where she died on 6 July 1962. A memorial service was held for her in San Francisco. (**A, AN, TT**)

MARX, FANNY, was born **FREYDEL MARX** on 4 July 1821 in *Surbourg*, Bas-Rhin, France, to **LIEBMANN MARX**, a native of the town, and his wife **BRUNETTE/BRUNEL/SOPHIE KLOTZ**, born in *Soultz-sous-Forêts*, Bas-Rhin. Freydel, called "Fanny" in the United States, immigrated to New Orleans, Orleans Parish, LA, ca. 1851, a reliable record for which we were unable to find. She was married to SAMUEL LOB, a native of Bavaria on 9 January 1855 in the city. Samuel was a dry goods merchant who kept a store on Annunciation

Street. Two daughters were born to the couple before the 1860 federal census: Amelie (b. 1856) and Nanette (b. 1858). Tragically, the girls did not live to be enumerated with their parents. Samuel and Fanny Low [*sic*], the former, a dry goods merchant from Germany, and the latter, his wife from France, were living alone at the time of the 1860 federal census. Two more daughters, Augustina (b. 1860), and Albertine (b. 1862), were born in New Orleans before the family left the city and returned to Europe. They came back to the United States via New York on 5 September 1863 aboard the Hamburg-America lines ship *Bavaria*. Samuel made his way to occupied New Orleans to reopen his shop on Annunciation Street. He appeared on the Civil War tax rolls in New Orleans for 1863, 1864 and 1865 doing business as a retail dealer. It is not likely that Fanny and the girls accompanied him back to the city while the Union and Confederacy were still at war. However, all were reunited in New Orleans at the time of the 1870 federal census. Samuel died in New Orleans on 21 February 1873 and was buried there in Hebrew Rest Cemetery #1. Fanny lived with her daughter, Albertine, and the latter's husband, **MOISE WALDHORN** (See entry), until her death in New Orleans on 22 December 1911. She was buried there in Hebrew Rest Cemetery #1. Note: Fanny's niece, Flora Marx, came to Louisiana in 1883 to become the second wife of **LEOPOLD GOUDCHAUX** (See entry) of Big Cane, St. Landry Parish, LA. (**A, AN, G, GB**)

MARX, FLORA,(*Surbourg*) See entry for **LEOPOLD GOUDCHAUX**

MARX, HENRY/HERZ, was born **NEPHTALI MARX** on 12 October 1835 in *Ingwiller*, Bas-Rhin, France, to **ELIE MARX**, a native of the town, and his first wife, **ZIBORA/SOPHIE LEVI**, born in *Saverne*, Bas-Rhin. According to the 1900 federal census for New Orleans, Orleans Parish, LA, Henry immigrated to America ca. 1858. We were unable to verify this using existing ship's records. He was enumerated for the first time in the 1860 federal census for New Orleans as a twenty-four-year-old clerk from France. He married MENA/MINNIE FRANCK/FRANK, a native of New Orleans ca. 1866, a record of which we were unable to find. Henry and Minnie were the parents of nine children: Sophie (b. 1868), Aron (b. 1869), Henriette (b. 1872), Tena (b. 1874), Alexander (b. 1877), Simon (b. 1880), Esther (b. 1881), Morris (b. 1884), and Hilda (b. 1886). Henry was a retail dry goods merchant, who, with the exception of a few years in the late 1870s into the early 1880s when he moved to Thibodaux, Lafourche Parish, LA, remained in New Orleans to raise his family. Minnie Marx died on 13 December 1907 in New Orleans and was interred there in Gates of Prayer Cemetery #2 (Joseph Street). Henry died in the city on 15 September 1909 and was buried with his wife. **(A, AN, G, GB)**

MARX, NANETTE, was born **NANNETTE MARX** on 26 August 1862 in *Surbourg*, Bas-Rhin, France, to **MORTIER/MARX MARX** and his wife, **FANNY LEVI**, both natives of the town. Nanette's twin, Elise Marx, died in *Surbourg* at the age of seven months. Nanette followed her sister **FLORA MARX** (See entry for **LEOPOLD GOUDCHAUX**) to Louisiana ca. 1890. She married SAMUEL HOCHWALD/HOCKWALD, a native of Galveston, Galveston Co., TX, who was of Austrian parentage, ca. 1899. We could find no records of Nanette's immigration or her marriage. In the 1900 federal census for Big Cane, St. Landry Parish, LA, Nanette was enumerated in the household of her sister and brother-in-law, Leopold and Flora Marx Goudchaux and their six children. Her husband, Samuel Hochwald, was living in the same town, but sharing his quarters with an unmarried male boarder, William Fisher. It is probable that Nanette, who had no children of her own, was helping to take care of her sister's large family. Samuel Hochwald died in Alexandria, Rapides Parish, LA, on 4 June 1912. At the time of his death he had been working as a butcher on a local Southern Pacific Railway line which operated between Alexandria and Lafayette. He was buried in the Jewish Cemetery in Pineville, Rapides Parish, LA, where he shares a headstone with Sylvan L. Goudchaux, son of his widow's sister, Flora Marx Goudchaux. Nanette Hochwald returned to live in Alsace, France where she was still living at the time of her sister Flora Goudchaux's death on 26 April 1923. **(A, AN, FS, GB)**

MAYER, MADLAINE, was born on 17 June 1808 in *Drachenbronn*, Bas-Rhin, France, to **DAVID MAYER** (bef. 1808 **ABRAHAM BENJAMIN**), a native of *Gunstett*, Bas-Rhin, and his wife **FROMETTE/SARA FRANK**, born in *Drachenbronn*, Bas-Rhin. Madlaine came to Louisiana before 1839, a record for which we were unable to find. She married ABRAHAM MEYER HEYMANN who was born on 6 May 1805 in Phalsbourg, Haut-Rhin, France to MAYER ISAAC HEYMANN and SARA DENNERY, natives of Mittelbronn, Haut-Rhin, France. We could not find a record for Abraham's marriage to Madlaine either. Abraham Heymann was naturalized in Clinton, East Feliciana Parish, LA on 1 May 1845 in East Feliciana Parish, LA. Four children were born to the couple in Louisiana: Meyer (b. 1839), Jacob (b. 1840), Benjamin (b. 1846), and Isaac (b.1848). Madlaine was always called "Emelie or "Emily" in the four census records between 1850-1880 in Clinton where her husband was a merchant and the owner of a hotel for almost forty years. Abraham died on 2 July 1879 in Clinton and was buried there in the Jewish Cemetery. His wife passed away at Clinton on 23 January 1888, where she had been living with her son, Isaac, a grocer. She was buried there in the Jewish Cemetery as well. While the date of birth on the tombstone records her birth as "July 8, 1808 in Drachabronn [*sic*], Alsace" civil records preserved at *Drachenbronn* show the 17 June date. It is worth noting that her birth was also given as 8 July 1808 by her father when registering his family at the time of the 1808 census of Jews taken at *Drachenbronn*. (**A, AN, B1808, ES**)

MAYER, MELANIE, was born on 16 May 1844 in *Niederbronn-les-Bains*, Bas-Rhin, France, to **JEANNETTE/ BABETTE VOGEL** (See entry), a native of the town, and her twenty-seven year old husband **MEYER MAYER**, of which nothing is known. Babette and her daughter, Melanie, appear in the 1846 census for *Niederbronn*, living with her parents. Babette was married but her husband was not present in the household. There is an immigration record for a twenty-seven-year-old **MEYER MEYER** who arrived from France in New Orleans on 24 October 1844 aboard the ship *Frances Depau*. We could find no more records for him in Louisiana. According to U.S. census records Babette and Melanie immigrated to Louisiana ca. 1846 a date that could not be verified by any existing ship's records. We know that Babette married **SAMUEL BLUM** (See entry) in Donaldsonville, Ascension Parish, LA, on 8 April 1854. Babette's daughter, Melanie Mayer, married JOSEPH BLUM, a native of Louisiana, on 1 November 1860. Their only child, Jacob, was born in 1862. Melanie's husband died the following year. Melanie remained all her life in Donaldsonville where she worked as a milliner. She stayed with her step-father **SAMUEL BLUM** (See entry) and mother, Babette, as long as they lived. She never remarried. Melanie died on 28 June 1931 and was buried in Bikur Sholim Jewish Cemetery in Donaldsonville. (**A, AN, E, G**)

MEYER, ABRAHAM, was born on 10 December 1852 in *Oberlauterbach*, Bas-Rhin, France, to **LEOPOLD MEYER (LÖB ISAAC ABRAHAM** before 1808) and his wife, **BABETTE/BARBE MARX/HIRSCH**, both natives of the town. According to a naturalization record filed in Shreveport, Caddo Parish, LA, Abraham arrived in Louisiana in 1874, a date which we could not verify using any available ship's record. He became a citizen in 1879. Abraham was enumerated with his brother, **MARX MEYER** (See entry) in the 1880 federal census for Shreveport. Abe, as he was known in Louisiana, was working as a merchant, while his brother Marx worked as his clerk. As they prospered, Abe and Marx began buying up local real estate. They developed farming interests and also went into the banking business. Abe, Marx, and a friend, Captain Peter C. Youree, a Missourian who had fought for the Confederacy, formed a bank which was eventually named the City Savings Bank and Trust Co., one of the oldest in Shreveport. Abe married ROSA HALFF, a native of Galveston, Galveston Co., TX, on 3 September 1890 in Houston, Harris Co., TX. He brought her back to Shreveport where their three children were born: Beulah Julia (b. 1891), Lionel Leopold (b. 1892), and Alvin Felix (b. 1894). By the time of the 1900 federal census, Abe had given up the retail business to concentrate on real estate. He was also vice-president of the bank he had helped found. He died in Shreveport on 4 January 1930 and was buried there in Hebrew Rest Cemetery #2 (Texas Ave.). Rosa died on 9 October 1940 in Shreveport and was buried with her husband. (**A, AN, G**)

MEYER/MYERS, ARON/JOHN, was born **ARON MEYER** on 27 August 1822 in *Niederroedern*, Bas-Rhin, France, to **SAMUEL MEYER**, le jeune, a native of the town and **AMALIE/MADELEINE AUSCHER**, born in *Oberlauterbach*, Bas-Rhin. He was mistakenly identified in the birth record as a female child, but was correctly identified as a boy in the 1836 and 1841 census records for the town. He appears to have been the first of his brothers and sisters to immigrate to Louisiana, arriving in New Orleans, Orleans Parish, LA, on 13 October 1846 aboard the ship *Leodes*. He began using, or was given the name JOHN MEYER, which was used on his marriage record to BABETTE SCHWARTZ, a native of Zweibrucken, Germany, which took place on 22 August 1850 in New Orleans. Thereafter he was known as John Meyer or "Myers," the latter spelling his brother, **JACOB MEYER/MYERS** (See entry), and two of his sisters, **ROSALIE MEYER/MYERS** (See entry for **MOISE LEVY** b. 1823) and **GERTRUDE/MARY MYERS** (See entry) always used. John was a retail grocer in New Orleans. He and Babette raised five children: Julia (b. 1854), Leon (b. 1855), Clara (b. 1857), Mathilde/Tillie (b. 1861) and Fanny (b. 1863). John Myers died on 27 June 1881 in New Orleans and was buried there in Hebrew Rest Cemetery #1. Babette died on 17 September 1894 and was buried with him. (**A, AN, E, G, GB, TT**)

MEYER, CAROLINE, was born **THÉRÈSE CAROLINE MEYER** on 27 March 1849 in *Oberlauterbach*, Bas-Rhin, France, to **LEOPOLD MEYER (LÖB ISAAC ABRAHAM** before 1808) and his wife, **BABETTE/BARBE MARX/HIRSCH**, both natives of the town. According to the 1900 federal census, Caroline immigrated ca. 1880 to Shreveport, Caddo Parish, LA. She may have been the thirty-two-year-old "Caroline Meier" who arrived in New York on 27 July 1881 from Bremen, Germany, aboard the SS *Nurnberg*. Caroline lived with her brothers, **ABRAHAM** and **MARX MEYER** (See entries), until her marriage on 3 January 1887 in Rapides Parish to HENRY D. BRENNER, an Austrian immigrant. The Brenners settled in Shreveport where Henry was a local retail grocer. The couple were the parents of four children: Bertha Meyer (b. 1887), twins Alphonse and Charles M. (b. 1889), and Leon (b. 1894; died 1902). Henry Brenner died on 8 May 1916 in Shreveport and was buried in Hebrew Rest Cemetery #2 (Texas Ave.) After her husband's death, Caroline made her home with her bachelor brother, Marx Meyer, until her death on 23 January 1927. She was interred with her husband and son, Leon, in the Brenner family plot in Hebrew Rest Cemetery #2 (Texas Ave.) in Shreveport. (**A, AN, G**)

MEYER, EMANUEL H., was born **EMANUEL MEYER** on 26 March 1855 in *Schweighouse-sur-Moder*, Bas-Rhin, France, to **DAVID MEYER,** a native of the town, and his wife, **FANNIE CERF**, born in *Haguenau*, Bas-Rhin. According to information given in the 1920 federal census, Emanuel immigrated to Louisiana in 1871, where he joined his sister, **MARY MEYER** MEYER (See entry) in St. Francisville, West Feliciana Parish, LA. We were unable to find a reliable ship's record for his arrival in America. He married ESTELLE COHN (COHEN) on 18 April 1882 in West Feliciana Parish. Estelle was a Louisiana native, born to St. Francisville dry goods merchant, LOUIS D. COHEN, a Prussian immigrant. Emanuel and Estelle were the parents of three children: Pearl (b. 1885), David (b. 1886), and

Lionel (b. 1889). Emanuel Meyer moved his family to nearby Baton Rouge, East Baton Rouge Parish, LA, ca. 1900 where he worked as a dry goods merchant. Estelle died on 26 June 1933 in Baton Rouge and was buried there in the Jewish Cemetery. Emanuel H. Mayer died on 20 January 1937 in New Orleans where he went to seek treatment. His remains were returned to Baton Rouge where they were interred with those of his wife. Note: As with all the MAYER/MEYER confusion, Emanuel's name is spelled both ways in various census and vital records. The six surviving children of the eleven born to David Meyer and Fannie Cerf immigrated to America: Four of them settled in Louisiana: **MARIE**, **HENRIETTE**, **JUSTINE** (See entries) and Emanuel. Adelaide and Sophie Meyer lived in Mississippi **(A, AN, G, GB)**

MEYER, FANNIE, was born on 4 December 1854 in *Wolfisheim*, Bas-Rhin, France, to **MOÏSE MEYER,** a native of the town, and his wife, **RÉGINE WOOG**, born in *Marckolsheim*, Bas-Rhin. Seventeen-year-old Fannie immigrated to America, arriving in New Orleans, Orleans Parish, LA, on 14 October 1872 aboard the SS *Saxonia*. She married LAZARD BLUMENTHAL, a sixty-eight-year-old widower with six children, on 20 October 1881 in Convent, St. James Parish, LA. Lazard, a native of Hesse-Cassel, Germany, had lived in the United States since ca. 1848, first in New Orleans, then during and after the Civil War, in Cincinnati, Hamilton Co., OH. He and his first wife, BABETTE LOEB, also a German native, had returned to Louisiana ca. 1870, to live in Donaldsonville, Ascension Parish, LA. Babette died in Bayou Lafourche in 1876 and was buried in Bikur Sholim Cemetery in Donaldsonville. After Lazard's remarriage in 1881 he continued to work as a dry goods merchant in the River Parishes of Louisiana, but later ran a boarding house in Plaquemine, Iberville Parish, LA. He and Fannie were the parents of three surviving children: Meyer (b. 1884), Henrietta (b. 1885) and Moses (b. 1892). Eighty-six-year-old Lazard was enumerated in the 1900 federal census for Plaquemine with his wife, Fannie, and son, Moses, who was only seven years of age. The couple's two older children were living in Napoleonville, Assumption Parish, LA, with the family of **SALOMON KLOTZ** (See entry for Salomon Klotz b. 1854 in *Urhwiller*). Meyer and Henrietta Blumenthal were cousins through Salomon Klotz's mother, **RACHEL MEYER** of *Wolfisheim*. Lazard Blumenthal died on 5 June 1906, in Plaquemine, and was buried there in the Jewish Cemetery. Fannie Meyer

Blumenthal died on 29 March 1911, and was buried with her husband. (**A, AN, G, GB, TT**)

MEYER/MYERS, GERTRUDE MARY, was born ca. 1832 in *Niederroedern*, Bas-Rhin, France, to **SAMUEL MEYER**, le jeune, a native of the town, and **AMALI/MADELEINE AUSCHER**, born in *Oberlauterbach*, Bas-Rhin. We were unable to find a birth record for Gertrude or Mary Meyer in *Niederroedern*, however she did appear as six-year-old "Gertrude Meyer" in the 1836 census for the town. Gertrude emigrated from France on the same passport with her sister **ROSALIE MEYER**, the latter's husband **MOÏSE LEVY** (See entry), and their three children in 1868. What is puzzling is that she did not appear with them on the ship's manifest of the SS *Holsatia* which docked in New York on 8 December 1868. Gertrude, however, always lived in the Moïse Levy household. She worked as a seamstress and a milliner. Mary "Myers" was enumerated with the Levy family in the 1870 federal census for Forest, Scott Co., MS, and again in 1880 after the family relocated to Evergreen, Avoyelles Parish, LA. She never married. Mary died on 20 January 1881 in Evergreen and was buried as Gertrude "Myers" in the Jewish Cemetery in Pineville, Rapides Parish, LA. Two of her brothers, **ARON/JOHN MEYER/MYERS** (See entry) and **JACOB MEYER/MYERS** (See entry) were residents of New Orleans. (**A, AN, AP, E, FS, TT**)

MEYER, HATTIE, was born **HENRIETTE MEYER** on 23 June 1861 in *Schweighouse-sur-Moder*, Bas-Rhin, France, to **DAVID MEYER**, a native of the town, and his wife, **FANNIE CERF**, born in *Haguenau*, Bas-Rhin. We believe that Hattie immigrated as "Henriette Meyer," and was accompanied by her widowed mother, **FANNY MEYER** (See entry), on board the SS *France*, which docked in New York from Le Havre, France, on 9 May 1877. Henriette, or "Hattie," as she was called in Louisiana, followed her sister, **MARIE MEYER** MEYER (See entry), to St. Francisville, West Feliciana Parish, LA. Hattie married WILLIAM HARTSON, a native of Hamburg, Germany, on 22 June 1880 in West Feliciana Parish. Hartson was a local dry goods merchant. The couple had three children: Corinne (b. 1881), David (b. 1883) and Florence (b. 1887). WILLIAM HARTSON died on 18 August 1894 and was buried in Hebrew Rest Cemetery in St. Francisville. Hattie continued in business in town as a dry goods merchant, with the help of her son, David. She retired to New Orleans, Orleans Parish, LA, just before 1910 to live with her daughter, Corinne

Hartson, who had married her first cousin, Isidore Hiller, the son of Adele Meyer, Corinne's aunt, who lived in Canton, Madison Co., MS. Hattie Hartson's sister, Mary Meyer, had moved from St. Francisville as well and was also enumerated with the Hiller-Hartson family in the 1910 federal census in New Orleans. In 1920 Hattie and Mary were enumerated with Hattie's other daughter, Florence, the wife of Alphonse B. Hiller, a native of Magnolia, Pike Co., MS. Hattie lived with the Hillers for the rest of her life. She died on 19 July 1940 in New Orleans and was buried there in Hebrew Rest Cemetery # 2. Note: The six surviving children of the eleven born to David Meyer and Fannie Cerf immigrated to America: Four of them settled in Louisiana: **MARIE, EMANUEL, JUSTINE** (See entries) and Hattie/Henriette. Adelaide and Sophie Meyer lived in Mississippi. **(A, AN, G, GB)**

MEYER, HENRI, was born **ISIDORE HENRI MEYER** on 15 January 1871 in *Muttersholtz,* Bas-Rhin, France, to JOSEPH MEYER, born in Bollwiller, Haut-Rhin, France, and his wife PAULINE MEYER, a native of Baden, Germany. Henri immigrated to New York from Antwerp, Belgium, arriving on 29 August 1890 aboard the SS *Waesland*. After a short stay in New Mexico where he worked as a clerk, he settled in Lake Charles, Calcasieu Parish, LA. He was employed by SAMUEL KAUFMAN, a local Jewish merchant. He married MIRIAM/MIRA REIMS, the Louisiana born daughter of **DAVID REIMS** (See entry), on 20 March 1901 at the Reims home in Lake Charles. Henri and Mira were the parents of two daughters: Aline (b. 1904) and Selma (b. 1905). Henry was a general merchant associated with the firm of Mendel & Meyer. He also had an interest in the Lake Charles Furniture Co. After their retirement Henri and Mira lived briefly in Los Angeles, Los Angeles Co., CA, where they were enumerated in the 1940 federal census living with their widowed daughter Selma Kahn, and her two children. Shortly thereafter, they relocated to Tulsa, Tulsa Co., OK where Henry died on 5 August 1946. Mira died there as well on 4 January 1975. Their final resting places are unknown at this time. **(A, AN, G)**

MEYER, HENRIETTE (*Lembach*), See entry for her father, **LEOPOLD MEYER**

MEYER, HENRY, was born on 20 June 1865 at *Herrlisheim*, Bas-Rhin, France, to **ABRAHAM MEYER**, a native of the town, and his wife, **ROSALIE RUF**, born in *Schirrhoffen*, Bas-Rhin. Nineteen-year-old Henry Meyer emigrated from Le Havre, France, to New York, arriving on 9 August 1882, aboard the SS *St. Laurent*. He was naturalized in Mayersville, Issaquena Co., MS, in 1889. Henry married **HERMANCE DREYFUS**, a native of Mulhouse, Haut-Rhin, France, on 21 May 1899 in New Orleans, Orleans Parish, LA. The couple never had children. Henry worked for his brothers-in-law, **JULES** and **LEON DREYFUS** in New Iberia, Iberia Parish, LA, at Jules Dreyfus & Co., Wholesale Grocers. In 1922 he and his wife joined his brother, **MYRTIL MEYER** (See entry), and Myrtil's wife, Louise Bendel, on a trip back to France to see relatives. Henry died on 23 January 1935 in New Iberia and was buried there in Temple Gates of Prayer Cemetery (the Jewish section of Rosehill Cemetery). When his wife, Hermance, died on 9 February 1956 she was interred there as well. A double stone marks their resting place. (**A, AN, F, G**)

MEYER, ISAAC, was born in *Lembach*, Bas-Rhin, France on 17 July 1824 to **CHARLES MEYER**, a native of the town, and his wife, **SOPHIE KLOTZ**, born in *Uhrwiller*, Bas-Rhin. We believe that Isaac Meyer arrived as twenty-three-year-old "Isador Meyer," a French immigrant who landed in New Orleans, Orleans Parish, La, from Le Havre, France, on 10 April 1847 aboard the ship *Jane H. Glidden*. Not long after his arrival in Louisiana, he died in or near Clinton, East Feliciana Parish, LA, on 5 September 1853 and was buried in the Clinton Jewish Cemetery. He was listed as one of the dead from Clinton in that year's yellow fever epidemic in the New Orleans, LA *Daily Picayune* published on 26 October 1853. (**A, AN, ES, GB**)

MEYER/MYERS, JACOB, was born **JACQUES MEYER** on 16 October 1833 in *Niederroedern*, Bas-Rhin, France, to **SAMUEL MEYER**, le jeune, a native of the town, and **AMALIE/MADELEINE AUSCHER**, born in *Oberlauterbach*, Bas-Rhin. We believe that the twenty-one-year-old "Jacques" Meyer who arrived in New Orleans, Orleans Parish, LA, on 28 December 1854 aboard the *Mortimer Livingston* out of Le Havre, France, is the same person as Jacob Myers who was enumerated in the 1860 federal census with his brother, **ARON/JOHN MEYER/MYERS** (See entry) in New Orleans. Jacob was working as a clerk in a store. He took out a license to marry **PAULINE MORITZ**, a native of Bavaria, on 31 December 1860 in New Orleans. The couple were the parents of eleven children: Salomon Victor (b. 1861), Leon Louis (b. 1863), Mathilde Laurel "Delia" (b. 1865; died 1867), Estelle/Esther (b. 1867), Moritz Marx (b. 1869),

David Marks (b. 1871), Rosa (b. 1872), Julia (b. 1874), Rebecca (b. 1876), Aron (b. 1878; died 1880) and Leonora (b. 1880; died 1907). Jacob was a partner in the firm C.B. Block & Co., wholesale tobacco dealers. He later opened his own tobacco business and lived with his large family on Magazine Street in New Orleans. Pauline Myers died on 31 December 1888 in New Orleans, and was buried there in Hebrew Rest Cemetery #1. Jacob died on 29 September 1892, after he fell out of a second story window at his residence. His lifeless body was found by his family after a maid, hearing a loud thud and then moans, discovered him in the alley behind the house. Jacob was buried in Hebrew Rest Cemetery #1 with his wife. (**A, AN, G, GB, TT**)

MEYER, JUSTINE, was born on 6 August 1859 in *Schweighouse-sur-Moder*, Bas-Rhin, France, to **DAVID MEYER,** a native of the town, and his wife, **FANNIE CERF,** born in *Haguenau*, Bas-Rhin. She came to Louisiana ca. 1880, a record for which we were unable to find. She joined her sister, **MARY MEYER** (See entry), who was living in St. Francisville, West Feliciana Parish, LA, with her husband, JOSEPH MEYER. Justine married ADOLPH TEUTSCH, a furniture dealer and native of Venningen, Rheinpfalz, Germany, on 22 May1883 in West Feliciana Parish, LA. The couple had no children. Adolph died on 13 March 1900 and was buried in Hebrew Rest Cemetery in St. Francisville, West Feliciana Parish, LA. Several years later, Justine married Adolph's cousin, RUDOLF TEUTSCH, six years her junior, a record for which we were unable to find. There were no children from this marriage either. Justine died on 6 May 1908 at Touro Infirmary where she had gone for treatment. Her remains were brought back to Hebrew Rest Cemetery in St. Francisville where she was buried near her first husband. Note: The six surviving children of the eleven born to David Meyer and Fannie Cerf immigrated to America: Four of them settled in Louisiana: **MARIE, EMANUEL, HENRIETTE** (See entries) and Justine. Adelaide and Sophie Meyer lived in Mississippi (**A, AN, G**)

MEYER, LEHMANN, was born on 10 June 1842 in *Dauendorf,* Bas-Rhin, France, to **JOSUÉ MEYER,** said to be a native of *Uhlwiller,* a small village just outside of *Dauendorf,* in several death records of his children, and his wife, MINDEL/MINETTE BLOCH, born in Grussenheim, Haut-Rhin, France. Lehmann immigrated to New Orleans, Orleans Parish, LA, from Le Havre France, aboard the ship *Nuremberg* with fellow townsman **DAVID/KAUFFMANN KLING**

(See entry).They arrived together on 23 March 1861, less than a month before the start of the Civil War. Lehmann settled in Thibodaux, Lafourche Parish, LA. He first appeared in American records in the 1870 federal census as twenty-five-year-old "Leahman Meyer," a retail merchant from France owning $5000 in personal property. He married Thibodaux native HENRIETTE "HARRIET" LEVY on 25 August 1873 in Lafourche Parish, LA. Henriette died less than a year later, on 3 August 1874, leaving him with one child, Julius, born that year. Harriet Levy Meyer was interred in Bikur Sholim Jewish Cemetery in Donaldsonville, Ascension Parish, LA. Lehmann married FLORENCE DREYFUS, a native of Jackson, Hinds Co., MS, on 17 March 1880 in New Orleans. Florence had married and been widowed by Auguste J. Kern in 1876. Lehmann took his bride back to Thibodaux to live. They were enumerated in the 1880 federal census at Thibodaux with his son, Julius, a cousin, Alfred Meyer, and fourteen-year-old Joseph Meyer, the son of his brother **SELIGMANN/SOLOMON MEYER** (See entry). Joseph and Alfred were working as clerks in his store. That same year Lehmann filed a claim with the French & American Claims Commission, which took testimony beginning in 1880 from French citizens who sought reparations for goods seized by the Union Army during the Civil War. Lehmann sought payment for cattle taken by General Cameron on 20 June 1863, as well as sugar and molasses taken by Captain Fuller on 16 November 1862, and compensation for his arrest and imprisonment during the Union army occupation of Thibodaux after the battle of Labadieville. The claims were eventually disallowed for want of jurisdiction. Lehmann and Florence never had children. Florence died on 28 May 1893 aboard the SS *La Champagne* just before it landed in Le Havre, Seine-Maritime, France. Her father, **JOSEPH DREYFUS** (See entry), a native of *Westhouse*, Bas-Rhin, France, who was accompanying her on the trip, had her remains brought ashore. Her place of burial has not been discovered. Previous to her death, Florence and her husband, Lehmann, had relocated to St. Louis, MO, where he died on 12 July 1893, just seven weeks after his wife's demise. He was interred at New Mount Sinai Cemetery & Mausoleum in Affton, St. Louis Co., MO. (**A, AN, G, TT**)

MEYER, LÉONARD, (*Lembach*) See entry for his father, **LEOPOLD MEYER**

MEYER, LEOPOLD, was born on 14 January 1806, at *Lembach*, Bas-Rhin, France, to **LEVY MEYER**, a native of the town, and his wife, **EVE MEYER**, whose parentage and place of birth were unknown to the person who registered her death at *Lembach* on 24 December 1848. Leopold Meyer married **ZIPPOPRA/SOPHIE LEOPOLD**, born in *Büswiller*, Bas-Rhin, France, on 21 December 1842 in *Lembach*. The bride was the daughter of **ABRAHAM LEOPOLD**, a native of *Büswiller*, Bas-Rhin, and his wife, **SARA LANDAUER**, born in *Wintzenheim*, Bas-Rhin. The couple boarded the immigrant ship *Luna*, with their two children, Léonard, born 13 June 1844, and Henriette, born 8 January 1846, which left Le Havre on the evening of 6 February 1860. Unable to make its way out of the English Channel to the open waters of the Atlantic Ocean, on account of gale winds and a snow storm, the ship foundered on the rocks, in full sight of horrified witnesses near Barfleur the next day. Leopold, Sophie, and their two children, perished along with their *Lembach* neighbors, **SALOMON** and **MINETTE LEHMANN** (See entry) on the morning of 17 February 1860. Their bodies were never found amongst those that eventually washed ashore. **(A, AN)**

MEYER, LOUIS/LAZARUS, was born **LAZARE MEYER** on 11 March 1834 in *Lembach*, Bas-Rhin, France, to SALOMON MEYER, a native of Niederhochstadt, Bavaria, and his wife **FRÉDÉRIQUE MOOG**, born in *Lembach,* Bas-Rhin, France. Nineteen-year-old Louis Meyer died at Clinton, East Feliciana Parish, LA, on 25 October 1853 during the yellow fever epidemic. Information on his tombstone in the Clinton Jewish Cemetery identified him as "Lewis Meyer, born March 11, 1834 at Lembach, Alsace Fr. Died at Clinton, La. Octbr. 25, 1853 aged 19 yrs, 7 m's, and 14 dys." This gave us the necessary information to find his birth record at *Lembach*. We were unable to find a reliable immigration record for him.**(A, ES)**

MEYER, LUCIEN, was born on 25 July 1875 in *Odratzheim*, Bas-Rhin, France, to JOSEPH MEYER, born in Bollwiller, Haut-Rhin, France, and his wife, PAULINE MEYER, a native of Baden, Germany. Lucien immigrated to America, arriving at New York, on 16 May 1893 from Antwerp, Belgium, on the SS *Friesland.* He joined his brother, **HENRI MEYER** (See entry), at Lake Charles, Calcasieu Parish, LA. Lucien married CAROLINE/CARRIE REIMS, the Louisiana born daughter of **DAVID REIMS** (See entry) on 21 February 1904 in Lake Charles. Henri's wife, Mira Reims, was Carrie's sister. Lucien and Carrie moved to Jennings, Jefferson Davis Parish, LA, ca. 1905 where their son Paul Reims Meyer was born. Lucien worked as a merchant.

He registered for the World War I draft in Lafayette, Lafayette Parish, LA, in 1918, where the family had settled. He owned and operated a variety, novelty and magazine store in town. Lucien died on 12 April 1944, and was buried in the Jewish Cemetery in Lafayette. Their son, Paul, became a physician and practiced in Port Arthur, Jefferson Co., TX. After her husband's death Carrie Reims moved to Texas and died in Port Arthur on 26 January 1988 at the age of 103. (**A, AN, G, GB, HJL**)

MEYER, MANFRED, was born **MANASSÈS MEYER** on 17 February 1852 in *Sarre-Union*, Bas-Rhin, France, to **MEYER MEYER** and his wife, **PAULINE ARON**, both natives of the town. According to his 1891 application for a U.S. passport, Manfred stated that he immigrated to America in August 1872 aboard the SS *Ville-de-Paris*, a record we could not verify. No one by that name was listed on the ship's manifest which landed in New York on 30 August 1872.There is, however, a record for an eighteen-year-old M. Meir, a German national, who sailed from Liverpool, England arriving in New York on 20 June 1871 aboard the RMS *City of Paris*, which is worthy of consideration. Manfred worked for seven years as a clerk in Natchez, Adams Co., MS, then went to Newellton, Tensas Parish, LA, where he was enumerated in the 1880 federal census as a twenty-five year old clerk from France. He also worked in Lake Providence, East Carroll Parish, LA, before finally settling in New Orleans, Orleans Parish, LA, where he formed a partnership with Charles Gerber selling wholesale hats and caps, then with Elias Landauer, at which time Landauer & Meyer expanded into trunks and rubber goods as well. He was also Secretary-Treasurer of J. Rosenberg & Co., wholesalers of fancy goods, notions and novelties. He married **EVA WEILMAN**, a New Orleans native, on 30 June 1881 in New Orleans. They were the parents of four children: Camille (b. 1883), Maurice Weilman (b. 1884), Elsa (b. 1885) and Simm (b. 1887). Eva and Manfred retired to Manhattan, New York, where both their daughters had settled with their husbands. Eva died on 29 February 1912 in Manhattan. Her place of burial is unknown. Manfred Meyer died on 5 August 1934 and was buried in Mount Carmel Cemetery in Flushing, Queens Co., NY. (**A, AN, G, GB, HJL**)

MEYER, MARIE, was born on 21 April 1849 in *Schweighouse-sur-Moder*, Bas-Rhin, France to **DAVID MEYER**, a native of the town, and his wife, **FANNIE CERF**, born in *Haguenau*, Bas-Rhin. She immigrated to Louisiana at the age of twenty ca. 1869, a reliable record for which we were unable to find. JOSEPH MEYER, a native of Freisbach (District of Germersheim) Rheinpfalz, Germany, took out a license to marry Mary Meyer on 8 May 1871 in New Orleans, Orleans Parish, LA. The couple settled in St. Francisville, West Feliciana Parish, LA, where Joseph was a dry goods merchant, and later a grocer. The couple had no children. Joseph died on 25 April 1907 in St. Francisville and was buried there in Hebrew Rest Cemetery. Marie, always called "Mary" in Louisiana, went to live with her widowed sister, **HENRIETTE MEYER** HARTSON (See entry), in New Orleans, where she died on 28 June 1923.She was interred at Hebrew Rest Cemetery in St. Francisville next to her late husband. Note: The six surviving children of the eleven born to David Meyer and Fannie Cerf immigrated to America: Four of them settled in Louisiana: **HENRIETTE, EMANUEL, JUSTINE** (See entries) and Marie. Adelaide and Sophie Meyer lived in Mississippi **(A, AN, G)**

MEYER, MARX, was born on 12 November 1861 in *Oberlauterbach*, Bas-Rhin, France, to **LEOPOLD MEYER (LÖB ISAAC ABRAHAM** before 1808) and his wife, **BABETTE/BARBE MARX/HIRSCH**, both natives of the town. Marx immigrated to America ca. 1878, a record for which we were unable to find. In his 1910 petition for naturalization Marx had affirmed that he arrived in New Orleans, Orleans Parish, LA, on 21 October 1880, on the ship *Nurnberg*, which was clearly a mistake, since he was enumerated in Shreveport, Caddo Parish, LA on 7 June 1880 at the home of his older brother, **ABRAHAM MEYER** (See entry), a local merchant. Marx (also commonly spelled "Marks" in Louisiana) was employed as his brother's clerk. Marks Meyer never married. He became a prosperous local merchant. He joined his brother, Abe, and a friend, Captain Peter C. Youree, a Missourian who had fought for the Confederacy, to form a bank which was eventually named the City Savings Bank and Trust Co., one of the oldest in Shreveport. Marks bought up land in Caddo, Bossier, and Red River Parishes, which he had planted in cotton and other local crops. He was also a vice-president of the Alphonse Brenner Co., selling both new and used furniture. Marks lived in a large house he had constructed for himself on Jordan Street in Shreveport. He was enumerated in the 1900 federal census in Shreveport where he lived with his sister, **CAROLINE MEYER** (See entry), her husband HENRY BRENNER, and their four children. Marks was naturalized on 2 November 1911 in Caddo Parish. After Caroline Brenner's death in 1927, her son, Charles Brenner, her widowed daughter, Bertha Brenner

Florsheim, and Bertha's only child, Sigmund Emmanuel Florsheim lived with Marks on Jordan Street. Marks managed his real estate holdings and was active until several years before his death, at the age of ninety-seven, on 4 July 1958. He was interred in Forest Park East Cemetery in Shreveport. (**A, AN, G**)

MEYER, MYRTIL, was born on 23 November 1876 at *Herrlisheim*, Bas-Rhin, France, to **ABRAHAM MEYER**, a native of the town, and his wife, **ROSALIE RUF,** born in *Schirrhoffen*, Bas-Rhin. Seventeen-year-old Myrtil immigrated to the United States, arriving at New York on 2 October 1893 aboard the SS *La Bretagne* from Le Havre, France. He travelled to Louisiana where an older brother, **HENRY MEYER** (See entry), was working in New Iberia, Iberia Parish, LA. Twenty-four-year-old Myrtil was enumerated in the 1900 federal census for St. James Parish, living alone and working as a merchant. He moved to Lafayette, Lafayette Parish, LA ca. 1903 to work for the family of his bride, **LOUISE BENDEL**, a native of Lafayette, whom he wed on 8 February of that year. Louise's mother, Mary Plonsky, the widow of Austrian-born merchant, William Louis Bendel, had married Benjamin Falk a year after the Louise's birth in 1875. The Falk dry goods store was incorporated as the Falk Mercantile Co., Ltd. in April 1903, two years after Benjamin Falk's death in 1901. Mary Plonsky Falk was president of the firm. Isaac Bendel, her son, was its vice-president, and Myrtil Meyer, her daughter Louise's new husband, was its secretary-treasurer. Myrtil and Louise never had children. They travelled extensively, going to New York to buy for their clothing firm and to visit Louise's brother, the famous Fifth Avenue milliner and department store owner, **HENRI BENDEL**, who had started his first shop in New Iberia, Iberia Parish, LA. Myrtil and Henry Meyer travelled to Europe with their wives in the summer of 1922, returning to New York early in September of that year. Myrtil died on 24 November 1928 in Lafayette. He was interred in the Lafayette Jewish Cemetery. After his death Louise retired from business. She lived with her brother, Isaac Bendel, in a home built for her by her brother Henri. Isaac concentrated on his real estate holdings, which after Henri's death in 1936, included the beautiful Bendel Gardens subdivision in Lafayette. Louise died on 14 February 1949 in Lafayette and was buried with her husband. (**A, AN, CA, G, GB**)

MEYER, RACHEL, (*Wolfisheim*) See entry for **DAVID KLOTZ**

MEYER/MYERS, ROSALIE/ROSETTE, (*Niederroedern*) (See entry for MOÏSE LEVY (*Niederbronn-les-Bains*).

MEYER, SALOMON/SOLOMON, was born **SELIGMANN MEYER** on 23 April 1838 in *Dauendorf*, Bas-Rhin, France, to **JOSUÉ MEYER**, according to several death records of his children said to be a native of *Uhlwiller*, Bas-Rhin, a small village just outside of *Dauendorf*, and his wife, MINDEL/MINETTE BLOCH, born in Grussenheim, Haut-Rhin, France. Seventeen-year-old Seligmann immigrated to New Orleans, Orleans Parish, LA, from Le Havre, France, arriving on 2 April 1855 aboard the ship *Desdemona*. He settled in the town of Thibodaux, Lafourche Parish, LA, where he was enumerated in the 1860 federal census as a twenty-two-year-old merchant trader with $1700 in personal property. Solomon, as he was known in Louisiana, married FLORIDA "FLORA" PERRILLOUX, a Thibodaux native from a large Catholic family, on 31 July 1861 at a civil ceremony in Thibodaux. They moved to Chackbay, Lafourche Parish, just outside of Thibodaux where Solomon opened a general store and raised horses and mules. He joined the Confederate cause subsequent to his 1861 marriage, signing on as Corporal in the Lafourche Parish Regiment of the Louisiana Militia. According to family accounts he was captured by the Union Army under General Godfrey Weitzel at the battle of Labadieville, Lafourche Parish, on 27 October 1862 and taken prisoner, but soon released, as was the custom early in the war. Solomon later filed a claim with the French and American Claims Commission which took testimony beginning in 1880 from French citizens who sought reparations for goods seized by the Union Army during the Civil War. He petitioned for payment of $51,730 on account of horses, mules, and sugar taken from his premises by Major Lewis in 1862. His claim was dismissed in 1882 for want of jurisdiction. Solomon and Florida were the parents of eight children: Sarah (b. 1864), Joseph (b. 1866), Leon (b. 1870), Matilda (b. 1873), twins Marie Henriette and Isidore (b. 1875), Jules (b. 1878), and Clara (b. 1881). Solomon Meyer worked as a merchant in Chackbay until his death ca. June 1883. His exact date of death and place of burial remain a mystery. His widow, Florida, opened an inn/boarding house in Thibodaux, where she worked to support her children. Mrs. Solomon Meyers [*sic*] was enumerated in the 1900 federal census in Lafourche Parish, living with her son Isidore who supported them while working as a farm laborer. Mrs. Solomon Meyer last appeared in a census record in 1920 where she was enumerated as a seventy-three-year-old servant working in the household of Lafourche Parish resident Ernest Roger, Jr. She died on 5 January 1924 in Thibodaux, Lafourche Parish. Her place of burial is unknown at this time. Her son Jules, who died at age nineteen, was interred in the Trosclair Graveyard at Chackbay. Both she and her husband may lie there in unmarked graves. (Note: See entry for Solomon's brother, **LEHMANN MEYER**) (**A, AN, G, R, TT**)

MICHEL, JACOB, was born **JACQUES MICHEL** on 21 April 1831 in *Struth,* Bas-Rhin, France, to ABRAHAM MICHEL, a native of Metz, Moselle, France, and his wife, **JEANNETTE/CHRISTINE NEUBURGER**, born in *Struth*, Bas-Rhin. According to a naturalization record, he arrived in America on 22 September 1853. In fact, twenty-two-year-old Jacques Michel arrived at New York on 13 September 1853 from Le Havre, France, aboard the ship *Hope Goodwin.* In 1860 he was enumerated as a single male in the household of Pointe Coupée merchant **NATHAN KERN** (See entry) and his wife **ROSINE MICHEL**, Jacob's sister. He married ADELE LEVY (b. 1833), a native of Belfort, Haut-Rhin, France on 28 September 1863 in Wilkinson Co., MS. Two children were born to them: Abraham (b. 1865) and David (b. 1867). Jacob relocated his family to Bayou Sara, West Feliciana Parish, LA, where Adele died on 18 October 1868. He married Adele's sister, born HENRIETTE, but known in Louisiana as CÉCILE H. LEVY (b. 1841), on 24 June 1869 in New Orleans. They returned to live and work in Bayou Sara, where five children were born: Harriet (1871-1875, buried Clinton Jewish Cemetery, East Feliciana Parish), Maurice (b. 1873), Ralph (b. 1876), Rose (b. 1878) and Armand Simon (b. 1880). While his store was spared when a whole block of Bayou Sara went up in flames in 1880, he had severe losses in 1886 after another fire, with only partial insurance. He died in May 1888 at Bayou Sara, and was interred in the Jewish Cemetery in Baton Rouge, East Baton Rouge Parish, LA. His wife, Cécile, who had later moved to New Orleans to live whith her daughter, Rose Michel Ries, died there on 1 April 1920 and was interred in Gates of Prayer Cemetery #2 (Joseph Street). Note: Michel is misspelled as "Mitchell," "Michael," and "Michell" in various American records. (**A, AN, F, G, GB, TT**)

MICHEL, MEYER, was born **MEYER LEVI MICHEL** on 13 January 1826 in *Struth,* Bas-Rhin, France, to ABRAHAM MICHEL, a native of Metz, Moselle, France, and his wife, **JEANNETTE/ CHRISTINE NEUBURGER**, born in *Struth*, Bas-Rhin. He immigrated to America ca. 1850, a reliable record for which we were unable to find. Meyer spent some time in Tennessee, before relocating to Waterloo, Pointe Coupée Parish, LA, to be nearer to his brother, **JACOB MICHEL** (See entry), and his sister **ROSINE MICHEL KERN** (See entry). He married ROSALIE/ROSINE LEVY, about whom we know very little except that she was a victim of the yellow fever epidemic of 1867. She died on 21 September of that year. She was buried in Hebrew Rest Cemetery #1 in New Orleans, Orleans Parish, LA. Meyer and Rosalie had five children. Henriette was was born ca. 1854 in Tennessee. Melanie (b. 1857), Abraham (b. 1858), Estelle (b. 1862), and Henry (b. 1866), were all born in Waterloo. Less than a year after his first wife's death, Meyer married ROSINA MEYER HESS, a widow of German extraction, on 29 June 1868 in New Orleans. Four children were born to Meyer and Rosina Hess in Waterloo: Lazard (b. 1869), Jacob (b. 1871), Rachel (b. 1872), and Herman (b. 1875). Meyer was the owner of two general merchandise stores. His first, The Alsace Store, was located just west of Waterloo, and The Evening Star Store which he opened in the mid-1880s was located in town. Meyer died on 8 March 1888 in Waterloo. He was buried in Hebrew Rest Cemetery # 1 in New Orleans. Rosina moved to New Orleans, shortly after his death, passing away five years later on 21 January 1893. She was buried in the same cemetery. (**A, AN, BC G, GB, TT**)

MICHEL, ROSINE (*Struth*) See entry for **NATHAN KERN**

MOCH, BERTHA, was born on 12 December 1875 in *Ingwiller,* Bas-Rhin, France to **ELIE/ELIAS MOCH** (See entry), a native of *Mertzwiller*, Bas-Rhin, France and his wife, **FANNY HAAS**, born in *Ingwiller*, Bas-Rhin. According to information given in the 1900 federal census for Eola, Avoyelles Parish, LA, Bertha immigrated to Louisiana with her mother and sister, Laura, ca. 1899, information that we were unable to verify using any available ship's records. She married ISAAC E. SILVERBERG, a New York native, who was a jeweler in Alexandria, Rapides Parish, LA. They wed on 18 June 1902 in Eola and returned to Alexandria to live. Twenty-nine-year-old Bertha died on 2 March 1904. She was laid to rest in the Jewish Cemetery in Pineville, Rapides Parish. LA. (**A, AN, AP, FS**)

MOCH, ELIE/ELIAS, was born on 21 December 1845 in *Mertzwiller*, Bas-Rhin, France, to **HERMANN MOCH**, a native of the town, and his wife, **SARA FRANK**, born in *Niederseebach*, Bas-Rhin. Elie married **FANNY HAAS** on 27 April 1874 in *Ingwiller*, Bas-Rhin. Fanny was born on 28 July 1848 in *Ingwiller*, Bas-Rhin, France, to **SAMUEL HAAS**, a native of *Rothbach*, Bas-Rhin, France, and his second wife, **ZERLINA WOLFF**, born in *Weinbourg*, Bas-Rhin. Elie and Fanny were the parents of four children all born at *Ingwiller*: Bertha (b. 1875), Zuline (b. 1877; died 1891 in *Ingwiller*), Henry (b. 1881; died at 7 months in 1881 in *Ingwiller*), and Sara/Laura (b. 1883). Thirty-seven-year-old "Elie Moch," a German national, arrived at New York, from Liverpool, England, on 21 May 1883 aboard the SS *Furnessia*. He was set up in business by Fanny's half-brothers, **SAMUEL** and **ALEXANDRE HAAS** (See entries). Elie became a successful dry goods merchant in the little town of Eola in Avoyelles Parish, LA. Fanny followed him to Eola in 1899 with her two surviving children, **BERTHA** and **SARA/LAURA MOCH** (See entries) after the death of her mother, **ZERLINA WOLFF HAAS**, at *Ingwiller* in 1897. After over two decades in business in Eola, Elie Moch moved his family to Alexandria, Rapides Parish, LA in 1908 to live with his daughter Laura and her husband, Joseph Goldberg. Elie died on 1 February 1928 in Alexandria and was buried in the Jewish Cemetery in Pineville, Rapides Parish, LA. Fanny died at Alexandria on 24 May 1930 and was buried with her husband. (**A, AN, AP, G,**)

MOCH, HARRIET/HENRIETTE, (*Mommenheim*), See entry for **NATHAN WEIL**

MOCH, HARRIET/JANNETE, (*Mertzwiller*), See entry for **SAMUEL WOLF**

MOCH, LAURA was born **SARA MOCH** on 25 January 1883 in *Ingwiller*, Bas-Rhin, France, to **ELIE/ELIAS MOCH** (See entry), a native of *Mertzwiller*, Bas-Rhin, France, and his wife, **FANNY HAAS,** born in *Ingwiller*, Bas-Rhin. According to information given in the 1900 federal census for Eola, Avoyelles Parish, LA, Laura immigrated to Louisiana with her mother and sister, Bertha, in 1899, information that we were unable to verify using any available ship's records. Laura married her deceased sister's late husband's business partner, Polish immigrant, JOSEPH M. GOLDBERG, on 24 November 1908 in Eola. They returned to Alexandria where Joseph was the proprietor of a jewelry store. Two children were born to the couple: Elaine (b. 1909) and Beryl (b. 1911). Joseph died on 23 May 1942 and was buried in the

Jewish Cemetery in Pineville, Rapides Parish, LA. His wife, Laura followed on 2 March 1951 and was buried with him. (A, AN, AP, FS)

MOCH, MARX, was born on 23 October 1841 in *Mommenheim*, Bas-Rhin, France, to **DANIEL MOCH**, a native of the town, and his wife, **JEANNE/HANNE KAHN**, born in *Niederbronn-les-Bains*, Bas-Rhin. Eighteen-year-old Marx Moch immigrated to America on the SS *John Merrick,* arriving in New Orleans on 24 January 1860. Six months later he was enumerated in the federal census for Shreveport, Caddo Parish, LA, working as a shoe maker. By 1870 he had become a successful merchant in Shreveport with personal property and real estate worth $4,000. He married **DINA LEVY** on 19 November 1875 in Caddo Parish. Dina was born **THÉRÈSE LEVY** on 25 June 1850 in *Schleithal*, Bas-Rhin, France, to **MARX LEVY**, a native of *Niederseebach*, Bas-Rhin, and his second wife, **FROMMIT WEILLER**, born in *Dauendorf*, Bas-Rhin. Her brothers, **SIMON, BERNARD, EMANUEL,** and half-brother, **SAMUEL LEVY** (See entries), were already residents of Shreveport when she arrived. We believe that she was listed as twenty-year-old "Dina Levy," an unmarried female, on board the SS *Holsatia* which arrived in New York on 14 September 1871. The 1866 census for the town of *Schleithal* confirms that she was known as "Dina," not "Thérèse." Marx and Dina were the parents of three children: Annie (b. 1876; see entry for **GUSTAVE KLEIN**), Fannie (b. 1878) and Daniel C. (b. 1879). Marx later became a dealer in horses and cattle in Shreveport, as well as the owner of a tannery. He died on 23 November 1918 and was buried in Hebrew Rest Cemetery #2 (Texas Ave.) in the city. Dina died on 10 December 1943, at the home of her grandson, Edward Klein, in Nashville, Davidson Co., TN. Her remains were returned to Shreveport where she was interred with her husband and son, Daniel C. Moch, in Hebrew Rest Cemetery #2 (Texas Ave.). (**A, AN, E, F, G**)

MOCH, SARA, (*Mommenheim*), See entry for **SAMUEL WEIL**.

MOCH, SOLOMON, was born on 21 March 1843 in *Scherwiller*, Bas-Rhin, France, to **MOÏSE MOCH**, a native of the town and his wife, JOSEPHINE WILLIG, born in Horbourg-Wihr, Haut-Rhin, France. He immigrated to Louisiana before 1870, a reliable record for which, we were unable to find. Solomon settled in Brashear City (now Morgan City), St. Mary Parish, LA, where he was enumerated in the 1870 federal census as a twenty-six-year-old retail grocer from France.

He married **JULIA GOUGENHEIM** on 17 March 1873 in St. Mary Parish. Julia was born **JULIE GUGENHEIM** on 13 October 1853 in *Obernai*, Bas-Rhin, France, to **JYCHAE LOUIS GUGENHEIM**, a native of *Zellwiller*, Bas-Rhin (See entry), and his wife, SARA WORMS, born in Boulay, Moselle, France. Julia immigrated with her mother and three sisters to Louisiana, via New York, arriving on 18 October 1855 aboard the ship *Switzerland*. She was raised in Morgan City, St. Mary Parish, LA, where her parents settled down to raise their family. Solomon and Julia Moch were the parents of five children: Maurice (b. 1875), Samuel (b. 1878), Abraham (b. 1879), Josephine (b. 1885), and William (b. 1891). Solomon died on 21 August 1898 in Morgan City and was buried in the Morgan City Cemetery and Mausoleum. After her husband's death, Julia moved to New Orleans, Orleans Parish, LA, where she lived with or near her sons, William and Samuel. She died on 9 February 1940 in New Orleans and her body was returned for burial to the Morgan City Cemetery and Mausoleum in Morgan City, LA. **(A, AN, F, G, GB)**

MOCK, JEANNETTE, was born **JEANNETTE MOG** in *Riedseltz*, Bas-Rhin, France, on 25 June 1817 to **MOYSE MOOG** and **ZWIE BLOCH,** both natives of the town. Jeannette immigrated to New Orleans, Orleans Parish, LA, ca. 1845, a reliable record for which we were unable to find. She married AUGUST ROSE/ROOS, a native of Speyer, Rheinpfalz, Germany ca. 1847, a record for which we were also unable to find. Jeannette and August were the parents of one son, Daniel August Rose, born on 4 July 1847. August was a merchant in New Orleans before his death on 4 July 1859 at the age of forty. He was buried at the now-demolished Gates of Mercy Cemetery. In 1957 the remains of those buried there were reinterred in Hebrew Rest #1 and a memorial plaque was installed which lists August Rose as one of those having been moved. His widow Jeannette lived with her son until her death in New Orleans on 27 February 1899. She was buried in Hebrew Rest Cemetery #1 the next day. **(A, AN, L, TT)**

MOCK, MAX/MARX, was born **MARTIN MOCH** on 20 March 1852 in *Mertzwille*r, Bas-Rhin, France, to twenty-year-old **MARIE/ MINETTE MOCH**, a native of the town. The maternal grandparents were **JOSEPH/HIRZEL MOCH** and his wife **HENRIETTE/ JEANNETTE/HANNE STORCK,** both natives of *Mertzwiller*. Seventeen-year-old Martin Moch immigrated to New Orleans, Orleans

Parish, LA, arriving on 22 November 1869 from Bremen, Germany, aboard the ship *Hermann*. He worked as a travelling salesman (drummer). Marx married SARAH SCHWARTZ, a native of Ingenheim, Rheinpfalz, Germany, on 16 September 1874 at New Orleans. They were the parents of six children: Benjamin Wolf (b. 1877), Hattie (b. 1879), Sidney (b. 1883), Rosa (b. 1884), Cleveland Lazard (b. 1885), and Elsie Carrie (b. 1887). Thirty-six-year-old "Max" Mock died in New Orleans on 14 August 1888. He was buried in Dispersed of Judah Cemetery in the city. Sarah followed on 4 September 1917 and was buried in the same cemetery. Note: The spelling "Mock" instead of "Moch" was consistently used by this family in Louisiana. Marx Moch appears in American records as both "Marx" and "Max." (**A, AN, GB**)

MOOCK/MOCK, BABETTE, (*Hatten*) See entry for **HERMANN HIRSCH**

MOSSER, JULIE/GITTEL, (*Surbourg*) See entry for **DAVID TRAUTMANN**

MÜLLER, ISIDORE, was born on 27 February 1847 in *Dehlingen*, Bas-Rhin, France, to **LOEB MÜLLER**, a native of the town, and his wife, AMÉLIE/MÉLINE CAHEN/KAHN, born in Forbach, Moselle France. Isidore immigrated to Louisiana after the Franco-Prussian War. We believe that twenty-four-year-old "Isador Muller," a German immigrant, arrived in New York from Liverpool, England, on 24 May 1871 aboard the SS *China*. Isidore married **JULIE KAUFMAN** on 21 May 1877 in New Orleans, Orleans Parish, LA. Julie was born **JULIE KAUFFMANN** on 11 September 1853 in *Gundershoffen*, Bas-Rhin, France to **JACQUES/JACOB KAUFFMANN**, a native of the town, and his wife, **JEANNETTE LEVI**, born in *Minversheim*, Bas-Rhin. Sixteen-year-old, Julie Kaufman immigrated to Louisiana, arriving in New Orleans, Orleans Parish, LA, on 6 April 1870 aboard the SS *Hannover*. Her occupation was listed as "dressmaker." She was enumerated two months later in the 1870 federal census living with her brother, Joseph, at Convent, St. James Parish, LA. **ROSALIE FRAENCKEL**, the widow of **SAMUEL RAAS** (See entry), was their next-door neighbor. Several years after their marriage, Isidore and Julie moved to Donaldsonville, Ascension Parish, LA. They were the parents of two children. Maurice was born in Labadieville, Assumption Parish, LA in March 1878. Isidore Müller died on 9 October 1878 during the yellow fever epidemic and was buried in Bikur Sholim Jewish Cemetery in Donaldsonville, Ascension Parish, LA. Their second child, Isadora "Dora" Müller, was born posthumously in May 1879 in Labadieville. Julie returned with her son and daughter to New Orleans where she worked as a dressmaker. In 1882 she decided to join her cousin, **LEOPOLD KAUFMANN** (See entry), in Lake Charles, Calcasieu Parish, LA. Her small dressmaking business was slowly transformed into Muller's Department Store, which was a Lake Charles fixture through the 1980s. Julie married a second time, to Louisiana native, **SIMON MARX**, in 1892 and had three more children: Helen (b. 1894), Sophie (b. 1896), and Adolph (b. 1897). Simon ran Muller's Department Store until his death on 20 December 1901 at the age of thirty-eight. Thereafter, Julie's son, Maurice J. Müller took over the business. Julie died on 9 April 1924 and was buried with her second husband in Graceland, the Jewish section of Orange Grove Cemetery, in Lake Charles. (**A, AN, G, GB, GW, TT**)

NETTER, ADOLPHE, was born on 24 May 1855 in *Ingwiller*, Bas-Rhin, France, to **THÉOPHILE NETTER**, a native of the town, and his wife, **BABETTE ISRAËL**, born in *Romanswiller*, Bas-Rhin. Fifteen-year-old Adolphe immigrated to America with his brother, **HENRY NETTER** (See entry), on the SS *Teutonia,* a ship out of Hamburg, Germany and Le Havre, France, which arrived at New Orleans, Orleans Parish, LA, on 10 April 1870. He and his brother Henry were lifelong residents of Donaldsonville, founding one of the largest dry goods stores in the town. They were associated for a time with their brother, **MEYER NETTER** (See entry), who eventually moved away. Adolph was also politically active, being a member of the school board, and the representative for Donaldsonville to the Ascension Parish Police Jury, of which he was also the president. In 1911 over half of the wooden structures in the town burned, including Netter & Co. Undeterred, Adolphe rebuilt a bigger brick structure that stretched from Mississippi Street through to Lessard St. which cost an estimated $100,000. Fifty-eight-year-old Adolphe Netter married thirty-one year old LUCILLE ÉLOÏSE MAURIN on 19 June 1913. She was the daughter of Antoine Maurin, manager of the Voiron Plantation, and granddaughter of sugar planter, Robert Maurin, who had owned the Ville du Bois plantation. Before her marriage she worked as a saleslady for Netter & Co. The wedding ceremony was conducted, by a Catholic Priest at the home of the bride's mother, Marie Maurin. The couple had two children: Babette (b. 1914) and Adolphe Antoine (b. 1916).

Adolphe Netter died on 16 April 1933 and was buried in the Ascension of Our Lord Catholic Church Cemetery in Donaldsonville in the family vault. His wife, Lucille Maurin Netter died ca. 8 November 1939 and was interred with him. Their son, Adolphe (d. 1996), and the latter's wife, Constance McFarland (d. 1976) were interred there as well. The plaque on the family vault is engraved with the four names. A Star of David is carved above Adolphe Netter's inscription. **(A, AN, G, GB)**

NETTER, ARON, was born on 20 May 1854 in *Schwindratzheim*, Bas-Rhin, France, to **SAMUEL CERF/HIRSCH NETTER**, a native of the town, and his wife, **ROSALIE/MINETTE BLOCH**, born in *Dauendorf*, Bas-Rhin. Aron immigrated to New Orleans, arriving on 14 October 1872, from Le Havre, France, aboard the SS *Saxonia*. He settled in East Baton Rouge Parish, LA, and worked as a general merchant in both Port Hickey and Port Hudson, villages only two miles apart. After a trip back to Alsace in early 1889, Aron married CORA LEOPOLD, a native of New Orleans, on 20 November 1889 in the city. Their two children, Gerald (b. 1891), and Bessie (b. 1894), were born in Port Hudson, East Baton Rouge Parish, LA. Aron gave up his dry goods business and moved his family to New Orleans ca. 1900, where he was one of the organizers of the Southern Paper Company, along with fellow Alsatian, **DAVID WOLBRETTE** (See entry). Aron served as secretary-treasurer of the company until his death on 30 December 1903. He was buried the next day in Gates of Prayer Cemetery #2 (Joseph Street) in New Orleans. Cora died on 24 January 1926 and was buried in the same cemetery. **(A, AN, G, GB)**

NETTER, CAROLINE, was born on 12 May 1857 in *Ingwiller*, Bas-Rhin, France, to **THÉOPHILE NETTER**, a native of the town, and his wife, **BABETTE ISRAËL**, born in *Romanswiller*, Bas-Rhin. She followed three of her brothers, **ADOLPHE, HENRY**, and **MEYER NETTER** (See entries), to Louisiana ca. 1875, a reliable record for which we were unable to find. Caroline married BERTRAND BEER, a native of New Orleans, whose parents were of German origin. Caroline and Bertrand were wed on 6 February 1878 in the city. Bertrand was a highly successfully cotton merchant in New Orleans. He had established his firm in 1872 with his brother-in-law and cousin, HENRY BEER, a native of Ingenheim, Rheinpfalz, Germany, his sister Virginia's husband. The firm, H. & B. Beer, later expanded taking on Edgar Bright as a partner. They handled not only cotton, cotton futures, but grains, provisions and coffee as well. Bertrand and Caroline were the parents of four children: Abraham Rayfield (b. 1879), Beatrice (b. 1882; died 1884), Sarah (b. 1885) and Gladys (b. 1891; died December 1891 at eight months). The couple and their children divided their time between New York, where Bertrand was the oldest southern member of the New York Cotton Exchange, and a home on St. Charles Avenue in New Orleans. They were enumerated in the 1910 federal census living both on 81st Street in Manhattan, and at 4035 St. Charles Avenue in New Orleans. Ill health forced Bertrand's retirement in 1905, but the firm carried on with their daughter Sarah Beer's first husband, Gus Worms, joining Edgar Bright and Henry Beer. Bertrand and Caroline traveled extensively during his retirement until his death on 16 February 1923 in New Orleans. Bertrand was buried in Hebrew Rest Cemetery #1 in the city. Caroline Netter Beer died on 17 February 1933 in New York City. Her remains were returned to New Orleans where she was interred with her husband. (**A, AN, G, GB**)

NETTER, EMILE, was born on 15 August 1869 in *Schirrhoffen*, Bas-Rhin, France, to **SAMUEL NETTER** and his wife **HANNAH/ HENRIETTE WEILL** (See entry), both natives of the town. In his March 1903 naturalization record filed in St. James Parish, LA, Emile stated that he had arrived in America on 8 June 1885, an assertion which we were not able to verify using any available ship's records. He worked as a peddler and clerk to make enough money to start his own business. He married FRANCES NEWMAN, an Alabama native, on 10 February 1896 in St. John the Baptist Parish, LA. Their only son, Alvin, was born the next year in White Castle, Iberville Parish, LA. By the turn of the twentieth Century the family had settled in Lutcher, St. James Parish, LA, where Emile was the proprietor of a grocery business. During their residence in Lutcher, Emile's mother, **HANNAH/HENRIETTE WEILL** (See entry), immigrated to America and lived with them there until her death in 1913. Several years later the couple and their son moved to Alexandria, Rapides Parish, LA, where Emile and his business partner, Morris Meyer, opened Meyer & Netter, a clothing store. Emile Netter died on 15 March 1941 in Alexandria, and was buried in the Jewish Cemetery in Pineville, Rapides Parish, LA. His wife died on 1 January 1944 and was buried in Pineville as well. (A, AN, G, GB)

NETTER, HENRY, was born **JACQUES NETTER** on 19 July 1852 in *Ingwiller*, Bas-Rhin, France, to **THÉOPHILE NETTER**, a native of the town, and his wife, **BABETTE ISRAËL**, born in *Romanswiller*,

Bas-Rhin. In the 1856 town census, the child, now four years old was enumerated as Jacques, but in the 1856 census he appeared as "Henry," age nine. Eighteen-year-old Henry immigrated to New Orleans, Orleans Parish, LA, with his brother, Adolphe, on the SS *Teutonia,* a ship out of Hamburg, Germany, and Le Havre, France, which arrived on 12 April 1870. He lived and worked the rest of his life in Donaldsonville, Assumption Parish, LA, for Netter & Co., one of the largest dry goods stores in town, which he and his brothers **MEYER** and **ADOLPHE NETTER** (See entries) started. In 1880 all three brothers were living together in Donaldsonville. All were unmarried. Subsequently Henry and Adolph boarded with **MELANIE MAYER** (See Entry), the widow of JOSEPH BLUM. Although Adolph eventually moved out, Henry stayed on, boarding with the widow Blum until his death on 30 November 1925. He was buried in Bikur Sholim Jewish Cemetery in Donaldsonville (**A, AN, E, G, GB**).

NETTER, MEYER, was born **MARC NETTER** on 16 December 1853 in *Ingwiller*, Bas-Rhin, France, to **THÉOPHILE NETTER**, a native of the town, and his wife, **BABETTE ISRAËL**, born in *Romanswiller*, Bas-Rhin. In the 1856 town census, the two-year-old child was enumerated as Marx, but in the 1856 census he appeared as seven-year-old "Meyer." He followed his two brothers, **ADOLPHE** and **HENRY NETTER** (See entries), to Louisiana ca. 1871, a date he gave at the time of the 1900 federal census. We have not been able to find a reliable immigration record for him. Meyer and his brothers worked together to make Netter & Co. one of the largest, and most successful dry goods stores in Donaldsonville, Ascension Parish, LA. Meyer married ELISE STERNE on 8 February 1881 in Donaldsonville. Elise was a New York native, whose mother Susanna had been born in Louisiana, The couple had four daughters: Adeline (b. 1881), Leonora (b. 1883), Ray (b. 1887) and Ethel (b. 1889). The 1911 fire which destroyed Netter & Co., drove Meyer and his family from Donaldsonville. He left Adolphe and Henry to pick up the pieces and moved to New Orleans, Orleans Parish, LA, then to Galveston, Galveston Co., TX, then back to New Orleans, where he and Elise were enumerated in the 1920 federal census, and finally to Austin, Travis Co., TX, where two of his daughters, Adeline Netter, and Leonora Netter Williams lived. Meyer worked in Texas as a dry good merchant. Elise died on 16 December 1920 and was buried in the Jewish section of Oakwood Cemetery, known as Beth Israël Cemetery #2, in Austin,

TX. Meyer died on 30 September 1939 and was buried there as well. (**A, AN, E, G, GB**)

RAAS, ISAAC, was born **ISAAC RAS** on 19 March 1825 in *Niedernai*, Bas Rhin, France, to **ELIE RAS**, the cantor at the local synagogue, born in 1800 at *Mutzig*, Bas-Rhin, France, and his wife, ROSINE HIRTZ, a native of Wintzenheim, Haut-Rhin, France. Twenty-one-year-old Isaac Raas was enumerated with his family in the 1846 *Niedernai* town census, but was missing from the 1851 census. We believe that he arrived in New Orleans, Orleans Parish, LA, as twenty-three-year-old [*sic*]"Isidore Ras",on 24 October 1846 from Le Havre, France, on board the ship *Taglione*. Isaac remained in New Orleans where he worked as a jeweler and watchmaker. He married **SARA KAUFMAN,** a native of *Gundershoffen,* Bas-Rhin, France, on 27 April 1854 in New Orleans. Sara was born **SARA KAUFFMANN** on 11 January 1822, along with a twin brother **RAPHAEL,** to **ABRAHAM KAUFFMANN**, a native of *Gundershoffen,* Bas-Rhin, France, and his second wife, **PAULINE/BÉLINE LOEB,** born in *Reichshoffen*, Bas-Rhin. We could find no reliable record for Sara's entry into the United States. Isaac and Sara were the parents of three children: Abraham (b. 1855), Pauline (b. 1857), and Julia (b. 1860), all born in New Orleans. Sara died on 26 September 1899 in New Orleans and was buried there in Hebrew Rest Cemetery # 1. After his wife's death, Isaac moved to Lake Charles, Calcasieu Parish, LA, to be near his daughter, Pauline. He died there on 3 May 1902. His remains were returned to New Orleans where they were interred with those of his wife in Hebrew Rest Cemetery # 1. (**A, AN, E, F, G**)

RAAS, SAMUEL, was born **SAMUEL RAS** on 6 June 1837 in *Niedernai*, Bas-Rhin, France, to **ELIE RAS,** the cantor at the local synagogue, born in 1800 at *Mutzig***,** Bas-Rhin, France, and his wife**,** ROSINE HIRTZ, a native of Wintzenheim, Haut-Rhin, France. Samuel arrived in New Orleans, Orleans Parish, LA, on 6 December 1858 from Le Havre, France, on the ship *Mataro.* He went to work as a clerk for his brother, **ISAAC RAAS** (See entry), who had a shop in New Orleans. Several years later he went out on his own and opened a store in Convent, St. James Parish, LA. He served with the French Company of St. James Parish, a Louisiana militia, during the American Civil War. Samuel married **ROSALIE FRAENCKEL** on 19 February 1866 in New Orleans. Rosalie was born on 11 March 1838 in *Rothbach*, Bas-Rhin, France, to **MARX FRAENCKEL**, a native of the town, and his wife, **JEANNETTE BECKER**, born in *Minversheim*, Bas-Rhin. We could not find a reliable record for the arrival of Rosalie Fraenckel in America. Samuel and Rosalie were the parents of two children: Isaac (b. 1867), and Samuel, who was born on 9 July 1869 after his father's death on 28 November 1868. Samuel was buried in Hebrew Rest Cemetery #1 in New Orleans. Rosalie remained in Convent, St. James Parish, LA, after her husband's death, where she and her two young boys, Isaac and Samuel, were enumerated at the time of the 1870 federal census. She moved to Baton Rouge, East Baton Rouge Parish, LA, to live with her brother **FELIX FRAENCKEL** (See entry) and his family some time before 1880. Her eighteen-year-old son Samuel died there on 17 September 1887 and was buried in the Baton Rouge Jewish Cemetery. After her brother Felix died in 1888, she went to live with her son Isaac and his family in Shreveport, Caddo Parish, LA, where she died on 3 April 1916. She was buried there in Hebrew Rest Cemetery #2 (Texas Avenue). (**A, AN, G**)

RAAS, SARA, (*Niedernai*) See entry for **JOSEPH BLUM**

REBLAUB, ROSINA/ROSALIE, (*Weinbourg*) See entry for **SAMUEL LEVY** (b. 1823)

REIMS, DAVID, was born on 23 December 1853 in *Ringendorf*, Bas-Rhin, France, to **SALOMON REIMS/RENS/REINS**, a native of *Haguenau*, Bas-Rhin, France, and his wife, **ELLEN/ÉLISE HERZOG**, born in *Ringendorf* Bas-Rhin. In an 1891 application for a United States passport, David wrote that he had immigrated to Louisiana, arriving aboard the SS *Saxonia* on 12 September 1871 from Le Havre, France. A search, however, of the passenger manifest for the SS *Saxonia* which landed in New York on 25 September 1871, did not include his name, nor could we find any other likely record for him. David married JULIA RAAS, the daughter of Alsatian natives **ISAAC RAAS** (See entry) and **SARAH KAUFFMANN** (See entry), on 6 June 1875 in New Orleans, Orleans Parish, LA, where the couple lived until 1883. They moved to Lake Charles, Calcasieu Parish, LA, that year where David opened up his own butcher shop. David and Julia were the parents of six children: Rosa (b. 1876), Bella (b. 1878), Miriam/Mira (b. 1880- See entry for **HENRY MEYER**), Armand (b. 1881), Carrie (b. 1884) and Blanche (b. 1889). David was naturalized in Lake Charles on 2 February 1891. He welcomed his sister, Marie's sons,

ERNEST and ACHILLE JAUDEL (See entries), into his home when they, too, emigrated from Alsace. David's wife, Julia, died on 23 July 1925 in Lake Charles and was buried there in Graceland, the Jewish section of Orange Grove Cemetery. David Reims died on 13 February 1930 and was buried there as well. (**A, AN, G**)

RIES, BENJAMIN, was born on 26 February 1820 in *Obernai*, Bas-Rhin, France, to MOÏSE/MOSES RIES/RYS, a native of Schopfloch, District of Ansbach, Bavaria, and his wife **ÉLÉONORE/ELLA/ELLEN SALOMON** (See entry), born in *Obernai*, Bas-Rhin. Fourteen-year-old Benjamin Ries immigrated with his parents and siblings to New Orleans, Orleans Parish, LA, arriving on 15 January 1835 from Le Havre, France, aboard the brig *Dido*. Seventeen-year-old Benjamin "Rees" [*sic*] died on 18 September 1837. His name appears on a list of those people buried at the Gates of Mercy Cemetery at Jackson and Saratoga Streets which was razed in the 1950s. The list was taken from records and a visual seach of the cemetery in the mid-nineteenth century. (**A, AN, R, TT**)

RIES, JEANNETTE, was born **JEANETTE RIES** on 6 February 1818 in *Obernai* Bas-Rhin, France, to MOÏSE/MOSES RIES/RYS, a native of Schopfloch, District of Ansbach, Bavaria, and his wife **ÉLÉONORE/ELLA/ELLEN SALOMON** (See entry), born in *Obernai*, Bas-Rhin. "Jannet," the name which appears on the ship's manifest, was said to be sixteen years old when she immigrated with her parents and siblings to New Orleans, Orleans Parish, LA, arriving on 15 January 1835 from Le Havre, France, aboard the brig *Dido*. She was married on 25 April 1835 to JACOB MAYER LEVI (aka. JOHN MAYER), a native of Landau, Rheinpfalz, Germany, in the parlor of her father's home, by her father, " the Rev Moses S. Reas," who had been a cantor and Hebrew teacher in both *Ingwiller* and *Obernai*. The celebration was a double wedding, with an older sister, **MINETTE RIES** (See entry) taking BINELL/PINAL LEVY as her husband. This event was so unusual that it was recorded in both French and English in the bilingual newspaper, *The New Orleans Bee (L'Abeille de la Nouvelle Orléans)*, on 5 May 1835. Jeannette and John were the parents of fourteen sons and daughters, eleven of whom survived to adulthood. Their first three children were born in New Orleans: Maurice (b. 1836), Emma (b. 1837) and Simon (b. 1839). The Mayer family relocated to Natchez, Adams Co., MS. ca. 1840 where they added eleven other children to their family: Caroline (b. 1841), Ophelia (b. 1843), Henry

Clay (b. 1845), Clementine (b. 1848; died 1849), Melanie (b. 1849), Adelaide (b. 1850; died 1852), Theresa (b. 1852), Benjamin Raphael (b. 1855), John, Jr. (b. 1858; died 1859), Eleanora Louisa (b. 1861) and Joseph Eggleston Johnston (b. 1862 in Washington, Adams Co., MS). John Mayer and his wife were respected citizens of Natchez for over forty years, where he was one of the leading merchants. He died in Natchez on 26 May 1882 and was buried in the Jewish Section of Natchez City Cemetery. Jeannette died on 12 August 1883 and was buried with him. (**A, AN, F, G, GB, TT**)

RIES, MINETTE, was born **MICHELETTE RIES** on 19 October 1814 in *Obernai* Bas-Rhin, France, to MOÏSE/MOSES RIES/RYS, a native of Schopfloch, District of Ansbach, Bavaria, and his wife **ÉLÉONORE/ELLA/ELLEN SALOMON** (See entry), born in *Obernai*, Bas-Rhin. "Minot," the name which appears on the ship's manifest, was said to be nineteen-years-old when she immigrated with her parents and siblings to New Orleans, Orleans Parish, LA, arriving on 15 January 1835 from Le Havre, France, aboard the brig *Dido*. She was married on 25 April 1835 to BINELL/PINAL LEVY, a native of Lixheim, Meurthe, France, in the parlor of her father's home, by her father, "the Rev Moses S. Reas," who had been a cantor and Hebrew teacher in both *Ingwiller* and *Obernai*. The celebration was a double wedding, with a younger sister, **JEANNETTE RIES** (See entry), taking JACOB MAYER LEVI (aka. JOHN MAYER) as her husband. This event was so unusual that it was recorded in both French and English in the bilingual newspaper, *The New Orleans Bee (L'Abeille de la Nouvelle Orléans*), on 5 May 1835. Binell and Minette were the parents of ten children: Albert (b. 1837), Morris (b. 1839), Bertha (b. 1841), Henry (b. 1842), Félicie (b. 1844; See entry for **LÉON. LEVY**), Nancy (b. 1845), Alexander (b. 1850), Louis (b. 1852), Émile (b. 1854) and Eleonora (b. 1856). Binell Levy owned a very successful clothing store in New Orleans He died on 12 September 1866 in New Orleans and was buried there in Hebrew Rest Cemetery #1. Minette died on 20 August 1869 in the city and was buried with her husband. (**A, AN, F, G, GB, TT**)

RIES, NANETTE, was born **NANNETTE MOÏSE** on 3 May 1807 in *Ingwiller*, Bas-Rhin, France, to MOÏSE/MOSES RIES/RYS, a native of Schopfloch, District of Ansbach, Bavaria, and his wife **ÉLÉONORE/ ELLA/ELLEN SALOMON** (See entry), born in *Obernai*, Bas-Rhin. Nanette was said to be twenty-five-years-old when she immigrated with her parents and siblings to New Orleans, Orleans Parish, LA, arriving on 15 January 1835 from Le Havre, France, aboard the brig *Dido*. Her name was recorded as "Hariet" on the ship's manifest. A notarial act dated 12 April 1845, filed after the death of PHINIAS DEPASS, indicated that Nanette Ries was his second wife. There were, apparently, no children who survived from this marriage. Nanette "Depose" [*sic*] married DANIEL LEMLE, a native of Baden, Germany, on 8 March 1848 in Natchez, Adams Co., MS. Twenty-five-year-old Daniel "Lammle" had immigrated on the ship *Austerlitz* which arrived at New Orleans, from Le Havre, France, on 29 September 1842. Daniel was a clothing merchant who had a store on Tchoupitoulas Street in New Orleans. According to the 1850 federal census, Daniel and Nanette were living together with her mother, Ellen Ries, in Lafayette, Jefferson Parish, LA (now part of uptown New Orleans). Ten years later, forty-three-year-old Daniel, and fifty-year-old Nanette had moved into New Orleans. No children were living with the couple. Nanette died on 7 April 1864 in New Orleans. There is no record of her place of burial. Daniel Lemle remarried and was the father of eleven children with JOHANNAH LOEB, a native of Alsace , France, or Bavaria, records for which, so far are conflicting. Daniel died in Mississippi on 30 July 1895 and was interred at Hebrew Union Cemetery in Greenville, Washington Co., MS. (**A, AN, G, TT**)

RIES/POLINE/PAULINE, was born **SIBILLE RIES** on 3 July 1812 in *Obernai*, Bas-Rhin, France, to MOÏSE/MOSES RIES/RYS, a native of Schopfloch, District of Ansbach, Bavaria, and his wife **ÉLÉONORE/ELLA/ELLEN SALOMON** (See entry), born in *Obernai*, Bas-Rhin. "Polin," the name which appears on the ship's manifest was said to be twenty-two-years-old when she immigrated with her parents and siblings to New Orleans, Orleans Parish, LA, arriving on 15 January 1835 from Le Havre, France, aboard the brig *Dido*. She married ELIAS EMSHEIMER, a native of Göcklingen, Rheinpfalz, Germany ca. 1836, a record of which cannot be located. Their only child, Ellen, was born on 30 August 1837. Elias died thirteen days later on 12 September 1837. Polin married JOHN WORMS, a native of Landau, Rheinpfalz, Germany, in New Orleans ca. 1840-1841, where their first child, Morris, was born ca. 1841. There were five more children born to the couple in Natchez, Adams Co., MS: Rosalie (b. 1843), Henry (b. abt. 1844), Julius (b. abt. 1846), Rachel (b. abt. 1847) and Theresa (b. abt. 1852). The Wormses had relocated to Natchez, perhaps to be close to John's friend, Jacob Meyer

Levi (aka. John Mayer), another immigrant from Landau, who had married Pauline's sister, **JEANNETTE RIES** (See entry). By 1860 the Worms family had moved to Waterloo, Seneca Co., NY. Pauline Ries Worms died on 28 April 1868 in New York State from consumption and was buried in Mount Hope Cemetery in Rochester, Monroe Co., NY. John Worms died in April 1885 and was buried with her. (**A, AN, G, TT**)

RIES, SALOMON, was born **SALOMON MOYSES** on 2 January 1805 to MOÏSE/MOSES RIES/RYSS/RIS, a native of Schopfloch, District of Ansbach, Bavaria, and his wife **ÉLÉONORE/ELLA/ELLEN SALOMON** (See entry), born in *Obernai*, Bas-Rhin. At the time of the 1808 census of Jews, during which all Jewish heads of household were obligated to take a surname, MOYSES SALOMON, then living in *Ingwiller*, Bas-Rhin, who took the name RIESS as a last name, identified his son, formerly SALOMON MOYSES, as having been born on 20 January 1805 in *Ingwiller*. There is, however, no record of a birth in *Ingwiller* for either a "Salomon Moyses" or a "Salomon Ries(s)." According to Salomon's 1840 Orleans Parish naturalization record, he asserted that he had been born in *Obernai*. Unfortunately there is no birth record for him in *Obernai* either. Salomon immigrated to New Orleans, Orleans Parish, LA, ahead of his parents ca. December 1832, for whose arrival we have no record. He married JULIE/JULIA/JUDITH MESSERITZ, a native of Amsterdam, Holland, ca. 1835 (an estimation based on the birth of a first child) in New Orleans. They were the parents of twelve children: Nancy (b. 1836), Morris (b. 1838), Henry (b. 1840) Therezia (b. 1842), Melanie (b. 1844), Jules (b. 1846), Mina (b. 1848), Pauline (b. 1849; died as a child), Bernard (b. 1852), Emma (b. 1855), Edward (b. 1857) and Ella (b. 1860). Solomon worked as a clerk and merchant in New Orleans. He died on 17 March 1875 in the city and was buried in Hebrew Rest Cemetery #1. Julie died on 15 October 1900 at Houston, Harris Co., TX, and was buried in Beth Israel Cemetery in Houston. (**A, AN, B1808, G, GB, TT**)

ROES, HEYMAN, was born **HEYMANN ROESS** on 9 February 1867 in *Herrlisheim*, Bas-Rhin, France, to **ISAAC/SIMON/JEAN ROESS**, a native of the town, and his wife, **NANETTE LEVY**, born in *Niederroedern*, Bas-Rhin. Heyman Roes wrote in a 1910 application for a U.S. passport that he had immigrated to New York City aboard the SS *La Bourgogne*, arriving on 3 December 1883. We believe, however, that the record for seventeen-year-old "Mr. H. Roess," a merchant from Alsace, who arrived on 28 May 1884 at New York, from Le Havre, France, aboard the SS *St. Laurent* is actually his arrival here in the United States. Heyman was naturalized in New York City on 24 October 1889 where he was working as a butcher and living at 318 East Houston Street. Heyman moved to Louisiana several years before he married FLORENCE MAAS on 4 September 1901 in Donaldsonville, Ascension Parish, LA. Florence's father, LEOPOLD MAAS was a well-known Donaldsonville merchant originally from Rheinpfalz, Germany. Heyman worked as a merchant at the Germania-Elise sugar plantation in Hohen Solms, Ascension Parish, LA, near Donaldsonville where his three children, Nanette (b. 1903), Leonard Heyman (b. 1904), and Bertha (b. 1905) were born. Heyman was appointed the postmaster at Hohen Solms in 1906. A year or so later, the family moved to Morgan City, St. Mary Parish, LA, where they were enumerated together in the 1910 federal census. Heyman was a merchant in a Morgan City dry goods store, owned by his father-in-law, Leopold Maas. Heyman's brother, **JOSEPH ROES** (See entry), had joined him there and was working as a salesman. The Roes-Maas business partnership was formalized in Baton Rouge, East Baton Rouge Parish, LA, in July 1914 when a charter was filed for Roes & Maas, wholesale and retail dealers in dry goods, clothing, shoes and general merchandise. Heyman was its president, with brothers-in-law, Albert Maas as vice-president, Charles Maas as secretary and Meyer Maas as treasurer. Heyman and Florence Roes and their children divided their time between Morgan City and Baton Rouge where the Leopold Maas family had relocated after Leopold's retirement from business. Heyman moved his family to New Orleans, Orleans Parish, LA, ca. 1930 where they were all enumerated in that year's census. Heyman Roes died in New Orleans on 18 February 1943 and was interred there at Hebrew Rest Cemetery #2. His wife, Florence, died on 1 February 1958 and was buried with him. Note: At the time of the 1808 name-taking census of Jews in 1808 in Alsace, only one family headed by JOSEPH HEYMAN, a resident of *Herrlisheim*, took the name ROESS as a family surname. Alternative spellings of REHS, ROESS and RESS were used throughout *Herrlisheim* civil records to designate this family. RESS was the spelling of choice in the *Herrlisheim* census taken in 1851. Heymann and Joseph used the spelling ROES in America. Their brother, EMILE ROES, a resident of New York City, was born EMIL REHS on 9 February 1872, although he used ROES in

New York, where he worked as a butcher. (**A, AN, B1808, B1851, G, GB**)

ROES, JOSEPH, was born **JOSEPH ROESS** on 15 February 1870 in *Herrlisheim*, Bas-Rhin, France, to **ISAAC/SIMON/JEAN ROESS**, a native of the town, and his wife, **NANETTE LEVY**, born in *Niederroedern*, Bas-Rhin. We believe that the twenty-year-old Joseph "Roesch," who arrived in New York on 2 December 1889 from Le Havre, France, aboard the SS *Champagne*, is likely his record of entry into the United States. He probably stayed for some time with his brother, Emile, a butcher, who had made New York City his home. Joseph relocated to Louisiana to work for another brother, **HEYMAN ROES** (See entry), at some time before the 1910 federal census where he was enumerated that year with Heyman in Morgan City, St. Mary Parish, LA, as a thirty-nine-year old unmarried salesman in a dry goods store. Forty-three-year-old Joseph Roes was married on 7 September 1913 at Baton Rouge, East Baton Rouge Parish, La, to his sister-in-law, CARRIE MAAS. The couple never had children. Joseph and Carrie remained in Morgan City until Heyman Roes retired and relocated to New Orleans, Orleans Parish, LA. Joseph and Carrie followed soon after. Both families were enumerated in the 1930 federal census living together at 2275 State Street. Joseph Roes died on 3 or 4 September 1933. His exact date of death will never be known. His wife left on Sunday 3 September 1933 on an outing with family members and did not return until the next day, at which time she found her husband in the bathroom with a gunshot wound to the mouth. The death was ruled a suicide and he was buried on 5 September 1933 at Hebrew Rest Cemetery #1 in New Orleans. Carrie Maas Roes died on 23 June 1944 at Vicksburg, Warren Co., MS. Her remains were returned to New Orleans where they were interred with those of her husband. (**A, AN, G, GB**)

ROOS, ADOLPHE, was born **MOYSE ROOS** on 17 December 1836 in *Wissembourg*, Bas-Rhin, France, to **NATHAN ROOS**, a native of the town, and his wife, ROSINE CAHEN, born in Landau Rheinpfalz, Germany. In a 1913 passport application, Adolphe stated that he had immigrated on or about 5 March 1854 to New Orleans, Orleans Parish, LA, aboard the ship *Humphrey Purrington*. In fact, seventeen-year-old Adolph Raas [*sic*], misidentified as Adolph "Bass" in the manifest transcription at *Ancestry.com*, arrived in New Orleans on 1 May 1854 aboard that ship. He and his brothers, **DAVID** and **HENRY ROOS**

(See entries) settled in Opelousas, St. Landry Parish, LA, where they were enumerated together in the 1860 federal census. David and Adolphe were working as merchants, with Henry employed as their clerk. Adolphe relocated to New Orleans, Orleans Parish, LA, after the Civil War. He took out a license to marry SUSAN BEER, a native of Ingenheim, Germany, in New Orleans on 16 October 1865. He was naturalized on 20 July 1868 in New Orleans, where he was a member of the firm A. Roos & Co., consisting of himself and his brother Henry, who had relocated his family to New Orleans as well. Adolphe and Susan never had children. The couple moved to San Francisco ca. 1876, where David made a fortune as a wine merchant. They returned to France to live in August 1904. Susan died on 5 September 1910 and was buried in Montparnasse Cemetery in Paris. Adolphe Roos died on 23 January 1919 in Montreux, Vaud, Switzerland. His remains were returned to Paris where they were buried with those of his wife. (**A, AN, G, GB, TT**)

ROOS, ARMAND WEILER, was born **ARON ARMAND ROOS** on 20 July 1888 in *Dauendorf*, Bas-Rhin France, to **MOSES/ RAPHAEL ROOS**, a native of *Ettendorf*, Bas-Rhin, and his wife **DELPHINE WEILLER**, born in *Dauendorf*, Bas-Rhin. Fifteen-year-old Armand Roos arrived in New York on 3 September 1903 aboard the Hamburg-Amerika Line SS *Blücher*. He went directly to Shreveport, Caddo, Parish, LA, to join his maternal uncles **DAVID** and **FELIX WEILLER** (See entries). Armand began working as a salesman in a dry goods store. In the 1910 federal census for Shreveport he was enumerated as a boarder in the house of Prussian native, Leopold Wolff, and his family. Armand was naturalized in Shreveport on 27 November 1911. After a trip back to France in the fall of 1912 to visit his parents, he returned to marry VALERIE KAHN, a native of Milliken's Bend, Madison Parish, LA, on 5 March 1913 in Vicksburg, Warren Co., MS. Valerie was the granddaughter of **MARCUS FEIST** (See entry), a native of *Trimbach*, Bas-Rhin, who lived in Milliken's Bend, LA, and later in Vicksburg, MS. Armand and Valerie were the parents of three children: Armand, Jr. (b. 1914), Henry Kahn (b. 1917), and Floyd David (b. 1925). Armand owned and operated Roos Bros., a general merchandise store, in Shreveport for over twenty years, in partnership with his brother **DAVID T. ROOS** (See entry). Armand died on 20 December 1931 and was buried in Hebrew Rest Cemetery #2 (Texas Ave.) in Shreveport. His wife, Valerie, and brother, David, remained in the mercantile business as

Roos & Roos until David died in 1960. Valerie died on 8 July 1982 and was interred with her husband and brother-in-law. (**A, AN, G, GB**)

ROOS, DAVID, was born on 13 February 1835 in *Wissembourg*, Bas-Rhin, France, to **NATHAN ROOS**, a native of the town, and his wife, ROSINE CAHEN, born in Landau Rheinpfalz, Germany. According to information given in the 1910 federal census, David indicated that he had immigrated to America in 1852. We believe, however, that he may have been the seventeen-year-old [*sic*] David Roos who arrived in New Orleans, Orleans Parish, La, on 30 March 1855 from Le Havre, France, aboard the ship *Ashland*. He and two of his brothers, **ADOLPHE** and **HENRY ROOS** (See entries) settled in Opelousas, St. Landry Parish,LA, where they were enumerated together in the 1860 federal census. David and Adolphe were working as merchants, with Henry employed as their clerk. David married ELISE/ALICE MARKS, a native of Germany, in New Orleans, Orleans Parish, LA, on 27 May 1861. They were the parents of seven children, all born in Opelousas: Rosalie (b. 1865), Isaac (b. 1866), Leonce (b. 1869), Nathan (b. 1871), Jonas (b. 1873), Jeannette (b. 1875), and Mary (b. 1877). David was a merchant in Opelousas for over fifty years. He advertised that he was a dealer in dry goods, notions, boots, shoes, hats, clothing, crockery, saddlery, hardware, groceries, tobacco and general plantation supplies. Two of his daughters, Jeannette and Mary, married sons of fellow Alsatian immigrant **SAMUEL CERF HAAS** (See entry). Elise Roos died on 3 November 1887 and was buried in Gemiluth Chassodim Jewish Cemetery in Opelousas. David Roos died on 13 October 1918 and was buried with his wife. (**A, AN, AP, G, GB**)

ROOS, DAVID THEODORE, was born on 13 August 1895 in *Dauendorf,* Bas-Rhin France, to **MOSES/ RAPHAEL ROOS**, a native of *Ettendorf,* Bas-Rhin, and his wife **DELPHINE WEILLER**, born in *Dauendorf*, Bas-Rhin. Sixteen-year-old David Roos arrived in New York on 2 July 1911 from Le Havre, France, aboard the SS *La Touraine*. He travelled to Shreveport, Caddo Parish, LA, to join his brother **ARMAND WEILLER ROOS** (See entry). He and Armand operated the Roos Bros. general merchandise store in Shreveport. David was naturalized on 19 April 1920. He went back to visit his parents who were living in *Haguenau*, Bas-Rhin, France, that same year. David, who never married, lived with Armand and his family, and after Armand died, with his brother's widow, Valerie Kahn, with whom he became a partner in Roos & Roos, a general merchandise store.

David died on 15 February 1960 in Shreveport and was buried there with his brother in Hebrew Rest Cemetery # 2 (Texas Ave.) Note: *Dauendorf* civil records have not been made available after 1892. We have therefore relied on David's declarations on his naturalization record and his application for a U.S. passport for his date and place of birth. (**A, AN, G**)

ROOS, HENRY, was born on 18 May 1842 in *Wissembourg*, Bas-Rhin, France, to **NATHAN ROOS**, a native of the town, and his wife, ROSINE CAHEN, born in Landau Rheinpfalz, Germany. He and two of his brothers, **ADOLPHE** and **DAVID ROOS** (See entries) immigrated to Louisiana and settled in Opelousas, St. Landry Parish where they were enumerated together in the 1860 federal census. We were unable to find a reliable record for Henry's entry into the United States. Henry, the youngest of the three, worked as a clerk in their brothers' general merchandise store. After the Civil War he relocated to New Orleans, Orleans Parish, LA, with his brother Adolphe. He was associated with A. Roos & Co., a wholesale clothing firm, at the corner of Customhouse and Exchange Place. Henry took out a license to marry BERTHA KLOTZ in New Orleans on 19 June 1869. Bertha was the Louisiana born daughter of **HENRI KLOTZ** of *Lauterbourg*, Bas-Rhin, France (See entry). The couple were the parents of six children: Rosa (b. 1870), Horace Nathan (b. 1872), Bella (b. 1873), Juliette (b. 1875), Rebecca (b. 1876), and Leona (b. 1881). Henry expanded his holdings, buying property in Crowley, Acadia Parish, LA, where he set up two of his sons-in-law, Rosa's husband JACOB MEYER and Bella's husband DANIEL BLUM in the grocery and dry goods business there. The firm in Crowley was known as H. Roos & Co. He also shared business interests with his brother David in St. Landry Parish, being the Vice-President of the St. Landry Mercantile Co. He died unexpectedly while on a business trip in Wilkes-Barre, Luzerne Co., PA, on 8 October 1897. His remains were returned to Louisiana for interment in Hebrew Rest Cemetery #1 in New Orleans. His wife, Bertha, died on 6 February 1920 in New Orleans and was buried with him. (**A, AN, G, GB, TT**)

ROOS, JACOB, was born **JACQUES ROOS** on 8 December 1842 in *Büswiller*, Bas-Rhin, France, to **MOÏSE ROOS**, born in *Ettendorf*, Bas-Rhin, France, and **MARIE LEVY**, a native of *Büswiller*, Bas-Rhin. He immigrated to Louisiana after his enumeration in the 1866 *Büswiller* town census. There are no records for him other than his untimely death on 2 August 1878 in Shreveport, Caddo Parish, LA. He was likely a victim of that year's deadly yellow fever epidemic, which took the lives of many immigrants who had no immunity to the disease. He was buried in Hebrew Rest Cemetery #1 (Jewish Section of Oakland Cemetery). His tombstone is cracked through the center, obscuring part of the name of his town of birth. It has been recorded, in error, as *Buschweiler*, the German spelling for *Bouxwiller*, while the stone was actually carved with the town name, "*Bueswiller*," an accepted alternative spelling for this much smaller village in Alsace. Fortunately Jacob's correct birth date was inscribed on his marker. (**A, AN, E, G**)

ROSENTHAL, CAROLINE, was born on 10 June 1845 to ISAÏAS ROSENTHAL, an immigrant to *Oberlauterbach*, Bas-Rhin, France, from Mlawa, Plock Province, Poland, and his second wife, **ROSALIE WALTHER** (b. 1809), a native of *Surbourg*, Bas-Rhin. Twenty-year-old Caroline Rosenthal immigrated to Louisiana after the Civil War, arriving in New York on 4 December 1866 from France, via London, England, aboard the ship *Cella*. She was accompanied by her twenty-four-year-old sister, **ESTHER ROSENTHAL** (See entry).Caroline lived with her brother, **JONAS ROSENTHAL** (See entry),a resident of Alexandria, Rapides Parish, LA, until she was married there on 16 March 1874 to SIMON WEINBERG/WINBARG, an immigrant from Kempen, Prussia, who was a widower with one daughter. The couple moved to Natchitoches, Natchitoches Parish, LA, where Simon was a merchant, They were the parents of six children: Rosina (b. 1875), Eugene (b. 1877), Louis (b. 1880), Harold (b. 1883), Albert (b. 1886) and Howard (b. 1891). Simon Weinberg died on 2 June 1910 in Natchitoches and was buried there in the Jewish Cemetery. Caroline died on 24 December 1930 in Natchitoches. We have not been able to find her place of burial. (**A, AN, F**)

ROSENTHAL, ESTHER, was born on 23 January 1842 to ISAÏAS ROSENTHAL, an immigrant to *Oberlauterbach*, Bas-Rhin, France, from Mlawa, Plock Province, Poland, and his second wife, **ROSALIE WALTHER** (b. 1809), a native of *Surbourg*, Bas-Rhin. Twenty-four-year-old Esther Rosenthal immigrated to Louisiana after the Civil War, arriving in New York on 4 December 1866 from France, via London, England, aboard the ship *Cella*. She was accompanied by her twenty-year-old sister, **CAROLINE ROSENTHAL** (See entry). Esther was enumerated in the 1870 federal census for Alexandria, Rapides Parish,

LA, living in the household with her siblings and half-siblings, **JONAS, MOSES**, and **MIRES ROSENTHAL** (See entries), and their families She married JACOB CASPER, a native of Prussia/Poland, on 12 January 1873 in New Orleans, Orleans Parish, LA. They had no children. Esther Rosenthal Casper died on 31 March 1875 in New Orleans. We were unable to find her place of burial, nor was there any obituary in the local newspapers. The death certificate for "Mrs. Esther Casper"revealed little else other than she was the daughter of Isaïas Rosenthal and that she died of what was termed as a "remittant abscess." Jacob Casper married, KATE COHEN on 6 January 1878 in New Orleans where he made a living as a peddler and dry goods merchant. The couple had no children. According to her New Orleans *Daily Picayune* obituary, Kate was the only Irish Jewess in New Orleans, having been born in Dublin, Ireland. Kate died on 30 March 1913 in New Orleans and was interred there in Dispersed of Judah Cemetery. Jacob Casper died on 1 September 1922 and was buried in the same cemetery. (**A, AN, G, GB, L**)

ROSENTHAL, ISAAC, was born **ISAC ROSENTHAL** on 10 July 1830 in *Oberlauterbach*, Bas-Rhin, France, to ISAÏAS ROSENTHAL, an immigrant to *Oberlauterbac*h from Mlawa, Plock Province, Poland, born on 8 January 1797, and his first wife, **SARA MEYER**, born on 10 January 1809 at *Oberlauterbach*, Bas-Rhin. Isaac followed his brothers, **MOSES** and **MIRES ROSENTHAL** (See entries), to Alexandria, Rapides Parish, LA, arriving in New Orleans, Orleans Parish, LA, from Le Havre, France, on 14 June 1850 aboard the ship *Pyramid*. By 1860 he was in business with William Gray, then with Marks Lisso, working as a merchant and sometimes drummer (peddler). A bachelor, he died on 1 November 1867, and was buried in the Jewish Cemetery in Pineville, Rapides Parish, LA. (**A, AN, F, FS**)

ROSENTHAL, JONAS, was born on 21 June 1843 in *Oberlauterbach*, Bas-Rhin, France, to ISAÏAS ROSENTHAL, an immigrant to *Oberlauterbach*, Bas-Rhin, France, from Mlawa, Plock Province, Poland, born there on 8 January 1797, and his second wife, **ROSALIE WALTHER** (b. 1809), a native of *Surbourg*, Bas-Rhin. Seventeen-year-old Jonas Rosenthal arrived in New Orleans, Orleans Parish, LA, on 25 June 1860 from Le Havre, France, aboard the ship *Lemuel Dyer*. He immediately left to join his half-brothers, **MOSES, MIRES** and **ISAAC ROSENTHAL** (See entries) in Alexandria, Rapides Parish, LA, arriving there aboard the steamer *Homer*. In April

1862 he joined Company K, Third Louisiana Cavalry, under Capt. **SAMUEL HAAS** (See entry), an Alsatian immigrant from *Rothbach*, Bas-Rhin. He served the entire war as a scout and guide for various Confederate divisions, including Colonel Gilling's Texas regiment. After the war he opened a general merchandise store. He married JEANETTE WEIL, a twenty-two-year-old immigrant from Ingenheim, Bavaria, on 20 September 1873 in Alexandria. They had eight children, all born in Alexandria: Eugene (b. 1874), Augusta (b. 1879), Rosa (b. 1880), Essie (b. 1883), Bella (b. 1885), Juliette (b. 1887), Bernard (b. 1889), and Beulah (b. 1892). In 1892 he joined Moses and Mires in the retail grocery business. He was President of the Rapides Parish School Board for many years. Jeannette died on 12 November 1907 in Alexandria and was buried in the Jewish Cemetery in Pineville, Rapides Parish, LA. Jonas died on 21 January 1930 in Alexandria, and was buried with her. **(A, AN, F, FS)**

ROSENTHAL, MIRES, was born **MEYER ROSENTHAL** on 30 December 1834 in *Oberlauterbach*, Bas-Rhin, France, to ISAÏAS ROSENTHAL, an immigrant to *Oberlauterbach* from Mlawa, Plock Province, Poland, born there on 8 January 1797, and his first wife, **SARA MEYER**, b. 10 January 1809, a native of *Oberlauterbach*, Bas-Rhin. Fifteen-year-old "Mayer Rouenthal," [*sic*] a native of France, whose destination was New Orleans, Orleans Parish, LA, arrived there on 25 June 1849, aboard the ship *J.H. Glidden*. In 1850 he was enumerated with two of his brothers, **MOSES** and **ISAAC ROSENTHAL** (See entries), who were living in Alexandria, Rapides Parish, LA. His business partnership with his brothers was interrupted by his service in the Confederate Army as a private in Company B, 2nd LA. Infantry (Moore Guards), an outfit from Rapides Parish which he joined in April 1861. He was wounded in July 1862 at the Battle of Malvern Hill which took place in Henrico Co., VA. He was treated there, and sent home, but the lead bullet was never extracted from his shoulder. Mires was paroled in May 1865 at Alexandria. He married CAROLINE AARON on 13 November 1866. Caroline was a native of Alexandria, born to a Prussian Jewish immigrant, MICHAEL AARON (d. 1853 of yellow fever), and his French Catholic wife, Justine Dupuy/Dupuis (b. 1828, Avoyelles, Parish, LA). Mires and Caroline had twelve children: Abraham (b. 1867), Sallie (b. 1868), Hannah (b. 1870), Bella (b. 1872), Isaiah (b. 1876), Mamie (b. 1877), Rosalie (b. 1879), Julius (b. 1881), Laurant Isaac (b. 1883), Esther (b. 1884), Aaron Mires (b. 1886) and Eva (b. 1891). He was partners with his brother, Moses, in a cotton brokerage firm. He also worked as a dry goods merchant, and later in life managed a grocery store for his stepfather-in-law, Julius Levin. He died on 22 May 1897 in Alexandria and was buried in the Jewish Cemetery at Pineville, Rapides Parish, LA. Family members suspected that lead poisoning, from the bullet he received at Malvern Hill in 1862 contributed to a lifetime of ill health and ultimately to his death. His wife, Caroline, died on 20 December 1903 and was buried with him. (**A, AN, F, FS**)

ROSENTHAL, MOSES, was born **MOÏSE ROSENTHAL** on 27 August 1828 in *Oberlauterbach,* Bas-Rhin, France, to ISAÏAS ROSENTHAL, an immigrant to *Oberlauterbac*h from Mlawa, Plock Province, Poland, born there on 8 January 1797, and his first wife, **SARA MEYER**, born on 10 January 1809 in *Oberlauterbach,* Bas-Rhin.. Eighteen-year-old Moïse Rosenthal immigrated to New Orleans, Orleans Parish, LA, arriving on 24 December 1846 aboard the ship *J.N. Cooper*. He moved to Alexandria, Rapides Parish, LA, then to Cotile Landing, Rapides Parish, before serving in the Confederate Army as a First Sergeant in Capt. Todd's Independent Co. (Prairie Rangers), then as Sergeant in Co. K. 3rd La. Cavalry. He was paroled at Merdian MS. in 1865 and returned to New Orleans where he married REGINA BLOOM on 28 October 1865. Regina was a twenty-two-year-old immigrant from Ingenheim, Bavaria. They returned to live in Alexandria, LA where he became a cotton broker as well as the leading grocer in the city. The couple had nine children all born in Alexandria: Sarah (b. 1866), Gertrude (b. 1868), Pauline (b. 1869), Benjamin (b. 1872), Isaac (b. 1875), Bertha (b. 1876), Esther (b. 1880), Emile (b. 1881), and Gilbert (b. 1884). Moses served as the treasurer for Rapides Parish. He was also elected to the Alexandria City Council, and was the president of Congregation Gemiluth Chassodim for two years. Moses Rosenthal died on 7 September 1898, and was buried in the Jewish Cemetery in Pineville (Rapides Parish), LA. His wife, Regina, died on 14 February 1927 and was buried with him. (**A, AN, F, FS**)

SALOMON, CHARLES GOUDCHAUX, was born **GUTSCHU SALOMON** on 4 March 1821 in *Scherwiller,* Bas-Rhin, France, to **MEYER SALOMON,** a native of the town, and his wife ROSETTE BLOCH. Although the family was enumerated in the 1819 *Scherwiller* town census, no record of the couple's marriage could be found there. We believe that Meyer Salomon died on 10 April 1821, just over a month after his son was born. Although his wife was not mentioned in his death record, a fact which is usually, but not always, included, he died in house #352, the same house where his two children, Nathan (b. 1819), and Gutschu were recorded to have been born. Meyer's widow Rosette Bloch may have taken the two children back to live with her parents, and subsequently remarried, as there is no more information about her or the children in *Scherwiller*. Charles/Gutschu Salomon immigrated to New Orleans, Orleans Parish, LA, a reliable record for which we were unable to find. He took out a license to marry ESTHER CLELY CAZÉRES, a native of Bordeaux, France, on 31 March 1853. Charles died on 23 August 1853 during the worst yellow fever epidemic that Louisiana had even seen. He was buried in Dispersed of Judah Cemetery in New Orleans. His only child, CHARLES GOUDCHAUX SALOMON, Jr., was born on 11 January 1854 and died on 29 July 1864. The child was buried in Dispersed of Judah Cemetery with his father. Charles's widow, Esther Cazéres, married ULYSSE HAÏM LOPEZ-SILVA ca. 1855, a record of which were were unable to find. Ulysse was a native of Bayonne, France, and owned a cigar store in the city. They were the parents of six children: Sarah Zélia (b. 1858), Edouard (b. 1859), Aron Alphonse (b. 1864), Lilie Mariam (b. 1866), Leah (b. 1868), and Aline Rachel (b. 1874). Esther died on 1 May 1877 in New Orleans and was buried in Dispersed of Judah Cemetery. Ulysse Haïm Lopez-Silva died on 12 February 1898 and was buried there as well. (Note: See pp12-13) (**A, AN, E, G, GB**)

SALOMON, ÉLÉONORE/ELLA/ELLEN, was born between 1777-. 1780 to **NAFTALY/CERF/HERTZ SALOMON**, a native of *Obernai* (*Obereinheim*), Bas-Rhin, France, and his wife TERTZE/TERTIA /THÉRÈSE WEYL, the daughter of ALEXANDRE (SENDER) JACOB WEYL and his wife, BELLE BLIEN, who lived in Metz, Moselle, France. The few records we have indicate that Ella was probably born in *Obernai* where she, her parents, and three brothers, were enumerated in the 1784 census of Jews in the Bas-Rhin. Ella married MOÏSE/MOSES RIES/RYSS/RIS, a native of Schopfloch, district of Ansbach, Bavaria ca. 1804. We have no record of their marriage, which may have taken place in Bavaria. Their first child, Salomon/Solomon (See entry), was born ca. 1805 in *Obernai* according to his naturalization record filed in New Orleans in 1840. His father, however, asserted at the time of the 1808 census of Jews in *Ingwiller*, Bas-Rhin, that Salomon had been born in *Ingwiller*. The couple's next two children, Nanette (b. 1807; See entry) and Henry (b. 1808; died

1816 in *Obernai*), were born in *Ingwiller*, Bas-Rhin, where Moïse was the cantor in the local synagogue. Moïse and Ella's last four children were born in *Obernai*: Sibille/Pauline (b. 1812; See entry), Michelette/Minette (b. 1814 ; See entry), Jeannette (b. 1818; See entry) and Benjamin (b. 1820; See entry). The couple, accompanied by five of their six surviving children arrived in New Orleans, Orleans Parish, LA, on 15 January 1835 from Le Havre, France, aboard the brig *Dido*. Their son, **SALOMON RIES** (See entry), had immigrated three years previously. Moïse Ries did not live out the year, dying in New Orleans on 6 September 1835. He was buried in Gates of Mercy (Shanarai Chasset) Cemetery at Jackson & Saratoga Streets which was razed in 1957. Ella Ries followed two of her married children, Salomon and Nanette, to Lafayette, Jefferson Parish, LA (now part of uptown New Orleans), where she died on 19 November 1855. She was buried with Moses and her young son Benjamin in Gates of Mercy Cemetery in New Orleans. (**A, AN, B1784, B1808, F, TT**)

SALOMON, MARIE/BABETTE, (*Obernai*) See entry for **GOTTLIEB/GEORGE DREYFUS**

SALOMON, PAULINE, was born **BABET SALOMON** on 27 September 1827 in *Obernai*, Bas-Rhin, France, to **MOÏSE SALOMON**, a native of the town, and his wife **MARIE ANNE/ MARIANNE LEVY**, born in *Epfig*, Bas-Rhin. She was enumerated as "Pauline Salomon, age twenty-two" at *Obernai* in the 1851 town census as the head of household working as a second-hand dealer, living with her two younger siblings, seventeen-year-old Jacques, also a second-hand dealer, and eleven-year-old Thérèse. Pauline's father had died in 1840, and her mother had followed in 1848. Pauline and Thérèse immigrated to New Orleans, Orleans Parish, LA, arriving on 30 June 1852, from Le Havre, France, aboard the ship *Venice*. Pauline's aunt, **ELEANOR SALOMON** (See entry), the widow of MOSES RIES, who lived in Lafayette, Jefferson Parish, LA (now uptown New Orleans), would have certainly been there to greet the girls. Efforts to trace Thérèse have been unsuccessful. DANIEL LEVY, a native of Bourscheid, Moselle, France, took out a license to marry Pauline Salomon on 13 March 1854 in New Orleans. Daniel and Pauline settled in Plaquemine, Iberville Parish, LA, where they were the parents of eight children: Henrietta (b. 1855), Meline (b. 1857), Moïse Lionel (b. 1859) John (b. 1860; died before 1870), Henry Julian (b. 1864), Leontin (b. 1867), Rebecca (b. 1869), and Simon (b. 1873). Daniel was initially a grocer, and later a dry goods merchant at Plaquemine. Pauline Salomon Levy died on 22 June 1890 in Plaquemine and was interred there the next day at the Jewish Cemetery. Daniel Levy died on 12 April 1897 at the home of his daughter, Rebecca Levy Bluestein. He was interred with his wife at the Plaquemine Jewish Cemetery (**A, AN, B1851, G, GB, TT**)

SCHRAM, ADÈLE, was born **ADÈLE SCHRAMM** on 8 November 1853 in *Schweighouse-sur-Moder*, Bas-Rhin, France, to **FÉLIX/ FAVRE SCHRAMM**, a native of the town, and his wife, **THÉRÈSE BERG**, born in *Mertzwiller*, Bas-Rhin. She followed an uncle, **MARC MEYER SCHRAM** (See entry), who had immigrated to Louisiana, twenty years previously, and who had settled for a time in Donaldsonville, Ascension Parish, LA. Nineteen-year-old Adèle arrived in New York from Le Havre, France, on 11 September 1873, accompanied by her fifteen-year-old brother, **MARTIN SCHRAM** (See entry), on the SS *Europe*. Although her uncle, **MARC MEYER SCHRAM** (See entry) had moved to Texas, Adele settled in Donaldsonville. She died there five years later at the age of twenty-four, on 2 October 1878. She was interred in Bikur Sholim Cemetery in Donaldsonville. Although her cause of death was not recorded, she died during a widespread yellow fever epidemic, which took the lives of many immigrants who had no immunity to the disease. (**A, AN**)

SCHRAM, MARC MEYER, was born on 28 November 1830 in *Schweighouse-sur-Moder*, Bas-Rhin, France, to BARUCH SCHRAM, a native of Erlenbach, Baden-Württemberg, Germany, and his wife, **RÉGINE/FRÉDÉRIQUE MEYER**, born in *Schweighouse*, Bas-Rhin. Meyer, or Morris, as he was often called in America, arrived in Louisiana ca. 1852, a date he gave on his 4 November 1857 declaration of intention to become a citizen in Ascension Parish, LA. We have not been able to find a reliable ship's record for his arrival in America. He settled in Donaldsonville, Ascension Parish, LA, where he married LETTIE MAYER/MEYER on 22 October 1855. Lettie, also known as Julia or Henrietta, was a native of Germany. The couple were the parents of four children, born in Donaldsonville, where Meyer was a dry goods and grocery merchant: Felix (b. 1856), Flora (b. 1858), Estelle (b. 1862), and David (b. 1865). After the end of the Civil War, Meyer moved his family to Galveston, Galveston Co., TX, to escape the rigors of Reconstruction and the economic depression which followed in Louisiana. Four more children were born to the couple in

Galveston: Cecile (b. 1867), Bella (b. 1869), Tenny (b. 1872), and Benny/ Benjamin (b. 1877). Meyer opened up a retail crockery store, and later a retail dry goods and gent's furnishings business, which put him in continual financial trouble, ending in bankruptcy, only months before a powerful hurricane struck Galveston Island on 8 September 1900, resulting in between 6,000 and 8,000 deaths. All eight members of the family survived the ordeal unscathed, although Meyer was forced to declare bankruptcy, once again, two years later. Henrietta Schram died on 25 October 1905 in Galveston, three days after celebrating her fiftieth wedding anniversary. Meyer followed on 14 April 1924, also in Galveston. We were unable to ascertain where they were buried. (**A, AN, GB, TT**)

SCHRAM. MARTIN, was born on 14 December 1857 in *Mertzwiller*, Bas-Rhin, France, to **FÉLIX/FAVRE SCHRAMM**, a native of *Schweighouse-sur-Moder*, Bas-Rhin, France, and his wife, **THÉRÈSE BERG**, born in *Mertzwiller*, Bas-Rhin. The family had moved from *Schweighouse-sur-Moder* to *Mertzwiller,* where Martin's birth was recorded. They did not appear, however, in the 1861 censuses for either *Mertzwiller* or *Schweighouse*. Fifteen-year-old Martin arrived in New York from Le Havre, France, on 11 September 1873, accompanied by his nineteen-year-old sister, **ADÈLE SCHRAM** (See entry), on the SS *Europe*. We assume that he came with her to Louisiana. But other than this ship's record we can find no trace of him in the United States. (**A, AN, E, GB**)

SIESS, DAVID, was born **DAVID SÜSS** on 31 May 1835 in Mühlheim, Rheinpfalz, Germany, to MICHAEL SÜSS, a native of Albsheim, Rheinpfalz, Germany, and his wife, **MINDEL/MINETTE LOB/THALSHEIMER**, born at Heiligenmoschel, commune of Niederkirschen, Canton Otterberg, Dept. Mont Tonnerre, France (Germany after 1814). David was raised by his step-father, **SALOMON LEHMANN** (See entry), and mother, Minette, in *Lembach*, Bas-Rhin, France. He immigrated to Louisiana from Le Havre, France, as "David Suss" on the ship *Suffolk,* which arrived in New Orleans, Orleans Parish, LA, on 29 December 1854. He joined his brothers, **SIMON** and **LEOPOLD SIESS** (See entries) at Mansura, Avoyelles Parish, LA, where they had opened a mercantile business under the name of S. Siess & Bros. Ultimately conscripted for service in the Civil War, David served only briefly, taking up the defense of Fort DeRussy in March 1863. He remained in Mansura, trying to keep his business together, until the death of his half-brother, **ISAAC LEHMANN** (See entry) in April 1864, at which time he fled to Alexandria, Rapides Parish, LA, for his own safety. Scarcely a month later, he joined Union forces and became a guide for General Nathaniel Banks whose armies were retreating from two disastrous battles at Mansfield and Pleasant Hill. He escorted the Union troops through Rapides and Avoyelles Parishes to Simmesport, Avoyelles Parish, LA, where, after crossing the Atchafalaya River, the whole company marched to New Orleans. David remained with his brother, Simon, who had left the parish in the summer of 1863, for almost a year. David returned to Avoyelles Parish at the conclusion of the Civil War to rebuild his life. He married CLARA COCHRANE, a native of Cottonport, Avoyelles Parish, LA, on 13 January 1868. They were the parents of five children: Mathilde (b. 1868), Eugénie (b. 1872), Caroline (b. 1877), Alice (b. 1878; died 1887), and Harry James (b. 1882). David and Simon were partners in the general store, and owned a cotton gin and sawmill, as well as a small farm where they planted cotton and other crops. A squabble between the brothers erupted in 1876, followed by a bitter court battle for ownership of the store, mills and farm. Simon moved his family to nearby Marksville, Avoyelles Parish, LA. David stayed in Mansura. He tended to his store and farmed well into the twentieth century. He was the Mayor of Mansura in 1870, 1886, 1888-92, 1895, and 1905. David was also for many years the postmaster at Mansura. David died on 7 April 1925 at his home. He was buried in the Jewish Cemetery in Pineville, Rapides Parish, LA. His wife, Clara, died on 5 July 1928. She had both Catholic and Jewish services and was buried in the Jewish Cemetery alongside her husband. (**A, AN, AP, G, GB**)

SIESS, LEOPOLD, was born **LEOPOLD SÜSS** on 5 January 1833 in Mühlheim, Rheinpfalz, Germany, to MICHAEL SÜSS, a native of Albsheim, Rheinpfalz, Germany, and his wife, **MINDEL/MINETTE LOB/THALSHEIMER**, born at Heiligenmoschel, commune of Niederkirschen, Canton Otterberg, Dept. Mont Tonnerre, France (Germany after 1814). Leopold was raised by his step-father, **SALOMON LEHMANN** (See entry), and mother, Minette, in *Lembach*, Bas-Rhin, France. According to his naturalization record, he arrived in New Orleans, Orleans Parish, LA, on 1 May 1854, an assertion which cannot be verified by any available ship's records. He joined his brother, **SIMON SIESS** (See entry for **FANNY CERF**), in Mansura, Avoyelles Parish, where they sold their wares in anticipation of buying a place on which to set up a general store. Several years after their younger brother, **DAVID SIESS** (See entry), arrived in 1854, the three brothers were able to buy land from Edmond Chatelain to fulfill that dream. Leopold had, however, decided to marry outside the faith. Edmond Chatelain's sister Josette, widowed at the age of sixteen, consented to the union so long as Leopold would convert to Catholicism. His decision to follow through with the marriage resulted in the dissolution of the Simon Siess & Bros. partnership in July 1857. Leopold converted to Catholicism the following month, registered his earmark and brand as a cattle owner, and became an American citizen before he and Josette were married in a Catholic ceremony on 5 November 1857. He started a small farm on land owned by his wife's family. To make ends meet, he also worked as a butcher in partnership with another of Josette's brothers, Ludger Chatelain. Leopold and Josette were the parents of six children: Auger (b. 1859), Florestine (b. 1860), Hermina (b. 1863), Emanuel (b. 1866), Isaac Edouard (b. 1871), and Louis Preston (b. 1875). He was conscripted as a private in Co. I, 18th Louisiana Infantry for service to the Confederacy in the Civil War. His last assignment was as a provost guard in Vermilionville (now Lafayette), Lafayette Parish, LA, in August 1863, after which he deserted the cause and joined the "Home Guard" as a lieutenant under Capt. F. W. Masters. These men called "jayhawkers" were part of an underground movement which supported a Union victory. In April 1864, after a skirmish with Confederates resulted in his capture and escape, as well as the death of his half-brother, **ISAAC LEHMANN** (See entry), he and his men continued to live under cover, doing what they could to harass Confederate troops until the end of hostilities. Leopold returned to his farm after the war. To make ends meet, he hired himself out to work for his brother David at the cotton gin and sawmill. He also sought occasional employment with **LEOPOLD GOUDCHAUX** (See entry) at Big Cane, St. Landry Parish. In 1882, after his eldest son, Auger, married a Jewish girl from Alexandria, Rapides Parish, LA, and settled there, Leopold left his family in Avoyelles Parish and went to live and work in Alexandria. In late January 1885 he became seriously ill while on a trip to Orange, Orange Co., TX. His son, Auger, went immediately by train to bring his father back. Leopold died on 4 February 1885 in Alexandria and was buried that same afternoon in the Jewish Cemetery in Pineville, Rapides Parish, LA. Josette Siess died in Mansura, Avoyelles Parish, LA, on 13 June 1914, and was buried there in St. Paul's Catholic Cemetery. (**A, AN, AP, CA, G**,)

SIESS, SIMON, (Mühlheim, Rheinpfalz, Germany/ *Lembach,* Bas-Rhin, France). See entry for **FANNY CERF**.

SOLOMON, NATHAN/ SOL, was born **ADAM SALOMON** on 27 June 1844 in *Bischheim*, Bas-Rhin, France, to **SELIGMANN SALOMON**, a native of *Scherwiller*, Bas-Rhin, France, and his first wife **HINDEL/HENRIETTE LEVY**, born in *Surbourg*, Bas-Rhin. Seligmann was widowed in 1846. He remarried soon after, fathering three more children, before he died in December 1851. His children with Hindel, Adam and Rachel, who appeared in the 1851 *Bischheim* census as Nathan and Rachel, disappeared from the 1856 census, where his second wife, **BABETTE KAHN**, a native of *Kolbsheim*, Bas-Rhin, was living with seven-year-old Samuel Salomon. According to the 1910 federal census, Nathan indicated that he had arrived in America in 1866, a date which cannot be verified by any existing ship's record. Adam/Nathan was enumerated for the first time in the 1870 census for New Iberia, Iberia Parish, LA. He was working there as a store clerk. Nathan married ADELE GOUGENHEIM in St. Mary Parish on 17 September 1872. We believe that Adele was born ca. June 1847 in Vaudreching, a few miles from Boulay, Moselle, France, to **JYCHAE LOUIS GUGENHEIM**, a native of *Zellwiller*, Bas-Rhin, France (See entry), and his wife, SARA WORMS, born in Boulay, Moselle, France. Eight-year-old Adele immigrated with her mother and three sisters to Louisiana, via New York, arriving on 18 October 1855 aboard the ship *Switzerland*. She was raised in Morgan City, St. Mary Parish, LA where her parents had settled. Nathan, usually called "Sol" in Louisiana, and Adèle were the parents of three children: Samuel (b. 1873;died bef. 1900), Sylvan (b. 1876), and Benjamin Charles (b. 1880). Nathan Solomon worked as a bar keep in Morgan City, then switched to the profession of liquor merchant, after moving to Lake Charles, Calcasieu Parish, LA, before 1900. Another move before 1910 brought Nathan, Adèle and their two surviving children, Sylvan and Benjamin, to New Orleans, Orleans Parish, LA, where Nathan worked as a traveling liquor dealer. Adele died in New Orleans on 9 July 1919 and was buried there in Gates of Prayer Cemetery #2 (Joseph Street). Nathan Solomon died on 8 December 1927 in New Orleans and was buried with his wife. Note: Although the name "Solomon" is usually spelled with an initial "o" in English, the French name is spelled with an initial "a." (**A, AN, B1851, E, G, GB**)

SOMMER, LEOPOLD, **"LEP,"** was born on 20 November 1874 in *Schirrhoffen*, Bas-Rhin, France, to **ADOLPH SOMMER** and his wife, **VALERIE BRAUN**, both natives of the town. We believe that he emigrated as seventeen-year-old "S. Sommer" from Antwerp, Belgium, arriving in New York on 20 August 1891 aboard the SS *Westernland*. He may have spent some time with his brother, **SYLVAN SOMMER** (See entry), who immigrated the following year, in Hawkinsville, Pulaski Co., GA, where they both worked as clerks in a dry goods store. Leopold Sommer appeared in the 1900 Federal Census using the name "Sylvain Sommer," as a boarder in the home of **ABRAHAM KLOTZ** (See entry), a native of *Uhrwiller*, Bas-Rhin, France, who had large commercial holdings and farming interests in Klotzville, Assumption Parish, LA. Lep, as he was familiarly known, was one of five clerks employed at the Klotz enterprise. At the time of his enumeration in 1900 in Klotzville, Lep gave his date of immigration as 1891 and his name as "Sylvain." His brother, born "Sylvain," had been enumerated a day earlier on 12 June 1900 as "Sylvain Sommer," at Kahns, West Baton Rouge Parish, LA. Several years later Lep Sommer began working in Hohen Solms, Ascension Parish, LA, where he was employed at the time of his marriage. He wed HENRIETTE "HATTIE" MOYSE, a native of Donaldsonville, Ascension Parish, LA, on 18 June 1902 at St. Gabriel, Ascension Parish, LA. They moved to Torras, Pointe Coupée Parish, LA, ca. 1903 where he opened The Leader Store, a general merchandise operation. Lep and Hattie were the parents of two daughters born at Torras: Lydie (b. 1903) and Rachel "Ray" (b. 1906). Lep was joined at Torras by his brother and sister-in-law, **SYLVAN** and **MARGUERITE KAHN SOMMER** (See entry for Sylvan Sommer), in 1905. The brothers carried dry goods, shoes, groceries, farm implements and other sundries in their store. They extended credit to the local farmers, accepting payment in cotton or cash. Sylvan moved his family to Kahns, West Baton Rouge Parish in 1911. After the town of Torras was washed away in the 1912 flood, Lep, the leading merchant in the town, stayed on for a year, but finally moved his family to Baton Rouge, East Baton Rouge Parish, where he opened Lep Sommer Mens Clothing on Main Street which eventually expanded into the two-story Sommer's Department Store. He started specializing in women's apparel in the 1920s after moving his operation to North Street where he opened The Fashion Store. His two daughters, who were LSU graduates, never married. Lep died on 11 December 1932 at his home in Baton Rouge, and was buried there in the Jewish Cemetery. Hattie Moyse Sommer died on 6 November 1973 and was interred beside him. (**A, AN, BC, G, GB**)

SOMMER, MARX, was born on 14 May 1876 in *Herrlisheim*, Bas-Rhin, France, to **ARON SOMMER**, a native of the town, and his wife, **SARA LEVY**, born in *Goersdorf*, Bas-Rhin. Sixteen-year-old "M. Sommer, a German national, whose destination was New Orleans, Orleans Parish, LA, landed in New York on 8 September 1892 from Le Havre, France. He settled in Rayne, Acadia Parish, LA, and was naturalized at Crowley, Acadia Parish, LA, on 27 June 1899. Marx went to work for David Levy's Acadia Cash Emporium, one of the most popular stores in town. Twenty-eight-year-old Marx Sommer, who had worked there for almost ten years died suddenly on 8 May 1904 from a hemorrhage due to a stomach ulcer. His body was shipped by train to Berwick, St. Mary Parish, LA, where it was interred there in the Hebrew Cemetery. (**A, AN, GB**)

SOMMER, SYLVAN, was born **SYLVAIN SOMMER** on 9 September 1876 at *Schirrhoffen*, Bas-Rhin, France, to **ADOLPH SOMMER** and his wife, **VALERIE BRAUN**, both natives of the town. Sixteen-year-old Sylvain Sommer arrived in New York aboard the SS *La Champagne* from Le Havre, France, on 21 November 1892. Sylvan spent the first six years in Mississippi, then moved in 1898 to Kahns, West Baton Rouge Parish, LA, to work for the Kahn Brothers, who were *Schirrhoffen* natives as well. Shortly thereafter he moved on to Port Allen, West Baton Rouge Parish, LA, to work for Welsh & Levy (See entry for **JACQUES WELSCH**). In 1905 Sylvan returned to France where he married **MARGUERITE KAHN**. Marguerite was born **MARIE KAHN** on 16 December 1886 in *Schirrhoffen*, Bas-Rhin, France to **HEYMANN KAHN,** a native of the town, and his second wife, **RACHEL DREYFUSS**. Marguerite was the half-sister of **GUS, CHARLES** and **SOL KAHN** (See entries), and the sister **of REINE KAHN** (See entry). Sylvan, his mother, **VALERIE BRAUN SOMMER** (See entry), and his nineteen-year-old bride, Marguerite, arrived back in New York on 22 November 1905 aboard the SS *Kaiser Wilhelm der Grosse*. They settled at Torras, Pointe Coupée Parish, LA, where their only child, Adolph, was born in 1906. Sylvan joined his older brother, **LEOPOLD "LEP" SOMMER** (See entry) who had opened up a dry goods store there in 1903. A year before the great Mississippi River flood of 1912 wiped out the town of Torras, Sylvan moved his family back to Kahns, West Baton Rouge Parish, LA, to work with his wife's brothers. In 1911 he was appointed postmaster at Kahns. They remained there until 1927, when they moved to Rayne, Acadia Parish, LA, to live and work with other Kahn family members. Sylvan died on 6 March 1962 and was buried in the Jewish Cemetery in Baton Rouge, East Baton Rouge Parish, LA. Marguerite died on 23 July 1976 at Rayne, Acadia Parish, LA, and was buried with her husband. (**A, AN, BC, G, GB**)

STEIN, JACOB, was born **JACQUES STEIN** on 17 November 1846 in *Oberlauterbach*, Bas-Rhin, France, to **ISAAC STEIN**, a native of *Salmbach*, Bas-Rhin, France and his wife, **ANNE/NANETTE/ JEANNETTE BLOCH**, born in *Trimbach*, Bas-Rhin. In his 1900 request for a United States passport, Jacob Stein wrote that he had immigrated to America from Le Havre, France, aboard the ship *William Penn* in June 1866. Although he had been enumerated as "Jacques" Stein in 1866 in the *Oberlauterbach* town census, where he lived with his parents and siblings, he and his sister, Henriette, known in America as Lena, were listed on the *William Penn*'s manifest as nineteen-year-old Jacob Stein and twenty-one-year-old Henriette Stein, natives of France. The brother and sister arrived in New York on 28 June 1866. Jacob, as he was always called in Louisiana, settled in Carroll Parish, LA, He was naturalized at Lake Providence, at the Carroll Parish Courthouse during the November term of 1872. (Note: Carroll Parish was divided into East and West Carroll Parishes in 1877). At the bottom of his affirmation of naturalization recorded in 1873, his name and place of birth, "*Oberlauterbach*, Canton Seltz," were written at the bottom in his own hand. Twenty-three year old Jacob Stein, an immigrant from France, appeared as J. Stein, in the 1870 federal census for Bell Place, Ward 1, Carroll Parish, LA. He was operating a general merchandise store with the help of Ewell [sic] Mayer, his partner, a twenty-seven year old immigrant from Germany, whom we ascertained was EMANUEL MEYER, the future husband of Jacob's sister Henriette (See entry for **LENA STEIN**), but known as "Lena" Stein in the United States. The partners were subsequently enumerated in the 1880 census for East Carroll Parish, Louisiana, living at Alsatia Plantation which consisted of the J. Stein plantation store and houses to shelter the mostly African-American tenant farmers working the land. The store was located behind a twenty foot levee (earthen dam) on the Louisiana side of the Mississippi opposite Vicksburg, Warren Co., MS. Thirty-eight-year-old Emanuel Meyer was enumerated as head of the household, living with his thirty-four-year-old wife, Lena, their four children, and his two brothers-in-law, thirty-three-year-old Jacob Stein and twenty-five-year-old Melville [*sic*] Stein (See entry for **MICHEL STEIN**), the latter two both immigrants from France. Emanuel Meyer and his family divided their time between the plantation and his business in St. Louis, MO, leaving his partner, Jacob Stein, still unmarried, to tend the store and run the farm. East and West Carroll Parishes, during the period of Reconstruction after the civil war, were rife with violence, murders, and occasional anti-Semitic attacks, reason enough for a married man with a family to leave his unmarried business partner to manage the store and plantation. Jacob Stein was appointed to the Police Jury (Parish Council) for East Carroll Parish in 1886. He was also a member of the Fifth District Levee Board which saw to the building and maintenance of levees along the Mississippi River that protected the farmland and villages sheltered behind them. On 25 April 1896 Jacob Stein cheated death when his plantation manager, Fritz Bowie, was shot and killed in front of Jacob in the Stein store by an irate African-American man in a dispute over wages. In 1901 Jacob was appointed postmaster at Alsatia. The Jacob Stein store and Alsatia Plantation are still known for one particular event, the arrival of President Theodore Roosevelt who hunted for black bear in the canebrakes of northern Louisiana in October 1907. Roosevelt and his party arrived by train at the Alsatia station of the Iron Mountain Railway and stopped at the J. Stein & Co. general store. A photo of the store whose gallery (porch) was crowded with people appeared in the 4 October 1907 edition of the New Orleans *Daily Picayune*. After two weeks in Louisiana, Roosevelt shot his bear. Not soon after that event, Jacob Stein fell ill. In the spring of 1909 Jacob was taken across the river to Vicksburg, Warren Co., MS for medical treatment. When he showed no signs of recovery he was transported by train to St. Louis, MO, where he died on 28 June 1909. A brief newspaper account of his death reported that he was a wealthy store and plantation owner at Alsatia, Louisiana, whose only family was his sister, Mrs. Meyer, of St. Louis. Jacob was interred at New Mount Sinai Cemetery and Mausoleum in Affton, St. Louis Co., Mo. (Note: The New Mount Sinai on-line death register has Jacob Stein listed in error as "Jacob Stern." (See: http://www.newmtsinaicemetery.org/death_registers.asp) (**A, AN, E, F, GB, TT**) See also pp 21,22 of this book.

STEIN, LENA, was born **MINA STEIN** on 24 June 1845 in *Oberlauterbach*, Bass-Rhin France, to **ISAAC STEIN**, a native of *Salmbach*, Bas-Rhin, and his wife, **ANNE/NANETTE/JEANNETTE**

BLOCH, born in *Trimbach*, Bas-Rhin. Mina was enumerated with her family in both the 1856 and 1866 censuses for the village of *Oberlauterbach* as "Henriette" Stein. Henriette, known in America as "Lena," was listed with her brother, **JACOB STEIN** (See entry) as twenty-one-year-old Henriette Stein, a native of France, on the manifest for the ship *William Penn*, which arrived in New York on 28 June 1866. She married Jacob's business partner, EMANUEL MEYER/ MAYER, an immigrant from Bavaria on 6 October 1871 in St. Louis, MO. Emanuel took Lena back to Alsatia, East Carroll Parish, LA, where they were enumerated on 5 June 1880 in that year's federal census. They were the parents of nine children. Fanny (b. 1872), Sidney (b. 1874), Celeste "Lessie" (b. 1875) and Julius (b. 1877) were born at Alsatia. The family, however, also maintained a residence in St. Louis, where they were enumerated, yet again, on 14 June 1880. In the St. Louis Census, unlike the Alsatia census, their fifth child, Sigmund, a two year old boy born in Bavaria, appeared with the family. Leo (b. 1881), twins Aron and Carrye (b. 1883), and Evelyn (b. 1886) were born in St. Louis where Emanuel ran E. Mayer & Co. selling hats wholesale and retail. Emanuel Meyer died on 15 October 1885, without ever seeing his last born child. He was interred at New Mount Sinai Cemetery & Mausoleum in Affton, St. Louis Co., Mo. "Lena H. Mayer, (widow Emanuel)" appeared in the 1899 St. Louis telephone directory living at 5122 Fairmount Ave. Lena remained in St. Louis with her children and died there on 30 October 1926. She was interred with her husband. (**A, AN, E, F, G, TT**)

STEIN, MICHEL, was born on 18 June 1854 in *Oberlauterbach*, Bass-Rhin France, to **ISAAC STEIN**, a native of *Salmbach*, Bas-Rhin, and his wife, **ANNE/NANETTE/JEANNETTE BLOCH**, born in *Trimbach*, Bas-Rhin. Eighteen-year-old Michel immigrated to the United States, arriving in New York on 14 October 1872 aboard the SS *Saxonia*. He was enumerated in the 1880 federal census for Alsatia, East Carroll Parish, LA, as "Melville" Stein, living in the household of his brother-in-law, Emanuel Meyer, his sister, Mina/Lena's husband. He and another brother, **JACOB STEIN** (See entry), were working as clerks in the Alsatia plantation store. Melville, as he was called in the handful of records concerning his short life, died on 24 February 1889 in Vicksburg, Warren Co., MS. His remains were sent to St. Louis, MO where his sister Lena Stein Meyer had them interred near those of her husband in New Mount Sinai Cemetery and Mausoleum located at Affton, St. Louis Co., MO. He had never married. (**A, AN, E**)

STRAUSS, BERNARD, was born **JACQUES STRAUS** on 28 June 1838 in *Gundershoffen*, Bas-Rhin, France, to **ISAAC STRAUS**, le jeune, a sixty-one-year-old widower, and his twenty-six-year-old second wife, **ROSALIE HIMMLER**, both natives of the town. Bernard immigrated to New Orleans, Orleans Parish, LA, from Le Havre, France, arriving on 1 October 1857 aboard the *Kate Dyer,* just months behind a maternal aunt, **MARIE HIMMLER EHRMANN** (See entry for **NATHAN EHRMANN**). Bernard was enumerated in the 1860 federal census, working in the Block, Firnberg & Co. dry goods store in Opelousas, St. Landry Parish, LA. Julie Strauss, the mother of one of the partners, **JOSEPH BLOCH** (See entry), was Bernard's paternal aunt, so his presence in Opelousas was not surprising. Bernard Strauss registered the birth of a child, JOSEPH CLEOPHA STRAUSS, on 23 July 1861 in New Orleans, Orleans Parish, LA, born to him at Opelousas, St. Landry Parish, LA, the legitimate issue of his marriage with JOSEPHINE CHOÜTE/ CHOATE, a person of color. At the time, whether a free person of color, or slave, Josephine could not have been his legal wife due to the laws against miscegenation in Louisiana. An 1864 Civil War register listed Bernard as an unmarried native of France with no prior military service who was working as a clerk in the town of Plaquemine, Iberville Parish, LA. By the time of the 1870 federal census Bernard was enumerated in New Orleans, living with his bride, **MARY/MARIE/MINETTE ROS/ROSS/ROOS**, a native of *Romanswiller*, Bas-Rhin, France. The couple had married on 6 January 1870. Mary had been previously married to a man identified as GEORGE or OSCAR STONE (aka. OSCAR STEIN), a native of Germany, who died on 13 January 1869 about fifty miles above New Orleans as a result of a boiler explosion on the steamer *Glide*. There had been no children from this marriage. Identifying **MARY ROOS** was particularly difficult. There were two possible candidates: young cousins, MINETTE ROOS born on 29 November 1829, to **MOISE ROOS**, a native of *Romanswiller*, and his wife, **MADELEINE/ MELANIE KAHN**, or **MUNDEL ROOS**, born on 10 August 1832, to Moise's brother, **JOSEPH ROOS**, a native of *Romanswiller* and his second wife, **FRÉDÉRIQUE BLUM**, born in *Pfaffenhoffen*, Bas-Rhin. Neither Minette nor Mundel appeared to have married or died in *Romanswiller*, and neither of them appeared in any census of *Romanswiller* after 1851. Two girls, both identified as MINETTE ROS, one twenty-two-years-old, the other, nineteen, immigrated together on the ship *Edward Everett,* out of Le Havre, France, arriving in New

Orleans on 5 April 1852. Bernard Strauss' wife, Mary Roos, was remembered as having immigrated at the age of seventeen, so was she the younger Minette (born Mundel) in 1832? In the 1900 federal census her date of birth was given as November 1834. The older girl, Minette, was born in November, but in 1829. It is more likely that, despite the obvious disparity in the year of birth, persons of that era were more likely to remember their birth month rather than their birth year. Mary's identification was finally confirmed by a piece of crucial information found in a copy of her last will and testament which was located at *FamilySearch.org*. It was filed under the name "Mary Rose Strouss,"In it she named two nephews, **EMANUEL** and **SOLOMON KAHN** (See entries), executors to her estate, and left personal items to her grand-nieces, Ella and Gertrude Kahn, two of their children, as well as a small amount of cash to two nieces, Melanie Levy and Melanie Wild [*sic*], both of whom were living in Europe. A check of *Romanswiller* vital records revealed that Fanny Roos, mother of Solomon and Emmanuel Kahn, and Mary Roos, wife of Bernard Strauss, were sisters, born to Moïse Roos and Madeleine/Melanie Kahn. Mary, now identified as Minette Roos, born in 1829, and her husband Bernard Strauss lived in New Orleans continuously for over fifty years. They never had any children. Originally Bernard was enumerated as a dry goods clerk, but as the years wore on he became a steamboat agent. Mary died on 17 March 1912, in New Orleans. At that time she was said to be seventy-seven years of age, a native of *Romanswiller*, Alsace, a resident of New Orleans for sixty years, and the wife of Captain Bernard Strauss, employed by the Mississippi Packet Company. She was buried in Hebrew Rest Cemetery #2 in New Orleans. Bernard died on 2 November 1916, in New Orleans. Upon his passing, practically all the steamboats along the river front flew their flags at half-mast for the man said to be one of the oldest steamboat agents in the country. He was interred in Gates of Prayer Cemetery #1 (Canal Street) in the city. Bernard's only descendant, Joseph Cleopha Strauss, married twice and fathered fourteen children. He lived and farmed along the Vermilion River, eight miles from Carencro in Lafayette Parish, LA. (**A, AN, F, G, GB, TT**)

STRAUSS, ELISE, was born on 20 October 1886 in *Niederroedern*, Bas-Rhin, France, to **DANIEL STRAUSS**, a native of the town, and his wife, **PAULINE CAHN**, born in *Soultz-sous-Fôrets*, Bas-Rhin. Elise immigrated to New York aboard the SS *La Savoie*, arriving on 3 September 1904 from Le Havre, France. She gave her destination as

Reserve, St. John the Baptist Parish, LA, where she was to meet her brother, **SOLOMON STRAUSS** (See entry). Elise joined her brother in Reserve, then moved with his family to New Orleans, Orleans Parish, LA, in 1912 where she lived with them on Magazine Street. She worked as a clerk at S. Strauss dry goods, her brother's store until her marriage on 7 September 1919 to HEYMAN ISAACS. The groom, a native of Louisiana, born to Polish parents, was an accountant for H.P. Wall Co. When he and Elise were enumerated in the 1930 federal census he had become the owner a gentlemen's furnishings shop on Royal Street in New Orleans, where the couple lived. Heyman and Elise never had children. He died on 28 May 1972 in New Orleans and was buried there in Gates of Prayer Cemetery #2 (Joseph Street). Elise died on 27 April 1979 and was buried with him. (**A, AN, G, GB, TT**)

STRAUSS, MOÏSE, was born **MOSES STRAUSS** on 18 March 1873 in *Niederroedern*, Bas-Rhin, France, to **DANIEL STRAUSS**, a native of the town, and his wife, **PAULINE CAHN**, born in *Soultz-sous-Fôrets*, Bas-Rhin. Fifteen-year-old Moïse Strauss arrived with his fourteen-year-old brother, **SOLOMON STRAUSS** (See entry), at New York aboard the SS *La Bretagne*, from Le Havre, France, on 25 February 1889. Moïse sought work in Louisiana, where he was naturalized in St. Charles Parish, on 21 February 1896. Twenty-seven-year-old Moïse was enumerated in the 1900 federal census living alone in Hahnville, St. Charles Parish, LA, where he worked as a grocery salesman. By the time of the 1910 federal census, Moïse had joined his brother, Sol, and sister, **ELISE STRAUSS** (See entry), in Reserve, St. John the Baptist Parish, LA, where they were living together with Sol's wife, Henriette, and son, Alvin. Sol and Moïse were in the retail dry goods business. Moïse relocated to New Orleans, Orleans Parish, Louisiana, before the 1920 federal census. He lived in a boarding house on Jackson Avenue and worked as a clerk in a local dry goods store through the 1930s until his retirement. Moïse never married. He died on 30 April 1948 in New Orleans and was interred there in Gates of Prayer Cemetery #2 (Joseph Street) with his brother, Sol, and sister-in-law, Henriette Feitel. (**A, AN, G, GB, TT**)

STRAUSS, NATHAN/ "NAT", was born **NATHAN STRAUS** on 10 October 1834 in *Wissembourg*, Bas-Rhin, France, to **DAVID STRAUS**, born in *Drachenbronn*, Bas-Rhin, and his wife **GENENTEL/FANNY HIRSCH**, a native of *Wissembourg*, Bas-Rhin. He immigrated to New Orleans, Orleans Parish, La, arriving on 4

November 1851 aboard the ship *Isaac Bell*. After a brief stay in Jackson, Hinds Co., MS, he moved to Clinton, East Feliciana Parish, LA, where he was naturalized on 21 October 1857. He is said to have joined the Confederate Army while in the parish, and to have had an illustrious career under Generals Braxton Bragg and Miller. Unfortunately we could find no record of his service. After the war, Nathan relocated to Mobile, Mobile Co. AL, where he became a wholesale grocer and dry goods merchant, as well as an auctioneer. He married FRANCES KOCH, a native of Hesse-Darmstadt, Germany, on 2 December 1868 in Mobile. They were the parents of four children: Edward (b. 1870), Violet (b. 1872), Harry (b. 1874) and David (b. 1877). Nat Strauss was also active in politics, having been elected to several terms in the Alabama legislature. Upon retirement, the couple followed their children back to New Orleans, where they had all eventually moved. Frances died on 11 April 1899 and was buried in Hebrew Rest Cemetery #1 in the city. Nathan was the grand secretary of Lodge #7, International order of B'nai B'rith, as well as one of the oldest members of the board of Touro Infirmary and the Jewish Widows' and Orphans' Home in New Orleans. He died on 2 November 1915 and was buried with his wife. (**A, AN, G, GB, HJL**)

STRAUSS, SOLOMON "SOL," was born **SALOMON STRAUSS** on 26 December 1874 in *Niederroedern*, Bas-Rhin, France, to **DANIEL STRAUSS**, a native of the town, and his wife, **PAULINE CAHN**, born in *Soultz-sous-Fôrets*, Bas-Rhin. Fourteen-year-old Solomon Strauss arrived on 25 February 1889 at New York with his fifteen-year-old brother, **MOÏSE STRAUSS** (See entry), aboard the SS *La Bretagne*, from Le Havre, France. He and his brother went to work as clerks in a dry goods store in Hahnville, St. Charles Parish, LA. Sol was naturalized in Hahnville on 11 February 1896. Shortly before the turn of the twentieth century, Sol went into partnership with RAPHAEL SINGER, a native of Frankenthal, Germany, in a dry goods store in Donaldsonville, Ascension Parish, LA. He was enumerated in the Singer family household in the 1900 federal census. Sol was married to HENRIETTA FEITEL, a Louisiana native, on 2 September 1901 at Donaldsonville. They were the parents of one child, Henry Alvin Strauss (b. 1904). Sol and his brother, Moïse, opened a dry goods store in Reserve, St. John the Baptist Parish, LA, ca. 1905. They were enumerated there in the 1910 federal census, along with Sol's wife and son, and their unmarried sister, **ELISE STRAUSS** (See entry). Sol and his family relocated to New Orleans, Orleans Parish, LA, ca. 1912 where he opened a dry goods store on Magazine Street. Sol died in New Orleans on 29 January 1940 and was buried there in Gates of Prayer Cemetery #2 (Joseph Street). Henrietta followed two years later on 31 December 1942 and was buried with him. (**A, AN, G, GB, TT**)

STROLITZ, BERNARD, was born on 14 March 1846 in *Duppigheim*, Bas-Rhin, France, to HEYMANN STROLITZ, a native of Warsaw, Poland, and his second wife, **MADELEINE ADLER**, born in *Fegersheim*, Bas-Rhin. Bernard probably immigrated to Louisiana ca. 1865, following his half-sister, **SARAH STROLITZ** (See entry), although we were unable to find a reliable ship's record for his entry into the United States. Twenty-one-year-old Bernard Strolitz was struck down by yellow fever and died on 17 September 1867 in New Orleans, Orleans Parish, LA. He was buried there in Hebrew Rest Cemetery #1. (**A, AN**)

STROLITZ, ROSALIE, was born on 15 March 1850 in *Duppigheim*, Bas-Rhin, France, to HEYMANN STROLITZ, a native of Warsaw, Poland, and his second wife, **MADELEINE ADLER**, born in *Fegersheim*, Bas-Rhin. Rosalie immigrated to America on the SS *Köln* out of Bremen and Havana, arriving in New Orleans, Orleans Parish, LA, on 25 January 1871. She married MOSES LEHMAN, a native of Bavaria, on 19 August 1872 in New Orleans. The couple settled near Bayou Sara, West Feliciana Parish, LA, where Moses worked as a clerk in a store. Four of their five children were born in West Feliciana Parish: Mathias (b. 1874), Melanie (b. 1877), Celine (b. 1879) and Julius (b. 1881). The family moved to Corsicana, Navarro Co., TX, ca. 1886, where Moses became a local dry goods merchant. The couple's last child, Cécile, was born there two years later. Rosalie died on 11 January 1901 in Corsicana and was buried there in the local Hebrew Cemetery. Moses died in Mineral Wells, Palo Pinto Co., TX on 4 November 1926. His remains were returned to Corsicana where they were buried with those of his wife. (**A, AN, G**)

STROLITZ, SARAH, was born **SAARA STROLITZ** on 8 December 1832 in *Duppigheim*, Bas-Rhin, France, to HEYMANN STROLITZ, a native of Warsaw, Poland, and his first wife, **BRUNETTE/ BRIGITTE FALK**, born in *Duppigheim*, Bas-Rhin. She was probably the same as twenty-seven-year-old Sarah Strolitz who immigrated to the United States aboard the SS *Teutonia*, which left out of Hamburg, Germany, and arrived in New York on 8 May 1860. She married

LEON LEHMAN, a native of Böchingen, Rheinpfalz, Germany, ca. 1864. We have been unable to find a marriage record for the couple. According to all federal census records between 1870 and 1920, their first child, Henry, was born in California in 1866. Their second child, Moïse/Maurice, was born in Louisiana in 1868. The family was living in New Orleans, Orleans Parish, LA, at the time of the 1870 federal census with their three sons: Henry, Moïse, and Jonathan/Joe born in November 1869. Leon was working as a clerk in a store to support his family. By 1880 the family had relocated to Bayou Sara, West Feliciana Parish, LA, where Sarah's sister Rosalie lived with her husband, MOSES LEHMAN. Leon opened up a grocery store in the small community. The family now included three more children: Blanche (b. 1872), Matt/Max (b. 1875) and Achille (b. 1879). The family moved once again, this time to Hanson City, near present-day Kenner, Jefferson Parish, LA ca. 1890. They bought two lots of ground on which they had built a single cottage containing a store, five rooms and a shed. Leon operated a small grocery store there with the help of two sons, Henry and Joe. Leon died on 12 February 1902 at Touro Infirmary in New Orleans, and was buried there in Gates of Prayer Cemetery #2 (Joseph Street). Sarah died on 30 April 1912 in Kenner, Jefferson Parish, LA, and was buried with her husband. (**A, AN, F, G, GB, TT**)

THEODORE, CLARISSE, was born **CAROLINE THEODORE** on 25 July 1867 in *Marmoutier*, Bas-Rhin, France, to **HERMANN/ ISAAC THEODORE**, a native of the town, and his wife, **MARIE ROOS**, born in *Romanswiller*, Bas-Rhin. Clarisse immigrated to New York, arriving with her first cousin, **ROSA THEODORE** (See entry), on 28 October 1889 aboard the SS *La Bretagne*. Clarisse was listed in the 1895 *New Orleans City Directory* boarding at #724 Baronne St., and was employed as a clerk. She married EMILE SASSOWSKY, a native of Romania, in New Orleans, Orleans Parish, LA, on 27 March 1895. Emile and Clarisse were enumerated in Franklin, St. Mary Parish, La in 1900, with their first two children, Jonas (b. 1896) and Lawrence (b. 1898). Emile worked in Franklin as a watch maker. Ten years later, Emile and Clarisse were living in Thibodaux, Lafourche Parish, LA. Two more children had been born to them since the last census, Rose (b. 1900), and Leon (b. 1903). Later that year Clarisse, Rose and Leon went back to France for a visit, returning to New York on 26 October 1910, aboard the SS *Chicago*. Clarisse, using her maiden name, Theodore, was enumerated in the 1930 federal census in

Manhattan, New York with her two youngest children, Leon and Rose Theodore. Said to be a widow, her twenty-seven year old daughter Rose was working as a typist. Clarisse continued to use her maiden name, Theodore, in a 1932 border crossing from the United States to Canada. She gave her age as sixty-five years and birthplace as *Marmoutier*, France. She listed her next of kin as her son, Leon, who lived in Chicago, Cook Co., IL. The final record found for Clarisse Theodore was a listing in the *Alexandria, VA City Directory* for 1938. Clarisse lived at 138 Glebe Road with her daughter, Rose, who worked as a stenographer, and her sons Leon and Lawrence Theodore, the latter a member of the United States Marine Corps. Lawrence's wife, Anne, also lived at the same address. On the other hand, Emile and his sons, Jonas and Lawrence, were listed in a 1915 Jersey City, Hudson Co., NJ directory at 124 Woodward Ave. Emile and Jonas worked as watchmakers, while Lawrence was a book keeper. Jonas registered for the World War I draft on 17 June 1917 from Jersey City. He listed his occupation as commercial artist and indicated he was supporting his mother. Emile Sassowsky subsequently moved to upstate New York. In April 1916 he opened up a watch and clock repair shop in Binghamton, Broome Co., NY. An article in the local paper reported that he had trained in France and Germany. In 1920 he was enumerated in the federal census for Union, Broome Co. NY, where he lived alone in a boarding house. His occupation was "mechanic in clock factory." We have not been able to ascertain a date or place of death for either Emile Sassowsky or Clarisse Theodore. (**A, AN, F, FPC**)

THEODORE, ROSA, was born **ROSE THEODORE** on 29 October 1864 in *Marmoutier*, Bas-Rhin, France, to **HENRI THEODORE**, a native of the town, and his wife, ADELAÏDE AMSELL, born in Bacourt, Meurthe-et-Moselle, France. Rosa immigrated to New York, arriving with her first cousin, **CAROLINE/CLARISSE THEODORE** (See entry), on 28 October 1889 aboard the SS *La Bretagne*. Rosa was listed in the 1895 New Orleans City Directory boarding at #724 Baronne St., and was said to be employed as a clerk. Her engagement to SIMON ISAACSON, aka SIMON ITZIGSOHN, a native of Germany, was announced on 4 July 1897. They were married on 12 August 1897 in New Orleans, Orleans Parish, LA. The couple returned to Palmetto, St. Landry Parish, LA, where Simon owned a general merchandise store. Rosa died in St. Landry Parish and was interred in the Jewish Cemetery in Washington, St. Landry Parish, LA. There was little legible information on her tombstone, which is very degraded, except her name and the name of her husband. The date, 1898, at the bottom of her marker was probably her year of death. Simon remarried in New Orleans on 18 July 1900 to BABETTE GERNSBACHER, a New York native. The couple, who lived in Palmetto, raised two children: Juliet Sydney (b. 1906) and Joseph Louis (b. 1911). Simon died on 16 November 1934 in Metairie, Jefferson Parish, LA, and was buried in Hebrew Rest Cemetery #2 in New Orleans. Simon had been a resident of Palmetto for over fifty years. His wife, Babette, died on 10 January 1955, and was buried with her husband. (**A, AN, GB**)

TRAUTMANN, DAVID, was born on 6 May 1819 in *Kutzenhausen*, Bas-Rhin, France, to **JACQUES TRAUTMANN** and **JEANNETTE JUNG**, both natives of the town. He immigrated to New Orleans, Orleans Parish, LA, ca. 1852, a reliable record for which we have not been able to find. He married **JULIE MOSSER** on 25 January 1854 in the city. She was born **GITTEL MOSSER** on 12 May 1824 in *Surbourg*, Bas-Rhin, France, to **ADÈLE/EDEL MOSSER** (See entry for **DAVID MOYSE GRADWOHL**), the twenty-two year old single daughter of **JOSEPH MOSSER** and his wife **ELIA KLEIN**. According to the 1900 federal census, Julie came to New Orleans, Orleans Parish, LA, in 1852 as well, but we could find no reliable ship's record for her arrival. David and Julie raised four children in New Orleans: Jacques (b. 1854), Joseph (b. 1856), Isidore (b. 1859), and Adeline (b. 1862). David was a successful clothing merchant, later joining his sons in the flour and grain business, Jac. Trautman & Co. David died on 22 November 1893 in New Orleans and was buried there in Hebrew Rest Cemetery #1. Julie died from pneumonia on 20 September 1916, and was buried in the same cemetery. (**A, AN, G, GB, L, TT**)

TRAUTMANN, SOPHIE, was born on 12 March 1845 in *Kutzenhausen*, Bas-Rhin, France, to **ISAAC TRAUTMANN**, born in *Lembach*, Bas-Rhin, France, and his wife, **RIFFGEN MOSSER,** born in *Kutzenhausen*, Bas-Rhin. Sophie immigrated to New Orleans, following her uncle **DAVID TRAUTMANN** (See entry) and his wife, **JULIE MOSSER**, her second cousin, arriving on 31 May 1861 on the ship *Stephen Crowell*. She married NATHAN MEYER, a native of Bavaria, Germany, on 23 August 1867 in New Orleans. Nathan was a dry goods dealer, and, later on in life, worked as a crockery drummer (travelling salesman) in the city. He and Sophie were the parents of six children: Abraham (b. 1869), Jeannette (b. 1870), Celina (b. 1876),

Jacob (b. 1878), Rosa (b. 1881), and Rita (b. 1886). Nathan died from dysentery on 10 July 1901 in New Orleans and was buried there in Hebrew Rest Cemetery #1. Sophie died on 2 April 1924 and was buried in the same cemetery. (**A, AN, GB, L, TT**)

UHRY, HEYMAN, was born on 2 September 1866 in *Schirrhoffen*, Bas-Rhin, France, to **ABRAHAM UHRY** and his wife, **MARIE ANNE KAHN**, both natives of the town. In a 1904 U.S. passport application, Heyman stated that he had immigrated to the United States aboard the SS *Amérique* in September 1883. A search of the passenger manifest for the SS *Amérique*, which arrived in New York on 13 September 1883 did not reveal an entry for him, nor did he appear on any other ship's manifest for the *Amérique* in 1883. There was, however, a record for a seventeen-year-old "Émile Uhry," a German national, who arrived on 8 May 1884 at New York from Le Havre, France, aboard the SS *Amérique* which is worthy of consideration. Heyman spent his first years in Georgia, becoming a citizen in July 1890 in Macon, Bibb Co., GA. He relocated to Plaquemine, Iberville Parish, LA, shortly thereafter, where he operated a dry goods store. Heyman married JULIA KRAUSS on 10 April 1900 in New Orleans, Orleans Parish, LA, and they returned to Plaquemine to live. Julia, a native of Leimersheim, Rheinpfalz, was a niece of LEON FELLMAN, who, with her four brothers, Leopold, Max, Alfred, and Fritz, had founded Krauss Co., Ltd., a department store at the corner of Canal & Basin Streets, which opened its doors in 1903. Julia and Heyman moved to New Orleans that year to work in the family business. They were the parents of two children: Marie (b. 1903) and Leon (b. 1906). As late as 1920, Heyman, his wife and two children were living together with the four Krauss brothers on State Street in uptown New Orleans. Heyman died suddenly on 17 November 1927, succumbing to a stroke in a Canal Street restaurant where he had been dining. At the time he was the secretary of the Joseph Cahn Manufacturing Co. Estranged from his wife, he had been living with friends on Prytania Street. Julia Uhry died on 25 June 1959 in the city and was buried at Metairie-Lakelawn Cemetery in New Orleans. Krauss Department Store closed its doors on Canal Street in 1994. (**A, AN, G, GB, TT**)

UHRY, HIPPOLYTE, was born on 16 August 1870 in *Schirrhoffen*, Bas-Rhin, France, to **ABRAHAM UHRY** and his wife, **MARIE ANNE KAHN**, both natives of the town. He immigrated to the United States aboard the SS *Normandie*, arriving in New York on 13

September 1886 at the age of sixteen years. His brother, **HEYMAN UHRY** (See entry), who had helped pay his passage, met him in New Orleans. Hippolyte was naturalized in Port Allen, West Baton Rouge Parish, LA on 1 April 1892, where he also declared that he had immigrated in 1886. He moved shortly afterwards to Plaquemine, Iberville Parish, LA, where Heyman and his wife, Julia, were operating a clothing store. Hippolyte married DORA KAHN, a native of Plaquemine, on 15 October 1903 in New Orleans. They were the parents of three children: Ralph (b. 1904), Marjorie (b. 1906) and Julian (b. 1914). After Heyman moved his family to New Orleans, ca. 1903, to help establish the Krauss Department Store, Hippolyte and another brother, **MOÏSE UHRY** (See entry), operated a clothing store in Napoleonville, Assumption Parish, LA, called The Hub, for almost two decades. When Moïse and his family moved to Lake Charles, Calcasieu Parish, LA, to start another business, Hippolyte and Dora followed. They lived there for several years before relocating ca. 1920 to operate a branch of their store, H. & M. Uhry, in Beaumont, Jefferson Co., TX. Hippolyte died on 28 November 1920 in Beaumont, after being struck by an automobile while attempting to cross a street. He was buried in Hebrew Rest Cemetery in Beaumont. Dora died on 15 September 1938 in Atlanta, Fulton Co., GA. Her remains were returned to Beaumont, where they were interred there in Hebrew Rest Cemetery. **(A, AN, G, GB, TT)**

UHRY, MOÏSE, was born **MORITZ UHRY** on 27 August 1874 in *Schirrhoffen*, Bas-Rhin, France, to **ABRAHAM UHRY** and his wife, **MARIE ANNE KAHN**, both natives of the town. According to his naturalization record dated 12 February 1900, filed in Napoleonville, Assumption Parish, LA, where he had opened up a dry goods store, Moïse wrote that he had immigrated to Louisiana on 20 February 1892. His brother **HIPPOLYTE UHRY** (See entry) was a witness to this record. Moise, may have been, however, the same as the twenty-six year-old [*sic*]"Moise Uhry" who arrived in New York on 24 December 1894 aboard the SS *Bretagne* from Le Havre, France, although the age is incorrect by five years. Moïse married EMILIE KAHN, a native of Louisiana, on 4 February 1903 in New Orleans, Orleans Parish, LA. They were the parents of four children, all born in Napoleonville: Myrtle (b. 1905), Marion (b. 1907), Aline (b. 1909) and Albert (b. 1911). Moïse operated The Hub dry goods store for almost two decades in Napoleonville, before he relocated his family to Lake Charles, Calcasieu Parish, LA, ca. 1917. He opened up a Hub dry goods store in

Lake Charles, doing business as M. Uhry, Inc. He served as the president of the firm, while his wife, Emilie, served as the treasurer. Their eldest daughter, Myrtle, was the firm's secretary, and another daughter, Marion, was a saleslady at the store. Hippolyte Uhry, his brother, initially Moïse's partner in Lake Charles, decided to open up a branch location in Beaumont, Jefferson Co., TX, where he moved his family before the 1920 federal census enumeration. Moïse and his family remained in Lake Charles through the 1930s, at which time they relocated once again, this time to retire near their daughter, Marion, who had married GEORGE LAUTERSTEIN, a merchant in LaGrange, Fayette Co., TX. Moïse died in LaGrange on 11 December 1949 and was buried there in the City Cemetery. Emilie died in Colorado Co., TX, on 12 June 1977, and was buried with her husband in LaGrange. (**A, AN, GB**)

UHRY, SARA/HENRIETTE, (*Ingwiller*) Se entry for **MOÏSE LEVY** (b. 1808)

VOGEL, BABETTE, (*Niederbronn-les-Bains*) See entry for **SAMUEL BLUM**

WALDHORN, MOÏSE, was born on 12 October 1852 in *Goersdorf*, Bas-Rhin, France, to **NAHUM WALDHORN**, a native of the town, and his wife, **JULIE LEVI**, born in *Niederbronn-les-Bains*, Bas-Rhin. He immigrated to American, arriving in New York on 14 October 1872 aboard the SS *Saxonia*. Moïse settled in New Orleans, Orleans Parish, LA, and worked until he was able to save enough money to start a business. In 1880, with the help of several partners, he established the People's Loan Office at the corner of Royal and Conti Streets in the French Quarter. During the difficult days of Reconstruction he bought and sold antiques and jewelry in order to keep many Creole families afloat until they could recover from the impoverishment visited upon them during the Civil War. Moïse married ALBERTINE LÖB, a native of New Orleans, on 30 January 1884 in New Orleans. The couple had four children: Augusta (b. 1886), Elsie (b. 1888), Samuel L. (b. 1890), and Ruth Constance (b. 1894). Moïse's pawn shop grew, slowly transforming itself into the high-end antique and jewelry business which, still to this day, is located on the same corner in the French Quarter, now known as Waldhorn & Adler. It continues to be owned by descendants of the Waldhorn family. Not only a respected merchant, Moïse was, for a time, president of Touro Synagogue. Suffering from years of bad health, Moïse took his own life in a furniture factory he owned on 31 October 1910. He was buried in Hebrew Rest Cemetery #2 in New Orleans. Albertine died on 3 October 1921, and was interred in the same cemetery. Note: See also entry for **FANNY MARX**, Albertine Lob's mother. (**A, N, G, GB**)

WEIL, ABRAHAM, was born on 1 July 1845 in *Brumath*, Bas-Rhin, France, to **JOSEPH WEIL**, a native of *Eckwersheim*, Bas-Rhin, and his wife, **SARA LEVI**, born in *Brumath,* Bas-Rhin. According to a 1914 application for a U.S. passport, which he made while temporarily residing at *Brumath*, he had immigrated to Louisiana in October 1866 from Le Havre, France, a record of which we have not been able to find. Abraham took out a license to marry SOPHIE RINDFOOS/ RINDFUSS, a native of Billigheim, Rheinpfalz, Germany, in New Orleans, Orleans Parish, LA, on 16 December 1868. Their only child, Leopold, was born in New Orleans on 12 September 1870. Abraham was naturalized on 21 October 1876 in New Orleans where he worked as a boot and shoemaker with a shop at #886 Magazine Street. The Abraham Weil family was enumerated in St. Joseph, Tensas, Parish, LA, in 1880 where he continued to work as a shoemaker. Sophie died on 17 December 1881 in New Orleans and was interred in Gates of Prayer Cemetery #2 (Joseph Street). Abraham married RACHEL SWITZER in New Orleans on 12 April 1882. Their first child, Cecilia, was born on 27 January 1883 in New Orleans. Shortly thereafter the family moved to Natchez, Adams Co., MS, where three more children were born: Carrie (b. 1885), Hilda (b. 1886; died at six months and interred in the Natchez City Cemetery), and Clara (b. 1888). Abraham appeared in the 1892 *Natchez City Directory* as a shoe and clothing salesman living on Franklin St. and was enumerated in the 1886 Natchez city census as a forty-year-old shoemaker from Germany. The family returned to New Orleans in time for their inclusion the 1900 federal census. Rachel died there on 23 August 1906 and was interred at Gates of Prayer Cemetery #2 (Joseph Street). Abraham died on 26 August 1922 and was buried with her. (**A, AN, G, GB, N, NB, TT**)

WEIL, A.B. "ALEX,**"** was born **BARUCH WEIL** on 10 October 1842 in *Lichtenberg*, Bas-Rhin, France, to **JOËL/JOSEPH WEIL**, a native of *Reichshoffen*, Bas-Rhin, France, and his wife, **HENNELÉ MOSES**, also called **FRÉDÉRIQUE/HINEL/RÉGINE HIRSCH/ HERTZ**, who was born in *Rothbach*, Bas-Rhin, France. We believe that Baruch Weil arrived in New Orleans, Orleans Parish, LA, on 27

January 1857 aboard the ship *Robert C. Winthrop* from Le Havre, France. He was, however, mistakenly recorded on the passenger manifest as a female. When Baruch enlisted on 9 May 1861 in New Orleans, Orleans Parish, LA, with Company I, 2nd LA Infantry, CSA, under the name "Alex" Weil, he reported that Homer, Claiborne Parish, LA was his usual residence. Alex was wounded at the Battle of Antietam in Sharpsburg, Washington Co., MD, in September 1862, captured at Gettysburg on 5 July 1863, shipped to New York as a prisoner, and exchanged in Virginia in September 1863. He fought his way back to Louisiana and was at the Battle of Mansfield (DeSoto Parish) in April 1864. He was paroled in Shreveport, Caddo Parish, in 1865. That same year he joined his brother, **MOÏSE WEIL** (See entry), in Memphis, Shelby Co, TN, where he was enumerated as an unmarried man, working as a clerk. After Moïse's death in 1868, Alex brought his brother's widow, Babette, and her five children to Shreveport, where he became a successful merchant. He was also the first president of the local I.O.B.B. (Independent Order of B'nai B'rith). He married **SOPHIE/SOPHIA LEADMAN** on 12 January 1870 in Shreveport. Sophia was born **CÉRINE LEDERMANN** in *Fegersheim*, Bas-Rhin, France, on 30 March 1852 to **ARON LEDERMANN** (See entry), a native of the town, and his wife, **JEANNETTE/ HENRIETTE WEINMANN** (See entry for **FELIX CAHN**), born in *Brumath*, Bas-Rhin. She immigrated to America with her parents on 7 November 1853 aboard the SS *Globe*. Sophie Ledermann Weil died on 20 December 1870 at the age of eighteen years and eleven days after giving birth to the couple's only child, Sophie. Her little girl followed her to the grave on 17 May 1871. They were both buried in Hebrew Rest Cemetery # 1 (the Jewish Section of Oakland Cemetery) in Shreveport. Alex died two years later on 12 June 1873, probably from yellow fever, and was buried with his wife and child. Note: In the 1851 and 1856 censuses of *Lichtenberg*, Alex B. was enumerated as "Auguste." (**A, AN, B1851, E, G**)

WEIL, ALPHONSE B., was born **ALPHONSE WEIL** on 11 April 1874 in *Reichshoffen*, Bas-Rhin, France, to **SIMON WEIL**, a native of the town, and his wife, **FREDERICKA SICHEL**, born in *La Walck*, Bas-Rhin. He immigrated to America, arriving in New York on 13 July 1891 from Le Havre, France, aboard the SS *La Champagne*. He came to Louisiana and began working for and living in the household of Alsace native, **ABRAHAM KLOTZ** (See entry), a merchant-planter residing in Klotzville (la ville de Klotz), the town named after him in

Assumption Parish, LA. Alphonse was a clerk, then bookkeeper for Klotz, and when the store and planting interests were incorporated in 1907 he became secretary of the Abraham Klotz Planting and Mercantile Co., Ltd. After Klotz's death in 1907 he remained there for over twelve years. He was still unmarried in 1910 and lived with Abraham Klotz's son, Edmond, and Eugene Abraham, Edmond's maternal uncle. Alphonse married ROSINE DREYFUS, a native of Livonia, Pointe Coupée Parish, LA, in 1915. Their two children Flora (b. 1916) and Simon (b. 1918) were born in Assumption Parish, where Alphonse had become the director of the Bank of Paincourtville in Klotzville. The family relocated to Livonia, in Rosine's home parish in the late 1920s, where Alphonse worked in the grocery business with his wife's family. In 1938 he became a director of the Bank of Maringouin, in Pointe Coupée Parish and retired at Livonia in 1970 as the oldest known notary and bank president in the United States. He died in a hospital in Baton Rouge, East Baton Rouge Parish, LA, on 14 April 1972 at the age of ninety-eight. He was buried in Baton Rouge in the Jewish Cemetery. His wife followed him in death on 3 July 1974 and was buried by his side. (**A, AN, G, GB**)

WEIL, BENJAMIN, was born on 2 January 1823 in *Bouxwiller*, Bas-Rhin, France, to **MARX/MARC WEIL**, a native of *Uhrwiller*, Bas-Rhin, and his wife, **JUDITH REICHSHOFFER**, a native of *Bouxwiller*, Bas-Rhin. In a claim that Benjamin Weil filed against the Mexican government for having seized a shipment of his cotton during the Civil War, he indicated that he had arrived in New Orleans, Orleans Parish, LA, on 12 June 1850. We believe, however, that he may have been the twenty-four-year-old "Bejamin [*sic*] Weil" who arrived in New Orleans, Orleans Parish, LA, from Le Havre, France, on 26 June 1846 aboard the ship *Damascus*. Since all 278 passengers on the ship had been recorded as German farmers headed for Mississippi, we have concluded that the captain of the *Damascus*, Mr. Bliss, cared little for the accuracy of his ship's manifest. Twenty-seven-year-old Benjamin Weil was enumerated on 30 September 1850 in that year's federal census for the Western District, Lafayette Parish, LA as a merchant from France. Thirty-five-year-old Benjamin Weil was enumerated in the 1860 federal census as an unmarried merchant from France, at Alexandria, Rapides Parish, LA. He shared lodgings with **ISAAC LEVY** (See entry), who later would become his brother-in-law. Levy and Weil, along with Isaac's brother, **JACOB LEVY** (See entry), and a cousin Marx Levy, whom we have not been able to identify, were business partners in Isaac Levy & Co. as general and commission merchants. In 1862 Ben Weil and Isaac Levy enrolled in the First Louisiana Cavalry, Company D, the Rapides Rangers, for service in the War Between the States. Nothing is known of Benjamin's service, but from other records we have gathered, we know that he continued to engage in the mercantile business in Alexandria, Rapides Parish, Opelousas, St. Landry Parish, and Texas. In March 1863 Isaac Levy & Co. branched out to facilitate their business, forming a new partnership with Bloch, Firnberg & Co. of Opelousas under the name of Levy Bloch & Co. Benjamin Weil and Marx Levy had a contract with the State of Louisiana to import arms and ammunition from Europe through Mexico, and to export cotton back in payment. The co-partnership with Bloch Firnberg & Co was dissolved in 1865 at the close of the Civil War. Shortly thereafter Benjamin Weil took a trip back to France. He returned on 22 June 1866 from Le Havre, France, to New York, aboard the SS *Lafayette*. Accompanying him on the voyage were his eighteen-year-old bride, ALICE BLOCH, an eleven-year-old relative, Camille Weil, both natives of Meurthe, Lorraine, France, and his twenty-eight-year-old sister, **SARA WEIL**, destined to marry his business partner, Isaac Levy. Benjamin Weil was granted American citizenship on 4 November 1869 in Rapides Parish, LA. Shortly afterwards, Ben and his bride, Alice Bloch Weil relocated to New Orleans where he worked as a cotton commission merchant, with offices on Gravier Street, The couple was enumerated there in the 1870 federal census along with Camille Weil, and forty-eight-year-old Rosa Bloch, who may have been Ben's mother-in-law. Ben and Alice were the parents of a son, George, born in New Orleans in 1873. Benjamin Weil was involved in two well-known lawsuits stemming from his activities during the Civil War. After his return from France, he had presented fifteen certificates of indebtedness to Louisiana Governor James Madison Wells (1865-67) alleging that he, Weil, had supplied the Confederate government with merchandise including guns and ammunition for a total of $140,894, which Wells had approved. The claim worked its way slowly through the Louisiana legislature where it was finally approved in 1870. Ben Weil, however, had already sold his interest in the claim to Thomas Anderson of St. Landry Parish, who collected the money. In 1872 Anderson and Governor Henry Clay Warmoth, who would be impeached later that year, were sued by the State of Louisiana for the same amount, alleging that its payment was illegal. In 1869 Ben Weil filed a second claim, this one against the government of Mexico, in a case which dragged on for almost twenty years, long after his death. He alleged that 957,000 pounds of cotton, worth over $340,000, were seized by the Mexican government in September 1864 between Piedras Negras and Laredo, Mexico. The cotton, in a large wagon train, had been headed for Matamoros, where duty was to be paid at the Mexican Custom's House and the goods shipped abroad. With interest accruing to the debt from 1864 to 1876 when the claim was settled, it was worth half a million dollars, which was awarded him that year. By then Ben, his wife, and child had returned to France, where they were living when he died on 27 April 1877 at the Charenton Asylum in the suburbs of Paris. His widow filed succession papers in New Orleans on 6 July 1877. The government of Mexico paid an installment of $300,000, which was transferred to the United States on behalf of Weil, but shortly thereafter Mexico sued to recoup the money stating that after a thorough examination the whole case was deemed to be fraudulent. Attorneys for the Mexican government alleged that letters between the business partners of Isaac Levy & Co and Bloch, Firnberg & Co. never discussed the loss of 1900 bales of cotton, nor could Ben Weil have ever been in possession of that much cotton on his own account. In the meantime the American government took the stand that it would not pay the money to Ben Weil's estate on the grounds that his loss occurred while he was an agent of the Confederacy, and that the shipment of cotton to Mexico during the Civil War was unlawful. Alice Weil appointed Lambert B. Cain, a native of Thiaucourt-Regniéville, Meurthe, France, and Adolph Marks, both New Orleans liquor merchants, to look after her interests. An agreement had been made that Cain would receive one-half of the proceeds of the Mexican claim, along with expenses. Cain hired lawyers who finally collected $171,889.61, but Cain died in 1881, leaving his widow to seek payment for his share. While Weil's estate was finally worth $185,409.71, it was alleged by the widow, Caroline Kahn Cain, that after her husband paid out $122,878 in attorney's fees and additional amounts for other expenses, the Weil estate was indebted to the Cain estate in the amount of $16,887.87, and further, as the executrix of his estate she reserved the right to sue for an additional $58,000 in fees owed to her. As late as December 1900 the United States Senate was still debating whether or not to reimburse Mexico for the $171,889.61 which had been finally paid out to the estate of Benjamin Weil. (**A, AN, GB, TT**)

WEIL CAROLINE, was born **JEANNETTE WEIL** on 5 May 1831 in *Surbourg*, Bas-Rhin, France, to **ALEXANDRE WEIL** and his second wife, **EVE/CAROLINE MOSSER (MOISIS GOELLEN** before 1808), both natives of the town. We believe that she arrived on June 14, 1850 as "Caroline Weil" in New Orleans, Orleans Parish, LA, on the ship *Pyramid* from Le Havre, France. Caroline married EMANUEL FRANK, a native of Prussia, a record for which we have been unable to find although we believe that the wedding probably took place in New Orleans. Emanuel and Caroline moved to Lockhart, Caldwell Co., TX, shortly after the wedding. Five of the couple's six children were born in Texas: Simon (b. 1855; died of consumption in 1889 at Victoria, Tamaulipas, Mexico), Melina/Marline (b. 1857), Joseph (b. 1860), Anna (b. 1862), Elise (b. 1865, San Antonio, Bexar Co., TX; died 1869 San Antonio). Caroline's last child, Pauline Camorita was born in New Orleans on 3 April 1868 where the family had returned and where they were enumerated together in the 1870 federal census. Forty-one-year old Emanuel was running a grocery store, and his thirty-eight-year-old wife, Caroline, was caring for their five surviving children, Simon, Melina, Joseph, Anna and Pauline. Caroline Frank died on 4 June 1876 in New Orleans and was buried there at Hebrew Rest Cemetery # 1. Emanuel died four years later, on 6 September 1880, and was buried in the same cemetery. Note: The remains of Elise, who died in San Antonio, and Simon, who died in Mexico, were also interred in Hebrew Rest Cemetery #1 in New Orleans. (**A, AN, G, GB, TT**)

WEIL, CAROLINE, was born **JEANNETTE WEIL** on 3 July 1838 in *Lichtenberg*, Bas-Rhin, France, to **JOËL/JOSEPH WEIL**, a native of *Reichshoffen*, Bas-Rhin, France, and his wife **HENNELÉ MOSES**, also called **FRÉDÉRIQUE/HINEL/RÉGINE HIRSCH/HERTZ**, born in *Rothbach*, Bas-Rhin. She appears to have immigrated ca. 1860 to Louisiana, to join her brothers, **SAMUEL, ALEX. B.** and **NATHAN WEIL** (See entries) who had settled in Shreveport, Caddo Parish, LA. We were unable to find a reliable record for her arrival in the United States. She married MARX ISRAEL ca. 1869. Marx was born in Ennery, near Metz, Moselle France, in 1838. He had immigrated to New Orleans, Orleans Parish, LA, before the Civil War, serving as a private in the 5th Co., 3rd Regiment, LA European Brigade, known as the Garde Française. He and Caroline settled in New Orleans, where Marx worked as a dry goods merchant. The couple moved to Shreveport, Caddo Parish, LA, ca. 1877 where Marx opened up another mercantile establishment. Marx and Caroline never had children. He died on 22 May 1896 in Shreveport and was buried in Hebrew Rest

Cemetery # 2 (Texas Ave.). Caroline died on 8 April 1899 and was buried there as well. (**A, AN, G, GB**)

WEIL, DAVID, was born on15 May 1828 in *Surbourg*, Bas-Rhin, France, the youngest son of **JOSEPH WEIL** and his wife **CAROLINE/GERTRUDE GROSS**, both natives of the town. We believe that nineteen-year-old [*sic*] David Weil immigrated to America, landing in New York on 22 December 1849 aboard the ship *New York*. Even though his age is a bit inaccurate and he, as were all the other passengers, was identified as "German," his occupation was listed as "engraver." David was enumerated in the 1850 federal census for Grand Coteau, St. Landry Parish, LA, where he had joined his brother, **JONAS WEIL** (see entry). He was identified there in error as David "Wells," an unmarried man, born in France, working as a "trader." He joined his brother, **JONAS WEIL** (See entry), and sisters, **MARLINE**, **MIRIAM** and **MELANIE WEIL** (See entries), in Alexandria, Rapides Parish, LA, after the Civil War, where he worked as a merchant for a brief time. He was, however, a lithographer by trade, and was enumerated in the 1870 federal census in New Orleans, Orleans Parish, LA, as a thirty-eight-year-old unmarried lithographer from France. He appeared throughout the 1870s in various New Orleans directories as a lithographer with a shop at #80 Exchange Place in the city. David died at Touro Infirmary in New Orleans on 29 June 1900. His remains were returned to the Jewish Cemetery in Pineville, Rapides Parish, for burial next to those of his brother, **NOCHIM WEIL** (See entry). David never married. According to his obituary, which appeared in the New Orleans *Daily Picayune* on 30 June 1900, David had once owned a lithograph company in New Orleans and was to be brought back the next day to Alexandria, for burial in the cemetery in Pine Hill [*sic*]. Note: His date of death was recorded erroneously on his tombstone as 29 July 1900. (**A, AN, FS, G, GB**)

WEIL, DAVID K., was born **KAUFMANN WEIL** on 10 March 1846 in *Lichtenberg*, Bas-Rhin, France, to **JOËL/JOSEPH WEIL**, a native of *Reichshoffen*, Bas-Rhin, France, and his wife **HENNELÉ MOSES**, also called **FRÉDÉRIQUE/HINEL/RÉGINE HIRSCII/HERTZ**, born in *Rothbach*, Bas-Rhin, France. Twenty-year-old David was the only child left in the household of Joël Weil in the 1866 census of *Lichtenberg*. However, he did not appear in the 1870 federal census for Louisiana. We believe that he may have been the David Weil who arrived on 3 September 1872 at New York, from Bremen, Germany aboard the SS *Bremen*. He joined his brothers, **ALEX B.**, **NATHAN**, **SAMUEL**, and sister **CAROLINE** (See entries) in Shreveport, Caddo Parish, LA. Twenty-seven-year-old David died from typhoid fever on 10 September 1873, three months after his brother Alex's demise. David was buried in Shreveport at Hebrew Rest Cemetery # 1 (Jewish Section of Oakland Cemetery). (**A, AN, E, G**)

WEIL, ERNEST, was born on 6 April 1861 in *Mackenheim*, Bas-Rhin, France, to **SAMUEL WEIL**, dit **SAPHEL**, born in the town, and his wife, **FANNY MARX**, a native of *Kutzenhausen*, Bas-Rhin. Sixteen-year-old Ernest Weil arrived in New York on 14 June 1877 from Le Havre, France, aboard the SS *France*. He settled in Marksville, Avoyelles Parish, LA, where he was employed as a clerk in the store of Mississippi born merchant, Elie Hiller. When Hiller closed down in Marksville, Ernest spent several years working in Shreveport, Caddo Parish, LA. He returned to Marksville and was betrothed to MATHILDE SIESS, the daughter of **SIMON SIESS**, a local merchant and his wife **FANNY CERF** (See Entry). The couple married on 17 October 1888 at the Congregation Gates of Prayer in New Orleans, Orleans Parish, LA. Mathilde and Ernest had three children: Flora (b. 1891), Jeanne (b. 1893), and Elise (b. 1896). The latter two were born in Florence, Fremont Co., CO where the family had gone out west to seek their fortune. Although Ernest invested in several mining ventures, he did not strike it rich. They left for Denver, Arapahoe Co., CO, where Ernest became active in the Woodmen of the World, founded by Joseph Cullen Root, a fraternal organization that also sold life and accident insurance. The job took the family to Minneapolis, Hennepin Co., MN. Ernest was soon promoted to the position of Sovereign Manager of Wisconsin, Minnesota and the two Dakotas. In 1907 Ernest was promoted again, to develop the Woodmen membership in Louisiana. After a short stay in Shreveport, he moved the family to New Orleans, Orleans Parish, LA, where he grew the Woodmen membership to over 22,000. He became the President of the Woodmen Mutual Health and Casualty Co. of Louisiana, as well as a permanent board member. He joined the board of Touro Infirmary, was President of the New Orleans B'nai Brith and a trustee of the Congregation Gates of Prayer. Fifty-five-year-old Ernest died on 3 December 1916 and was buried in Gates of Prayer Cemetery #2 (Joseph Street). Mathilde died on 22 June 1931 in Jackson, Hinds Co., MS where she had been living with her daughter, Flora Kahn. Her remains were returned to New Orleans to be buried with those of her husband. (**A, AN, AP, G, GB**)

WEIL, FANNY, was born **FANNI WEIL** on 11 January 1850 in *Quatzenheim*, Bas-Rhin, France, to **EPHRAÏM WEIL,** a native of the town, and his wife, **MARIE LEHMANN**, born in *Illkirch-Graffenstaden*, Bas-Rhin. She immigrated with her brother, **ISAÏE WEIL** (See entry), on the SS *Hammonia*, arriving in New Orleans from Le Havre, France, on 4 December 1871. She died less than two years later, on 24 September 1873, in Shreveport, Caddo Parish, LA, a victim of the yellow fever epidemic that swept the city in that year. She was buried in Hebrew Rest Cemetery #1 (Jewish Section of Oakland Cemetery) the next day. (**A, AN, E, G**)

WEIL, GERTRUDE/CAROLINE, was born **GERDRUTHE WEIL** on 15 January 1825 in *Reichshoffen* Bas-Rhin, France, to thirty-seven-year-old **ISAAC WEIL**, a native of the town, and forty-year-old **MADELEINE/JULIE LEVI**, the widow of **LAZARE HEYMANN**, who had died on 6 February 1814. The father was not named in Gertrude's birth record, but she was given the surname "Weil." Isaac, Julie, and Gertrude were enumerated together as a family in the 1836 census for *Reichshoffen*. Madeleine Levy, a native of *Reichshoffen*, died there on 26 January 1847. Although Madeleine was not recorded as the wife of Isaac Weil, Isaac was the first witness listed on her death certificate. He declared that his relationship to her was "husband." In the 1851 census for *Reichshoffen*, sixty-one-year-old Isaac, a "widower," was living with twenty-six-year-old Gertrude who worked as a dressmaker. Isaac Weil died on 28 March 1859 in *Reichshoffen*. His death record indicated that he was "unmarried." We were unable to find a likely record for Gertrude's immigration to America, which surely took place subsequent to the American Civil War, and, perhaps much later. She died on 29 November 1892 in Klotzville, Assumption Parish, LA, and was buried in Bikur Sholim Jewish Cemetery in Donaldsonville, Ascension Parish, LA. An article in the *Assumption Pioneer* dated 3 December 1892 announced the November 29th death of Miss "Caroline" Weil from *Reichshoffen,* at the home of **ABRAHAM KLOTZ** (See entry) of Klotzville. She was said to be the "adopted mother" of **PAULINE ABRAHAM**, wife of ABRAHAM KLOTZ. We could find nothing more about her in any census or vital records. (**A, AN, B1851, E, TL**)

WEIL, ISAAC/ISIDORE, was born **ISAAC WEIL** on 10 February 1849 in *Oberlauterbach*, Bas-Rhin, France, to **DAVID WEIL**, a native of the town, and his wife **CAROLINE LEVY**, born in *Niederbronn-*

les-Bains, Bas-Rhin. He was the twin brother of **MOSES/MOÏSE WEIL** (See entry) who died in Shreveport, Caddo Parish, LA, in 1873 during the yellow fever epidemic. We believe that the entry for an eighteen-year-old "Isidore Weil," a French national, who arrived on 6 April 1867 at New York, from Le Havre, France, aboard the SS *Bellona* is likely his. He applied for a passport on 8 March 1875, using the name Isidore Weil. Isaac gave evidence to prove that he had been naturalized in Caddo Parish the year before. He did not return to the United States. Isaac made his home, first in *Strasbourg*, then in *Haguenau*, where he married Guillemette Levi, a native of *Goersdorf*, Bas-Rhin, on 20 November 1876. One of their children, Maurice Charles (Moritz Carl) Weil, later immigrated to Brazil. (**A, AN, TT**)

WEIL, ISAÏE, was born on 4 July 1852 in *Quatzenheim*, Bas-Rhin, France, to **EPHRAÏM WEIL,** a native of the town, and his wife, **MARIE LEHMANN**, born in *Illkirch-Graffenstaden*, Bas-Rhin. He followed his brother, **JACOB WEIL** (See Entry) to Louisiana. Isaïe immigrated with his sister, **FANNY WEIL** (See entry), on the SS *Hammonia*, arriving in New Orleans from Le Havre, France, on 4 December 1871. After his sister's death in 1873 in Shreveport, he relocated permanently to Alexandria, Rapides Parish, LA, to be near his brother. He married REBECCA WARSHAUER, a Polish immigrant, on 19 November 1879 in Alexandria, where he worked as a butcher. They were the parents of eight children: Solomon (b. 1880), Yetta (b. 1882), Jacques J. (b. 1884), Ephraïm (b. 1887), Albert Joseph (b. 1889), Fannie Augusta (b. 1892), May Rose (b. 1894), and Hortense E. (b. 1897; died at three months). Isaïe died on 22 May 1928 in Alexandria, and was buried in the Jewish Cemetery in Pineville, Rapides Parish, LA. His wife died on 25 October 1932 and was buried with him in Pineville. (**A, AN, E, FS, G**)

WEIL, JACOB, was born **JACQUES WEYL** on 25 December 1827 in *Ingwiller*, Bas-Rhin, France, to **SAMUEL WEYL**, a native of the town, and his wife, **CAROLINE OPPENHEIM**, born in *Haguenau*, Bas-Rhin. Twenty-one-year-old Jacob Weil arrived in New Orleans, Orleans Parish, LA, on 18 May 1852 from Le Havre, France, aboard the ship *Tirrell*. He took out a license to marry JANNETT/SCHANETT LEMLE, a native of Ingenheim, Germany, on 4 April 1854 in New Orleans. They were the parents of three children, all born in the city: Fanny (b. 1857), Samuel (b. 1859), and Julia (b. 1862). Jacob worked as a merchant in New Orleans in partnership with his brother,

LEOPOLD WEIL (See entry) who arrived in 1854. After the Civil War, Jacob and Leopold were joined by another brother, **MARX WEIL** (See entry). They formed a clothing manufacturing partnership on Chartres Street, which was dissolved upon Jacob's death on 15 March 1871. Jacob was buried in New Orleans at Gates of Prayer Cemetery #2 (Joseph Street). Jeanette Lemle Weil died on 21 December 1915 and was buried with her husband. (**A, AN, TT**)

WEIL, JACOB, was born **JACQUES WEIL** on 2 September 1847 in *Quatzenheim*, Bas-Rhin, France, to **EPHRAÏM WEIL**, a native of the town, and his wife, **MARIE LEHMANN**, born in *Illkirch-Graffenstaden*, Bas-Rhin. He was the first of three siblings to immigrate to Louisiana. (See entries for **FANNY** and **ISAÏE WEIL**) We believe that he may have arrived as seventeen-year-old "Jacques Weill" at New York on 18 January 1865 aboard the ship *William Frothingham*. Twenty-three-year-old Jacob was enumerated in the 1870 federal census at Alexandria, Rapides Parish, LA, where he was working as a clerk in a store. He married JULIA WOLF, a native of Covington, Kenton Co., KY, on 17 June 1872 in Alexandria. They had no children. Jacob and Julia were merchants in Alexandria most of their lives, They lived for a short while in Groesbeck, Limestone Co., TX, but soon returned to Louisiana. For many years the couple operated a millinery establishment in Alexandria known as the Fashion Bazaar. Julia died on 10 November 1907 in Alexandria, and was buried in the Jewish Cemetery in Pineville, Rapides Parish, LA. Jacob died on 18 June 1914 and was buried with her. (**A, AN, FS, G**)

WEIL, JONAS, was born **JEAN WEIL** on 1 April 1826 in *Surbourg*, Bas-Rhin, France, to **JOSEPH WEIL** and his wife, **CAROLINE GROSS**, both natives of *Surbourg*. According to his obituary he had immigrated to America in 1848. We believe, however, that he may have been the twenty-three-year-old "Jean Wheil" [*sic*] who arrived in New Orleans, Orleans Parish, LA, on 30 November 1849 from Bordeaux, France, aboard the ship *Massachusetts*. He settled in Grand Coteau, St. Landry Parish, LA, where he married JULIA OCTAVIA LOPEZ on 15 May 1850 in a civil ceremony. A Catholic ceremony was performed on 13 March 1851 at St. Charles Borromeo Church in Grand Coteau. Julia, a St. Martin parish native, was born on 12 April 1832 to François Lopez and his wife Julia Marcelline Garrio. Jonas and Julia had, at least seven children born in Grand Coteau: Jonas D'Azincourt (b. 22 Feb 1851), Julie Melanie (b. 9 Feb 1852), Mary (b. 1855), Rosa

(b. 1857), Estelle (b. 1859) and Joseph (b. 1861). Jonas worked as a cattle trader, and supplied the local Confederate units with beef during the Civil War. After the war, and the death of his brother, **NOCHIM WEIL** (See entry), he and his family moved to Alexandria, Rapides Parish, LA, to be near his four siblings who lived there. He worked as a general merchant. Two other children were born in Alexandria: Augusta (b. 1867) and Nochim (b. 1870). His wife, thirty-eight-year-old Octavia (called Rebecca in the 1870 census), died on 18 August 1871 and was buried in the Jewish Cemetery in Pineville, Rapides Parish, LA, as "Rebecca, wife of Jonas Weil." Jonas died on 19 February 1883 in Alexandria and was buried in Pineville as well. (**A, AN, FS, G, SWLR**)

WEIL, JONAS, was born on 15 January 1858 in *Dambach-la-Ville*, Bas-Rhin, France, to **SELIGMAN WEIL**, a native of *Rosheim*, Bas-Rhin, and his wife, BABETTE SÜSSKIND, born in Moselle, France. We believe he is the same person as "J. Weill," a seventeen-year-old merchant, who arrived at New York on 11 August 1875 aboard the SS *France* from Le Havre, France. Jonas was enumerated in the 1880 federal census in Assumption Parish working as a clerk in a dry goods store. He was naturalized in New Orleans, Orleans Parish, LA, on 23 November 1882. On 3 July 1888, while staying in Mexico City, Mexico, he applied for an American passport in order to travel abroad. He identified himself as a native of Alsace, Germany, having been born there on 15 January 1858. Still unmarried in 1900 he was back in the United States, working as a dry goods salesman in Rayne, Acadia Parish, LA. He married SYLVIA PHILLIPS on 9 September 1902 in New Orleans. Sylvia was a Louisiana native, whose father had been born in Jamaica, British West Indies. Jonas settled down in New Orleans to raise a family and work as the secretary of Krauss Co., Ltd., a department store located on Canal Street in the city. Jonas and Sylvia were the parents of three children: Elinor (b. 1904) and twins Mercedes and Jules Simon (b. 1914). When Jonas's nephew, **SELIGMAN HENRI WEIL** (See entry), immigrated to Louisiana in 1908, he became a permanent part of the household. Jonas and his family, accompanied by his nephew, moved to Baton Rouge, East Baton Rouge Parish, LA, in 1919 where Jonas was employed as secretary of the Rosenfeld Dry Goods Co., Ltd. By 1930 he was vice-president of the firm. Jonas died on 8 November 1933 in Baton Rouge. His remains were transported to New Orleans where they were buried in Dispersed of Judah Cemetery. Sylvia died at Washington D.C. on 24 December

1936. Her remains were brought back to New Orleans for interment with those of her husband. (**A, AN, GB**)

WEIL, LAZARD, was born **LAZARUS WEIL** on 24 April 1880 in *Lingolsheim*, Bas-Rhin, France, to **ABRAHAM WEIL**, a native of the town, and his wife, **MARIE WOLF/WOLFF**, born in *Wolfisheim*, Bas-Rhin. We believe that he immigrated to the United States as "L. Weil" aboard the SS *Kaiser Wilhelm Der Grosse*, arriving in New York from Cherbourg on 20 December 1905. He settled in New Orleans, Orleans Parish, LA, where he was naturalized on 14 January 1911 as a thirty-year-old unmarried immigrant from France. He took a job as a merchant at Reserve, St. John the Baptist Parish, LA, where he worked in the commissary at Leon Godchaux Co., a sugar refinery. Forty-four-year-old Lazard died at Reserve on 16 October 1924. He was interred at Gates of Prayer Cemetery #1 (Canal Street) in New Orleans, Orleans Parish, LA. He never married. (**A, AN, G, GB**)

WEIL, LEOPOLD, was born on 12 July 1836 in *Ingwiller*, Bas-Rhin, France, to **SAMUEL WEIL**, a native of the town, and his wife, **CAROLINE OPPENHEIM**, born in *Haguenau*, Bas-Rhin. Leopold emigrated from Le Havre, France, aboard the ship *Wurtemberg* which arrived at New Orleans, Orleans Parish, LA, on 23 January 1854. He started out as a peddler in the city and soon made enough money to go into business with his brother **JACOB WEIL** (See entry), who had come to New Orleans two years earlier. They opened a small clothing business on Tchoupitoulas Street. Leopold took out a license to marry BENA MEYER/MAIER, a native of Bermersheim (now Bermersheim vor der Höhe), Rheinpfalz, Germany, on 29 July 1856. They were wed two days later. Leopold and Bena were the parents of nine children, all born in New Orleans: Clara (b. 1858), Samuel (b. 1860), Jacob (b. 1861), David (b. 1863), William L. (b. 1865), Caroline (b. 1868), Emanuel L. (b. 1870), Salomon (b. 1872), and Isaac (b. 1874). The family stayed on in the city during the Union occupation of New Orleans during the Civil War. After the conclusion of hostilities, Jacob and Leopold joined their brother **MARX WEIL** (See entry), and another partner, Emile Traub, in the clothing manufacturing business. The death of Jacob in 1871 forced the closing of the enterprise. Leopold remained in the wholesale clothing business on Chartres Street in the French Quarter. His success allowed him to put resources into real estate. The Leopold Weil Building and Improvement Company was incorporated in 1903. His mercantile business was incorporated the same year as the Leopold Weil Company, Ltd. Leopold was a past vice president of the Congregation Gates of Prayer, a member of Temple Sinai and a life-long member of the Jewish Widows and Orphans Home, Touro Infirmary and the Hebrew Benevolent Society. He died at his home on St. Charles Avenue on 20 February 1905 and was interred in Hebrew Rest Cemetery #2 in New Orleans. His wife, Bena, died on 20 October 1908 and was buried with her husband. (**A, AN, GB, TT**)

WEIL, MARLINE, was born ca. 1812 in *Surbourg*, Bas-Rhin, France, to **JOSEPH WEIL** and his wife ,**CAROLINE/GERTRUDE GROSS**, both natives of *Surbourg*. We could find no birth record for "Marline," probably born as "**MERLEN**," a first name which was commonly used by families in the town at the time. The first half of the birth records for that year (No. 1-39) are missing from the available records on line, however the 1812 index is intact and does not show an entry for her. Marline appeared as the twenty-four-year-old unmarried daughter of Joseph and his wife, Gertrude Gross, in the 1836 *Surbourg* town census. She was enumerated in the 1851 census for *Surbourg* with her widowed mother, Caroline Roos [*sic*], as a thirty-four-year-old unmarried female. We could find no record of her immigration to the United States. There are only two records for her in Louisiana. In the 1880 federal census, she was enumerated as seventy-year-old Mary Weil, an unmarried woman living in Alexandria, Rapides Parish, LA, with her sister, Melanie Weil Ehrstein (See entry for **BARUCH EHRSTEIN**). She was buried as "Marline" Weil, ca. 1884, in the Jewish Cemetery at Pineville, Rapides Parish, LA, Her tombstone indicates only that she was born in *Surbourg* and died at age seventy-two. We could find no civil record for her death. (**A, AN, B1851, E, FS, G**)

WEIL, MARX/MAX, was born **MARX WEYL** on 6 October 1825 in *Ingwiller*, Bas-Rhin, France, to **SAMUEL WEYL**, a native of the town, and his wife, **CAROLINE OPPENHEIM**, born in *Haguenau*, Bas-Rhin. According to his obituary, he arrived in America during the California Gold Rush (1848-1855). We have not been able to locate any written trace of his presence out West or a possible record for his immigration. He came to New Orleans, Orleans Parish, LA, at the conclusion of the Civil War in 1865 and married **CELESTINE EHRLICH**, a record of which we were unable to find. Celestine was born on 21 April 1849 in *Wissembourg*, Bas-Rhin, France, to **LION/LEON ERLICH**, a native of the town, and his wife,

REINE/REBECQUE LEVY, born in Busenberg, Germany. Celestine immigrated to New York, arriving on 4 September 1860, aboard the ship *Fulton*. Marx and Celestine were the parents of five children all born in New Orleans: Samuel (b. 1866), Jules (b. 1867), David (b. 1868), Carrie (b. 1872), and Sarah (b. 1875). After working for several years with his two brothers, **JACOB** and **LEOPOLD WEIL** (See entries), in the wholesale clothing business, the death of Jacob in 1871 forced the closing of the firm. Marx soon opened a very successfully wholesale crockery business in the city. Celestine's sister, **CAROLINE EHRLICH**, born on 17 July 1851 in *Wissembourg*, Bas-Rhin, appeared as an eighteen-year-old member of the household in the 1870 federal census. We have uncovered no further records of Caroline's presence in Louisiana or elsewhere. Ninety-two-year-old Marx Weil died on 8 February 1918 in New Orleans, and was buried in Hebrew Rest Cemetery #2 in the city. Celestine died on 28 March 1928 and was buried in the same cemetery. Note: EHRLICH is often spelled ERLICH in records. Marx was known as Max in Louisiana records, but his crockery business was called Marx Weil & Son. (**A, AN, G, GB, TT**)

WEIL, MELANIE, (*Surbourg*) See entry for **BARUCH/BERNARD EHRSTEIN**

WEIL, MIRIAM, (*Surbourg*), See entry for **DAVID KUHNAGEL**

WEIL, MOSES, was born **MOÏSE WEIL** on 10 February 1849 in *Oberlauterbach*, Bas-Rhin, France, to **DAVID WEIL**, a native of the town, and his wife **CAROLINE LEVY**, born in *Niederbronn-les-Bains*, Bas-Rhin. Moses appeared in the 1866 town census for *Oberlauterbach*, at the home of his sister, Henriette Weil Levy. He was not enumerated in Shreveport, Caddo Parish, LA, or anywhere else in Louisiana in the 1870 federal census. We were unable to find a reliable record for his immigration to America. Twenty-four-year-old Moses Weil died on 10 September 1873, another victim of the raging yellow fever epidemic which struck Shreveport that year. He was buried in Hebrew Rest Cemetery #1 (Jewish Section of Oakland Cemetery). Note: See entry for his twin brother **ISAAC/ISIDORE WEIL**. (**A, AN, E, G**)

WEIL, MOSES/MOÏSE, was born **HERTZEL WEIL** on 25 October 1828 in *Lichtenberg*, Bas-Rhin, France, to **JOËL/JOSEPH WEIL**, a native of *Reichshoffen*, Bas-Rhin, France, and his wife **HENNELÉ MOSES**, also called **FRÉDÉRIQUE/HINEL/RÉGINE HIRSCH/ HERTZ,** , born in *Rothbach*, Bas-Rhin. Her name was given as **RENÉ** [*sic*] **LEOPOLDEN** in Moïse's birth record. As this couple's eldest son, Moïse may have been the first to arrive in Louisiana, however, we were unable to find a reliable record for his immigration to America. He settled in Shreveport, Caddo Parish, LA. Moses married BABETTE WEILL, a native of Sarrebourg, Moselle, France, on 30 January 1860 in Shreveport. They were the parents of five children: Rosa (b. 1861), Cora (b. 1863), Charlotte (b. 1866), Charles (b. 1867), and Henry (b. 1868). The family relocated to Memphis, Shelby Co., TN ca. 1865, where he was enumerated as "Herrel Weill," a head of household, in the Memphis city census for that year. He was working as a peddler. Moses died on 18 September 1868 in Memphis. He was buried in Temple Israel Cemetery in the city. His tombstone reads: "Moïse Herrel Weil, Born at *Lichtenberg*, Bas-Rhin, France, Oct. 25,1828; Died Sept. 18, 1868." Babette raised her children in Shreveport, living first with her brother-in-law, **ALEX B. WEIL** (See entry), until his death in 1873. Afterwards, she stayed on her own in the city, until her daughter Cora married Henry Bodenheimer in 1880. Henry was a native of Bellevue, Bossier Parish, LA. Babette lived with Cora's young family until her death on 5 June 1910. She was buried in Hebrew Rest Cemetery # 2 (Texas Ave.) in Shreveport. (**A, AN, TT**)

WEIL, NATHAN, was born on 25 December 1834 in *Lichtenberg*, Bas-Rhin, France, to **JOËL/JOSEPH WEIL**, a native of *Reichshoffen*, Bas-Rhin, France, and his wife **HENNELÉ MOSES**, also called **FRÉDÉRIQUE/HINEL/RÉGINE HIRSCH/HERTZ**, born in *Rothbach*, Bas-Rhin. We believe that eighteen-year-old [*sic*] Nathan Weil immigrated to Louisiana, arriving in New Orleans, Orleans Parish, LA, on 25 October 1854 from Le Havre France, aboard the ship *Ashland*. He settled in Shreveport, Caddo Parish, Louisiana, and fought, just as his brothers Samuel and Alex had, in the Civil War. He enlisted as a private in Company K, 11th LA Infantry, the "Shreveport Rebels." After the war he married **HARRIET/HENRIETTE MOCH**, his brother Samuel's wife's sister. She was born **HETCHEN MOCH** on 26 January 1840 in *Mommenheim*, Bas-Rhin, France, to **DANIEL MOCH**, a native of the town and his wife, **JEANNE/HANNE KAHN**, born in *Niederbronn-les-Bains*, Bas-Rhin. Nathan and Harriet were wed on 3 December 1867 in Shreveport, where Nathan continued to work as a merchant. Harriet was one of the many victims of the terrible yellow fever epidemic in Shreveport in 1873. She died on 17 September 1873 and was buried in Hebrew Rest Cemetery #1 (Jewish Section of Oakland Cemetery). They had no children and Nathan never remarried. He remained in Shreveport, boarding with strangers and working as a store clerk. In 1889 he sued MARX ISRAEL, his sister Caroline's husband, claiming $5000 damages for false imprisonment. We could find no more about this family problem. Nathan died on 17 December 1901 in Shreveport and was buried near his wife in Hebrew Rest Cemetery #1. Note: See also entry for **CAROLINE WEIL**. (**A, AN, E, G, GB**,)

WEIL, NOCHIM, was born on 3 January 1814 in *Surbourg*, Bas-Rhin, France, to **JOSEPH WEIL** and his wife, **CAROLINE/ GERTRUDE GROSS**, both natives of the town. We believe the record for thirty-six-year-old "Nachem Weil," a French immigrant, who left from Le Havre, France, and arrived at New Orleans, Orleans Parish, LA, on 18 March 1853 aboard the ship *Wurtemberg* is likely his record, despite a small discrepancy in age. He and his brothers-in-law **BERNARD EHRSTEIN** (See entry), **DAVID KUHNAGEL** (See entry), and their wives, his sisters Melanie and Miriam Weil, were enumerated in the 1860 federal census in Newton, Newton Co., TX, where they operated the merchandising firm of N. Weil & Co. They remained in Texas for the duration of the Civil War, returning to Louisiana ca. 1865. Nochim died shortly afterwards on 12 May 1865 in Opelousas, St. Landry Parish, LA. His body was returned to Pineville, Rapides Parish, LA, where it was interred in the Jewish Cemetery. He lies next to his brother, **DAVID WEIL** (See entry), who died in 1900. His tombstone indicates that he was born in *Surbourg*, and succumbed at Opelousas at the age of fifty-two. He never married. (**A, AN, FS, G, TT**)

WEIL, SAMUEL, was born on 23 February 1832 in *Lichtenberg*, Bas-Rhin, France, to **JOËL/JOSEPH WEIL**, a native of *Reichshoffen*, Bas-Rhin, France, and his wife **HENNELÉ MOSES**, also called **FRÉDÉRIQUE/IIINEL/RÉGINE HIRSCH/HERTZ**, born in *Rothbach*, Bas-Rhin. Since he appeared in the 1851 census for *Lichtenberg*, but not in the 1856 census for the same town, we believe that he immigrated between 1851 and 1856 to Louisiana following his brother, **NATHAN WEIL** (see entry). There is an entry for twenty-one-year-old Samuel Weil, a French national, who landed in New Orleans, Orleans Parish, LA, from Le Havre, France, on 23 January

1854 aboard the ship *Wurtemberg*, which may be a record of his arrival. He fought in the Civil War, serving as a private in Co. G, 3rd LA. Infantry, and was paroled in Shreveport, Caddo Parish, La, on 7 June 1865. He married **SARA MOCH** on 7 February 1866 in Caddo Parish. Sara was born on 2 September 1837 in *Mommenheim* Bas-Rhin, France, to **DANIEL MOCH**, a native of *Mommenheim*, and his wife, **JEANNE/HANNE KAHN**, born in *Niederbronn-les-Bains*, Bas-Rhin. Samuel was a merchant, and later a butcher in Shreveport. The couple had no children. Samuel died on 29 August 1897 and was buried in Hebrew Rest Cemetery #1 (Jewish Section of Oakland Cemetery). Sara followed on 10 May 1901 and was buried beside him. (**A, AN, B1851, E, G**)

WEIL/WEYL, SARA (*Bouxwiller*) See entry for **ISAAC LEVY** (*Marmoutier*)

WEIL, SARAH, was born **SORLÉ WEIL** on 22 February 1832 in *Ingwiller*, Bas-Rhin, France, to **SAMUEL WEIL**, a native of the town, and his wife, **CAROLINE OPPENHEIM**, born in *Haguenau*, Bas-Rhin. We believe that three of Sarah's brothers, **MARX**, **JACQUES/JACOB**, and **LEOPOLD WEIL** (See entries), preceded her to America. There is a ship's record for a twenty-one-year-old "Suzanne Weill," a French national, who arrived at New Orleans, Orleans Parish, La, on 30 December 1854 from Le Havre, France, aboard the ship *John Hancock* which is worthy of consideration. Sarah married AARON WOLF, a native of Speyer, Rheinpfalz, Germany ca. 1855, a record of which we have not been able to find. Aaron and Sarah were the parents of six children, all born in New Orleans: Elizabeth/Lisette (b. 1856), Fanny (b. 1858), Regina/Rachel (b. 1860), Pauline (b. 1863), Samuel (b. 1864), and Abraham (b. 1866). Aaron was a prosperous merchant, and before the Civil War, a slave owner, who had a crockery store on Magazine Street in New Orleans. Sarah Weil Wolf died on 21 December 1890 in New Orleans and was interred there in Hebrew Rest Cemetery #1. Ninety-three-year-old Aaron Wolf died on 19 October 1919 and was buried in the same cemetery. (**A, AN, G, GB, TT**)

WEIL SELIGMAN HENRI, "H.S.," was born **SELIGMAN WEIL** on 20 February 1886 in *Dambach-la-Ville*, Bas-Rhin, France, to **HENRI WEIL**, a native of the town, and his wife, CLÉMENTINE SCHILL, born in Neunkirch-lès-Sarreguemines, Moselle, France.

Seligman arrived in New York on 14 November 1908 aboard the SS *La Savoie* from Le Havre, France. He was listed on the passenger manifest as a twenty-two-year-old tailor, whose last address was in Sarreguemines, Germany. He traveled to New Orleans, Orleans Parish, LA, where he boarded with his uncle, **JONAS WEIL** (See entry). Seligman was granted U.S. citizenship in 1914 at New Orleans where he was working as a clerk in a clothing company. He registered for the World War I draft in 1918 at New Orleans where he was employed as a traveling salesman for Arthur A. Katten clothing manufacturers. When Seligman's uncle moved to Baton Rouge, East Baton Rouge Parish, LA, ca. 1920, he followed, and was enumerated there in the 1920 federal census as "H.S. Weil," a thirty-seven-year-old nephew in the household of Jonas Weil. He worked in Baton Rouge as a clerk at Rosenfeld Dry Goods Co., Ltd., where Jonas was secretary of the firm. Seligman left that same year for France, where he took up "temporary" residence in Paris. Attached to his *Dambach-la-Ville* birth record is a notation that he married MADELEINE ELIZABETH DUMARD on 23 December 1937. The couple fled Paris when it fell to the Nazi occupation in 1940 and sought refuge in the Limousin mountains at Ahun, Creuse, France. Seligman died there on 30 September 1942. He was buried at the Cimetière des Batignolles in Paris. (**A, AN, GN**)

WEIL, SIMON, was born **SIMON WEILL** on 23 March 1838 in *Bischheim*, Bas-Rhin, France, to **LEOPOLD WEILL**, a native of the town, and his wife, **SARA HAUSSER**, born in *Strasbourg*, Bas-Rhin. Fourteen-year-old Simon emigrated from Le Havre, France, arriving in New Orleans, Orleans Parish, LA, on 29 December 1854 aboard the ship *Suffolk*. We believe that he started his career in Mississippi, working as a peddler and occasionally as a clerk in mercantile establishments where he was enumerated as "S. Weil" in the 1860 federal census at Yazoo City, Yazoo Co., MS and Brownsville, Hinds Co., MS only a month apart in the fall of that year. Simon Weil paid federal taxes in 1864 at New Orleans, Orleans Parish, LA, where he was working as a retail dealer. A year later, in December 1865, he paid taxes as a retail dealer living in Vicksburg, Warren Co., MS. While in New Orleans he met his future wife, eighteen-year-old JANE M. PICARD, whose father, Henry, was a native of Colmar, Haut-Rhin, France. Simon took out a license to marry Jane on 13 June 1864 at New Orleans, where their only child, Caroline "Carrie" Weil, was born on 8 June 1865. The following year, Simon, his wife and child, along with his father-in-law, Henry Picard, and the latter's wife, Henrietta

Markstein, moved to Bayou Sara, West Feliciana Parish. Simon and Henry opened a wholesale and retail establishment known as Picard & Weil at Bayou Sara. The two families were enumerated living next door to one another there in both the 1870 and 1880 federal censuses. Simon was naturalized in West Feliciana Parish, LA, on 12 March 1872. Simon, a respected merchant at Bayou Sara for eighteen years, died there on 26 April 1884. He was interred in New Orleans at Hebrew Rest Cemetery #1. Henry Picard remained in Bayou Sara until his retirement from business in 1889. Simon's widow, Jane Picard Weil, married JULIUS PICARD, a New York native, on 11 May 1886 in West Feliciana Parish. Henry Picard was enumerated in New Orleans in the 1900 federal census with his daughter, Jane, her second husband, Julius, his granddaughter, Carrie, her husband, Albert Kaiser and Carrie's child from her first marriage, Gustave Levy Kaiser (aka. Gordon Kay). Jane's husband, Julius Picard started the New Orleans firm of Picard, Kaiser & Co, with his step-daughter Carrie Weil's second husband, Albert Henry Kaiser. Jane's father, Henry Picard, died in New Orleans on 24 June 1902 and was interred in Hebrew Rest Cemetery #1 in New Orleans. Julius Picard passed away less than a year later, on 13 April 1903 and was buried there as well. His widow, Jane, moved to Manhattan, New York ca. 1911, where she died on 22 March 1918. We have not been able to locate her place of burial(**A, AN, G, GB, TT**)

WEILL, ADRIEN, was born on 18 August 1903 in *Osthoffen*, Bas-Rhin, France, to **LEON WEILL**, whom we have not been able to trace, and his wife **HERMANCE**, née **WEILL**. She was born **HERMINE WEILL** on 8 March 1877 at *Schirrhoffen*, Bas-Rhin, France to **MICHEL WEILL**, a native of the town, and his wife, **SOPHIE WEILL**, born in *Westhoffen*, Bas-Rhin. Since Adrien was born at the beginning of the twentieth century we have taken his birth date, and names of his parents, from his 17 May 1927 naturalization record, filed at New Orleans, Orleans Parish, LA. Adrien and his brother **ROGER MARCEL WEILL** (See entry) immigrated to America, arriving in New York from Le Havre, France, on 21 January 1920 aboard the SS *Lafayette*. Adrien travelled to Lutcher, St. James Parish, LA with Roger to join their uncle, **JONAS WEILL** (b. 1878; See entry), at his dry goods store. Roger worked as the bookkeeper, and Adrien was a travelling salesman. Adrien relocated to Biloxi, Harrison Co., MS, where he spent the rest of his life. He started his career with a small shoe store and leveraged it into a large business which enabled him to invest in real estate. He opened the first drive-in restaurant on the Mississippi coast, developed the first shopping center, and opened a drive-in theater. He was also a partner in the Avelez Hotel Corporation which owned the Avelez and Riviera Hotels on Biloxi Beach. He married JEANNETTE DEES, an Alabama native, ca. 1936, a record for which we were unable to find. They were the parents of four children: Jolene (b. 1938), Jacqueline (b. 1940), Adrian Michael (b. 1943), and Donna Lynn (b. 1953). Adrien died on 21 February 1971 at Biloxi and was interred there at Southern Memorial Park. Jeannette died on 16 April 2002 at Biloxi and was buried with her husband. Note: Adrien's mother, sixty-nine-year-old Hermine Weill arrived at New York on 20 November 1946 from Cherbourg, France aboard the SS *Ile-de-France*. She died at Biloxi on 5 January 1947 and was buried there in the Biloxi City Cemetery. (**A, AN, G, GB**)

WEILL, ARTHUR GASTON, was born on 1 July 1845 in *Strasbourg*, Bas-Rhin, France, to **DAVID WEILL** and his wife, **SOPHIE CERF**, both natives of *Strasbourg*. Arthur Weill arrived in New York on 8 August 1864 from Liverpool, England, aboard the *City of London*. He apparently made his way south into West Feliciana Parish, LA, during some of the heaviest fighting in the War Between the States. In an 1890 Veteran's Schedule for West Feliciana Parish, he was shown to have enlisted in 1865 to fight for the Confederacy, and discharged the same year at the end of hostilities. He may have spent several years in New Orleans where he opted for French citizenship on 4 July 1872 at the conclusion of the Franco-Prussian War. Afterwards he returned to St. Francisville, West Feliciana Parish, where he was naturalized on 24 March 1876 as Arthur Gaeton [*sic*] Weill. He remained in St. Francisville for the rest of his life. He worked as a clerk in a store and never married. Arthur Weill died on 26 January 1902 in St. Francisville and was buried there in Hebrew Rest Cemetery. (**A, AN, G, TT**)

WEILL, BLANCHE, (*Schirrhoffen*) See entry for **JULES/JULIUS WEILL**

WEILL, CAROLINE, (*Bischheim*) See pages 27-40

WEILL, CÉLINE, was born **CELESTINE WEILL** on 23 March 1889 in *Schirrhoffen*, Bas-Rhin, France, to **CHARLES WEILL** and his wife, **EMILIE KAHN**, both natives of the town. She immigrated to

America, arriving in New York on 30 August 1910 from Bremen, Germany, aboard the SS *Kaiser Wilhelm II,* with her older sister **PAULINE WEILL** (See entry). Their brother, **JACOB WEILL** (See entry) met them in New York and brought them by train to Louisiana. Céline stayed with Jacob until her marriage to JULIAN KAHN, a native of Rayne, Acadia Parish, LA, on 1 March 1917 in Rayne. The couple had one daughter, Fleurette, born in 1918. Julian kept a general store, and, in later years, owned and operated a hardware store in the town of his birth. Julian and Céline both died at Rayne, he on 22 November 1959 and she, on 29 January 1985. We have not been able to locate a place of burial for the couple. **(A, AN, G, TT)**

WEILL, CHARLES, was born on 1 March 1851 in *Schirrhoffen*, Bas-Rhin, France, to **ABRAHAM WEILL,** a native of the town, and his second wife, **EMILIE/ELISA WEILL**, whose birthplace we were unable to find. He may have been the twenty-one-year-old Charles Weill who arrived in New York on 6 August 1872 from Le Havre, France, aboard the SS *Russia*. He settled in Donaldsonville, Ascension Parish, LA, near his half-sister **MARIE ANNE WEILL** Tobias (See entry). Twenty-six-year-old Charles Weill died on 25 October 1878 in Ascension Parish, at the end of one of the most deadly epidemics of yellow fever ever to visit the area. He was buried in Bikur Sholim Jewish Cemetery in Donaldsonville. **(A, AN, G)**

WEILL, FANNY, was born on 3 July 1879 in *Schirrhoffen*, Bas-Rhin, France, to **CHARLES WEILL** and his wife, **EMILIE KAHN**, both natives of the town. Fanny's brother, **JULES WEILL** (See entry), returned to France to bring her back to Louisiana. They arrived in New York from Le Havre, France, aboard the SS *La Lorraine* on 29 August 1903. Fanny settled in Napoleonville, Assumption Parish, LA, where Jules was living at the time. Fanny married HERMAN WEISS, a native of Ungvar, Hungary (now Uzhorod, Ukraine) on 28 February 1907 in Bunkie, Avoyelles Parish, LA, where the groom was a local merchant, associated with his brothers, Joe and Sam, and father, Martin Weiss. Shortly after the wedding, he moved his bride to Robeline, Natchitoches Parish, LA, where he opened up a dry goods store. They were the parents of two sons: Mervin (b. 1907) and Charles (b. 1912). After Charles's birth in Robeline, Herman moved his family to Alexandria, Rapides Parish, LA, where he operated a dry goods store independently of his brothers, who owned Weiss Bros. and Weiss & Goldring in the same town. Herman died on 31 August 1937 in

Alexandria, and was buried in the Jewish Cemetery in Pineville, Rapides Parish, LA. Fanny followed her sons, Mervin and Charles, to New York where they had gone to work for their cousin, David Weiss, at Weiss Bros., Inc., a national chain headquartered in Manhattan. Fanny died in Forest Hills, Queens, New York, on 1 July 1964. We were not able to locate her final resting place. (**A, AN, TT**)

WEILL, FELIX, was born on 19 May 1881 in *Schirrhoffen*, Bas-Rhin, France, to **CHARLES WEILL** and his wife, **EMILIE KAHN**, both natives of the town. Sixteen-year-old Felix Weill arrived in New York from Le Havre, France, on 4 September 1897 aboard the SS *La Touraine*. He followed his brothers, **JACOB**, **JONAS**, and **JULES WEILL** (See entries), to Louisiana, where they all worked for a short time in Atchafalaya, St. Martin Parish, LA. Eighteen-year-old Felix died at Rosa, St. Landry Parish, LA, from typhoid fever on 29 September 1899. His body was taken to the Jewish Cemetery in Opelousas, St. Landry Parish, where it was interred. (**A, AN, TT**)

WEILL, FELIX, was born **FELIX WEIL** on 13 November 1888 in *Brumath*, Bas-Rhin, France, to **BENJAMIN WEIL**, a native of the town, and his wife RÉGINE KAUFFMANN, born in Malsh, Baden-Württemberg, Germany. Felix immigrated to America with his brother **JULES/JULIUS JOSEPH WEILL** (See entry), arriving in New York from Le Havre, France, on 23 April 1904 aboard the SS *La Savoie*. He took up residence in Napoleonville, Assumption Parish, LA, and worked as a clerk in the firm of M. Levy, Inc. He married JULIA LEVY, a native of Galveston, Galveston Co., TX, ca. 1916, a record for which we were unable to find. The couple's only child, Felice Rose was born in 1919 in Galveston. In 1924 Félix made a trip home to Alsace to visit his relatives, indicating that he had lived continuously for twenty years in Napoleonville. Upon his return, he moved his family back to his wife's home town, where he became the manager of an upholstery company. He died in Galveston on 5 May 1933 and was buried in the local Hebrew Benevolent Society Cemetery. His wife died twenty years later on 11 February 1953 and was buried with him. (**A, AN, G**)

WEILL, GUSTAVE "GUS," was born **GODCHAUX WEILL** on 20 November 1864 in *Schirrhoffen*, Bas-Rhin, France, to **JOSEPH WEILL**, a native of the town, and his wife **SARA SAMUEL**, born in *Trimbach*, Bas-Rhin. He immigrated to Louisiana, sailing on board the

SS *La France* which arrived in New York on 3 November 1882. He was listed on the passenger manifest as "Gottchard Weil." Gustave or "Gus" as he was familiarly known in Louisiana, started out in St. James Parish, LA, but soon relocated to White Castle, Iberville Parish, LA, where he operated a dry goods store. He married HERMINA WEIL, a native of Grünstadt, Germany, on 10 December 1890 in New Orleans, Orleans Parish, LA. Four children were born to the couple in White Castle: Ray (b. 1892), Julius (b. 1893), Bernice (b. 1898; later the wife of **LEOPOLD WEILL** - See entry), and Lester Isaac (b. 1899; died 1918). Five years before his death, the couple retired to Baton Rouge, East Baton Rouge Parish, LA, where Guss (usual spelling) died on 22 November 1925. He was interred next to his son Lester in Bikur Sholim Jewish Cemetery in Donaldsonville, Ascension Parish, LA. Gus Weill's original store at White Castle became one of a chain of thirteen South Louisiana department stores, which included Weill's Department Store at New Roads, Pointe Coupée Parish, LA, in operation there on West Main Street from 1936-1963. The store was relocated to the New Roads Shopping Center on Olinde Street where it closed in 1985. His chain of stores was later purchased by the Bart-Well Corporation of Baton Rouge. Hermina died on 18 November 1933 at her daughter's home in Donaldsonville, and was buried with her husband and son. (**A, AN, BC, G, GB, TT**)

WEILL, HANNAH/HENRIETTE, was born **HARIETE WEIL** on 17 June 1838 in *Schirrhoffen*, Bas-Rhin, France, to **ABRAHAM WEILL**, a native of the town, and his first wife, **BARBE/BRIGITTE LEVY,** born in *Drachenbronn*, Bas-Rhin. Hannah married **SAMUEL NETTER**, also a native of *Schirrhoffen* on 31 October 1868. Samuel was the son of **ELIE NETTER**, a native of *Bouxwiller*, Bas-Rhin, France, and his second wife, **SARA KLEIN,** born in *Niederroedern*, Bas-Rhin. Seventy-one-year-old Hannah/Henriette Netter followed her son, **EMILE NETTER** (See entry), to America, arriving on 21 September 1909 at New York, from Bremen, Germany, aboard the SS *Kaiser Wilhelm II*. She settled in Lutcher, St. James Parish, LA, with him. Henriette died there on 15 January 1913, and was buried with her sister, **MARIE ANNE WEILL** (See entry), in Bikur Sholim Jewish Cemetery in Donaldsonville, Ascension Parish, LA. (**A, AN, G**)

WEILL, HERMINE, (*Schirrhoffen*) See entry for **ADRIEN WEILL**

WEILL, JACOB, was born on 20 October 1875 in *Schirrhoffen*, Bas-Rhin, France, to **CHARLES WEILL** and his wife, **EMILIE KAHN**, both natives of the town. He followed his brother, **JULES WEILL** (See entry), to America, arriving in New York from Le Havre, France, on 10 August 1890, aboard the SS *La Gascogne*. He started his career with his half grand-uncle, **LEOPOLD GOUDCHAUX** (See entry), in Big Cane, St. Landry Parish, LA. From there he moved on to Atchafalaya, St. Martin Parish, LA, where he worked with his brothers, **FELIX** and **JONAS WEILL** (See entries), until the former's death in 1899. He returned to Big Cane to work as a merchant, having met his future wife, MAE WOLFF, at the funeral of his brother, Felix, the year before. Mae was a native of nearby Washington, St. Landry Parish, LA. The couple married on 6 January 1909 at Washington. The bride's father, **LEON WOLFF** (See entry), was a relative of Leopold Goudchaux's good friend **SAMUEL CERF HAAS** (See entry) of Bayou Chicot, St. Landry Parish, LA. Jacob and Mae settled in Abbeville, Vermillion Parish, LA, near his brother **JULES WEILL** (See entry) where he was a dry goods merchant. Jacob and Mae had two daughters: Emilie (b. 1909) and Sara (b. 1914). Jacob died on 19 December 1957 in Abbeville, and was taken for burial to the Jewish Cemetery in Lafayette, Lafayette Parish, LA. Mae died on 10 October 1968 in Baton Rouge, East Baton Rouge Parish, LA, at the home of her daughter Sara Kantrow. She was buried with her husband in the Lafayette Jewish Cemetery. (**A, AN, G, GB, TT**)

WEILL, JONAS, was born on 7 September 1877 in *Schirrhoffen*, Bas-Rhin, France, to **CHARLES WEILL** and his wife, **EMILIE KAHN**, both natives of the town. His naturalization record, witnessed by his brother Jacob and brother-in-law Samuel Weiss, showed that he had immigrated to Louisiana in October 1892. We believe however that he was the sixteen-year-old Jonas Weill who arrived in New York on 27 November 1893 from Le Havre, France, aboard the SS *La Bretagne*. Like his brothers before him, he started out in Louisiana in the employ of his half grand-uncle, **LEOPOLD GOUDCHAUX** (See entry), in Big Cane, St. Landry Parish, LA. He joined his brothers, **JACOB** and **FELIX WEILL** (See entries), a few years later to work in Atchafalaya, St. Martin Parish, LA. Shortly thereafter he and Jacob joined their sister **FANNY WEILL** (See entry) and her husband, Samuel Weiss, in Abbeville, Vermillion Parish, La, where Jonas was naturalized in October 1892. Jonas returned to Big Cane, and was enumerated there in the 1900 federal census. After the death of his brother Felix in 1899, he returned to Abbeville, to join his brother, **JULES WEILL** (See entry). Jonas met, **GERTRUDE SOKOLOSKI**, a local girl of German ancestry. They were married on 29 January 1908 in Abbeville at the local hotel. Jonas and Gertrude were the parents of five sons: Carl (b. 1911), Herbert (b. 1913), Leonard (b. 1915), Robert (b. 1918), and William (b. 1921; died 1944 in Italy, a casualty of WWII). Jonas was a planter, cotton broker, and later the superintendent of a cotton gin in his adopted town. He died on 4 August 1963 in Abbeville. His wife followed on 5 October 1971. They were buried in the Jewish Cemetery in Lafayette, Lafayette Parish, LA. (**A, AN, GB, TT**)

WEILL, JONAS, was born on 3 December 1878 in *Schirrhoffen*, Bas-Rhin, France, to **MICHEL WEILL**, a native of the town, and his wife, **SOPHIE WEIL**, born in *Westhoffen*, Bas-Rhin. Sixteen-year-old Jonas Weill immigrated to New York, arriving from Hamburg, Germany, accompanied by his twenty-five-year-old brother, **LEON WEILL** (See entry), on 9 November 1895 aboard the SS *Patria.* He joined Leon and another brother, **JULIUS WEILL** (See entry), in Burnside, Ascension Parish, LA, where they operated a general merchandise store and a ginnery. Jonas remained in Burnside until after World War I, after which he moved to Lutcher, St. James Parish, LA, where his brother, Julius, had relocated previously. He opened a dry goods store in partnership with William Venus, his brother Julius's former clerk. In 1920 he welcomed two nephews, sons of his sister, **HERMANCE/ HERMINE WEILL,** and her husband, **LEON WEILL**, to Louisiana. **ROGER MARCEL** and **ADRIEN WEILL** (See entries), joined Jonas in business in Lutcher. Roger worked as the bookkeeper at the store, and Adrian was a travelling salesman. Jonas retired from business ca. 1940, and went to live in New Orleans, Orleans Parish, with his brother Julius Weill's widow, **BERTHA LEVY**. He died in New Orleans on 23 May 1942 and was buried in Hebrew Rest Cemetery #1 in the city. He never married. (**A, AN, GB**)

WEILL, JOSEPHINE, was born on 15 May 1868 in *Schirrhoffen*, Bas-Rhin, France, to **CHARLES WEILL** and his wife, **EMILIE KAHN**, both natives of the town. She came to Louisiana ca. 1891, a record of which we were unable to find, to be married to her half first cousin once removed, JACOB LEHMAN GOUDCHAUX, born in Big Cane, St. Landry Parish, LA. They were wed on 25 March 1892 at the Opelousas Courthouse in Opelousas, St. Landry Parish, LA. Jacob started out as a merchant in Big Cane, working with his father,

LEOPOLD GOUDCHAUX (See entry).Three children were born to the couple: Charlotte "Lottie" (b. 1893), Callie (b. 1896; died 1898) and Eugene Weill (b. 1899). Jacob later moved the family to Bunkie, Avoyelles Parish, LA, then to Lake Charles, Calcasieu Parish, LA, where he owned a drugstore, and finally back to St. Landry Parish, to the town of Lemoyne where he owned a farm. Jacob died there on 20 January 1937 and was buried in the Jewish Cemetery in Opelousas. Josephine died on 25 August 1939 at Rayne, Acadia Parish, LA, and was buried with her husband in Opelousas. (**A, AN, TT**)

WEILL, JULES, was born **JUDAS WEIL** on 11 December 1820 in *Haguenau*, Bas-Rhin, France, to **BARUCH WEIL**, a male nurse and resident of the town, and his wife, **PHILIPPINE ROOS/ROSE** (**FEGELE** before 1808), born in *Haguenau*, Bas-Rhin. By 1836 the family had disappeared from the town census for *Haguenau* taken that year, and may have moved on to Paris. Jules Weill married **HANNAH/HARRIET/HENRIETTE FRANCK** ca. 1840, a record of which we have not been able to find. Hannah was born **HANA FRANCK** on 4 April 1819 in *Soultz-sous-Fôrets*, Bas-Rhin, France, to **AUSCHER ELIAS** (also called **DOTTERLÉ**) **FRANCK**, and his wife **ZIBORA WEIL**, both natives of the town. Three of their first four children were known to have been born in France, Rachel (b. 1841), Pauline (b. 1846 at Paris, Ile-de-France, France), and David Theodore (b. 1848 at Paris, Ile-de-France, France). Three of Hannah's siblings had preceded her to Louisiana. **MICHEL FRANCK** (See entry) arrived in 1843 and settled in Clinton, East Feliciana Parish, LA. **MATILDA/MADELEINE FRANCK** (See entry) arrived in 1846, married Gabriel Brown and settled in Iberville Parish, LA. **JACOB FRANCK** (See entry) left for Louisiana in 1847 and settled in St. Helena Parish, LA. Although we have been unable to find a ship's record for the Jules Weill family, they first appeared in the 1850 federal census for Iberville Parish, LA. They were enumerated there in the household of twenty-four-year-old Gabriel Brown, a merchant from Prussia and his wife "Madam Brown," better known as Matilda Franck, Hannah's sister. Thirty-year-old merchant, Jules Weil, his twenty-eight-year-old wife Harriet, and children, nine-year-old Rachel, four-year-old Pauline, two-year-old David, and one-year-old Matilda, were all said to be from France. Jules was employed as a grocer. Matilda does not appear in any subsequent census records and may have died as a baby. At least two more children were born to the couple in Iberville Parish: Abraham (b. 1852), and Rosalie (b. 1856). Jules Weil died on

25 May 1859 at Plaquemine, Iberville Parish, LA, and was buried there in the Jewish Cemetery. Hannah continued to keep the grocery store after her husband's death, where her son David was working as a clerk as early as 1860. Hannah, her children David, Abraham, and Rosalie were enumerated again in 1870 in Plaquemine. Hannah was still running the grocery with the help of her sons, twenty-two-year-old David and sixteen-year-old Abraham. Her married daughter, Pauline, was living nearby with her husband, **LEON LEVY**, a meat vendor, and their three children, Henrietta (b. 1864), Rosalie (b. 1866), and Jules (b. 1868). Hannah relocated to Clinton, East Feliciana Parish, LA, perhaps as early as 1873. Her late brother **JACOB/JACQUES FRANCK** had once lived there and was buried there in the Jewish Cemetery. Her daughter, Rosalie Weill, who had married **ISAAC STARN** ca. 1873, had died at Clinton, a year later, weeks shy of her nineteenth birthday and was also buried in the Clinton Jewish Cemetery. Hannah was enumerated in Clinton in the 1880 federal census with her daughter Pauline Weill Levy, who was working as a seamstress, son Abraham Weill, who was clerking in a store, and her three Levy grandchildren. Hannah's son, David T. Weill and his wife Ada Oppenheimer had also settled at Clinton and were enumerated there with their children in 1880. Hannah died at Clinton on 1 September 1885 and was interred in the Clinton Jewish Cemetery. Her son, Abraham, survived his mother by only two months, dying on 4 November 1885. He was interred at Clinton as well. (**A, AN, G, GB, L, TT**)

WEILL, JULES, was born **JOSUÉ WEILL** on 9 October 1869 in *Schirrhoffen*, Bas-Rhin, France, to **CHARLES WEILL** and his wife, **EMILIE KAHN**, both natives of the town. He immigrated to Louisiana, arriving in New Orleans, Orleans Parish, LA, from Le Havre, France, on 26 March 1888 aboard the SS *La Gascogne*. He got his start with his half grand-uncle, **LEOPOLD GOUDCHAUX** (See entry), at Big Cane, St. Landry Parish, LA. He spent some time in St. John the Baptist Parish as a merchant, then moved on to Napoleonville, Assumption Parish, where he applied for a passport to return to France for a few months. Upon his return, he married BELLA BADT, a Texas native of Polish and German extraction, on 12 January 1904 in New Orleans, Orleans Parish, LA. Their first child, Henry Badt Weill, was born in White Castle, Iberville Parish, LA. The family finally settled down in Abbeville, Vermillion Parish, LA, where Jules owned a dry goods store. Four more children were born to the couple: Esther (b.

1908), Emeline (b. 1912), Freda (b. 1915), and Mathilde (b. 1919). Jules also ran a stable and was a horse dealer in Abbeville. He died in Abbeville on 20 December 1950, and was buried in the Jewish Cemetery in Lafayette, Lafayette Parish, LA. Bella died on 1 April 1962 and was interred with him. Note: See entries for his siblings: **JOSEPHINE, JACOB, JONAS, FANNY, PAULINE, CÉLINE MARGUERITE,** and **FELIX WEILL**) (A, AN, G, GB, TT)

WEILL, JULES/JULIUS, was born **JULIUS JOSEPH WEILL** on 15 August 1887 in *Brumath*, Bas-Rhin, France, to **BENJAMIN WEIL,** a native of the town, and his wife RÉGINE KAUFFMANN, born in Malsh, Baden-Württemberg, Germany. Jules immigrated to America with his brother **FELIX WEILL** (See entry), arriving in New York from Le Havre, France, aboard the SS *La Savoie* on 23 April 1904. He settled in Baton Rouge, East Baton Rouge Parish, LA, where he was enumerated in the 1910 federal census working as a clerk in a store. Jules registered for the World War I draft in 1917 at Kenner, Jefferson Parish, LA, and stated that he was unmarried and employed as a clerk in the Felix & Bloch mercantile store, which had been opened in the late nineteenth century by **REBECCA KAUFFMAN FELIX** (See entry for **MARX FELIX**). Jules married **BLANCHE WEILL** on 24 July 1919 in New Orleans, Orleans Parish, LA. Blanche was born **PAULINE WEILL** on 23 February 1890 in *Schirrhoffen*, Bas-Rhin, France, to **EUGENE/JONAS WEILL,** a native of the town, and his wife, **CAROLINE BECKER,** born in *Niederbronn-les-Bains*, Bas-Rhin. Blanche emigrated from Bremen, Germany to New York, arriving aboard the SS *Kaiser Wilhelm der Grosse* on 5 September 1906. She was sixteen years old and accompanied by her uncle, **GUSTAVE/GUS WEILL** (See entry), his wife and children. She went with her uncle's family back to White Castle, Iberville, Parish, LA, where she was enumerated with them in the 1910 federal census. After his marriage to Blanche, Jules Weill went to work as a clerk in a department store in White Castle, LA, where he and his bride were enumerated together in the 1920 federal census. They were the parents of a daughter, Rae Caroline, born in August 1920. Ten years later the family had relocated to Leesville, Vernon Parish, LA, where Jules was employed as a dealer in hides. By 1940 they had moved to Natchez, Adams Co., MS, where Jules was running a retail ladies ready to wear shop. His wife worked with him in the store as a saleslady. Blanche died in Natchez on 27 November 1967 and was buried in the Jewish section of the Natchez City Cemetery. Jules died in Natchez on 31 July

1968 and was buried with her. Note: Blanche's mother, Caroline Becker was the sister of **NATHAN BECKER** (See entry), a longtime resident of White Castle, LA. (**A, AN, TT**)

WEILL, JULIUS, was born on 4 February 1875 in *Schirrhoffen*, Bas-Rhin, France, to **MICHEL WEILL**, a native of *Schirrhoffen*, Bas-Rhin, and his wife, **SOPHIE WEIL**, born in *Westhoffen*, Bas-Rhin. He immigrated to America, arriving in New York on 8 September 1890 aboard the SS *La Champagne* to join his brother, **LEON WEILL** (See entry), in Burnside, Ascension Parish, LA. He relocated to Lutcher, St. James Parish, LA, before 1900 where his aunt **HENRIETTE WEILL NETTER** (See entry) was living. Julius opened up a grocery store there, remaining in Lutcher through the 1920s. He married **BERTHA LEVY** a native of *Marckolsheim*, Bas-Rhin, France on 15 May 1911 in Manhattan, New York. Bertha was born on 14 February 1889, to **DAVID LEVY**, and his wife **PAULINE**, née, **LEVY,** residents of the town, about whom we have no more information. According to what was written in the 1920 federal census Bertha immigrated to Louisiana in 1911, the same year as her marriage. Twenty-two-year-old "Berthe Levy" arrived in New York on 25 March 1911 from Le Havre, France, aboard the SS *La Savoie*. Her town of birth, *Marckolsheim*, and her father's name "David Levy," also appeared on the passenger manifest to identify her. Since Julius had gone back to France, having applied for a U.S. passport in May 1910, we believe that the marriage had been arranged at that time. After their New York wedding, the couple returned to Lutcher where their three children were born: Leon (b. 1912), Aline (b. 1913), and Sylvia (b. 1922). They moved permanently to New Orleans, Orleans Parish, LA ca. 1925, where Julius owned a dry goods store. He died on 22 February 1937 and was buried in Hebrew Rest Cemetery #1 in New Orleans. His widow, Bertha Weill was enumerated in the 1940 federal census in New Orleans. She was living with her unmarried children, Leon, a dealer in furs, and Sylvia. Also enumerated in the household was her sixty-year-old brother-in-law, Jonas Weill, who had retired from business. Bertha died on 29 August 1972, and was buried in Hebrew Rest Cemetery # 1 with her husband. Note: Their tombstone in Hebrew Rest shows their accurate dates and places of birth. (**A, AN, G, GB, I**)

WEILL, LEON, was born on 11 August 1870 in *Westhoffen*, Bas-Rhin, France, to **MICHEL WEILL**, a native of *Schirrhoffen*, Bas-Rhin, and his wife, **SOPHIE WEIL**, born in *Westhoffen*. Sixteen-year-old Leon Weill emigrated from Le Havre, France, arriving in New York on 13 September 1886 aboard the SS *Normandie*. He settled in Burnside, Ascension Parish, LA, near his aunts, **HENRIETTE WEILL NETTER** and **MARIE ANNE WEILL TOBIAS** (See entries). Leon was joined by his brother, **JULIUS WEILL** (See entry), where they worked together as merchants and planters in Burnside. Leon and later, Jonas, also operated a public cotton gin in the parish, under the name of Leon Weill & Bro. Leon made three trips back to Alsace to visit relatives. On the second, in 1895, he brought his young sixteen-year-old brother, **JONAS WEILL** (See entry), back with him. He went back to France for the last time, in 1902. On 27 March 1903, while superintending the work in the cotton gin, he got hopelessly tangled in the machinery. His brothers and a local physician rushed him to Hotel Dieu Hospital in New Orleans, Orleans Parish, LA, where he died the next day. He was buried in Hebrew Rest Cemetery # 1 in New Orleans. (Note: Burnside was one of the closest settlements to Tezcuco Plantation.) **(A, AN, GB)**

WEILL, LEOPOLD, was born on 24 June 1885 in *Schirrhoffen*, Bas-Rhin, France, to **CHARLES WEILL** and his wife, **EMILIE KAHN**, both natives of the town. Twenty-year-old Leopold immigrated to the United States, arriving in New York on 13 August 1905, accompanied by his thirty-year-old brother **JACOB WEILL** (See entry), aboard the SS *Etruria* from Liverpool, England. Jacob and Leopold returned to Abbeville, Vermillion Parish, LA where the former had settled. Leopold subsequently took a job as a salesman in a store in Donaldsonville, Ascension Parish, LA. Several years later he moved permanently to Lafayette, Lafayette Parish, LA. He married BERNICE WEILL, a native of White Castle, Iberville Parish, LA, on 25 June 1919 at the Hotel Gruenwald (now Hotel Roosevelt) in New Orleans. The couple returned to Lafayette where Leopold was a livestock dealer. Four children were born to them: Emelie L. (b. 1921), Ray S. (b. 1924), Leopold, Jr. (b. 1925), and Gus (b. 1934). Leopold later went into the real estate business and was one of the developers of Bendel Gardens, a high-end subdivision in Lafayette. Both father and son were active in politics. Gus Weill later became the executive secretary to Louisiana Governor John McKeithen (1964 -72). Leopold died in Lafayette on 23 November 1964. Bernice followed on 1 August 1983. They were buried together in the Jewish Cemetery in Lafayette. **(A, AN, GB, TT)**

WEILL, MARGUERITE, was born **MARGARETHA WEILL** on 22 April 1891 in *Schirrhoffen*, Bas-Rhin, France, to **CHARLES WEILL** and his wife, **EMILIE KAHN**, both natives of the town. Twenty-one-year-old Marguerite immigrated as "Margareta Weill," arriving in New York from Bremen, Germany, on 3 September 1912 aboard the SS *Grosser Kurfurst*. Her destination was Abbeville, Vermillion Parish, La, to join her brothers, **JULES** and **JACOB WEILL** (See entries). She married ARNOLD KAHN, a native of Rayne, Acadia Parish, LA, on 30 November 1919, in his hometown. Arnold was a druggist who owned and operated his own pharmacy. Two children were born to the couple: Alfred Karl (b. 1921) and Emelie Marion (b. 1925). Marguerite died on 13 October 1947 in Rayne, and was interred in the Jewish Cemetery in Lafayette, Lafayette Parish, LA. Arnold married a second time, to Lizzie C. Cherry, in 1958. He died on 17 July 1973 in Rayne, and was buried with his first wife in the Jewish Cemetery in Lafayette. (**A, AN, G, TT**)

WEILL, MARIE ANNE was born on 3 February 1831 in *Schirrhoffen*, Bas-Rhin, France, to **ABRAHAM WEILL** a native of the town and his wife **BARBE/BRIGITTE LEVY** born in *Drachenbronn,* Bas-Rhin. Marie Anne immigrated to Louisiana in the 1850s, a record for which we were unable to find. She married MAAS/MOSES TOBIAS, a Polish immigrant ca. 1856, also a record which is not available. The couple settled in Donaldsonville, Ascension Parish, LA, where Maas opened a dry goods and grocery business. The couple raised six children there: Sylvan (b. 1857), Jonas (b. 1860), Michel (b. 1865), Bertha (b. 1866), Jasmin (b. 1868) and Adela (b. 1869). Marie Anne died in Donaldsonville on 9 February 1887 and was buried there in the Bikur Sholim Jewish Cemetery. Maas Tobias died on 10 October 1891 and was buried with his wife. Note: Goldie, daughter of Sylvan Tobias, married **PAUL KAHN** (See entry**).** See also the entry for **SAMUEL NETTER**, husband of Mary Anne's sister, **HENRIETTE WEILL. (A, AN, G)**

WEILL, PAULINE, (*Schirrhoffen*) See entry for **NATHAN BECKER.**

WEILL, PAULINE, was born on 7 November 1887 in *Schirrhoffen*, Bas-Rhin, France, to **CHARLES WEILL** and his wife, **EMILIE KAHN**, both natives of the town. She accompanied her sister **CÉLINE WEILL** (See entry), arriving in New York from Bremen, Germany, on

30 August 1910 aboard the SS *Kaiser Wilhelm II*. Her brother, **JACOB WEILL** (See entry), met them in New York, and they took the train to Louisiana. She stayed with her brother, **JULES WEILL** (See entry), in Abbeville, Acadia Parish, LA, until her marriage ca. 1917 to JACK LEAVY, a native of Great Britain, who had settled in Texas and worked as a travelling salesman. The couple settled in Beaumont, Jefferson Co., TX, where Jack filled out a World War I Draft Registration Card in 1918. They moved back to Lafayette, Lafayette Parish, LA, before 1930 where they opened up a millinery shop, which soon closed. They were enumerated in Port Neches, Jefferson Co., TX, at the time of the 1940 federal census. Jack owned a retail dry goods store where he and his wife both worked. The couple never had children. Pauline died in Rayne, Acadia Parish, LA, on 24 July 1952 and was buried in the Jewish Cemetery in Lafayette, Lafayette Parish, LA. Jack died on 9 March 1968 in Waco, McLennan Co., TX, where he had been living for a little over two years. His remains were returned to the Lafayette Jewish Cemetery to be interred next to those of his wife. (**A, AN, G, TT**)

WEILL, ROGER MARCEL, was born on 2 July 1902 in *Osthoffen*, Bas-Rhin, France, to **LEON WEILL**, whom we have not been able to trace, and his wife **HERMANCE**, née **WEILL**. She was born **HERMINE WEILL** (See entry for **ADRIEN WEILL**) on 8 March 1877 at *Schirrhoffen*, Bas-Rhin, France, to **MICHEL WEILL**, a native of the town, and his wife, **SOPHIE WEILL**, born in *Westhoffen*, Bas-Rhin. Since Roger was born at the beginning of the twentieth century we have taken his birth date, and names of his parents, from his 19 May 1927 naturalization record, filed at New Orleans, Orleans Parish, LA. Roger and his brother Adrien Weill immigrated to America, arriving in New York from Le Havre, France, on 21 January 1920 aboard the SS *Lafayette*. Roger travelled to Lutcher, St. James Parish, LA, with Adrien to join their uncle, **JONAS WEILL** (b. 1878; See entry), at his dry goods store. Roger worked as the bookkeeper, and Adrien was a travelling salesman. Roger and Adrien relocated permanently to Biloxi, Harrison Co., MS, ca. 1930. Roger was the proprietor of a men's clothing store there. He married AGNES BROUSSARD, a native of Jeanerette, Iberia Parish, LA, ca. 1936 in Mississippi. They were the parents of three children: Leon J (b. 1937), Sonja Rose (b. 1938), and Roger Marcel, Jr. (b. 1940). Roger died at Biloxi on 18 January 1988 and was interred there in Southern Memorial Park. Agnes died on 10 October 1996 at Biloxi and was interred with her husband. Note:

Roger's mother, sixty-nine-year-old Hermine Weill arrived at New York on 20 November 1946 from Cherbourg, France aboard the SS *Ile-de-France*. She died at Biloxi on 5 January 1947 and was buried there in the Biloxi City Cemetery (**A, AN, G, GB**)

WEILLER, DAVID, was born on 18 October 1861 in *Dauendorf*, Bas-Rhin, France, to **BARUCH WEILLER**, a native of the town, and his wife, **JEANNETTE/HENRIETTE BLUM**, born in *Rothbach*, Bas-Rhin. He immigrated to America from Le Havre, France, on the SS *St. Germain*, landing in New York on 18 July 1883. He journeyed to Louisiana and settled in Shreveport, Caddo Parish, LA, to be near his brother **FELIX WEILLER** (See entry). He married EDDAH BERNSTEIN, his brother Felix's wife's sister, on 12 February 1896 in Shreveport. The couple had no children. David worked as a dry goods merchant until his death on 25 May 1911 in Shreveport. He was buried there in Hebrew Rest Cemetery #2 (Texas Ave.). Eddah remarried five months later to HERMAN ABRAMS, a Prussian hat merchant. There were no children from that marriage either. Eddah died on 10 July 1938 in Shreveport, and was buried in Hebrew Rest Cemetery #2 (Texas Ave.) with her second husband, Herman, who had died on 12 June 1935. (**A, AN, G**)

WEILLER, FÉLIX, was born on 30 June 1854 in *Dauendorf*, Bas-Rhin, France, to **BARUCH WEILLER**, a native of the town, and his wife, **JEANNETTE/HENRIETTE BLUM**, born in *Rothbach*, Bas-Rhin. "F. Weiler" [*sic*], from *Dauendorf*, immigrated to America, arriving in New Orleans, Orleans Parish, LA, from Le Havre, France, on 14 October 1872 aboard the SS *Saxonia*. He settled in Shreveport, Caddo Parish, LA, where he worked as a dry goods merchant, and where he was naturalized on 20 April 1889. He married FLORENCE/FLORA BERNSTEIN, a native of Plaquemine, Iberville Parish, LA, in Shreveport, on 4 June 1879. They were the parents of one child, Eunice, born on 22 March 1880 in Shreveport. Flora Bernstein died on 1 April 1916 in Shreveport and was buried there in Hebrew Rest Cemetery #2 (Texas Ave.). Felix died on 4 December 1935 in Shreveport and was buried with her. (A, AN, G)

WEINMANN, JEANNETTE/HENRIETTE/HARRIET, (*Brumath*) See entries for **ARON LEDERMANN** and **FÉLIX CAHN**.

WEISS, LEOPOLD, was born **LÉOPOLD WEIS** on 19 July 1850 in *Ingwiller*, Bas-Rhin, France, to **SALOMON WEIS/WEISS** and **ADELE/JEANNETTE KLEIN**, both natives of the town. Léopold emigrated from Hamburg, Germany, to New York, arriving on 9 November 1870 aboard the SS *Thuringia*. He first appeared in Louisiana records in the 1880 federal census at Vermilionville (now Lafayette), Lafayette Parish, LA. Still unmarried, he was living in a boarding house and working locally as a merchant. He married ADELINE/ADA LEVY, a native of New Orleans, on 22 March 1882 in New Orleans, Orleans Parish, LA, where the family would spend the rest of their lives. Leopold and Ada had one child, Bertha, born in December 1882. Leopold started a clothing manufacturing business in New Orleans, specializing in men's shirts. He died on 27 October 1895 in New Orleans and was buried there in Hebrew Rest Cemetery #1. The business was taken over by his brother, **THÉOPHILE/THEODORE WEISS** (See entry), who had joined him in New Orleans from his home in Farmerville, Union Parish, LA. Leopold's widow, Ada, lived with her daughter Bertha and the latter's husband, David M. Davis, in New Orleans, until her death on 29 April 1943. She was interred with her husband in Hebrew Rest Cemetery #1. Note: Leopold Weiss and Ada Levy were first cousins once removed. Ada Levy was Jeannette Klein Weiss' sister, Sara Klein Levy's granddaughter. (**A, AN, TT**)

WEISS, THÉOPHILE/THEODORE, was born **THÉOPHILE WEISS** on 17 February 1857 in *Ingwiller*, Bas-Rhin, France, to **SALOMON WEIS/WEISS** and **ADELE/JEANNETTE KLEIN**, both natives of the town. He emigrated from Le Havre, France, to New York, arriving on 12 August 1873 aboard the SS *Pereire*. He took a job at Farmerville, Union Parish, LA, in the general store of DANIEL STEIN (See entry for **PAULINE BLUM**, wife of SIMON STEIN), where he worked as a clerk. Theodore, a name which he would use exclusively in Louisiana, was enumerated in the 1880 federal census as a twenty-three-year-old boarder in the household of Daniel Stein. (Note: His last name was misspelled as "Wise" in this census.). Theodore married LENA SILVERSTEIN, a Louisiana native, on 19 January 1882 at New Orleans, Orleans Parish, LA. The couple returned to Farmerville where their two children, Leon Charles (b. 1882) and Salomon (b. 1885) were born. Theodore was naturalized at Farmerville on 7 November 1882. The family moved to New Orleans, Orleans Parish, LA, ca. 1892, where Theodore's brother, **LEOPOLD WEISS** (See entry) had opened a shirt manufacturing business on Chartres

Street in the French Quarter. After his brother's death in 1895, Theodore took over the business and renamed it Theo Weiss & Co. He took on David Ettinger and Samuel Reisfeld as partners. Theodore and his family lived in a comfortable house in uptown New Orleans at #1731 Robert Street. Theodore's wife, Lena, died on 7 December 1926 at Clifton Springs, Ontario Co., NY, a location noted for its sulfur springs which was a popular health spa at the time. Her remains were returned to New Orleans where they were buried at Hebrew Rest Cemetery # 1. Theodore died on 18 August 1929 while visiting at Bethlehem, Grafton Co, NH. His remains were returned to New Orleans where they were interred with those of his wife. (**A, AN, GB**)

WELSCH, CAROLINE, was born on 21 September 1846 in *Schirrhoffen*, Bas-Rhin, France, to **GOTTLIEB WELSCH,** a native of the town (See entry), and his wife, **ROSALIE OPPENHEIM,** born in *Haguenau,* Bas-Rhin. Caroline immigrated with her parents to America, arriving in New Orleans, Orleans Parish, LA, on 26 October 1849 from Le Havre France, aboard the ship *Brunswick*. She married JACOB LEOPOLD, a native of Albisheim, Rheinpfalz, Germany, on 29 August 1865 in New Orleans, Orleans Parish, LA. Jacob was a dry goods merchant in New Orleans. Three children were born to the couple: Bertha (b. 1866), Isabelle (b. 1869) and Gustave (b. 1871). Caroline died on 12 April 1876 and was buried in Gates of Prayer Cemetery #2 (Joseph Street) in New Orleans. Her husband, Jacob, died on 26 January 1907 and was buried in the same cemetery. (**A, AN, G**)

WELSCH, CLAIRE/CLARA, (*Schirrhoffen*) See entry for **ISAAC HEYMANN.**

WELSCH, CLEMENTINE, was born on 14 February 1869 in *Schirrhoffen*, Bas-Rhin, France, to **ISAAK WELSCH** and his wife **HENRIETTE LEVY**, both natives of the town. Sixteen-year-old Clemetine Welsch immigrated to America, arriving in New York from Le Havre, France, on 20 August 1885 aboard the SS *Amérique*. She married SAM BENJAMIN, a Polish immigrant and they settled in Shreveport, Caddo Parish, LA, where their only child, Herbert, was born in 1898. Sam died three months after his son's birth. Clementine lived thereafter with her brother, **JACQUES "JACOB" WELSCH**, and other cousins from *Schirrhoffen*, in Port Allen, West Baton Rouge Parish and finally at Baton Rouge, East Baton Rouge Parish, LA, where she died on 28 October 1939. She was buried in the Jewish Cemetery in

Baton Rouge. Note: WELSCH is almost always spelled WELSH in American civil records. (**A, AN, F, G, GB, L**)

WELSCH, EMANUEL/MANNIE, was born **KAUFFMANN WELSCH** on 30 September 1872 in *Schirrhoffen*, Bas-Rhin, France, to **ISAAK WELSCH** and his wife **HENRIETTE LEVY**, both natives of the town. He immigrated to the United States as "Kauffman Welsch," arriving in New York on 12 August 1889 from Le Havre, France, aboard the SS *La Champagne* with his first cousin, **AARON LEVY** (See entry). Emanuel travelled to Galveston, Galveston Co., TX, where he worked for the firm of Levy & Welsh started by his uncle, **THÉOPHILE/GOTTLIEB WELSCH**. He appeared as "Mannie Welsh" in the 1896 *Galveston City Directory* as a boarder in the home of Joseph Levy, his uncle's business partner. Emanuel moved to Louisiana ca. 1897 in order to work for his brother **JACOB/ JACQUES WELSCH** (See entry) in Port Allen, West Baton Rouge Parish, LA, as a salesman for Welsh & Levy. He was naturalized as "Mannie Welsh" at Port Allen on 2 February 1904. Thirty-seven-year-old "Emanuel Welsh." was enumerated in the 1910 federal census for Port Allen in the household of his widowed sister, **CLEMENTINE WELSCH** BENJAMIN (See entry), and brother Jacques Welsh. Still unmarried, he was working as a clerk in the family's general store. In April 1912 while still living at Port Allen, he applied for a U.S. passport under the name of "Mannie Welsh" to return to France for two months. Nothing further is known of him. (**A, AN**)

WELSCH, FELIX, was born on 5 May 1841 in *Schirrhoffen*, Bas-Rhin, France, to **ARON WELSCH,** a native of the town, and his wife, **ELIZABETH HEYMANN**, born in *Haguenau*, Bas-Rhin. According to his 1897 application for a U.S. passport, Felix wrote that he immigrated to America from Liverpool, England, arriving on 28 July 1866. We were, however, not able to find a reliable record for him on ships arriving in New York or New Orleans. Felix married another *Schirrhoffen* resident, **MARIE HEYMANN,** born there on 28 February 1849 to **ISAAC HEYMANN** and his wife **SARA WELSCH**, both natives of the town. Marie is probably the same as "Marie Heymann" who immigrated to New York, arriving from Le Havre, France, on 14 December 1866 aboard the SS *William Penn.* Her marriage to Felix took place on 10 October 1868 in New Orleans, Orleans Parish, LA. They were the parents of twelve children: Isidore (b. 1868), Fannie (b. 1870), Rachel (b. 1872), Leopold (b. 1875), Henry

(b. 1876), Louis (b. 1878), Maurice/Moses (b. 1880), Pauline (b. 1882), Ella (b. 1884), Clara (b. 1885), Rosalie (b. 1889) and Jacob Joseph (b. 1894). Although he started out as a peddler in New Orleans, Felix eventually had clothing stores on Baronne Street, and then moved to Poydras Street where he went into partnership with his sons. Félix was in business in New Orleans for over thirty-five years. He died on 29 July 1909 in New Orleans and was buried there in Gates of Prayer Cemetery #2 (Joseph Street). His wife, Marie Heymann Welsch died on 10 June 1934 and was buried in the same cemetery. Note: With a few exceptions, the New Orleans Branch of this family retained the "c" in spelling the family name, unlike their Baton Rouge cousins. (**A, AN, G, GB**)

WELSCH, GOTTLIEB, was born **GOËTSCHEL WELSCH** on 9 March 1815 in *Schirrhoffen*, Bas-Rhin, France, to **SAMUEL WELSCH** and **MERLÉ/MARYANNE HEYMANN**, both natives of *Schirrhoffen*. He married **ROSALIE OPPENHEIM** on 8 July 1845 in *Schirrhoffen*. Rosalie was born on 16 September 1816 in *Haguenau*, Bas-Rhin, France, to **JOSEPH OPPENHEIM** and his wife, **JUDITH KAHN**, both natives of *Haguenau*. Gottlieb and Rosalie had one child, a daughter, **CAROLINE WELSCH** (See entry), born on 21 September 1846 in *Schirrhoffen*. Thirty-two-year-old Gottlieb Welsch immigrated with his thirty-two-year-old wife "Roseli," and their two-year-old daughter "Carolina," arriving in New Orleans, Orleans Parish, LA, on 26 October 1846 aboard the Ship *Brunswick* from Le Havre, France. They settled in New Orleans where Gottlieb was a junk dealer. Gottlieb Welsch was the sexton of the Gates of Prayer Synagogue, and during the great yellow fever epidemic of 1853 saw to forty-five burials of the 137 members that were struck down by the disease. Gottlieb died on 1 August 1870 in New Orleans and was buried there in Gates of Prayer Cemetery #2 (Joseph Street). Rosalie died on 5 August 1895 in New Orleans and was buried in the same cemetery. (**A, AN, G, GB**)

WELSCH, GOTTLIEB "GABE," was born **GODSCHAUX WELSCH** on 7 January 1846 in *Schirrhoffen*, Bas-Rhin, France, to **ARON WELSCH**, a native of the town, and his wife, **ELIZABETH HEYMANN**, born in *Haguenau*, Bas-Rhin. We were unable to find a reliable ship's record for his arrival in America. He was first enumerated in the 1880 federal census working as a clerk in the store owned by *Schirrhoffen* native, **HENRY COHN, JR.** (See entry) in Brusly Landing, West Baton Rouge Parish. He later moved to New

Orleans, Orleans Parish, LA, where he worked with his brother, **FELIX WELSCH** (See entry), as a clerk and salesman. Never married, he died on 1 September 1908 in New Orleans and was buried there in Gates of Prayer Cemetery #2 (Joseph Street). (**A, AN, G, GB**)

WELSCH, HANNAH, was born **HENRIETTE WELSCH** on 22 April 1836 in *Schirrhofen*, Bas-Rhin, France, to **ARON WELSCH**, a native of the town, and his wife, **ELIZABETH HEYMANN**, born in *Haguenau*, Bas-Rhin. Henriette was the sister of immigrants **GOTTLIEB** and **FÉLIX WELSCH** (See entries) She married CHARLES KAHN, a native of Heidelberg, Baden, Germany on 27 May 1862 in *Schirrhoffen*. They had four children all born in *Hatten*, Bas-Rhin, France, where Charles was working as a merchant: Léopold/Leon (b. 1867; See entry), Louis (b. 1868; See entry), Henry (b. 1870; See entry), and Fanny (b. 1874; See entry). Hannah followed her three sons to Louisiana, immigrating with her daughter Fanny ca. 1893, according to the 1910 federal census for Algiers, Orleans Parish, LA. We were unable to find a reliable record for their arrival. Hannah lived with her daughter, **FANNY KAHN** BODENGER (See entry), in Algiers until her death on 28 June 1914. She was buried in Gates of Prayer Cemetery #2 (Joseph Street) in New Orleans. (**A, AN, G, GB**)

WELSCH, HENRIETTE, was born **ELIZABETHE WELSCH** on 24 June 1823 in *Schirrhoffen*, Bas-Rhin, France, to **SAMUEL WELSCH** and **MERLÉ/MARYANNE HEYMANN**, both natives of *Schirrhoffen*. In 1836 she appeared in the *Schirrhoffen* census as twelve-year-old "Dousette Welsch." She did not appear in the 1841 census, when she would have been seventeen. At that age she could have been working in another town. We believe she is the same as "Henriette Welsch" who emigrated from Le Havre, France, on the Ship *Sharon,* arriving on 16 October 1849 at New Orleans, Orleans Parish, LA. She became the second wife of ABRAHAM SCHWARZSCHILD, a native of Germany. Abraham's first wife, Rosa, also a German native, died on 3 August 1853 in New Orleans. Although there is no marriage record available for Abraham, a New Orleans merchant, and Henriette Welsch, there are three birth records for their children: Mary (b. 2 December 1854), Caroline (b. 8 March 1856) and Fanny (b. 2 December 1857), the last record of which identified Henriette as a native of *Schirrhoffen*. Thirty-six-year-old Henriette Welsch Schwarzschild died in New Orleans on 27 June 1858 and was buried there in Gates of Prayer Cemetery #2 (Joseph Street). **(A, AN, E, L, TT)**

WELSCH, JACQUES, was born **JAKOB WELSCH** on 23 August 1874 in *Schirrhoffen*, Bas-Rhin, France, to **ISAAK WELSCH** and his wife **HENRIETTE LEVY**, both natives of the town. He followed his elder sister, Clementine, and brother, Emanuel, to Louisiana in 1891. In a 1906 application for a U.S. passport, Jacques wrote that he had arrived on 15 August 1891 at New York from Le Havre, France, aboard the SS *La Bourgogne*. Sixteen-year-old "Jacob Welsch" actually arrived in New York on 14 September 1891 from Le Havre, France, aboard the SS *La Bretagne*. Jacques, as he was known in Louisiana, was in business with his brother, **EMANUEL WELSCH** (See entry), and another cousin, **EMANUEL LEVY** (See entry), in a dry goods business in Port Allen, West Baton Rouge Parish, LA, which was called Welsh & Levy. In 1900 Jacques Welsch, Emanuel Levy and **SYLVAN SOMMER** (See entry), all former residents of *Schirrhoffen*, were all living and working together in Port Allen. Although a branch of the store had recently been opened in Baton Rouge, Jacques was staying with his sister **CLEMENTINE BENJAMIN**, her son, HERBERT BENJAMIN, his brother, Emanuel Welsch, and his partner and first cousin, Emanuel Levy, in Port Allen at the time of the 1910 federal census. The dry goods firm of Welsh & Levy moved permanently to Baton Rouge, East Baton Rouge Parish, LA, in April 1915, after the partners disposed of their holdings in Port Allen. That same year Jacques Welsch married **SUZANNE COHN (**See entry**)** who had immigrated with her parents from *Bischwiller,* Bas-Rhin, France, at the age of six, and who was raised in Lorman, Jefferson Co., MS. Jacques died two years later, on 29 December 1917 at Touro Infirmary in New Orleans, Orleans Parish, LA, and was buried in the Jewish Cemetery in Baton Rouge, East Baton Rouge Parish, LA. The couple had had no children. Note: The Baton Rouge branch of this family spelled their name "Welsh." Jacques appeared in many newspaper articles in Louisiana as "Jake Welsh" **(A, AN, G, GB, L)**

WELSCH, MARIE/MARY, (*Schirrhoffen*) See entry for **ISAAC KLEIN**

WELSCH, SAMUEL, was born on 3 May 1789 in *Schirrhoffen*, Bas-Rhin, France, to **HILAIRE/HIRTZEL WELSCH**, a native of the town and his wife **BLUME/SABINE HIRTZEL**, born in *Büswiller*,

Bas-Rhin. Samuel married **MERLÉ/MARIE HEYMANN**, also a native of *Schirrhoffen*, Bas-Rhin, on 2 July 1813. Marie was the daughter of **SCHLUMEL/ SALOMON HEYMANN,** a native of the town, and **CLAIRE ISAAC** (Breinle before 1808), about whom we know nothing. Merlé Heymann died in *Schirrhoffen* on 10 July 1847. Their children, Gottlieb, Claire, Elizabethe, aka Henriette, and Marie all immigrated to Louisiana (See individual entries). Marie, the last to come, was accompanied by her elderly father, Samuel. They probably arrived at some time between their enumeration together in the 1851 census for the town of *Schirrhoffen*, and their appearance in the 1860 federal census for New Orleans, Orleans Parish, La. We were unable to find a reliable ship's record for either of them. In 1860, Samuel, age seventy-five, was enumerated, living in New Orleans next door to his newly married daughter, **MARIE WELSCH** (See entry), and her husband **ISAAC KLEIN**, and his daughter, **CLAIRE WELSCH**, and her husband, **ISAAC HEYMAN** (See entry). Samuel died on 24 April 1868 in New Orleans and was buried there in Gates of Prayer Cemetery # 2 (Joseph Street). **(A, AN, B1851, G, GB, L, TT)**

WEYL, CAROLINE, was born **CAROLINA WEYL** on 31 July 1868 in *Westhouse*, Bas-Rhin, France, to **SELIGMANN WEYL**, a native of the town, and his wife, **ROSALIE LEVY**, born in *Mutzig*, Bas-Rhin. Seventeen-year-old Caroline Weyl emigrated from Le Havre, France, aboard the SS *St. Laurent*, which arrived at New York on 12 February 1886. Caroline gave her destination as New Orleans. She married NATHAN SILVERMAN on 25 February 1894 in New Orleans, Orleans Parish, LA. The couple settled in Franklin, St. Mary Parish. LA. They were enumerated there in the 1900 federal census living next door to Nathan's brother, Abe Silverman. Both men were clothing merchants from Poland. Caroline and Nathan were the parents of three children: Daniel Nathan (b. 1894), Pearl (b. 1897) and Albert (1902). Caroline's brother, **JEROME WEYL** (See entry), a watchmaker, also lived in the household in 1900. Nathan and Caroline raised their children in Franklin, and lived there for over half a century. Caroline died on 4 August 1953 and was buried in Temple Gates of Prayer Cemetery (Rosehill Cemetery - Jewish Section) in New Iberia, Iberia Parish, LA. Nathan followed on 12 April 1958 and was buried with her. **(A, AN, G, GB)**

WEYL, JEROME, was born **HYERONIMUS WEYL** on 13 October 1877 in *Westhouse,* Bas-Rhin, France, to **SELIGMANN WEYL**, a native of the town, and his wife, **ROSALIE LEVY**, born in *Mutzig*, Bas-Rhin. Jerome immigrated to the United States, arriving in New York on 15 December 1897 aboard the SS *La Champagne*. He joined his sister, **CAROLINE WEYL** (See entry), the wife of NATHAN SILVERMAN, in Franklin, St. Mary Parish, LA, where they were all enumerated in the 1900 federal census. Jerome was a watchmaker by trade, and worked in the town as a jeweler. By the time of the 1910 federal census for Franklin, St. Mary Parish, thirty-four-year-old Jerome was living with another sister, **MARIE/MARGUERITE WEYL** (See entry), and her husband, ISAAC POPKIN, a jeweler from Russia. Jerome was still unmarried and was working with his brother-in-law in the latter's jewelry store in town. Jerome made enough money to set up his own shop in nearby Patterson, St. Mary Parish, LA, ca. 1915. He registered for the World War I draft from there on 12 September 1918 indicating that he was self-employed as a jeweler and watchmaker. Jerome was enumerated at Patterson as a forty-year-old unmarried jeweler in the 1920 federal census. He lived in a boarding house and operated his own jewelry store. Still in Patterson at his jewelry store at the time of the 1930 federal census, Jerome had since married HELEN AARON ca. 1921. She had at least one child from a previous marriage, a fifteen-year-old son identified as Bobbie Weyl, who was enumerated with them. The couple also had two children of their own: Paul (b. 1922) and Jane (b. 1924). Helen Aaron, who was not Jewish, was born in Amite Co.MS, in 1892. Jerome and Helen spent their final years in Houma, Terrebonne Parish, LA. Jerome died there on 5 February 1949 and was buried in Garden of Memories Cemetery in Gray, Terrebonne Parish, LA. Helen died on 4 November 1973 and was buried with him. (**A, AN, G, GB, TT**)

WEYL, MARIE/MARGUERITE, was born **MARIA WEYL** on 13 January 1875 in *Westhouse*, Bas-Rhin, France, to **SELIGMANN WEYL**, a native of the town, and his wife, **ROSALIE LEVY**, born in *Mutzig*, Bas-Rhin. She arrived in New York on 19 November 1894 aboard the SS *La Touraine* from Le Havre France. Marie, always known as Marguerite in U.S. census records, joined her sister, **CAROLINE WEYL** (See entry) and brother-in-law, Nathan Silverman, who had settled in Franklin, St. Mary Parish, LA. Marguerite married ISAAC DAVID POPKIN ca. 1897, a record for which we were unable to find. Isaac, a native of Russia, had opened up a jewelry store in Franklin just before the turn of the twentieth century. Isaac and Marguerite were the parents of five children: Reuben (b.

1898), Lionel (b. 1899), Oscar (b. 1902), Hugo Jacob (b. 1903), and Dora (b. 1907). Marguerite's brother, **JEROME WEYL** (See entry), also a jeweler, joined his brother-in-law in business and lived with the family. He was enumerated with the Popkins and their children in the 1910 federal census for Franklin. Isaac and Marguerite remained in Franklin for almost a half-century. Isaac ran the jewelry store with the help of his sons Reuben and Oscar. Isaac died on 16 May 1946 at Franklin and was interred in Gates of Prayer Cemetery #1 (Canal Street) in New Orleans, Orleans Parish, LA. Marguerite died on 17 November 1954 at Franklin and was interred with her husband. (**A, AN, G, GB**)

WILDENSTEIN, JACQUES, was born **JAQUES WILTENSTEIN** on 11 December 1842 in *Fegersheim*, Bas-Rhin, France, to **ABRAHAM WILTENSTEIN**, a native of the town, and his wife **CELESTINE/ODILE MEYER/MAYER,** born in *Duttlenheim*, Bas-Rhin. Jacques immigrated to New Orleans, ca. 1869, a date which appears in both the 1900 and 1910 federal census records for the family. We were unable, however, to find a reliable record for his arrival in the U.S. Jacques settled in Jeanerette, Iberia Parish, LA. He started out as a grocer in town. Jacques married MINA/MINETTE FELIX/FALK (see entry for **MARX FELIX**), a Louisiana native, on 2 April 1879 in New Orleans, Orleans Parish, LA. They returned to Jeanerette to live where they had five children: Celestine (b. 1880), Hanna/Nanna (b. 1881), Carrie (b. 1884), Gustave (b. 1886), and Marx (b. 1888). Jacques, who was, by 1900, a successful dry goods merchant in Jeanerette, sought to move to New Orleans to open a new business. He partnered with his son-in-law, **CHARLES LEVY** (See entry), and they opened a wholesale liquor distributorship. His wife, Mina, died on 31 July 1918, and was buried in Gates of Prayer Cemetery # 1 (Canal Street). Jacques followed on 25 October 1927, and was buried with her. (**A, AN, G, GB**)

WOLBRETTE, DAVID, was born **DAVID WOLLBRET** on 20 December 1853 in *Schwenheim*, Bas-Rhin, France, to SAMUEL **WOLBRETTE,** also known as **DAVID SAMUEL,** born in *Reichshoffen*, Bas-Rhin, France, and his wife, **LEYEN/LOUISE MARX**, a native of *Schwenheim*, Bas-Rhin. Eighteen-year-old "David Volbrette [*sic*]," arrived in New Orleans, Orleans Parish, LA, from Le Havre, France, on 14 October 1872 aboard the SS *Saxonia*. He started out as a dry goods merchant in Assumption Parish, LA. David married

ANNA MOYSE, a native of Nancy, Meurthe-et-Moselle, France, in 1878, a record for which we have been unable to find. David moved to Plaquemine, Iberville Parish, LA, where he was enumerated in the 1880 federal census with his wife Anna, and first child, Samuel (b. 1879).The couple were the parents of seven more children, all born in Iberville Parish: Thérèse (b. 1881), Jules (b. 1885), Sidney Moyse (b. 1886), Bertha (b. 1888), Louise (b. 1890), Henri (b. 1891), and Hermance Sarah (b, 1892). David was naturalized in Iberville Parish on 5 June 1889. He and his family moved to New Orleans just before his wife's untimely death in 1898. She was interred there in Gates of Prayer Cemetery # 2 (Joseph Street). David organized the Southern Paper Co., in 1902 and was its first president. He died on 13 November 1920 at Colorado Springs, CO. where he had gone to recover from an operation. His remains were returned to New Orleans where they were buried at Gates of Prayer Cemetery # 2 (Joseph Street) with those of his wife. **(A, AN, G, GB)**

WOLBRETTE, LAZARE, was born **LAZARE DAVID** on 14 November 1857 in *Schwenheim*, Bas-Rhin, France to SAMUEL **WOLBRETTE,** also known as **DAVID SAMUEL**, born in *Reichshoffen*, Bas-Rhin, France, and his wife, **LEYEN/LOUISE MARX**, a native of *Schwenheim*. Of the four children born to the couple, his birth record was the only one where the adopted 1808 surname, Wolbrette, was not used. Lazare immigrated to Louisiana after the Franco-Prussian War to join his brother, **DAVID WOLBRETTE** (See entry). We were unable to find a record for his arrival in America. Twenty-year-old Lazare died from the "stranger's disease," yellow fever, at Bayou Lafourche on 8 September 1878, during one of the worst epidemics of the nineteenth century. He was buried in Bikur Sholim Jewish Cemetery in Donaldsonville, Ascension Parish, LA. **(A, AN)**

WOLF, SAMUEL, was born **SAMUEL WOLFF** on 25 May 1824 in *Büswiller*, Bas-Rhin, France, to **David WOLFF,** a native of the town, and his wife, **JOSEPHINE WELSCH,** born in *Schirrhoffen*, Bas-Rhin. Samuel was an early immigrant to Mississippi, however, we were unable to find a likely record for his arrival in America. He married **HARRIET MOCK,** born **JANNETE MOCH,** on 18 June 1828 in *Mertzwiller*, Bas-Rhin, France, to **LIENHARD MOCH,** a cattle dealer, and his wife, **CAROLINE STORCK,** both natives of the town. Samuel and Harriet were married in Amite County MS, on 7 July 1851.

They and their five children, Delphine (b. 1852), Meyer (b. 1857), Fanny (b. 1859), Harry (b.1863) and Leon (b.1868) made their home in Osyka, Pike County, Mississippi, where Sam Wolf was a dry goods merchant. They were enumerated there in the 1870 federal census living next door to Isaïe Cerf and his family. Four members of the Wolf family were buried in Louisiana in the Jewish Section of the Old German Cemetery in Kirksville, Tangipahoa Parish, Louisiana (a third of a mile into Louisiana from the Mississippi border). The parents were predeceased by two sons: Henry/Harry who died on 10 October 1878, and Meyer/Myer who died on 24 October 1878, both in Osyka, no doubt in that year's yellow fever epidemic. Samuel Wolf died on 26 June 1899 in Osyka, and his wife died in New Orleans on 23 March 1906. Both were buried with their two sons at Kirksville. Note: Samuel's brother **LAZAR,** born **LEMAN WOLFF** on 11 February 1826, in *Büswiller,* Bas-Rhin, married Mina, an immigrant from Lambsheim, Bavaria. The family also lived in Osyka, MS. Lazar died on 14 August 1900 and was buried at the cemetery at Kirksville, Tangipahoa Parish, LA along with his wife, who had died on 31 August 1896. (**A, AN, G**)

WOLFF, CERF, was born **ISAAC WOLFF** on 7 August 1824 in *Neuwiller-lès-Saverne*, Bas-Rhin, France, to **ISAAC WOLFF**, a native of the town, and his wife, THÉRÈSE MORHANGE, born in Metz, Moselle, France. In the 1836 census for *Neuwiller*, twelve-year-old Isaac was enumerated as "Cerf Isaac" confirming the name he used in Louisiana. According to his 1857 American naturalization record, Cerf arrived in Louisiana in 1852. We believe he was the twenty-seven-year-old "Isaac Wolff" who arrived in New Orleans, Orleans Parish, LA, on 1 October 1852 from Le Havre, France, aboard the ship *Eastern Queen*. He settled in Waterloo, Pointe Coupée Parish, LA, where he opened up a general store. The following year he took out a bond to marry CAROLINE LEVY, about whom nothing is known. There is no license on file and no record of a marriage ever having taken place. Cerf wed **SARAH ZACHARIAS** on 9 December 1858. Their marriage record included the information that she had been born in 1838 in *Struth,* Bas-Rhin, France, to NATHAN ZACHARIAS, a native of Hoffenheim, Baden, Germany, and his wife **MATHILDE WEIL**, born in *Haguenau*, Bas-Rhin, France. While there is no birth record for her in *Struth*, there are death records for both of her parents in that town. Her sister, Babette, was born on 14 June 1826 in Haguenau, Bas-Rhin, France. A one-year-old brother, Aron, died in *(Wald)Hambach*, Bas-

Rhin in 1830, where, another sister, Caroline, was born the following year. Fifteen-year-old Sarah, her father, Nathan (who was recorded in error as Zacharias Nathan, reversing the first and last names), and her mother Mathilde were enumerated together in the 1851 town census for *(Wald)Hambach*. Because her father was a cantor and teacher it is clear that the family moved around more than most Jewish couples during that time. So far we have not been able to ascertain where Sarah was actually born, only where she lived before she immigrated. Cerf and Sarah Zacharias Wolff had eight children: Helena/Ellen (b. 1860) and Isidore (b. 1862) were born before Cerf enlisted as a second Lieutenant in Co. D of the Pointe Coupée Regiment, Louisiana Militia, in the summer of 1862 at the start of the Civil War. The couple had six more children after the war: Rachel (b. 1866), Cornelia (b. 1868), and Theresa/Théresine (b. 1870), were probably born at New Roads (formerly False River) where Cerf operated a general store with his partner, Pierre Langlois, on Main Street ca. 1866-1870. His son Lazard (b. 1872) was probably born at Hermitage, Pointe Coupée Parish, where the family had moved before the 1870 federal census. Later on in the 1870s Cerf operated the Alma Store at Alma Plantation at Lakeland, Pointe Coupée Parish where Leopold (b. 1876), and Maurice (b. 1879) were born. Before his death in 1884, Cerf had opened the Burnt Bridge Store at Bayou Cirier, not far from the Alma Store at Lakeland This latter establishment was taken over by his wife and children in 1884. His son, Lazard, remained in the parish into the early twentieth century to operate the Burnt Bridge Store, probably until the devastating 1912 flood. Cerf Wolff died on 4 December 1884 in Pointe Coupée Parish and was buried in the Jewish Cemetery in Baton Rouge, East Baton Rouge Parish, LA. (Note: His tombstone is inscribed in French with his places of birth and death.) His wife, Sarah, moved to New Orleans in 1893 where she died on 18 May 1904. She was buried there in Gates of Prayer Cemetery #2 (Joseph Street). (**A, AN, BC, B1851, G, GB, TT**)

WOLFF, HENRIETTA, was born **HENRIETTE WOLFF** on 26 January 1845 in *Oberbronn*, Bas-Rhin, France, to **RAPHAEL WOLFF**, a native of *Offwiller*, Bas-Rhin, and his wife, HENRIETTE/NANETTE BLUM, born in Rheinpfalz, Germany. Henrietta was married in Karlsruhe, Baden-Württemberg, Germany, on 7 February 1867 to ALEXANDER/ALEX WEIL, a native of Albersweiler, Rheinpfalz, Germany, according to information given in the *Biographical and Historical Memoirs of Northwest Louisiana*, published by the Southern Publishing Company, Chicago & Nashville, in 1890. This same source indicated that Alexander Weil had immigrated to Louisiana, arriving on 19 March 1850 at New Orleans, Orleans Parish, LA. We believe that the ship's record for an Alexander Weil, who arrived at New Orleans from Vera Cruz, Mexico, on 20 March 1850 aboard the ship *Lemuel Dyer,* is, in fact, his record. Alex was first enumerated in Homer, Claiborne Parish, LA, in 1860 as a twenty-nine-year-old clerk working in a store owned by an elder brother, Michael Weil. At the outbreak of the Civil War Alex enlisted in the Second Louisiana Infantry, Company F, the Claiborne Guards. This regiment saw action at Malvern Hill, second Manassas (Bull Run), and the battle of Sharpsburg (Antietam) where Alex was wounded in the leg. He returned from the hospital at Richmond to participate in the capture of Harper's Ferry, the battles of the Wilderness and Gettysburg, where he was, at this latter place, shot in the head, but survived to wear the bullet removed from his skull as a watch charm. Still suffering from a head wound that refused to heal, he returned to Germany in 1866 to seek treatment and where he was married. Alex and his bride, Henrietta Wolff returned to Louisiana from Europe ca. 1867, a record for which we were unable to find. Their five daughters were born in Homer, Claiborne Parish, LA: Carrie Justine (b. 1868), Lily (b. 1869; died 1870), Camille (b. 1871), Omega (b. 1874), and Blanche (b. 1877). After having worked at Homer as a dry goods merchant for almost thirty years, Alex moved his family to New Orleans, where he spent his remaining time as an insurance agent. He died on 26 May 1900 at New Orleans and was buried there in Hebrew Rest Cemetery #2. Henrietta Wolff Weil died on 20 September 1914 at Evergreen, Avoyelles Parish, LA, where her daughters, Carrie, who had married **SOLOMON LEVY** (See entry), and Omega, who had wed Sol's brother, **GUSTAVE LEVY** (See entry), were living. Henrietta's remains were returned to New Orleans where they were interred in Hebrew Rest Cemetery #2 with those of her husband. (**A, AN, AP, GB**)

WOLFF, JUSTINE, was born on 27 December 1849 in *Oberbronn*, Bas-Rhin, France, to **RAPHAEL WOLFF**, a native of *Offwiller*, Bas-Rhin, and his wife, HENRIETTE/NANETTE BLUM, born in Rheinpfalz, Germany. Twenty-four-year-old Justine emigrated from Germany, where her parents had moved when she was a child, arriving in New York from Bremen, Germany, on 1 November 1873 aboard the SS *Smidt*. Justine settled in New Orleans, Orleans Parish, LA, where she became the Superintendent /Matron at Touro Infirmary. She was forced to give up the job in the early 1890s when trained nurses were introduced into the hospital's staff. Justine subsequently opened up a boarding house on St. Charles Avenue, where she was enumerated in the 1900 federal census. Overtaken by illness at the age of fifty-four, she died at the home of her sister, **HENRIETTA WOLFF** (See entry), on 18 April 1904. She had never married. Justine was interred at Hebrew Rest Cemetery #2 in New Orleans. (**A, AN, G, GB**)

WOLFF, LAZAR/LEMAN, (*Büswiller*) See entry for **SAMUEL WOLF**

WOLFF, LEON, was born **LEOPOLD WOLFF** on 18 May 1850 in *Weinbourg*, Bas-Rhin, France, to **HIRTZEL/CERF WOLFF**, a native of the town, and his wife, **SARA WEIL,** born in *Saverne*, Bas-Rhin. Leon immigrated with his first cousin, **SOLOMON HAAS** (See entry) arriving in New York on 29 August 1871 aboard the SS *Denmark*. They travelled to Louisiana to join his cousin's half-brothers, **SAMUEL** and **ALEXANDRE HAAS** (See entries) in St. Landry Parish, LA. Leon, whose aunt, Zerlina Wolff, was the Haas brother's stepmother, followed Solomon to Bayou Chicot, St. Landry (now Evangeline) Parish, LA, where the two young men started their careers, learning English on the steps of the Baptist Church from the local schoolmaster. Leon, with the help of Sam Haas, set up a mercantile business in nearby Washington, St. Landry Parish, where he spent the rest of his life. Leon married LENA HEYMANN, a native of New River, Ascension Parish, LA, the daughter of German immigrants. They were wed on 2 March 1880 in New Orleans, Orleans Parish, LA. Six children were born to the couple: Rosetta (b. 1880), Michel (b. 1882), Florence (b. 1883), Mae (b. 1885; See entry for **JACOB WEILL**), Caroline (b. 1886) and Aaron (b. 1888). Lena died in Washington on 23 August 1888 and was buried there in Hebrew Rest Cemetery. Two years later, Leon travelled to Alexandria, Rapides Parish, LA, to marry REBECCA WEIL, a Louisiana native of German extraction. She was a childless widow, whose first husband, German-born, Sol Mayer, had drowned in a riverboat accident on 5 December 1878, three years after their marriage. Leon and Rebecca were wed on 27 March 1890. They returned to Washington where their three children were born: Sylvan (b. 1891), Edouard (b. 1892) and Julien Édouard (b. 1897). Leon was one of the most prominent men in town. He ran a successful general store and was an officer of the local bank. He was elected mayor of Washington in 1891 and served for two years.

Leon also participated in many of the business deals that enriched his relatives, Sam and Alex Haas, including the development of the Shell Canal in St. Landry Parish. Rebecca Weil Wolff died on 9 July 1927 at Washington and was buried there in Hebrew Rest Cemetery. Leon died on 19 September 1937 at Washington and was interred with his wife. Engraved on his tombstone were the words "Leon Wolff, A Native of *Ingwiller*, Alsace, France, June 10 1850 – September 19, 1937." He was, in fact, born three weeks earlier and several miles away in *Weinbourg,* where the family was enumerated together in the 1851 census for the town. Note: It took several years to find the Haas and Wolff immigration record. Their names were erroneously transcribed as "Jane Wolff" and "Salamona Heuss." (**A, AN, AP, B1851, G, GB**)

WOLFF, SAMUEL, was born on 26 September 1830 in *Neuwiller-lès-Saverne*, Bas-Rhin, France, to **ISAAC WOLFF**, a native of the town and his wife, THÉRÈSE MORHANGE, born in Metz, Moselle, France. He was enumerated with his widowed mother in the 1851 census for *Neuwiller-lès-Saverne* as a twenty year old peddler. We have not found any reliable record of his immigration to Louisiana. Samuel Wolff was issued a license to marry **BABETTE LEVY** at New Orleans, Orleans Parish, LA, on 20 May 1859. Babette was born **BABETTE LEVI** on 22 March 1833 in *Niederbronn-les-Bains*, Bas-Rhin, France, to **ELIE/ELIAS LEVI/LEVY**, a native of the town, and his wife, RÉGINE/REINE EBERHARDT, born in Burrweiler, Rheinpfalz, Germany. Twenty-two-year-old Babette Levy arrived in New Orleans, Orleans Parish, LA, with a younger brother, **LÉON LEVY** (See entry), from Le Havre, France, on 7 December 1857 aboard the ship *Nuremberg*. Samuel and Babette settled in Waterloo, Pointe Coupée Parish, LA, a few houses down from Samuel's older brother, **CERF WOLFF** (See entry), where they were enumerated in the 1860 federal census with their three year old son, Isidore, born on 22 March 1860. Samuel Wolff was working as a baker at Waterloo. Twenty-one-year-old **LEON LEVY** (See entry), Babette's brother, was living next door. One more child was born to the couple, a son, Marcen M./MASSEY/MM, who was registered as having been born in New Orleans on 27 May 1861. No trace of the couple can be found until the reappearance of the forty-four-year-old widow "B. Wolf" in the 1880 federal census for New Orleans, where she was enumerated living on Melpomene Street with her two sons, twenty-one-year-old Isidore, a grocery clerk, and "Massey," a nineteen-year-old employee in a clothing store. When and where Samuel Wolff died is still a mystery. It is possible that he did not survive long after the birth of his second son, succumbing to one of the many epidemics which took the lives of so many immigrants. "Babetta Wolf" died at Touro Infirmary on 21 March 1881 and was interred the next day at Hebrew Rest Cemetery #1 (Canal Street) in New Orleans. Note: We have based the identification of Samuel Wolff on his having settled near Cerf Wolff in Waterloo, Pointe Coupée Parish, as well as the fact that both men had children named Isidore. Unfortunately Samuel's New Orleans Justice of the Peace marriage record gave no clue as to his birthplace, and his brother Cerf, was not a witness or a bondsman at the time of the marriage. Moreover, since there was no death or marriage record for Samuel in *Neuwiller-lès-Saverne*, we have concluded that he had immigrated to join his brother in Louisiana. (**A, AN, B1851, G, GB, TT**)

WORMSER, CHARLES, was born on 13 March 1865 in *Marmoutier*, Bas-Rhin, France, to **JOSEPH WORMSER**, a native of the town, and his wife, **MADELEINE/MINETTE LEVY**, born in *Birkenwald*, Bas-Rhin. He immigrated to the United States aboard the SS *France* from Le Havre, France, arriving in New York on 3 November 1882 to join his brothers **LAZARE** and **MEYER WORMSER** (See entries) in Iberia Parish. He married CARRIE GUGENHEIM, a native of New Orleans of German extraction, in St. Charles Parish, ca. 1891, a record of which we were unable to find. Carrie's sisters, Rosa and Mathilde, were already married to Charles's brothers, Lazard and Meyer Wormser. Charles was naturalized at New Iberia, Iberia Parish, LA, on 12 March 1894. The three brothers, married to three sisters, eventually settled in Jeanerette, Iberia Parish, LA, where they were enumerated in the 1900 federal census living next door to one another Charles and Carrie were the parents of two children: Joseph Charles (b. 1892) and Gertrude (b. 1895). The Wormser brothers owned and operated stores in Jeanerette and New Iberia. Charles Wormser was a also a director of the Citizens Bank of Jeanerette. Carrie Wormser died on 10 April 1931 in a hospital in Philadelphia, Pennsylvania. Her remains were returned to New Orleans, Orleans Parish, La, where they were interred in Hebrew Rest Cemetery # 2 in the city. Charles died on 23 December 1951 in Jeanerette and was buried in Hebrew Rest Cemetery #2 in New Orleans with his wife. (**A, AN, F, G, GB**)

WORMSER, JUSTIN, was born **JUSTIN JOSEF WORMSER** on 29 January 1886 in *Marmoutier*, Bas-Rhin, France, to **MOISE/**

JOSEPH WORMSER and his wife ERNESTINE LEVY, both natives of the town. Justin's father, Moise, was the brother of LAZARE, CHARLES and MEYER WORMSER (see entries) who settled in Jeanerette, Iberia Parish, LA. Justin immigrated to Louisiana aboard the SS *La Savoie* from Le Havre, France, arriving in New York on 8 November 1907. He joined his brother, LOUIS WORMSER (See entry), in Baldwin, St. Mary Parish, LA, where Louis was operating a dry goods store. Justin married his first cousin, MINA WORMSER, his Uncle Meyer's daughter, on 26 April 1911 in Gulfport, Harrison Co., MS. The wedding took place out-of-state as Louisiana had recently outlawed first cousin marriages. Justin and Mina were the parents of two children: Harold Justin (b. 1914) and Lorraine (b. 1922). Justin's father-in-law, Meyer, came to live with the couple and their children in Jeanerette, after Meyer's wife, Tillie, died in 1928. Justin Wormser was responsible for the expansion of Wormser's Department Store which is, to this day, still operated in New Iberia by his grandson, JOHN WORMSER. Justin Wormser died in Jeanerette on 23 February 1963 and was buried in Hebrew Rest Cemetery #2 in New Orleans, Orleans Parish, LA. Mina died the following year, on 13 September 1964 in Jeanerette, and was buried with her husband. The three buildings which comprise the present Wormser's Department Store, a fine example of art deco architecture developed by Justin Wormser, were added to the U.S. National Register of Historic Places in 1995. (A, AN, F, G, GB)

WORMSER, LAZARE, was born on 7 September 1850 in *Marmoutier*, Bas-Rhin, France, to JOSEPH WORMSER, a native of the town, and his wife, MADELEINE/MINETTE LEVY, born in *Birkenwald*, Bas-Rhin. According to his naturalization papers which were filed in New Iberia, Iberia Parish, LA, on 30 March 1899, Lazare arrived in Louisiana on 5 January 1873. We believe, however, that he probably was the same as "Louis Wormser" who arrived in New York on 10 September 1872 from Le Havre, France, aboard the SS *Denmark*. Lazare worked as itinerant dry goods merchant in St. James Parish, LA. After his brother, MEYER WORMSER (See entry), joined him in 1879, they opened a small store in the parish. Lazare married ROSA GUGENHEIM, a native of New Orleans of German extraction, on 30 January 1884 in nearby St. Charles Parish. They were the parents of six children who survived to adulthood: Joseph Lazard (b. 1884), Sarah (b. 1886), Mina/Mena (b. 1887; See entries for PAULINE and ADELE BLUM of *Dettwiller*), Aline (b. 1889), Jonas (b. 1891) and Fannie (b. 1892). Lazare and his family eventually settled in Jeanerette, Iberia

Parish, LA, with his brothers, Meyer and **CHARLES WORMSER** (See entry), where they operated a lucrative general merchandise store with branches in New Iberia, Iberia Parish, and Franklin, St. Mary Parish, LA. Lazare died in Jeanerette on 3 March 1916, and was buried in Hebrew Rest Cemetery #1 in New Orleans, Orleans Parish, LA. His wife, Rosa, died in Berwick, St. Mary Parish, LA, on 20 November 1930 and was buried in the same cemetery. (**A, AN, G, GB**)

WORMSER, LOUIS, was born **LUDWIG ARON WORMSER** on 20 December 1887 in *Marmoutier*, Bas-Rhin, France, to **MOISE/JOSEPH WORMSER** and his wife **ERNESTINE LEVY**, both natives of the town. Louis's father, Moise, was the brother of **LAZARE, CHARLES** and **MEYER WORMSER** (see entries). Sixteen-year-old Louis Wormser arrived in New York from Le Havre, France, on 3 September 1904 aboard the SS *La Savoie*. He indicated on the passenger manifest that he was going to Jeanerette, LA, to meet his uncle, Lazare Wormser. Louis opened a dry goods store in Baldwin, St. Mary Parish, LA, where, three years later, he was joined by his brother, **JUSTIN WORMSER** (See entry). The brothers lived together in Baldwin until the late 1920s, when Justin took his family to Jeanerette to join his uncles in business. Louis remained in St. Mary Parish at the Baldwin store and boarded with a family in nearby Franklin, the St. Mary Parish seat. He died in Franklin on 26 December 1953, and was buried with other family members in Hebrew Rest Cemetery #2 in New Orleans, Orleans Parish, LA. He never married. (**A, AN, G, GB**)

WORMSER, MEYER/MAYER, was born **MICHEL WORMSER** on 21 June 1862 in *Marmoutier*, Bas-Rhin, France, to **JOSEPH WORMSER**, a native of the town, and his wife, **MADELEINE/ MINETTE LEVY**, born in *Birkenwald*, Bas-Rhin. According to his naturalization papers which were filed in New Iberia, Iberia Parish, LA, on 30 March 1899, Meyer arrived in Louisiana on 15 October 1879. We were not able to verify that date using existing ship's records. Meyer joined his brother, Lazare Wormser, who was working as a dry goods merchant in St. James Parish. They were enumerated together there in 1880. Meyer, the younger of the two, was acting as his brother's clerk in a dry goods store. Meyer married **MATHILDE/ TILLIE GUGENHEIM**, a Louisiana native of German extraction, on 3 September 1889 in New Orleans, Orleans Parish, LA. Tillie's sister, Rosa, was already married to Meyer's brother, Lazare. Meyer and Tillie were the parents of three daughters all born in Jeanerette, Iberia Parish,

LA: Mina (b. 1890), Sophie (b. 1892) and Bella (b. 1894). Meyer and his family settled in Jeanerette to live near his brothers **LAZARE** and **CHARLES WORMSER** (See entries) where they operated a lucrative general merchandise store with branches in other towns and parishes in Acadiana. Tillie died on 26 July 1928 in Jeanerette, and was buried in Hebrew Rest Cemetery #2 in New Orleans, Orleans Parish, LA. Meyer died in Jeanerette on 2 March 1935 and was buried with his wife. (**A, AN, F, G, GB**)

ZACHARIAS, SARAH (*Struth*) See entry for **CERF WOLFF**

PART V

ILLUSTRATIONS, MAPS AND INDICES

CAROLINE AARON, WIFE OF DAVID LEVY, BORN IN BOUXVILLER.
ALSACE. MAR 22, 1842 – DIED JAN. 15, 1921 (Caroline was born 27
March 1842)
GATES OF PRAYER CEMETERY #2 (JOSEPH STREET), NEW
ORLEANS, ORLEANS PARISH, LA
(PHOTO COURTESY OF TERI D. TILLMAN)

RAPHAEL BLOCK BORN HERRLISHEIM – HEBREW REST
CEMETERY # 1, NEW ORLEANS, ORLEANS PARISH, LA
(PHOTO COURTESY OF DEBBIE NATHAN)

ERNEST BLOCK – BORN IN DUTTLENIIEIN [sic] GERMANY FEB 17, 1877 DIED JAN 7, 1902
(Ernest was born on 17 January 1877)
JEWISH CEMETERY, PINEVILLE, RAPIDES PARISH, LA

MIRIAM BLUM – BELOVED WIFE OF H.P. FORTIN
BORN IN DETTWEILER, ALSACE, JAN. 10, 1842- DIED IN
BERWICK, LA, FEB. 17, 1907
(Marie Blum was born on 10 January 1840)
DETAIL OF TOMBSTONE ON FRONT COVER
JEWISH CEMETERY, BERWICK, ST. MARY PARISH, LA

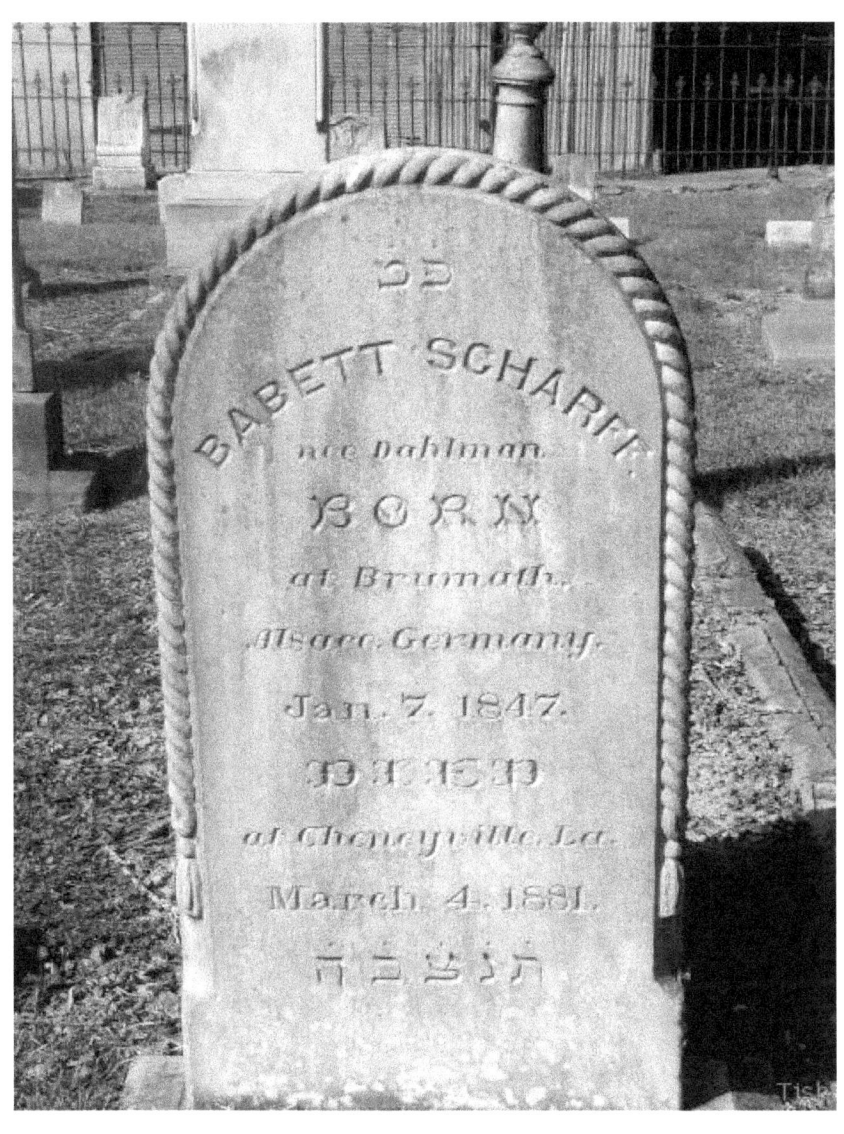

BABETT SCHARFF, NÉE DAHLMAN. BORN AT BRUMATH, ALSACE, GERMANY JAN. 7, 1847.
DIED AT CHENEYVILLE, LA MARCH 4, 1881
(Babette Dahlmann was born on 29 January 1846)
JEWISH CEMETERY, PINEVILLE, RAPIDES PARISH, LA

SACRED TO THE MEMORY OF LOUIS GIRST [sic]
BORN IN NIEDERBRONN, FRANCE, MAY 1, 1837.
DIED IN ALEXANDRIA, LA, SEPT. 25, 1866
JEWISH CEMETERY, PINEVILLE, RAPIDES PARISH, LA

CHARLOTTE FLONACHER, NÉE HIRSCH
BORN AT NIEDERROEDERN, ELSACE, GERMANY
OCT. 25, 1845
DIED FEB. 11, 1893 (Date of Interment)
JEWISH CEMETERY, CLINTON, EAST FELICIANA PARISH, LA

MOTHER
RACHEL KLEIN, BORN IN HOEMHEIM [sic], ALSACE
AUG. 7, 1849
FEB. 12, 1931
JEWISH CEMETERY, PINEVILLE, RAPIDES PARISH, LA

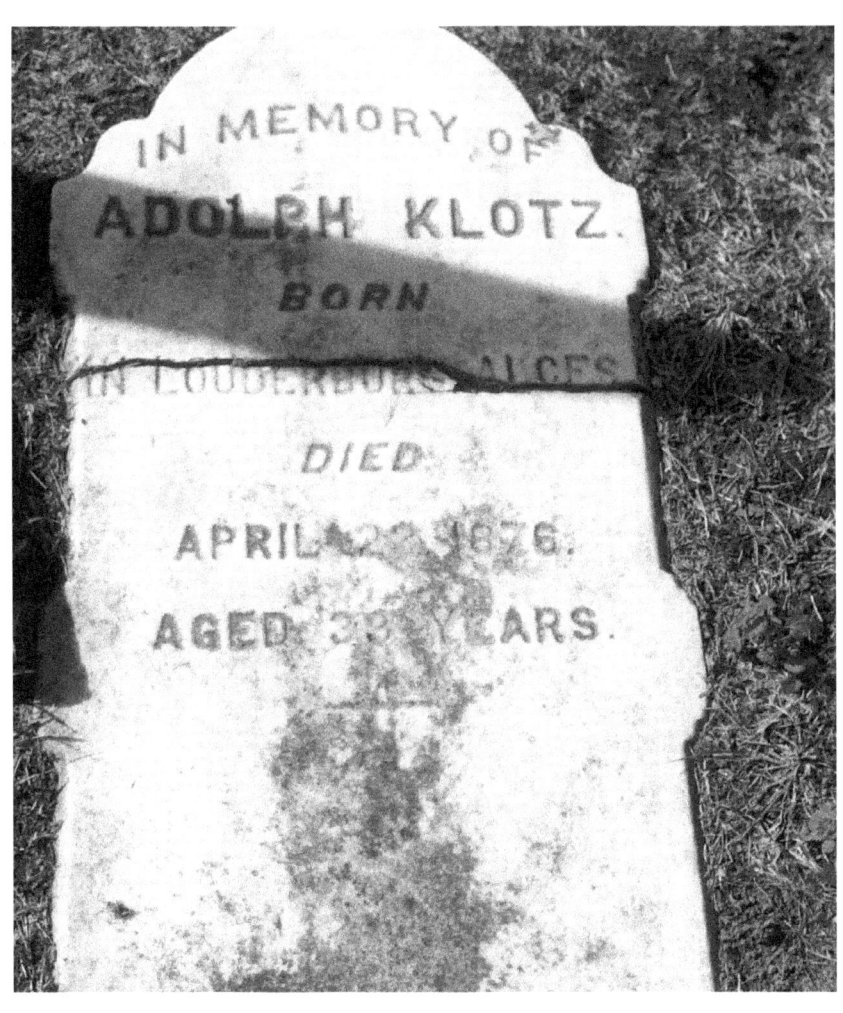

IN MEMORY OF ADOLPH KLOTZ
BORN IN LOUDERBURG ALCES [sic]
DIED APRIL 22, 1876. AGED 33 YEARS
GATES OF PRAYER CEMETERY #2 (JOSEPH STREET), NEW ORLEANS, ORLEANS PARISH, LA
(PHOTO COURTESY OF TERI D. TILLMAN)

EDARD [sic]LEVY (ÉDOUARD LEVY). BORN IN LANDERSBURG [sic]
SEPT. 23, 1817. DIED MAY 3, 1881
(Édouard Levy was born on 18 October 1817 at Frankfort-am-Main,
Germany)
JEWISH CEMETERY, PINEVILLE, RAPIDES PARISH, LA

ISRAEL LEVY
BORN AT BOUXVILLER, ALSACE
DIED AT OPELOUSAS, LA, JULY 19, 1881
CEMILUTH CHASSODIM JEWISH CEMETERY, OPELOUSAS, ST. LANDRY PARISH, LA

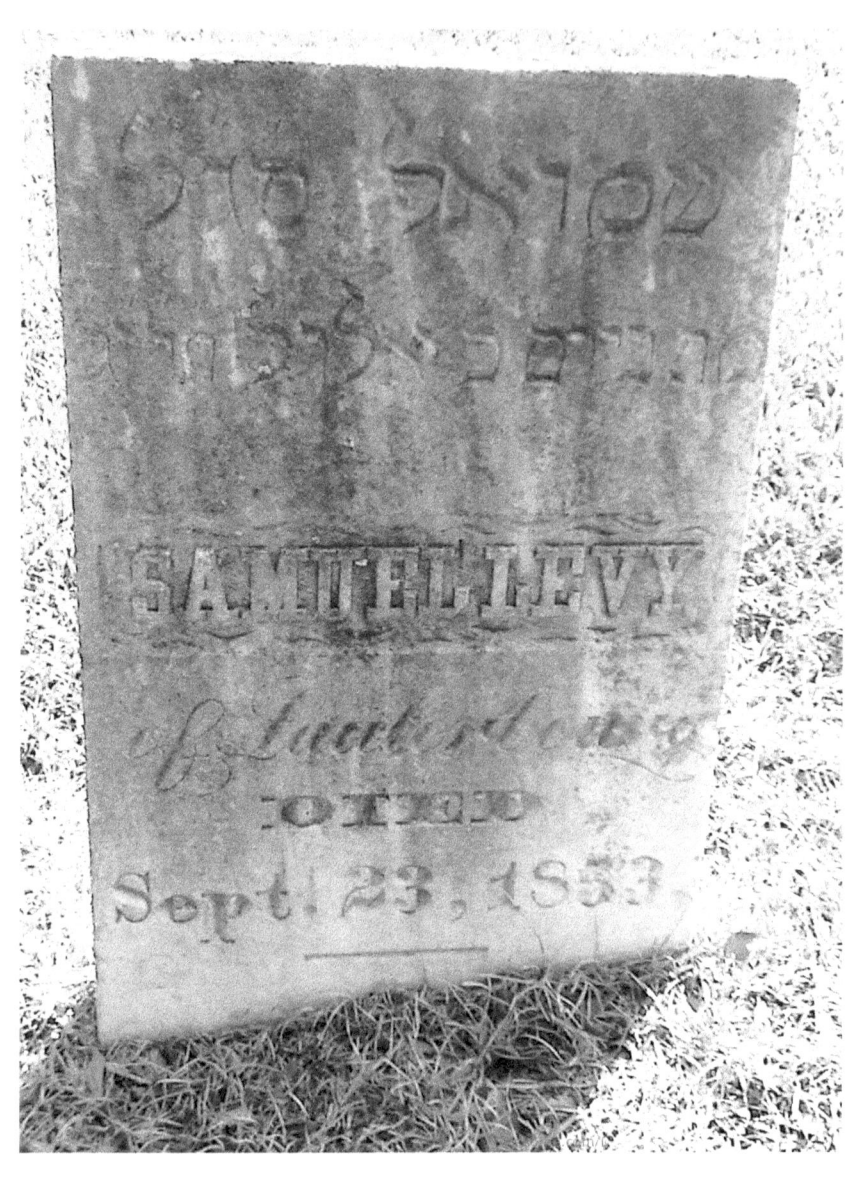

SAMUEL LEVY OF LAUTERBOURG
DIED Sept. 23, 1853
JEWISH CEMETERY, PINEVILLE, RAPIDES PARISH, LA

SIMON LEVY of LAUTERBOURG
DIED Oct. 3, 1853
JEWISH CEMETERY, PINEVILLE, RAPIDES PARISH, LA

EMILY HEYMAN, NÉE MEYER. BORN IN DRACHABRON [sic],
ALSACE, JULY 8, 1808. DIED IN CLINTON, LA, JAN'Y 23, 1888
(She was born Madlaine Mayer on 17 June 1808)
JEWISH CEMETERY, CLINTON, EAST FELICIANA PARISH, LA

I. MAYER [sic] (See MEYER, ISAAC)
BORN
IN LAMBACH [sic]
DIED SEPT. 5, 1853
AGED 28 YEARS
JEWISH CEMETERY, CLINTON, EAST FELICIANA PARISH, LA

IN LOVING MEMORY JUSTINE M. TEUTSCH- WIFE OF RUDOLPH TEUTSCH - BORN IN SCHWEIGHAUSEN, ALSACE, GERMANY AUG. 6, 1859. DIED MAY 6, 1908
GELEBT & GELITTEN (Lived & Suffered)
HEBREW REST CEMETERY, ST. FRANCISVILLE, WEST FELICIANA PARISH, LA

SACRED TO THE MEMORY OF LEWIS MEYER
BORN MARCH 11, 1834, AT LEMBACH, ALSACE, FR.
DIED AT CLINTON, LA. OCTBR. 25, 1853
AGED 19 YRS. 7 M'S, and 14 DY'S
JEWISH CEMETERY, CLINTON, EAST FELICIANA PARISH, LA

MOSES ROSENTHAL. BORN IN OBERLAUTERBACH, ALSACE AUGUST 28, 1828. DIED SEPTEMBER 7, 1898 EARTH HAS NO SORROW THAT HEAVEN CANNOT HEAL
(Moïse was born on 27 August 1828)

JEWISH CEMETERY, PINEVILLE, RAPIDES PARISH, LA

DAVID SIESS
BORN IN LEMBACH, STRASBURG, FRANCE
JUNE 3, 1836 – APR. 7, 1925
AGE 88 YRS. 10 MOS. 4 DAYS
FATHER WE MISS THEE
(David Siess was born on 31 May 1835 at Mühlheim, Dist. Frankenthal, Rheinpfalz, Germany)
JEWISH CEMETERY, PINEVILLE, RAPIDES PARISH, LA

NACHIM [sic] WEIL. BORN IN SAUBOURG [sic], ALSACE, DIED IN OPELOUSAS. MAY 12, 1865. AGED 52 YEARS
JEWISH CEMETERY, PINEVILLE, RAPIDES PARISH, LA

SIMON WEIL. BORN IN BISCHHEIM, ALSACE,
MARCH 28, 1838. DIED IN BAYOU SARA, LA. APRIL 26, 1884
(Simon Weill was born on 23 March 1838)

HEBREW REST CEMETERY # 1, NEW ORLEANS, ORLEANS
PARISH, LA
(*PHOTO COURTESY OF TERI D. TILLMAN*)

LEON WOLFF. A NATIVE OF INGWILLER, ALSACE, FRANCE
JUNE 10, 1850
SEPT. 18, 1937
(Leon was born on 18 May 1850 at Weinbourg)

JEWISH CEMETERY, WASHINGTON, ST. LANDRY PARISH, LA

RAILROAD COLLAPSE NEAR LEP SOMMER'S LEADER STORE DURING 1912 FLOOD AT TORRAS, POINTE COUPÉE PARISH, LA
(*PHOTO COURTESY OF BRIAN COSTELLO*)

Photo of Lep Sommer from *Beautiful Pointe Coupee and her Prominent Citizens*, published in 1906 and reprinted in 1999 by the Pointe Coupee Historical Society
(*PHOTO COURTESY OF BRIAN COSTELLO*)

Mr. Godchaux
Mobile Merchant at Waterloo, Pointe Coupée Parish, LA

(*PHOTO COURTESY OF JUDY RIFFEL- Le Comité des Archives de la Louisiane – PHOTO ENHANCEMENT COURTESY OF STELLA CARLINE TANOOS*)

Interior of Lep & Sylvan Sommer's Leader Store, Torras, Pointe Coupée Parish, LA
Photo from *Beautiful Pointe Coupee and her Prominent Citizens*, published in 1906 and reprinted in 1999 by the Pointe Coupee Historical Society
Courtesy of Brian Costello

MAP OF BAS-RHIN, FRANCE

LOCATION OF BAS- RHIN IN FRANCE
(Dark shaded area)

INDEX OF TOWNS IN THE BAS-RHIN APPEARING IN THIS BOOK

Balbronn 208, 263

Batzendorf 61, 155, 156, 161, 163, 174

Benfeld 166, 167

Birkenwald 239, 255, 263, 392-394

Bischheim 2, 3, 14, 15, 25, 28, 29-35 71, 73-75, 78, 80, 83, 132, 147, 187, 202, 203, 218-221, 255, 276, 326, 361, 363, 417

Bischwiller (Bischweiler) 44, 45, 101, 187, 189, 382

Bouxwiller (Buchsweiler) 3, 41, 48, 51, 96, 98, 116, 118, 120, 121, 156, 167, 168, 203, 227, 236, 245, 246, 248, 249, 264, 274, 275, 278, 316, 345, 360, 366, 397, 407

Brumath 9, 85, 88, 91, 102, 111, 112, 126, 130, 136-141, 149-152, 169, 170, 172, 176, 178, 180, 181-186, 216, 217 237, 241, 343, 344, 365, 371, 376, 401

Büswiller (Busweiler) 51, 248, 264, 290, 315, 316, 382, 386, 390

Dambach-la-Ville 54, 55, 261, 354, 360, 361

Dauendorf 74, 104, 105, 200, 201, 205, 212, 236, 239, 271, 273, 288, 294, 298, 302, 313-315, 376,

Dehlingen 158-160, 257, 258, 300

Dettwiller (Dettweiler) 45, 46, 70, 73, 75-77, 81, 190, 238, 248, 274, 394, 400

Diebolsheim 67, 108

Dossenheim-sur-Zinzel 104, 155

Drachenbronn (now Drachenbronn-Birlenbach) 280, 281, 334, 366, 374, 410

Duppighcim (Düppigheim) 56, 58, 59, 62, 66, 113, 126, 128-132, 161, 232, 233, 240, 241, 255-257, 260-262, 266, 268, 336

Duttlenheim (Düttlenheim) 56, 58, 59, 62, 65, 69, 70, 129, 130, 166, 385, 399

Eckwersheim 343

Epfig 321

Ettendorf 51, 74, 127, 162, 199, 200, 202, 214, 215, 313, 314-316

Fegersheim 216-218, 336, 344, 385

Froeschwiller (Fröschweiler) 96, 158

Goersdorf (Görsdorf) 154, 162, 328, 342, 352

Gundershoffen (Gundershofen) 58, 61, 63, 65-67, 72, 74, 75, 87, 89, 118-124, 131, 153, 154, 191-193, 194, 234, 256, 300, 305, 332

Gunstett 72, 280

Haguenau (Hagenau) 61, 79, 96, 98, 119, 127, 133, 153, 156. 165, 194, 200, 283, 285, 288, 291, 306, 314, 352, 352, 355, 356, 360, 369, 378-381, 388

Hambach (Became Waldhambach in 1891) 388

Harskirchen 51, 52, 150

Hatten 59, 60, 157, 158, 159, 161-164, 174, 176, 180-182, 205, 263, 300, 381

Herrlisheim (Herlisheim) 49, 56, 67, 68, 101, 213, 286, 293, 310-312, 328, 398

Hochfelden 82, 85, 86, 117, 265

Hoenheim (Hönheim) 147, 194, 202, 221, 404

Illkirch-Graffenstaden (Illkirch-Grafenstaden) 220, 221, 223, 351-353, 354

Ingwiller (Ingweiler) 4, 31, 50, 67, 125, 126, 143, 145, 146, 203, 218, 222-224, 233-235, 243-245, 248, 250, 251, 258, 262-265, 276, 279, 296-298, 301-304, 307, 308, 310, 320, 321, 342, 352, 355, 356, 360, 377, 391

Kolbsheim 326

Krautergersheim 56, 92, 110, 211

Kuttolsheim 22, 23, 53, 54, 85, 86, 235, 236, 244, 259, 265, 267, 274

Kutzenhausen 339, 340, 350

Langensoultzbach (Langensulzbach) 127, 152, 233, 247

Lauterbourg (Lauterburg) 93-95, 107, 165, 207, 208-210-212, 214, 216, 238, 249, 250, 254, 266, 269, 270, 272, 315, 405, 408, 409

La Walck (Walk) 45, 46, 176, 344

Lembach 5, 43, 44, 97, 131, 224, 226, 227, 228-230, 276, 277, 286-290, 323-326, 339, 411, 413, 415

Lichtenberg 163, 343, 344, 348, 349, 357-359

Lingolsheim 355

Mackenheim 350

Marckolsheim (Markolsheim) 237, 284, 372

Marmoutier (Maursmünster) 4, 228, 233, 236, 239, 243, 245, 250-252, 255, 262, 337, 338, 360, 392-394

Matzenheim 116, 118

Mertzwiller (Merzweiler) 5, 67, 68, 96, 98, 114, 116, 117, 153, 155, 196-200, 207, 209-212, 296-299, 300, 322, 323, 386

Minversheim 49, 133, 149, 163, 300, 306

Mommenheim 77, 92, 169, 180, 206, 207, 220, 221, 223, 297-299, 358, 360

Mulhausen (Mühlhausen) 3, 72, 243

Muttersholtz (Müttersholz) 554, 55, 286

Mutzig 24, 25, 74, 202, 305, 308, 383, 384

Neuwiller-lès-Saverne (Neuweiler) 50, 67, 116, 195, 233, 247, 257, 387, 391, 392

Niederbronn-les-Bains (Bad Niederbronn) 77, 79, 136, 149, 181, 185, 202, 236, 242, 252, 258, 261, 262, 264, 265, 271, 273, 274, 275, 278, 281, 294, 298, 342, 351, 357-360, 371, 391, 402

Niedernai (Niedereinheim) 4, 74, 305, 306

Niederroedern (Niederrödern) 30, 33, 82, 91, 98, 154, 155, 160, 161, 164, 174, 242, 261, 264, 273, 282, 285, 287, 294, 310, 312, 333-335, 366, 403

Niederseebach (now Seebach) 86, 236, 239, 265, 271, 273, 274, 297, 298

Oberbronn 123, 165, 388, 389

Oberlauterbach 21, 22, 264, 282, 283, 285, 287, 292, 316-319, 329, 330, 351, 357, 414

Obernai (Obereinheim) 4, 109-111, 113, 114, 141-143, 167, 168, 204, 224-228, 239, 258, 264, 299, 307-310, 320, 321

Oberschaeffolsheim (Oberschäffolsheim) 87, 88, 118, 234, 256

Oberseebach (now Seebach) 130

Odratzheim 42, 56, 57, 62, 69, 131, 254, 290

Offendorf 68, 87-90, 169,

Offwiller (Offweiler) 48, 126, 127, 162, 388, 389

Osthoffen (Osthofen) 161, 182, 183, 206, 230, 232, 362, 375

Osthouse (Osthausen) 201, 217

Pfaffenhoffen (Pfaffenhofen) 79, 332

Quatzenheim 32, 72, 88, 351-353

Reichshoffen (Reichshofen) 23, 42, 43, 74, 127, 206-208 237, 241, 248, 275, 276, 278, 305, 343, 344, 348, 349, 351, 352, 358-360, 385, 386

Riedseltz (Riedselz) 60, 63, 84, 168, 170, 181, 185, 186, 193, 246, 299

Ringendorf 166, 167, 214-216, 306

Romanswiller (Romansweiler)47, 48, 69, 153, 161, 165, 166, 173, 188, 224, 228, 229, 235, 259, 301, 303, 304, 332, 333, 337

Rosheim 87, 89, 190, 200, 201, 354

Rothbach 72, 118-124, 132, 133, 143, 145, 146, 155, 162, 194, 297, 305, 318, 343, 348, 349, 358-360, 376
Salmbach 22, 329, 330,

Sarre-Union (Sarreunion) 291
Saverne (Zabern) 57, 61-63, 69, 83, 85, 86, 90, 92, 156, 163, 279, 390,

Schaffhouse-sur-Zorn (Schaffhausen) 72, 240, 266,

Scherwiller (Scherweiler) 96, 98, 147, 298, 319, 320, 326

Schirrhoffen (Schirrhofen) 9, 49, 56, 61, 62, 66, 67, 68, 90, 99, 100, 101, 126, 148, 149, 153, 154, 158, 170-182, 184, 185, 187, 188, 202, 231, 239, 242, 270, 272, 273, 286, 293, 303, 327, 328, 340, 341, 362, 363-368, 370-375, 378-383, 386,

Schleithal 236, 237, 239, 273, 298,

Schweighouse-sur-Moder (Schweighausen) 4, 49, 96, 174, 189, 283, 285, 288, 291, 322, 323, 412

Schwenheim (Schweinheim) 70, 76, 77, 81, 218, 222, 223, 238, 239, 255, 385, 386

Schwindratzheim 154, 155, 160, 161, 164, 302

Sélestat (Schlettstadt) 109, 110, 113, 133, 147, 237, 241, 270,

Soultz-les-Bains (Sulzbad) 44, 45

Soultz-sous-Forêts (Sulz unter dem Wald) 3, 60, 109, 112, 115, 129, 132-135, 165, 238, 249, 269, 276, 278, 333, 335, 369

Strasbourg (Strasburg) 4, 22, 54, 71, 73, 74, 78, 80, 83, 90, 117, 118, 218-221, 223, 251, 256, 257, 345, 352, 361, 363

Struth 103-105, 123, 125, 190, 194-196, 230, 295, 296, 387, 395

Surbourg (Surburg) 63, 102, 103, 125, 140, 143, 186, 204, 205, 214-216, 278-280, 300, 316-318, 326, 339, 347, 349, 353, 356-360, 416

Tieffenbach 103-105, 230, 247

Trimbach 22, 49, 63, 114, 130, 186, 313, 329, 331, 365

Uhlwiller (Uhlweiler) 205, 288, 294
Uhrwiller (Uhrweiler) 207, 209, 211-214, 246, 284, 287, 327, 345

Waldhambach (Hambach before 1891) 387, 388

Waltenheim-sur-Zorn 177, 178, 183, 184, 187

Weinbourg (Weinburg) 125, 125, 146, 270, 297, 306, 390, 391

Weiterswiller (Weitersweiler) 110, 133, 237, 241, 269

Westhoffen (Westhofen) 42, 362, 368, 372, 373, 375

Westhouse (Westhausen) 23-25, 108-111, 113, 114-116, 133, 166, 167, 201, 241, 270, 289, 383, 384

Wingersheim 23, 42, 43, 53, 54, 131, 155, 161, 169, 208

Wintzenheim-Koscherberg 4, 74, 236, 244, 267, 274, 290,

Wissembourg (Weissenburg) 60, 84, 105-109, 112, 115, 118, 124, 157, 158, 160, 163, 164, 169, 224, 265, 266, 274, 312, 314, 315, 334, 356, 357

Wittersheim 189, 206, 207

Woerth-sur-L'Ill (Werde) 116, 118, 247

Wolfisheim 108, 211, 213, 284, 293, 355

Zellwiller (Zellweiler) 141, 142, 224, 225, 227, 228, 299, 326

Zinswiller (Zinsweiler) 143, 192

PARISH MAP OF LOUISIANA

INDEX OF LOUISIANA TOWNS AND PLANTATIONS APPEARING IN THIS BOOK

Note: The parish (county) is in parenthesis. Also note that this index does not include New Orleans (Orleans) because it appears on almost every page in this book.

Abbeville, (Vermillion) 367, 368, 370, 373-375

Abita Springs (St. Tammany) 188, 189

Alexandria (Rapides) 47, 48, 62, 84, 94, 125, 126, 136, 148, 150-152, 160, 161, 166, 203, 205, 207, 211, 212, 215, 216, 218-223, 238, 239, 245, 246, 249-252, 254, 255, 261, 267, 269, 272, 280, 296, 297, 303, 316-319, 324, 325, 338, 345, 346, 349, 350, 352-357, 364, 365, 390, 402

Algiers (Orleans) 174, 381

Alma Plantation (Pointe Coupée) 388

Alsatia Plantation (East Carroll) 329-331

Ama (St. Charles) 161

Atchafalaya (St. Martin) 365, 367, 368

Attakapas (St. Martin) 20, 119, 120, 122 - 124,

Azima Plantation (St. Mary) 236

Baldwin (St. Mary) 393, 394

Bastrop (Morehouse) 109, 112, 113, 115, 233, 236, 239, 241, 243, 252, 255, 262, 263

Baton Rouge (East Baton Rouge) ix, 19, 25, 61, 68, 72, 82, 90, 99, 100-102, 104, 105, 133, 138, 152, 153, 164, 170-178, 180, 181, 184, 185, 187, 198, 205, 217, 220, 232, 240, 242, 263, 272, 273, 284, 295, 296, 306, 311, 312, 327, 329, 345, 354, 361, 366, 367, 371, 378, 379, 380, 382, 383, 388

Bayou Chicot (St. Landry, now Evangeline) 145, 146, 194, 367, 390

Bayou Cirier (Pointe Coupée) 388

Bayou Fordoche (Pointe Coupée) 247

Bayou Goula (Iberville) 72
Bayou Jack (St. Landry) 140

Bayou Lafourche (Lafourche) 192, 284, 386

Bayou Sara (West Feliciana) 195, 222, 295, 336, 337, 362, 417

Belle Rose (Assumption) 114, 196-199

Bellevue (Bossier) 359

Bell Place (West Carroll Parish) 329

Belmont (St. James) 173

Berwick (St. Mary) 56, 70, 71, 76-78, 81, 82, 142, 166, 183, 207, 213, 238, 239, 328, 394, 400

Big Cane (St. Landry) 138, 139, 150, 261, 280, 325, 367-369, 370

Bonnet Carré (St. John the Baptist) 121

Brashear City (St. Mary) [Renamed Morgan City in 1876] 142, 182, 206, 231, 298

Brickhern Plantation (Lafourche) 43

Brusly Landing (West Baton Rouge) 99, 171, 175, 178, 380

Bunkie (Avoyelles) 64, 65, 144-146, 364, 369

Burnside (Ascension) 368, 372, 373

Calumet (St. Mary) 260

Campti (Morehouse) 233, 262

Carencro (Lafayette) 74, 333

Chackbay (Lafourche) 294, 295

Chamberlin (West Baton Rouge) 272, 273

Cheneyville (Rapides) 102, 152, 401

Cinclare Sugar Plantation (West Baton Rouge) 99

Clayton (Concordia) 177

Clinton (East Feliciana) 128, 134, 135, 154, 156, 160, 196, 247, 281, 287, 290, 295, 335, 369, 370, 403, 410, 411, 413

Cloutierville (Natchitoches) 94

Colfax (Grant) 238, 249

Convent (St. James) 100, 179, 192, 232, 268, 284, 300, 305, 306

Cora Plantation (Iberville) 198

Cote Blanche Plantation (St. Mary) 236, 256

Cottonport (Avoyelles) 48, 324

Crowley (Acadia) 62, 63, 260, 315, 328

Cypress Hall Plantation (West Baton Rouge) 231

Delhi (Richland) 164, 165

Donaldsonville (Ascension) 15, 53, 54, 56, 58, 61, 62, 65-68, 71, 73, 75, 77-80, 83, 85, 102, 114, 147, 154, 157, 163, 164, 174, 197-199, 206, 207-214, 231, 281, 284, 289, 300-302, 304, 305, 311, 322, 323, 327, 335, 351, 364, 366, 367, 373, 374, 386

Elkinsville (St. Charles) 232

Elm Hall Plantation (Assumption) 263

Eola (Avoyelles) 143, 296, 297

Espenan, Charles Plantation (Lafourche) 147

Evergreen (Avoyelles) 63, 64, 82, 139, 143-146, 148, 242, 261, 265, 273, 285, 389

False River, now New Roads (Pointe Coupée) 195, 388

Farmerville (Union) 79, 81, 377

Franklin (St. Mary) 69, 95, 235-237, 255, 256, 260, 337, 383-385, 394,

Germania-Elise Plantation (Assumption) 263, 311

Glencoe (St. Mary) 237

Goldman (Tensas) 266

Gramercy (St. James) 268

Grand Coteau (St. Landry) 176, 349, 353

Grande Pointe (St. James) 268

Gray (Terrebonne) 384

Greensburg (St. Helena) 134
Gretna (Jefferson) 168

Haasville (Avoyelles) 144

Hahnville (St. Charles) 232, 334, 335

Hanson City (Jefferson) 337

Harrisonburg (Catahoula) 132, 179

Hermitage (Pointe Coupée) 388

Hohen Solms (Assumption) 263, 311, 327

Holmesville (Avoyelles) 227

Homer (Claiborne) 242, 273, 275, 276, 344, 389

Houma (Terrebonne) 53, 168, 169, 180, 204, 241, 244, 254, 274, 384

Irishtown, (Iberville) 128

Jackson (East Feliciana) 156, 160, 162, 239,

Jeanerette (Iberia) 153, 237, 241, 376, 385, 392-395

Jefferson City (now part of uptown New Orleans) 104

Jennings (Jefferson Davis) 189, 190, 290

Kahns (West Baton Rouge) 171, 175, 176, 187, 327, 328, 329

Kenner (Jefferson) 81, 89, 128, 132, 337, 371

Kennerville (Jefferson) – [Later Kenner] 128, 132

Kentwood (Tangipahoa) 98

Kessler (Assumption) 199

Kirksville (Tangipahoa) 98, 113, 387

Klotzville (Assumption) 42, 43, 196, 197, 199, 208, 327, 344, 345, 351

Labadieville (Assumption) 176, 182, 289, 294, 300,

Lafayette (Jefferson now part of uptown New Orleans) 309, 321, 322

Lafayette (Lafayette) 20, 92, 120, 182, 222, 280, 291, 293, 294, 367, 368, 371, 373-375 (See also Vermilionville)

Lake Charles (Calcasieu) 60, 63, 74, 143, 167, 189, 190, 192-194, 261, 286, 290, 301, 305-307, 326, 341, 342, 369

Lakeland (Pointe Coupée) 388

Lake Providence (East Carroll) 291, 329

Leesville (Vernon) 371

Lemoyne (St. Landry) 369

Live Oak Plantation (Lafourche) 180

Livonia (Pointe Coupée) 345

Logansport (Desoto) 49

Longview (St. James) 268

Lutcher (St. James) 49, 147, 268, 303, 362, 368, 372, 375,

Mangham (Richland) 95

Mansfield (DeSoto) 324, 344

Mansura (Avoyelles) 97, 226, 323-325

Marco (Natchitoches) 238, 249

Marengo Plantation- See Cinclare Sugar Plantation

Marksville (Avoyelles) 59, 64, 97, 139, 324, 350, 351

Marrero (Jefferson) 49

Melrose Plantation (Natchitoches) 43

Metairie (Jefferson) 168, 339,

Millikin's Bend (Madison) 85, 131, 169, 313

Monroe (Ouachita) 44 -47, 71, 79, 80, 93-95, 109, 113, 115, 127, 155, 162, 163, 165, 177, 213, 236, 253,

Morgan City (St. Mary) 50, 83, 141, 142, 167, 176, 177, 180-183, 206, 213, 225-228, 230, 299, 311, 312, 326,

Morganza (Pointe Coupée) 137, 138

Napoleonville (Assumption) 46, 167, 197, 198, 208, 210, 213, 214, 230, 231, 233, 248, 263, 284, 341, 364, 365, 370

Natchitoches (Natchitoches) 43, 93-96, 165, 166, 177, 182, 238, 250, 316, 317

Newellton (Tensas) 291

New Iberia (New Iberia) 53, 102, 119, 120, 122-124, 237, 241, 287, 293, 326, 383, 392- 394

New River (Ascension) 83, 210, 390

New Roads (Pointe Coupée) 138, 195, 278, 366, 388

Oak Ridge (Morehouse) 45

Opelousas (St. Landry) 15, 51, 63, 74, 75, 84, 107, 108, 140, 143, 145, 146, 192, 234, 245, 249, 251, 256, 261, 313-315, 332, 346, 359, 360, 365, 368, 407

Orange Grove Plantation (West Baton Rouge) 231

Paincourtville (Assumption) 212, 345

Palmetto (St. Landry) 338, 339

Patterson (St. Mary) 69, 76, 77, 384

Pearl River (St. Tammany) 278

Pineville (Rapides) 47, 48, 62, 65, 102, 125,136, 140, 151,203, 212, 216, 219, 221-223, 239, 249, 254, 265, 270, 272, 280, 285, 298, 298, 303, 317-320, 324, 325, 349, 350, 352-356, 357, 359, 365, 399, 401, 402, 404, 406, 408, 409, 414-416

Pine Woods (Catahoula) 132

Plantersville (Morehouse) 112

Plaquemine (Iberville) 111, 112, 128, 135, 137, 139-141, 143, 150, 170, 171, 174, 181, 182, 185-187,195, 284, 321, 322, 332, 340, 341, 370, 376, 386

Plattenville (Assumption) 211, 213

Pointe-à-la-Hâche (Plaquemines) 48

Ponchatoula (Tangipahoa) 233, 248

Port Allen (West Baton Rouge) 99, 231, 232, 240, 242, 328, 341, 379, 382,

Port Hickey (East Baton Rouge) 302

Port Hudson (East Baton Rouge) 156, 302

Prairie Mer Rouge (Morehouse) 109

Provençal (Natchitoches) 165, 166, 254, 261

Raceland (Lafourche) 43, 197

Rayne (Acadia) 171, 176, 181, 182, 187, 222, 328, 329, 354, 364, 369, 374, 375

Rayville, (Richland) 93, 95, 164

Reserve (St. John the Baptist) 87, 121, 334, 335, 355

Rice (Jefferson) 161

Robeline, (Natchitoches) 364

Rosa (St. Landry) 365
Rosedale (Iberville) 232

Rosedale (West Baton Rouge) 99

Seidenbach Plantation (West Baton Rouge) 231

Sellers (St. Charles) 69, 87, 89

Shreveport (Caddo) 43, 44, 55, 58, 59, 65, 67, 77, 86, 91, 92, 95, 109, 111, 113, 114, 116-118, 133, 153, 154, 168, 169, 171, 177-179, 183-185, 187, 188, 199-202, 217, 218, 236, 237, 239, 242, 243, 265, 266, 271-276, 282, 283, 292, 293, 298, 306, 313-316, 344, 348, 350-352, 353, 357-360, 376, 378,

Sicily Island (Catahoula) 177

Simmesport (Avoyelles) 324

St. Francisville (West Feliciana) 248, 283, 285, 286, 288, 292, 346, 363, 364, 412

St. Gabriel (Ascension) 327

St. Joseph (Tensas) 73, 240, 255, 266, 267, 343

St. Rose (St. Charles) 232

St. Sophie (Plaquemines) 48

Stein's Bluff (Union) 79, 80

Tallulah (Madison) 82

Tezcuco Plantation (Ascension) 373

Theresa Plantation (Lafourche) 43

Thibodaux (Lafourche) 54, 65, 75, 83, 84, 206, 230, 280, 289, 294, 295, 338

Tiger Bend (Avoyelles) 144
Torras (Pointe Coupée) 90, 327, 328,

Vermilionville (Lafayette)-[Renamed Lafayette in 1884] 57, 62, 92, 120, 136, 325, 377

Vidalia (Concordia) 90, 91, 127, 165, 269

Ville du Bois Plantation (Ascension) 301

Voiron Plantation (Ascension) 231, 301

Washington (St. Landry) 192-194, 272, 338, 339, 367, 390, 391, 418

Waterloo (Pointe Coupée) 60, 137, 195, 258, 296, 387, 391, 392, 420

Waterproof (Tensas) 266

White Castle (Iberville) 49, 50, 171, 198, 303, 366, 370, 371, 372, 374

Winnsboro (Franklin) 95, 164

www.ingramcontent.com/pod-product-compliance
Lightning Source LLC
Chambersburg PA
CBHW071234300426
44116CB00008B/1029